MW01064873

Microsoft®

Microsoft® Windows® 2000 Security Technical Reference

Internet Security Systems, Inc.

PUBLISHED BY
Microsoft Press
A Division of Microsoft Corporation
One Microsoft Way
Redmond, Washington 98052-6399

Chapter 3 was written by Linda Locher, Chapters 5 and 7 were written by Tom Fronckowiak, and Chapter 11 was written by Craig Zacker.

Library of Congress Cataloging-in-Publication Data
Microsoft Windows 2000 Security Technical Reference / Internet Security Systems, Inc.
p. cm.
Includes index.
ISBN 0-7356-0858-X
1. Computer security 2. Microsoft Windows (Computer file). I. Internet Security Systems, Inc.

QA76.9.A25 M56 2000
005.8--dc21 00-041827

Printed and bound in the United States of America.

1 2 3 4 5 6 7 8 9 WCWC 5 4 3 2 1 0

Distributed in Canada by Penguin Books Canada Limited.

A CIP catalogue record for this book is available from the British Library.

Microsoft Press books are available through booksellers and distributors worldwide. For further information about international editions, contact your local Microsoft Corporation office or contact Microsoft Press International directly at fax (425) 936-7329. Visit our Web site at mspress.microsoft.com. Send comments to *mspinput@microsoft.com.*

Acquisitions Editor: David Clark
Project Editor: Maureen Williams Zimmerman
Technical Editor: Jim Fuchs

Contents

4 Active Directory 89

5 Authentication 153

6 Cryptography and Microsoft Public Key Infrastructure 175

List of Tables

Preface

When David Clark and Anne Hamilton first asked me to undertake this project, Windows 2000 was still at beta 2. I had previously written detailed security documentation on Windows NT 4.0, and I thought I knew the scale of the work involved. I could not have been more wrong. As Windows 2000 evolved during the development process, some features were added and others changed. The interface underwent a series of changes—some fairly major, others less so. During testing we found issues, some of which were subsequently identified as bugs and fixed. Working with a product still in development was challenging. We learned a great deal the hard way, and it took more time than I had expected. Other members of the Knowledge Services team at Internet Security Systems were called in to help, and many a long evening was spent testing or trying to resolve a particular problem.

The book could not have been written without the help of two team members in particular: Ivan Phillips and Dimitris Tsapakidis. Their collective expertise and hard work were invaluable.

Thanks must also go to Tom Fronckowiak, Linda J. Locher, and Craig Zacher for their collaboration on several chapters in an effort to get us past the finishing post.

Last, but by no means least, my thanks to Maureen Zimmerman for guiding the book, and me, through the editing process to completion.

I learned a great deal during the development of this book. I hope readers find it both educational and a useful reference. Microsoft has provided a wealth of security functionality in Windows 2000. This book is intended to help readers get the most out of it.

John Hayday
Director of Knowledge Services
Internet Information Services, Inc.

Chapter 1
Overview of Security Changes in Windows 2000

Microsoft Windows 2000 represents a major step forward by Microsoft in the evolution of the Microsoft Windows NT product line. While some of the core remains, much has been added to provide the additional functionality required by the industry. A great deal of attention has been paid to security, which is now fully integrated with the new Active Directory directory service structure. In terms of scalability, Windows 2000 is designed to scale effectively from the laptop—with full support for Plug and Play and the Advanced Configuration and Power Interface (ACPI)—to the server and across architectures, with support for load balancing and clustering. Interoperability has been improved, with greater support for heterogeneous environments including NetWare, UNIX, MVS, and AS400, and the use of well-defined standards, including the Lightweight Directory Access Protocol (LDAP), the Kerberos v5 Protocol, and the Domain Name System (DNS). Windows 2000 has also been designed to be more reliable than previous versions of Windows. Manageability has improved, with more flexible management tools and Data Center improvements.

On the hardware front, improvements include support for the ACPI, Universal Serial Bus (USB), IEEE 1394 (FireWire), Accelerated Graphics Port (AGP), multiple display support, Digital Versatile Disc or Digital Video Disc (DVD), Plug and Play, and the Win32 driver model (WDM). Support for the WDM allows hardware manufacturers to write one driver for both Windows 2000 and Windows 95/98 platforms.

File system changes include support for the Universal Disk Format (UDF), FAT 32 (allowing users to dual boot Windows 2000 and Windows 95/98), disk defragmentation, improved backup, and the introduction of the NTFS file system for Windows 2000. The version of NTFS used in Windows 2000 introduces Encrypting File System (EFS), the concept of property sets, disk quotas, and improved volume management.

The management infrastructure has been improved with the introduction of Active Directory and the inclusion of new facilities such as Service Pack Slipstreaming, the Windows Installation service, Diagnostic booting options, Windows Management Instrumentation (WMI), and the Microsoft Management Console (MMC).

Several new areas of security functionality exist, with Active Directory at the core of many. With careful planning, the building blocks of Active Directory allow you to model your business in a manner that supports the most effective use of these technologies.

Windows 2000 Versions

Windows 2000 shipped in four versions:

- **Windows 2000 Professional.** Replacing Windows NT 4.0 Workstation, Windows 2000 Professional is intended to serve as the standard corporate operating system for desktop and mobile users. To aid the transition—while preserving user information—upgrading from Windows NT 3.51/4.0, Windows 3.*x*, and Windows 95/98 is possible via the new Setup Manager. Windows 2000 Professional includes improved hardware support, PCMCIA card hot-swapping, and support for ACPI and APM. Deployment ability is aided by the inclusion of the SysPrep utility, which allows a single master disk image to be securely prepared for duplication. Support for offline folders makes network files available offline, while EFS ensures the protection of sensitive data on mobile systems should the system be stolen.
- **Windows 2000 Server.** Replacing Windows NT 4.0 Server, Windows 2000 Server is intended to become the mainstream workgroup and departmental business server, supporting infrastructure services, file/print and Web services, application services, and communications services. It supports four-way symmetric multiprocessing (SMP) and introduces Active Directory. Management is simplified through the consolidation of administrative tasks into the MMC and the introduction of the Group Policy. The inclusion of Terminal Services allows continued support for legacy desktop hardware.
- **Windows 2000 Advanced Server.** Replacing Windows NT 4.0 Server Enterprise Edition, Windows 2000 Advanced Server is meant to serve as a midrange server solution, offering all the features found in the standard version of Windows 2000 Server and additionally supporting eight-way SMP, Enterprise Memory Architecture (EMA), clustering, and load balancing.
- **Windows 2000 Datacenter Server.** New to Windows 2000, Datacenter Server offers the highest levels of performance and supports 32-way SMP. Datacenter Server also has all the features of the standard version of Windows 2000 Server, but is optimized for enterprise deployment and solutions.

Security Features New to Windows 2000

This book will explore the range of new security functionality in Windows 2000 as well as the areas of the operating system that have had more subtle security changes. In this chapter, we'll outline the following major new areas of security-relevant functionality. We'll discuss each area in detail in later chapters.

- **Active Directory.** Active Directory is the core of the flexibility and scalability of the Windows 2000 security model, providing information about all objects on the network and simplifying common administrative tasks.

- **Kerberos.** Kerberos has replaced NTLM as the default authentication protocol within or across domains. It provides mutual authentication of workstations and servers and offers interoperability improvement in heterogeneous environments.
- **Public Key Infrastructure.** The Windows 2000 Public Key Infrastructure (PKI) is the core of much of the new security functionality in Windows 2000, making extensive use of certificates for many security-related functions.
- **Group Policy objects.** The new Group Policy model allows for centralized control of a security policy, while at the same time providing flexibility by permitting various security-related settings to be controlled in a more decentralized manner.
- **Internet Protocol Security Protocol.** The Internet Protocol Security Protocol (IPSec) provides advanced network security, ensuring the integrity, authentication, and—optionally—confidentiality of data.
- **Encrypting File System.** Encrypting File System (EFS) allows the optional encryption of data on a system's hard disk, ensuring confidentiality should the disk be stolen or otherwise compromised.
- **Security Configuration Tool Set.** The Security Configuration Tool Set comprises a range of tools designed to centralize the design, application, and monitoring of a security policy.

Active Directory

New to Windows 2000, Active Directory directory service is the core of the system's security. It provides a secure, distributed, scalable, and replicated hierarchical directory service that is completely integrated with Windows 2000. Active Directory replaces the security accounts manager (SAM) database area of the registry on domain controllers—found in earlier versions of Windows NT—as the primary repository for security information, including user accounts, groups, and passwords. As such, Active Directory forms a trusted component of the Local Security Authority (LSA). Active Directory stores both user credentials to support authentication and access control information to support authorization to access system resources. Member servers and workstations retain the local SAM database for locally defined users and groups.

Integrating the Internet Domain Name System (DNS) concept of a namespace with the operating system's directory services, Active Directory can serve to help unify and manage multiple existing namespaces, providing a single point of administration for all resources. Active Directory is not an X.500 directory. Rather, it uses the Lightweight Directory Access Protocol (LDAP) as the core access protocol and supports the X.500 information model. As with Windows NT 4.0, the domain remains the primary security and administrative unit. At the highest hierarchical level, you can connect multiple domains into a tree structure, while at the lower levels you can establish a hierarchy of organizational units (OUs) to reflect the organization's internal structure. The resulting hierarchical structure forms a namespace served by the DNS locator service. This provides unique names for all objects in the directory. Integration between Active Directory and DNS also allows Active Directory to register server location information in DNS server location records. Thus these records can be used to identify domain controllers during the logon process, something that in Windows NT 4.0 necessitated that the Netlogon service use a NetBIOS broadcast. Kerberos protocol-specific server location records additionally enable a client to locate servers that run the Kerberos v5 Key Distribution Center (KDC) service.

Domains are still served by domain controllers, but the concept of a primary domain controller (PDC) and a backup domain controller (BDC)—in which all updates had to be made on the PDC—has been largely replaced. Servers in the domain are now either domain controllers (DCs)—hosting a copy of Active Directory—or member servers. Active Directory uses DCs only, and all DCs are peers. An administrator can make changes to any DC, and the updates (to Active Directory) will be automatically replicated on all other DCs within the site via remote procedure calls (RPCs). This provides for more resilience and load balancing in the domain. While changes can be written to all DCs, a PDC emulator role—present when the domain is operating in mixed (Windows 2000/Windows NT 4.0) mode—retains some functions in a full native Windows 2000 mode. In a mixed Windows 2000/Windows NT 4.0 network, the PDC emulator acts as the PDC to the Windows NT 4.0 BDCs. The continued presence of the PDC emulator in native mode provides for integrity of the schema (directory structure) and ensures that where critical, replication delays do not adversely affect the system's security functions. A password can be changed on any DC, but is then preferentially replicated to the DC holding the PDC emulator role (by default the first DC in the domain). If a subsequent authentication request fails because of a bad password at a particular DC, the request is also forwarded to the PDC emulator—in case the password has recently been changed—before the authentication attempt is rejected. Account lockout is also processed on the PDC emulator.

The hierarchical nature of Active Directory allows for a fine-grained administration structure that is ideally suited for decentralized administration without compromising security. Support for transitive trusts eases the administration of multiple domains. If each domain acts as a security boundary, multiple security boundaries are therefore possible. At the highest level, administrators from domain A are not automatically administrators in domain B. Within the domain, the default scope of administration is the whole domain, and the domain's administrator has authority over every object and service within that domain. Active Directory allows privileges to be granted (delegated) to users based on the specific functions they must perform within a given scope. In Windows 2000, administrative scope can include the entire domain (the default) or a subtree of OUs within the domain, or it can be limited to a single OU. This flexibility eliminates the need to grant users extensive administrative privileges over large areas of the user population simply to perform a single administrative function—such as resetting a user's password—within a particular business unit. You can model the business unit as an individual or as a hierarchy of organizational units (OUs), and you can grant the user the privilege to reset a user's password only within the scope of a particular OU. You can delegate and restrict specific permissions within Active Directory in scope in this manner. The Delegation of Control Wizard significantly simplifies setting up delegation options.

Within Active Directory, access control lists (ACLs) protect all objects in the same manner that files and folders are protected when using NTFS. ACLs form part of the object's security descriptor, along with information on the level of auditing required for specific object access events. An ACL consists of a number of access control entries (ACEs). ACLs on directory objects contain both ACEs that apply to the object as a whole and also ACEs that apply to the individual attributes of the object. Each ACE identifies a particular user's or group's access to a given object or particular object's attributes. Active Directory automatically implements inheritance of ACLs; thus, ACLs applied to a container object will automatically propagate down to all child objects and subcontainers. This has the additional benefit of reducing replication traffic, as only a single right needs to be replicated to other Active Directory replicas; each replica subsequently propagates the inherited ACL permissions locally. Using ACLs within Active Directory allows an administrator to control not only whether users can see a given object, but also which individual properties of the object can be seen. For example, all users might be permitted to see other users' basic details, but prevented from seeing other users' home address details. This level of access might be restricted to the individual concerned and to members of the human resources department. The delegation of administrative privilege is controlled by the use of ACLs in the same manner.

Domains

Active Directory is made up of one or more domains, each constituting an administrative and security boundary within the Windows 2000 network. A domain can span more than one physical location. Every domain has its own security policies and settings, including administrative and user rights, EFS policy, and ACLs. Each domain might also have security relationships (trusts) with other domains. When multiple domains are connected by trust relationships and share a common schema, configuration, and global catalog, they constitute a domain tree. Multiple domain trees can be connected together into a forest.

In Windows NT 4.0, the size of the registry limited the number of user accounts in a domain. Larger organizations therefore found it necessary to artificially divide their infrastructures into multiple domains, each with its own directory and user accounts. In Windows 2000, Active Directory is capable of scaling to a much larger capacity to store user, group, and computer accounts. Therefore, organizations might in principle consolidate all user accounts and resources into a single domain. In practice, organizations might decide to retain multiple domains for security or other reasons.

Trees and Forests

A domain tree consists of several domains that share a common schema and configuration, forming a contiguous namespace within Active Directory. All domains within a tree are linked by transitive trust relationships. A hierarchy of domains allows for finer granularity of administration without compromising security. To accommodate organizational change, you can move user and group accounts from one domain to another.

A forest is a set of one or more trees that do not form a contiguous namespace. All trees in a forest share a common schema, configuration, and global catalog. All trees in a given forest trust each other via two-way transitive trust relationships. Unlike a tree, a forest does not need a distinct name—an organization can include Windows 2000 domains with disjointed DNS names.

Organizational Units

Within the hierarchy of Active Directory, OUs are logical containers that exist below the level of the domain, and into which you can place users, groups, computers, and other OUs. A domain can have any number of OUs that are themselves organized in a hierarchical namespace. These OUs can be modeled to reflect the departments and organizations in the company. A well-defined OU structure will greatly simplify security management and delegation of administrative control. You can easily rename OUs within the domain tree and you can also move them to a different location if necessary.

Permissions can flow down the tree; you can grant permissions to users (as well as permissions to a group of users) on an OU basis.

Domain Trust Relationships

The Windows 2000 domains can be organized into a domain tree. The trust relationships between domains allow users with accounts defined in one domain to be authenticated by resource servers in another domain. In a Windows NT 4.0 multiple domain environment, domains were logically classed as either account domains or resource domains. One-way interdomain trust relationships were typically defined from the resource domains to the account domain or domains. User accounts created in the account domains were trusted by all resource domains, whereas user accounts created in resource domains were not trusted outside of those domains. Managing trust relationships between account domains and resource domains on a large network was a complex task, and in an enterprise multimaster domain model could result in hundreds of one-way trust relationships.

Unlike Windows NT 4.0, Windows 2000 automatically creates two-way transitive trusts between domains as you add each domain to the domain tree. Like Windows NT 4.0, this trust is defined on the basis of a secret key shared by both domains, which is updated on a regular basis. When you create the first domain controller in a domain, you are given the option of adding the domain to an existing domain tree. Choosing to do so results in the automatic creation of a parent-child trust relationship with the parent domain specified (and for which you must provide domain administrative credentials). All domains thereby implicitly trust other domains in the tree. Trust relationships are used by the Kerberos v5 authentication protocol when clients and servers are in separate domains in the forest.

As Figure 1-1 illustrates, Windows NT 4.0 trusts are either one-way, or two-way and nontransitive; that is, domain A trusts domain B and domain B might also trust domain A, but if domain C has a separate trust relationship with domain B, domain A has no relationship with domain C. All Windows 2000 trust relationships—within a forest—are by default two-way and transitive: If domain A has a two-way trust with domain B and domain B has a two-way trust with domain C, domain A trusts domain C and domain C trusts domain A. Explicit one-way or two-way nontransitive trust relationships can be established to Windows NT 4.0 domains, or Windows 2000 domains in another forest if required. For organizations with multiple domains, the overall number of explicit one-way trust relationships is therefore significantly reduced.

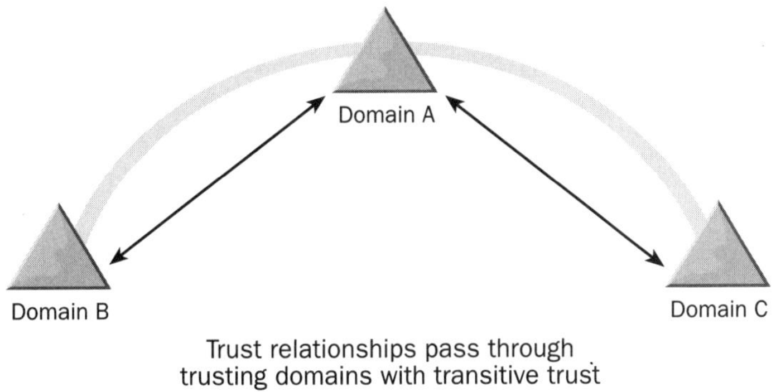

Figure 1-1. *Windows trust relationships.*

Kerberos

The Kerberos authentication protocol was developed at the Massachusetts Institute of Technology during the 1980s as part of Project Athena. Project Athena examined the design, implementation, and administration of distributed networks. Kerberos has been implemented on many UNIX platforms, in which the Distributed Computing Environment (DCE) Security Services are layered on the Kerberos protocol. The latest Kerberos v5 protocol has been implemented on a variety of platforms and is used to provide a single authentication service in a distributed network. The Internet Engineering Task Force (IETF) has adopted Kerberos v5 in the form of RFC 1510. The Windows 2000 implementation of Kerberos complies with this and the Generic Security Service KRB5 token format to provide interoperability with operating systems other than Windows 2000. A client running an operating system other than Windows 2000 can therefore successfully request and subsequently use a service ticket from a Windows 2000 network authentication service known as a Key Distribution Center (KDC). A Windows 2000 Professional desktop can also be configured to use a UNIX KDC—users can log on to the desktop using an account defined on the UNIX KDC. Windows 95, Windows 98, and Windows NT 4.0 clients can be upgraded to support Kerberos logon authentication.

The Kerberos authentication protocol defines the security interactions between a client, a resource, and a KDC. In Windows 2000, a KDC is implemented as the authentication service on each DC. The Windows 2000 domain becomes the equivalent of a Kerberos realm, using Active Directory as the account database for users (principals) and groups. The Kerberos protocol is fully integrated with the Winlogon single sign-on architecture to provide authentication and access control. In Windows 2000, Kerberos v5 is the default, or primary network authentication protocol. If a password is used to log on to a domain account, Windows 2000 uses Kerberos for authentication. Alternatively, if a user logs on by using a smart card, Kerberos authentication with certificates is used. The Kerberos KDC Service is responsible for generating session keys and granting service tickets for mutual client/server authentication. For further discussion of Kerberos KDC Service, see Chapter 3, "Windows 2000 Security Model and Subsystems."

The Kerberos protocol also supports the concept of impersonation, which allows a client to connect to a service and that service then to impersonate the client when connecting to another service. Likewise, the second service could also impersonate the client if required. This provides for a more robust and scalable authentication model in multitier client/server application architectures.

While the Kerberos protocol is the default for network authentication, you can also use Secure Socket Layer /Transport Layer Security (SSL/TLS) authentication. Windows NTLM authentication is also retained for compatibility with Window NT 4.0 systems.

Public Key Cryptography

As networks open up to provide businesses with intranets, Internet presences, and extranets that encompass suppliers, partners, or clients, the network user population grows significantly. As the network grows physically and logically larger, the potential opportunities for unauthorized users to obtain access to data also increase. To securely distribute and manage user credentials across such an organization requires a well-planned Public Key Infrastructure (PKI). A PKI is a system consisting of digital certificates—certificate authorities that verify and authenticate the validity of each party involved in an electronic transaction by means of public key cryptography.

Windows 2000 PKI

Windows 2000 introduces the tools necessary to build a comprehensive standards-based PKI. Central to this infrastructure is Microsoft Certificate Services, which allows the deployment of one or more enterprise certificate authorities (CAs) to support an organization's business needs. The CAs let an organization establish and vouch for the identity of certificate holders by managing the issuing and revocation of X.509 public key certificates. Certificate Services are integrated with Active Directory in a manner that uses the directory service to publish information about certificate services, including the locations of user certificates and certificate revocation lists.

Microsoft Certificate Services provides a scalable hierarchical CA model for supporting different uses of certificate services. In its simplest form the CA hierarchy can consist of a single CA, but larger organizations would typically deploy a PKI consisting of multiple CAs with a clearly defined certificate path. The root CA at the top of the hierarchy could exist outside of the organization, and would be provided by a third party. However, there is no requirement that all CAs share a common top-level CA parent.

A separate component of Certificate Services is the certification Web enrollment pages, which let certificate requesters make their requests using a Web browser. This Web-based interface is customizable, allowing an organization to tailor the interface to its specific requirements.

You can use Windows 2000 Group Policy objects (GPOs) to automatically distribute certificates to computers, establish certificate trust lists, and identify common trusted certificate authorities. GPOs also control the management of recovery policies, based on certificates, for EFS.

Once an organization is able to manage digital certificates, a range of enhanced security options becomes available to cover such technologies as e-mail, Secure Web Communications, Digitally Signed Software, EFS, IP Security, and Smart Card Security.

Secure E-mail

Standard Internet mail is not secure. It is sent over open networks as plain text. The very nature of Internet mail increases the risk that unauthorized persons can monitor your mail—which might contain confidential or proprietary information—without ever entering your organization's premises.

Caution It's important to consider the nature of your organization's electronic communication. How many employees forward their office e-mail to personal Internet mail accounts? How many have inadvertently sent proprietary e-mail to the wrong address? E-mail is also susceptible to impersonation. Anyone can impersonate the sender of a mail message by using readily available tools to counterfeit the e-mail's originating IP address and mail header.

To counter potential vulnerabilities, the Secure/Multipurpose Internet Mail Extensions (S/MIME) working group of the IETF has developed the open S/MIME standard. The standard allows digital signing and encryption of e-mail. Clients operating on any platform that utilizes S/MIME can send secure e-mail to each other over the Internet regardless of which servers handle the messages, because all cryptographic functions are performed on the mail clients. Most leading mail-client vendors—including Microsoft—support S/MIME. Secure e-mail with S/MIME uses the industry-standard X.509 digital certificates and public key technology. S/MIME assures senders that only the intended recipients can read the contents of the encrypted mail. Recipients are also assured that the message is genuine. Each mail client must have a valid certificate for the secure mail to function correctly.

Best Practice You can deploy Microsoft Certificate Services to issue secure mail certificates that will work with S/MIME-compliant secure mail clients such as Microsoft Outlook 98 or 2000. Web enrollment pages can also facilitate users' request and receipt of secure mail certificates.

Secure Web Communication

All Web-based communication utilizing the Hypertext Transfer Protocol (HTTP), Telnet, or File Transfer Protocol (FTP) over the Transport Control Protocol/Internet Protocol (TCP/IP) is not secure because all information is sent as clear text. Confidential or sensitive information can be easily intercepted and read. This inherent lack of encryption is compounded by the lack of authentication of the Web server when using standard HTTP, opening the way for the introduction of a rogue Web server. Such a server could passively attempt to obtain information from the client or actively attempt to introduce malicious software to the client.

A variety of secure communications standards exists using public key technologies. Two of the most popular protocols, Secure Sockets Layer 3.0 and the open Transport Layer Security (based on SSL), are widely deployed by businesses to provide secure channels for confidential communication on the Web. Limitations on the strength of cryptography allowed for export are dealt with during the initial phase of any transaction, when both client and server negotiate the strength of the cryptography to be used. The server chooses the strongest cryptographic strength supported by both client and server. The highest level of security is therefore available only when both client and server support strong export-controlled cryptography.

Where strong encryption technology is required—to protect financial transactions, for example—other specialized cryptographic protocols (as permitted by current cryptography export regulations) have been developed, such as the Secure Electronic Transaction (SET) protocol and the Server Gated Cryptography (SGC) protocol. Microsoft Internet Information Server (IIS) supports SGC, and Microsoft Internet Explorer 5 (utilizing the Microsoft Wallet) supports SET. You can use Microsoft Certificate Services to issue client and server authentication certificates for use with Internet Explorer and IIS along with other third-party products. User authentication certificates can also be used to control access to IIS resources. IIS authenticates users on the basis of certificates, which are then mapped to user accounts. Such mapping can be accomplished on a one-to-one or one-to-many basis. In the latter case, the mapping is between certificates issued by a particular CA to a single user account. This might be appropriate when a particular partner's employees require access to a Web-based stock management application. The partner has its own Microsoft certificate authority, which it uses to issue authentication certificates to employees. Rather than map individual certificates to specific user accounts on the Web server, you could decide to map any valid authentication certificate issued by the partner's CA to a single user account.

Digitally Signed Software

To counter the threat of viruses or other malicious code contained in programs downloaded from the Internet, Microsoft developed Authenticode technology, which enables developers to digitally sign software using standard X.509 certificates. Once software is signed, any modification will invalidate the digital signature. The presence of a valid digital signature ensures that the user can verify both the software's origin and that the software has remained unaltered since it was signed. Windows 2000 public key group policies can be configured to specify CAs trusted by your organization for code signing, so that software from publishers using certificates provided by these CAs can be downloaded automatically without reference to the users. You can configure Internet Explorer to prevent users from downloading and running unsigned software.

Smart Cards

Smart cards, which contain a small integrated circuit, are tamperproof and can be used to store users' certificates and public keys. Protected by a personal identification number (PIN), smart cards provide stronger security for user authentication and nonrepudiation. Because the cryptographic operations are isolated from the operating system, they are not susceptible to attacks on the operating system. A general-purpose smart card interface has been used to integrate cryptographic smart cards as part of the smart card logon support in Windows 2000. To use the card, the user must insert it into the smart card reader attached to the system and, when prompted, enter his or her PIN. The smart card thus requires two-factor identification: the possession of the card and the knowledge of the PIN. Windows 2000 supports use of smart cards for network logon and remote access authentication using the EAP-TLS extension to the Point-to-Point Tunneling Protocol (PPTP).

Note You can use Microsoft Certificate Services to issue smart card certificates.

The Microsoft CryptoAPI provides an architecture for supporting cryptographic functionality in applications. It separates the applications that use the cryptography from the implementation of the cryptographic algorithms. CryptoAPI architecture is designed to support installable cryptographic service providers (CSPs). These CSPs might be software-based or take advantage of cryptographic hardware devices. Through the CryptoAPI, support for PK-based applications is provided uniformly on workstations and servers running Windows NT and Windows 2000 as well as workstations running Windows 95/98.

Group Policy Objects

In Windows NT 4.0, the System Policy Editor tool configured user and computer settings stored in the Windows NT registry database. In Windows 2000, the concept of Group Policy objects has replaced that functionality. Group Policies are used to centrally define system and application settings for groups of users and computers. These settings include software policies, scripts (computer startup and shutdown and user logon and logoff), user documents and settings, application deployment, and security settings. Group Policies are defined as a property of a domain or OU using the Active Directory Users And Computers administration tool. The Group Policy defines information contained in a Group Policy object (GPO). The GPO is associated with one or more Active Directory objects, such as a site, domain, or OU, allowing for centralized or decentralized management of policy options. Decentralized management is aided by the ability of administrators to delegate control of GPOs. By default, a GPO will affect all computers and users in the scope to which it is applied. This behavior can be modified, however, by the application of filters (system access control lists, or SACLs) based on users' or computers' membership in a Windows 2000 Security Group. ACLs are also used to control the delegation of access to the Group Policy Editor.

The Group Policy Editor and its extensions let you define Group Policy options for managed desktop configurations for computers and users. With the Group Policy editor you can specify settings for

- **Software policies.** You can use software policies to mandate registry settings on the desktop, including those affecting operating system components and applications.
- **Scripts.** You can control scripts—such as computer startup and shutdown and logon and logoff—via group policy.
- **Software management options.** Software management options can control which applications are available to users and which appear on the desktop. Administrators can install, assign, publish, update, repair, and remove software for groups of users and computers through these options
- **User documents and settings.** User documents and settings can add files, folders, or shortcuts to special folders that represent the user's desktop. Special folders are located under the user profiles in the \Documents And Settings folder. These settings control the ability to redirect the user's My Documents folders to a network location.
- **Security settings.** You can import security settings from a security template and apply them automatically. The same template can be used by the Security Configuration Tool Set to analyze a system's current security configuration.

The GPO for computers is applied at system startup. The GPO affecting users is applied when the user logs on. The deployment of applications occurs only during system startup or when the user logs on, rather than on a periodic basis. By default, GPOs will be reapplied every 8 hours (configurable between 7 seconds and 45 days).

Local Security Policy Settings

The security policy in effect on a particular system is viewable to administrators via the Security Settings option in the Control Panel. The "secpol" MMC Snap-In permits the administrator to view both the local policy settings and the effective settings. When an effective setting is the result of a GPO, the local settings will have no effect. When there is no GPO-enforced setting, the local administrator can set an effective local policy setting. This permits domain administrators to define certain security policy options centrally and apply them uniformly across the GPO's scope, while allowing local administrators to set other security policy options on an individual per-system basis.

Internet Protocol Security

Windows 2000 includes an implementation of the IETF's Internet Protocol security (IPSec) for advanced network security, providing the integrity, authentication, and confidentiality of network data. IPSec exists below the transport level, so its security services are transparently inherited by applications. IPSec is equally suited to protecting sensitive data travelling over the sections of the internal network, between clients and a particular application server, or between individual hosts (or sites) forming a Virtual Private Network (VPN) over an insecure network. The IPSec Policy Agent Service provides IPSec facilities and is responsible for managing the IPSec policy and starting the ISAKMP/Oakley (IKE) and the IPSec driver.

Designed by the IETF for the Internet Protocol, Windows 2000 IPSec uses industry-standard encryption algorithms and authentication techniques. IPSec is an open industry standard, defined in several RFCs. Multiple companies working on IPSec implementations test interoperability against the standard to ensure greater interoperability across their products compared to existing proprietary IP encryption technologies.

As defined by the IETF, IPSec uses an IP Authentication Header (AH) and an IP Encapsulated Security Payload (ESP). The AH provides for integrity, source authentication, and anti-replay using an algorithm to compute a Hash Message Authentication Code for each IP packet. The ESP provides confidentiality, in addition to authentication and integrity, by using the Data Encryption Standard algorithm in the Cipher Block Chaining (DES-CBC) algorithm. Windows 2000 IPSec implements the Internet Key Exchange protocol to automatically manage integrity and encryption keys. Administrators can choose either AH or ESP depending upon the sensitivity of the information they are protecting and the relative vulnerability of the network. Of course, there is processing overhead associated with the ESP encryption.

A Windows 2000 IPSec policy is configured using the IP Security Policy MMC Snap-In. With the snap-in, you can design IPSec policies centrally and then assign them to either individual computers or groups of computers using OUs in Active Directory. IPSec policies are built around the concept of negotiation policies and IP filters. Negotiation policies determine the security services that you want to include—for example, those that require confidentiality and those that do not. You can set multiple security services for each negotiation policy, with the ISAKMP/Oakley service responsible for negotiating a policy that both parties to the security association can accept. Filtering permits the negotiation policy to be applied to different computers. IP filters determine which actions to take, based upon either individual or ranges of source and destination IP address, protocol type, and if appropriate, IP protocol ports for individual IP datagrams. You can define an IPSec policy to provide IPSec services to a datagram, to allow it to pass unmodified, or to discard it.

Encrypting File System

By providing on-disk data encryption using public key cryptography, Encrypting File System (EFS) included with Windows 2000 permits files and folders on a user's system to be secured against unauthorized access. This level of protection is necessary to prevent access to sensitive data when Windows 2000 cannot provide security using the standard

NTFS ACLs. This would be the case if a hard disk was stolen and placed into another system, or if the original system was booted onto a floppy disk containing an alternative operating system. Tools that allow access to files on NTFS formatted volumes irrespective of any NTFS permissions are freely available for both MS-DOS and UNIX operating systems.

Encrypting data raises the issue of data recovery should an employee who has encrypted some sensitive data leave the organization or lose his or her encryption keys. To protect against the inability to access company data, a data-recovery plan is considered essential for most business environments.

EFS has been designed to be simple to use, enabling a user to encrypt a folder (and its current and future contents) or an individual file by selecting the Encrypt Contents To Secure Data option from the folder or files advanced properties option in Windows Explorer. If a folder is marked as encrypted, all files copied into or created within the folder will automatically be encrypted. Additionally, files copied from an encrypted folder remain encrypted, as do those archived using a Windows 2000 aware backup program. Files or folders copied to a floppy disk or other non-NTFS volume will lose their encryption.

The initial release of EFS does not support file sharing between users, but the EFS architecture is designed to facilitate this functionality at a later release. The current release is therefore best suited to providing protection for sensitive data on hand-held mobile systems, or for data required by only a single user.

The protection is accomplished using public-key encryption and takes advantage of the CryptoAPI architecture in Windows 2000. When enabled, files are encrypted with a fast symmetric encryption algorithm using a randomly generated file encryption key (FEK). The initial release of EFS uses the expanded Data Encryption Standard (DESX) as the encryption algorithm. The randomly generated file encryption key is then itself encrypted with one or more public keys, including those of the user and the key recovery agent. Because the FEK is totally independent of a user's public/private key pair, the recovery agent can decrypt the file's contents without compromising the user's private key. EFS supports encryption and decryption of files stored on local drives as well as those stored on remote file servers. EFS is tightly integrated with NTFS, providing a high-performance system in which users should notice little difference between reading an encrypted or a decrypted file.

Because encryption occurs automatically during read and write operations, an encrypted file is decrypted when read from the disk prior to being sent to a remote system, where it is then re-encrypted when written to the local disk. EFS therefore offers no protection for data in transit. You must use other network security protocols, such as IPSec, for this purpose.

You can define your organization's Windows 2000 EFS recovery policy in the Active Directory Default Domain Policy and mandate the policy for all computers in the domain. Alternatively, you can define a policy covering individual OUs. By default, the domain administrator controls the EFS recovery policy. He or she can delegate that control to designated security administrators. This allows your organization a high level of control and flexibility regarding who is authorized to recover potentially sensitive encrypted data. EFS also supports the use of multiple recovery agents, allowing organizations a level of redundancy and flexibility in implementing their recovery procedures.

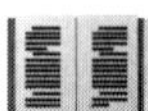

More Info In a home environment, the EFS automatically generates a recovery key when the local administrator first logs on, making the local administrator the default recovery agent.

Security Configuration Tool Set

The Security Configuration Tool Set provides a single point of administration for Windows 2000–based system security settings. The Tool Set permits an administrator to

- Configure security settings on one or more Windows 2000–based computers.
- Perform security analysis on one or more Windows 2000–based computers.
- Use a security configuration as part of Group Policy.

Configurable Security Settings

Given the scale and diversity of configurable security parameters in Windows 2000, securing a Windows 2000–based network can be complex and detailed in terms of the system components involved and the level of change that might be required. The Security Configuration Tool Set allows configuration at a macro level, enabling the administrator to define a number of security settings in a security template and then have those settings automatically implemented across the domain. The Security Configuration Tool Set therefore complements other, more specific security tools that address particular aspects of system security. The following components underlie the Tool Set:

- **Secedit.exe.** You can use the command-line tool Secedit.exe to apply a security policy or initiate an analysis. However, the Security Configuration Manager is required to display the results.
- **Security Configuration and Analysis.** The Security Configuration and Analysis MMC Snap-In allows security configuration templates defined in the Security Templates MMC Snap-In to be imported into a security database (either the Local Computer Policy database or any private database). Importing configurations builds a machine-specific security database, which you can then apply to the system. Additionally, you can analyze the system against the settings held in the database and differences displayed in the GUI.
- **Security Configuration Service.** The Security Configuration Service is the core engine of the Security Configuration Tool Set. It runs on every Windows 2000–based system and is responsible for all security configuration and analysis functionality provided by the Tool Set.

- **Security settings extension to the Group Policy Editor.** As part of the Group Policy Editor, an administrator uses the Security Configuration Tool Set to define security settings as part of a GPO. A GPO can then be assigned with domain or OU scope or to a specific computer in Active Directory. The GPO can be reapplied periodically to ensure that the system continues to adhere to given corporate security policy. Security configuration settings, stored as templates, can be imported and exported between the Security Configuration Manager and the Group Policy Editor.
- **Security Templates.** The Security Templates Snap-In to the Microsoft Management Console (MMC) allows the administrator to define computer-independent security configurations (text-based .inf template files).
- **Setup Security.** During a clean installation of the Windows 2000 operating system, the security configuration service performs the initial security configurations using predefined configurations that ship with the system, thus creating an initial security database (called the Local Computer Policy database).

The Security Configuration MMC Snap-In permits the administrator to define security templates covering the following areas:

- **Account policies.** This template holds security settings covering password policy, account lockout policy and Kerberos policies (DC only).
- **Directory objects.** This template holds security configuration settings for Active Directory objects (DC only).
- **Event log.** This template holds configuration settings for the Event Logs.
- **Local file system.** This template holds access control settings for the local file system.
- **Local policies.** This template holds security settings covering audit policy, user rights assignment, and computer security options.
- **Registry keys.** This template holds access control settings and values for local registry keys.
- **Restricted groups.** This template holds security settings covering the management of group memberships for selected groups that might be considered sensitive, such as local Administrators or Backup operators.
- **System services.** This template holds security startup settings for all local or network system services. This area is designed such that independent software vendors (ISVs) can build attachments for configuration and analysis of specific system services.

In the case of directory, registry, and local file systems, the security templates hold security settings for object-based security descriptors, including object ownership, the ACL, and auditing information.

Default Security Settings

With the release of Windows 2000, Microsoft has taken the opportunity to review operating system security in respect to the access permissions and privileges granted to the three main user groups—Administrators, Power Users, and Users. Microsoft has attempted to more clearly define the roles of these groups in terms of the functions they are expected to perform and hence their level of system access. Administrators are defined as users who can

- Install the operating system.
- Install Service Packs and Hotfixes.
- Install Windows Updates.
- Upgrade the operating system.
- Repair the operating system.
- Configure critical machine-wide operating system parameters.

The default Windows 2000 permissions do not therefore restrict Administrative access to any registry or file system object. Administrators can perform all functions supported by the operating system. In addition, they can grant themselves any right that they do not have by default.

Users should not be able to compromise the integrity of the operating system or installed applications. Users are prevented from modifying machine-wide registry settings, operating system files, and program files. They cannot install programs that can be run by other users, nor can they run programs installed by other users (this restriction is to prevent Trojan horses). Users should be able to run any application that has been previously installed by an Administrator, Power User, or themselves. In practice, users might not be able to run legacy applications because those applications were not designed with operating security in mind.

Power Users should ideally be able to perform any task except for the administrative tasks listed above. They should be able to perform per-machine installations and uninstallations of applications that do not install system services. They should also be able to customize system-wide resources (including System Time, Display Settings, Power Configuration, and Printers). In practice, Power Users might not be able to install legacy applications because those applications attempt to replace operating system files during the setup process.

Default access control settings have also been significantly overhauled for Windows 2000, with the groups such as Everyone and Authenticated Users—whose membership is automatically configured by the operating system—no longer being used to assign permissions (with some exceptions for backward compatibility). Instead, only those groups whose membership can be controlled by the administrator are used.

The newly defined default access control settings—available following a clean installation of Windows 2000—provide for a standard secure Windows 2000 environment. Once applications that satisfy the Windows 2000 Application Specification have been deployed, security can be further increased by effectively removing the need to make users members of the Power Users Group.

Summary

In this chapter, we've introduced some of the more important new security functionality of the Windows 2000 distributed security model. This functionality consists of a variety of security enhancements unavailable in previous versions of Microsoft operating systems that should serve to make Windows 2000 the most secure widely deployed operating system. Correctly deployed and administered, Windows 2000 can help improve your existing network and communications security solutions and processes.

Chapter 2
Windows NT 4.0 Security Review

While Windows 2000 has much new security functionality, and many dialogs have changed, many of the existing underlying security structures remain unaltered. This chapter will offer a helpful review of the main security features of Windows NT 4.0, allowing you to clearly see both the differences and the similarities between Windows NT 4.0 and Windows 2000. You'll also see the security evolution of the Windows NT product family. In later chapters, we'll examine these differences in more detail. In this way we hope to ease the transition for those migrating from Windows NT 4.0 to Windows 2000. In later chapters we'll point out Windows 2000 features that have a Windows NT 4.0 equivalent.

Overall System Security Design

The Windows NT security architecture can be broken down into a number of interrelated components. Figure 2-1 on the following page presents an overview of the architecture.

As you can see in the figure, the architecture is divided into two modes: *kernel mode,* where highly privileged code requiring direct access to memory and hardware operates; and *user mode,* where applications and windows subsystems reside.

In user mode, the operating system allocates memory space, and applications and subsystems are protected from each other and from the privileged operating system code. While much of the security subsystem resides in user mode, the two components that ultimately control access to all system resources—the Security Reference Monitor and Object Manager—reside in kernel mode.

Secure Logon Process

Access to a system is enforced by means of a mandatory logon. This is a fundamental security requirement, and one amplified by the C2 requirements of the U.S. Trusted Computer Security Evaluation Criteria (TCSEC). This identification and authentication is the foundation of the Windows NT security system. Without identifying and authenticating the user logging on to the system, access to objects cannot be controlled, user rights and abilities cannot be enforced, and accountability cannot be maintained via auditing. For these reasons Windows 95 and Windows 98 can never be considered secure operating systems. For Windows NT, however, security was a primary design requirement. This requirement manifests itself throughout the operating system, and is first evident to the user during the logon process. The logon process differs slightly depending on whether the user is attempting to log on to the local system or on to a domain.

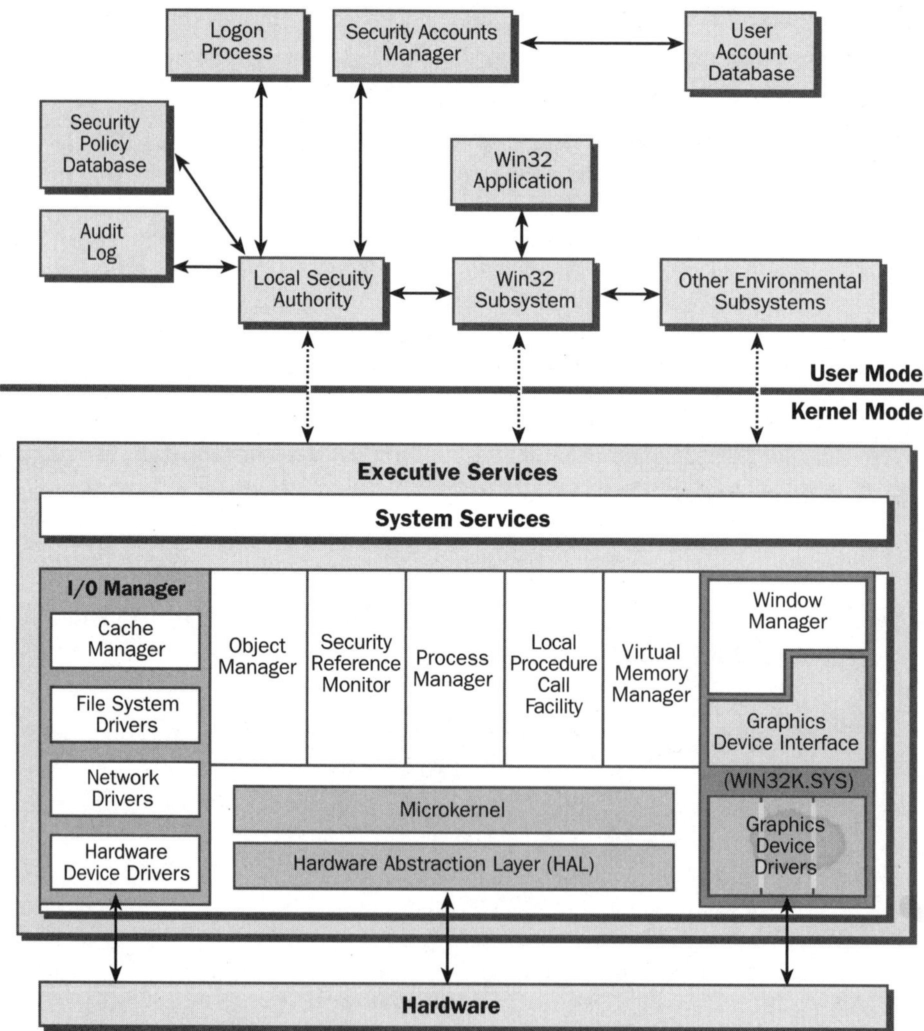

Figure 2-1. *Windows NT 4.0 security architecture.*

Winlogon

At the heart of the authentication process, Winlogon authenticates and logs on the interactive user. Winlogon is part of an interactive logon model that consists of three components: the Winlogon executable, a Graphical Identification and Authentication (GINA) dynamic-link library, and a number of network providers.

The Winlogon executable handles both nonuser interface functions and functions that are independent of authentication policy. Winlogon has the following responsibilities in providing authentication facilities to Windows NT and Windows 2000:

- **Window station and desktop protection.** Winlogon sets the protection of the window station and corresponding desktops to ensure each is properly accessible.
- **Standard secure attention sequence (SAS) recognition.** Winlogon has special hooks that allow it to monitor Ctrl+Alt+Del as a secure attention sequence. Winlogon makes this special relationship available to GINAs to use as their SAS or as part of their SAS.
- **SAS routine dispatching.** When Winlogon encounters a standard SAS or when GINA delivers a SAS to Winlogon, Winlogon sets the appropriate state, changes to the Winlogon desktop, and dispatches to one of GINA's SAS processing routines.
- **User profile loading.** Following successful logon, but before activation of the shell for the newly logged-on user, Winlogon loads the appropriate user profile into the registry under the HKEY_LOCAL_USER key.
- **Assignment of security to user shell.** When a user logs on, Winlogon provides a service for GINA in which the newly logged-on user's security is applied to one or more initial processes created for that user.
- **Screen saver control.** Winlogon is responsible for monitoring keyboard and mouse activity to determine when to activate and terminate a screen saver. If the screen saver is marked as secure, Winlogon treats the workstation as locked. When there is mouse or keyboard activity, Winlogon invokes a GINA function and normally locked workstation behavior resumes. If the screen saver is not secure, any keyboard or mouse activity terminates the screen saver without notification to GINA.
- **Multiple network provider support.** Multiple networks installed on a Windows NT system, such as Novell, can be included in the authentication process and in password-updating operations. When a logon process such as Winlogon is logging on or changing the password for an account, it can make this information available to additional networks for identification and authentication purposes. These additional networks might need to perform secondary authentication.

Winlogon exists in three states, with associated desktops:

- **Logged-off.** The Winlogon desktop is used for interactive identification and authentication and other secure dialog boxes. Winlogon switches to this desktop automatically once it receives a SAS. At this point, users are prompted to identify themselves and provide authentication information. If correctly identified, and assuming there are no restrictions to prevent it, the user is logged on and a shell program is activated in the user's context. Winlogon changes to the logged-on state.
- **Logged-on.** Once a user has successfully logged on, an application desktop is created from which users can interact with the shell (Windows Explorer), activate additional applications, and generally perform their work. This desktop is protected so that nothing but the system and the particular instance of the interactive logon session can access it. If the interactive user also activates a process using the service controller, that service application will not be able to access the application desktop. From the logged-on state, users can either stop all work and log off, or lock their workstations. If the user decides to log off, Winlogon will terminate all processes associated with that logon session and the system will be available for another user. If the user decides to lock the workstation, a secure desktop is displayed.
- **Workstation-locked.** When in the workstation-locked state, the secure desktop is displayed either until the user unlocks the workstation or until an administrator forces a logoff. If the workstation is unlocked, the user's typical desktop is again displayed and work can resume. If, however, an administrator unlocks the workstation, the logged-on user's processes are terminated and the system becomes available for another user to log on.

Graphical Identification and Authentication

GINA is a replaceable dynamic link library (DLL) component loaded by the Winlogon executable. Windows NT is shipped to load and execute the standard Microsoft GINA (MSGINA.DLL). GINA implements the authentication policy of the interactive logon model and performs all identification and authentication user interactions. GINA is replaceable, and provides export functions that independent software vendors (ISVs) and developers can use to modify their interactive logon models. Using this facility, you can use smart cards, biometrics, or other authentication mechanisms in place of the standard Windows NT username and password authentication. The Microsoft GINA (MSGINA) provides the following functionality.

Legal Notification Dialog Box

MSGINA provides for company-specific messages to be displayed before normal logon. These messages, controlled by the contents of two registry keys, are displayed in a Legal

Notice dialog box displayed before the normal Welcome screen. The caption of the dialog box is taken from one of these key values, while its message is taken from the other.

Don't Display Last Username

By default, the MSGINA logon screen displays the name of the last user to successfully log on to a computer. This behavior is controlled by a registry key value that—when set to 1—will ensure that the logon dialog box doesn't display any usernames.

AutoAdmin Logon

This MSGINA feature allows a Windows NT or Windows 2000 system to log on a user automatically, either for the duration of a single session (in which case the user must have a null password), or every time that the system boots or the user logs off. Both the specified user account and its password are stored in the registry. The absence of a password indicates a one-time-only logon. By default, MSGINA overrides autologon and provides standard authentication interactively. You can disable this behavior.

Allow Unauthenticated Shutdown

You can configure MSGINA to include a Shutdown button in the logon dialog box, permitting users to shut down the system without first logging on.

Userinit.exe Activation

MSGINA activates the Userinit.exe application at user logon time, running the application in the newly logged-on user's context and on the user's desktop. Its purpose is to set up the user's environment by restoring net uses, establishing profile settings, and running logon scripts, including those of network providers. MSGINA then activates the user shell program or programs—Windows Explorer by default—that inherit the environment that Userinit.exe sets up.

Logged-On Security Options

If a user enters a SAS while logged on, he or she is presented with the following range of security options. An alternative GINA can also present these options when a SAS is provided while a user is logged on.

- Shut down the system.
- Log off.
- Change your password.
- Go to the task list.
- Lock the workstation.

Interactive Logon to Local Machine

When a user attempts to log on to a local system, the sequence of events illustrated in Figure 2-2 (shown on the following page) occurs.

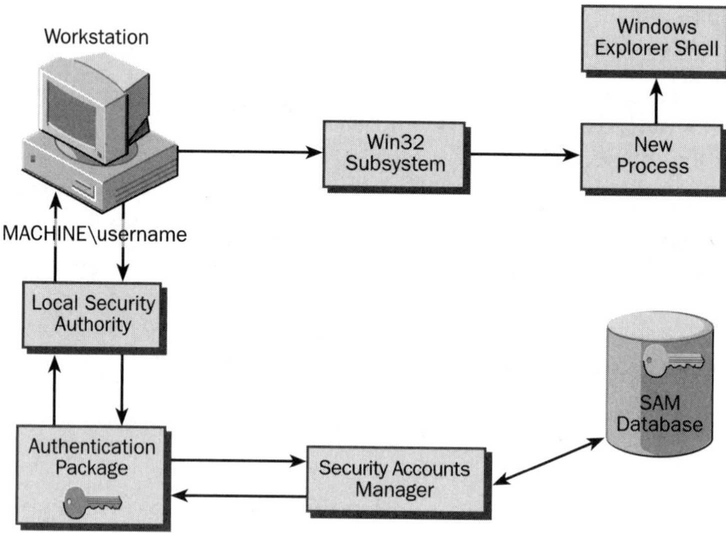

Figure 2-2. *Interactive logon using a local account.*

1. The user presses Ctrl+Alt+Delete to display a logon dialog box. This provides a trusted path to the operating system and ensures that a Trojan horse program (a program designed to look like a logon dialog and thus capture user passwords) is not running.
2. The user provides a username and password. In a system that is part of a domain, the local machine name must also be selected in the logon dialog.
3. The logon process hashes the password, using a LAN Manager One-Way Function (OWF) and the Windows NT OWF, and sends it to the Local Security Authority (LSA).
4. The LSA calls the MSV1_0 authentication package. This is split into two halves: The top half executes on the machine that the user is logging onto (or connecting to); the bottom half executes on the machine containing the user account. In the case of an interactive logon, the top half talks directly to the bottom half, which checks the SAM database. If the user account details are found and the hashed passwords match, the SAM returns the user's security identifier (SID) together with any group SIDs that the user is a member of.
5. The authentication package then creates a logon session and passes the SIDs to the LSA.
6. The LSA creates a security access token using the SIDs returned by the authentication package and other built-in group SIDs. (We'll discuss these later in this chapter.)

7. A handle to the access token is returned to the logon process with a success status. The logon session calls the Win32 subsystem to create a process and attach the access token, thus creating a subject for the user account.
8. If the logon is rejected, the logon session is deleted and an error is returned to the logon process.

Interactive Logon to a Domain User Account

If the user is going to log on to the computer using an account defined in a Windows NT domain, the sequence of events illustrated in Figure 2-3 occurs.

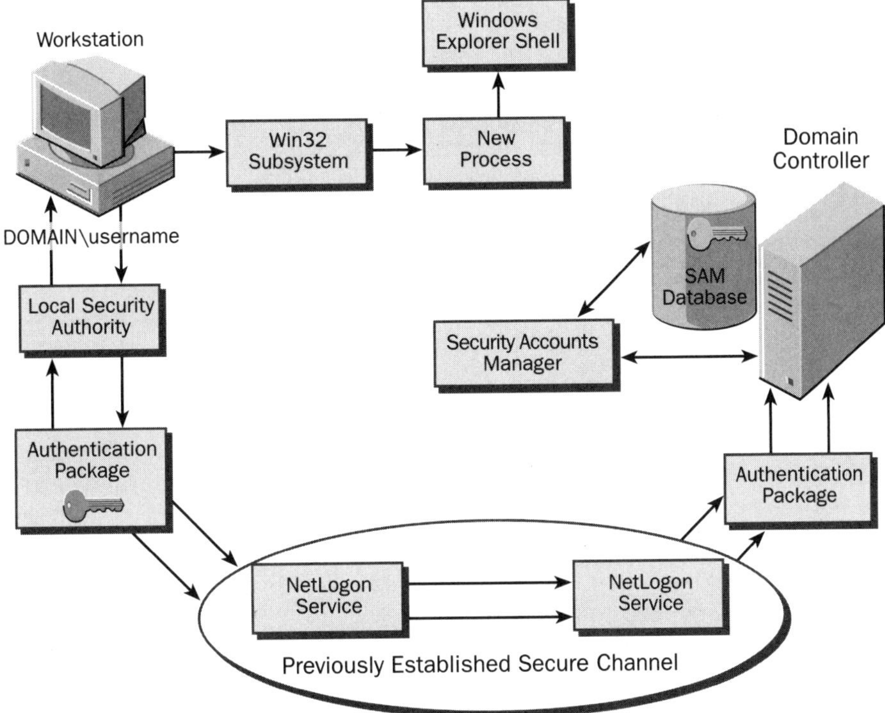

Figure 2-3. *Interactive logon using a domain account.*

1. The user presses Ctrl+Alt+Delete to display a logon dialog box. This provides a trusted path to the operating system and ensures that a Trojan horse program is not running.
2. The user provides a username and password, along with the name of a domain against which the user wants to be authenticated.

3. The logon process hashes the password using a LAN Manager OWF and Windows NT OWF and sends it to the LSA.
4. The LSA runs the appropriate authentication package—normally MSV1_0. Because the domain name provided by the user is different from the local computer name, the top half of the authentication package calls the NetLogon service to forward the user logon information to a domain controller for the specified domain. The NetLogon service already has a secure connection with a domain controller for the domain the computer is joined to. The user's name and encrypted password hash are forwarded to the NetLogon service on the domain controller for verification.
5. The NetLogon service on the domain controller calls the bottom half of the MSV1_0 authentication package locally with the user's details to obtain the correct hashed password from its SAM database. If the user account details are found and the hashed passwords match, the SAM returns the user's SID together with any group SIDs that the user is a member of. This information is returned to the NetLogon service on the domain controller, which returns the information over the secure connection to the NetLogon service on the user's workstation.
6. NetLogon on the workstation returns the SIDs to the authentication package MSV1_0. The local authentication package then creates a logon session and passes the SIDs to the LSA.
7. The LSA creates an access token using the SIDs returned by the domain controller's authentication package, along with other built-in group and local group SIDs. The LSA also saves a protected copy of the LAN Manager OWF and Windows NT OWF in memory to use later if the user attempts to make network connections to remote servers.
8. The handle to the access token is returned to the logon process with a success status. The logon session calls the Win32 subsystem to create a process and attach the access token, thus creating a subject for the user account. In an interactive session, the Win32 subsystem starts the Windows Explorer shell.
9. By default, the Windows NT workstation caches the authentication information of the last 10 users who successfully logged on. The username and domain information is saved with an encrypted copy of the users' Windows NT password hash. The cached logon information is stored in the Security portion of the local registry, in what are known as LSA secrets. This technique allows a user to log on to the local workstation using the domain account information when a domain controller for the domain is not available.
10. If the logon is rejected, the logon session is deleted and an error is returned to the logon process.

Network Logon

Network logon happens when a user attempts to connect to a remote server on a network that is also a member of the same Windows NT domain or a trusted domain. Network logon occurs when a client connects to a server. It happens "under the covers" in most cases. Figure 2-4 illustrates the sequence of events in a network logon.

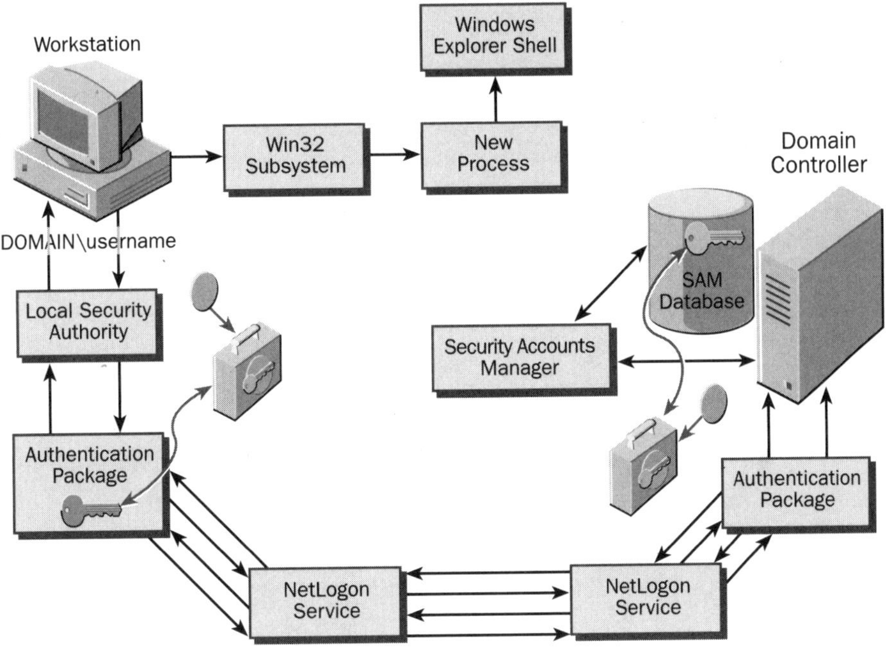

Figure 2-4. *Network logon.*

The user does not need to do another interactive logon. A good example of a network logon is connecting to a remote file server. When the network connection to the remote file server is created, the NTLM challenge/response occurs. The steps are as follows:

1. The user attempts to connect to network share by mapping a network drive—without entering in alternate username/password information.
2. The file system redirector attempts to connect to the file server service.
3. The file server generates a nonce (a server-specified data string) to use for NTLM authentication and sends the nonce to the client.
4. The client signs the nonce in the LSA using the saved password hashes from the successful interactive logon.

5. The client returns the signed nonce to the server.
6. The server takes the client's domain, username, challenge (a nonce generated when the user logged on), and signed nonce, and calls LSA for authentication.
7. LSA calls the MSV1_0 authentication package, passing in the network authentication information. MSV1_0 looks at the domain name. If it is the domain for the local computer, MSV1_0 verifies the signed nonce using the user account hash from the local SAM.
8. If the domain name is different from the local computer, MSV1_0 passes logon information to the NetLogon service. The NetLogon service forwards the logon information to the NetLogon service on the domain controller. The NetLogon service on the domain controller calls the local authentication package, MSV1_0, passing in the user logon information. MSV1_0 on the domain controller verifies the signed nonce using the password stored in the SAM on the domain controller.
9. If logon information is verified, MSV1_0 on the domain controller returns SIDs to the NetLogon service on the domain controller, which in turn returns them to the NetLogon service on the server.
10. MSV1_0 on the file server passes the SIDs to LSA, which builds an impersonation access token that represents the client, or user, initiating the network connection.
11. The file server thread handling the remote client request then impersonates the user and attempts to complete any file operations. These operations either succeed or fail based on access permissions in the file system for that user.

The network authentication protocol we just described remains in Windows 2000 for backward compatibility. For example, Windows 2000 workstations will go through this same network authentication sequence when connecting to a Windows NT 4.0 server. In Windows 2000, the default network authentication protocol has changed to Kerberos v5 authentication.

Pass-through Authentication

Pass-through authentication usually occurs when a user attempts to authenticate to a domain that is not the domain that the user's computer belongs to (in other words, the computer that the user's account is registered on). In this case, the computer's domain controller checks whether the domain is a trusted domain. If it is, the NetLogon service on the initial workstation passes the logon information to the NetLogon service on the first domain controller, which forwards it to the NetLogon service on the second domain controller (in the trusted domain where the user's account resides). The NetLogon service on the account (trusted) domain uses the MSV1_0 authentication package to validate the account information and return the appropriate SIDs to the NetLogon service on the first domain controller (in the computer's domain). In turn, the computer's domain returns the information to the workstation. If the computer being connected to is a backup domain controller (BDC)—in which the user account is defined but the password differs—the BDC forwards the logon request to the primary domain controller (PDC) in the same domain. This scenario will take care of a situation in which a password change has not been replicated to the BDC. If the user attempts to make a connection to a computer in a domain that is not trusted, the logon proceeds as if the user were connecting to an account on the remote computer. If the user can't be authenticated against the desired domain or computer, the logon fails.

Impersonation

Windows NT supports the ability for servers to impersonate a remote user, or client, by adopting that user's token. This ability is important in a distributed environment in which, for example, a server might want to use Windows NT access control for determining which operations the user is allowed to perform.

To further clarify, consider that most services are running with the privileges of the local system account. When the service running as a local system attempts to access a file, that service would automatically have full access. However, the user account interacting with the service might not. To ensure that the file is protected as its owner intended, the service therefore impersonates the user: the user's Impersonation Access Token is compared to the access control list on the file.

Local Security Authority

The Local Security Authority (LSA) is one of the central components of the security subsystem. The LSA is responsible for validating all local and remote user logons, generating security access tokens, and managing the local security policy, including controlling the audit policy. The LSA is also responsible for writing to the event logs any audit messages produced by the Security Reference Monitor.

Security Reference Monitor

The Security Reference Monitor (SRM), which runs within the kernel, is responsible for enforcing all access validation and audit policies within the local security policy. As such it prevents direct access to objects by any user or process, thereby ensuring that any protection is provided uniformly to objects within the system. The SRM works in conjunction with the Object Manager to validate access to objects and generate any audit messages required. When access to an object is requested, the SRM compares the contents of the object's ACL with the contents of the user's access token. If access is granted to the object, the SRM allocates a handle to the process and this handle is used for all other similar access requests, negating the need for further access checking.

Object Manager

The Object Manager is responsible for the naming, security, allocation, and disposal of Windows NT objects on the system. Windows NT objects include the following components, along with other system objects used in system programming:

- devices
- directories
- files
- network shares
- ports
- printers
- processes
- symbolic links
- threads
- windows

Security Accounts Manager

The security accounts manager (SAM) is responsible for the control and maintenance of the SAM database. The SAM database is located in a part of the registry that is protected by ACLs that only allow the system and administrators access. The SAM database contains account information for all user and group accounts and provides this information to support user validation during logon. It compares the cryptographic hash of the password given during logon with the hashed value password stored in the SAM database. It then provides the user's SID—as well as the SIDs for any groups the user belongs to—back to the LSA. The SIDs are then used to create a security access token for that user's current session.

Every Windows NT system has a local SAM database. Each workstation or server has a SAM database for local users and groups specific to that computer. Every domain controller has a SAM database that identifies users and groups available for use on all computers in the domain. The SAM database on backup domain controllers is an identical read-only copy of the SAM database on the primary domain controller. In this case, the SAM database from the PDC is replicated to all BDCs, allowing any DC to respond to authentication requests.

The SAM database stores two cryptographic hashes of each user's password:

- **LAN Manager password.** This is stored for backward compatibility with LAN Manager Servers. LAN Manager file servers were used for PC file servers in the mid-to-late 1980s and early 1990s and were available on many different operating systems. Windows 95 and Windows 98 implement LAN Manager authentication. It is based on the standard OEM character set, is not case-sensitive, and can be a maximum of 14 characters long. The LAN Manager password is encrypted using the Data Encryption Standard (DES) algorithm. Because they lack case sensitivity, LAN Manager passwords are much easier to attack via the brute force approach than are Windows NT passwords—the password space (number of possible permutations) is much reduced. Additionally, a weakness in the algorithm permits a password longer than seven characters to be attacked in seven-character chunks. This occurs because all seven characters of the password are individually used to encrypt a known constant to produce both the first eight and last eight bytes of the encrypted password. Any password of seven characters or less in length is immediately identifiable as such from the encrypted version (the second eight bytes of the encrypted password will always be AAD3B4435B51404EE if the second seven characters in the password are null).

- **Windows NT password.** This password is based on the Unicode character set, and is case-sensitive. The Windows NT password is encrypted using the Message Digest 4 (MD4) algorithm.

Comparing Security Between LAN Manager and Windows NT Passwords

Comparing the possible LAN Manager passwords and the number of Windows NT passwords reveals the following.

LAN Manager

The password is effectively 2 × 7 character strings represented by 2 × 8 byte DES encrypted values. Each can be attached independently; each is limited to the original equipment manufacturer character set; and none are case-sensitive.

- Possible characters = 36 (numbers and letters)
- 7-character password = 2 x 36^7 = 2 x 78 billion combinations

Windows NT

The password is a single 16-byte digest of a variable-length string (effectively limited to 14 characters), computed using the RSA MD-4 encryption algorithm. Windows NT passwords are case-sensitive and can be a mix of upper/lowercase characters, numbers, and punctuation.

- Possible characters = 96 (upper/lowercase characters, numbers, and 34 punctuation)
- 14 character password = 96^{14} = 5 billion billion billion combinations

The area of the registry holding the Windows NT and LAN Manager hashed passwords is reversibly encrypted with a derived key; the user's relative ID (RID) is essentially obfuscated as further protection. Access to this area of the registry is also protected by an ACL, effectively denying access to all user accounts except those of an administrator. Security can be further increased, replacing the original obfuscation with stronger 128-bit encryption available in Windows NT 4.0 Service Pack 4.

Discretionary Access Controls

Discretionary access controls (DACs) provide object owners with the ability to control access to the object as well as the level of access available to particular users or groups. You can control access to objects—folders, files, printers, registry keys, and so on—either through GUI-based tools (Windows Explorer, Print Manager, User Manager, and Server Manager) or via the command line. The type of access that you can grant to specific users or groups depends on the type of object concerned. We'll discuss object access in later chapters of this book. Access to objects is normally granted to local groups. Users or global groups requiring access to the resources protected by the ACL can be added to the local group as appropriate.

Underlying the concept of DACs and ACLs is the security descriptor. The security descriptor on an object can contain the following security information:

- Security identifiers (SIDs) for the owner and primary group of the object
- A DACL that specifies the access rights allowed or denied to particular users or groups
- A SACL that specifies the types of access attempts that generate audit records for the object
- A set of control bits that qualify the meaning of a security descriptor or its individual members

Windows NT provides a rich set of security permissions. Irrespective of object type, generic access rights provide the basic building block. These rights are mapped to standard and object-specific access rights. Table 2-1 shows the meaning of each generic access right.

Table 2-1. Generic access rights.

Generic Access Right	Meaning
GENERIC_ALL	read, write, and execute access
GENERIC_EXECUTE	execute access
GENERIC_READ	read access
GENERIC_WRITE	write access

Each object has a set of access rights that corresponds to operations specific to that type of object. In addition to these object-specific access rights, a set of standard access rights corresponds to operations common to most types of objects that can be secured. Table 2-2 shows the meaning for each of the standard access rights.

Table 2-2. Standard access rights.

Standard Access Right	Meaning
DELETE	The right to delete the object
READ_CONTROL	The right to read the information in the object's security descriptor except for the information in the SACL
SYNCHRONIZE	The right to use the object for synchronization
WRITE_DAC	The right to modify the DACL in the object's security descriptor
WRITE_OWNER	The right to change the owner in the object's security descriptor

In addition to the standard access rights, combinations of standard access rights are also defined as shown in Table 2-3.

Table 2-3. Standard access right combinations.

Standard Access Right Combinations	Meaning
STANDARD_RIGHTS_ALL	Combines DELETE, READ_CONTROL, WRITE_DAC, WRITE_OWNER, and SYNCHRONIZE access
STANDARD_RIGHTS_EXECUTE	READ_CONTROL
STANDARD_RIGHTS_READ	READ_CONTROL
STANDARD_RIGHTS_REQUIRED	Combines DELETE, READ_CONTROL, WRITE_DAC, and WRITE_OWNER access
STANDARD_RIGHTS_WRITE	READ_CONTROL

It is a principle of DAC that, by default, the owner of an object (Creator/Owner in Windows NT terms) is the only person able to set access controls. Therefore, a user can exclude the administrator from access to certain objects. Windows NT permits a user to allow another user to take ownership of an object. This is a two-stage process: the original owner must allow a user to take ownership of the object; the second user then takes ownership. To conform to the principle but still allow the administrator to retain ultimate control of the system, the administrator can always take ownership of an object. However, having done so, the administrator cannot give the ownership back to the original owner. Thus the act of taking ownership should be visible to the original owner.

Security Identifiers

Windows NT uses security identifiers (SIDs) to uniquely identify security principals. Security principals are users, groups, machines, and domains within the system. A SID is constructed of an issuing authority and a unique identifier. Thus, with the exception of well-known SIDs, each SID is guaranteed to be unique.

When a number of user accounts have the same access requirements, groups make it easier to control access to resources. A user account placed in a group obtains the rights and permissions granted to the entire group. Windows NT provides a number of built-in groups (which have predefined RIDs), with predefined rights and permissions. You can create additional groups as required. You can add user accounts to these groups as necessary. A number of special groups—to which the system controls membership—also exist.

Built-in groups have predefined RIDs, which means the relative group ID within the domain is the same, but the SID is unique for each computer or domain. For example, the Administrators group has a constant RID, but the SID for Administrators is different on every computer. The special groups have predefined SIDs that are the same on every computer. For example, the SID for the Everyone group is the same on every computer.

Understanding these special groups is essential to making full use of the security available on the system. While only the system can allocate users to these groups, the groups can be used to set ACLs on objects. For example, you can grant an Interactive user account access to a file and at the same time deny remote network access to the same user account.

Creator/Owner

Creator/Owner is used on an inherited ACE to refer to the SID of the user who created the object. The SID is not assigned to any user—that is, users are not added to the group, nor is Creator/Owner added to the access token.

Interactive

Interactive is a constant SID added to the security access token that identifies that this token represents a user who is interactively logged onto the machine. When used to grant permissions, Interactive means that only users who are interactively logged on will be allowed access.

Network

Network is a constant SID added to the access token associated with a network logon. When used to grant permissions, Network means that any authenticated user via a remote network connection will be allowed access.

Everyone

Everyone is added to all access tokens. When used to grant permissions, Everyone means that all authenticated users—as well as any anonymous or unauthenticated network connections—are granted permissions.

System

System is the operating system components and any Windows NT system service, or application service, running as the local system.

Authenticated Users

Authenticated Users was introduced in Service Pack 3 to identify users who are authenticated to the system by interactive or network authentication—and to differentiate from Everyone, which includes anonymous network connections.

Security Access Token

The LSA creates a security access token as part of the interactive or network logon process. Access tokens are associated with application processes and identify the user who initiated the process activity. Every process on the system has an associated access token. When the user logs off, all processes associated with the user terminate and the access token is destroyed. An access token contains the following information:

- User's SID
- Group SIDs to which the user belongs
- A logon SID that identifies the current logon session
- User or Group privileges
- Owner SID (to be assigned to any object created during the current session)
- Primary Group SID (for POSIX use)
- The default DACL that the system uses when the user creates a securable object without specifying a security descriptor
- The source of the access token
- Whether the token is a primary or impersonation token
- An optional list of restricting SIDs
- Current impersonation levels

The security access token ensures that processes running on a user's behalf do not have greater access to an object than the user does; in other words, they operate in the *security context* of that user. A *subject* is the combination of a user's security access token and the process acting on behalf of the user. To accommodate a client-server model, Windows NT supports two types of subjects:

- **A simple subject.** The user's primary security access token—issued to the user at logon—is used to control the security context the process operates under.
- **A server subject.** The process has been implemented as a protected server process and can have multiple subjects as clients. The process has its own primary security access token describing its own security context. When a client connects to a protected server, the server can use the appropriate user's security access token to perform actions in the client's security context, rather than the server's own security context.

When a server needs to act in a client's security context, it will usually use a technique called impersonation, in which a particular thread of the server process has an impersonation security access token that identifies the client. Using the impersonation token, the process thread can check the client's access to specific securable objects and generate audit events, thereby correctly identifying the client. Alternatively, the server can get the client's credentials and log the client on to the server's computer. This client logon session is normally only necessary if the server needs to use the client's security context to access network resources.

Think of the security access token as an ID card that details an individual's level of access, as shown in Figure 2-5.

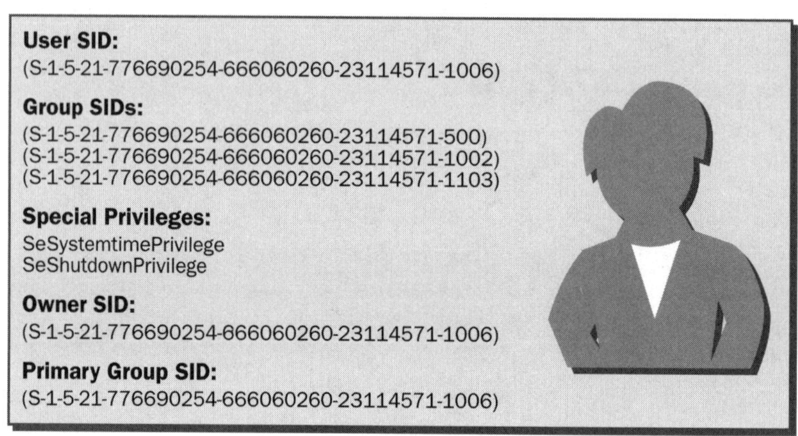

Figure 2-5. *Security access token.*

Access Control Lists

Objects within a Windows NT system can be protected by a security descriptor that contains an access control list (ACL). ACLs contain access control entries (ACEs) detailing the type of access granted to a particular group or user for the given object (for a DACL) or the type of auditing required (for a SACL). The lack of an ACE in a DACL means all requests for access to that object will be denied, except in special cases relating to the object's owner or the system administrators.

Access permissions identified by ACEs are cumulative—except for No Access—so a user granted read permission by virtue of his or her SID and write permission by virtue of his or her membership in a group would have both read and write permissions to the object. If the user is a member of a third group that had been explicitly denied access, the denial overrides any other access permissions.

Windows NT 4.0 supports both access-allowed and access-denied ACEs. The user interface for setting security permissions does not expose the ability to set access-denied ACEs, although programs could use Win32 security APIs to define deny permissions.

Here is a sample ACL (produced by using Checkacl.exe) for the file Test.txt:

```
Owner: BUILTIN\Administrators (alias)
       excess size(*pOwner) == 15 bytes
       Administrators (unknown type)
Group: Test1\None (group)
       None (unknown type)
DACL: 3 ACEs
  DACL, entry 0
    ACE type: access-denied
    Trustee:
      Guests (group)
    Inheritance:
      NO_INHERITANCE
    Permissions:  0000 0000  0001 1111 - 0000 0001  1111 1111
      DELETE
      READ_CONTROL
      WRITE_DAC
      WRITE_OWNER
      SYNCHRONIZE
      STANDARD_RIGHTS_REQUIRED
      STANDARD_RIGHTS_ALL
  DACL, entry 1
    ACE type: access-allowed-set
    Trustee:
      Administrators (group)
    Inheritance:
      NO_INHERITANCE
    Permissions:  0000 0000  0001 1111 - 0000 0001  1111 1111
      DELETE
      READ_CONTROL
      WRITE_DAC
      WRITE_OWNER
      SYNCHRONIZE
      STANDARD_RIGHTS_REQUIRED
      STANDARD_RIGHTS_ALL
  DACL, entry 2
    ACE type: access-allowed-set
    Trustee:
      Everyone (group)
    Inheritance:
      NO_INHERITANCE
    Permissions:  0000 0000  0001 0010 - 0000 0000  1010 1001
      READ_CONTROL
      SYNCHRONIZE
```

```
SACL: 1 ACEs
  SACL, entry 0
    ACE type: audit-success
    Trustee:
      Everyone (group)
    Inheritance:
      NO_INHERITANCE
    Permissions:  0000 0001  0001 1111 - 0000 0001  1011 1111
      DELETE
      READ_CONTROL
      WRITE_DAC
      WRITE_OWNER
      SYNCHRONIZE
      ACCESS_SYSTEM_SECURITY
      STANDARD_RIGHTS_REQUIRED
      STANDARD_RIGHTS_ALL
```

The file's DACL contains three ACEs: Guest, which has no access; Administrators, which has full control; and Everyone, which has read access. Notice that the access-denied ACE is always placed at the top of the DACL to ensure that it is the first comparison made. Also notice that there is no inheritance set, as a file is a noncontainer object.

The file's SACL contains one ACE: Everyone. Auditing has been placed on this file for all successful access by the Everyone group.

Accessing an Object

Examining the process of accessing an object shows us how the various security components interact in a typical process. The user logs on to the system and, after completing the logon process, the system creates a security access token and associates the token with all processing activity the user initiates. This access token is attached to any process the user runs on the system concerned (in our example, Microsoft Word). The process requires read access to an object (in this case a file). NTFS reads the file's SID. The file system also obtains a handle to the process token for the Word process running for this user. NTFS calls the SRM, passing in the handle to the access token and a copy of the SID for the file. The SRM implements the access verification routine that determines if the user—or any groups the user is a member of—is granted the desired permissions (read or write). The access verification compares each ACE in the object's ACL against SID information in the user's access token. If the user or a group is explicitly denied access or has insufficient access rights for the required operation, an access-denied message is returned to the process. If the required level of access is permitted, the SRM permits the Object Manager to return a handle to the process, via which it can access the object. The handle will remain valid while the process requires read access to the object. Figure 2-6 illustrates the process.

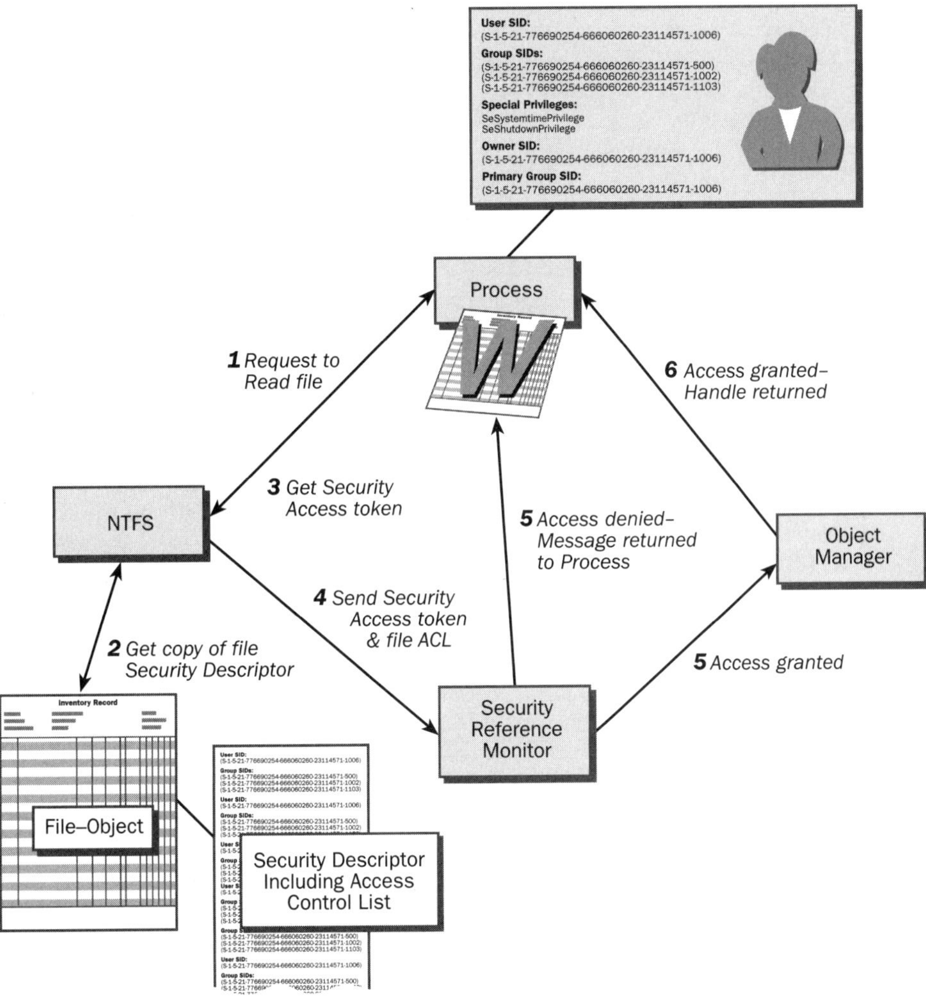

Figure 2-6. *Accessing an object.*

Workgroups, Domains, and Trust Relationships

For the small office, Windows NT provides peer resource sharing, in which the user of an individual system can share the local resources on his or her computer. As the number of users grows, this style of interworking becomes increasingly difficult to manage. Centralizing the administration of the network in a domain offers the next level in scalability. Again, as the network becomes larger, we can use trust relationships to create and link multiple domains. While this model offers a reasonable degree of scalability, the largest organizations will find the lack of a directory structure and the inability to delegate privileges problematic. Windows 2000 attempts to address these and other scalability issues.

Workgroups

A workgroup is a small collection of Windows NT systems that do not share any user or group account information. In such a configuration, each system in the workgroup utilizes only its own SAM database for authentication. Therefore, when the user attempts to access another system, either the guest account must be enabled or an identical user account and password must exist. This configuration is difficult to administer in all but the smallest environments and lacks central control. However, workgroups are sometimes used within a larger installation to tightly control access to an individual machine.

Joining a Domain

Before being permitted to participate in a domain, a computer must be added to the domain's SAM database and have an account password created. In a multidomain environment, computers are usually added to the resource domains. Joining a computer to a domain is accomplished in the Network section of the Control Panel. An appropriate set of user credentials—those of a domain administrator or other user with necessary privileges—is required to authenticate to the domain controller as part of the joining process (unless a computer account has already been created at the domain controller).

Once the computer has joined the domain, the NetLogon service uses the computer account and password to authenticate to a domain controller at startup, before a user starts an interactive logon. NetLogon changes the computer password automatically every seven days. Once authenticated, a secure channel (and trust relationship) is created with the domain controller. User authentication requests sent from the computer to the domain controller are sent over the secure channel. These secure channel messages were authenticated in Windows NT 4.0. Service Pack 4 also introduced encryption and integrity on all NetLogon messages. If the domain has a trust relationship to other domains, the local computer has a trust path that extends to its domain controller and then on to other domain controllers in any trusted domains (using pass-through authentication).

Domains

A Windows NT Domain defines the administrative scope of a security boundary for users, groups, and computer accounts. A Windows NT 4.0 domain is a collection of computers with a central security authority—the primary domain controller (PDC). Thus a domain must consist of a minimum of a PDC and zero or more workstations or member servers. In practice, a backup domain controller (BDC) would be provided for all but the smallest or least mission-critical installations. BDCs provide multiple identical copies of the domain-wide SAM database to increase availability and distributed authentication service to multiple servers.

The presence of a BDC provides distributed authentication and a degree of load balancing. A domain allows a common user-account database and common security policy to be shared and eliminates the need for every computer to provide its own authentication service. Once a user has been authenticated to a domain using the authentication service of either the PDC or a BDC, that user can access resources anywhere within the domain, subject to his or her having the necessary permissions.

Trust Relationships

Windows NT uses trusts to define relationships between domains. Trusts allow domains to share resources, and they can ease administration. Trust relationships allow distributed networks to grow in size and scope by allowing users from one domain to make authenticated network connections to servers located in other domains.

Trusts consist of two entities, a *trusted domain* and a *trusting domain*. A trusted domain (sometimes called the accounts domain) is a domain where user accounts that the trusting domain accepts as valid reside. In diagrams of domain models, an arrow points to the trusted domain; you can think of it as pointing toward people you can trust. A trusting domain (sometimes called the resource domain) contains the resources the user is accessing.

Thus, by default, a trust exists only in one direction (one-way trust). Trusts can, however, be established in both directions (as two one-way trusts) if required. In those cases, both domains trust each other, and user accounts and global groups from either domain can be granted access to resources in the other domain. Figure 2-7 illustrates a one-way trust relationship.

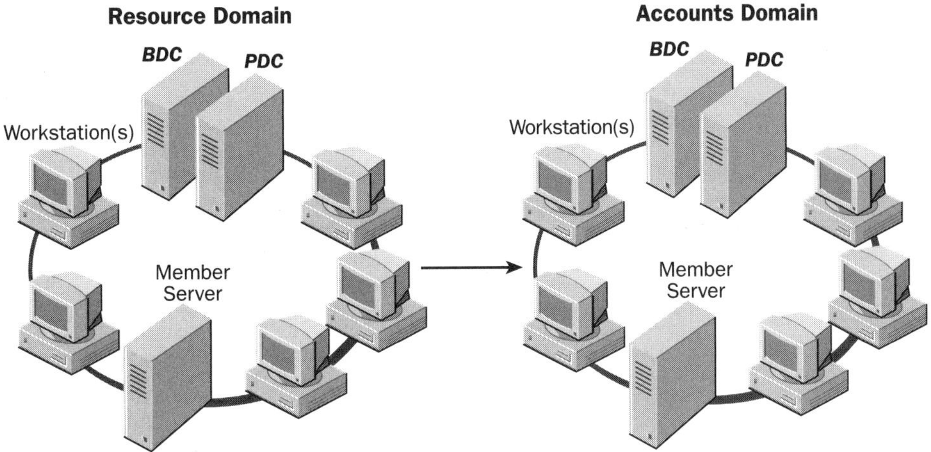

Figure 2-7. *The one-way trust relationship.*

In the figure, the Resource domain trusts the Accounts domain. Thus user accounts in the Accounts domain can receive access to resources in the Resource domain. However, users in the Resource domain are not trusted in the Accounts domain. That means that user accounts defined in the Resource domain will fail to make authenticated network connections to server computers in the Accounts domain. This might present a problem if user accounts in the Resource domain are used to manage access permissions to local resources. Users in the Resource domain might be attempting to look up account information in the Accounts domain—perhaps to establish an ACL on a file or folder. To add user or global groups from the Accounts domain to the ACL, the system requires access to the Accounts domain user account database. This access can often be accomplished using an account defined in the Accounts domain. But a user account in the Resource domain is not trusted to complete this request. This problem is resolved by permitting users in the Resource domain to access information in the Accounts domain as anonymous users. As such, they have read-only access to the user account database. This functionality permits everyone—whether or not they have an account on the Accounts domain—the same level of access. Anonymous access can be restricted, but not without an impact on certain types of domain models.

You can create several domain models using the basic concept of trusts. Each model has particular advantages in a given environment.

Single Domain Model

The single domain model is suited for small organizations that have a centralized organizational structure. Administration is simplified, no trust relationships are required, and definition of groups is easier than in more complex domain models.

Master Domain Model

The master domain model is intended for companies that require centralized control of user accounts and security administration, but whose resources must be managed in a decentralized manner. All user accounts are defined in the master domain, which is often referred to as the Master Account Domain or Master User Domain. Resources—such as file and print servers or database applications—are placed in one or more resource domains. Users are placed in global groups in the master domain and these groups are added to local groups in the appropriate resource domains. The Domain Administrator for the Master Account Domain manages user accounts. The Domain Administrators for each of the Resource domains manage the resource servers and the access permissions to those resources. Figure 2-8 illustrates this model.

The advantage of the master domain model is the centralized administration of user accounts, with a common policy for accounts and passwords. Administrators who manage user accounts do not have administrative control over resources, and resource administrators are not permitted to create new user accounts that have access to anything other than local information. The creation of user accounts in the resource domain is, however, discouraged. The master domain model provides Windows NT users single sign-on with a single user account to all Windows NT services available in the resource domains.

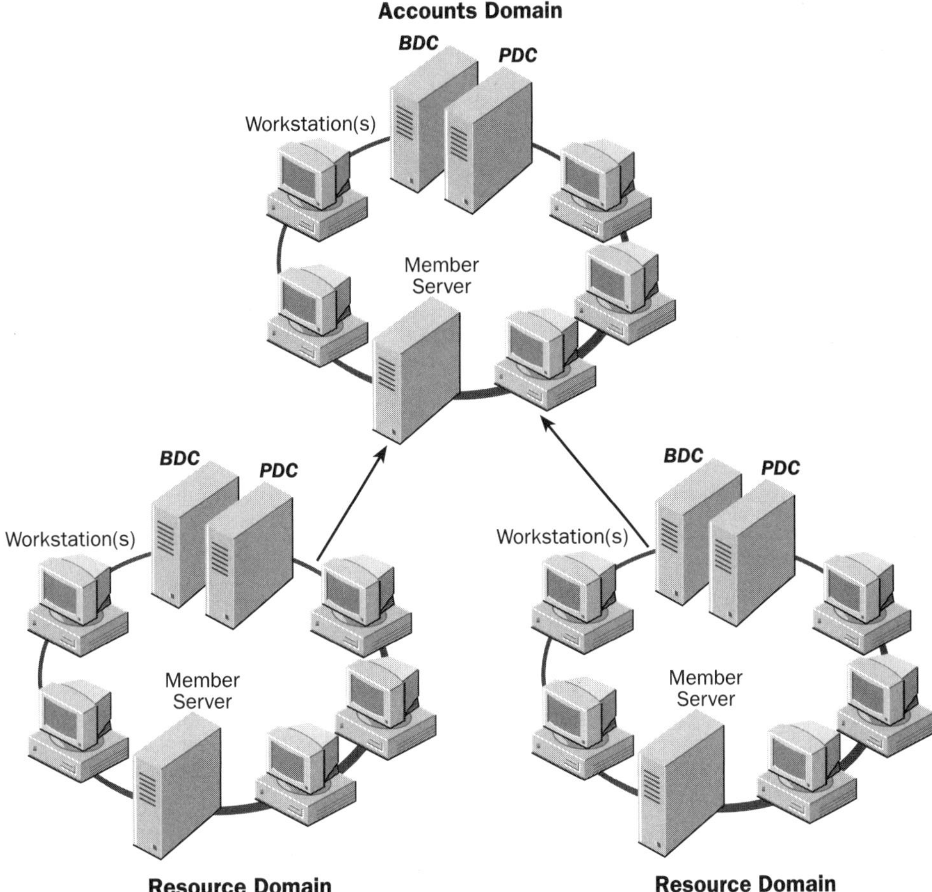

Figure 2-8. *The master domain model.*

Multiple Master Domain Model

The multiple master domain model supports companies comprised of major divisions or diverse geographic locations that need to manage their own user accounts. The model consists of a small number of master domains, each with a two-way trust between them, and a number of resource domains. Thus a user account can be created in any one of the master domains and use resources in any of the trusting resource domains. In other respects the model behaves similarly to the single master domain model; however, it offers far greater flexibility and scalability. Figure 2-9 illustrates the multiple master domain model.

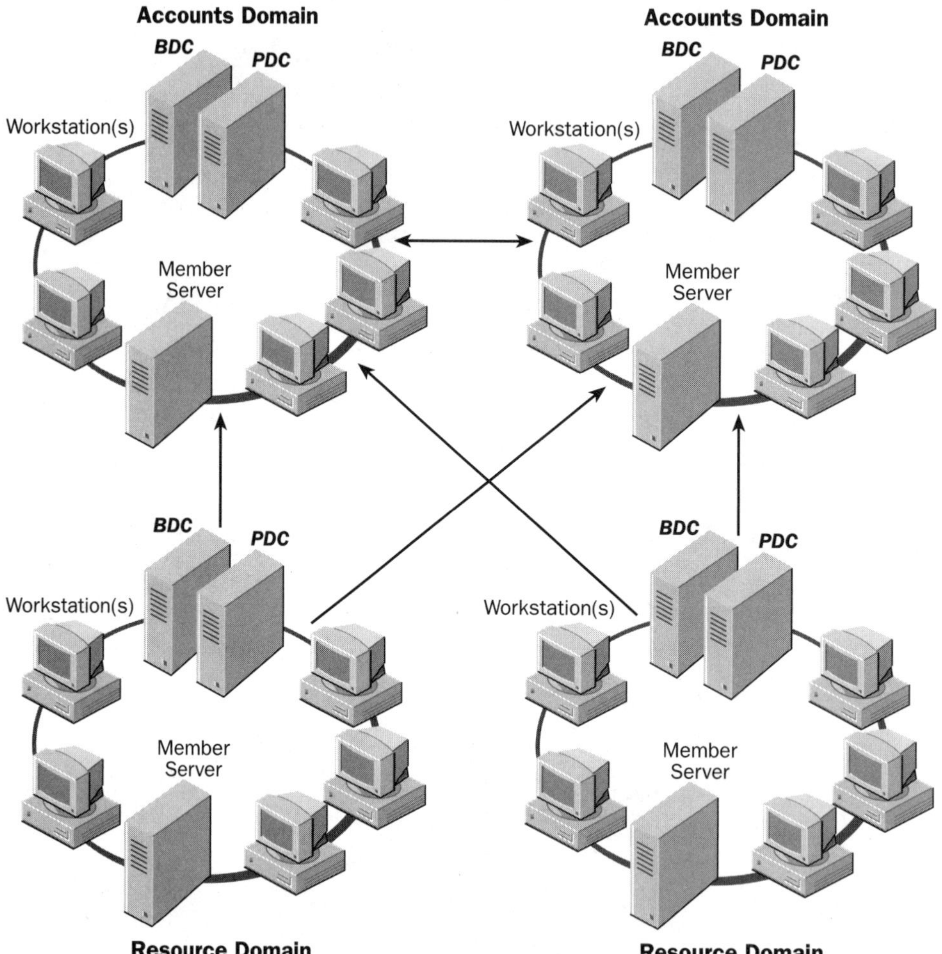

Figure 2-9. *The multiple master domain model.*

The advantage of the multiple master domain model is that different operating divisions or geographic locations (for example, North America, Europe, the Middle East, Asia, and so on) can independently manage their user account databases. However, users from any master account domain can access shared resources available in any trusting resource domain.

Complete Trust Model

The complete trust model offers no centralization of user accounts or security administration. Resource management is also decentralized. Each department maintains its own domain, managing user accounts and resources as required. This model is often used in organizations that need their departments to maintain their own independence. An adequate level of security can be achieved in this model only if there is complete cooperation among administrators. Each department must abide by the corporate security policy to prevent one domain from becoming the weak link. Figure 2-10 illustrates the complete trust model.

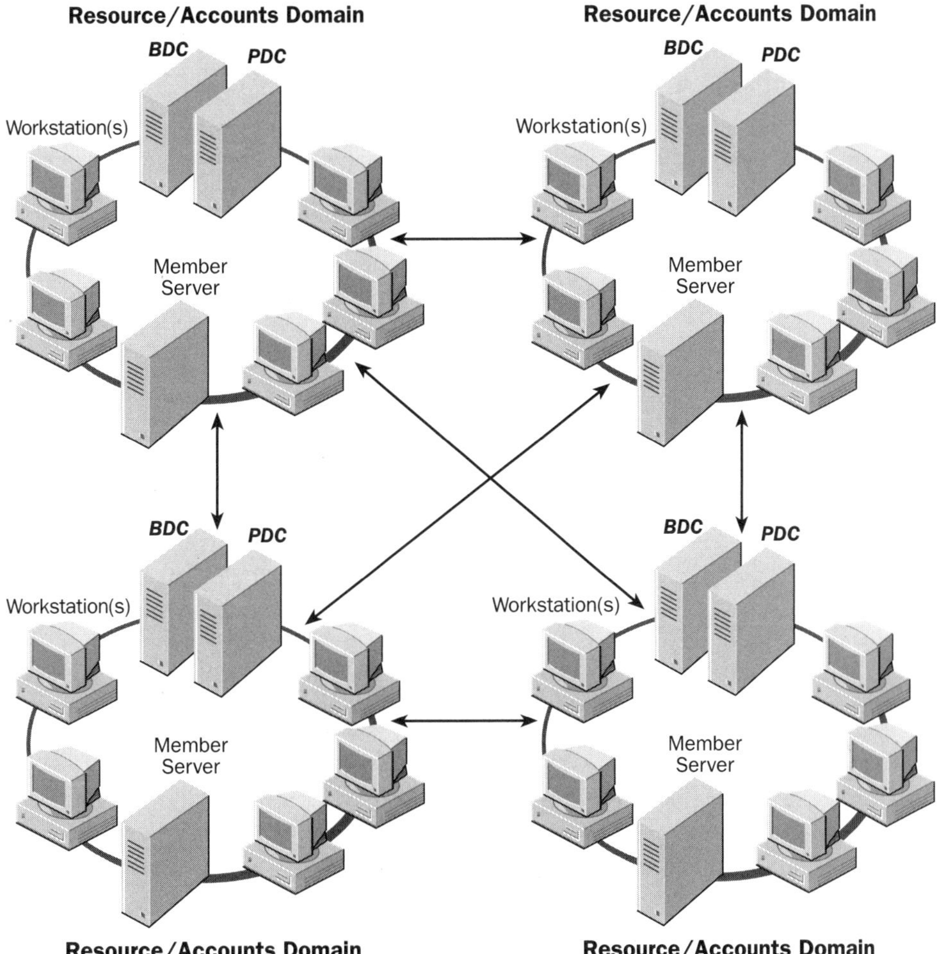

Figure 2-10. *The complete trust model.*

The advantage of the complete trust model is that it lends itself to a less structured relationship between different groups in an organization and allows users from any department to access any available resource. The number of trust relationships to support the complete trust model can grow quickly, depending on the number of domains involved.

Security Considerations

Trust relationships allow organizations to attempt to match their IT infrastructures to their organizational structures. In large corporations, multiple master domains with perhaps hundreds of resource domains are common. In some cases, the number of master domains is intentional; in other cases they are due to size constraints on the SAM database on the Windows NT 4.0 domain's PDC.

Caution As the number of master domains increases—each with a two-way trust to the others—it is increasingly important for all domains to operate the same centrally mandated security policy. Otherwise, domain administrators have no assurance that each domain is operating a similar security posture. A security weakness in one domain can result in an increased level of vulnerability in others.

The need to establish and maintain trusts between domains becomes an administrative problem as the number of domains increases. This is exacerbated by the absence of transitive trusts between domains: in the case of three domains, domain A trusts domain B, and domain B trusts domain C, but domain A does not implicitly trust domain C. This lack of transitive trusts prevents Windows NT 4.0 domains from being structured into a hierarchy, offering only a two-level domain model. Therefore, you cannot build a multi-level tree of domains.

Some resource domains are planned centrally; most are departmental servers used for projects or departmental computing needs. As such they are "unmanaged" by central IT staff. In terms of the central policy, their administrators are not considered trusted and the servers don't need to have two-way trust relationships to the account domains. One advantage of resource domains comes precisely from the difficulty of socially, organizationally, and technically implementing a central security policy everywhere. Lots of users buy a system to support a project and don't want someone from central staff thousands of miles away telling them what they can do with it. The downfall of this model comes when resource domain administrators start creating local domain accounts and establishing trust relationships to other resource domains, thereby effectively bypassing the centralized control and security policy.

The Windows 2000 approach is to remove the current limitation on domain sizing and to provide an enterprise directory to support a full hierarchical domain structure. This model allows for both centralized decision-making and decentralized administration; it also supports interoperability with Windows NT 4.0.

Access Control

The access control model in Windows NT 4.0 (part of the design of Windows NT since the 3.1 release), based upon the user's security access token and the ACL protecting the object, offers a sound basis for security. The user interface to this flexible, object-based security model provides a simple means of managing an object's security properties—and applying security settings—without too much richness or complexity in the implementation.

To further aid and simplify the secure propagation of access controls, Windows NT supports ACE inheritance on objects. Objects are defined as either container objects or noncontainer objects. Container objects can hold other objects (container or noncontainer).

Optionally, all objects within the container can inherit ACEs on container objects. This inheritance is accomplished at the time that the object is created within the container, or optionally when the container's ACL is changed.

File System Access Control

Access control for the file system—which will only function if the volume has been formatted as NTFS—is controlled from the File or Directory permissions dialogs.

File Permissions

For files, the permission dialog offers this high-level grouping of permissions: No Access, Read, Change ("Modify" in Windows 2000), and Full Control. Table 2-4 details these permissions.

Table 2-4. Standard file permissions.

Access Type	No Access	Read (RX)	Change (RWXD)	Full Control
Display file data		X	X	X
Display file attributes		X	X	X
Run file if program		X	X	X
Display file owner and permissions		X	X	X
Change file attributes			X	X
Change data in and append data to file			X	X
Delete file			X	X
Change file owner and permissions				X

Special File Access Permissions

On some occasions the standard file permissions do not provide access permissions granular enough to provide the required level of protection. On those occasions, the underlying permissions (No Access, Read, Write, Execute, Delete, Change Permissions, and Take Ownership) can be assigned in specific combinations by making use of the "Special Access..." option. Table 2-5 gives details of the special access permissions.

Table 2-5. Special file access permissions.

Access Type	No Access	R	W	X	D	P	O	FC
Display file data		X						X
Display file attributes		X		X				X
Run file if program				X				X
Display file owner and permissions		X	X	X				X
Change file attributes			X					X
Change data in and append data to file			X					X
Delete file					X			X
Change file owner							X	X
Change file permissions						X		X

Directory Permissions

As with file permissions, Windows NT supports a comprehensive range of directory access permissions.

The standard dialog offers the high-level groupings of permissions: No Access, List, Read, Add, Read & Add, Change, and Full Control. Table 2-6 details these permissions.

Table 2-6. Standard directory permissions.

Access Type	No Access	List	Read	Add	Read & Add	Change	Full Control
Display directory filenames		X	X		X	X	X
Display directory attributes		X	X	X	X	X	X
Change to subdirectory		X	X	X	X	X	X
Change directory attributes				X	X	X	X
Create subdirectory and add files				X	X	X	X
Display directory owner and permissions		X	X	X	X	X	X
Delete directory and subdirectory						X	X
Change directory permissions							X
Take ownership of directory							X

Special Directory Access: Special File Access

Directories are container objects and therefore have two associated sets of permissions: the permissions on the directory itself, and the permissions that will be inherited by files created within the directory. Subdirectories (container objects) will always inherit all the permissions from the higher-level directory. By default when setting directory permissions using the standard dialog, file permissions are set as shown in Table 2-7. Special Directory Access and Special File Access—available from the standard Directory Permissions dialog—permit these defaults to be changed.

Table 2-7. Standard inherited permissions.

Access Type	Directory Permissions	File Permissions
No Access	None	None
List	RX	Not specified
Read	RX	RX
Add	WX	Not specified
Add and Read	RWX	RX
Change	RWXD	RWXD
Full Control	All	All

The file permissions will be inherited by any file created in the directory after you set the permissions. You can also set these permissions on existing files and subdirectories if required. When access to files is shown as Access Not Specified, users cannot access those files in the directory unless access is granted by another means, such as by setting access permissions on the individual files.

When you copy a file, its permissions are inherited from the directory you copy it into. When you move a file, it retains its original permissions. Files with permissions different from the directories they're stored in can lead to security problems. Though Windows 2000 is based on the Windows NT 4.0 model, it offers the ability to enforce a more robust ACL policy.

New to Windows 2000 is the concept of automatic inheritance. Unlike Windows NT 4.0, Windows 2000 supports automatic inheritance of inheritable ACEs and can differentiate between inherited ACEs and those applied directly to the object. In Windows NT 4.0, an object could inherit ACEs only when it was being created or when a new ACL was being applied to the object. Windows 2000 introduces a new inheritance model in which directly applied ACEs have precedence over inherited ACEs. The system implements this precedence by placing directly applied ACEs ahead of inherited ACEs in a DACL. A file on a Windows 2000 NTFS file system can automatically inherit ACEs from the folder that contains it. Similarly, a registry subkey can inherit ACEs from the key above it in the registry hierarchy. Windows 2000 allows an object to protect itself from inherited ACEs, which was not possible in Windows NT 4.0.

Further changes have been made to the Access Control Editor, which consists of a set of property sheets and property pages that enables the user to view and modify the components of an object's security descriptor. The editor now consists of a basic property page—which provides a simple interface and allows a user to edit an object's ACEs in its DACL—along with an advanced property sheet, which enables the user to edit the object's SACL, change the object's owner, or perform advanced editing of the object's DACL.

Share-Level Security

Directories must be shared to make them available for network client access. The default permission when a share is created is Full Control to the group Everyone. Share-level permissions effectively sit in front of directory and file permissions for network access. As such, they are not as fine-grained and are restricted to No Access, Read, Change, and Full Control. You'll need NTFS permissions if you want to achieve a finer level of control. Used together, share and directory/file permissions permit a high degree of control and are particularly useful in the situation that requires differing access controls, depending on whether a file is being accessed locally or across the network.

Real World Share Levels

An administrator creates a folder on the NTFS file system on a resource server. The folder has several subfolders and multiple files. The two highest subfolders have different but related user communities, each requiring some level of access to the other's folders. The administrator first has to decide whether to create a single share at the highest level or two shares at the next level down the folder hierarchy (either option is possible, depending on several factors and the administrator's personal preference). Let's say your administrator decides to create a single share. Once the share option has been decided, the administrator decides to implement folder and file security as shown in Table 2-8.

Table 2-8. Sample use of folder and file access permissions.

Folder/Files	Security Permissions
Parent Folder-R&D	Share Permissions: Research, Development-Change Folder Permissions: Research-List Development-List
Subfolder-Research	Folder Permissions: Research-Full Control Development-No Access
Subfolder-Development	Folder Permissions: Development-Full Control Research-Read

Even with this simple example, you can see that ACLs provide a rich level of functionality with which to control access to objects. Using the more advanced features available in Windows 2000, you can meet the most demanding of businesses access control policies.

Registry Access Control

Access control to the Windows NT and Windows 2000 registry follows a model similar to that for the file system, except there's only one level of access control—there is no equivalent to the differing file and directory permissions within the file system. The standard Registry Key Permissions dialog exposes only Read, Full Control, and Special Access options. As in the file system, a new registry key created under an existing key will inherit its permissions and, when changing the permissions on a higher-level key, the permissions on its subkeys can also be reset.

As you can see in Table 2-9, the "Special Access Option..." allows access to more fine-grained control.

Table 2-9. Registry access control.

Access Type	Description
Query Value	Read the settings of a value entry in a subkey
Set Value	Set the value in a subkey
Create Subkey	Create a new key or subkey within a selected key or subkey
Enumerate Subkeys	Identify all subkeys within a key or subkey
Notify	Receive audit notifications generated by the subkey
Create Link	Create symbolic links to the subkey(s)
Delete	Delete selected keys or subkeys
Write DAC	Modify the DACL for the key
Write Owner	Take ownership of the selected key or subkey
Read Control	Read security information within selected subkey

Printer Access Control

Printers, like the file system and registry, are also protected by an ACL. Printer permissions are set via the individual printer property page. The printer permission dialog shows settings for group or user access to a particular printer.

There are four sets of permissions allowable: No Access, Print, Manage Documents, and Full Control. Table 2-10 on the following page shows the actions available for each type of permission. New users can, by default, print and manage their own print jobs (because they pick up Creator/Owner permissions), but they can't manage other users' documents. Control of printer availability is configurable separately. A printer can be shared on the network, with the printer's ACL controlling both local and remote access. There is no separate printer-share ACL.

Table 2-10. Printer access control.

Action	No Access	Print	Manage Documents	Full Control
Print documents		X		X
Control settings for documents			X	X
Pause, resume, restart, and delete documents			X	X
Change the printing order of documents				X
Pause, resume, purge printer				X
Change printer properties				X
Delete printer				X
Change printer permissions				X

Security Event Logging

Windows NT 4.0 has comprehensive auditing capabilities. Once a security auditing policy has been established, auditing can be set on most security-related operations within the operating system. While security-specific auditing is limited to the events generated for the security event log, installed applications can provide additional auditing to the application log. System-related events, which are also often useful from a security perspective, are stored in the system event log. Table 2-11 describes the three event logs.

Table 2-11. Windows NT audit logs.

Log Type	Detail
System	Holds information on hardware and operating system events. Also holds print auditing information, if enabled.
Application	Used by applications to record various information. The level of information in this log is heavily application-dependent.
Security	Records security-related actions that the system administrator has chosen to audit (log on, log off, read file, delete file, and so on).

The security audit policy controls whether the following security event categories will be audited:

- File and Object Access
- Logon and Logoff
- Restart, Shutdown, and System
- Security Policy Changes
- Use of User Rights
- User and Group Management

At the policy level, options are provided to record both success and failure for each auditing category. Within each category there are multiple security events. For example, File and Object Access will log Open Handle events when someone attempts to open a file, as well as Close Handle events when someone closes the file. In the case of File and Object Access, enabling the policy provides little in the way of auditing, until specific auditing is enabled for each object type; for example, through the file system, registry, or print manager. Establishing auditing therefore requires a two-step process: first set a policy in User Manager, and then set detailed auditing requirements on particular objects.

As we mentioned earlier, the LSA controls auditing. Enabling (success or failure) auditing categories causes the LSA to generate the corresponding security events to the event log subsystem.

The configuration of all audit logs can be set independently. Windows 2000 extends the Windows NT 4.0 audit facilities to include event logs for the Directory Service, DNS Server, and File Replication Service. In the case of auditing access to objects, Windows 2000 also exposes more granular auditing control.

Users and Groups

To manage users, Windows NT 4.0 uses local user accounts and local and global group accounts. Local users and groups are created in the SAM database on the local computer. When you first install a workstation or standalone server, Windows NT creates a number of predefined users and local groups. When you install a domain controller, Windows NT creates a number of domain groups. Local user and group accounts only have scope on the system on which they are created, while global groups have scope across the domain in which they are created. Windows NT creates only two user accounts by default—the local administrator account and the guest account.

User Rights and Privileges

User rights and privileges provide the means for the local administrator to control who is allowed certain types of access or to perform specific system operations. For example, user rights describe who is allowed to interactively log on to the computer or who is allowed to make a network connection to the computer. Privileges are required for specific operations—such as the ability to back up or restore files, change the system time, or run a program that is part of the trusted computer base of the operating system. Once granted, these privileges are contained in a user's security access token. While granted, privileges are normally only invoked by the specific program requiring them to perform particular tasks that the default security policy would not permit; for example, to back up or restore files. Each local group has associated privileges—as shown in Tables 2-12 and 2-13 on pages 54 and 55—allocated by the system and which cannot be altered.

Table 2-12. Domain controller: built-in abilities.

Built-in Abilities	Administrators	Server Operators	Account Operators	Print Operators	Backup Operators	Users	Guests	Everyone
Manage auditing	X							
Create and manage user accounts	X		X[1]					
Create and manage global groups	X		X[1]					
Create and manage local groups	X		X[1]			X[2]		
Assign user rights	X							
Lock the server	X	X						X[3]
Override the lock of the server	X							
Format server's hard disk	X							
Create common groups	X	X						
Share and stop sharing directories	X	X						
Share and stop sharing printers	X	X		X				

Notes:

[1] Account operators cannot modify the accounts of Administrators, nor can they modify the Domain Admins global group or the Administrators, Servers, Account Operators, Print Operators, or Backup Operators local groups.

[2] Even though users have the right to create local groups on a server, they will not be able to do so unless they have been allowed to log on locally at the server or have access to the User Manager For Domains.

[3] Even though members of the Everyone group have the right to lock the server, only those users also able to log on locally at the server will actually be able to lock it.

Table 2-13. Workstation and standalone server: built-in abilities.

Built-in Abilities	Administrators	Power Users	Users	Guests	Everyone
Manage auditing	X				
Create and manage user accounts	X	X[1]			
Create and manage local groups	X	X[2]	X[3]		
Assign user rights	X				
Lock the workstation	X	X		X	
Override the lock of the workstation	X				
Format workstation's hard disk	X				
Create common groups	X	X			
Share and stop sharing directories	X	X			
Share and stop sharing printers	X	X			

Notes:

[1] A member of the Power Users group can create user accounts, but can modify and delete only those accounts so created.

[2] A member of the Power Users group can create local groups and add and delete users from those groups. A member of the Power Users group can also add and delete users in the Power Users, Users, and Guests local groups. Members of the Power Users group cannot modify the Administrators group.

[3] A member of the Users group can create local groups, but can modify only those local groups so created.

In addition, a number of rights, both standard (as shown in Table 2-14 on page 56) and advanced (as shown in Table 2-15 on page 57) can be allocated independently of a group's abilities.

Table 2-14. Standard user rights.

Standard User Rights	Default Rights on Windows NT Workstation and Standalone Server	Default Rights on Windows NT Domain Controller
Log on locally (*SeInteractiveLogonRight*)	Administrators, Everyone, Guests, Power Users, Users, Backup Operators	Administrators, Account Operators, Backup Operators, Server Operators, Print Operators
Access this computer from the network (*SeNetworkLogonRight*)	Administrators, Everyone, Power Users	Administrators, Everyone
Take ownership of files or other objects (*SeTakeOwnershipPrivilege*)	Administrators	Administrators
Manage auditing and security log (*SeSecurityPrivilege*)	Administrators	Administrators
Change the system time (*SeSystemTimePrivilege*)	Administrators, Power Users (Question Power Users)	Administrators, Server Operators
Shut down the system (*SeShutdownPrivilege*)	Administrators, Everyone, Guests, Power Users, Users	Administrators, Account Operators, Backup Operators, Server Operators, Print Operators
Force shutdown from a remote system (*SeRemoteShutdownPrivilege*)	Administrators, Power Users (Question Power Users)	Administrators, Server Operators
Back up files and directories (*SeBackupPrivilege*)	Administrators, Backup Operators, Server Operators	Administrators, Backup Operators, Server Operators
Restore files and directories (*SeRestorePrivilege*)	Administrators, Backup Operators	Administrators, Server Operators, Backup Operators
Load and unload device drivers (*SeLoadDriverPrivilege*)	Administrators	Administrators
Add workstations to the domain (*SeMachineAccountPrivilege*)	(N/A)	(None)

Table 2-15. Advanced user rights.

Advanced User Rights	Default Rights on Windows NT Workstation and Standalone Server	Default Rights on Windows NT Domain Controller
Act as part of the operating system (*SeTcbPrivilege*)	(None)	(None)
Bypass traverse checking (*SeChangeNotifyPrivilege*)	Everyone	Everyone
Create a paging file (*SeCreatePagefilePrivilege*)	Administrators	Administrators
Create a token object (*SeCreateTokenPrivilege*)	(None)	(None)
Create permanent shared objects (*SeCreatePermanentPrivilege*)	(None)	(None)
Debug programs (*SeDebugPrivilege*)	Administrators	Administrators
Generate security audits (*SeAuditPrivilege*)	(None)	(None)
Increase quotas (*SeIncreaseQuotaPrivilege*)	Administrators	Administrators
Increase scheduling priority (*SeIncreaseBasePriorityPrivilege*)	Administrators	Administrators
Lock pages in memory (*SeLockMemoryPrivilege*).	(None)	(None)
Log on as a batch job (*SeBatchLogonRight*)	(None)	(None)
Log on as a service (*SeServiceLogonRight*)	(None)	(None)
Modify firmware environment variables (*SeSystemEnvironmentPrivilege*)	Administrators	Administrators
Profile single process (*SeProfSingleProcess*)	Administrators	Administrators
Profile system performance (*SeSystemProfilePrivilege*)	Administrators	Administrators
Replace a process-level token (*SeAssignPrimaryTokenPrivilege*)	(None)	(None)
Add workstations to the domain (*SeMachineAccountPrivilege*)	(None)	(N/A)

Note In Windows 2000, the concept of standard and advanced rights has been replaced with a single grouping of user privileges. The Windows NT rights map to Windows 2000 privileges, with the following two additions: Enable computer and user accounts to be trusted for delegation *(SeEnableDelegationPrivilege)*, and remove computer from docking station *(SeUndockPrivilege)*.

Not all abilities are matched by corresponding rights; therefore, it is not possible to completely match a built-in group's abilities by use of rights.

The predefined allocation of abilities to specific groups and the inability to replicate all abilities as rights make it difficult to separate roles and thus enforce the concept of least privilege. The lack of a security structure below the level of a domain also makes the delegation of administrative functions difficult. The introduction of Active Directory in Windows 2000 now allows for separation of roles and delegation of administrative responsibility down the domain and organization hierarchy. A number of new groups have also been added.

Account Policy

An account policy can be defined on a domain-wide basis. It can control the following properties:

- Account lockout policy
- Password length
- Password minimum and maximum age
- Password uniqueness

Additionally, you can add password filtering (providing password content control, such as forcing users to use both characters and numbers in their passwords), as an optional dynamic-link library. On a per-user basis, logon hours and workstations accessed can also be controlled. While offering a superset of the account policy options found in Windows NT 4.0, Windows 2000 has the added ability to control, via the Group Policy, where a policy is to be applied: the site, a domain, or an organizational unit level. Thus, you can enforce multiple account policies across the enterprise.

Policies

A System Policy consists of a set of registry settings that defines the computer resources available to a user or group of users. System Policies—which you create with the System Policy Editor—can be defined for specific users, groups of users, computers, or for all users. Policies control various aspects of the user environment, such as which applications are available, which options appear in the Start menu, who can configure the desktop, and so on.

The System Policy Editor creates a file that contains registry settings. At logon these settings are applied to the user or local machine portions of the registry. The concept of a System Policy has been taken much further in Windows 2000, in the shape of Group Policies. These offer a true superset of the configurable options available in Windows NT 4.0 and include the ability to control most security policy settings. As we've mentioned, a Group Policy object can be applied at the site, a domain, or an organizational unit level, allowing the enforcement of multiple policies across the enterprise.

Summary

Although much has changed in the transition from Windows NT to Windows 2000, the core security functionality remains. On top of this core, Windows 2000 offers much that is new. Underneath the new GUI, anyone familiar with Windows NT security will see the same underlying security concepts of access control lists, security access tokens, SIDs, and so on. The largest architectural change—and one that has a major impact on security—is the introduction of Active Directory. Understanding the security implications of this change—and successfully deploying Active Directory across the enterprise—is critical to the security of a Windows 2000 installation. As you progress through the remainder of this book, you will learn what is new in terms of Windows 2000 security functionality and how you can use it to successfully secure your network.

Chapter 3
Windows 2000 Security Model and Subsystems

This chapter introduces the concepts of the Windows 2000 security model and its subsystems. Subsequent chapters will cover these concepts in greater detail.

Introducing the Security Model

A fundamental relationship exists between Active Directory directory service and the incorporated Windows 2000 security model. Active Directory stores all the domain's security policy information—such as domain-wide password restrictions—that has a direct bearing on the use of the system. Active Directory also stores security policy information for overall domain management. The fundamental relationship is achieved only by completely integrating Active Directory with the Windows 2000 operating system.

Windows 2000 provides a security model that consistently implements access control to all domain resources based on group membership. The Windows 2000 security model enables you to define permissions down to the level of an individual directory object attribute. You can delegate administrative tasks as necessary to various trusted users.

Windows 2000 Server implements an object-based security model and fine-grained access control for all objects contained in Active Directory. Objects with associated security attributes are called *securable objects*. Examples of securable objects include files, user objects, and registry keys. A security descriptor defines the security attributes of securable objects. You implement access control by assigning a unique security descriptor to each Active Directory object. The security descriptor contains information about the owner of the object and the object's primary group. The security descriptor contains two access control lists (ACLs). The discretionary ACL, or DACL, describes who should have access to a particular object and what type of access to grant. The system ACL, or SACL, defines what type of auditing to record for an object. In other words, the SACL contains information about various access events to audit for an object, such as a successful access or a failure to access the particular object.

Administrators can manage properties on objects by monitoring user access, setting permissions, and assigning ownership. In addition to controlling access to a specific object, administrators also control access to specific attributes of that object. For example, when an administrator properly configures the object's security descriptor, a specific user might be allowed access to a subset of information (as illustrated in Figure 3-1), such as reading employees' e-mail addresses but not their home addresses.

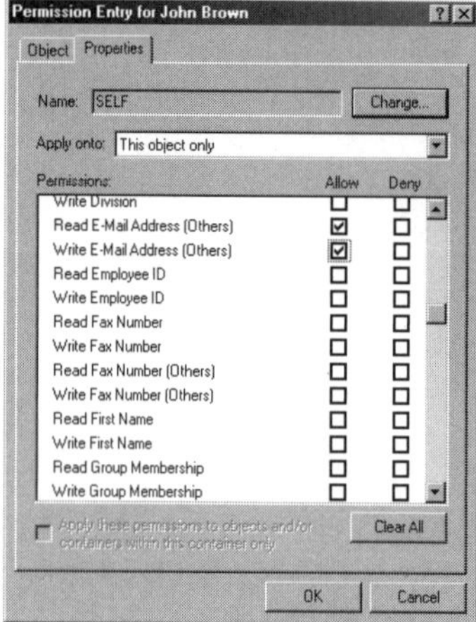

Figure 3-1. *Administrators can allow access to a subset of a security descriptor's information.*

Understanding Security Principals

Active Directory represents physical entities, such as persons and computers, as user accounts and computer accounts. Groups, user accounts, and computer accounts are directory objects called *security principals*. Active Directory automatically assigns security identifiers (SIDs) to these objects for logon authentication and also to enable access to domain resources. A domain controller in the domain where the object is located authenticates the security principal object.

User Accounts and Computer Accounts

Active Directory uses user accounts and computer accounts to perform the following functions:

- Authenticating users and computers
- Administering security principals
- Allowing or denying access to domain resources
- Auditing actions performed with user accounts and computer accounts

When the administrator establishes a trust relationship between a Windows 2000 domain within a particular forest and a Windows 2000 domain outside that particular forest, the administrator can grant access to resources within the internal domain to the security principals from the external domain.

Each security principal from the trusted external domain is represented by a *foreign security principal* created by the trusting domain's Active Directory. Administrators should not manually alter these foreign security principals.

Foreign security principals can become members of domain local groups of the trusting domain. These local groups can in turn have members from other domains outside the forest. You can view foreign security principal objects by enabling Advanced Features on Active Directory Users And Computers.

To enable Advanced Features

1. Choose Active Directory Users And Computers from the Administrative Tools menu.
2. Expand the domain node in the console tree.
3. Choose Advanced Features on the View menu.
4. Click ForeignSecurityPrincipals on the console tree to view the list of foreign security principals available for the domain. Figure 3-2 illustrates this screen.

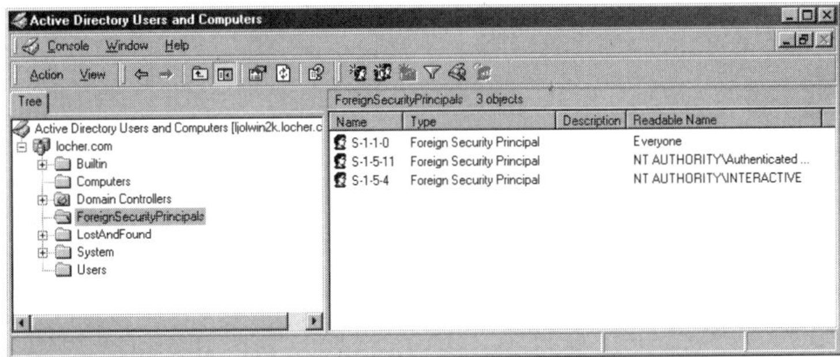

Figure 3-2. *The foreign security principal objects list found under the Active Directory Users And Computers console.*

Naming Security Principals

A security principal name uniquely identifies a user, group, or computer within a single domain. Security principal names must be unique within their own domains, but they are not unique across domains. You can rename, move, or contain security principal objects within a nested domain hierarchy.

Security principal object names must adhere to the following guidelines:

- The security principal object name must be unique to any computer, user, or group name within the domain.
- All leading spaces and periods are cropped from security principal object names.
- Security principal object names cannot consist solely of spaces or periods.

- You cannot use the following characters in a security principal object name: front slash (/), backslash (\), brackets ([ ]), colon (:), semi-colon (;) pipe (|), equal sign (=), comma (,), plus sign (+), asterisk (*), question mark (?), left angle bracket (<), or right angle bracket (>).
- Computer account names can consist of no more than 15 characters. The name can include uppercase and lowercase letters, numbers, and hyphens, but it cannot contain spaces or periods. The name cannot consist entirely of numbers.
- User account names can consist of no more than 20 characters.
- Group account names can consist of no more than 63 characters.

User Accounts

Each user who logs on to the network should be assigned a unique user account and password so that you and the network can both identify that user. This user account and password enables a user to log on to computers and domains with a unique identity that can be authenticated and authorized for domain resources access. Use Active Directory Users And Computers on the Administrative Tools menu to create, disable, delete, and maintain individual user accounts for users who log on to your network.

Predefined User Accounts

When you install the Windows 2000 operating system, you'll be provided with two predefined default user accounts that enable you to log on to a computer locally. You'll use the default accounts primarily for the initial logon and configuration of a local Windows 2000 machine and for access to resources on the local computer. There are two predefined accounts:

- **Administrator local account.** The Administrator account has extensive rights and permissions that permit you (or your organization's administrator) to make changes to any file system or registry object on the local machine. These permissions include the following:
  - Installation of Service Packs, Hotfixes, and operating system components, such as drivers for hardware
  - Upgrades to the operating system
  - Repairs to the operating system
  - Installation and running of legacy Windows-based applications
- **Guest local account.** The Guest account has limited permissions and rights that restrict users to operating and saving documents to the local computer.

The Administrator and Guest user accounts are also used to log on to a domain; therefore, you need to modify these accounts on local machines. To keep your network secure, you should at the very least ensure that the local Administrator password is different from the domain Administrator password and is known only by the network administrators. Depending on the structure of your organization, you might also want to disable the Guest account on local machines. It is important to ensure that each user account and group is appropriate for your network and assigned only the necessary resources.

Computer Accounts

A domain administrator creates a unique computer account for each computer that joins the Windows 2000 domain. The purpose of a computer account is to provide a means for authenticating and auditing the computer's access to the network and to the domain resources. By default, any computer account that the domain administrator creates is automatically added to the Domain Computers group. You can create, disable, delete, and maintain computer accounts using Active Directory Users And Computers on the Administrative Tools menu. The machine's role in the domain, the machine's operating system, and membership information are all stored in the computer account, as illustrated in Figure 3-3.

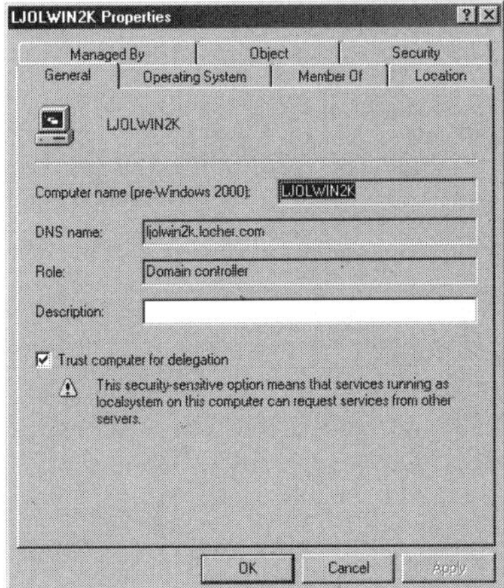

Figure 3-3. *The computer account information found in the Properties dialog box.*

Each computer also receives a SID when the account is first created. The internal processes of Windows 2000 refer to the SID rather than to the computer account's name. This way, if you delete a particular account and then at a later date create an account with the same name, the new account will not receive the rights or permissions previously granted to the old account: the new account is assigned a new SID.

Note Every account on the network—user, computer, and group—is issued a unique SID that identifies it when the account is first created.

Computer accounts create trust relationships with a domain controller. These trust relationships use Microsoft Remote Procedure Call to establish secure channels. The Local Security Authority (LSA) uses secure channels to pass the user's authentication request to a domain controller in a Windows 2000 domain.

Creating a Computer Account

A user with administrator privileges on a local computer can enter the initial computer account name on that computer during the Windows 2000 installation process. However, a user must be a member of the domain administrators group to add the computer account name to a domain controller in a Windows 2000 domain. The computer joins the domain when the domain administrator creates the computer account name at the domain controller. A domain administrator can create the computer account name on the domain controller in two ways. (Creating a computer account on the domain controller is not recommended.)

The user can create the computer account name during the installation process of Windows 2000. If the computer account name does not yet exist on the domain controller, the user requests a valid domain administrator account name and password. The user cannot create the computer account name on the domain controller if valid domain administrator credentials are not presented.

The second way the domain administrator can create the computer account name is through the Active Directory Users And Computers console on the Windows 2000 domain controller.

When an administrator creates a computer account name, he or she needs to consider the following two restrictions:

- To remain consistent with Windows NT and Windows 2000 account management utilities, the computer account name should be in all uppercase letters.
- The maximum length for a computer name is 15 characters.

Once the domain administrator has named the computer in one of the two ways mentioned earlier in this section, the system takes over. A trailing dollar sign ($) always appears at the end of the computer account name. This trailing dollar sign is not included in the 15-character maximum.

The default password assigned for a new computer account is the lowercase representation of the computer account name, minus the dollar sign. The maximum length of the password is 14; the password is truncated if the computer account name exceeds this length. When the computer account becomes active on the domain, the password provided at creation time becomes invalid and a new random password is established in its place.

What Happens When a Computer Joins a Domain

When a Windows 2000 computer joins a domain, the following steps occur:

1. The domain name the computer is trying to join is validated.
2. After the domain name is validated, the local machine locates a domain controller in that domain.
3. A session is established between the machine and the domain controller (located in step 2), using the security context of the passed-in credentials

supplied in the Network Identification tab on the System Properties dialog box in Control Panel.

4. The computer account is enabled at this point and the computer account is created on the domain controller.
5. An object is created for the computer. Appending a dollar sign to the name of the computer account generates the computer object name. The name of the computer object consists of uppercase letters only.
6. The password for this account is created in the LSA. The default password assigned upon creation is changed to a random password. This password changes, by default, every 28 days via a secure channel between the local computer and a domain controller.
7. The local primary domain information LSA policy is set to refer to the domain the computer joins. The LSA policy for a Windows 2000–based client consists of the domain name, domain SID, DNS domain name, DNS forest name, and domain GUID.
8. The system updates the name of the DNS name assigned to the local machine.
9. The Domain Admins group is added to the Local Accounts Administrator group on the local machine.
10. The system initializes the Net Logon trusted domain cache to the trusted domains domain list.
11. The Windows Time Service is enabled and started.
12. The system starts the Net Logon service.

Netlogon

Once the domain administrator creates a computer account on the domain controller, the computer attempts to validate its computer account. It does this by first sending a local Netlogon request, and then sending a unicast Netlogon request to all the domain controllers in the master domain list.

The computer establishes a secure channel connection with the first domain controller that validates its Netlogon request. The secure channel is established only after both the computer and the domain controller are satisfied that the other has correctly identified itself through its computer account. After the secure channel is established, user account logon requests can pass from the computer to the domain controller.

Group Accounts

Group accounts are Active Directory or local computer objects that are collections of users, computers, contacts, and miscellaneous other groups. A group typically consists of all the resources necessary to run a specific service or application; a group is owned by a single node at any point in time. With groups, you can create e-mail distribution lists, filter group policy settings, and manage access to shared resources.

Group Types

Windows 2000 Active Directory includes two group types: *Security groups* and *e-mail Distribution groups*. Figure 3-4 shows these group types in the New Object–Group dialog box.

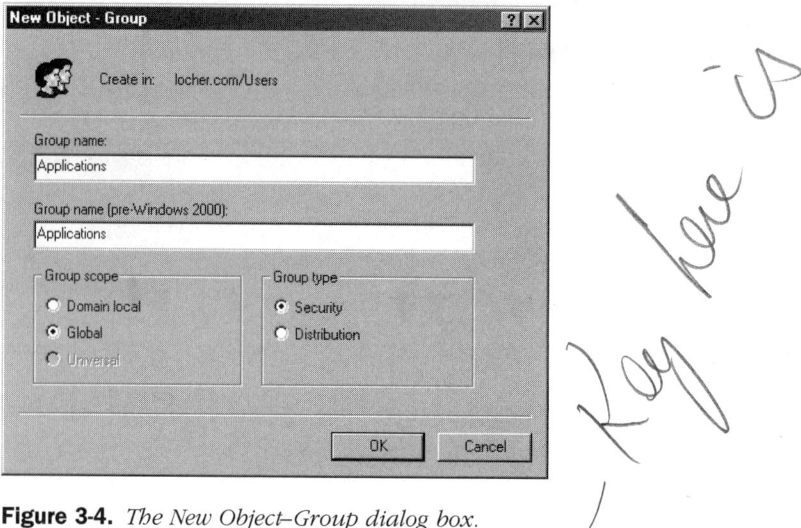

Figure 3-4. *The New Object–Group dialog box.*

Security groups are used for both e-mail distribution lists and to grant access to resources and objects. Security groups gain their access permissions in DACLs. These DACLs define resource and object permissions. The DACL is the part of the security descriptor that denotes which users and groups are permitted to access an object and the types of permissions granted to those users and groups.

When you assign permissions for resources, you're better off assigning those permissions to a security group rather than assigning them individually to users. Because you assign rights once to a group (rather than many times to each individual user), this approach simplifies network administration and saves time.

There are three reasons why you can use distribution groups solely for e-mail distribution lists: They cannot be included in DACLs used to assign permissions on objects and resources, they are not security-enabled, and they cannot be used to filter Group Policy settings. You can use distribution groups only with e-mail applications—such as Microsoft Exchange—to send e-mail messages to groups of users.

Security Group Scopes

Each security and distribution group is assigned a subgroup, or scope, that identifies the extent to which the group participates in the domain tree or forest. This section details the four types of scopes in Windows 2000. Groups with Universal Scopes are new in Windows 2000; the other three scopes are inherited from Windows NT.

Local Groups Based on Security Accounts Manager

Windows 2000 desktops and servers that are not domain controllers store their Local Groups in the security accounts manager (SAM) of the local machine. Groups installed by default on these systems are stored in the SAM's built-in database. These default groups have inherent system privileges. For example, the Account Operators group can administer domain user and group accounts in a domain.

Domain Local Scope Groups

Domain local groups can include accounts and groups from a Windows 2000 domain. These groups are equivalent to the SAM-based local groups, but you can use them only to grant users permissions within a domain. Local groups are stored in Active Directory. These local groups are different from Windows NT 4.0 SAM-based groups. You could only use NT 4.0 local groups on primary domain controllers (PDCs) or backup domain controllers (BDCs) because the SAM was identical on those machines. You can use Windows 2000 domain local groups on any computer in the Windows 2000 domain where they are defined.

You can nest domain local groups into other domain local groups. The domain local group can be granted permissions only in the same domain. You can convert domain local groups to a universal group only in native mode domains and only if the domain local group doesn't already have another domain local group as its member.

Global Scope Groups

Global groups have no inherent system privileges. They are meant to be an administrator's main means for securing access to security objects in a Windows 2000 domain. A global group can include accounts and groups only from the domain where the group is defined. You can convert a global group to a universal group only in native mode domains, and only if the domain local group is not a member of any other global group.

Universal Scope Groups

Universal groups are disabled until the domain is upgraded to a native mode domain. Universal groups have no inherited system privileges. A universal group can include accounts and groups from any Windows 2000 domain in the domain tree or forest. You can grant universal groups permissions in any domain in the domain tree or forest.

When the domain is in native mode, universal groups can be nested into other groups and they can be assigned permissions in any domain. You can't convert universal groups to any other type of group.

Built-in and Predefined Groups

When you install a Windows 2000 domain controller, you'll find several default groups installed in the Built-in and Users folders of the Active Directory Users And Computers console. These default groups are security groups that contain common sets of rights and permissions. You can use these default security groups to grant certain permissions, roles, and rights to accounts and groups that you want to include in the default groups.

Default Groups for Standalone and Member Servers

The default groups installed on a machine depend upon the role the machine plays. If the machine is a standalone server or a workstation, the following default groups are installed during a clean installation:

- Administrators
- Backup Operators
- Guests
- Print Operators
- Replicator
- Users

If the server is a member server in the domain, the following default groups are installed during a clean installation:

- Account Operators
- Pre-Windows 2000 Compatible Access
- Print Operators
- Server Operators

Built-in Groups

The Built-in folder contains default groups with domain local scope. The groups in this folder are primarily used to assign default sets of permissions to users who have some administrative functions in that domain.

The following list describes all the built-in groups for member servers, domain controllers, standalone servers, and workstations:

- **Account Operators.** The Account Operators group can administer domain user and group accounts in a domain. Specifically, Account Operators can create, modify, and delete user, group, and computer accounts of Active Directory (except for the built-in groups themselves). This group does not have permission to alter the Administrators and Domain Admins groups or members of those groups. By default, the Account Operators group has no members.
- **Administrators.** This group is granted a broad set of administrative authority over all resources and accounts within a domain. Members of this group have full and unlimited access locally to the computer and to the domain. Because of this unlimited power, keep membership in this group to a bare minimum. Administrators should have a second account that they normally use and only use their account in the Administrators group when they need to perform any of the following functions:
  - Upgrades to the operating system
  - Installation of Service Packs and Hotfixes

- Installation of hardware drivers
- Installation of system services
- Configuration of system parameters, such as password policies

Initially, the only member of the Administrators group is the Administrator account. However, when a member of the Administrators group creates an object, the Administrators group becomes the default owner of that object. When a computer joins a domain, the Domain Admins group is added to the Administrators group of the joining computer. The Enterprise Admins group is added to the Administrators group of the joining server when a server becomes a domain controller.

- **Backup Operators.** Backup Operators are granted permission to override security restrictions to back up and restore all files on a machine, regardless of any permissions that might protect those files. Backup Operators are also granted permission to log on to a computer and shut it down. By default, this group has no members.
- **Guests.** By default, members of the Guests group are granted the same access as members of the Users group. The Guests group is meant to provide occasional or one-time users with limited privileges to a computer's built-in guest account.
- **Power Users.** Members of the Power Users group have more power than the average user, but less power than members of the Administrators group. For example, Power Users can install applications to a Windows 2000 system, but not if the application needs to install any system services. Only members of the Administrators group can add system services. Power Users can create user accounts, but can't alter or delete user accounts they did not create. Members of this group can also create local groups and remove members from local groups they have created. Power Users can also modify system-wide settings such as Shares, Printers, Power Configuration, and System Time.
- **Pre-Windows 2000 Compatible Access.** This group is backward-compatible. It allows read access on all users and groups within the domain. Initially, the only member of this group is the Everyone entity.
- **Print Operators.** Members within this group are granted permission to administer domain printers. Print Operators are permitted to manage printers and document queues. The only member, by default, is the Domain Users group.
- **Replicator.** The File Replication service on Windows NT domain controllers uses the Replicator group to support file replication in an NT domain. The Replicator group is not used in Windows 2000 machines.
- **Server Operators.** Members of the Server Operators group are granted permission to administer domain servers. Specifically, members of this group can log on to a server interactively, shut down the server, start and stop services, format the hard disk of the computer, create and delete network shares, and back up and restore files. This group has no members by default.

- **Users.** Members in the Users group are restricted from making accidental or intentional system-wide changes. Members in this group are also restricted from running most legacy applications. Members of this group can perform tasks such as using local and network printers, locking the computer, running applications on the computer, and shutting down the computer. If the installation program of an application permits per-user installation, users can install applications that only they are permitted to use. Initially, the only member of this group is the Authenticated Users group.

Predefined Groups

The Users folder in the Active Directory Users And Computers console contains predefined groups that possess global scope. These predefined groups are installed on domain controllers during a clean installation and include the following:

- **Cert Publishers.** This group includes as its members all computers that run an enterprise certificate authority. The Cert Publishers members are authorized to publish certificates for User objects in Active Directory.
- **Domain Admins.** Members of this group are authorized to administer the domain. The Domain Admins group is, by default, a member of the Administrators group on all computers that have joined the domain, including all of the domain controllers. Any object created in Active Directory by any member of the Domain Admins group has as its default owner, the Domain Admins group. Objects other than those created in Active Directory by members of the Domain Admins group—such as files—have the Administrators group as a default owner. You add accounts to this group if you want an account to have broad administrative rights in one or more domains.
- **Domain Computers.** This group contains all of the computers that have joined a particular domain, excluding domain controllers.
- **Domain Controllers.** The Domain Controllers group contains all of the domain controllers in the domain. As new domain controllers join the domain, they are automatically added to this group.
- **Domain Guests.** This group is, by default, a member of the Guests group of the same domain. The default member of this group is the domain's Guest built-in user account.
- **Domain Users.** This group, by default, includes as its members all user accounts in a domain. Every time you create a user account, it is automatically added to this group.
- **Enterprise Admins.** This group exists only in the root domain of an Active Directory forest of domains. The forest root domain is the first domain created in the forest. Members of this group automatically receive permission to log on to any of the domain controllers in the forest. Members of the Enterprise Admins group are also authorized to make forest-wide changes in Active Directory, such as adding child domains. If the domain is a native-mode domain, the Enterprise Admins group is a universal group. If the domain is a mixed-mode domain, the

Enterprise Admins group is a global group. The only member of this group, by default, is the Administrator account for the forest root domain.

- **Group Policy Creator Owners.** Members of this group are authorized to create new Group Policy objects (GPOs) in the Active Directory. Usually, the default owner of a new GPO is the user who created it. The default member of this group is the Administrator user account.
- **Schema Admins.** This group exists only in the root domain of an Active Directory forest of domains. Members of this group are authorized to make changes to the schema in Active Directory. If the domain is in native mode, Schema Admins is a universal group. If the domain is in mixed mode, Schema Admins is a global group. The only member of this group, by default, is the Administrator account for the forest root domain.

Converting Security and Distribution Groups

As long as the Windows 2000 domain is in native mode, you can convert groups from a security group to a distribution group and vice versa. *Native mode* is the condition to which all domain controllers in the Windows 2000 domain have been upgraded. The administrator enables Windows 2000 native-mode operation through Active Directory Domains And Trusts.

When your Windows 2000 domain consists of both Windows NT and Windows 2000 domain controllers, your domain is referred to as a *mixed-mode* domain. You cannot convert groups while the Windows 2000 domain remains in mixed mode. Mixed-mode domains do not support the nested and universal group features of Windows 2000.

To convert a group in a native mode Windows 2000 domain

1. Choose Active Directory Domains And Trusts from the Administrative Tools menu.
2. Expand the domain node in the console tree.
3. Double-click the folder that contains the group you want to convert.
4. In the details pane on the right-hand side of the window, right-click the group, and then choose Properties from the context menu.
5. Select the group type for the conversion on the General tab, under Group type. Click OK.

Domain Trusts

A *domain trust* is an established relationship between two domains that enables users in one domain—their logon domain, or the trusted domain—to be authenticated by a domain controller in another domain (the trusting domain). Each type of domain trust relationship has only two domains—the trusted domain and the trusting domain. Before a user is allowed to access resources in another domain, Windows 2000 security must determine whether the trusting domain—the domain containing the resources the user is attempting to access—has a trust relationship with the trusted domain.

The rest of this section describes the four types of domain trust relationships: the three types of one-way trust and the nontransitive trust.

One-Way Trusts

A *one-way trust* is a single one-way trust relationship in which Domain A trusts Domain B, but Domain B does not trust Domain A. Authentication requests can only be passed from the trusting domain to the trusted domain. A Windows 2000 domain can establish a one-way trust in the following three ways:

- Through Windows 2000 domains located in a different forest
- Through Windows NT 4.0 domains
- Through MIT Kerberos v5 realms. Kerberos v5 is the primary security protocol for authentication within a Windows 2000 domain. This protocol verifies the identities of both the network services and of the user.

Note A transitive trust links all Windows 2000 domains in the same forest; users in Domain A can access resources in Domain B and Domain C—as long as they are granted the proper permissions.

Caution In a Windows 2000 forest, it is not possible to have nontransitive trusts between domains that are included in the same Windows 2000 forest.

Nontransitive Trusts

A *nontransitive trust* is formed between two domains in the trust relationship; this kind of trust relationship does not extend to any other domains in the forest. By default, nontransitive trusts are one-way. An administrator can create a two-way trust relationship by creating two one-way trusts.

All trust relationships established between domains that are not both Windows 2000 domains within the same forest are nontransitive. For example, a trust relationship between a Windows 2000 domain and a Windows NT domain is a nontransitive trust.

Note All trust relationships between Windows NT and Windows 2000 domains are nontransitive. In a mixed-mode environment, all Windows NT trusts within the forest are nontransitive.

Distributed Security Features

Distributed security features secure access to resources and to the network; these features also ensure the integrity and privacy of data and communications within the enterprise network. This section covers several key distributed security features: user authentication, impersonation, access token, access control, and Public Key Infrastructure.

User Authentication

To provide access for legitimate users on your network, you must authenticate all user access to system resources. Authentication for domain users depends on user accounts in Active Directory. You manage these accounts by using the Active Directory Users And Computers console. The default location for domain user accounts is the Users folder of the Active Directory Users And Computers console.

Instead of creating numerous accounts on different servers and application databases throughout the network, the administrator creates a single account for each user. The domain authentication service and the enterprise directory are integrated. What this means to you is that—in addition to providing access to network services—each single user account is also a directory entry for global address book information. As a result, the user needs only one password to log on to any client workstation in the domain.

Windows 2000 supports single sign-on for users within a domain forest. Trust relationships in a Windows 2000 forest are, by default, bidirectional. Therefore, authentication in one domain of the forest is sufficient for pass-through authentication to the resources in other domains in the forest. After the user logs on interactively, network security protocols such as Kerberos transparently authenticate the user's identity to all requested network services.

Interactive Logon

When you log on at the keyboard of a Windows 2000 computer, Winlogon displays a dialog box asking for your account identification. You are also required to select, from a drop-down menu, either the domain or the local machine you want to log on to. You further substantiate your claim to being the account holder by entering your password. Winlogon collects and packages the proof of identity you supply into a data structure, and then passes everything to the LSA to verify your identity. If the LSA determines that your account is valid and that you are the actual account holder, Winlogon sets up an interactive session on the computer. If the LSA cannot verify all the account information, you are denied access to the computer. The clear text password is not transmitted in the proof of identity.

The manner in which LSA verifies your account identity depends upon where your account was issued. If the local machine's LSA itself issued your account, that machine can check its own account database to validate the information. If either local domain LSA or the trusted domain LSA in the network issued the account, the local LSA must contact the LSA that issued the account for the account to be verified as valid and to determine whether you are the account holder.

Impersonation

Impersonation gives a thread the ability to execute in a security context other than the context of the process that actually owns the thread. In other words, impersonation is a thread's ability to use an access token that represents the client's credentials to obtain access to objects that the client has access to. Each process possesses a primary token that describes the actual security context of the user account associated with that process.

For example, you might be running an application that needs to access files protected by a security descriptor. In this case, the application can impersonate the client before accessing the necessary files, thus ensuring that the client can obtain only authorized access to information stored in those files.

During impersonation, the service is considered to be running in a client's security context. The purpose of the impersonation design is to allow application services to carry out an operation in a "least-privileged" mode when responding to network requests on behalf of client programs.

The main reason for the impersonation design is to trigger access checks against the client's identity. Because the client's identity is in use, access to objects such as remote files is based on permissions granted to the user or group the user is a member of, rather than on the server's security identity . Thus the access is either expanded or restricted, depending upon the permissions of the client.

Service Accounts

Windows 2000 services can run under the security context of a domain user account. The services installed with the Windows 2000 operating system run under the Local System account. You can configure services installed at a later date to run as Local System, or you can start them using a separate account on the local system or on a domain account defined in Active Directory.

A service's primary token identifies the service's account, the privileges granted to the account, and the groups associated with the account. The information contained in the primary token is used during access checks, when the service requests access to objects necessary for it to function.

Impersonation Levels

Impersonation levels allow the client to control to what level a service is permitted to act as the client. The client assigns the impersonation level when the client process connects to the service. The user does not select impersonation levels; instead, they are specified within the code for applications as Security Quality of Service (SqoS) information. There are four levels of impersonation.

Anonymous

In the anonymous level of impersonation, the service impersonates the client but remains anonymous to the service because the impersonation token doesn't contain any information about the client.

Identify

The identify level of impersonation means that a service can use the identity of the client in its own security mechanism, but at this level of impersonation the service cannot impersonate the client.

Impersonate

In the impersonate level of impersonation, the service is permitted to impersonate the client. When the service is located on the same local computer as the client process, the service can act as the client to access network resources.

Delegate

At the delegate level of impersonation, the service can impersonate the client when it accesses resources both on the service's computer and on other computers in the network. Windows NT and Windows 2000 do not natively support the delegation-impersonation level, but the security package might have the ability to provide this level of impersonation. In the current implementation, Remote Procedure Call always requests delegation-level security context from the security package for unauthenticated transports. The server maps the requested level to the native level for authenticated transports (named pipes and LRPC).

Access Token

The access token is an object that includes information about the identity and privileges of an account associated with a particular process or thread. Each process that occurs on the system has a primary token associated with it. The token describes the security context of the user account associated with the process.

When a user logs on, the system verifies the user's password by comparing it with the information stored in a security database. The system creates an access token for the user account if the password is authenticated. Each process executed on behalf of the user receives a copy of this access token. When a thread interacts with a securable object or a user attempts to perform a task that requires privileges, the system uses the token to identify the user.

A thread can impersonate a client account. When this happens, the thread is permitted to interact with securable objects by using the security context of the client. Therefore, a thread that impersonates a client is assigned both a primary and an impersonation token.

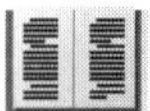

More Info A *primary access token* represents the security context of a process. An *impersonation access token* is used to temporarily adopt a different security context for a thread within a services process, such as when a thread impersonates a client account.

Access tokens contain the following information:

- The SID for the user's account.
- A list of SIDs for security groups that include the user as a member.
- A list of the user's privileges and the user's security groups privileges held on the local computer.
- The SID for the user or security group that owns an object. When a user or a security group either creates or takes ownership of an object, that user or security group becomes the owner of that object.

- The SID for the user's primary security group.
- A default DACL that contains a built-in set of permissions that the operation system applies to objects created by the user if the user does not specify a security descriptor.
- The source of the access token, such as Session Manager.
- A value that specifies whether the access token is a primary token or an impersonation token.
- The value of the current impersonation level.
- Information about the access token that the operating system uses internally.
- An optional list of restricting SIDs that limit access to securable objects.
- A Session ID value that indicates whether the token is associated with the Terminal Services client session.

Access Control

To fully understand access control, you first need to understand the definition of a thread. A *thread* is a sequential portion of program code, or more simply put, a thread is a piece of program code executing on the computer. Threads are the real agents of action on a computer. The Windows 2000 operating system coordinates the execution of the threads by assigning each thread a scheduling priority for execution on the processor. A process can have several threads associated with it.

A thread must identify itself to the operating system's LSA to gain access to an object. Because a thread does not have a security identity, it must borrow one from a security principal, such as a user. When a user logs on, the user's security identity is encased in an access token associated with that user's logon session. When the user begins an application, the application runs as a process within the logon session. A copy of the user's access token is presented to the application process and also with each of the application's threads of execution. When an application's thread needs to open a file, for example, the thread identifies itself as the user's agent by presenting the user's access token.

Before the operating system allows the thread's execution to proceed, it performs an access check on the thread to determine whether the security principal (such as a user) is permitted the level of access requested by the thread. The access check compares the information contained in the thread's access token to the information contained within the object's security descriptor.

The security subsystem steps through each access control entry (ACE) in the object's DACL until it finds an ACE that either allows or denies access to the user or one of the user's groups, or until it has checked all ACEs. If the security subsystem reaches the end of the list and has not been explicitly denied or permitted the desired access, the security subsystem denies access to the object.

ACEs are listed in canonical order in the DACL, which means that the Deny ACEs all come before the Allow ACEs. This order is necessary because an object's DACL might contain an ACE that permits access to a group, but denies access to an individual user who happens to be a member of that group. If, during an access check, the ACE is reached that allows access to the user's group before the check reaches the ACE that actually denies access to the user, the user will be permitted access to the object. This order of processing would most certainly be a problem because a user might improperly get access to a resource.

Public Key Infrastructure

Public Key Infrastructure (PKI) is a system made up of registration authorities such as certification authorities (CAs) and digital certificates that use public key cryptography to authenticate and verify the validity of each client involved in an electronic transaction. Standards for PKI are constantly evolving to meet the needs of electronic commerce.

The rest of this section describes the features in Windows 2000 that can assist your organization in implementing a PKI.

Certificates

A *certificate* is a collection of digitally signed data issued by an authority that vouches for the identity of the certificate holder. Certificates are used to authenticate the user, data integrity, and the secure exchange of information across nonsecure networks, such as the Internet. A certificate securely binds a public encryption key to the identity of the person, computer, or service that holds the corresponding private encryption key.

Windows 2000 certificate-based processes use X.509v3 as the standard certificate format. The X.509v3 certificate includes information about the entity to which the certificate is issued, optional information about the CA issuing the certificate, and information about the certificate itself. This information can include the entity's name, public key, and public key algorithm. Administrators can manage certificates through the Certificates MMC console.

Certificate Services

In Windows 2000, the Certificate Services component creates and manages CAs. The responsibilities of a CA include establishing and vouching for the certificate holders' identity. A CA is also responsible for revoking certificates once they are no longer considered valid. The CA publishes certificate revocation lists (CRLs) for use by certificate verifiers. Administrators can manage Certificate Services through the Certification Authority MMC console.

Smart Card Support

Smart cards provide security solutions in a tamper-resistant, portable way. Windows 2000 supports the use of smart cards to store certificates used for public key cryptography–related activities such as secure e-mail, Web authentication, and logging on to a Windows 2000 domain.

Smart cards provide the following features:

- Isolation of computations critical to security that involve features such as authentication and key exchange
- Portability of credentials as well as other personal information between computers at work, on the road, or at home

Public Key Policies

The administrator can use the Windows 2000 Group Policy MMC to automatically distribute certificates to computers, to manage recovery policies for the Encrypting File System, and to establish common trusted CAs and certificate trust lists.

Understanding Encrypting File System

Encrypting File System (EFS) enables users to store data securely on their local systems by encrypting and decrypting data in selected NTFS files and folders as needed. The EFS is designed to store information for an individual on a local computer and therefore does not support sharing encrypted files.

Caution You cannot encrypt or decrypt files and the contents of folders on FAT volumes.

EFS is tightly integrated with the NTFS file system, making encryption easy to manage and transparent to the user. Users work with encrypted files and the encrypted contents of folders just as they would work with any other files and folders. When the user who originally encrypted a file accesses it at a later date, EFS file contents are decrypted as file blocks are read from the disk into the object cache. The entire file is not decrypted to a temporary file for the "user session." This process is completed seamlessly, without the user needing to remember a separate password for the encrypted file.

More Info If the user copies or moves the encrypted file or folder to a file system other than a Windows 2000 NTFS volume, encryption is removed and the file is copied as clear text. There is one exception to this: files and folders stored by Windows 2000 Backup remain encrypted on the backup media.

When intruders attempt to access those same encrypted files and folders, they are prevented from doing so. Using EFS is particularly useful for securing data on hardware that might be vulnerable to theft, such as external disk drives and laptops.

Note Only the contents of a folder or subfolder are encrypted, not the folder or subfolder themselves.

How EFS Works

EFS automatically generates an encryption key pair for a user if one does not already exist. The encryption key pair is composed of the public and private key of each user. If an encryption key pair needs to be generated, and the user is logged on to a domain, the generation occurs on a domain controller. If the user is logged on to a workgroup, the generation occurs on the local computer.

The computer or domain controller will implement symmetric key encryption and public key encryption. (Public key encryption is not more secure or stronger than symmetric key encryption. It is slower but more versatile.) The computer system asks EFS to generate a pseudo-random number for the file, known as the file encryption key (FEK). The FEK is used later to decrypt the file's data. The extended Data Encryption Standard (DESX) encryption algorithm uses the FEK to generate the encrypted file. The encrypted file is then stored on disk. At this point, the secret key algorithm has been implemented.

However, this process has more steps. To tighten security of the FEK, the FEK itself is encrypted with the user's public key, thereby ensuring that users do not share the same decryption key. Because the slower public key encryption method is used only on the smaller FEK, system performance is not affected. The newly ciphered FEK is then stored with the encrypted file. Both the FEK and the file are secured at this point.

Note It is not possible for other system accounts that have permissions for the encrypted file, such as the Take Ownership permission, to open the file without the encryptor's or the recovery agent's private key. However, some other permissions remain unaffected. For example, an administrator with delete permissions for the encrypted file can still delete that user's encrypted file, even though the administrator cannot open and read it.

The user who encrypted the file can decrypt the ciphered FEK with that user's private key, which must match the public key. Decrypting the FEK also enables a recovery agent by using the recovery agent's private key. The administrator assigns the recovery agent through the Group Policy Snap-In. The purpose of the recovery agent is to recover data for an encrypted file in the event that the private key becomes accidentally deleted or corrupted, or if an employee leaves the company and the administrator then needs to recover an encrypted file. The recovery agent administrator is issued a public key certificate to decrypt files and folders for the purpose of recovering user data encrypted with EFS.

Once the FEK is decrypted, it is used to decrypt the data in the file, enabling the user to work with the encrypted files just as he or she would work with unencrypted files. This decryption process is transparent to the user. Without the decryption of the ciphered FEK, the actual file itself cannot be decrypted. If the user does not possess a valid private key to the file, an "Access is denied" message appears when he or she tries to open the file.

Caution To address a known vulnerability, it is essential that the recovery agent's private key is removed from any portable computer.

Introducing New Local Security Features

The new features in Windows 2000 will enhance security on your local machine. These features include a new version of NTFS and the secondary logon.

NTFS

Windows 2000 includes the latest, improved version of the NTFS file system, NTFS version 5. To use the new features of NTFS, such as EFS, you must update from Windows NT 4.0 to the newest Windows 2000 NTFS format.

NTFS uses ACLs that determine whether a specific user or group is permitted access to a resource (such as a file). Information taken from the security token associated with the logged-on user is compared to the information with the ACL associated with that resource. An ACL lists ACEs that contain information such as user names and groups; an ACL also includes which permissions the users and groups have for each resource.

Caution To use ACLs on files, you must be using NTFS.

File permissions for groups and users include Full Control, Modify, Read and Execute, Read, and Write. Folder permissions for groups and users include Full Control, Modify, Read and Execute, List Folder Contents, Read, and Write.

Secondary Logon

Generally, it's not a good practice for administrators to go about their daily work while logged on using their administrative accounts, because even administrators can make mistakes, such as unintentionally deleting objects. Fortunately, Windows 2000 comes with a Secondary Logon Service (SLS)—also known as the RunAs service—that enables administrators to use a standard user account for logon and to launch an administrative console with elevated permissions to perform administrative tasks when necessary. To avoid security breaches (as with any administrative tool or user account), don't leave the administrative console unattended while you are not using it.

You access the RunAs service in two ways. You can access it by right-clicking on the Administrative Tool application and then selecting RunAs from the context menu. Figure 3-5 illustrates the RunAs dialog box.

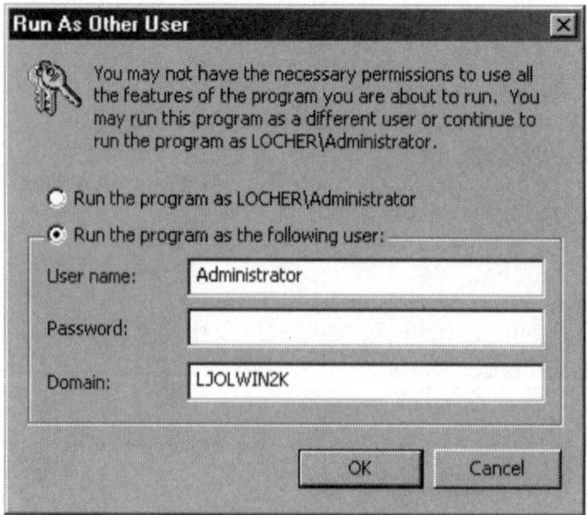

Figure 3-5. *The RunAs dialog box.*

You can also access the service from a command line, as shown in Figure 3-6.

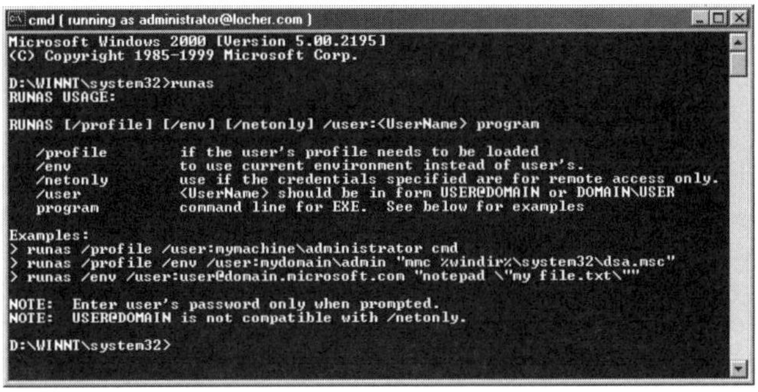

```
cmd ( running as administrator@locher.com )
Microsoft Windows 2000 [Version 5.00.2195]
(C) Copyright 1985-1999 Microsoft Corp.

D:\WINNT\system32>runas
RUNAS USAGE:

RUNAS [/profile] [/env] [/netonly] /user:<UserName> program

   /profile         if the user's profile needs to be loaded
   /env             to use current environment instead of user's.
   /netonly         use if the credentials specified are for remote access only.
   /user            <UserName> should be in form USER@DOMAIN or DOMAIN\USER
   program          command line for EXE.  See below for examples

Examples:
> runas /profile /user:mymachine\administrator cmd
> runas /profile /env /user:mydomain\admin "mmc %windir%\system32\dsa.msc"
> runas /env /user:user@domain.microsoft.com "notepad \"my file.txt\""

NOTE:  Enter user's password only when prompted.
NOTE:  USER@DOMAIN is not compatible with /netonly.

D:\WINNT\system32>
```

Figure 3-6. *Command-line execution of RunAs.*

The RunAs syntax is

```
RUNAS [/profile] [/environment] [/netonly] /user:<UserName>
    program
```

Definitions for the switches are as follows:

```
/profile - Use if the user's profile needs loaded
/env - To use the current environment instead of the user's environment.
/netonly - Use this switch if the credentials specified are for remote
/ access only.
/user - The [UserName] should be in the form of USER@DOMAIN or DOMAIN/USER
/program - Use the command line for EXE.
```

One way you can use the SLS is to open a command console window using RunAs and launch applications from there. To accomplish this, open a command prompt window and type *runas /u:administrator@<company.com> cmd*. As shown in Figure 3-7, when the command console window opens, the title bar displays the ID you used to open the window. From this command console window you can run applications such as the Active Directory Users And Computers console.

```
cmd ( running as administrator@locher.com )
Microsoft Windows 2000 [Version 5.00.2195]
(C) Copyright 1985-1999 Microsoft Corp.

D:\WINNT\system32>
```

Figure 3-7. *The RunAs command console title bar.*

Administrative Tools

Here are a few of the administrative tool applications you can run from the RunAs command console window:

- Active Directory Domains And Trusts (Domain.msc)
- Active Directory Sites And Services (Dssite.msc)
- Active Directory Users And Computers (Dsa.msc)
- Domain Controller Security Policy (Dcpol.msc)
- Domain Security Policy (Dompol.msc)

Note You can run any command line tool from the console, including scripts. You can run any MMC snap-in by simply starting MMC and adding a console, or you can run the administrative tools from the UI with RunAs—just right-click the tool on the Administrative Tools menu and then choose Run As from the context menu.

Introducing the Security Subsystem

The Windows 2000 security subsystem is made up of a set of security components that ensure that users and applications cannot access resources without proper identification and authentication. The security subsystem keeps track of the security policies and accounts in effect on any given computer system.

Policies and accounts stored on a domain controller where Active Directory is installed are the policies and accounts in effect for the particular domain where the domain controller is located. These policies and accounts are stored in Active Directory. The rest of this section describes the components included in the security subsystem. (Chapter 5, "Authentication", has more information about authentication and the Local Security Authority.)

User Rights

User rights enable users to perform specific actions, such as backing up information on computers. Administrators assign specific rights to group accounts and individual user accounts. User rights and access rights differ in that user rights apply to rights assigned at the local level to user accounts, while access rights apply to secured objects.

It is best to administer user rights on a group account basis. Administering user rights in this manner simplifies the task of user account administration and ensures that a user automatically inherits the rights associated with a particular group.

There are two types of user rights: privileges and logon rights.

Privileges

A privilege is the right of a user or group account to perform a variety of system-related operations on the local computer, such as loading device drivers. System administrators can use administrative tools, such as the Local Security Policy console under Local Policies, to add, remove, or modify privileges for user and group accounts. Figure 3-8 illustrates the Local Policies screen.

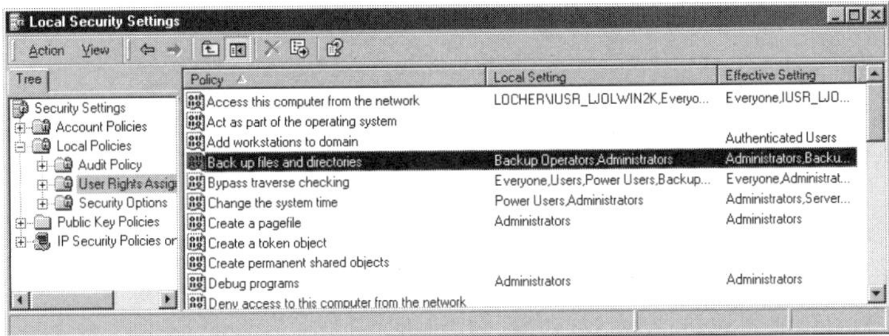

Figure 3-8. *Local Policies User Rights Assignment screen.*

Privileges and access rights differ in a couple of ways. *Access rights* control access to securable objects, such as registry keys. *Privileges* control access to system resources and system-related tasks. And while a system administrator assigns privileges to user and group accounts, access rights are granted or denied to securable objects based upon access rights granted in the ACEs in the object's DACL.

An account database is stored in the local LSA on each Windows 2000 system that contains the privileges held by user and group accounts for that computer. When a new user logs on, the system produces an access token. This access token contains a list of the user's privileges, including privileges (obtained from the account database) granted to the groups the user belongs to. These privileges apply to the local machine only. Administrators can grant different privileges to domain accounts on different computers throughout the domain.

When a user attempts to perform a privileged operation on the local machine, the system checks the user's access token for the necessary privileges. If the access token does show the necessary privileges, the system ensures that the privileges are enabled. Of course, if the user fails any of these checks, the system does not permit the user to perform the operation on the computer. *GetTokenInformation* is the Windows 2000 function that indicates the privileges held in an access token as well as which privileges are enabled.

Logon Rights

A logon right is a user right that determines how a user logs on to a system. System administrators can use the Local Security Policy console under Local Policies to manage these rights. The Windows 2000 logon rights are as follows:

- **Access this computer from the network.** This right permits a user to log on to the computer over a network. Administrators, Everyone, and Power Users are all granted this right by default.

- **Log on as a batch job.** By default, this right enables Administrators to log on to the computer using a batch-queue facility.
- **Log on as a service.** This right permits a security principal to log on to the computer as a service to establish a security context. By default no one is granted this right.
- **Log on locally.** This right allows users to log on locally at the computer's keyboard. This right is granted by default to Administrators, Account Operators, Backup Operators, Print Operators, and Server Operators.

Local Security Policy

Local policy information is stored by the LSA in a set of internal LSA Policy Objects. The local security policy identifies a number of items:

- Accounts that are assigned privileges
- The domains that can be trusted to authenticate logon attempts
- The type of security auditing to perform on the system
- The accounts that are permitted to access the system and the logon rights permitted, such as logging on as a service
- The default memory quotas

Refer to Chapter 9, "Security Configuration and Monitoring," for more detailed coverage of the Local Security Policy.

Group Policy

You use Group Policy to specify users' environments; you rely on the Windows 2000 operating system to enforce those policies afterward. A Group Policy object is not a profile because it is not an environment setting that the user can change. Administrators manage and maintain Group Policies through the Group Policy Editor Snap-In or through the Active Directory Users And Computers console.

When you configure a Group Policy in a site, domain, or organizational unit, all its users and computers are affected. Group Policies do not affect any of the other objects within that site, domain, or organizational unit, especially security groups.

Implementing Security Functionality with System Services

A service is a program, routine, or process that runs in the background of a Windows 2000 environment and performs a specific system function to support other programs. Administrators can publish services in Active Directory when they are provided over a network, resulting in the simplification of service-based usage and administration.

Services typically run under the System account, but you can also run them under a user-defined account. You must ensure that services are managed appropriately and that they do not present any security risks—they are critical to system security. To manage services, you must be a member of the Administrators or Server Operators group.

Services have three startup options: They can start up automatically when the system boots, they can be manually started and stopped by the administrator or server operators, or they can be disabled. You always want the critical services to start when the server is booted.

The Services and Applications node in the Computer Management console enables you to view and manage properties of any server service or application installed on the Windows 2000 server. To view or manage services, select Computer Management from the Administrative Tools menu. Open Services and Applications, and then click Services to display all available services on the server, as illustrated in Figure 3-9.

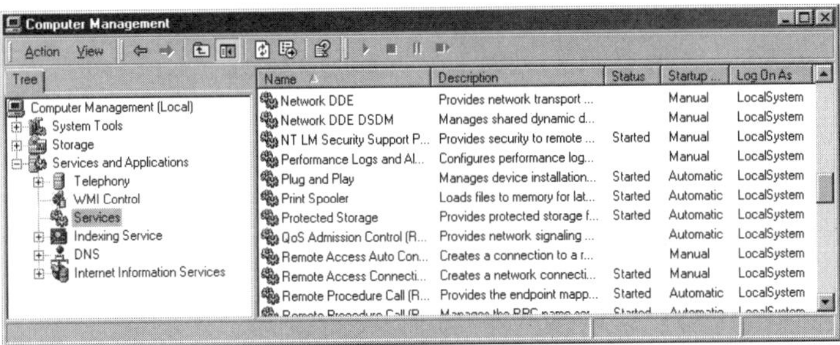

Figure 3-9. *The available services on a server.*

To view the properties of each individual service, right-click on the service and then choose Properties from the context menu. Figure 3-10 illustrates the Property sheet for a service.

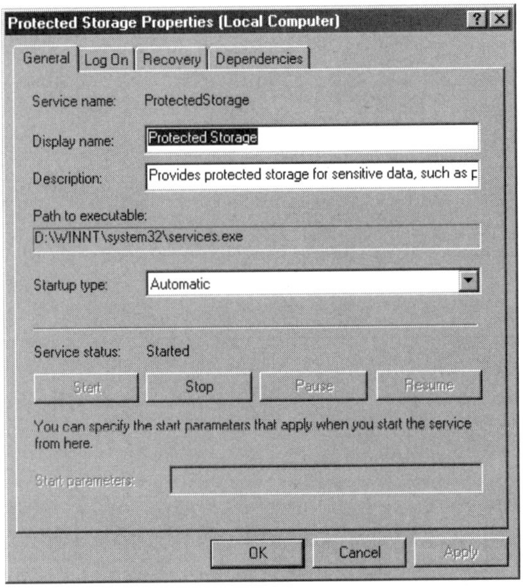

Figure 3-10. *Property sheet for the Protected Storage service.*

The Services list includes the following default security-related services:

- **Certificate Services.** This service revokes and issues X.509 certificates for public key cryptography. It requires the Protected Storage service.
- **Protected Storage.** This service prevents access by unauthorized users, processes, or services by providing protected storage for sensitive data. It requires Remote Procedure Call service.
- **Event Log.** This service records security events that you can view in Event Viewer.
- **Internet Authentication Service.** This service enables authentication, authorization, and accounting of VPN and dial-up users. It requires Remote Procedure Call service.
- **IPSec Policy Agent.** This service starts the IP security driver and the ISAKMP/Oakley (IKE) and manages the IP security policy. It requires Remote Procedure Call service.
- **Kerberos Key Distribution Center.** This provides client/server authentication by generating session keys and granting service tickets. It requires Remote Procedure Call service.
- **Netlogon.** The Netlogon service locates domain controllers and performs other directory service functions, such as updating the Domain Name System (DNS) resource records for domain controllers.
- **NTLM Security Support Provider.** In most cases this service is necessary because it provides security for Remote Procedure Call applications that use transports other than named pipes.
- **Remote Procedure Call.** This service provides a number of services, including the endpoint mapper. Protected Storage, Internet Authentication Service, IPSEC Policy Agent, and Kerberos Key Distribution Center are only a few of the services that depend upon Remote Procedure Call.
- **RunAs Service.** This process works in conjunction with the RunAs program and enables users to start processes under alternate credentials.
- **Security Accounts Manager.** This is the service that stores security information for local user accounts.

Summary

This chapter introduced you to the security model and its subsystems. You learned about the types of domain trust relationships that Windows 2000 Server supports and Security Principals such as user accounts, computer accounts, and groups. You also learned about distributed security features such as access control, PKI, and EFS; and features of the security subsystem, such as user rights, LSA, and system services. Before you begin to plan and implement security for your organization, you should be familiar with these basic security concepts. The subsequent chapters of this book cover these topics in more detail.

Chapter 4
Active Directory

Windows 2000 introduces the Active Directory infrastructure to the Windows platform. Active Directory is the basis for Windows 2000 distributed networking and also facilitates the use of centralized and decentralized management techniques, including the Group Policy and remote operating system installations. (For more information on Group Policy, refer to Chapter 8.)

Because Active Directory forms a central—though not compulsory—component of the Windows 2000 operating system (except in the case of Windows 2000 domain controllers, which require its installation), it is important to understand how it works. In this chapter we'll focus on Active Directory and its underlying technologies.

Active Directory and Directory Services: the Basics

Computing trends constantly move toward larger networks and more distributed computing, especially with the increasing number of telecommuters. This means that modern operating systems have to provide mechanisms to manage distributed resources, identities, and relationships. These systems must cope with users across geographically separated networks, intranets, and extranets; users working from home; and all the security implications that accompany these factors.

Windows 2000 achieves this level of functionality by implementing a directory service solution. A directory service provides a place to store information about network-based entities such as applications, files, printers, and users, and provides a consistent way in which to manage and secure that information. A directory service acts as a central authority that manages the identities and brokers the relationships between these distributed entities, enabling them to work together. For the directory service to supply these fundamental network operating system functions and to ensure the integrity and privacy of the network, it must be tightly integrated within the management and security mechanisms of the operating system.

Why Do We Need a Directory Service?

The explosive growth of networked computing and telecommuting has created the need for directory services. A user working at home needs to have the same level of potential access to resources as he or she would have if actually working on site at the company's offices.

Directory services enable users to search for network resources, using either names or attributes of objects. Directory services also permit the following benefits:

- Security can be enforced and defined by administrators.
- Directories can be distributed across many computers in a network.
- Directories can be replicated, making them more resistant to failure.
- Directories can be partitioned into multiple stores, allowing the storage of a large number of objects.

Active Directory allows the distribution of information between network resources and users and acts as the central authority for network security. This functionality allows the operating system to verify a user's identity and control the user's access to network resources using access control lists (ACLs). Active Directory acts as an integration point for management tasks and brings systems together, enabling organizations to apply standard business rules to distributed applications, network resources, and users without requiring administrators to maintain a variety of specialized directories.

Active Directory is an enterprise-class directory service that is scalable, built from the ground up using Internet-standard technologies, and fully integrated with the operating system. Thus it is designed to reduce the number of directories a computer uses and provide an infrastructure for isolating, migrating, and centrally managing network resources.

How Does Active Directory Work?

Active Directory stores information in a hierarchical, object-oriented fashion, providing multimaster replication support for distributed network environments. Active Directory uses objects to represent network resources such as users and groups, machines, devices, applications, and containers to represent organizations. Active Directory also uses objects to represent collections of related objects, such as printers. It organizes information into a tree structure made up of these objects and containers—similar to the way the Windows operating system uses folders and files to organize information on a computer.

Active Directory also provides a single, centralized view when it manages the relationships among objects and containers, making resources easier to find, manage, and use in a highly distributed network. The Active Directory hierarchy is flexible, allowing organizations to organize resources in a way that optimizes manageability.

Active Directory can nest containers to reflect a company's organizational structure. Grouping objects in the directory lets administrators manage objects as collections rather than as individual objects. This increases management efficiency and accuracy while letting organizations distribute network management in a style consistent with their particular business processes.

Object-Oriented Storage

As we mentioned, Active Directory stores information about network elements in the form of objects. These objects can be assigned attributes that describe specific characteristics about the object. Companies can then store a wide range of information in the directory and control access to it with ACLs. Object- and attribute-level security lets you precisely control access to information stored in the directory. Active Directory lets you assign access privileges for each attribute of the object, as well as at the entire object level.

Multimaster Replication

To provide high performance, availability, and flexibility in distributed environments, Active Directory uses multimaster replication. By installing domain controllers, you can create multiple copies of the directory—known as directory replicas—throughout the network. Changes made anywhere on the network are automatically replicated throughout the network. This is in contrast to single-master replication, in which all changes must be made to a single, authoritative directory database.

For example, you can make synchronized directory replicas available to each location in a Wide Area Network (WAN). Such a process can give users faster performance because they can locate resources by using the local directory service rather than by traversing the WAN. You can manage these same directories locally or remotely, depending on available administrative resources.

What Are the Benefits of Active Directory?

Because Active Directory is integrated with a Windows 2000 domain controller, it provides network administrators, developers, and users with access to a directory service with a wide range of benefits.

Simplified Management

Distributed systems can lead to time-consuming and redundant management. Active Directory allows companies to lower management costs by providing a single place through which to manage users, groups, and network resources, as well as to distribute software and to manage desktop configurations. Active Directory also provides a single point of management for Windows user accounts, clients, servers, and applications, along with the ability to synchronize with existing directory services. The ability to remotely install and distribute software reduces the amount of onsite work for support staff, thereby significantly cutting costs for an enterprise distributed over a wide scale. Active Directory allows you to delegate specific administrative privileges and tasks to individual users and groups, allowing the distribution of system administration tasks to localized or centralized administration depending on the available administration resources. Specific management tasks, such as resetting user passwords, can be delegated to the office administrators in the individual business units, while more privileged functions, such as creating a user, can be reserved for administrators in the centralized IT department.

Strengthened Security

Because Windows 2000 is targeted at distributed networking, consistent methods of authentication and authorization are required for both users within the intranet and legitimate users performing remote access from an extranet. Active Directory centralizes management and enforces role-based security consistent with an organization's business processes.

Active Directory also facilitates single sign-on to network resources by using integrated security services that are transparent to end users. Active Directory also includes built-in support for secure Internet-standard protocols and authentication mechanisms such as Kerberos, Public Key Infrastructure (PKI), and Lightweight Directory Access Protocol (LDAP) over the Secure Socket Layer (SSL). Strengthened security can speed deployment of e-business by letting you use the same tools and processes to manage access control and user privileges across internal desktop users, remote dial-up users, and external e-commerce customers.

Central Authority

Once a user is authenticated and logged on, all resources in the system are protected and access is granted or denied based on a single authorization model. Thus organizations don't have to protect resources in one way for users who log on via the intranet and another way for those who use digital certificates to access resources over the Internet.

Extended Interoperability

Many companies use a wide range of technologies that must work together—e-mail servers, applications, network devices, firewalls, and e-commerce applications—resulting in a diverse collection of directories. Active Directory provides a set of standard interfaces for application integration and open synchronization mechanisms to ensure Windows interoperability with a wide variety of applications and devices. Active Directory extends interoperability in the following ways:

- By consolidating multiple application directories management, using open interfaces, connectors, and synchronization mechanisms. Organizations can consolidate directories including Novell's NDS, LDAP, ERP, and e-mail.
- By allowing organizations to deploy directory-enabled networking, including support for network devices from vendors that use the directory to let administrators assign quality of service and allocate network bandwidth to users based on their role in the company.
- By allowing organizations to develop and deploy directory-enabled applications. Using the fully extensible directory architecture, developers can build applications that deliver functionality tailored to the needs of the end user.

Active Directory provides an integration point for diverse systems by exposing all of the Windows 2000 directory features through standards-based interfaces such as LDAP, ADSI, JADSI, and MAPI, thereby allowing companies to consolidate existing directories and develop directory-enabled applications and infrastructures. Active Directory also provides a development platform for directory-enabled applications, allowing application developers to control the behavior of an application based on the user's role in the company.

The benefits of Active Directory extend beyond the Windows environment. The open synchronization mechanisms within Active Directory ensure interoperability of the Windows platform with a wide variety of applications and devices. For example, native support for LDAP, DirSync, and ADSI interfaces enables leading vendors such as Cisco, SAP, BAAN, and 3COM to integrate with Active Directory and provide simplified and powerful management of their multiplatform products.

Policy-Based Administration

Group Policies are configuration settings that are applied to computers or users as they are initialized. (See Chapter 8 for more information on Group Policy.) All group policy settings are contained in Group Policy objects applied to Active Directory sites, domains, or organizational units. These settings determine who can access directory objects and domain resources, which domain resources are available to which users, and how these domain resources are configured for use.

Information Replication

As mentioned earlier, Active Directory uses multimaster replication, which allows the update of any directory from any domain controller. By using multiple domain controllers in one domain, you can introduce an element of load balancing and fault tolerance. If one domain controller slows, stops or fails, the other domain controller (or controllers) can take over, thereby maintaining the necessary directory access, as well as continuing to provide the distributed security facilities.

Active Directory Architecture

A *directory* is a hierarchical structure that stores information about objects on networks. Objects include users, computers, shared resources, and so on. A *directory service* combines the directory with the services required to make the directory's information available to users, usually concealing the physical network topology and protocols from the user. A user can access—and administrators can configure—any resource without knowing where or how it is connected.

Active Directory can only run on domain controllers. It provides a place to store data—along with services to make that data available.

Active Directory and Domain Name System (DNS)

Active Directory makes use of Internet Standard technologies, including the Domain Name System (DNS), which is required for its operation. Both DNS and Active Directory are *namespaces*—bounded areas in which a given name can be resolved. This name resolution is the process of translating a name into some object or information that the name represents. The integration of DNS and Active Directory is an important part of the

Windows 2000 operating system. However—although they share the same structure—they are not the same namespace. Both DNS and Active Directory domains use the same domain names for different namespaces.

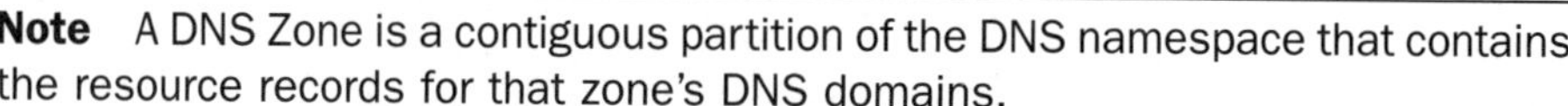

Note A DNS Zone is a contiguous partition of the DNS namespace that contains the resource records for that zone's DNS domains.

The domain names used by DNS and Active Directory are based on the DNS hierarchical naming structure, which in turn is based on the inverted tree structure. This consists of a single root domain with parent and child domains underneath as the nodes. Each parent domain or child domain can have further child domains attached beneath it. Every computer in a DNS domain is uniquely identified by its fully qualified domain name (FQDN). For example, the FQDN of a computer located in the domain child.parent.iss.net is *computername*.child.parent.iss.net.

Every Windows 2000 domain has a DNS name, and every Windows 2000–based computer has a DNS name. Thus computers and domains are represented as both Active Directory objects and DNS nodes, with DNS hierarchy nodes representing domains or computers. Both Active Directory and DNS use databases to resolve names.

DNS is a *name resolution service* that resolves names and computer names to IP addresses through requests sent from the DNS client to the DNS server as DNS queries, which are passed to the DNS database. The DNS server receives the name request and then either resolves the name query through locally stored files or consults another DNS server higher in the hierarchy.

Active Directory is a directory service, resolving domain object names to object records through the requests received by the domain controllers. The requests are then sent to the domain controllers as LDAP search requests to the Active Directory database. Active Directory clients use LDAP to send the queries to the Active Directory server. An Active Directory client queries DNS as a locator service and resolves the Active Directory domain, site, or service name to an IP address to locate the Active Directory server. Active Directory requires DNS to function, although the reverse is not true.

Active Directory has been designed to use DNS as a locator service to allow it to exist within the global Internet DNS namespace. If an organization that requires an Internet presence is running Windows 2000 as its operating system, the Active Directory namespace is maintained as a hierarchical Windows 2000 domain (or domains) beneath a DNS registered root domain as a DNS namespace. Even if the organization chooses not to be part of the Internet DNS namespace, the DNS is still required to locate Windows 2000–based computers.

The final point worth noting about the interrelationship of DNS and Active Directory is the use of SRV records. These are required for Active Directory to work; Active Directory maps the name of a service to the name of the server offering that service. Active Directory clients and servers use SRV resource records to determine IP addresses of domain controllers.

DNS servers should also provide support for dynamic update, which defines a protocol for dynamically updating a DNS server with new or changed values. Without this DNS dynamic update protocol, you must manually configure the records created by the domain controllers and stored by DNS servers.

Windows 2000 is compatible with other DNS servers. However, if you use a DNS server running on a platform other than Windows 2000, the server must support SRV or be upgraded to a version that does support it. If you use a legacy DNS server that supports SRV but not dynamic updates, you must manually update the resource records at the time that the Windows 2000 server is promoted to a domain controller.

Note You can update the resource records by using the Netlogon.dns file created by the Active Directory Installation Wizard. The file is located in the %systemroot%\System32\config folder.

Active Directory and Domain Controllers

Installing Active Directory converts a Windows 2000 server to a domain controller. While a domain can have many domain controllers within it, a domain controller can host only one domain.

What is a Windows 2000 domain controller? Specifically, it is a Windows 2000 server that has been configured using the Active Directory Installation Wizard (or using a member server that has been upgraded using the domain controller promotion program DCPromo.exe), which installs and configures components that in turn provide Active Directory directory services to the network computers and users. Domain controllers store domain-wide directory data (such as the system security policy), and manage user domain interactions, including user logon, authentication and directory searches.

By promoting a server to a domain controller, the installation wizard either creates a new Windows 2000 domain or assigns the domain controller to an existing domain. While Windows NT 4.0 had both primary domain controllers (PDCs) and backup domain controllers (BDCs), all domain controllers function as peers and support multimaster replication in Windows 2000. Active Directory information is thus replicated among the domain on all domain controllers.

Planning For convenience, you can upgrade to Windows 2000 from an existing Windows NT 4.0 domain structure in stages. Before you proceed, note that a Windows 2000 domain controller is a global catalog server and it holds the operations master roles.

Global Catalog

The Windows 2000 operating system introduces the global catalog (GC), a database kept on one or more domain controllers that performs two key Active Directory roles: logon and querying:

- **Logon.** Within a native-mode domain, the GC provides the universal group membership information during a logon request. Every object authenticating to

Active Directory must reference the GC server, including every computer that boots up. In a multidomain environment, at least one domain controller that contains the GC must be running and available for users to be able to log on. A GC server must also be available when a user logs on with a non-default UPN, or user principal name (UPN). (We'll explain UPNs later in this chapter.) If a GC is not available when a user initiates a network logon process, the user can log on only to the local computer and not onto the network. The only exception to this is for users who are members of the Domain Administrators group—they can log on to the network even when a GC is not available.

- **Querying.** In a forest that contains many domains, the GC allows users to search across all domains without having to search each domain individually. The GC makes directory structures within a forest transparent to end users seeking information. Most Active Directory network traffic is query-related: users, administrators, and programs all request information about directory objects. Queries occur much more frequently than do updates to the directory.

By default, Active Directory automatically creates a GC on the initial domain controller in the Windows 2000 forest. Each forest must have at least one GC. If you use multiple sites with native-mode domains, you might want to assign a domain controller in every site to hold GC, because a GC (which determines an account's group membership) is required to complete the logon authentication process. If you use mixed-mode domains, you do not require a GC query for logon. (For an explanation of mixed- and native-mode domains, please see the section on domains later in this chapter.)

You can move the GC's location to another domain controller within the same forest with the Active Directory Sites And Services Snap-In. You can configure any domain controller to host a GC based on your organization's requirements for servicing logon requests and search queries. The higher the number of GC servers, the quicker the response to user inquiries. However, as the number of GC servers increases, so does the replication traffic required. Hence, there is a tradeoff between hosting a high number of GC servers for faster logon and querying and handling high amounts of network traffic.

Operations Master Roles

Multimaster replication among peer domain controllers is impractical for some types of alterations to Active Directory; so only one domain controller—the operations master—accepts requests for such changes.

When you create the first domain within a new forest, at least five single operations master roles are assigned to the first domain controller in that domain by default. In a small Active Directory forest with only one domain and one domain controller, the domain controller continues to own all the operations master roles. In a larger network, whether with a single or multiple domains, you can reassign these roles to one or more of the other domain controllers. Some roles must appear in every forest. Other roles must appear in every domain in the forest.

The following two forest-wide operations master roles must be unique in the forest:

- **Schema master.** The domain controller holding the schema master role controls all updates and modifications to the schema. The schema defines each object, including the object's attributes that can be stored in the directory. To update the schema of a forest, you must have access to the schema master.
- **Domain naming master.** The domain controller holding the domain naming master role controls the addition or removal of domains in the forest.

The following three domain-wide operations master roles must be unique in each domain.

- **Relative ID (RID) master.** The RID master is responsible for allocating sequences of RIDs to each domain controller in its domain. Each time a domain controller creates a user, group, or computer object, it assigns the object a unique security identifier (SID). The SID consists of a domain security ID—which is the same for all SIDs created in the domain—and a relative ID, which is unique for each SID created in the domain. When the domain controller has exhausted its pool of RIDs, it requests another pool from the RID master.
- **PDC emulator.** If the domain contains computers operating without Windows 2000 client software, or if it contains Windows NT BDCs, the PDC emulator acts as a Windows NT PDC, processing password changes from clients and replicating updates to the BDCs. The PDC emulator receives preferential replication of password changes performed by other domain controllers in the domain. If a logon authentication fails at another domain controller because of a bad password, that domain controller forwards the authentication request to the PDC emulator before rejecting the logon attempt.
- **Infrastructure master.** The infrastructure master is responsible for updating all interdomain references whenever an object referenced by another object moves. For example, whenever the members of groups are renamed or changed, the infrastructure master updates the group-to-user references. When you rename or move a member of a group and that member resides in a different domain from the group, the group might temporarily appear not to contain that member. The infrastructure master of the group's domain is responsible for updating the group so that it knows the new name or location of the member. The infrastructure master distributes the update using multimaster replication. Unless only one domain controller is in the domain, do not assign the infrastructure master role to the domain controller that hosts the GC. If you do, the infrastructure master will not function. If all domain controllers in a domain also host the GC (including a situation in which only one domain controller exists), all domain controllers have current data and therefore the infrastructure master role is not needed.

Active Directory Objects

Active Directory objects are the entities that make up the network. An object is a set of distinct attributes that represent something concrete, such as a user or computer. When you create an Active Directory object, Active Directory generates values for some of the attributes and you must enter the others. An example of an attribute value entered by Active Directory is the globally unique identifier (GUID).

The Schema

The schema is a description of the object classes and the attributes for those object classes.

Note The *object class* is a blueprint for a specific kind of object that can be stored in the directory. An object class is a distinct, named set of attributes that represents something concrete, such as a user, a printer, or an application. The attributes hold data describing the thing that is identified by the directory object. Attributes of a user might include the user's given name, surname, and e-mail address. The terms *object class* and *class* are interchangeable.

For each class of object, the schema defines the attributes that object class must have, the additional attributes it can have, and the object class that can be its parent. Every Active Directory object is an instance of an object class. Each attribute is defined only once and can be used in multiple classes.

Active Directory stores the schema, whose definitions are also stored as objects: Class Schema objects and Attribute Schema objects. This storage system enables Active Directory to manage class and attribute objects in the same way that it manages other directory objects.

Applications that create or modify Active Directory objects use the schema to determine what attributes the object must or might have and what those attributes can look like in terms of data structures and syntax constraints.

Objects are either *container* objects or *leaf* objects (also called non-container objects). A container object can store other objects; a leaf object cannot. For example, a folder is a container object for files, which are leaf objects. Every class of object in the Active Directory schema has attributes that ensure the following criteria:

- Unique identification of each object in a directory data store
- For security principals (users, computers, or groups), compatibility with SIDs used in the Windows NT 4.0 operating system and earlier
- Compatibility with LDAP standards for directory object names

Schema Attributes and Querying

Using the Active Directory Schema tool, you can mark an attribute as indexed. Doing so adds all instances of that attribute to the index—not just the instances that are members of a particular class—and you can include attributes in the GC. Indexing an attribute helps queries to more quickly find objects that have that attribute. The GC contains a default set of attributes for every object in the forest; you can add your choices to these.

Schema Object Names

As we stated earlier, classes and attributes are both schema objects. Any schema object can be referenced by any of the following types of names:

- **LDAP display name.** The LDAP display name is globally unique for each schema object. The LDAP display name consists of one or more words. Each word after the first word has an initial capital. For example, mailAddress and machinePasswordChangeInterval are the LDAP display names for two schema attributes. Active Directory Schema and other Windows 2000 administrative tools show objects' LDAP display names. Programmers and administrators use the LDAP display name to reference the object programmatically.
- **Common name.** The common name for schema objects is also globally unique. You specify the common name when creating a new object class or attribute in the schema. The relative distinguished name (RDN) of the object in the schema represents the object class.
- **Object identifier (OID).** A schema object's identifier is a number issued by an issuing authority such as the International Organization for Standardization (ISO) or the American National Standards Institute (ANSI). For example, the OID for the SMTP-Mail-Address attribute is 1.2.840.113556.1.4.786. OIDs are guaranteed to be unique across all networks worldwide and form a hierarchy. Once you obtain a root OID from an issuing authority, you can use it to allocate additional OIDs.

Object Naming Conventions

Active Directory allows different formats for object names depending on the context in which you use them. If your organization has several domains, you can use the same user name or computer name in different domains. The SID, GUID, LDAP distinguished name (DN), and canonical name generated by Active Directory all uniquely identify each user or computer in the directory. If the user or computer object is renamed or moved to a different domain, the security ID, LDAP relative distinguished name (RDN), and canonical name all change, but the GUID generated by Active Directory does not.

Security Principal Names

A *security principal* is a Windows 2000 object managed by Active Directory that is automatically assigned a SID for logon authentication and for access to resources. A security principal can be a user account, a computer account, or a group; thus a *security principal name* is a name that uniquely identifies a user, computer, or group within a single domain. A *security principal object* must be authenticated by a domain controller in the domain in which the security principal object is located; the security principal object can be granted or denied access to network resources.

A security principal name is not unique across domains, but for backward compatibility it must be unique within its own domain. Security principal objects can be renamed, moved, or contained within a nested domain hierarchy.

Security Identifiers

A SID is a unique number created by the security subsystem of the Windows 2000 operating system, and assigned to security principal objects—that is, to user, group, and computer accounts. Every account on your network is issued a unique SID when that account is first created. Internal processes in the Windows 2000 operating system refer to an account's SID rather than to the account's user or group name.

Each Active Directory object is protected by an ACL that identifies which users or groups can access that object. Each ACL contains one or more access control entries (ACEs). Each ACE identifies a particular user or group by SID and defines the level of access that user or group is permitted to the object. For example, a user might have read-only access to certain objects, read access and write access to others, and no access to still others.

If you create an account, delete it, and then create an account with the same user name, the new account does not have the rights or permissions previously granted to the old account because the accounts will have different SIDs.

LDAP-Related Names

Active Directory is an LDAP-compliant directory service based on an X.500 directory structure. In the Windows 2000 operating system, all access to Active Directory objects occurs through LDAP. LDAP defines what operations you can perform to query and modify information in a directory and how you can securely access information in a directory. Therefore, you would use LDAP to find or enumerate directory objects and to query or administer Active Directory. You can query by LDAP distinguished name (an attribute of the object), but because these names are difficult to remember, LDAP also supports querying by other attributes (for example, by color to find color printers). Thus you can find an object without needing to know its distinguished name.

LDAP Distinguished Names and Relative Distinguished Names

LDAP provides DNs and RDNs for objects. Active Directory implements these LDAP naming conventions with the variations shown in Table 4-1.

Table 4-1. LDAP naming conventions and their Active Directory counterparts.

LDAP DN and RDN Naming Convention	Corresponding Active Directory Naming Convention
cn=common name	cn=common name
ou=organizational unit	ou=organizational unit
o=organization	dc=domain component
c=country	(not supported)

Every Active Directory object has an LDAP DN. Objects are located within Active Directory domains according to a hierarchical path that includes the labels of the Active Directory domain name and each level of container objects. The DN defines the full path to the object. The RDN is that segment of an object's DN that is an attribute of the object itself and defines the name of the object itself.

By using the full path to an object—including the object name and all parent objects to the root of the domain—the DN identifies a unique object within the domain hierarchy. Each RDN is stored in the Active Directory database and contains a reference to its parent. During an LDAP operation, the entire DN is constructed by following the references to the root. In a complete LDAP DN, the RDN of the object to be identified appears at the left with the name of the leaf and ends at the right with the name of the root, as shown here:

```
cn=JDoe, ou=Widgets, ou=Manufacturing, dc=USRegion, dcOrgName.dc=com
```

The RDN of the *JDoe* user object is cn=JDoe, the RDN of *Widgets* (the parent object of *JDoe*) is ou=Widgets, and so on.

Active Directory tools do not display the LDAP abbreviations for the naming attributes (dc=, ou=, or cn=). These abbreviations are shown only to illustrate how LDAP recognizes the portions of the DN. Most Active Directory tools display object names in canonical form, which we'll describe later in this chapter. The Windows 2000 operating system uses the DN to let an LDAP client retrieve an object's information from the directory, but no Windows 2000 user interface requires you to enter DNs. The explicit use of DNs, RDNs, and naming attributes is required only when you write LDAP-compliant programs or scripts.

LDAP URL Names

Active Directory supports access using the LDAP protocol from any LDAP-enabled client. LDAP URLs are also used in scripting. An LDAP URL begins with the prefix *LDAP*, and then names the server holding Active Directory services, followed by the attributed name of the object (the DN). For example:

```
LDAP://server1.USRegion.OrgName.com/cn=JDoe,ou=Widgets,
ou=Manufacturing,dc=USRegion,dcOrgName.dc=com
```

LDAP-based Active Directory Canonical Names

By default, Active Directory administrative tools display object names using the canonical name format, which lists the RDNs from the root downward and without the RFC 1779 naming attribute descriptors (dc=, ou=, or cn=). The canonical name uses the DNS domain name format—the constituents of the domain labels section of the name are separated by periods, as in USRegion.OrgName.com. Table 4-2 contrasts the LDAP DN with the same name in canonical name format.

Table 4-2. LDAP DN format contrasted with the canonical name format.

LDAP DN Name	cn=JDoe,ou=Widgets,ou=Manufacturing,dc=USRegion,dcOrgName.dc=com
Canonical Name	USRegion.OrgName.com/Manufacturing/Widgets/Jdoe

Object GUIDs

In addition to its LDAP DN, every object in Active Directory has a GUID: a 128-bit number assigned by the Directory System Agent when the object is created. The GUID—which you cannot alter or remove—is stored in an attribute required for every object: *objectGUID*. Unlike a DN or RDN, the GUID never changes.

When you store a reference to an Active Directory object in an external store, you should use the *objectGUID* value.

Logon Names: User Principal Names and Security Account Manager Account Names

As we described earlier, security principals are objects that Windows-based security is applied to for both logon authentication and resource access authorization. Users are one type of security principal. In the Windows 2000 operating system, user security principals require a unique logon name to gain access to a domain and its resources.

User Principal Name

In Active Directory, each user account has a user principal name (UPN) in the format <user>@<DNS-domain-name>. A UPN is a name—assigned by an administrator—that is shorter than the LDAP distinguished name used by the system and thus easier to remember. The UPN is independent of the user object's DN, so you can move or rename a user object without affecting the user logon name. When users log on using a UPN, they no longer have to choose a domain from a list on the logon dialog box.

The UPN consists of three parts: the UPN prefix (user logon name), the @ character, and the UPN suffix (usually a domain name). The default UPN suffix for a user account is the DNS name of the Active Directory domain in which the user account is located. The UPN is an attribute (*userPrincipalName*) of the security principal object. If a user object's UPN attribute has no value, the user object has a default UPN of userName@DnsDomainName.

If your organization has many domains that form a deep domain tree organized by department and region, default UPN names can become unwieldy. For example, the default UPN for a user might be sales.states.iss.net. The logon name for a user in that domain is user@sales.states.iss.net. Instead of accepting the default DNS domain name as the UPN suffix, you can simplify both administration and user logon processes by providing a single UPN suffix for all users. The UPN suffix is used only within the Windows 2000 domain and is not required to be a valid DNS domain name. You can choose to use your e-mail domain name as the UPN. The user in the previous example would thus have the UPN name user@iss.net.

For a UPN-based logon, a GC might be necessary, depending on the user logging on and the domain membership of the user's computer. A GC is needed if the user logs on with a non-default UPN and the user's machine account is in a different domain than the user's user account. That is, if instead of accepting the default DNS domain name as the UPN suffix (as in the example user@sales.states.iss.com), you provide a single UPN suffix for all users (so that the user becomes simply user@iss.net), a GC is required for logon.

You use the Active Directory Domains And Trusts Snap-In to manage UPN suffixes for a domain. UPNs are assigned at the time a user is created. If you have created additional suffixes for the domain, you can select from the list of available suffixes when you create the user or group account. The suffixes appear in the list in the following order:

- Alternate suffixes
- Root domain
- Current domain

Security Accounts Manager Account Name

A security accounts manager (SAM) account name is required for compatibility with Windows NT 3.*x* and Windows NT 4.0 domains. The Windows 2000 user interface refers to the SAM account name as the "User logon name (pre-Windows 2000)."

SAM account names are sometimes referred to as flat names because, unlike DNS names, SAM account names do not use hierarchical naming. Because SAM names are flat, each one must be unique in the domain.

Description of Active Directory Objects

The objects described in Table 4-3 are created during installation of Active Directory, either during a fresh installation or an upgrade of a Windows NT 4.0 domain.

Table 4-3. Default Active Directory objects.

Icon	Folder	Description
	Domain	The root node of the snap-in represents the domain being administered.
	Computers	Contains all computers running Windows NT and Windows 2000 that join a domain. If you upgrade from a previous version, Active Directory migrates the machine account to this folder. You can move these objects.
	System	Contains Active Directory systems and services information, such as RPC, WinSock, and other information.
	Users	Contains all the users in the domain. In an upgrade, all users from the previous domain will be migrated. Like computers, the user objects can be moved.

You can use Active Directory to create the objects described in Table 4-4.

Table 4-4. Active Directory objects.

Icon	Object	Description
	User	A user object is an object that is a security principal in the directory. A user can log on to the network with these credentials and access permissions can be granted to users.
	Contact	A contact object is an account that does not have any security permissions. You cannot log on to the network as a contact. Contacts are typically used to represent external users for the purpose of e-mail.
	Computer	This is an object that represents a computer on the network. For Windows NT workstations and servers, this is the machine account.
	Organizational Unit	Organizational units are used as containers to logically organize directory objects such as users, groups, and computers in much the same way that folders organize files on your hard disk.
	Group	Groups can contain users, computers, and other groups. Groups simplify the management of large numbers of objects.
	Shared Folder	A Shared Folder is a network share that has been published in the directory.
	Shared Printer	A Shared Printer is a network printer that has been published in the directory

Object Publishing

Publishing is the act of creating objects in the directory that either directly contain the information you want to make available or provide a reference to it. For example, a user object contains useful information about users, such as their telephone numbers and e-mail addresses, while a volume object contains a reference to a shared file system volume.

You should publish information in Active Directory when the information is useful or interesting to a large part of the user community or when it needs to be widely accessible. Information published in Active Directory has two major characteristics:

- **Relatively static.** Publish only information that changes infrequently such as telephone numbers and e-mail addresses.
- **Structured.** Publish information that is structured (such as a user's business address) and can therefore be represented as a set of discrete attributes.

Operational information used by applications is an excellent candidate for publishing in Active Directory, including global configuration information that applies to all instances of a given application.

Applications can also publish their connection points in Active Directory. Connection points are used for a client/server rendezvous. Active Directory defines architecture for integrated service administration using Service Administration Point objects and provides standard connection points for applications that use the Remote Procedure Call (RPC), Winsock, and Component Object Model (COM) interfaces. Applications that do not use the RPC or Winsock interfaces for publishing their connection points can explicitly publish Service Connection Point objects in Active Directory.

You can also publish application data in Active Directory using application-specific objects. Application-specific data should meet the criteria discussed above: it should be globally interesting, relatively nonvolatile, and structured.

Interoperability

Active Directory supports a number of standards to ensure interoperability of the Windows 2000 environment with other Microsoft products and with a wide variety of products from other vendors.

Active Directory uses LDAP to enable interoperability with other LDAP-compatible client applications. Given the appropriate permissions, you can use any LDAP-compatible client application to browse, query, add, modify, or delete information in Active Directory.

Internal and External References

You can create a cross-referenced object that points to a server in a directory external to the forest. When a user searches a subtree that contains this cross-referenced object, Active Directory returns a referral to that server as part of the result set, and the LDAP client then follows the referral to get the data requested by the user.

Internal references refer to external directories that appear within the Active Directory namespace as a child of an existing Active Directory object. *External references* refer to an external directory that does not appear within the Active Directory namespace as a child.

For both internal and external references, Active Directory contains the DNS name of the server, which holds a copy of the external directory. This server also stores the distinguished name of the root of the external directory, in order to allow search operations in the external directory.

The Role of Kerberos in Interoperability

The Windows 2000 operating system supports multiple configurations for cross-platform interoperability:

- **Clients.** A Windows 2000 domain controller can provide authentication for client systems running implementations of RFC 1510 Kerberos, including clients running an operating system other than Windows 2000. Windows 2000–based user and computer accounts can serve as Kerberos principals for UNIX-based services.

- **UNIX clients and services.** Within a Windows 2000 domain, UNIX clients and servers can have Active Directory accounts and can therefore obtain authentication from a domain controller. In this scenario, a Kerberos principal would be mapped to a Windows 2000 user or computer account.
- **Applications and operating systems.** Client applications for Win32 and operating systems other than Windows 2000 that are based on the Generic Security Service Application Program Interface (GSS-API) can obtain session tickets for services within a Windows 2000 domain. In an environment that already uses a Kerberos realm, the Windows 2000 operating system supports interoperability with the following Kerberos services:
  - **Kerberos realm.** Windows 2000–based systems can authenticate to an RFC 1510 Kerberos server within a realm with a single sign-on to both the server and a local Windows 2000 account.
  - **Trust relationships with Kerberos realms.** A trust relationship can be established between a domain and a Kerberos realm, meaning that a client in a Kerberos realm can authenticate to an Active Directory domain to access network resources in that domain.

Backward Compatibility with the Windows NT Operating System

A special type of interoperability maintains backward compatibility with earlier versions of the current operating system. By default, the Windows 2000 operating system installs in a mixed-mode network configuration. A mixed-mode domain is a networked set of computers running both Windows NT and Windows 2000 domain controllers. Because Active Directory supports a mixed-mode domain, you can upgrade domains and computers at whatever rate you choose, based on your organization's needs.

Active Directory supports the Windows NT LAN Manager (NTLM) authentication protocol used by the Windows NT operating system, which means that authorized Windows NT users and computers can log on to and access resources in a Windows 2000 domain. To Windows NT clients and Windows 95 or Windows 98 clients not running Active Directory client software, a Windows 2000 domain appears to be a Windows NT Server 4.0 domain.

Windows 2000 Domains

Active Directory is always made up of at least one domain. Promoting or creating the initial domain controller in a network also creates the domain. You cannot have a domain without at least one domain controller, and each domain in the directory is identified by a DNS domain name. You use the Active Directory Domains And Trusts Snap-In to manage domains. You use domains to accomplish the following network management goals:

- **Delimit security.** A Windows 2000 domain defines a security boundary. Security policies and settings (such as administrative rights and ACLs) do not cross from one domain to another. Active Directory can include one or more domains, each with its own security policies.

- **Replicate information.** A domain is a Windows 2000 directory partition that is a unit of replication. Each domain stores only the information about the objects located in that domain. All of a domain's domain controllers can receive changes made to objects and can replicate those changes to all other domain controllers in that domain.
- **Apply Group Policy.** A domain defines one possible scope for policy. (You can also apply Group Policy settings to OUs or sites.) Applying a Group Policy object (GPO) to the domain establishes how domain resources can be configured and used. For example, you can use Group Policy to control desktop settings, such as desktop lockdown and application deployment. These policies are applied only within the domain and not across domains.
- **Structure the network.** Because one Active Directory domain can span multiple sites and can contain millions of objects (as compared to earlier versions of Windows NT Server, in which the SAM database had a limit of about 40,000 objects per domain), most organizations do not need to create separate domains to reflect the company's divisions and departments. Therefore, you should never need to create additional domains to handle additional objects. However, some organizations do require more than one domain to accommodate (for example) independent or completely autonomous business units that do not want anyone external to the unit to have authority over their objects. Such organizations can create additional domains and organize them into an Active Directory forest. Another reason to split the network into separate domains is if two parts of your network are separated by a link so slow that you never want complete replication traffic to cross it. (For slow links that can still handle replication traffic on a less frequent schedule, you can configure a single domain with multiple sites.)
- **Delegate administrative authority.** In networks running Windows 2000, you can narrowly delegate administrative authority for individual OUs as well as for individual domains, reducing the number of administrators with wide administrative authority needed. Because a domain is a security boundary, administrative permissions for a domain are limited to the domain by default. For example, an administrator with permissions to set security policies in one domain is not automatically granted authority to set security policies in any other domain in the directory.

Mixed-Mode and Native-Mode Domains

Windows 2000 is capable of supporting Windows NT 4.0–based workstations and servers within Windows 2000 domains. This leaves us with two possible cases:

- **Mixed-mode domain.** A domain with Windows NT 4.0 (and Windows 95/98) domain controllers and Windows 2000 domain controllers.

- **Native-mode domain.** A domain containing solely Windows 2000 domain controllers.

Mixed-Mode Domains

From the moment the PDC is upgraded until you decide to switch the domain into Windows 2000 native mode, the domain is in mixed mode. Mixed mode provides maximum backward compatibility with earlier versions of the operating system. Note that mixed mode only relates to the authentication infrastructure of a domain—in other words, the domain controllers. Even when a domain has only Windows 2000 DCs and has been switched to native mode, clients and servers running earlier versions of Windows NT and clients running Windows 95/98, can exist within the domain. This is known as a mixed environment.

You can leave the domain operating in mixed mode indefinitely, even if you have upgraded all the BDCs in the domain as well as the PDC. There are only four reasons to remain in mixed mode:

- **You cannot upgrade BDCs.** In this scenario, you have BDCs that for some reason you cannot upgrade or demote to member servers. This might be because you have applications that must run on a BDC but for some reason will not run on Windows 2000.
- **Inadequate physical security of BDCs.** A fundamental aspect of security is the physical security of the machine itself. A consideration here could be the difference between single-master updating of the SAM by the PDC alone, and Active Directory multimaster updating of the account database by all domain controllers.
- **BDC Security.** Because of the single-master nature of Windows NT directory updates, you might be comfortable with comparatively relaxed security on your BDCs. If so, you need to consider this when upgrading the BDCs to Windows 2000 DCs. If you cannot appropriately upgrade security of your BDC, you might consider demoting the BDC to a member server during upgrade, adding a new Windows 2000 domain controller in a different location, or possibly even reconsidering your proposed domain structure.
- **Fallback to Windows NT remains necessary.** As you must realize by now, one feature of mixed mode is its degree of backward compatibility. Mixed mode has the benefit of allowing you to add new Windows NT BDCs to the domain if a problem arises. In this situation, once the BDC has joined the domain, you could force a resynchronization of the account database. Then, as long as no Windows 2000 domain controllers are in the domain, you could promote the BDC to PDC. You should plan for fallback or recovery, but at some point, you will want to switch over completely to the new environment.

Native-Mode Domains

Once you've upgraded all DCs, you can switch the domain from mixed mode to native mode. Several things happen during the switch:

- The domain uses only Active Directory multimaster replication between DCs, so support for Netlogon replication ceases.
- Because Netlogon replication is now switched off, you can no longer add new Windows NT BDCs to the domain.
- Because multimaster replication is enabled, the former PDC is no longer the master of the domain; all DCs can now perform directory updates. One point that sometimes causes confusion is the continued existence of the PDC Emulator role. Despite the multimaster nature of Active Directory, Windows 2000 has a number of roles designated as operations masters, and PDC Emulator is an operations master role. Usually, the former PDC will continue as PDC Emulator operations master holder, which in a native-mode environment means that password changes are replicated to the former PDC preferentially by other DCs.
- Windows 2000 group types, such as universal and domain local groups, are enabled, as is group nesting.

This switch to native mode is not performed automatically by running DCPromo; you must administer the change. You should make the switch to native mode as soon as possible.

Planning Changing the domain mode from mixed to native mode is easy to do but impossible to undo, so bear in mind all of the factors discussed previously to determine when to make the change. Do not change domain mode if you have—or will have—any Windows NT DCs. We'll discuss changing the domain mode in the section on using Active Directory later in this chapter.

Sites

A Windows 2000–based site is a set of computers in one or more IP subnets, connected using Local Area Network (LAN) technologies, or as a set of LANs connected by a high-speed backbone. Computers in a single site need to be well-connected, which is generally a characteristic of computers within a subnet. (*Well-connected* is typically defined as a subnet with adequate bandwidth for the purpose of the network.) In contrast, separate sites are connected by a link that is slower than LAN speed. Use the Active Directory Sites And Services Snap-In to configure connections both within a site and between sites.

In the Windows 2000 operating system, sites provide the following services:

- Clients can request service from a domain controller in the same site (if one exists).

- Active Directory spends minimal time between intrasite replication.
- Active Directory tries to minimize bandwidth consumption for intersite replication.
- Sites let you schedule intersite replication.

Users and services should be able to access directory information at any time from any computer in the forest. This means that additions, modifications, and deletions of directory data must be replicated from the originating domain controller to other domain controllers in the forest. However, the need to widely distribute directory information must be balanced against the need to optimize network performance. Active Directory sites help to maintain this balance.

It is important to understand that sites are independent of domains. Sites map the physical structure of your network, whereas domains typically map the logical structure of your organization. Logical and physical structures are independent of each other, which has the following consequences:

- There is no necessary connection between sites and domain namespaces.
- There is no necessary correlation between your network's physical structure and its domain structure. However, in many organizations, domains are set up to reflect physical network structure. This is because domains are partitions, and partitioning influences replication. Partitioning the forest into multiple, smaller domains can reduce the amount of replication traffic.
- Active Directory lets multiple domains appear in a single site and a single domain appear in multiple sites.

How Active Directory Uses Site Information

You specify site information using Active Directory Sites And Services, and then Active Directory uses this information to determine how best to use available network resources. Using sites makes the following types of operations more efficient:

- **Servicing client requests.** When a client requests a service from a domain controller, Active Directory directs the request to a domain controller in the same site, if one is available. Selecting a domain controller that is well connected to the client that placed the request makes handling the request more efficient. Attempting to use domain controllers in the client's site first localizes network traffic, increasing the efficiency of the authentication process.
- **Replicating directory data.** Sites enable the replication of directory data both within and among sites. Active Directory replicates information within a site more frequently than across sites, which means that the best-connected domain controllers, those most likely to need particular directory information, receive replications first. The domain controllers in other sites receive all changes to the directory, but less frequently, reducing network bandwidth consumption.

Default-First-Site-Name

A default first site named Default-First-Site-Name is set up automatically when you install Windows 2000 Server on the first domain controller in your enterprise by running the Domain Controller Promotion Wizard or DCPromo.exe. Default-First-Site-Name is shown in Figure 4-1. The promotion wizard is the preferred setup method. You can rename this site later if necessary.

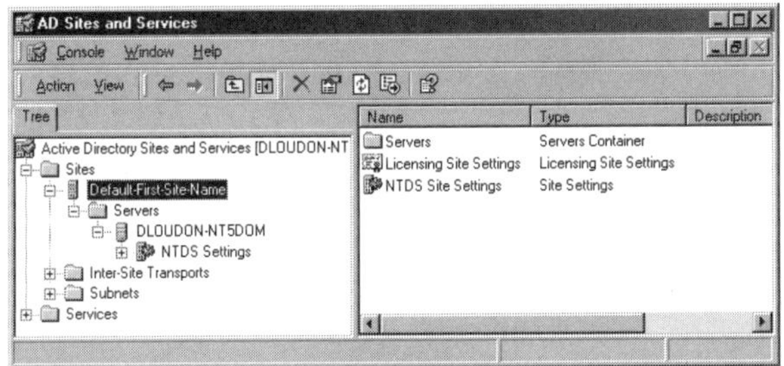

Figure 4-1. *The Default-First-Site-Name site information as displayed in the Sites And Services Manager Snap-In.*

The replication topology of sites on your network controls the following aspects of replication:

- **Where replication occurs.** For example, replication can occur when DCs communicate directly with which other DCs in the same site. Additionally, this topology controls how sites communicate with each other.
- **When replication occurs.** Replication between sites can be completely scheduled by the administrator. Replication between DCs inside the same site is notification based, where notifications are sent within five minutes of a change being made to an object in the domain.

All newly promoted domain controllers will be placed in the Site container that applies to them at time of install. For example, a server bound for Atlanta, Georgia might be initially built and configured in Reading, England, so the DC Promotion Wizard or DCPromo.exe will place the server in the Reading site. Once in Atlanta, the server object can be moved to the new site via the Sites and Services Manager Tool.

Organizational Units

New to the Windows 2000 operating system, OUs are a type of directory object into which you can place users, groups, computers, printers, shared folders, and other OUs within a single domain. An OU (represented by a folder in the Active Directory Users and Computers interface) lets you logically organize and store objects in the domain. If you have multiple domains, each domain can implement its own OU hierarchy. As Figure 4-2 illustrates, OUs can contain other OUs.

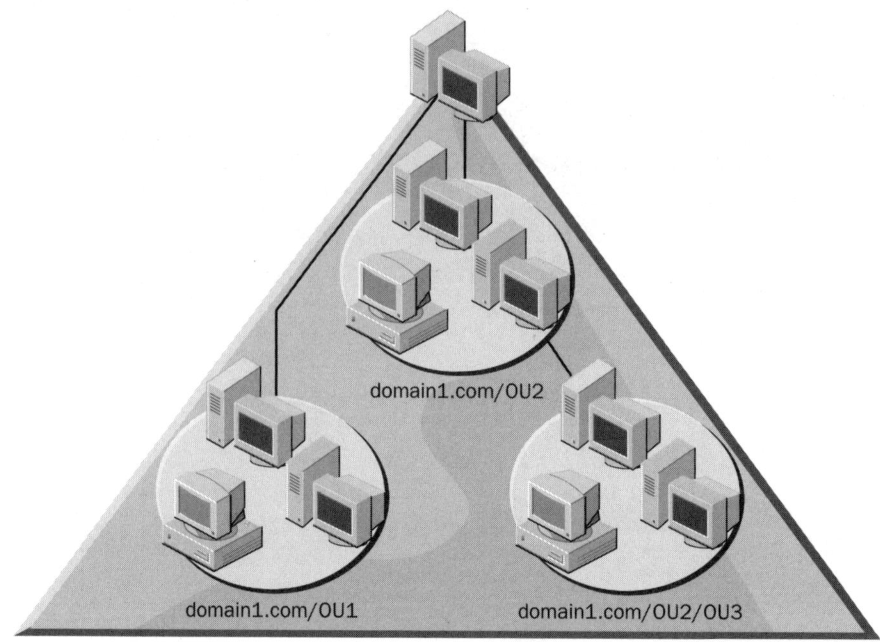

Figure 4-2. *The OU hierarchy inside a single domain.*

You use OUs primarily to delegate administrative authority over sets of users, groups, and resources. For example, you might create an OU to contain all user accounts for a particular business unit. After creating OUs to delegate administration, apply Group Policy settings to the OUs to define desktop configurations for users and computers. Because you use OUs to delegate administration, the structure you create will probably reflect your administrative model more than it reflects your business organization.

Although users can navigate a domain's OU structure when looking for resources, querying the GC to find resources is much more efficient. Therefore, you don't need to create an OU structure that appeals to end users. You can also create an OU structure that mirrors your business organization, but doing so can prove difficult and expensive to manage. Instead of creating an OU structure to reflect resource location or departmental organization, design OUs with administrative delegation and Group Policy settings in mind.

Active Directory Replication

The information stored in Active Directory on every domain controller is partitioned into three categories: domain, schema, and configuration data—even if the domain controller is not a GC server. Each of these categories is in a separate directory partition, which is also called a naming context. These directory partitions are the units of replication. The three directory partitions that each Active Directory server holds are defined as follows:

- **Domain data directory partition.** This partition contains all the objects in the directory for this domain. Domain data in each domain is replicated to every domain controller in that domain, but not beyond its domain.
- **Schema data directory partition.** This partition contains all object types (and their attributes) that you can create in Active Directory. This data is common to all domains in the domain tree or forest. Schema data is replicated to all domain controllers in the forest.
- **Configuration data directory partition.** This partition contains replication topology and related metadata. Active Directory–aware applications store information in the configuration directory partition. This data is common to all domains in the domain tree or forest. Configuration data is replicated to all domain controllers in the forest.

If the domain controller is a GC server, it also holds a fourth category of information:

- **Partial replica of domain data directory partition for all domains.** In addition to storing and replicating a complete set of all objects in the directory for its own host domain, a GC server stores and replicates a partial replica of the domain directory partition for all other domains in the forest. This partial replica, by definition, contains a subset of the properties for all objects in all domains in the forest. A partial replica is read-only, whereas a complete replica is read/write.

If a domain contains a GC, other domain controllers replicate all objects in that domain to the GC, and then partial replica replication takes place between GCs. If a domain has no GC, a regular domain controller serves as the source of the partial replica.

By default, the partial set of attributes stored in the GC includes those attributes most frequently used in search operations, because one of the GC's primary functions is to support clients queries to the directory. Using GCs to perform partial domain replication instead of doing full domain replication reduces WAN traffic.

Replication Within a Site

If your network consists of a single LAN or a set of LANs connected by a high-speed backbone, the entire network can be a single site. The first domain controller you install automatically creates the default first site, named Default-First-Site-Name. After installing the first domain controller, all additional domain controllers are automatically added to the same site as the original domain controller, with one exception: If at the time that you install a domain controller, its IP address falls within the subnet previously specified in an alternative site, the domain controller is added to this alternative site.

Directory information within a site is replicated frequently and automatically. Intrasite replication is tuned to minimize replication latency. Intrasite directory updates are not compressed, since uncompressed exchanges use more network resources but require less domain controller processing power.

Figure 4-3 illustrates replication within a site. Three domain controllers replicate the forest's schema data and configuration data, as well as all directory objects with a complete set of each object's attributes.

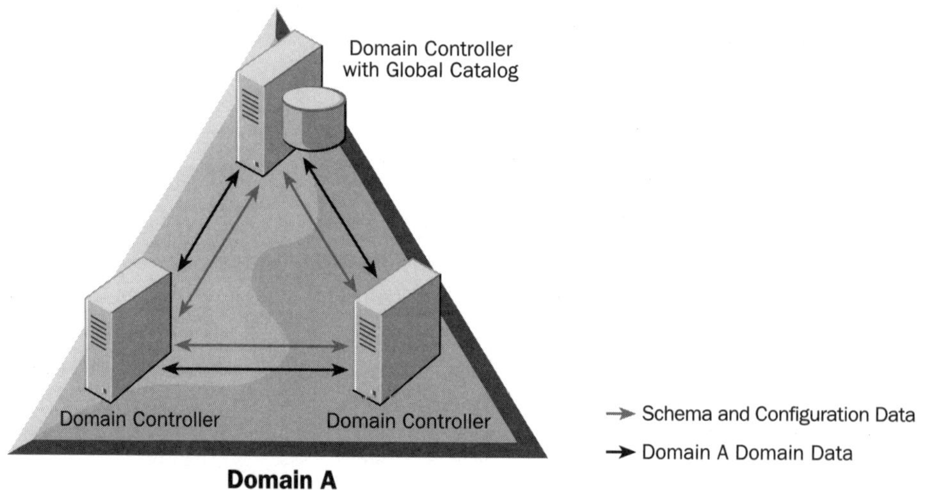

Figure 4-3. *Intrasite replication with a single domain.*

The configuration formed by the connections used to replicate directory information between domain controllers, called the *replication topology*, is automatically generated by the Knowledge Consistency Checker (KCC) service in Active Directory. Active Directory site topology is a logical representation of a physical network and is defined on a per-forest basis. Active Directory attempts to establish a topology that allows at least two connections to every domain controller, so that if a domain controller becomes unavailable, directory information can still reach all online domain controllers through the other connection.

Active Directory automatically evaluates and adjusts the replication topology to meet the changing state of the network. For example, when a domain controller is added to a site, the replication topology is adjusted to incorporate this new addition efficiently. Active Directory clients and servers use the forest's site topology to route query and replication traffic efficiently.

Replication Between Sites

Create multiple sites to optimize both server-to-server and client-to-server traffic over WAN links. In the Windows 2000 operating system, intersite replication automatically minimizes bandwidth consumption between sites.

How Sites Are Connected

Network connections between sites are represented by *site links*. A site link is a low-bandwidth or unreliable connection between two or more sites. A WAN that connects two fast networks is an example of a site link. Generally, any two networks connected by a link that is slower than LAN speed are probably connected by a site link. In addition, a fast link that is near capacity has a low effective bandwidth and is considered a site link. When you have multiple sites, sites connected by site links become part of the replication topology.

In a Windows 2000–based network, site links are not automatically generated—you must create them using the Active Directory Sites And Services Snap-In. By creating site links and configuring their replication availability, relative cost, and replication frequency, you provide Active Directory with information about which Connection objects to create to replicate directory data. Active Directory uses site links as indicators for where it should create Connection objects, and Connection objects use the actual network connections to exchange directory information.

A site link has an associated schedule that indicates at what times of day the link is available to carry replication traffic.

By default, site links are transitive, which means that a domain controller in one site can make replication connections with domain controllers in any other site. In other words, if site A is connected to site B, and site B is connected to site C, domain controllers in site A can communicate with domain controllers in site C. When you create a site, you might want to create additional links to enable specific connections between sites and customize existing site links connecting the sites.

Figure 4-4 on the following page shows two sites connected by a site link. Of the six domain controllers in the figure, two are bridgehead servers. (The system automatically assigns the bridgehead server role.)

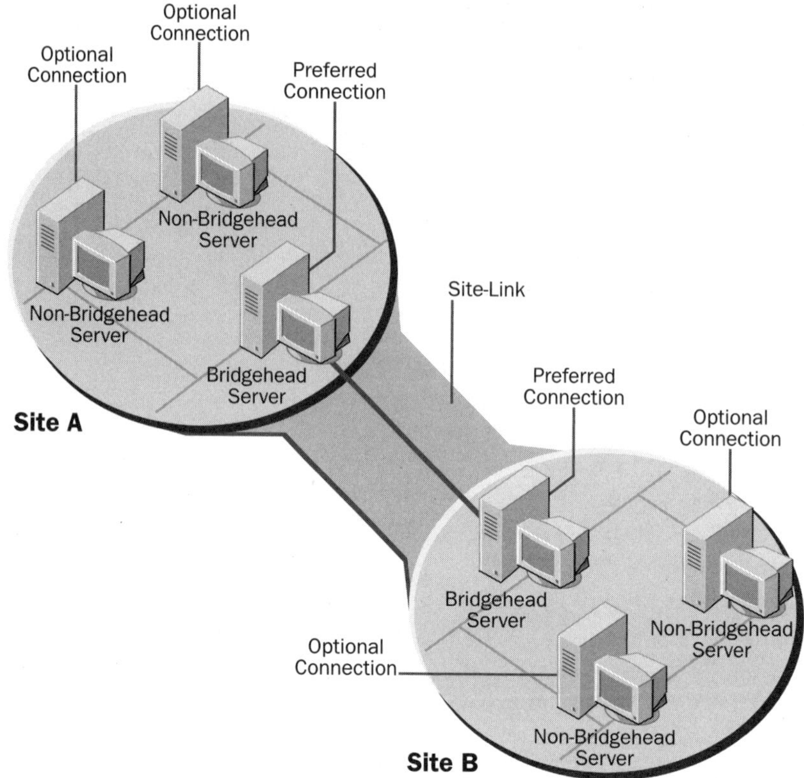

Figure 4-4. *Two sites connected by a site link. Each site's preferred bridgehead server is used preferentially for intersite information exchange.*

The bridgehead servers are the preferred servers for replication, but you can also configure the other domain controllers in the site to replicate directory changes between sites.

After updates are replicated from one site to the bridgehead server in the other site, the updates are then replicated to other domain controllers within the site through intrasite replication. Although a single domain controller receives the initial intersite directory update, all domain controllers service client requests.

Planning and Rollout Considerations

Planning the Active Directory infrastructure is a major consideration when upgrading to Windows 2000, and requires careful planning. In this section, we will outline some of the factors that you should take into account before deploying a Windows 2000 Active Directory.

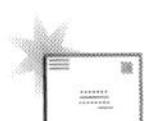

Note This section will only cover those aspects of Active Directory deployment which are related, either directly or indirectly, to the security of the Windows 2000 network. We will not cover other influences, such as cost or ease of use. For more information on deploying Windows 2000 systems, please see the following Microsoft documentation: the Deployment Planning Guide volume of the *Microsoft Windows 2000 Server Resource Kit* and the *Active Directory Services for Microsoft Windows 2000 Technical Reference.*

Planning for Active Directory

When working on your Active Directory plan, use the following design principles to guide your decision-making process:

- **Simplicity is the best investment.** Simple structures are easier to explain, easier to maintain, and easier to debug. Although some added complexity can add value, be sure to weigh the incremental added value against the potential maintenance costs in the future. For example, the maximum optimization of query and replication traffic might require a complex site topology. However, a complex site topology is generally harder to maintain than a simple site topology. In each case, you must consider the point at which the cost of maintaining the structure is greater than the cost of a wasted resource. Additionally, almost everything that you create will require some maintenance over its lifetime. A structure that you create without well-defined reasons will end up costing you more in the long run than any value it adds. Justify the existence of any structure you create.
- **End users care about data and administrators care about structure.** End users want to find files and data and locate people, and they want to know the easiest way to do this. They are not exposed to directory structures; they do not care how your structures are set up. Administrators care about how a directory is structured. The structure usually reflects who can create, delete, and manage objects.
- **Your business and your organization will always change.** The normal changes that occur at any organization—from employee moves to enterprise-wide reorganizations or acquisitions—will affect your Active Directory structure. When designing your structure, consider how these potential changes will affect end-user and administrator interaction with the directory. For example, consider the impact that your last major business reorganization would have had on the structures you've designed. Would the changes have required significant and expensive changes to the Active Directory structure?
- **Aim for the ideal design.** In your first design pass, design what you consider to be the ideal structure, even if it does not reflect your current domain or directory infrastructure. It is useful and practical to understand an ideal structure, even if it is not currently attainable.

- **Explore design alternatives.** Make more than one pass at each design. The value of a design becomes more evident when you compare it to other design ideas. Multiple designs will help you to evaluate and compare the functionality and reliability of each component of each design and combine the best of all designs into the plan that you will implement.

Active Directory represents the following network elements as objects:

- computers
- groups
- printers
- shared file folders
- users

In Active Directory, you can query objects, inspect them for information of interest, and update or delete them. An Active Directory plan is all about creating a structure around these objects that answers the following questions:

- Where will you place the objects?
- How will you define the objects?
- How will you discover the objects?
- Who will be able to access the properties of objects?
- Who will manage the objects?

Composing Your Active Directory Plan

Four basic components make up an Active Directory Structure: forests, domains, OUs, and sites. The objective is to create a planning document for each component of the structure, capturing important decisions and justifications along the way. These planning documents will then serve as a starting point for your next planning task, migration. Four planning documents make up the suggested Active Directory Structure Plan:

- Forest Plan
- Domain Plan for each forest
- OU Plan for each domain
- Site Topology Plan for each forest

Planning the Forest Structure

As you have seen, a forest is a collection of Active Directory domains with the following key characteristics:

- **Single schema.** The Active Directory schema defines the object classes and the attributes of object classes that can be created in the directory. The schema exists as a distinct naming context that is replicated to every domain controller in the forest. By default, the Schema Administrators group has full control over the schema.

- **Single configuration container.** The Active Directory configuration container is a distinct naming context that is replicated to every domain controller in the forest. Items in the configuration container include a definition of the site topology for the forest. By default, the Enterprise Administrators group has full control over the configuration container.
- **Complete trust.** When you create domains in Active Directory, the system automatically creates a spanning tree of two-way transitive trusts connecting the domains in that forest.
- **A single global catalog.** The global catalog contains a copy of every object from every domain in the forest, but only a select set of the attributes from each object.

Forest Planning Process

The primary steps to creating a Forest Plan for your organization are:

1. Determine the number of forests for your network.
2. Create a forest change control policy.
3. Understand the impact of changes to the Forest Plan after deployment.

You will have to make these decisions in conjunction with current domain administrators and your security team to ensure that you consider all factors considered the design phase.

Determining the Number of Forests for Your Network

When you begin to plan your forest model, start with a single forest, which will be sufficient for most situations. The purpose of creating forests is to enable collaboration between domains in the same forest. Within a single forest, users have a consistent view of directory data via the global catalog, and through transitive trust, users have the potential to be granted access to any resource in the forest.

A need for multiple forests can arise if you must isolate domains in one forest from domains in another forest. There are situations in which isolation between domains is both necessary and appropriate. Limited trust between two organizations on the same network infrastructure can occur for the following reasons:

- **The organizations do not want administrators from the other domains to manipulate the schema or configuration or to add new domains.** Domain administrators and enterprise administrators have similar security responsibilities. However, unlike the permissions of an enterprise administrator, a domain administrator has full access to all directory objects on an individual domain controller. Any domain administrator can take ownership of objects in the configuration and schema containers by running services on the domain controller that have full system access permissions.

- **The organizations do not trust each other's delegated administrators to refrain from flooding the global catalog.** A representation of every object in the forest resides in the global catalog. An administrator who has been delegated the ability to create objects can intentionally or unintentionally create a denial of service condition. You can create this condition by flooding the domain with objects, thereby flooding the global catalog, and flooding the network with replication.
- **The organizations cannot agree on a forest change policy.** Certain changes, such as schema changes, configuration changes, or the addition of new domains, have forest-wide impact. Each organization in the forest should agree on a process for implementing these changes, and agree on membership of the Schema Administrators and Enterprise Administrators group. If organizations cannot agree on a common policy, they should not share the same forest.
- **The organizations want to limit the scope of trust.** Every domain in a forest trusts every other domain in the forest. Every user in the forest can be included in a group membership or can appear on an ACL on any computer in the forest. If you want to prevent certain users from ever being granted permission to certain resources, those users must reside in a different forest than the forest where the resources reside. If necessary, you can use explicit trust to grant those users access to resources in specific domains.

All domain administrators for all domains in a forest have equal ability to modify configuration information that is replicated globally throughout the forest. For this reason, it is important that only *managed domains*—whose domain administrators are trustworthy members of the organization's administration staff—are joined to the forest. *Unmanaged domains*—whose domain administrators cannot be trusted with this responsibility—should not be joined to the domain forest. Instead, those domains can use accounts or services in the forest by configuring explicit one-way trust to specific domains.

Incremental Costs for an Additional Forest

For users in a forest to access objects in another forest, additional configuration is required. This additional configuration requires maintenance. Additional forests—should they ever need to interact with each other—incur an incremental cost that is usually proportionate to the level of interaction. The following are examples of additional configuration that lead to incremental costs:

- **Each additional forest must contain at least one domain.** This might require you to have more domains than you had originally planned for. The higher the number of domains, the greater the potential for a vulnerability to be discovered and exploited.
- **You must manage the forest-wide components of each forest separately.** For example, the schema and configuration container elements and their associated administration group memberships must all be managed separately—even if they are essentially the same.

- **You must create and maintain an explicit trust between domains in different forests.** The explicit trust between domains is one-way and nontransitive. Without established trust, users in one forest cannot be granted access to read or manipulate objects in another forest.
- **There are restrictions on the use of UPN-style logon between computers in different forests.**
- **By default, users in one forest are only aware of objects in the global catalog of their own forest.** To discover objects in a different forest, users must explicitly query domains that are outside their own forest. Alternatively, administrators can import data from other domains into the forest where the user resides. This can add cost for two reasons:
  - Users must be trained to understand the directory structure, so that they know where to direct queries when global catalog queries fail.
  - When you import data from a domain in a separate forest, you put a process in place to keep the imported data up to date when it changes in the source domain, thereby introducing a potential area of exploitation between the forests.

Creating a Forest Change Control Policy

Each forest you create should have an associated Forest Change Control Policy as part of your Forest Plan document. You will use this policy to guide changes that have forest-wide impact. The policy should include the following information:

- Who will be in the Enterprise Administrators group, and who will be allowed to change the membership of this group?
- Who in the organization will define the process for adding new domains to the forest?
- Who will define the configuration change process?
- Who will be in the Schema Administrators group, and who will be allowed to change the membership of this group?
- Who will define the schema change process?

Caution Since the forest-wide administrator groups have unlimited power over the forest, keep their membership small and closely controlled.

Planning the Domain Structure

You will need to consider the following key characteristics of a Windows 2000 domain when you begin creating your domain structure plan:

- **A partition of the forest.** An Active Directory forest is a distributed database; domains define the partitions of the database.

- **Service by domain controller servers.** A domain controller can host exactly one domain. You can make changes to objects in the domain on any domain controller of that domain. All the domain controllers in a given forest also host a copy of the Configuration and Schema containers for that forest.
- **A unit of authentication.** Each domain database contains security principal objects such as users, groups, and computers. Security principal objects are special in that they can be granted or denied access to the resources on a network. To prove its identity before accessing a resource, a security principal must be authenticated by a domain controller for the domain in which the security principal object is located.
- **A scope of administration.** Every domain has a Domain Administrators group, which has full control over every object in the domain database, by default. This means that regardless of the permissions currently set on an object, a domain administrator can take ownership of that object and arbitrarily reset the permissions. This capability allows domain administrators to recover from any possible situation that arises from misapplication of permissions.
- **A unit of domain user account security policy.** A small set of security policies that apply to domain user accounts can only be set on a per-domain basis (for example, Add Workstation To A Domain Privilege).
- **DNS domain names.** A domain is identified by a DNS name, which is hierarchical. The DNS name of an Active Directory domain indicates its position in the forest hierarchy.

Domain Planning Process

Each forest that you create will contain one or more domains. The steps to creating a Domain Plan for a forest are:

- Determine the number of domains in each forest.
- Choose a forest root domain.
- Assign a DNS name to each domain and create a domain hierarchy.
- Plan DNS server deployment.
- Optimize authentication with shortcut trusts.
- Understand the impact of changes to the Domain Plan after deployment.

Again, you'll need to consult your organization's domain administrators and security team, as well as those responsible for DNS and physical networking.

Creating a Multiple-Domain Forest

It is better to start by designing a single domain network and then justifying any additional domains—even if you currently have more than one NT4.0 domain—rather than starting with a multiple domain structure. This is because every domain that you create will introduce more overhead.

Consider these possible reasons for adding more domains in your domain structure:

- **Partitioning to scale the forest.** Depending on your network topology, it might be inefficient to carry the replication traffic of a single large domain to every location that needs a domain controller. By dividing the forest into multiple domains, you can reduce replication traffic and the forest will scale more easily over the entire network.
- **Organization requires autonomous domain administration supervision.** Normally, domain administrators in a given domain have complete control over all objects in that domain. If a subdivision in your organization will not accept an unknown administrator supervising its objects, place those objects in a separate domain. For example, for legal reasons, it might not be prudent for a subdivision of an organization that works on highly sensitive or secret projects to accept domain supervision from a central IT group. However, remember that all subdivisions in the forest must agree to share the configuration container and schema.
- **Preserve an existing Windows NT 4.0 domain.** If you already have Windows NT 4.0 domains in place today, you might want to keep them as they are instead of consolidating them into a smaller number of Active Directory domains.

Now consider the following reasons for not creating a new domain:

- **Security accounts manager size limitations.** In Windows NT 4.0, the SAM database had a practical limitation of about 40,000 security accounts per domain. Active Directory can scale easily to millions of objects per domain. For practical purposes, a single domain can accommodate all the objects in a forest, so it should never be necessary to create additional domains to handle more objects.
- **Primary domain controller (PDC) availability requirements.** In Windows NT 4.0, only a single domain controller, the PDC, could accept updates to the domain database. Organizations with large networks therefore found it difficult to ensure wide availability of the PDC, since a network outage could prevent administrators on one part of the network from being able to update the domain. To satisfy the availability requirement, you would create additional domains to distribute PDC servers throughout the network. This is no longer necessary in Windows 2000, since all Active Directory domain controllers can accept updates.
- **Delegation of administration.** In Windows NT 4.0, the only way to delegate administration over a set of objects was to put those objects into a different domain and make the administrators of those objects administrators in that separate domain. For example, to delegate the management of a set of users, you would create a new user domain. To delegate management of resource servers such as file or print servers, you would create resource domains. In Windows 2000, you can delegate administration within a domain using OUs, which are easier to create, delete, move, and modify than domains, and thus better suited to the delegation role.

Incremental Costs for an Additional Domain

Each domain in the forest will introduce some amount of management overhead. When debating whether to add a domain to your domain plan, weigh the following costs against the benefits you determined earlier in the chapter:

- **More domain administrators.** Domain administrators can initiate changes to the forest, and therefore must be trusted individuals. For each additional domain that you create, you must select members for the Domain Administrators group, and monitor and audit the group membership on a regular basis. In general, having fewer domain administrator groups means that you are less likely to experience a security breach or a mistake that has forest-wide consequences.
- **More domain controller hardware.** In Windows 2000, a domain controller can host only a single domain. Each new domain you create will require at least one computer, and in most cases will require two computers to meet reliability and availability requirements. Since all Windows 2000 domain controllers can accept and originate changes, you must physically guard them more carefully than you did Windows NT 4.0 BDCs, which were read-only. The administration delegation within Active Directory domains reduces the requirement for resource domains. Some remote locations that currently must host two domain controllers—a master user domain and a local resource domain—now require only one domain controller if you choose to consolidate to fewer Active Directory domains.
- **More trust links.** Trust between domains allows users and groups from one domain to be granted access to resources in another domain. For a domain controller in one domain to authenticate a user from another domain, it must be able to contact a domain controller within the second domain, thereby adding another possible point of failure. The more users and resources located in a single domain, the less an individual domain controller must rely on being able to communicate with other domain controllers to maintain service.
- **Greater chance of having to move a security principal between domains.** The more domains you have, the greater the chance that you'll have to move security principals, such as users and groups, between two domains. For example, a business reorganization or a job or location change for a particular user can create the need to move a user between domains. To end users and to administrators, moving a security principal between OUs inside a domain is a trivial and transparent operation. However, moving a security principal between domains is more involved and can have an impact on the end user.

Choosing a Forest Root Domain

Once you determine how many domains you will place in your forest, you need to decide which domain will be the forest root domain. The *forest root domain* is the first domain that you create in a forest. The two forest-wide groups—enterprise administrators and schema administrators—should reside in this domain.

Caution If all the domain controllers for the forest root domain are lost in a catastrophic event, the remaining domains in the forest will be affected. Therefore, you must be able to geographically disperse domain controllers for the forest root, or keep them in a safe, easily serviced location. If all the domain controllers are lost, you must restore at least one from backup to be able to continue. There is no way to reinstall the forest root domain.

If your forest contains only one domain, that domain will be the forest root. If your forest contains two or more domains, consider the following two approaches for selecting the forest root domain:

- **Use an existing domain that will be well protected.** Select a domain from the list of domains, and determine which operation is critical to your organization. Since you cannot afford to lose this domain, it will already require the kind of fault tolerance and recoverability that a forest root requires.
- **Create a structural root domain.** Creating an additional domain to serve solely as the forest root carries all the costs of an extra domain, but has certain benefits that might apply to your organization, such as:
    - The domain administrator in the forest root domain will be able to manipulate the membership of the Enterprise Administrators and Schema Administrators groups. You might have administrators who require domain administrator privilege for some part of their duties, but you do not want them to manipulate the forest-wide Administrators groups. By creating a separate domain, you avoid ever needing to place these administrators into the Domain Administrators group of the forest root domain.
    - Since the domain is small, you can easily replicate it anywhere on your network to provide protection against geographically centered catastrophes.
    - Since the only role the domain has is to serve as the forest root, it never risks becoming obsolete. In a situation in which you select a domain from your planned list of domains to be the forest root, there is always a chance that particular domain will become obsolete, perhaps because of a change in your organization. However, you will never be able to fully retire such a domain, since it must play the role of forest root.

Note You can add a domain to a forest only when you first create the domain. You can create a domain by promoting a Windows 2000 server to the Active Directory domain controller role, or by upgrading a Windows NT 3.51 or Windows NT 4.0 PDC to Windows 2000. You can remove a domain from a forest only by demoting all of the Windows 2000 domain controllers for that domain.

Planning the Organizational Unit Structure

Windows 2000 introduces the OU, which enables a company to structure its network to match more closely with its business processes. The OU is also useful from a security perspective—along with the use of security groups, the OU permits you to easily apply

Group Policy and other security configuration to specific subsets of the enterprise. For example, you could create an OU for all servers (there is a default OU for domain controllers) that would simplify the application of more secure security templates to secure the servers. (See Chapter 10 for more information on security templates.) Carefully planning the OU structure will aid in the security administration of the network.

Generally, you should create OUs that mirror your organization's functional or business structure. For example, create child OUs for individual business units. OUs enable you to model your organization in a meaningful and manageable way, and allow you to assign an appropriate local authority as administrator at any hierarchical level. As each domain can implement its own OU hierarchies, you can create OUs within each domain, independent of the structures in the other domains, further enhancing both domain management and security. Although someone can maliciously penetrate one domain and learn about its internal structure, other domains might have different structures, giving the hacker no obvious advantage in terms of knowledge about the internal structure of other domains.

Creating OUs to Delegate Administration

You can also use OUs to split up networks into areas that can be administered locally, thereby allowing you to distribute domain administration among localized administrators.

OUs are the smallest scope to which you can delegate administrative authority. Examples of resource administration include granting an individual the ability to manage printer queues and file resources located within an OU if that individual's account is also located within that OU. You can also grant an individual the authority to create and delete user accounts in an entire subtree of OUs.

By delegating administrative authority, you can eliminate the need to regularly log on with sweeping authority over an entire domain. Although you will still have an Administrator account and a Domain Administrators group with administrative authority over the entire domain, you can reserve these accounts for occasional use by a limited number of highly trusted administrators.

Creating OUs to Apply Group Policy/Secure computers

As you have seen, OUs are the smallest scope to which you can assign Group Policy settings, enabling you to determine access, configurations, and use of resources for the OU and any or all of its child objects (including other OUs). However, OUs are not security principals and do not have members. Their purpose is solely to organize and contain directory objects. Use group assignments to grant rights and permissions to users. Assigning group memberships should be your first step in account management. You can then use OUs to contain the Group objects and assign Group Policy settings.

You can also assign OUS to machines, depending on their configuration or purpose. This facilitates easy application of more secure configurations to high-risk machines such as servers or exposed workstations.

Domains or OUs

You might need to decide whether to split a particular part of your network into separate domains or separate OUs. We offer the following recommendations as guidelines:

- Split the network into separate domains if you have a decentralized organization in which different users and resources are managed by completely different sets of administrative personnel.
- Split the network into separate domains when two parts of your network are separated by a link so slow that you never want complete replication traffic to cross it. (For slow links that can still handle replication traffic on a less frequent schedule, you can configure a single domain with multiple sites.)
- Split a domain into OUs to reflect the structure or your organization.
- Split a domain into OUs to delegate administrative control over smaller groups of users, groups, and resources. The amount of administrative control you grant can be complete (such as creating users and changing passwords) or limited (such as maintaining print queues).
- Split a domain into OUs if a particular organizational structure in your company is likely to change later. When possible, organize domains so that you will not have to move them or split them in the future.

Planning the Site Structure

While sites are typically a group of well-connected computers, you might have considerations for the site structure other than the geographical location.

Determining the Number of Sites for Your Enterprise

When planning for replication of the directory, start with a single site structure, and then add sites depending on any bandwidth and connectivity constraints. If you have a single LAN, the entire network can be a single site, as LAN connections are typically fast.

While you can define multiple sites within one well-connected location, this choice has some potential drawbacks, including higher administration costs and less information exchange between domain controllers in the other well-connected sites. If you want a client to log on to a particular set of domain controllers, define your sites so that only those domain controllers—and not others in the same relative physical location—are in the same site as that client.

A fast, reliable connection is more common when computers are in close proximity. Having computers in the same subnet suggests that those computers are well connected and should be in the same site. However, regardless of physical locations, computers in different subnets could still be well connected by high bandwidth connections. In such a case, subnets and physical proximity should not necessarily determine the site assignment. A multihomed computer with subnet addresses in different sites can belong to only one of the sites, not all of them. It is a good idea to assign all the addresses for a multihomed computer to the same site.

Establishing separate sites provides the following benefits:

- Partitions client use of the network
- Further optimizes the exchange of directory information
- Facilitates administration by centralizing resources such as configuration information
- Fine-tunes replication behavior

Establish a separate site with its own domain controllers when you believe domain controllers are not responding fast enough to meet your users' needs. First you must decide whether the branch office needs a domain controller at all. If the branch office does not have a domain controller, there will be no replication traffic to the branch office. Clients could use one of the network connections to the main office to log on to the network. This option is acceptable if a fast, reliable network connection is available. More often, a network connection to a distant domain controller is relatively slow. Having no domain controller in a distant location is only acceptable for small branches with up to five computers, where the performance impact affects limited users. Larger branch offices are better configured as separate sites containing one or more local domain controllers. Placing a branch office into a domain within a separate site also permits localized administration, by delegating control to a trusted individual within the branch office.

If replication between all domain controllers must take place on the same schedule, it might seem wise to assign all those domain controllers to the same site. This configuration will achieve a uniform replication schedule, but it limits your ability to adjust directory replication behavior. By creating separate sites, you can fine-tune replication according to site conditions. If you have good connectivity between a group of servers and clients, create sites and establish bridgehead servers in each site to provide load balancing. You can divide the potential for client requests between servers by establishing separate sites. Even though one site might be well connected to other sites, replication is still reduced, since the server or servers in the site handle all requests for clients within the site.

When planning your sites, consider which domain controllers each computer should use for the logon process. During the logon process, a client attempts to find a domain controller in its local site. To ensure this process happens efficiently and reliably, your fast network connections need to map directly to low-cost site links in your site topology. Associating client subnets to sites they are in ensures efficient client access to resources because the clients will have good connectivity to the resources.

Within a site, each domain controller has the potential to act as a bridgehead server if needed. (The system automatically assigns bridgehead servers, which are the preferred servers for replication.) If you specify one or more computers to be your preferred bridgehead servers, only a single domain controller acts as the bridgehead server at any given time. Active Directory selects another preferred bridgehead server for use in the event of failure. However, while this rerouting takes place, there will be a period of time during which no intersite replication will occur.

Placing Domain Controllers and GC Servers

Access to a global catalog (GC) is required for successful logon attempts. A GC is necessary to determine group memberships during the logon process. If your network has any slow or unreliable links, enable at least one GC on each side of the link for maximum availability and fault tolerance.

Most of your Active Directory network traffic will be query-related: users, administrators, and programs requesting information about directory objects. Updates to the directory that cause directory replication traffic should occur much less frequently. To get the best network performance, place at least one domain controller in each site. With a domain controller in each site, all users can access a server that can service query requests over the fastest links available.

To help optimize network traffic at sites connected by slow links, you can also configure domain controllers to receive directory replication updates only during off-peak hours.

The best network performance comes when the domain controller at a site is also a GC. That way, that server can fulfill queries about objects in the entire forest. However, enabling many domain controllers as GCs can increase replication traffic on your network.

Planning the DNS structure

Several aspects of DNS structure require careful consideration at the planning stage. We will examine those aspects in this section.

Arranging Domains in a Tree

A tree is a set of one or more Windows 2000 domains with *contiguous* names. Figure 4-5 presents a single tree with a contiguous namespace. Since company.com does not have a parent domain, it is considered the tree root domain. The child domain of company.com is child.company.com, and the grandchild domain of company.com is grandchild.child.-company.com. These domain names are contiguous because each inherits the name of the domain ahead of it in the domain hierarchy.

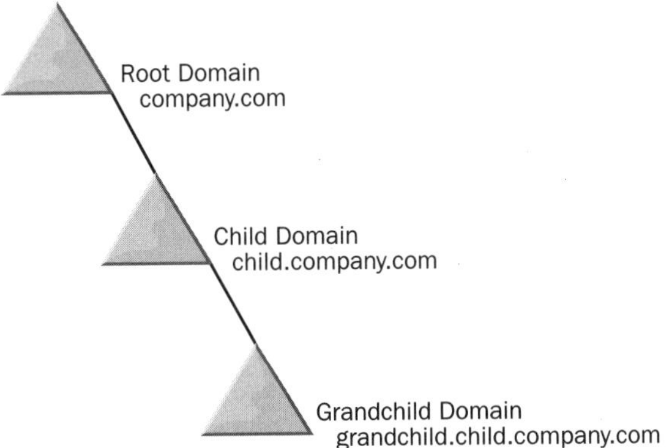

Figure 4-5. *Single tree with three domains forming a contiguous namespace.*

You can have more than one tree in a forest. Names are assigned arbitrarily when you create each domain. Creating more tree root domains increases the number of trees in a forest, as shown in Figure 4-6.

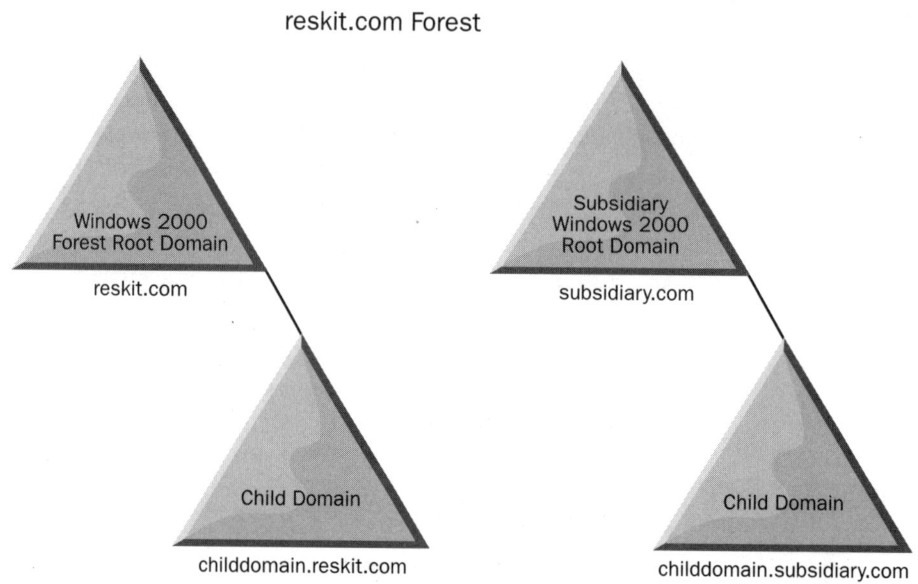

Figure 4-6. *Forest with multiple trees.*

The domain hierarchy in a forest determines the spanning tree of transitive trusts that connects each domain. If a forest has multiple trees, the forest root domain is at the top of the trust tree and all other tree roots are children, from a trust perspective. Figure 4-7 depicts the relationship of two trees in a transitive trust relationship.

Domain Naming Recommendations

To create the domain hierarchy in a forest, assign a DNS name to the first domain, and then decide if every subsequent domain is a child of an existing domain or a new tree root. Assign names accordingly.

Note The parent-child relationship is a naming relationship and trust relationship only. Administrators in a parent domain are not automatically administrators of a child domain. Policies set in a parent domain do not automatically apply to child domains.

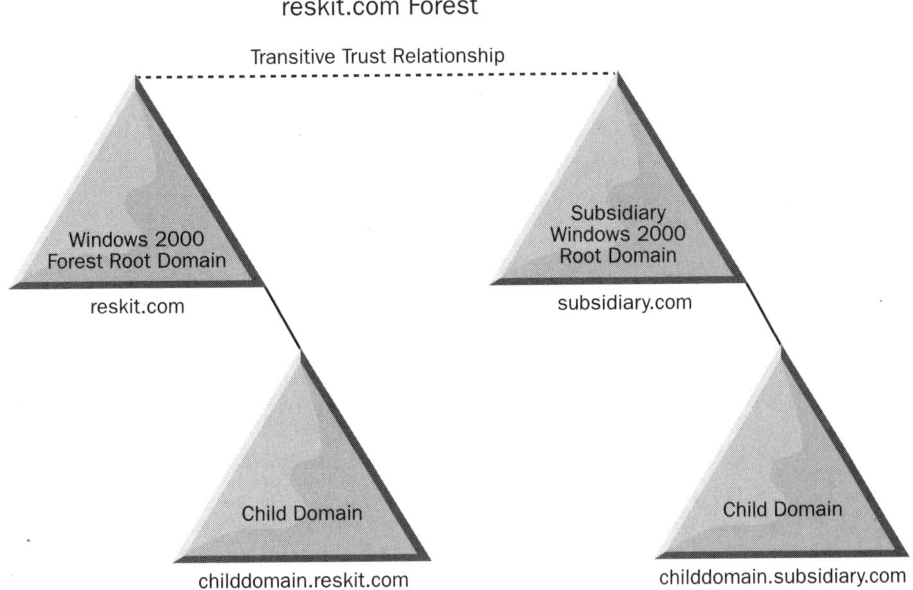

Figure 4-7. *Multiple tree forest with a transitive trust relationship.*

Planning DNS Server Deployment

To plan DNS server deployment to support your Active Directory domains, you must identify the DNS servers that will be authoritative for your domain names, and ensure these servers meet the requirements of the domain controller locator system.

Authority and Delegation in DNS

The DNS is a hierarchical, distributed database. The database itself consists of *resource records*. A resource record primarily consists of a DNS name, a record type, and data values associated with that record type. Like Active Directory, the DNS database is divided into partitions that enable the database to scale efficiently even on large networks. A partition of the DNS database is called a *zone,* which contains the records for a contiguous set of DNS names. A DNS server that loads a zone is said to be authoritative for the names in that zone.

DNS Server Requirements

If you do not already have DNS servers running on your network, we recommend that you deploy the DNS service provided with Windows 2000 Server. If you have existing

DNS servers, some of them must meet two requirements in order to support your Active Directory domains:

- **Service Location Record support.** The DNS servers that are authoritative for the locator records must support the SRV resource record type.
- **Dynamic Update Protocol support.** The DNS servers that are authoritative for the locator records and are the primary master servers for those zones should support the Dynamic Update Protocol as defined in RFC 2136.

The DNS service provided with Windows 2000 Server meets both these requirements and also offers two important additional features:

- **Active Directory integration.** Using this feature, the DNS service stores zone data in the directory. This makes DNS replication multimaster, and allows any DNS server to accept updates for a directory service–integrated zone.
- **Secure dynamic update.** Secure dynamic update is integrated with Windows security, allowing an administrator to precisely control which computers can update which names and thereby preventing rogue computers or domains from stealing existing names out of DNS.

Optimizing Authentication with Shortcut Trusts

Depending on the network location of the domain controllers for each domain, each extra authentication hop between two domains can increase the chance of failure, or increase the likelihood of authentication traffic having to cross a slow link. If this situation develops on your network, you can connect any two domains with a *shortcut trust*.

For example, if you have multiple trees in a forest, you might want to connect the group of tree roots in a complete mesh of trust. Remember that in the default arrangement, all tree roots are considered children of the forest root from a trust perspective. That means that authentication traffic between any two non-forest-root domains must pass through the forest root. Creating a complete mesh of trust allows any two tree root domains to directly communicate with each other.

Using Active Directory

You control Active Directory by using a series of Microsoft Management Console snap-ins:

- **Active Directory Domains And Trusts Snap-In.** This snap-in provides a graphical view of all domain trees in the forest.
- **Active Directory Sites And Services Snap-In.** This snap-in enables the management of sites within the enterprise structure.
- **Active Directory Users And Computers Snap-In.** This snap-in enables the creation and management of User, Group, Printer, Computer objects, and shared resources within Active Directory.

We will examine each of these tools in the following sections of this chapter.

Active Directory Domains And Trusts Snap-In

The Active Directory Domains And Trusts Snap-In enables you to manage the domains in the forest, manage the trust relationships that tie the domains and forests together, configure the mode of operation for each domain, and configure the alternative UPN suffixes for the forest.

To start the Active Directory Domains And Trusts Snap-In

1. Log on as an administrator. If you log on using an account that does not have administrative privileges, you might not be able to manage Active Directory.
2. Press Start, point to Programs, and then click on Administrative Tools.
3. Click on Active Directory Domains And Trusts. A window similar to Figure 4-8 appears.

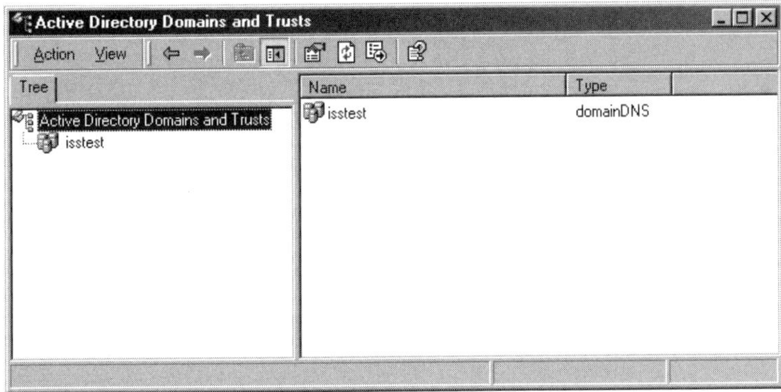

Figure 4-8. *Active Directory Domains And Trusts Snap-In.*

4. Add alternate User Principal Name suffixes. The UPN provides an easy-to-use naming style for users to log on to Active Directory. The default UPN suffix is the forest DNS name, which is the DNS name of the first domain in the first tree of the forest. In this example, the default UPN suffix is iss.net.
5. Right-click the root node of the Active Directory Domains And Trusts, and choose Properties from the context menu.
6. Add the UPN suffixes *ISSReading.net* and *ISSAtlanta.net.*
7. You can manage each of the domains shown in the tree view by starting the Active Directory Users And Computers Snap-In. Right-click the domain node for iss.net and choose Manage from the context menu.

Changing the Domain Mode

As you saw earlier, Windows 2000 domains operate in either mixed mode or native mode. When a domain is first installed, it is in mixed mode. You can change the mode of operation from mixed mode to native, but you can never change to mixed mode from native mode. Native mode does not support down-level Windows NT 4.0 DCs.

To switch to native mode

1. Make sure all domain controllers in your domain are running Windows 2000 Server.
2. Right-click the domain object and choose Properties from the context menu. A window similar to Figure 4-9 appears.

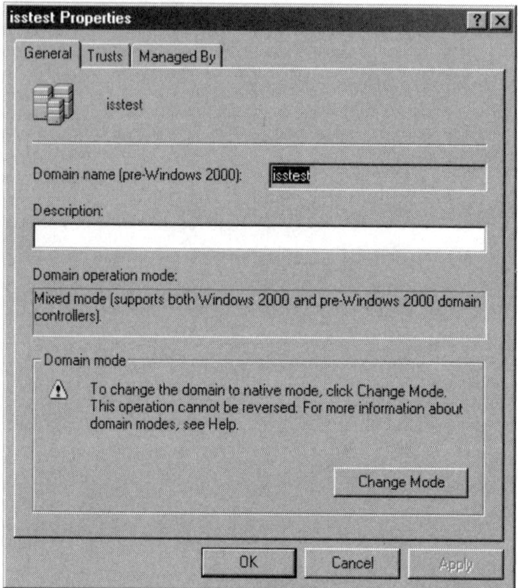

Figure 4-9. *Domain properties for isstest before domain mode conversion.*

3. Click Change Mode.
4. Restart the domain controller. Figure 4-10 shows the domain properties after the domain mode conversion.

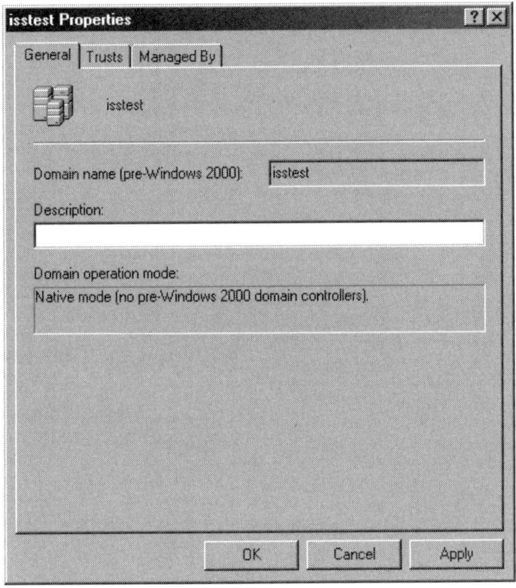

Figure 4-10. *Domain properties for isstest after domain mode conversion.*

The Active Directory Users And Computers Snap-In

The Active Directory Users And Computers Snap-In is used to create and manage users, computers, and other Active Directory objects.

Starting the Active Directory Users And Computers Snap-In

To use the Active Directory Users And Computers Snap-In you must be logged on as an Administrator. If you log on using an account that does not have administrative privileges, you might not be able to create several directory objects. There are several ways to start this snap-in:

- You can invoke the Active Directory Users And Computers Snap-In from the Active Directory Domains And Trusts Snap-In (as described in the previous section).
- Alternatively, you can load the snap-in from the Administrative Tools menu. Figure 4-11 on the following page shows the snap-in.

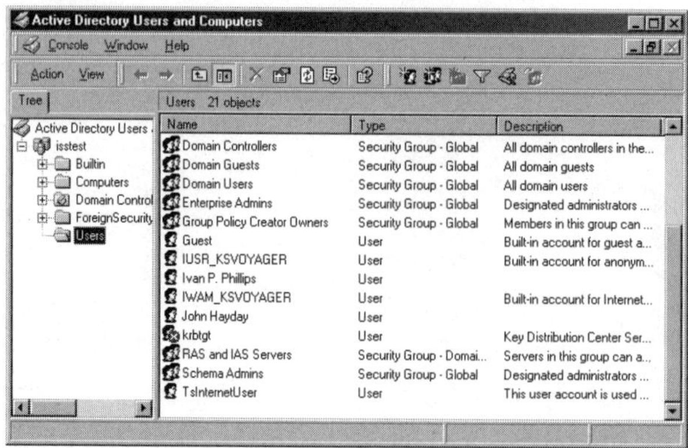

Figure 4-11. *The Active Directory Users And Computers Snap-In.*

The following sections will demonstrate operations such as create, move, and rename through an example on a given object class. You can use the same principles for any of the object classes.

Adding an Object: Organizational Unit

The following procedure creates an OU in the specified domain. Note that you can create nested OUs, and there is no limit to the nesting levels.

To add an OU

1. Right-click a domain object, click New and then click Organizational Unit. Or, click the New Organizational Unit toolbar button.
2. Type Business Model as the name of your new OU.
3. Click OK.

Creating a User Account

The following procedure creates the user account Ivan Phillips in the Business Model OU.

To create a new user account

1. Right-click the Business Model organizational unit, click New, and then click User. Or, click the New User toolbar button.
2. Type the user information shown in Figure 4-12, then click Next.

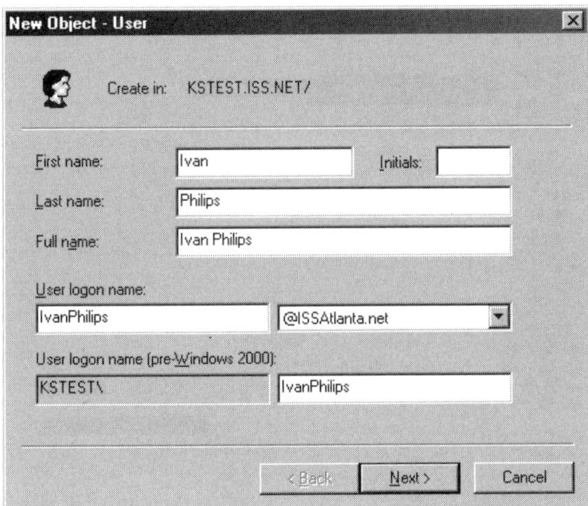

Figure 4-12. *New Object - User dialog box.*

3. Type a password in both the Password and Confirm Password boxes, and select the appropriate account options, shown in Figure 4-13.

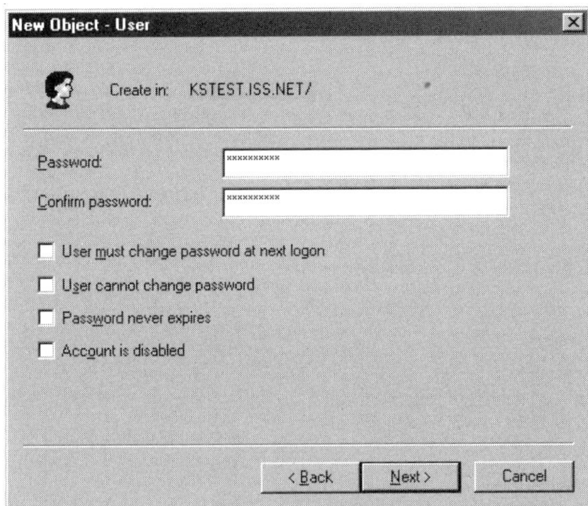

Figure 4-13. *New Object - User second dialog box.*

4. Click Next and then click Finish in the confirmation dialog. You have now created an account for Ivan Phillips in the Business Model organizational unit.

To add user information

1. Right-click the user object, and choose Properties from the context menu.
2. Fill in the desired information in the Properties sheet.
3. Click OK.

Moving a Object: User Account

You can move users, computers, and groups from one OU to another in the same domain or a different domain.

To move the user account

1. Select the Business Model organizational unit.
2. Right-click the Ivan Phillips user account and choose Move from the context menu.
3. Select the folder to which you want to move the account (Users in this example), and click OK.

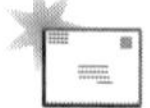

Note If you upgrade from a previous version of Windows NT Server, you might want to move existing users from the Users folder to some of the OUs that you create.

Creating a Group

To create a group

1. Right-click the Business Model organizational unit, click New, and then click Group. Or, click the Create New Group button on the toolbar.
2. In the Group Name text box, type *Local Machines*. It should appear as shown in Figure 4-14.
3. Select the appropriate Group type and Group scope:

Note The *Group type* indicates whether you can use the group to assign permissions to other network resources, such as files and printers. You can use both security and distribution groups for e-mail distribution lists. The *Group scope* determines the visibility of the group and what type of objects can be contained within the group, as described in Table 4-5.

Table 4-5. Group scopes.

Scope	Visibility	Can Contain
Domain Local	Domain	Users, global, or universal groups
Global	Tree	Users or global groups
Universal	Forest	Users, global, or universal groups

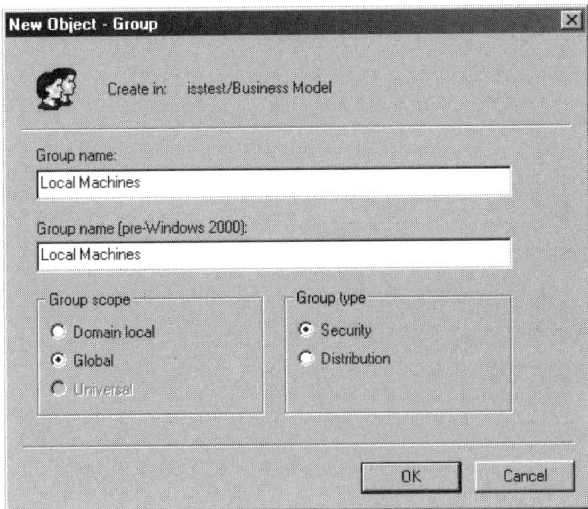

Figure 4-14. *New Object - Group dialog box.*

Adding a User to a Group

To add a new or existing user to a group

1. Right-click the Local Machines group, and then choose Properties from the context menu.
2. On the Members Tab, click Add. This will start the Select Users, Contacts, Or Computers dialog box shown in Figure 4-15. You can use this dialog box to scope your query to the forest, a specific domain, or an OU.

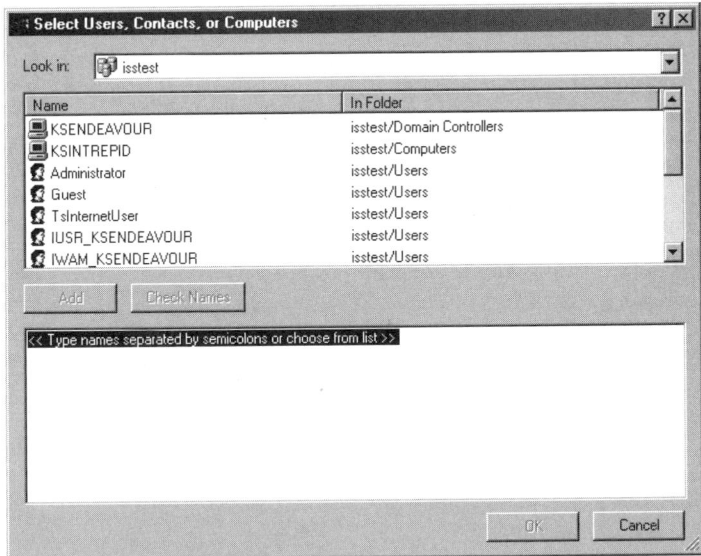

Figure 4-15. *The Select Users, Contacts, Or Computers dialog box.*

3. Click Ivan Phillips, and then click Add.
4. Alternatively, you can right-click the users from the results pane of the Active Directory Users And Computers Snap-In, and then choose Add Members To A Group from the context menu or click the Add Members To A Group toolbar button. This alternative might be more efficient for adding large numbers of members to a group.

Publishing a Shared Folder

You can publish any shared network folder—including a Distributed File System (DFS) folder—in the directory. Creating a shared folder object in the directory does not automatically share the folder. This is a two-step process: You must first share the folder, and then publish it in the directory.

To share a folder

1. Use Windows Explorer or the command line to create a new folder called Local Machines on one of your disk volumes.
2. In Windows Explorer, right-click the folder name, choose Properties from the context menu, click the Sharing tab, and click Share This Folder.
3. In the Share Name box, type *LM*.
4. Click OK.

To publish the shared folder in the directory

1. In the Active Directory Users And Computers Snap-In, right-click the Business Model Organizational Unit, click New, and then click Shared Folder. You'll see the dialog box shown in Figure 4-16.
2. In the Name box, type *Shared Folder*. Type *\\<your machine name>\LM* in the Network Path box. For example, type *\\KSENDEAVOUR.ISS.NET\LM*.

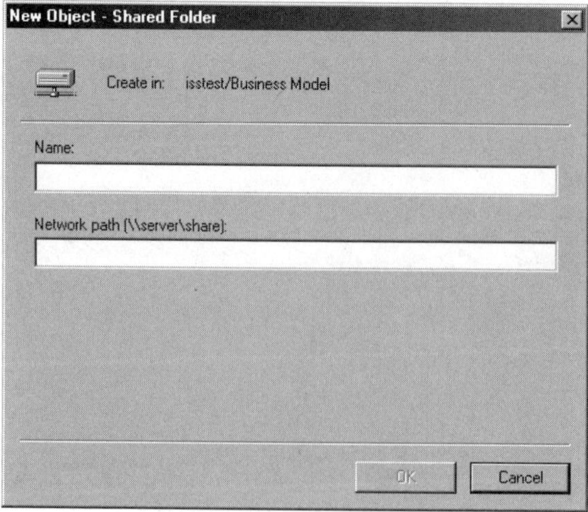

Figure 4-16. *The New Object - Shared Folder dialog box.*

3. Click OK.

   Users can now see this volume while browsing in the directory.

To browse the directory

1. From the desktop, open My Network Places.
2. Click Entire Network, then click Directory.
3. Click the domain name, and then click Business Model.
4. To view the files in the volume, click Shared Folder.

Creating a Computer Object

A computer object is created automatically when a computer joins a domain. You can also create the computer object before the computer joins a domain.

To create a computer object

1. In the Active Directory Users And Computers Snap-In, right-click the Business Model OU, click New, and then click Computer.
2. For the computer name, type *kangaroo*. Optionally, you can select which users are permitted to join a computer to the domain, thereby allowing yourself to create the computer account and also allowing someone with fewer permissions to install the computer and join it to the domain.
3. Click OK.

Managing Computers

Now that you've created the computer object, you might want to manage this computer remotely, diagnose the services running on this computer, look at the event viewer, and so forth.

To start the Computer Management Snap-In

1. In the Active Directory Users And Computers Snap-In, right-click the computer object and choose Manage from the context menu.
2. The Computer Management Snap-In will start for the selected computer.

Renaming, Moving, and Deleting Objects

You can rename and delete every object in the directory, and you can move most objects to different containers.

To move an object

1. In the Active Directory Users And Computers Snap-In, right-click the object, and then choose Move from the context menu.
2. The Directory Browser will appear. Select the destination container for the object that you are moving and click OK.

To delete an object

1. Right-click on the object you want to delete and choose Delete from the context menu.
2. Click OK in the confirmation dialog box.

Nested Groups

You can use nested groups if you are running Active Directory in native mode. Nested groups are easier to manage, and thus reduce administrative overhead.

To create a nested group

1. Create a new group. In Active Directory Users And Computers Snap-In, right-click the Business Model folder, click New, and then click Group. Type *All Marketing* as the name for the new group and click OK.
2. Right-click the Business Model folder, click New, and then click Group. Type *Press Liaison* as the name for the new group and click OK.
3. Right-click the Press Liaison folder, and choose Properties from the context menu.
4. Click the Member Of tab and click Add.
5. Select All Marketing and click Add to make the Press Liaison group a member of the All Marketing group.
6. Click OK. Figure 4-17 shows the completed properties page for the Press Liaison group.

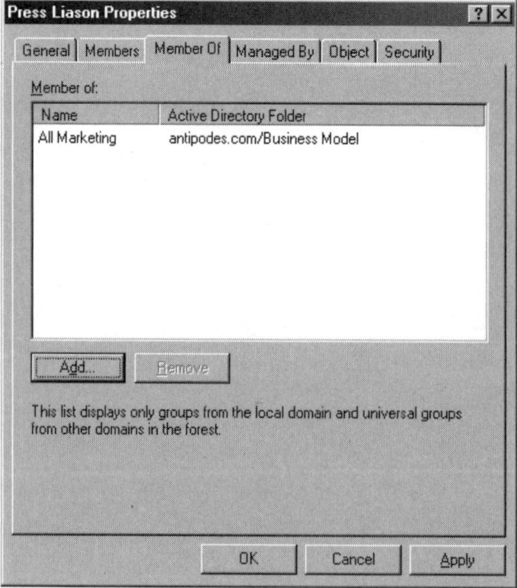

Figure 4-17. *The Press Liaison Properties page.*

To check the nested groups

1. Right-click All Marketing, choose Properties from the context menu, and then click the Membership tab. You will see Press Liaison as a member of All Marketing.
2. Double-click Press Liaison, and then click the Membership Of tab. You will see Press Liaison listed as a member of the group All Marketing.

Filtering a List of Objects

Filtering the list of returned objects can allow you to manage the directory more efficiently. The filtering option allows you to restrict the types of objects returned to the snap-in—for example, you can choose to view only users and groups, or you might want to create a more complex filter. In addition, if an OU has more than a specified number of objects, the filter dialog allows you to restrict the number of objects displayed in the results pane. You can use the Filter Options dialog box to configure this option.

To create the filter

1. Start the filter dialog box, shown in Figure 4-18, by either clicking the Set Filtering Options toolbar button in Active Directory Users And Computers Snap-In or by choosing Filter Options from the View menu.
2. Select the Show Only The Following Types Of Objects option, and then select Users And Groups.
3. Click OK.

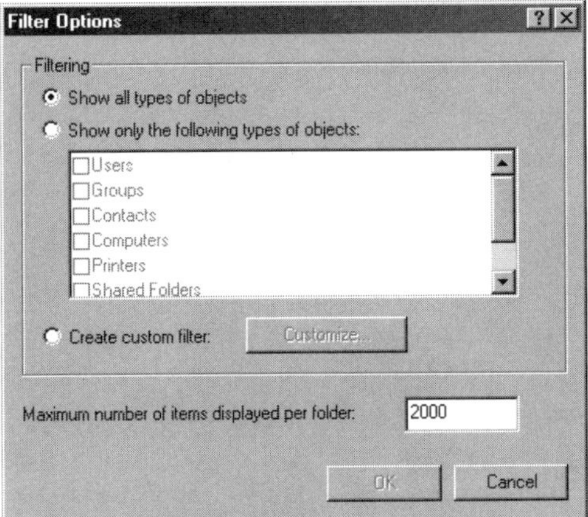

Figure 4-18. *Filter Options dialog box.*

After you click OK, whenever you view a container, the container will retrieve user and group objects only. If you also enable the description bar, you will also see a visual indication that a filter has been applied.

Setting ACL Permissions

You can apply access control to Active Directory objects as follows:

1. Ensure that you enable viewing of advanced features on the Active Directory Users And Computers Snap-In View menu.
2. For every Active Directory object there will be an additional tab named Security on the object's properties page. This tab enables you to set security and access control settings for that object, and also controls inheritance and propagation of the security settings to and from that object. Figure 4-19 shows the Security tab of an object's properties page.

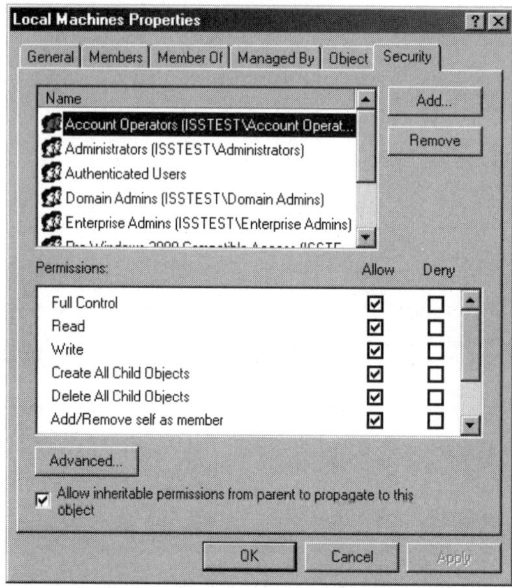

Figure 4-19. *The Security tab of an object's properties page.*

3. Use the Allow and Deny columns to set the security rights for each group listed. The Deny setting will override any conflicting Allow setting. You can add or remove additional users and groups by using the Ad0d and Remove buttons. (See Chapter 8, "Group Policy," and Chapter 9, "Security Configuration and Monitoring," for more details on setting ACLs and advanced security properties.)
4. The Allow Inheritable Permissions From Parent To Propagate To This Object setting controls where parent properties will affect the child object. The parent settings will overwrite all settings, including any Deny settings.
5. Click OK when you're done setting permissions.

The Active Directory Sites And Services Snap-In

The primary purpose of the Active Directory Sites And Services Snap-In is to administer the replication topology both within a site (in a LAN) and between sites (in a WAN) in your enterprise environment. The Sites portion of the Active Directory Sites And Services Manager enables you to:

- **Display the valid sites within an enterprise.** For example, *Default-First-Site-Name* might be a site name. You can create, delete, or rename sites.
- **Display the servers that participate in a site.** You can delete or move servers between sites.
- **Display the applications that use site knowledge.** The Active Directory topology is rooted at Sites\Default-First-Site-Name\Servers, which contains only those servers participating in a specific site, regardless of domain. To view the connections for any given server, display Sites\Default-First-Site-Name\Servers\{server}\NTDS Settings. Each server has connections and schedules that control replication to other servers in this site.
    - **Connections.** For two machines to have two-way replication, a connection must exist from the first machine to the second, and a complementary connection must exist from the second machine to the first.
    - **Schedules**. Within a site, pull replication of any new directory deltas occurs between servers approximately every five minutes. Schedules are significant within a site to force periodic notification to inbound partners in the event that a partner has a damaged connection object. This type of notification typically occurs every six hours. Additionally, schedules are significant in controlling pull replication between sites. (There is no automatic five-minute replication between sites.)
- **Display transports and links between sites.** Transports represent the protocols used to communicate between chosen sites (that is, IP).
- **Display subnets.** Subnets allow the administrator to associate ranges of IP addresses with sites.

Using the Sites Topology Tool

To run the Active Directory Sites And Services Snap-In

1. Click Programs on the Start menu.
2. Click Administrative Tools, and then click Active Directory Sites And Services.

   You'll see a console similar to that shown in Figure 4-20 on the following page.

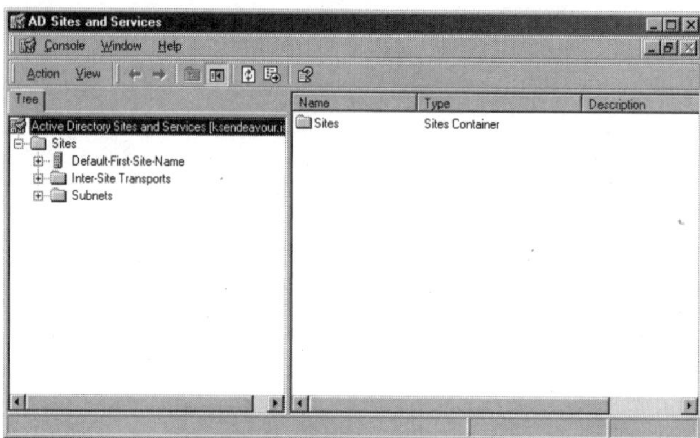

Figure 4-20. *Sample console.*

Likewise, the other computers have two configured connections. A sample topology is shown in Figure 4-21.

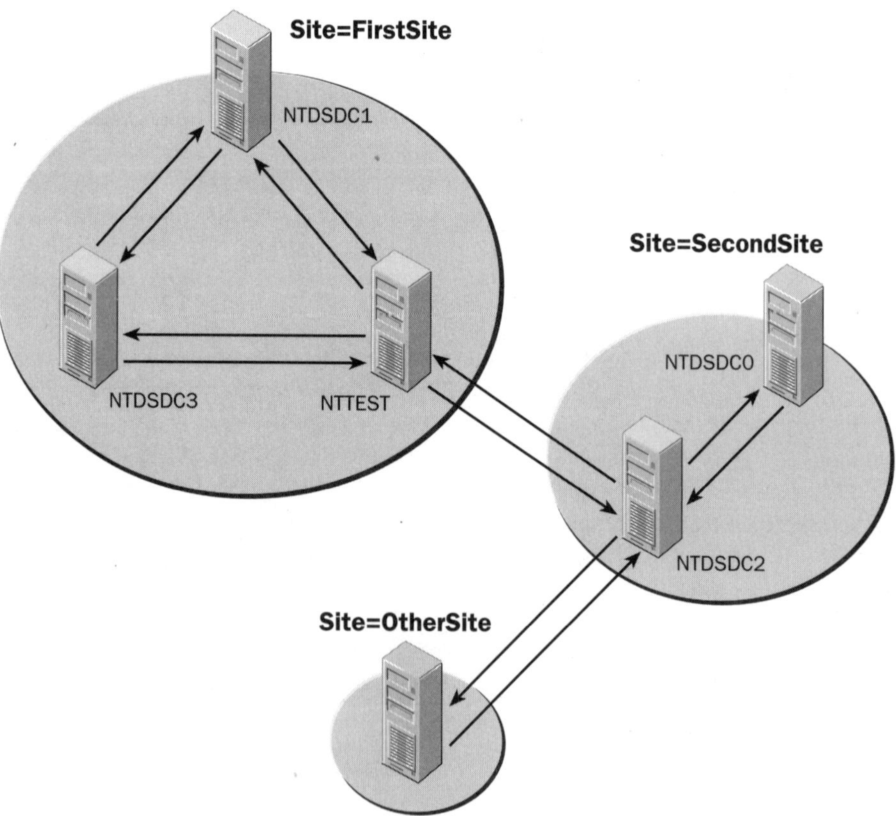

Figure 4-21. *Sample topology.*

To add new sites

1. Right-click Sites in the tree in the left pane of the console and Choose New Site from the context menu. You'll see the New Object - Site dialog box, shown in Figure 4-22.

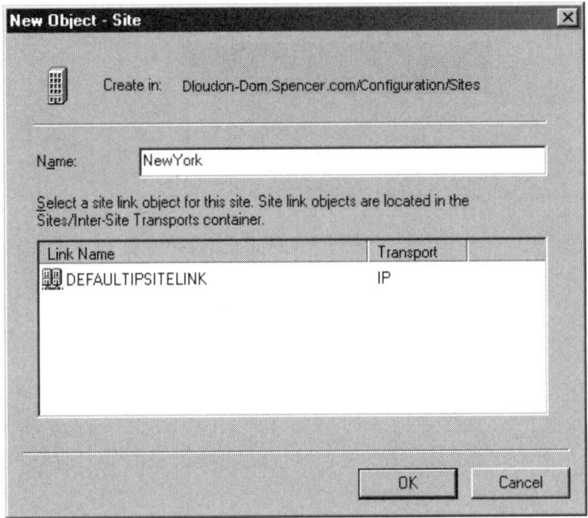

Figure 4-22. *Creating a site.*

2. Type in a name for the new site (*Reading,* for example).
3. Select a site link object for the site and click OK.
4. Click OK in the confirmation dialog box; we'll next cover the tasks mentioned in the confirmation dialog box.

To define subnets for a particular site

1. In the left pane of the console, right-click the Subnets item that appears under the site name.
2. From the Action menu, go to New, and then click Subnets.
3. In the Name box, type your subnet and subnet mask numbers (for example, *200.201.202.0/24*) as shown in Figure 4-23 on the following page. If you have correctly entered the subnet, it will appear in the Subnets folder.

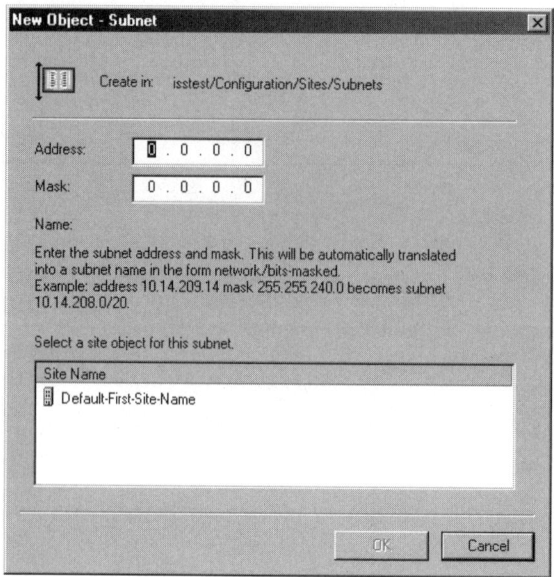

Figure 4-23. *Adding a subnet.*

To associate the subnet with a site

1. Right-click the subnet in the right pane of the console and Choose Properties from the context menu.
2. In the Site box, use the drop-down list to select a site to associate with this subnet.

Using the Services Tool

By default the Services node is hidden from the Active Directory Sites And Services tool.

To show the services node

1. Ensure that the Show Services Node option is selected on the Active Directory Sites And Services View menu
2. You'll see the services node in the left-hand side pane of the MMC, as shown in Figure 4-24.

You can set certain properties for each of the properties shown in the right-hand side pane of the MMC. You can create more objects within these containers, but that procedure is beyond the scope of this book.

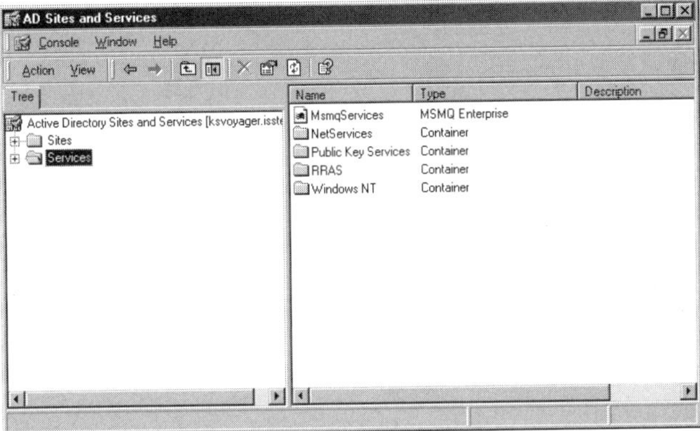

Figure 4-24. *Active Directory Sites And Services: Services node.*

Managing Active Directory

Various tools and wizards make the task of managing Windows 2000–based systems easier. We will now look at the tools that simplify the task of administering Active Directory and its distributed networks.

Delegation of Control

Because Active Directory is designed to support distributed networks, you might not need a single team of administrators to administer the whole enterprise. Active Directory allows you to delegate control for Active Directory objects and containers to trusted individuals, thereby allowing localized administration. For example, local administrators could be responsible for the creating of new user accounts for staff members who join their particular office, while the overall enterprise administrators would still be responsible for the Computer Policy, which is distributed from Group Policy via Active Directory to all computers within the enterprise.

Use Delegation and Group Policy with OUs, Domains, and Sites

You can delegate administrative permissions for—and associate Group Policy with—the following Active Directory containers:

- OUs
- domains
- sites

An OU is the smallest Windows 2000 container to which you can delegate authority or apply Group Policy. Both delegation and Group Policy are security features of the Windows 2000 operating system.

Note In addition to delegating authority over containers, you can also grant permissions (such as read/write) down to the attribute level of an object.

Assigning administrative authority over OUs, domains, or sites lets you delegate administration of users and resources. Assigning GPOs to any of these three types of containers allows you to set desktop configurations and security policy for the users and computers in the container. The next two sections discuss these topics in more detail.

Container Delegation

In the Windows 2000 operating system, delegation allows a higher administrative authority to grant specific administrative rights for OUs, domains, or sites to groups (or individuals). This feature greatly reduces the necessary number of administrators with sweeping authority over large segments of the user population. Delegating control of a container lets you specify who has permissions to access or modify that object or its child objects. Delegation is one of the most important security features of Active Directory.

Domain and OU Delegation

In the Windows NT 4.0 operating system, administrators sometimes delegate administration by creating multiple domains to have distinct sets of domain administrators. In the Windows 2000 operating system, OUs are easier to create, delete, move, and modify than are domains, and are thus better suited to the delegation role.

To delegate administrative authority (other than authority over sites, which we cover in the next section), you grant group specific rights over a domain or OU by modifying the container's DACL. By default, members of the domain administrators security group (Domain Admin) have authority over the entire domain, but you can restrict membership in this group to a limited number of highly trusted administrators. To establish administrators with lesser scope, you can delegate authority down to the lowest level of your organization by creating a tree of OUs within each domain and delegating authority for parts of the OU subtree.

Domain administrators have full control over every object in their domain. However, they do not have administrative rights over objects in other domains.

Note By default, the Enterprise Admins group is granted full control over all objects in a *forest*.

To delegate administration of a domain or OU

1. Right-click the domain or OU and choose Delegate Control from the context menu.

2. Add the groups (or users) to whom you want to delegate control, and then either delegate the listed common tasks or create a custom task to delegate. Table 4-6 lists the common tasks you can delegate.

Table 4-6. Commonly delegated tasks.

Domain Common Tasks You Can Delegate	OU Common Tasks You Can Delegate
Join a computer to a domain.	Create, delete, and manage user accounts.
Manage Group Policy links.	Reset passwords for user accounts.
	Read all user information.
	Create, delete, and manage groups.
	Modify the membership of a group.
	Manage printers.
	Create and delete printers.
	Manage Group Policy links.

Using a combination of OUs, groups, and permissions, you can define the most appropriate administrative scope for a particular group: an entire domain, a subtree of OUs, or a single OU. For example, you might want to create an OU that lets you grant administrative control for all user and computer accounts in all branches of a single department, such as an accounting department. Alternatively, you might want to grant administrative control only to some resources within the department, such as computer accounts. Or you might want to grant administrative control for the Accounting OU, but not to any OUs contained within the Accounting OU.

Because OUs are used for administrative delegation and are not security principals themselves, the parent OU of a user object indicates who manages the user object. It does not indicate which resources that particular user can access.

Site Delegation

Use the Active Directory Sites And Services Snap-In to delegate control for sites, server containers, intersite transports (IP or SMTP), or subnets. Delegating control of one of these entities gives the delegated administrator the ability to manipulate that entity, but the administrator doesn't have the ability to manage the users or computers located in the entity.

For example, when you delegate control of a site, you can choose to delegate control of all objects, or you can delegate control for one or more objects located in that site. The objects for which you can delegate control include User, Computer, Group, Printer, OU, Shared Folder, Site, Site Link, Site Link Bridge, and so on. You are prompted to select the scope of the permissions you want to delegate. If you specify general, you are are prompted to grant one or more of the following permissions: Full Control, Read, Write, Create All Child Objects, Delete All Child Objects, Read All Properties, or Write All Properties.

Summary

This chapter introduced Active Directory and its underlying architecture and concepts. A thorough understanding of these principles is vital to understanding Windows 2000 security, which to a large extent is built around Active Directory.

In Chapter 5, we'll discuss how Windows 2000 authenticates the identities of individuals and clients to prevent unauthorized access to network resources.

Chapter 5
Authentication

One of the more difficult tasks that a Windows 2000 server performs is controlling access to its resources. This isn't surprising, given that most networks are inherently insecure and support a range of users, each of whom has different access authorizations and resources with configurable permissions.

In the Windows 2000 security model, controlling resource availability is a dual-phase process. A server must first verify the identity of the individual or client requesting access to a particular resource. This verification prevents unknown users from accessing network resources. A server must validate clients in a way that prevents a user's identity from being impersonated by an unscrupulous person or a rogue application. At the same time, however, the server must ensure that service is not denied to authorized users.

Once the server validates the user's identity, Windows 2000 performs an access-control check based on the rights granted to that user and the permissions attached to the resource. This authorization check enables an administrator to assign different access privileges to different users.

This chapter deals with authentication and how the Windows 2000 security system implements this security function. Authentication is such a fundamental and encompassing aspect of Windows 2000 and network security that it is built into many features covered in this book, including the Microsoft Public Key Infrastructure, Internet protocol security, and virtual private networks.

Overview

While authentication refers to the general process of one entity identifying itself to another entity, the typical authentication scenario usually involves a user or client authenticating to a server for the purpose of accessing some service or resource. Since most transmissions occur over relatively insecure networks, servers must be restrictive in nature, granting access to only those users who can successfully prove their identities.

Windows 2000 user authentication consists of two distinct logon types. The first type, *interactive logon*, requires a user to log on to either a domain account or local computer account. The second type, *network authentication*, provides proof of identity to specific network services. For users logged on to a local computer account, network authentication is a manual process repeated for each requested network service. Domain account users benefit from the Windows 2000 feature known as single sign-on. Once a user logs on to a domain account, network authentication is done transparently each time the user requests a network service.

In real-life scenarios, proving one's identity might consist of handing a driver's license to a bank teller for validation or entering a bankcard and PIN into an ATM. Because operating systems deal with users in a virtual context, electronic authentication is not as obvious as these kinds of face-to-face encounters. Simple authentication mechanisms in the past used passwords to control access to computers and user accounts. In effect, the user confirmed his or her identity by providing a secret that only he or she knew. While shared secrets are still the basis for authentication, the mechanisms and protocols used to protect those secrets have changed. Effective authentication protocols make it hard for intermediaries to intercept logon credentials and impersonate other users or systems. Windows 2000 security systems support a number of authentication methods. Kerberos v5 is the primary mechanism for interactive logons and network authentication, while the authentication methods provided by NT LAN Manager (NTLM) are supported for compatibility with Windows NT 4.0 machines. Secure Sockets Layer (SSL) and Transport Layer Security (TLS) are public key–based protocols useful for two-way network authentication to secure Web servers.

Windows 2000 additionally supports the use of hardware tokens for authentication purposes. Hardware tokens, such as smart cards, decrease the vulnerability of secret keys by storing the keys on the device and protecting them with a personal identification number (PIN) or password. This procedure raises the assurance level of the requestor's identity—not only must a requestor provide the correct PIN, but he or she also must have physical possession of the token.

Interactive Logon and Network Authentication

Interactive logon refers to the act of a user entering logon credentials to authenticate to a local computer or domain account to access the Windows 2000 computing environment. These logon credentials correspond to a secret that the user or administrator has set for the local or domain account he or she is logging on to. The shared secret can be a traditional password or—given the advanced security features added to the basic Windows 2000 operating system—the secret might involve a key stored on a smart card and protected by a PIN. Since the interactive logon support for Windows 2000 contains replaceable libraries that can be swapped for higher security modules, the shared secret might even include other harder-to-replicate biometric identification such as fingerprints or retinal scans. As mentioned earlier, a user can interactively log on to either a local machine or a domain account. A successful logon to a local machine provides the user access to resources and services of that machine. A successful domain account logon also gives the user access to both the local machine and the domain's authentication service, which is used during network authentication for requesting access to server-based resources.

In general, network authentication is a noninteractive process that dynamically identifies users to network services. Network authentication doesn't require the user to enter any logon information. Rather, by virtue of the single sign-on feature, the authentication protocol validates the user with information obtained during the interactive logon.

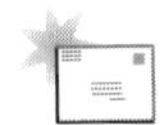

Note Some network logon scenarios do allow connections using alternative user names and authentication credentials. Mapping a network drive, for instance, allows a user to log on interactively using alternative credentials.

Interactive Logon

As it did in Window NT 4.0, Winlogon provides the interactive logon support for the Windows 2000 operating system. Interactive logon requires three system components: Winlogon.exe, Graphical Identification and Authentication DLL (GINA), and a network provider DLL.

Winlogon.exe

Aside from loading the other two components required by interactive logon, Winlogon.exe handles operations involving the user interface that are independent of the authentication policy. These operations include creating usable desktops, registering a secure attention sequence (SAS) with the OS, maintaining workstation states, and implementing time-out operations. In addition, Winlogon sends event notification messages to GINA and provides a variety of interface functions that GINA can call, such as queries, desktop operations, and message box handlers.

Graphical Identification and Authentication DLL (GINA)

This module performs user interactions specific to the authentication policy. GINA is a replaceable DLL that Winlogon loads early during the boot process. GINA provides a specific list of export functions that Winlogon uses to identify and authenticate the user. It must adhere to a set of integrity rules that ensures the safety of the system. Because the interactive logon model allows you to replace this DLL with other GINA modules, it supports customizable user identification and authentication. For instance, a custom-replacement GINA can provide functionality for biometric devices used to identify users.

Network Provider DLL

Winlogon can also load one or more network provider DLLs that provide secondary authentication through a standard protocol to other types of networks, such as Novell. The network provider translates a standard network provider interface to network-specific functions. Since Winlogon loads these modules, each network provider can collect user identification information needed for validation on that network during the logon procedure.

When Winlogon initializes, one of its first duties is to register a SAS with the system. The SAS provides a trusted path to the OS, ensuring that other applications can't hook this key sequence in an attempt to capture user passwords. The default SAS is Ctrl+Alt+Del.

Once Winlogon registers the SAS, it generates three desktops for system use. These desktops provide GINA with functionality necessary for user authentication:

- **Screen saver desktop.** This desktop is active during execution of a screen saver. The system has access to this desktop at all times. The interactive logon session has access to it only if a user is currently logged on.
- **Winlogon desktop.** Upon receipt of a SAS, Winlogon switches to the Winlogon desktop for user authentication. This desktop provides secure dialogs for identification information, such as usernames, domain names, and passwords. You'll recognize the Winlogon desktop as the familiar logon prompt you see when you reboot and type Ctrl+Alt+Del.
- **Application desktop.** This desktop, created whenever a user logs on, is available for the duration of the logon session. Also known as the user desktop, the application desktop is where all activity for the logged-on user takes place. Like the other desktop types, the application desktop is protected: only the system and logged-in user have access to it.

The authentication actions that GINA performs are state-specific. Depending on Winlogon's current state, GINA determines what actions are required. Each state can evoke a number of possible actions from GINA. Winlogon maintains three states

- **Logged-out state.** The logged-out state occurs during the absence of an interactive logon session. Winlogon prompts users for identity authentication information such as passwords or smart cards. Upon successful authentication by GINA, Winlogon changes from the logged-out state to the logged-on state.
- **Logged-on state.** The logged-on state allows users access to the application desktop, where they can run applications and perform whatever duties are necessary. This state provides a transition to either of the other two states (logged-out and workstation-locked). A user can close his or her applications and log off, in which case Winlogon terminates all remaining processes connected to that user's logon session and returns the state to logged-out. A user can also suspend work and lock the workstation for later use. In this situation, Winlogon changes to the workstation-locked state.
- **Workstation-locked state.** This state provides a secure desktop that requires either user authentication to switch to the logged-on state or administrator authentication to switch to the logged-off state. By providing his or her original

logon credentials, a user can unlock the workstation to reactivate the application desktop. An administrator can alternatively provide administrator account credentials to terminate the user's processes and return to the logged-out state.

Winlogon has the additional ability to implement time-out operations for the secure dialogs it provides to GINA, such as those found during the logged-out state and workstation-locked state. Winlogon notifies GINA of a dialog timeout by returning an appropriate dialog result code. Because of this notification system, and to maintain system integrity, it's important that GINA uses the secure dialogs provided by Winlogon rather than regular Win32 dialogs.

Authentication Package

Contained within a DLL, an authentication package accepts logon credentials as input, and determines—through its authentication routines—whether to permit a user to log on. Depending on the package, logon credentials might include passwords, cryptographic data, and even biometric readings.

The Local Security Authority (LSA), as described in the next section, links to package DLLs during system startup. Whenever the LSA needs to authenticate a user, it accesses the appropriate security package, feeding in the logon data. This process occurs during both phases of Windows 2000 authentication—interactive logon and network authentication.

In addition to authenticating the user, an authentication package has two responsibilities:

- Creating a new LSA logon session for the user
- Returning a set of security IDs (SIDs) that will be bundled into the user's security token.

Windows 2000 comes installed with two authentication packages, one for MSV1_0 and another for Kerberos v5. Additionally, Windows 2000 is extensible, allowing different types of user authentication processes through custom-built authentication packages. For packages other than the two Microsoft-installed DLLs, you must replace GINA with a GINA that calls that package.

Local Security Authority

GINA collects logon data from the user, packages it, and feeds it to the LSA. As a core security component of the Windows 2000 OS, the LSA is responsible for validating users for local and remote logons and maintaining the local security policy. As you can see in Figure 5-1 on the following page, the LSA accomplishes these responsibilities by calling specific authentication packages.

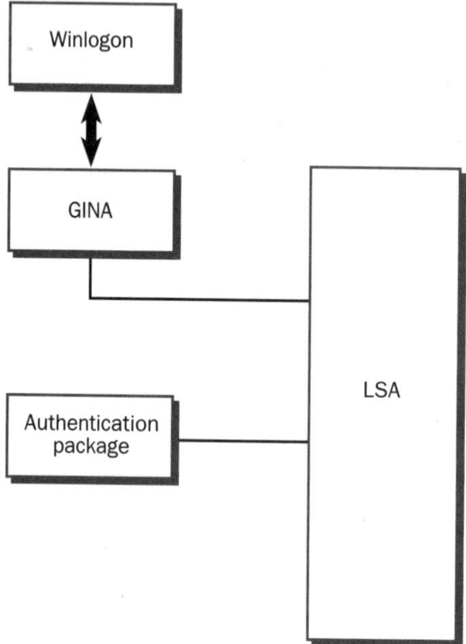

Figure 5-1. *The Local Security Authority.*

After the authentication package either accepts or rejects the logon data for user authentication, the result returns through the LSA to GINA, which displays the authentication success or failure to the user. GINA also returns the result to Winlogon. If the authentication package successfully authenticated the user, Winlogon creates a window station and desktop for the user and starts the shell process that the user will use to interact with the computer.

Interactive Logon to Local Machine

To log on to a local machine, each Windows 2000 user must have an account in the system's security accounts manager (SAM). The SAM is a protected subsystem that manages user and group information through security accounts stored in the local computer registry. When a user requests a local logon, the system compares the logon information against entries in the SAM database. Although Kerberos v5 is the default authentication mechanism for interactive domain logons, Kerberos does not process local logon requests. Windows 2000 uses the MSV1_0 authentication package for local machine logons. To initiate the logon procedure, a user types the SAS, normally Ctrl+Alt+Del. Upon receipt of the SAS, Winlogon switches to the Winlogon desktop, dispatches GINA, and displays the standard logon dialog, which consists of the username and password. For domain machines, the domain name is also required. Once the user enters this information, GINA passes it to the LSA for validation.

The LSA calls the appropriate authentication package—in this case MSV1_0—with the password in the form of a nonreversible secret key generated with a one-way hash function. The LSA interrogates the SAM database for the user's account details and matching key. If the SAM finds the account information, it returns the user's SID and the SIDs of any groups that the user is a member of to the MSV1_0 authentication package. The authentication package returns the user's SID and group membership SIDs to the LSA. The LSA uses these SIDs to create a security access token. The token handle and a logon confirmation are returned to Winlogon, and the user is presented with the application desktop. Figure 5-2 shows the components used during an interactive logon to a local machine.

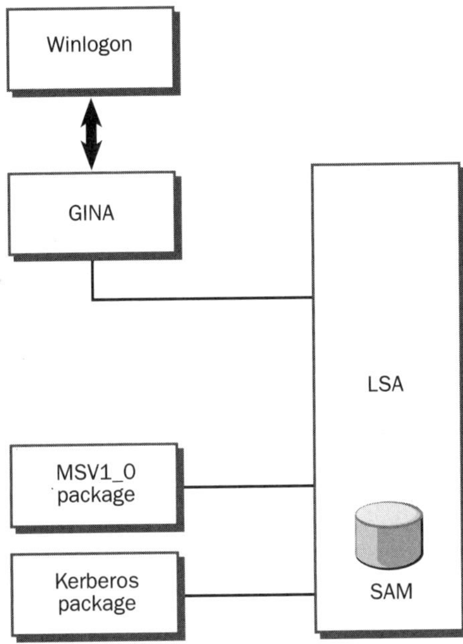

Figure 5-2. *Interactive logon components.*

Interactive Logon to a Domain Account

In contrast to local security accounts stored in the SAM database, domain user accounts are stored in the domain's Active Directory directory service. When a user logs on to a domain account from a Windows 2000 machine, what the user is essentially doing is requesting permission to use the local system services on that machine. You already know that any client requesting the use of any domain service must first authenticate to the domain before gaining access. Similarly, the user must first prove his or her identity before being allowed to use the local system services of a Windows 2000 machine.

Domain logon is a multistep process that uses, by default, the Kerberos v5 authentication protocol. (We'll explain Kerberos v5 in detail later in the chapter.) Kerberos v5 is a ticket-based system that provides mutual authentication between a client and server. Tickets are requested and granted for use of resources and services.

To authenticate to a domain account, a user first requests admission to the domain's ticket-granting service (TGS). Once granted, the user requests a session ticket for the computer he or she is logging on to. Finally, the user asks for admission to the local system services on that computer.

To initiate the logon procedure, a user types the SAS, normally Ctrl+Alt+Del. Upon receipt of the SAS, Winlogon switches to the Winlogon desktop, dispatches GINA, and displays the standard logon dialog, which consists of the user logon name, password, and domain name. For domain accounts, the user logon name follows the style of a user principal name (UPN). A UPN consists of a user account name and the name of the domain that contains the account, separated by an @ sign. For example, the UPN *user45@ntdev.microsoft.com* has a user account name of *user45* and a domain name (also called a UPN suffix) of *ntdev.microsoft.com*. Once the user enters his or her UPN and password and selects the correct domain, GINA passes this information to the LSA for validation.

When the LSA receives the user's logon information, it calculates a nonreversible secret key by sending the password through a one-way hashing function. The LSA stores the resulting hash in a credentials cache where the LSA can retrieve it later. The LSA uses the hash value for renewing ticket-granting tickets (TGTs) or when logging on to a non-Kerberos server where NTLM authentication is required.

Through the Kerberos authentication package, the LSA communicates with the Key Distribution Center (KDC) on the domain controller, as shown in Figure 5-3. Domain controllers register Kerberos v5 authentication protocol-specific SRV records in the Domain Name System (DNS). This allows clients to perform a DNS lookup to locate servers that run the KDC service. The Kerberos authentication package sends the KDC an authentication service request comprised of the client's identity information and pre-authentication data. Typically, the pre-authentication data is a time stamp encrypted with the key derived from the password hash. Upon receipt of the authentication service request, the KDC decrypts the pre-authentication data with its own version of the key. Validating the decrypted time stamp proves that the client indeed knows the password.

Once the KDC validates the user's identity, it returns a logon session key for the client (encrypted with the client's key) and a TGT (encrypted with the KDC's own key) to the Kerberos authentication package. The TGT allows the user to request tickets for domain services, including the system services on the target computer. The authentication package decrypts the session key and stores it, along with the TGT, in its credentials cache for later use.

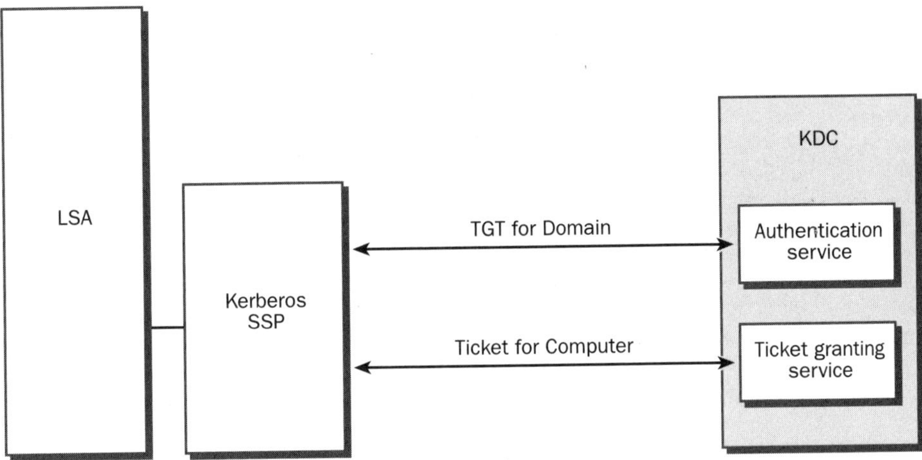

Figure 5-3. *Interactive domain account logon.*

The Kerberos authentication package sends a ticket request for the local machine to the KDC. The KDC responds with a session ticket that the user can present when requesting access to the computer's system services. The LSA then determines if the user is part of any local security groups and whether he or she has any special privileges on the machine. The resulting SIDs—along with the SIDs from the session ticket—are used to build the access token. The token handle and a logon confirmation are returned to Winlogon, and the user is presented with the application desktop.

Tip If a domain KDC is not available, Windows 2000 uses MSV1_0 to attempt a domain logon using pass-through authentication, as is done in Windows NT 4.0. If a domain controller is not available, MSV1_0 attempts a local logon with cached credentials. See Chapter 2, "Windows NT 4.0 Security Review," for a discussion of interactive logon using MSV1_0.

Just as each Windows 2000 server and workstation includes a Kerberos Security Support Provider (SSP), every domain controller provides a Kerberos v5 KDC for the domain. When a Kerberos client on a Windows 2000 computer wants to authenticate to the domain, the system refers to a DNS to find the nearest available domain controller for key distribution. The nearest domain controller becomes the preferred KDC and is used for the logon session. If, during the user's logon session, the preferred KDC becomes unavailable, the client uses DNS to locate an alternate KDC.

As stated earlier, if the Kerberos client can't find a domain controller for authentication, Windows 2000 can attempt to authenticate the user with MSV1_0. This type of authentication is accomplished by using logon credentials that the LSA might have cached in its volatile protected memory. MSV1_0 can use these credentials, if available, for authentication.

Security Support Provider

Another component of the Windows 2000 authentication model is the Security Support Provider (SSP). The SSP is used during noninteractive logons, such as network authentication, and makes one or more security packages available to the application. The SSP implements the network security protocol—such as NTLM or Kerberos—that authenticates the user who is making a network connection to a service somewhere on the network.

The SSP, in conjunction with the Security Support Provider Interface (SSPI), provides a common way for client applications to utilize security packages without having to know about the specific details of the security protocol. The SSPI provides generic functionality that allows transport-level applications and system services to query for available SSPs and to select an SSP for use in obtaining an authenticated connection.

Figure 5-4 shows the relationship of the SSPI and available SSPs to the LSA and security packages.

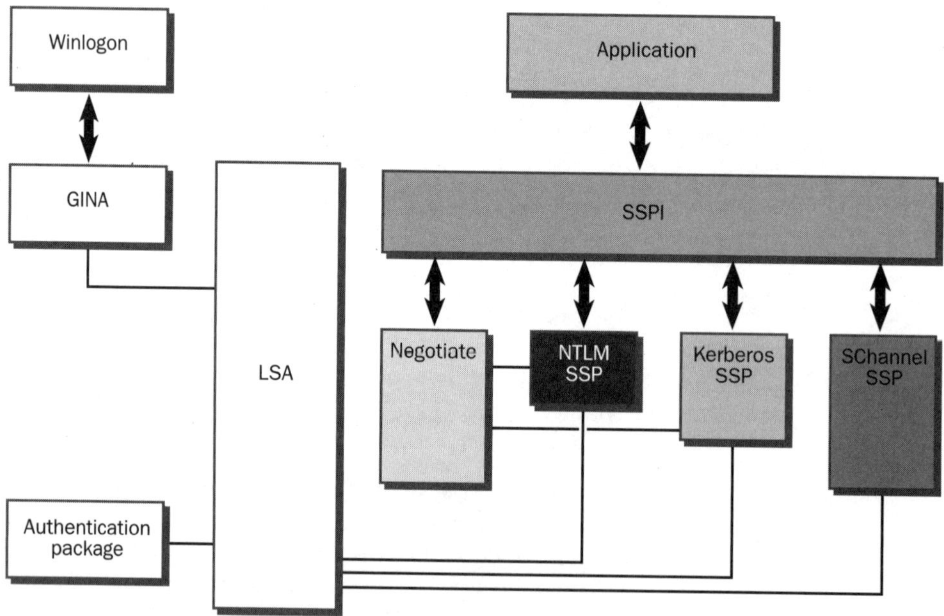

Figure 5-4. *Microsoft-installed SSPs.*

The SChannel SSP implements the SSL protocol. A standard developed by Netscape, SSL provides authentication over an encrypted channel. We'll discuss SSL at the end of this chapter.

Figure 5-4 also shows an SSP labeled Negotiate. Instead of specifying an SSP to use to process the authentication request, the application can specify Negotiate, which will analyze the request and route it to the SSP that fits best.

Network Authentication

In the scheme of the Windows 2000 single sign-on feature, network authentication depends upon a successful interactive domain account logon. When an application needs to use a network resource, the application indirectly accesses the necessary authentication package by calling the SSPI, as shown in Figure 5-5.

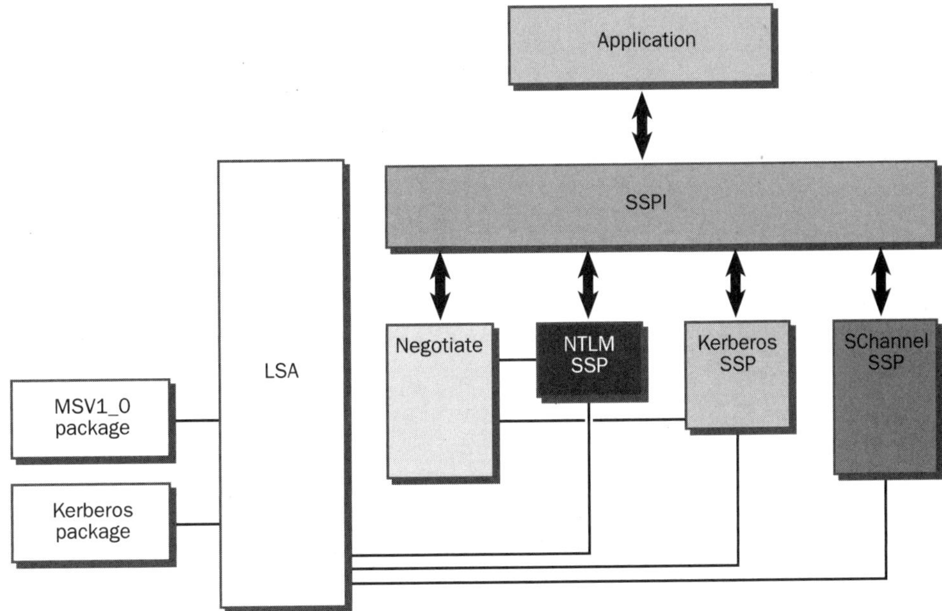

Figure 5-5. *Noninteractive logon components.*

From the security package, the user session presents the previously established TGT to the TGS on the KDC. The TGS issues a session ticket to that user for that service. The user presents the service ticket to the requested resource and is granted access.

In addition to using the issued ticket for immediate access, the LSA also stores the session ticket in a provided Kerberos ticket cache. The length of time that a ticket is valid is dictated by a setting in the Kerberos security policy known as maximum lifetime for service ticket. As long as a stored ticket has not expired, the LSA can retrieve it for reuse by the associated network-based service.

Although the initial domain account logon requires interaction from the user, all network authentications, including TGT renewal, are performed transparently. Figure 5-6 on the following page shows the order of events during a network authentication.

Network authentication involving a machine running an operating system other than Windows 2000 uses the NTLM protocol. For more information on network authentication using NTLM, see Chapter 4, "Active Directory."

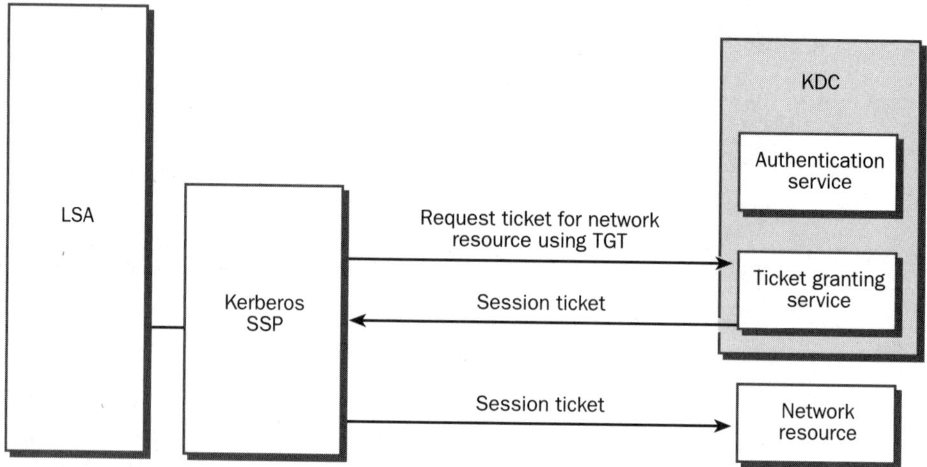

Figure 5-6. *Network authentication.*

Kerberos v5

Kerberos v5 is a standard Internet protocol that provides strong authentication of user and system identities. Because Kerberos v5 uses cryptographic mechanisms to encrypt passwords, you can use it over insecure networks to verify the identity of both parties during a network transaction. In Windows 2000 domains, these transactions typically involve clients requesting the use of network services such as file sharing or print sharing, and network services authenticating these clients before granting them access.

Kerberos v5 services have replaced NTLM as the primary authentication mechanism in Windows 2000. Kerberos v5 is available on all domain controllers, and each Windows 2000 workstation and server includes a Kerberos v5 client. You can therefore use the Kerberos v5 protocol for authentication between machines running Windows 2000, such as a Windows 2000 Professional client authenticating to a Windows 2000 domain controller. Authentication involving NT 4.0 (or earlier) domain controllers or workstations uses NTLM as the authentication protocol. Because Kerberos v5 is based on the RFC 1510 Kerberos reference implementation, Windows 2000 also interoperates with other Kerberos RFC 1510 servers and clients in certain scenarios, and even on machines with operating systems other than Windows 2000.

How Does Kerberos v5 Work?

The Kerberos protocol is a ticket-based system. Clients authenticate to the network and request tickets from the KDC for specific network resources. The KDC provides two services:

- **Authentication Service (AS).** AS authenticates users and issues TGTs that the client uses to request session tickets.

- **Ticket-Granting Service (TGS).** TGS issues session tickets for network services based on the TGT issued to a client.

Before clients can request session tickets for network services, those clients must be authenticated to the network. The AS confirms the user's identity by comparing the submitted logon credentials against the user's account in Active Directory. For password authentication, the logon credentials include a password-based hash that the AS verifies against the user's account. The Windows 2000 architecture also supports public-key authentication, as in the case of smart card logon. Using a Kerberos public-key extension that we'll discuss later, the AS performs a cryptographic verification using the client's public key stored in his or her domain account. Upon validation, the AS issues a TGT that the client uses to request session tickets.

The TGT is a persistent ticket that, by default, has a lifetime of 10 hours (600 minutes). The TGT is used each time a client wants to access a different network service. The client submits the TGT to the TGS along with the name of the service for which the client wants the ticket. Upon approval, the TGS issues a session ticket, which the client stores in its ticket cache.

Internal fields of the ticket restrict the period for which the session ticket is valid. For each requested use of a service, the client retrieves the ticket from its ticket cache and submits the ticket to the service for access. Figure 5-7 and the enumerated steps that follow illustrate the sequence of events in the Kerberos v5 network authentication process.

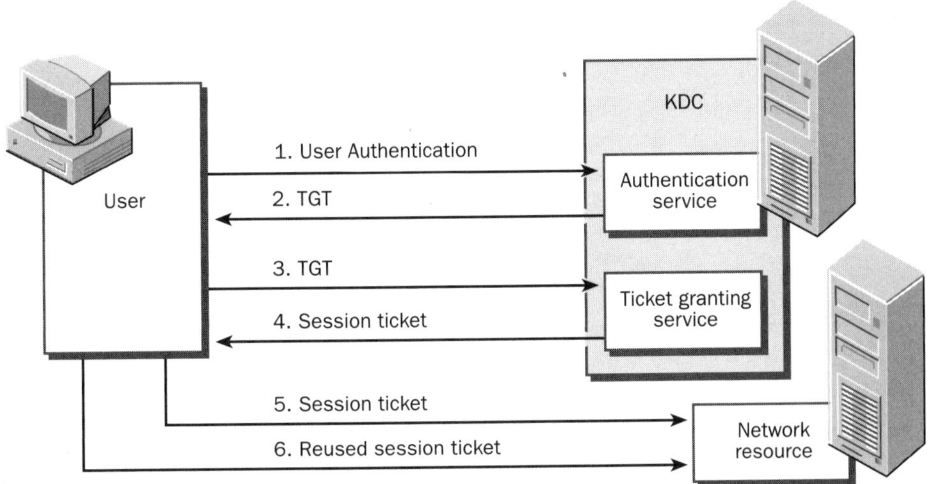

Figure 5-7. *Kerberos v5 authentication process.*

1. The user authenticates to the KDC through the AS.
2. The AS provides a TGT to the user.
3. When the user requires access to a network service for the first time, it sends the TGT to the TGS requesting a session ticket for that specific service.

4. The TGS issues a session ticket to the client for that service.
5. The client sends the session ticket to the network service for access.
6. When the client requires subsequent use of a service, it checks its ticket cache for a session ticket valid for that service. If the client finds a valid ticket, it presents the ticket for access. If the ticket has expired or the client does not have a ticket for that service, the client must return to the TGS to either renew an out-of-date ticket or request a new one.

What's in a Ticket?

For confidentiality, much of the data found in service tickets is encrypted with the server's secret key. Of course, for the client to manage its tickets, each ticket needs nonsensitive header information that any program can access without having to decrypt the ticket. The following ticket information is not encrypted:

- Ticket format version number
- Name of the domain that issued the ticket
- Name of the server for which the ticket is valid

The server's secret key protects the rest of the ticket information, which includes:

- The session key shared between the client and server for secure transmissions
- Name of the client's domain
- Client's name
- Time of the initial authentication and issuance of the TGT on which this ticket is based
- Validity time of the ticket (comprised of a start time and an end time)

Tip The time stamp provides a useful function: It keeps attackers from stealing the service ticket and reusing it at a later time. The requested service verifies that the time indicated by the time stamp is within an acceptable range of the current time.

Mutual Authentication

You already know that the identity of the user or client is important to the network service. The reverse is also true: the identity of the service is important to the user or client. Suppose you're copying a finance spreadsheet over an insecure network to a remote server. Yes, the transmission will be private, but you also want to ensure that the recipient—with whom you share this privacy—is genuine. One of the benefits of Kerberos v5 under Windows 2000 is that it provides mutual authentication. In other words, both parties are present and accounted for.

If, during the Kerberos authentication process, a client requests access to a specific network service by sending a session ticket, the client can also request that the server mutually authenticate itself. The server responds to the request by returning the embedded time stamp encrypted with the shared session key. The client decrypts and validates the known time stamp, proving that the server possesses the correct secret key to decrypt the token and obtain the shared session key.

Delegation of Authentication

Delegation is another feature supported by the Kerberos v5 protocol. In configurations involving multitiered client/server applications, a client might want to access a server that requires access to a second server. Just as the client uses a session ticket to authenticate to the first server, the first server needs a ticket to authenticate to the second server. However, the type of access the second server grants should be based on the client's authorizations, not the first server's authorizations. Delegation of authentication—which is a type of impersonation—allows the client to authorize the first server to represent it when accessing the second server. Sanctioned by the KDC, this type of impersonation allows the second server to have limited access to the first server based on the client's rights.

For the front-end server to obtain session tickets to the back-end server on behalf of the client, the client requests a forwardable TGT from the KDC, indicating in the request which server will act in its name. If the Kerberos policy permits forwarding, the KDC generates a TGT for the front-end server, sets the FORWARDABLE flag in the TGT, and sends the TGT to the client. The client then forwards the TGT to the front-end server. The front-end server can subsequently present this TGT to the KDC when requesting a session ticket to the back-end server.

For delegation of authentication to work, the client and both servers must be running on Windows 2000 machines, and both the client and service's accounts must be enabled for delegation.

Enabling Kerberos v5 Authentication

To use Kerberos v5 for authentication between servers that run network services and clients that need these services, both the client and server must be running Windows 2000. In some scenarios, either the client or the server can be running a compatible RFC 1510 Kerberos implementation. A domain controller running Windows 2000 can authenticate RFC 1510 Kerberos clients. Likewise, a server running an RFC 1510 Kerberos implementation can authenticate Windows 2000 Professional clients within an organization.

When you install Windows 2000, you automatically enable authentication using Kerberos v5. The Kerberos v5 services residing on the domain controller—such as the KDC and TGS—are installed using the Active Directory Installation Wizard. Once you install these services, the installation process starts the TGS and enables Kerberos authentication.

Kerberos v5 Policies

Like many other security features embedded in Windows 2000, Kerberos policies for domains are configurable. In a Windows 2000 domain, Kerberos settings are implemented through the domain's KDC. These settings are defined in the default domain group policy.

By default, only users belonging to the Domain Admins security group can update Kerberos settings. The following settings dictate Kerberos v5 behavior in a Windows 2000 domain:

- **Enforce user logon restrictions.** The overhead cost of validating a ticket request against the target computer's user rights policy slows down network access. This option is enabled by default. Turning it off is less secure, but can speed up access to the network service.
- **Maximum lifetime for a service ticket.** This option specifies how long a user can access a service with a given session ticket. This policy is set to 10 hours by default.
- **Maximum lifetime for a user ticket.** The KDC issues TGTs during logon. This setting, 10 hours by default, determines how long a user can use the TGT before renewing it or requesting a new one.
- **Maximum lifetime for user ticket renewal.** Ticket renewal lifetime refers to the length of time a continuously renewed TGT is valid. The default maximum is seven days.
- **Maximum tolerance for computer clock synchronization.** This setting exists because of the time inconsistencies between clocks on different machines. The Kerberos v5 protocol uses time checks to ensure that unauthorized users do not pirate valid tickets and use them at a later time. Set to five minutes by default, this setting determines the allowable difference between the client's clock and the server's clock.

Kerberos v5 Applications

You know that Windows 2000 uses Kerberos v5 for password and smart card interactive logon and network authentication. However, Windows 2000 uses the Kerberos protocol in many other system services. For example, Internet Protocol Security (IPSec), which provides packet-level protection of data between machines and is the chassis beneath virtual private networks (VPNs), uses Kerberos v5 as the default authentication method. (See Chapter 12, "Terminal Services," for more information on IPSec.) In addition, Kerberos v5 generates transitive trusts between domains for account authentication. Kerberos v5 is also used during server authentication for message queuing, and you can use it for print server security when submitting print jobs over your LAN or intranet.

NT LAN Manager

NT LAN Manager (NTLM) is the primary mechanism used for authentication in Windows NT 4.0 and earlier versions of Windows NT. NTLM is included with Windows 2000 to maintain compatibility when running in a mixed-mode network, which is the default configuration for Windows 2000. Mixed-mode networks can contain workstations and servers that run both Windows 2000 and Windows NT 4.0 (or earlier). NTLM is used as the authentication protocol when the authenticator, the requestor, or both are running

Windows NT 4.0 or earlier. For example, a configuration in which a Windows 2000 domain server needs to authenticate a Windows NT 4.0 workstation would use NTLM.

In addition, NTLM is used for authentication with Windows 2000 machines that are not part of a domain. Standalone servers use NTLM to authenticate clients. In networks that contain strictly Windows 2000 machines, the network configuration can be set to native mode on the domain controller. Native mode restricts the use of NTLM for network authentication.

As for Active Directory support for cross-domain service, computers from Windows NT domains can use NTLM to logon and access server-based resources from Windows 2000 domains.

The distinct advantage that the Kerberos protocol has over NTLM is in the way a server authenticates a client for resource access. With Kerberos, a client hands the server a ticket that cryptographically validates the user's identity. Under NTLM, however, the server must directly contact the domain controller and ask the domain authentication service to validate the user's credentials.

Smart Card Logon

In addition to password-based authentication, the Kerberos v5 protocol includes a public key extension that enables Windows 2000 to support smart card logons. While deploying smart cards in an organization increases administrative overhead and cost, hardware authentication provides an immeasurable security benefit over simple knowledge-based identities.

What Are Smart Cards?

A smart card is a device with a built-in electronic microchip used to store electronic data. The size of a conventional credit card, a smart card can also contain functionality allowing you to perform specified operations directly on the card itself.

Windows 2000 supports a type of smart card called a contact smart card. The front of a contact smart card has a gold plate exposing electrical connectors that provide a channel to the embedded microchip. A smart card reader—when connected to a smart card—makes contact with the card's gold plate and transfers data to and from the chip. The size and physical characteristics of smart cards are specified by ISO standards 7810 and 7816, respectively.

The Windows 2000 security model uses smart cards as cryptographic peripherals to store authentication credentials for network logon and remote access authentication. The Microsoft Public Key Infrastructure (PKI) utilizes a key pair for cryptographic operations such as authentication, data integrity, and encryption. The key pair consists of a private nondisclosed key and a public distributed key. Cryptographic service providers (CSPs) that expose smart card functionality allow for storage on smart cards of both private keys and public key certificates. The number of certificates and keys that a smart card can store depends on the individual manufacturer. In the interest of key protection, most smart card implementations will allow access to public key certificates but will not allow the reading or writing of the private keys except in an encrypted form.

What Are the Advantages of Smart Cards?

Smart cards provide a level of security beyond that of conventional password authentication. Additionally, smart cards supplement the private-key storage containers used by Microsoft's Cryptographic Application Program Interface (CryptoAPI) and can replace software tokens used in certain security-enabled applications that provide authentication, data integrity, or confidentiality. Private-key storage containers and software tokens, defined by the public key cryptography standard (PKCS #12), store sensitive private keys on the computer's hard disk. This section describes the advantages smart cards have over password authentication and nonremovable private key storage.

Secure Storage Device

While no cryptographic storage device is truly tamperproof, smart cards provide tamper-resistant storage of private key and public key certificates. Security features protect the electronic data stored on the card. Because the private keys are generated on the card and only wrapped versions of private keys leave the card, the user's private cryptographic material should never be externally exposed to any application or person. A PIN set by the entity entrusted to enable the card controls access to the card. If a user enters an invalid PIN for several consecutive logon attempts, the card will become inactive. Furthermore, unlike passwords that are sent through networks and can therefore be attacked, PINs are exclusive to a user and his or her smart card. International standards govern the smart card's physical properties, such as the flexibility and acceptable temperature thresholds of the card's plastic and the characteristics of the electrical contact.

Stronger Proof of Identity

While authentication protocols protect logon credentials during transit, the validity of a user's identity is still based on a single piece of knowledge—the password. Smart cards provide a second degree of security by requiring an additional identity possession. Not only must the user know the PIN required to access the smart card, but he or she must also possess the smart card itself. Someone who attempts to impersonate a smart card user with only the PIN or with only the smart card will be unsuccessful.

Cryptographic Operations Performed on the Card

The architecture of the Microsoft CryptoAPI allows for the installation of cryptographic modules. These modules (CSPs) can contain a variety of supported algorithms and key strengths. CSPs can be software-based, or they can interface with a particular smart card and support the cryptographic operations and data-storage features of that card. Smart card manufacturers will typically write CSPs for their smart cards that users can employ for any CryptoAPI compliant application. Smart card CSPs handle the logon and cryptographic operations. This process keeps the cryptographic operations and private key data from ever being exposed to the operating system. Unlike software-based cryptographic routines, smart cards are not vulnerable to system attacks.

Portability

Smart cards provide a distinct portability advantage over software-based keys stored on a hard disk. In the Windows 2000 environment, where network logon information is kept in Active Directory, passwords allow authentication from any machine in the Windows 2000 domain. Smart cards maintain this portability because you can remove a smart card from one card reader and insert it in another. In addition to authentication credentials, however, smart cards protect other private key information that can be useful outside the Windows 2000 domain.

Smart Card Readers

Currently, Windows 2000 interfaces with smart card readers through one of two ways: You can attach a smart card reader to an RS-232 serial port or you can insert a smart card reader into a PCMCIA type II slot. Upon detection of the hardware, Windows 2000 automatically installs the device drivers for the following RS-232 smart card readers:

- Smart TLP3 from Bull CP8
- GCR410P from Gemplus
- 220P from Litronic
- 3531 from Rainbow Technologies
- SwapSmart from SCM Microsystems

Windows 2000 also supports the following PCMCIA readers:

- GPR400 from Gemplus
- SwapSmart from SCM Microsystems

To install one of the card readers listed here, attach the reader to the Windows 2000 machine, restart the machine, and log on as the administrator. Installation will occur automatically, including copying the device drivers. Upon successful installation, an Unplug Or Eject Hardware icon will appear in the toolbar. The Unplug or Eject Hardware dialog box will include this smart card reader in a list of hardware devices.

For Plug and Play–compliant smart cards other than those listed in this section or available as part of the Windows 2000 installation, the Add/Remove Hardware Wizard will follow the administrator logon. Follow the installation directions through the wizard, using the manufacturer's setup instructions as an additional guide.

Enabling Smart Cards

Smart cards represent a piece of the Microsoft PKI. Before a user can utilize a smart card for authentication, the smart card has to be programmed, or enabled, with identity information and cryptographic material. During the enrollment process, the smart card generates a public and private key pair. It stores the private key internally and bundles the public key and user information in a certificate request that it sends to a CA. Upon authorization, the CA generates a public key certificate for the user that is ultimately retrieved by the requesting application and written to the smart card.

The Windows 2000 security suite includes a CA that administrators use to issue and maintain public key certificates. Under the Microsoft PKI, smart cards are enabled in one of two ways. In a low-assurance environment, users can request certificates and program smart cards by accessing a Certificate Services Web page. Since the Web page is tied to the CA, the user can complete the enrollment process interactively.

Alternatively, network administrators can employ a smart card enrollment station for higher levels of user assurance. By centralizing the enrollment process, administrators gain tighter control over how—and to whom—certificates are issued. The enrollment agent, who owns an enrollment agent certificate, uses the smart card station to request certificates on behalf of the user. How strict the agent is in validating the user's identity is a matter of company policy.

Chapter 7, "Access Control Model," provides in-depth information about Certificate Services and the PKI.

Using Smart Cards

Once you've installed a smart card reader and have an active smart card containing your logon credentials, you can log on to the Windows 2000 domain. Normally, you type Ctrl+Alt+Del to be prompted for your username, your password, and possibly your domain name. For smart card authentication, you instead insert the smart card into the reader and, when PIN prompt appears, you enter your PIN. This kicks off a certificate authentication sequence using Kerberos v5 as the authentication protocol.

Smart Card Interactive Logon

Interactive logon using smart cards is similar to the password-based logon process.With passwords, however, a single encryption key is derived using a one-way hash function. The Kerberos v5 protocol uses this key for both encryption and decryption of transmissions. Smart cards are a product of the public key world and operate on a two-key system. Windows 2000 implements a public key extension of Kerberos v5 to support smart cards. This extension modifies the initial exchange when the KDC authenticates the user and provides a logon session key and TGT. Instead of using the password-based symmetric key to encrypt the logon session key, the KDC employs the user's public key. The encrypted session key can only be decrypted with the user's private key found on his or her smart card.

As described previously, a user inserts the smart card into the reader to initiate the logon sequence. This produces a SAS, which is equivalent to typing Ctrl+Alt+Del. Upon receipt of the SAS, Winlogon switches to the Winlogon desktop, dispatches GINA, and displays the dialog that asks for the activation PIN. After the user enters the PIN, GINA passes the user's logon information to the LSA. Using the PIN, the LSA obtains the user's public key certificate. This certificate is sent to the KDC with the normal pre-authentication data.

The KDC responds, encrypting the session key with the public key found in the certificate. The LSA uses the private key on the smart card to decrypt the session key. Once this decryption takes place, the session key secures all other transmission between the two parties.

Secure Sockets Layer

While Kerberos v5 is the protocol of choice for authentication within and between Windows 2000 domains, not all authentications take place over a network-to-network connection. Windows 2000 includes Secure Sockets Layer (SSL) support for users who need to authenticate to a network via the Internet.

SSL is an open standard that combines public key technology and symmetric encryption to provide authentication, confidentiality, and message integrity to network or Internet transactions. SSL mutually allows clients and servers to authenticate to each other by trading public key certificates.

Figure 5-8 and the numbered steps that follow depict the SSL authentication and handshake process.

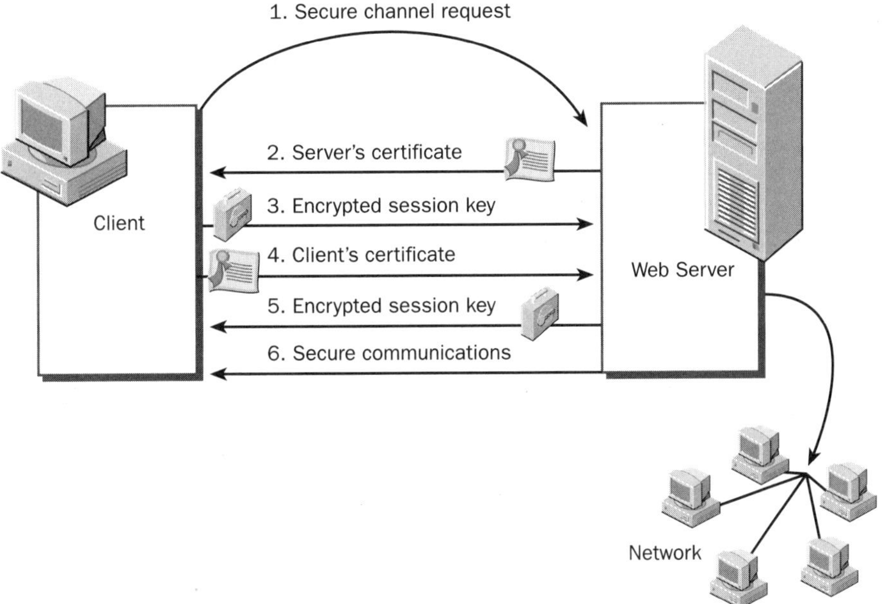

Figure 5-8. *Secure Sockets Layer.*

1. The client contacts the server and requests a secure channel.
2. The server responds with its public key certificate.
3. The client verifies the server's certificate and uses it to encrypt a session key. The encrypted session key is sent to the server.
4. The client additionally sends its public key certificate.
5. The server verifies the client's certificate and responds with a session key encrypted with the client's public key.
6. The client and server negotiate a cryptoalgorithm and communicate securely using the agreed session key.
7. After validating the client's identity, the server can log the user on to the domain using his or her Windows 2000 domain account.

With SSL, authentication is accomplished by virtue of the association between the public and private key pair. Public key certificates bind the identity of a user (or entity) to a public key. By encrypting handshake transmissions with public keys, both the requestor and authenticator's identities are assured. Only the user or entity whose name appears in a certificate possesses the private key needed to decrypt and read the transaction.

Being certificate-based, SSL authentication has administrative overhead that password-based Kerberos does not. However, as you learned earlier, the Windows 2000 architecture provides the necessary components to support a PKI. Using Web-based registration, users can request and retrieve public key certificates. Administrators can issue, manage, and revoke certificates using Windows 2000 Certificate Services. Finally, Active Directory acts as a repository for user certificates and stores certificate policy information.

The level of protection offered by SSL or any other cryptographic operation depends directly on the length of the encryption key used during the operation. SSL supports strong encryption, which uses keys of 128 bits or more, as well as encryption using weaker 40- or 56-bit keys. Export restrictions once prevented U.S. companies from distributing products using strong encryption to international customers. However, a regulation recently issued by the U.S. government now allows Microsoft to make strong encryption products available worldwide. The Windows 2000 operating system will include 128-bit encryption support for both domestic and international customers.

Like Kerberos, SSL not only acts as an authentication mechanism, but also provides a means for two parties to agree on security parameters and establish a secure channel for confidential communication.

Summary

Verifying the identity of users is an important function in the Windows 2000 security model. Together, the authentication and authorization security functions allow Windows 2000 to control access to network resources. These functions prevent unknown users from gaining unauthorized access to sensitive data or protected services. Chapter 7 discusses how Windows 2000 implements authorization through the access control model.

Chapter 6
Cryptography and Microsoft Public Key Infrastructure

This chapter introduces cryptography and Public Key Infrastructure (PKI) and explains why and how to deploy them in your Windows 2000 environment. The first part of the chapter explains the security services offered by cryptography, the building blocks of cryptography, the importance of key relationships and exchange, and the high-level cryptographic services available to applications and operating systems. The second part of the chapter describes how you can use PKIs in Windows 2000 and how to configure the certificate services in Windows 2000. The third part of the chapter discusses how to go about designing your PKI, whether provided by Microsoft or by third parties.

An Introduction to PKI

A PKI allows client and server applications to gain trust in each other's authentication credentials in a highly scalable and efficient manner. Applications can then employ those credentials to perform strong authentication and make use of end-to-end confidentiality and integrity services.

To show where a PKI might prove useful, let's look at the case study of a company called Exploration Air that wants its customers to have access to an internal Web server. Exploration Air expects a number of users in each customer organization to securely log on to the Web server. The challenge lies in managing authentication credentials for all those external users. If Exploration Air uses passwords, their IT department is expected to somehow identify those users, as well as process password changes for them. This solution does not scale well, and for a large number of users it becomes unmanageable. Attackers can also guess passwords, and passwords might not offer strong enough authentication for high-value transactions.

With a PKI, Exploration Air can delegate the issuing of authentication credentials to certification authorities run by the customers themselves, or to a commercial certification authority. This way, the company needs to configure its Web server only to trust those authorities. Those credentials also offer strong authentication because they cannot be guessed.

Now let's say that Exploration Air wants to exchange secure e-mail with users of the same customers. A password infrastructure is actually incapable of offering end-to-end secure e-mail among multiple users, and no such implementations exist. Technically, the servers that hold the passwords would have to get involved for every recipient, for every e-mail sent. The servers would also have access to either the contents of the e-mail or the secret key material that protects the confidentiality or integrity of messages. In contrast, public key–enabled e-mail clients can directly exchange secure e-mail using the authentication credentials of their users.

Windows 2000 PKI Offerings

Windows 2000 offers a comprehensive mechanism for issuing certificates that allows organizations to take full advantage of the PKI technology. Microsoft's adherence to industry standards means Windows 2000 will interoperate with any third-party public key–enabled software.

Windows 2000 will work equally well with certificate services offered by other PKI vendors. Windows 2000 can also participate in Internet-based commercial PKIs, such as the one offered by VeriSign.

Windows 2000 offers the following PKI features:

- A number of public key–enabled applications and services: Internet Information Server, Internet Explorer, Microsoft Outlook and Microsoft Outlook Express, Encrypted File System (EFS), IPSec, and smart card logon.
- Active Directory, which you can use as a publication point for certificates and certificate revocation lists (CRLs).
- Microsoft Certificate Services, which enable an organization to issue its own certificates and implement its own PKI.
- Support for smart cards in Windows 2000, which you can use for key storage and cryptographic operations (in addition to logons).
- Commercial certificate authority (CA) certificates preloaded in Windows 2000, which enable users and computers to participate in existing PKIs on the Internet.
- Public Key policies in the Group Policy, which allow administrators to control the external CAs that users and computers can trust.

These features are implemented on industry standards such as X.509, LDAP, SSL/TLS, S/MIME, IPSec, and the Public Key Extensions of Kerberos, enabling interoperability with third-party applications and PKIs.

Cryptographic Background

Cryptography provides the following security services to the operating system and applications. In this chapter, we use the term *entity* to refer to both users and servers.

Confidentiality

Confidentiality ensures that only authorized entities have access to information. This service is particularly useful when you must store sensitive data in vulnerable locations such as laptops, or transmit it across vulnerable networks, such as the Internet or an outsourced WAN. Cryptography then helps by turning big secrets (your data) into small secrets (the cryptographic keys). Keys are easier secrets to manage, especially since they can be exchanged in advance.

Entity Authentication

The entity authentication service proves one entity's identity to another, and it is commonly implemented by demonstrating the possession of a secret. Cryptography helps by keeping that secret private during the authentication process.

Data Integrity

The integrity or data authentication service assures that a chunk of data did indeed originate from an entity and that it remains unaltered. Cryptography helps by binding the data to its originator. In some contexts, integrity might be defined only as ensuring that data remain unaltered.

Nonrepudiation

Nonrepudiation enables users to digitally sign electronic documents and be legally bound by the signatures, as if those signatures were handwritten. Cryptography can provide evidence that a user signed a document, but a lot of conditions need to be met for a court to consider this legally binding. Some countries and some U.S. states legally recognize digital signatures. You can find more information on this issue at *http://www.mbc.com/ecommerce.html* and *http://cwis.kub.nl/~frw/people/hof/DS-lawsu.htm*.

PKI Basics

Entities can have one or more private-public key pairs and associated public key certificates. A certificate is a statement issued by a certification authority according to a policy that binds an entity's public key to its name for a period of time. (You'll learn more about policies later in the chapter.) Another entity that trusts this CA also trusts that the public key belongs to the named entity.

When entity A is presented with a certificate by entity B, entity A can tell from the certificate name that the certificate belongs to a legitimate user of the system. Entity B proves he or she is the legitimate holder of the certificate by proving his or her knowledge of the associated private key. Entity A can optionally check the certificate's current validity by looking it up on the CA's CRL.

Furthermore, entities A and B can now use end-to-end confidentiality and integrity services without the cooperation of any third entity. For example, users can exchange secure e-mail and securely access Web content on an intranet.

For certain applications, this security model presents some advantages when compared to a security model that forces all entities to share secret keys with central authorities. One advantage is that users and computers can authenticate thousands or millions of other entities in a scalable manner, without the immediate cooperation of a mediating server such as a Windows domain controller, a Kerberos Key Distribution Center (KDC), or a CA. For example, almost all Web browsers can authenticate a Web server bearing a certificate from VeriSign, a universally trusted commercial CA.

Another advantage to this model is that users and computers can efficiently use end-to-end security services between them, without the immediate cooperation of a mediating entity. For example, users can exchange confidential e-mail without sharing the contents or keys that protect the contents with mediating servers.

A third advantage is that private keys are typically 1024-bit-long strings and cannot be guessed the way that passwords can. Therefore, you can use certificates for strong authentication.

Finally, account databases need not store a secret for every user and computer. Active Directory actually stores hashed passwords for use by Kerberos and other authentication protocols.

Multiple CAs and Issuing Policies

An enterprise can have multiple issuing CAs to serve the different certificate needs of users and to implement different security policies.

Note that CAs also have a private-public key pair and the associated public key certificate. Multiple CAs are typically linked together in a hierarchy, with parent CAs issuing certificates to subordinate CAs. Trust in a CA implies trust in its subordinate CAs. Therefore, if you trust the root CA at the top of a hierarchy, you implicitly trust all CAs in it.

Users and computers are typically configured to trust root CAs. Therefore, they can efficiently authenticate entities bearing certificates from any subordinate CA. An organization's CA can even be certified by a universally trusted commercial CA, which could make the certificates it issues recognizable by other organizations.

The certification authority issuing policies we've mentioned so far describe a) how the CA identifies users and computer before issuing them a certificate; and b) what legal liabilities, if any, the CA accepts by issuing a certificate.

Policies, on the other hand, might be less important for certificates issued by an organization for internal use. A policy created for this situation could be equivalent to your policy for issuing user passwords. Policies are essential when you use certificates to communicate with other organizations—or when other organizations use them to communicate with you.

Policies are also essential when other organizations issue certificates to your organization and vice versa. Examples include having your own CA certified by a commercial CA, or issuing certificates to customers for use in an extranet application.

Cryptographic Services

This section introduces some building blocks in cryptography and the security services they offer. If you are familiar with cryptography, feel free to skip this section.

Symmetric Cryptographic Algorithms

Symmetric cryptography is the classic form of cryptography. People have relied on it for thousands of years to keep messages private.

Symmetric cryptography works by transforming (encrypting) the plaintext (the original data) to ciphertext (the protected data) in a way that makes it infeasible to reverse the process without the full knowledge of the transformation function. For a number of reasons the secret transformation is split into a constant part, the *cryptographic algorithm*, and a variable part, the *cryptographic key*. The algorithm can be widely deployed in software or devices that use cryptography, and in general it is not assumed to be secret. Therefore, all security lies in keeping the key secret.

By definition, the reverse process uses the same key—hence the name *symmetric* cryptography. The decryption transformation turns the ciphertext back into the plaintext. The transformation is split into a decryption algorithm and the same cryptographic key.

Symmetric keys are either random blocks of data or are derived from user passwords, and are usually 40 to 128 bits in length. Symmetric algorithms use symmetric keys and a block algorithm such as DES, DESX, RC2, or RC4 to encrypt and decrypt raw data.

Asymmetric Cryptographic Algorithms

Asymmetric, or *public key*, cryptography also turns plaintext into ciphertext using an algorithm and a key. The difference lies in the use of a different decryption key, hence the name asymmetric.

The decryption (private) key and the encryption (public) key are related to each other, but the former cannot feasibly be derived from the latter. Therefore, the encryption key need not be kept secret, and can even be made public. Instead, users of public keys need to trust that a given key does belong to a particular owner. This issue is addressed by the process of certification (described later in the chapter). Security lies in keeping the private key secret.

Asymmetric keys are randomly chosen from a set that has certain properties specific to the asymmetric algorithm, so that two users are unlikely to generate the same keys. Key sizes commonly range from 512 to 4096 bits. Asymmetric cryptographic algorithms, such as RSA, encrypt symmetric keys in key exchange protocols and in hybrid cryptographic systems.

Asymmetric Signing Algorithms

You can also reverse the one-way relationship between asymmetric keys to *sign* data with a private key and *verify* the signature with the public key. This is because the signature could only have been feasibly generated with its associated private key. Asymmetric cryptographic keys are used for digital signatures and Challenge-Response authentication. Some common asymmetric algorithms include RSA and Digital Signature Algorithm (DSA).

Asymmetric Key Exchange

Some public key algorithms, notably Diffie-Hellman, can directly generate a shared secret, given two private-public key pairs. This is in contrast to exchanging a previously generated secret by protecting it with an asymmetric cryptographic algorithm.

As with asymmetric keys, these keys are randomly chosen from a set that has certain properties specific to the asymmetric algorithm, so that two users are unlikely to generate the same keys. Key sizes commonly range from 512 to 4096 bits.

Hashing

A hash function is one-way transformation that efficiently turns arbitrary-length data into fixed-length data, and given some data or its hash value, it is computationally infeasible to find some other data that will hash into the same value. Some applications also require the hash function to be collision-resistant, so that it is hard to find any two inputs with the same hash value.

Therefore, if two documents hash into the same value, we can be certain that they are identical. So when we want to efficiently or privately compare two pieces of data, we can compare their hash values. For example, we can verify that a message was delivered intact by comparing its hash value before and after delivery. And we can securely compare two secrets by comparing their hash values.

Hash algorithms are commonly used for digital signatures, passphrases, integrity protection (for tasks such as software distribution), and Challenge-Response authentication. Hash algorithms such as MD5 and SHA-1 commonly use hash values from 128 to 160 bits long.

Cryptographic Services

Windows 2000 combines the cryptographic building blocks to provide cryptographic services to applications. When more than one entity is involved, you can assume that shared and public keys have been exchanged.

Hybrid Encryption

Applications frequently employ hybrid or bulk encryption when they are required to apply a confidentiality service to shared data. This protocol assumes that the receiver has a private-public key pair and that the sender has obtained the public key.

A typical example is that of the SSL/TLS protocol used in secure Web browsing: The browser software (the initiator) is preloaded with some CA public keys, and the Web server (the receiver) has an asymmetric key pair and a certificate issued to itself from one of those CAs.

The browser then can generate a random symmetric key, encrypt it with the public key, and send it to the server. This is now a shared secret key, and the operation is essentially a key exchange. Either party can now use the key to encrypt data with a symmetric encryption algorithm and send the data to the other party.

The symmetric encryption is used because asymmetric algorithms are many times slower than symmetric algorithms and therefore not typically used for bulk encryption of data.

SSL/TLS, S/MIME, secure e-mail in Microsoft Exchange, and EFS all use hybrid encryption to provide a confidentiality service.

Digital Signatures

Digital signatures offer a data authentication service, ensuring that a message did indeed originate from an entity, and that it is unaltered.

Digital signatures are also hybrid in nature, again for efficiency reasons: A hash function is first applied to the data to be signed, producing a hash value or *message digest.* Then an application applies the asymmetric signing algorithm to the digest, using the signer's private/signing key. The digital signature consists of this signed hash, and is appended to the message.

The verifier repeats the first step to obtain the hash of the message he or she received, and then applies the asymmetric signing algorithm to the digital signature, using the signer's public/verifying key, which yields the original hash, and compares the two.

Any changes to the received message will change its hash. Also, any intentional changes to the signed hash are computationally infeasible without access to the private/signing key.

Digital Signatures offer data authentication services to Authenticode, S/MIME, and secure e-mail in Microsoft Exchange.

Message Authentication Codes

Message Authentication Codes, or MACs, offer a data authentication service similar to digital signatures, but use a shared symmetric key. MACs are only meaningful to those who possess the signing/verifying key.

One category of MACs called HMACs uses *keyed hashes*. HMACs concatenate a symmetric key with the message before hashing. Therefore, only the key holders can compute the message digest.

Another method for calculating MACs involves symmetrically encrypting the message with a block cipher in cipher block chaining (CBC) mode. In that mode, each plaintext block is combined (XORed or binary added) with the previous ciphertext. The final ciphertext is the MAC. The most common implementation uses the DES algorithm in CBC mode.

MACs provide data authentication services to SSL/TLS and IPSec.

Challenge-Response Authentication

Challenge-Response authentication mechanisms offer an entity authentication service. They authenticate one entity to another by proving knowledge of a credential (shared secret or private-public key pair) while keeping that credential private.

The authenticator challenges the authenticated party with a challenge, or *nonce*. The authenticated party responds with a cryptographic function of both nonce and the credential. The authenticator can then verify the response using the shared secret or corresponding public key.

When the credential is a shared secret, the cryptographic function can be a symmetric encryption algorithm or a hash function (or a MAC). If the credential is a private-public key pair, an asymmetric signing algorithm is used.

Challenge-Response authentication protocols include NTLM, SSL/TLS client authentication, digest authentication in Microsoft Internet Explorer and Microsoft Internet Information Services (IIS), and Point-To-Point Tunneling Protocol (PPTP).

Certification and Key Exchange

To use any kind of cryptographic services with more than one entity, these entities first need to share a secret or each other's public keys to authenticate one another.

Note Authentication is necessary to protect against active "man-in-the-middle" attacks, in which an attacker masquerading as one of the legitimate parties can insert messages into the communications channel. Without authentication, it is still possible to preserve confidentiality and integrity, assuming only passive (eavesdropping) attacks are possible.

If only one entity makes a public key available to the other, *only that entity* can be authenticated—not the other. This is sufficient in some scenarios, such as a Web server proving its identity to Web browsers.

Windows 2000 actually has a native "secret-key" infrastructure (based on the user and computer passwords stored in Active Directory) and can also run and make use of a PKI.

These two infrastructures complement each other and solve different problems, as discussed in the Microsoft PKI section earlier in this chapter.

Secrets are shared in the following ways:

- Long-term secrets are typically established out-of-band (for example, outside the untrusted communication medium over which applications apply cryptographic services) between entities and central authorities. A typical example of this is the logon password that users share with Active Directory.
- Short-term secrets are intended to protect the contents of a session. They can be established through the process of key exchange if long-term secrets or public keys are already shared. (This process is described in the following section.)

Public keys are shared in the following manner:

- Users and computers obtain the public keys of certification authorities they trust in an out-of-band manner or over a secure channel. For example, in Windows 2000 public keys are either preloaded into the operating system or securely propagated in the Group Policy.
- Users can now obtain the public keys of other entities over untrusted channels, packaged in certificates issued by those certification authorities. The certificates allow them to trust that the public keys belong to the named entities.

Key Exchange

Key exchange, or key agreement, is a category of protocols that allows two entities that share a long-term secret or at least one public key to establish a short-term shared secret.

Key exchange protocols make use of the symmetric and asymmetric protocols described earlier in this chapter. Some Windows 2000 protocols that perform key exchange are Kerberos v5, SSL/TLS, and IPSec. For further information about these protocols, see Chapter 5, "Authentication."

Certification

Certification is the basis of a PKI. Certification binds a public key with the key holder's name and the intended key usage for a period of time. It is performed by a CA, and provides assurance (to entities who trust it) that the public key does indeed belong to the named entity. The resultant certified public key is called a digital or public key certificate, or simply a certificate. Certificates are sometimes published in a directory or distributed by their owners.

Users and computers who trust a CA and have its certificate can verify the certified public keys of other entities that have registered with it. Services (typically Web services such as IIS) can use certificates to identify users, map them into Windows accounts, and give them access to resources. The discretionary access control lists (DACLs) on the resources determine the users' authorization.

CAs can also set up *trust relationships* with each other. In a hierarchical CA model, such as the one in Windows 2000, the child (subordinate) authority would obtain its certificate from its parent CA. End users who trust a parent CA trust all its subordinates' CAs.

We'll discuss the hierarchical model further in the Microsoft PKI section later in this chapter. At this point it is worth mentioning that CAs at the top of hierarchies are called *root*, and only issue certificates to subordinate CAs, not to end users. Root CAs have by necessity *self-signed certificates*—in other words, they issue certificates to themselves by signing their public keys with their own private keys. By trusting a few root CAs, therefore, users and computers can efficiently verify the certificates of millions of other entities.

End users can also generate self-signed certificates when the users generate a key pair and no CA is available to enroll with. This typically happens when EFS is used in the absence of a Windows 2000 Enterprise CA. Such certificates are of value only to their owners, since other users cannot trust or verify them.

Technically, certification is performed by digitally signing the end user's public key together with identifying information (for example, name and e-mail address), using the CA's private/signing key. The CA's public key is widely distributed; users who choose to trust the public key can use it to verify its digital signatures on certificates.

Thus CAs are trusted for a number of things, including properly identifying key holders before issuing them a certificate, revoking this certificate when it is no longer valid, and keeping their own private/signing keys confidential. You need to document these issues in the CA's certificate practice statement (CPS), especially if you use its certificates to communicate with other organizations.

The next section describes why and how certificates are revoked.

Certificate Revocation

Revocation is the act of canceling a certificate, effectively recalling the issuer's signature on the combination of public key and user name.

The following situations can result in certificate revocation:

- The user changes his or her name.
- The user's private key is compromised; the user will enroll separately for a new certificate under a new key pair.
- The issuer's signing key is compromised. If other parties can now issue certificates on behalf of the issuer, all issued certificates are now invalid.
- The user leaves the organization or the part of the organization for which the CA is responsible.
- The computer owner of the certificate (computer owners can have keys, too) is replaced, compromised, or decommissioned.

Technically, revocation is performed by publishing the certificate's serial number in a CRL signed by the issuing CA.

A CA's certificate is revoked if its private key is compromised, because now other parties can issue certificates on its behalf. Therefore, all its certificates, including ones issued to subordinate CAs and their issued certificates, are also considered revoked.

Certificate Renewal

Renewal is the act of issuing a new certificate using the same name, a new serial number, and perhaps (but not necessarily) a new key pair. Renewal does not affect the validity of the old certificate.

You should renew user and computer certificates just before they are about to expire. For CA certificates, renewal should happen earlier, because for a certificate to be valid at any given time, the certificates of the issuing CA and its parents must also be valid. It would be unfortunate if a CA certificate expiration caused any issued certificates to expire. Therefore, Microsoft CAs implement *time nesting*, meaning that they will not issue certificates that will expire later than their own certificates. This time-nesting policy can cause problems toward the end of a CA's certificate lifetime. For example, if a CA issued certificates one month before its certificate expired, those issued certificates would need to have an expiration period of less than one month.

Therefore, you should renew a CA certificate when its remaining lifetime approaches the longest validity period of certificates it issued. For example, a CA that issues certificates valid for two years should have a lifetime of four years, and renew its certificate every eighteen months.

After renewal, an entity uses the new certificate and key pair, if any. The old set is archived to decrypt and verify old and even new documents.

Microsoft PKI

The Windows 2000 PKI consists of a number of components:

- **The public key–enabled applications and services.** These are IIS, IPSec, smart card logon, EFS, Internet Explorer, Outlook, and Outlook Express. These components interact with each other, and they make use of the cryptographic security services. Some of them also perform key management. They are all standards-based and can interoperate with non-Microsoft entities. They obtain the keys or certificates they need from their own user's or host's store, Active Directory, and Exchange.
- **The user and host certificate stores.** These store the entity's own certificate, if any, and a pointer to the cryptographic service provider that holds the private key. They also store the certificates of trusted CAs and other entities. These certificate stores are made available to the PK-enabled applications.

- **The Certificates MMC Snap-In for certificate management.** This snap-in allows users to browse the certificate stores, export private certificates and private keys, and perform certificate enrollment with Microsoft enterprise CAs.
- **The Public Key policies.** These policies specify which CA certificates populate the user and host stores and how these certificates are trusted. They also define automatic certificate enrollment and renewal behavior for hosts. PK policies are defined in the Group Policy objects.
- **The Certificate Services.** These services allow you to implement your own PKI using the enterprise and standalone Microsoft CAs. Enterprise CAs issue certificates to domain users and hosts and publish them in Active Directory; standalone CAs are generic CAs that can issue any type of certificate to anyone, including non-Windows entities.
- **Active Directory.** Active Directory is a certificate publication point for Microsoft CAs.

Behind the scenes you will also find the cryptographic service providers (CSPs), which are accessible through the Microsoft CryptoAPI. CSPs offer key generation and other crypto services to the PK-enabled client software and the Microsoft CAs. CSPs also provide an interface to smart cards.

The next section will concentrate on the Windows 2000 Certificate Services, key management for users and hosts, and Public Key policies. First we will explain the purpose of a PKI in Windows.

Why Use a PKI?

Both Windows NT and Windows 2000 have a secret key infrastructure of sorts. All domain users and workstations have a shared secret key (password) relationship with the domain controllers (DCs). Those passwords are typically used with Kerberos and NTLM to authenticate users to services and DCs, as well as to authenticate hosts to DCs. The passwords can also derive cryptographic keys that offer link confidentiality (with PPTP, for example) and integrity (for example, SMB signing).

The secret key infrastructure is well-suited to offer authentication services to the Windows 2000 domains found within a corporation. However, this model encounters trust and scalability problems as soon as you need other security services or your network needs to communicate with external users.

As we explained in the beginning of this chapter, the PKI enables entities across organizational boundaries to trust each other's credentials in an efficient manner. The PKI also enables end-to-end security services to be used between entities, and offers strong entity authentication. A PKI complements the Windows NT and Windows 2000 secret key infrastructure and allows you to exploit more security services across a more distributed environment.

Note that even if a Windows environment does not implement a PKI, the Windows 95, 98, NT, and 2000 clients already participate in some Internet-wide, commercial PKIs. Those clients come preloaded with a number of commercial CA certificates, allowing them to authenticate other participating entities. This is how Internet Explorer and other Web browsers can establish secure SSL/TLS connections with Internet Web servers or verify signed code (for example, ActiveX components and other software) downloaded from the Internet and your intranet. Users can also verify signed e-mail sent to them, and if they enroll with a commercial CA and obtain their own certificates, they can also send and receive signed and encrypted e-mail. Windows 2000 enables the management of this trust in external CAs through the Group Policy.

Certificate Services

Certificate Services allows you to implement your own PKI. This section describes their components and installation.

Microsoft Certificate Services

Microsoft Certificate Services is the certification authority service. Its job is to accept certificate requests, issue certificates, and publish the CRL.

There are two kinds of Microsoft CAs: enterprise and standalone. An enterprise CA is meant to issue certificates to domain users and computers according to some ACLs. Windows 2000 services, such as EFS and interactive logons with smart cards, can use these certificates, and they can be published to Active Directory. A standalone CA is meant to issue certificates to entities outside your Windows 2000 domains, such as customers and users of other organizations.

Some of the differences between the two CAs are evident in the way their policy and exit modules work. You can actually replace those modules with your own in a standalone CA. For example, you might want to define a policy that automatically issues certificates according to certain rules.

Since standalone CAs can issue certificates to any kind of entity—even non-Windows 2000 entities—they are more suited to be your root CAs. They are capable of operating offline, as they don't need to automatically authenticate the requestors like the enterprise ones do. You'll find more information on this topic later in the chapter.

Certificate Templates

Templates are profiles that define the contents of certificates issued by Microsoft enterprise CAs. Those contents include user information such as name and e-mail address obtained from Active Directory, expiration time, and intended certificate usage.

Each template is defined by its intended usage. For example, the user template called "User" allows its holder to use EFS, to encrypt e-mail, to sign e-mail, and to authenticate himself or herself to Web servers. The computer template called "WebServer" allows its holder to authenticate itself to Web browsers. Table 6-1 provides a list of templates.

Table 6-1. Certificate templates.

Certificate template name	Certificate purposes	Issued to users or computers
Administrator	Code signing, certificate trust list (CTL) signing, EFS, secure e-mail, client authentication	Users
Authenticated session	Client authentication	Users
Basic EFS	EFS	Users
Computer	Client authentication, server authentication	Computer
Code Signing	Code signing	Users
Domain Controller	Client authentication, server authentication	Computers
EFS Recovery Agent	File recovery	Users
Enrollment Agent	Certificate request agent	Users
Enrollment Agent (Offline request)	Certificate request agent	Users
IPSec (Offline request)	Internet Protocol security	Computers
IPSec	Internet Protocol security	Computers
Router (Offline request)	Client authentication	Computers/routers
Smart Card Logon	Client authentication	Users
Smart Card User	Client authentication, secure e-mail	Users
Subordinate certification authority	All	Computers
Trust List Signing	CTL signing	Users
User	EFS, secure e-mail, client authentication	Users
User Signature Only	Secure e-mail, client authentication	Users
Web Server	Server authentication	Computers

Each domain forest has a single set of certificate templates stored in Active Directory. You can examine them with the Active Directory Sites And Services Snap-In. To do so, start the Active Directory Sites And Services Snap-In, choose Show Service Node from the view menu, expand the Services node, expand the Public Key Services node, and then select the Certificate Templates, as shown in Figure 6-1.

Each template has an attached ACL that specifies which users and computers can enroll for it or access it otherwise. For example, Figure 6-2 shows that all authenticated (domain forest) users can enroll for certificates of the User template. You cannot edit templates through the user interface.

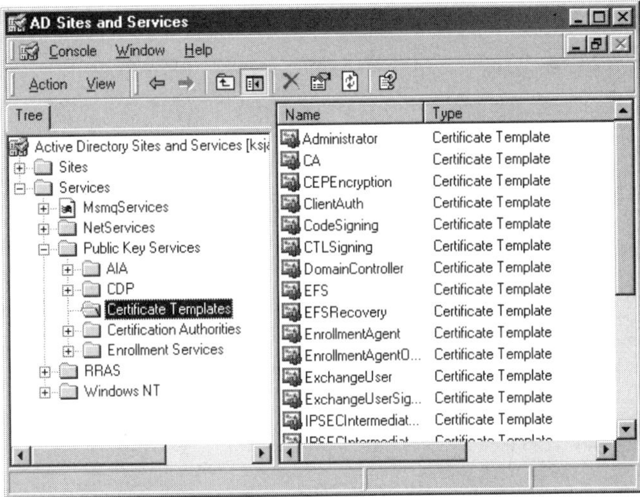

Figure 6-1. *Certificate Templates in Active Directory.*

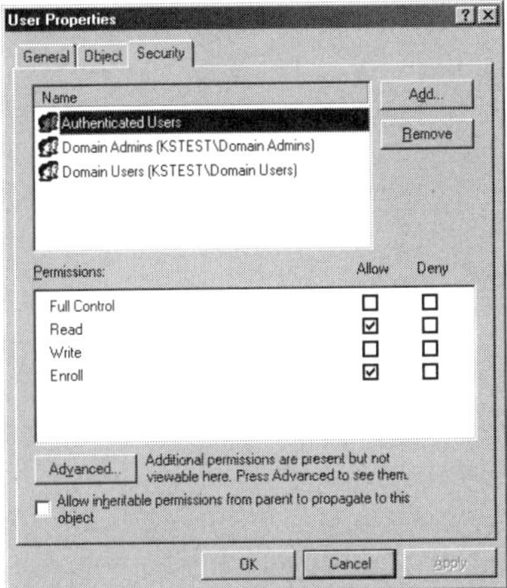

Figure 6-2. *Access control on Certificate Templates.*

You can configure each enterprise CA to issue only certificates of certain templates. For example, you might want to designate a CA to issue only Administrator certificates.

Standalone CAs also have certificate types, but they are not called templates, they cannot be examined through the user interface, and no ACL is attached to them.

Policy Module

The CA calls the policy module to decide whether a certificate should be issued, denied, or marked as pending for the CA administrator to review.

On an enterprise CA, the module provided with Windows 2000 will accept certificate requests from users with read and enroll access to the CA. The defining characteristic of an enterprise CA is that it authenticates the requesting entities using their domain accounts. By default, all authenticated (domain forest) users have such access, as indicated in Figure 6-3.

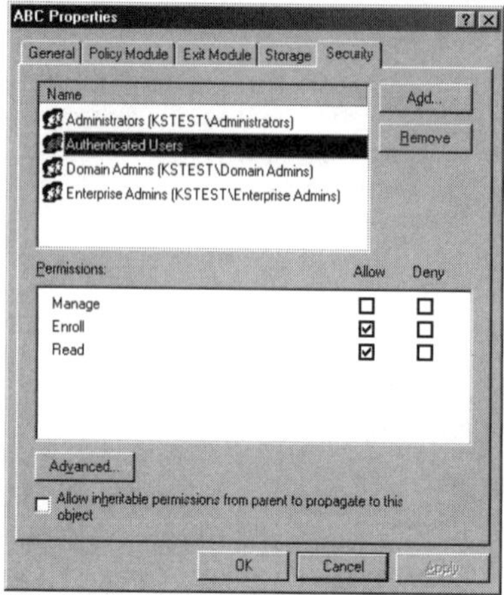

Figure 6-3. *Access control on an Enterprise Certification Authority.*

The module will then verify that the template against which the request was made is actually available for issuing by this CA, and then check that the user has enroll access to the template.

On a standalone CA, the policy module will accept requests from users with similar access to the CA, which by default is everyone, authenticated or not. It will then mark the requests as pending by default, or you can also configure it to issue them automatically. Templates are not defined for standalone CAs.

On both types of CA, the module will also add two X.509v3 extensions to the certificate with the following:

- **CRL distribution point (CDP) records.** These point to where the CA publishes its CRL.
- **Authority information access (AIA) records.** These point to where the CA's certificate is published.

Those pointers are in the form of a URL, and can point to Active Directory (LDAP), to the CA's Web interface (http) or to the CA's shared folder (file), if one is specified during installation. When forming those URLs, use the replaceable parameter syntax shown in Table 6-2.

Table 6-2. CA replaceable parameters.

Variable	Value
%1	DNS name of the certification authority server
%2	NetBIOS name of the certification authority server
%3	Name of the certification authority
%4	Renewal extension of the certification authority
%5	Location of the domain root in Active Directory
%6	Location of the configuration container in Active Directory
%7	The "sanitized" name of the certification authority, truncated to 32 characters with a hash on the end

Exit Module

The CA calls the exit module after it issues a certificate. The module's job is to publish the certificate in the location specified in the certificate request, typically Active Directory for enterprise CAs and the file system for standalone CAs. The module is also responsible for publishing the CRL.

Certification Authority Snap-In

The Certification Authority Snap-In—shown in Figure 6-4—allows you to view and manage certificates and requests, configure the CA, and manually publish the CA CRL.

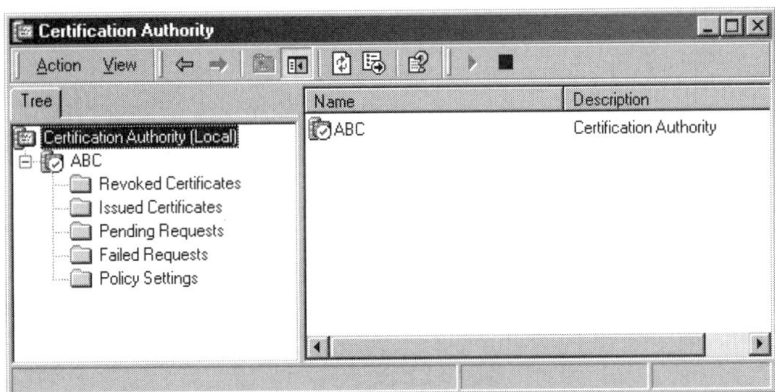

Figure 6-4. *The Certification Authority Snap-In.*

This snap-in allows you to do the following:

- View the revoked certificates and manually publish the CRL.
- View and revoke issued certificates.
- View, issue, and deny any pending requests. Such requests are only possible on standalone CAs.
- View failed requests. Requests can be failed by the policy module if the requestor is not authorized to enroll in the CA's ACL or by the CA administrator who reviews the pending requests.
- For enterprise CAs only: view, add, and remove Policy Settings (the certificate templates) the CA is allowed to issue. You can specify which entities can be issued which certificate templates in Active Directory.

By right-clicking on the CA's name and choosing Properties from the context menu, and clicking on the General tab you can access the Properties sheet shown in Figure 6-5.

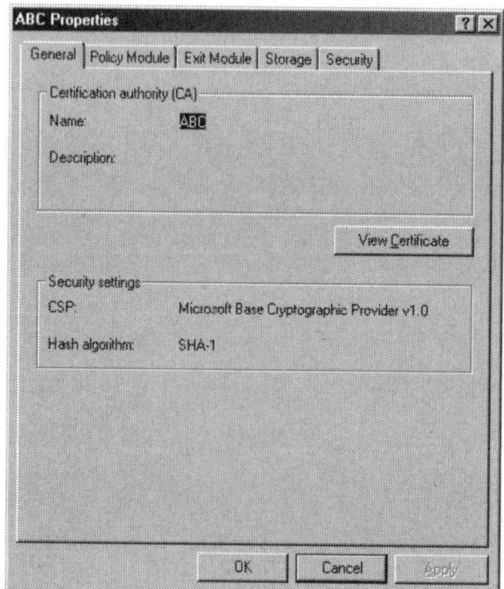

Figure 6-5. *The Certification Authority Properties sheet: General.*

With this sheet, you can do the following:

- **View the CA's general properties.** Those include the CA's certificate, as well as the CSP used for cryptographic operations, and the hash algorithm used for signing certificates.
- **Configure and change the policy module.** Options include the CDP and AIA extensions to be included in the published certificates, and whether requests are automatically accepted or made pending (standalone CAs only).
- **Configure and change the exit module.** You can view and modify the CRL publication points, as well as specify where the CA is allowed to publish certificates; this is specified in the request itself.

- **View the data storage locations.** These include the CA's configuration data, which are stored in Active Directory or a shared folder. You can also view the folders in which the Certificate database and the Request log are stored.
- **Set Access Control on the CA.** This allows you to specify who can manage it, enroll with it, and read its configuration information.

By right-clicking on the CA's name and choosing All Tasks from the context menu, you can perform the following tasks:

- **Start and stop the CA.** This is equivalent to starting and stopping the Certificate Services service from the Services Snap-In.
- **Back up and restore the CA.** You can choose to backup the CA's key pair as well as the issued certificate log and the pending request queue. You can also incrementally back up the latter two. Microsoft recommends that you use Windows 2000 Backup to back up the whole server. If you choose to use the CA Snap-In for backup, you should also use the IIS Snap-In to back up the IIS metabase. (The IIS metabase is required for the Certificate Services Web interface.)
- **Renew the CA certificate.** You can opt to generate a new key pair, too.

Installation

Before you set up a CA, you can create an issuer policy statement to be included or simply referenced in the CA's certificate. This will be visible with the Issuer Statement button whenever you view a certificate. The policy statement is defined in the CAPolicy.inf file that should be placed in the %systemroot% directory before you install the Certificate Services.

A user with local administrative privileges can install enterprise and standalone CAs from Control Panel. To do so, open the Add/Remove Programs tool, click Add/Remove Windows Components, select Certificate Services, click Next, and follow the onscreen prompts.

The wizard will prompt you for the CA type (enterprise or standalone; root or subordinate). See the "Designing Your Public Key Infrastructure" section later in this chapter to decide what kinds of CAs you need.

You can install enterprise CAs only on servers on Windows 2000 domains and only if you are a user with write access to Active Directory. You can find who has such access using the Active Directory Sites And Services Snap-In by inspecting the ACL in the Public Key Services node in the Services node. By default that is the forest root Domain Administrators. On a member server, though, this group is not by default a member of the local Administrators group, and you need to add it to perform any software installation.

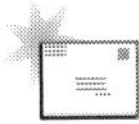

Note In the first release of Windows 2000, only users of this user's domain will be given enroll access to certificate templates. You might want to grant such access to the server's domain users, or even to authenticated users. The Knowledge Base article Q239452 documents this issue.

If you select the Advanced Options, you will be prompted for the following:

- A CSP that the CA will use for its cryptographic operations. The default is the Microsoft CSP, which you should not change unless you have a specific need to use another one.
- A hash algorithm to use in signing certificates (defaults to SHA-1).
- An existing key pair to use when restoring an existing CA.
- A key length for the size of the private and public keys, which for the Microsoft CSP defaults to 512 bits. Microsoft recommends a key length of at least 2048 bits. Of course, this option is not available if you chose to use existing keys.

Next you will be prompted for the CA's naming information, which appears on its certificates. The name fields are as follows:

- **CA Name.** This is the name by which your organization will identify the CA. This corresponds to the Common Name field of the X.509 certificate and the Active Directory object. You can use any characters in this name, but a sanitized version is used for operations that can't handle special characters (filenames and Active Directory objects, for example). The *certutil* command-line utility can display the sanitized name for a CA.
- **Organization.** The legal name of your organization.
- **Organizational Unit.** The division to which the CA belongs. This is not associated with the Active Directory Organizational Units (OUs).
- **Locality.** Your city.
- **State or Province**
- **Country.** A two-character country code, as defined in the X.500 standard. For example, the United States is US, Canada is CA, and the United Kingdom is GB.

If you are installing a root CA, you will be asked for its validity period. A typical value is 2 to 10 years. For a subordinate CA, this value is determined by its parent.

Next you will be asked for the location of the certificate database and its log. For a standalone CA you will have to specify a shared folder where the CA will publish information about itself, such as its certificate and CRL. For an enterprise CA or a standalone CA whose installer has write access to Active Directory, this information is published in the directory and therefore specifying a folder is optional.

If you are installing a subordinate CA, you will also be asked for a parent CA. You can automatically request a certificate by pointing to the computer that runs the parent CA, or you can generate a request into a file and submit it manually (for example, into the parent CA's Web interface). If you do that—or if the CA sets the automatic request to pending by the CA—you will have to import the certificate into the CA later to enable it.

Command-Line Utilities

The Certificate Services come with three command-line utilities that extend the capabilities provided by the user interface. They are meant to be run by developers and knowledgeable certification authority administrators.

CertSrv

To start the CA as a standalone application and display its actions on the console for diagnostic purposes, type the command *certutil –z* at a command prompt. You cannot run it while the CA is run as a normal service, so you have to stop that first.

You can start and stop the CA service either from the Certification Authority Snap-In, from the Services node in the Services And Applications node of the Computer Management Snap-In, or by typing *net start certsvc* and *net stop certsvc* at a command prompt.

CertReq

You use this utility to request certificates from CAs.

CertUtil

Use CertUtil to perform the following tasks:

- Display Certificate Services configuration information or a file containing a request, a certificate, a PKCS #7, or certificate revocation list.
- Get the certification authority configuration string.
- Retrieve the CA signing certificate.
- Revoke certificates.
- Publish or retrieve a certificate revocation list.
- Determine whether a certificate is valid or whether the encoding length is incompatible with old enrollment controls.
- Verify one or all levels of a certification path.
- Resubmit or deny pending requests.
- Set attributes or an integer or string value extension for a pending request.
- Verify a private-public key set.
- Decode files based on hexadecimal or base 64.
- Encode files to base 64.
- Shut down the server.
- Display the database schema.
- Convert a Certificate Server 1.0 database to a Certificate Services 2.0 database.
- Back up and restore the CA keys and database.
- Display certificates in a certificate store.

- Display error message text for a specified error code.
- Import issued certificates that are missing from the database.
- Set and display certification authority registry settings.
- Create or remove Certificate Services Web virtual roots and file shares.

Certificate Lifecycles

This section describes how entities (users and hosts) manage, store, and use certificates. We'll discuss both the Microsoft Certificate Services and third-party PKIs.

An entity's private-public key pair can be seen as another credential, in addition to the Windows password shared between it and the domain controller. Since an entity's private key is not shared with anyone else, it has different generation and storage requirements than a Windows password. Also, the public key has certification (authentication) and publication requirements. Entities can and sometimes do have more than one key pair and associated certificate.

User Keys

Users can browse, export, or enroll for certificates by using Internet Explorer (by going to Tools, then Internet Options, and then selecting Content) or by using the Certificates Snap-In.

Generation and Certification

Key generation and certification happen together, and are normally initiated by a user requesting a certificate from a CA. The user generates the keys (except for Smart Card Enrollment) using one of the Cryptographic Service Providers available to his or her system.

The following list describes several ways to invoke a certificate request (which will trigger the key generation).

- At the Certificates Snap-In, expand the Personal node and right-click on Certificates. Select All Tasks and then select Request New Certificate, as shown in Figure 6-6. Only enterprise CAs in the domain tree are visible through this method.
- Point Internet Explorer at a CA's Web interface. That can be any CA: enterprise, standalone, or a non-Microsoft CA.
- The administrator at a smart card enrollment station who generates keys and certificates in smart cards on behalf of users can invoke certificate requests. The administrator does this using an enterprise CA's Web interface and Internet Explorer. The administrator needs to have an Enrollment Agent certificate.
- If a user attempts to use EFS without an EFS certificate, the action automatically triggers a certificate request. If no enterprise CA is available in the domain tree, the certificate will be self-signed (signed by the user's private key).

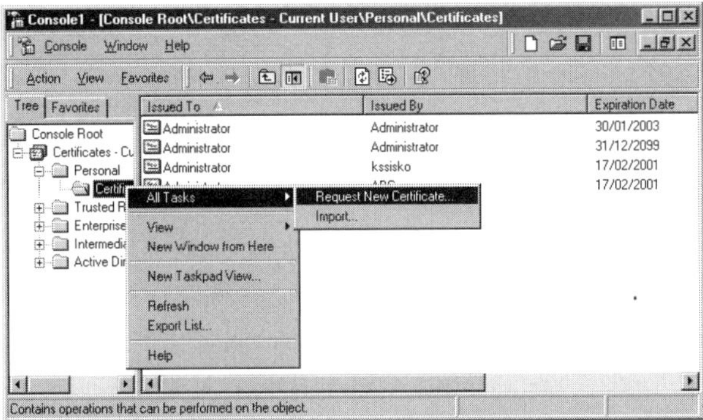

Figure 6-6. *Requesting a certificate with the Certificates Snap-In.*

In the first three cases, the user can choose a certificate template or type and—if using the snap-in—a friendly name for the certificate. By selecting Advanced Options, the user can also choose a CSP for key generation, enable strong protection for the private key, and with the snap-in, choose an enterprise CA. Using Web enrollment, the user can also choose the private key length and whether the key can be exported from its store once generated.

The Microsoft CAs also accept previously generated certificate requests in the PKCS #10 standard format used by Web servers and other applications.

Storage

The private key is managed by a CSP and stored in the user's profile or on a smart card. In the former case, the key's file permissions protect it. With strong protection enabled, you can encrypt the key with a password that must be entered every time an application needs the key. A private key stored on a smart card is protected by a PIN and by the physical properties of the smart card.

The public key is packaged into the certificate and also stored in the user's profile. Enterprise CAs will publish some types of certificates in Active Directory by default. Note that if you use roaming profiles, a user's certificate and private key is available on all domain Windows 2000 Professional workstations.

You can also import and export key pairs. You can mark private keys as exportable at generation or when you import them. Certificate export supports the DER X.509, CER X.509, and PKCS #7 standard formats. PKCS #12 is used when the private key is exported together with the certificate.

Publication

An enterprise CA automatically publishes some types of certificates on Active Directory. A standalone CA will not normally publish the certificate if requested using the methods described earlier. Third-party CA software might or might not publish certificates.

Note Standalone CAs can publish a certificate in a location specified in the request, but the request methods in Windows 2000 do not specify a location.

Usage

You can use user certificates issued by the Microsoft standalone CAs and third-party CAs to access secure Web servers with SSL/TLS client authentication and for secure e-mail. You can also use certificates issued by Microsoft enterprise CAs with EFS and for smart card interactive logon using Kerberos.

A password might be required if you need to use a private key that has strong protection enabled.

Revocation

The issuing CA can revoke user and computer certificates for a number of reasons discussed earlier in the chapter. Some non-Microsoft CAs will allow users to revoke their own certificates.

Renewal

Users can renew their certificates before or after they expire. They can choose to keep existing key pairs or generate a new one.

Host Keys

Users with local administrative privileges can manage host key pairs using the Certificates Snap-In. This section only highlights the differences with the user key lifecycle.

Generation and Certification

You can invoke the certificate request at the snap-in or at the Web interface of a CA, where you will have to select the "local machine store" option.

You can set hosts to automatically enroll and renew their keys. We'll describe this procedure in the next section.

Storage

The machine's key store stores the private key . Note that private keys are not typically protected, since services that use them run unattended, with no user intervention.

Publication

Host keys are published in the same manner as user keys.

Usage

IIS uses host keys to authenticate itself to Web browsers. Windows 2000 optionally uses host keys with IPSec to authenticate the host to others.

Revocation

Host keys are revoked in the same manner as user keys.

Renewal

You can perform renewal manually—as with user keys—or automatically, if specified in the public key policies.

Public Key Policies

The public key security policies are set in Group Policy Objects and the Local Policy Object. You'll find them in the Group Policy snap-in, in the Security Settings node of the Windows Settings node under Computer Configuration. Note that these are computer policies; therefore, you can only define which computers—but not which users—will receive them within a site, domain, or OU. See Chapter 8, "Group Policy," for a full discussion.

Automatic Certificate Request Settings Policy

This policy defines whether computers should automatically enroll for certificates and which enterprise CAs they should contact. Computers can only request computer-related certificate types, such as those of IPSec or Web (SSL).

Trusted Root CAs and Enterprise Trust Policies

These policies define the following:

- Which root CAs users can trust when verifying certificates.
- Whether users are allowed to trust additional CAs of their own choosing.
- The key usage for the certificates issued by each of those CAs (the purposes for which those certificates are valid).

Microsoft CAs within your domain forest are automatically added to those policies. To distribute the certificates of non-Microsoft CAs within your organization, use the Trusted Root CAs policy.

To distribute the certificate of CAs that belongs to other organizations or to commercial CAs, use the Enterprise Trust policy. This policy contains certificate trust lists (CTLs), which are digitally signed lists of certificates and allowed key usages. To construct one, you need a Trust List Signing certificate from an enterprise CA.

Encrypted Data Recovery Agents Policy

This is not really a PK policy —it's a policy about EFS, a client of PKI technology. It defines whether there is an EFS recovery policy within the scope of the Policy object. If a recovery policy is defined, it is populated with the certificates of the recovery agents. A defined but unpopulated policy means EFS is not available. See Chapter 9, "Security Configuration and Monitoring," for a full description of this policy.

Active Directory

In the previous sections we explained how Active Directory supports different components of the Microsoft Certificate Services, as well as PKI in Windows 2000 in general. In summary, Active Directory has the following properties:

- It is used as a publication point for issued certificates, CA certificates, and CRLs.
- It stores the Certificate Templates used by the enterprise CAs.

- It defines which Group Policies are in force across domains, part of which are the public key policies.
- You can employ it to map certificates to users. This mapping is primarily used when users authenticate themselves to IIS using a certificate.

Designing Your Public Key Infrastructure

You can implement your PKI by using the Microsoft Certificate Services and Active Directory or other compatible products. The issues discussed in this section are largely independent of the PKI products you choose to use.

Identify Your Certificate Requirements

Your certificate requirements are driven by the Public Key–enabled applications you use or plan to use. Identifying those requirements will let you decide which users and computers need what type of certificates. For each set of users you should identify the following criteria:

- the types of certificates they need
- private key size
- cryptoalgorithms allowed
- key lifetime
- private key storage (on smart cards, for example)
- private key exportability

Then you can identify how many and what kind of CAs you need. Your options include:

- Microsoft enterprise CAs, which can automatically issue a certificate to a user or computer with a Windows 2000 domain account.
- Microsoft standalone CAs, which typically require an administrator to manually issue certificates.
- Third-party CA software.
- Commercial CA services on the Internet, such as those provided by VeriSign and Thawte. These have the advantage of preloaded certificates in most client software, and can be a common point of trust among organizations. The downside to these services is that the private key that directly or indirectly signs your certificates is not under your direct control—a private key compromise at the commercial CA also compromises all of your certificates.

CAs issue certificates for users and computers. If you have any number of CAs, it is likely that you will want to organize them into a hierarchy. This organizing is done by introducing root and intermediate CAs (also chosen from the preceding list), whose job is to certify the intermediate and issuing CAs, respectively. For an explanation of why and how to achieve this, see the information on trust strategies later in this section.

Secure E-mail

A secure e-mail service offers confidentiality and data authentication services by implementing encryption and digital signatures mechanisms. All users of secure e-mail need to have a key pair with an enabled certificate. The industry standard for secure e-mail is S/MIME. You can obtain S/MIME certificates from either Microsoft or commercial CAs.

One issue to consider is whether you intend to exchange secure e-mail with other organizations. If so, you will need to establish a key relationship with them. In other words, both organizations need to obtain a certified copy of each other's CA public key that issues e-mail certificates, or the key of one of its parent CAs. One solution is to have those CAs be subordinate to (have their public keys signed by) a commercial CA that most organizations trust.

Secure e-mail certificates are available from commercial CAs, Microsoft standalone CAs, and Microsoft enterprise CAs under the Administrator, Smart Card User, User, and User Signature Only templates.

If you use Exchange as your server, and don't intend to exchange secure e-mail with other organizations, you can also issue certificates with its Key Management Server (KMS). The KMS will be integrated into the Certificate Services and Active Directory in the next releases.

Secure Web Servers with SSL/TLS

This is the most widely deployed implementation of public key technology, in which the server uses a certificate to authenticate itself to browsers. Both external and internal Web servers can obtain their certificates from a commercial CA, whose certificate is already preloaded into browsers. Internal Web servers could also obtain certificates from your own CAs that are trusted by intranet browsers.

Server authentication certificates are available from commercial CAs, standalone CAs, and under the Computer, Domain Controller, and Web Server templates.

Secure Web Servers with SSL/TLS Client Authentication

Web applications that have a strong requirement for authentication can be configured to authenticate users (through Web browsers), using the users' certificates. Again, you can issue your own certificates or outsource them to a commercial CA.

Client authentication certificates are available from commercial CAs, standalone CAs, and under the Administrator, Authenticated Session, User, and User Signature Only templates.

Code Signing with Authenticode

Code signing is a data-authentication mechanism that allows entities to verify that software and documents have indeed been released by their authors, and that they haven't been tampered with. Microsoft's implementation of this technology is Authenticode.

Authors digitally sign their codes or documents using a key pair, and users verify this signature using the corresponding certificate.

Code-signing certificates are available from commercial CAs, standalone CAs, and under the Administrator and Code Signing templates.

Smart Card Authentication to Windows 2000 Hosts

You can use smart cards to provide strong authentication for interactive logons. You can obtain appropriate certificates only from Microsoft enterprise CAs using the Smart Card Logon and Smart Card User templates.

IPSec Without Kerberos

IPSec provides a confidentiality, integrity, and authentication service to TCP/IP. Windows 2000 computers use Kerberos with their computer account passwords for authentication within their domains.

Non-Windows 2000 computers and devices (routers, for example) cannot have computer accounts with the domain controllers and therefore cannot use Kerberos for IPSec authentication. In a similar manner, Windows 2000 computers that need to establish IPSec connections with other machines cannot have computer accounts with the domain controllers and therefore cannot use Kerberos for IPSec authentication. Instead, they can use a private-public key pair for authentication.

IPSec certificates are available from commercial CAs, standalone CAs, and under the IPSec template.

EFS

EFS provides a confidentiality service to NTFS. It employs user key pairs to encrypt and decrypt files and recovery agent key pairs for file recovery purposes. An agent key (for the Administrator) is created at installation, and then user keys are automatically generated the first time they encrypt a file with EFS.

EFS and EFS recovery certificates are available only from enterprise CAs under the Basic EFS and EFS Recovery Agent templates, respectively.

In an environment with no Microsoft enterprise CAs, all EFS certificates are self-signed.

Custom PK–Enabled Applications

You can write custom applications that make use of X.509 certificates. This feature permits developers to utilize the strong authentication provided by certificates in their own applications.

Define Certificate-Issuing Practices

If you decide to run your own CAs, you will need to draw a CPS specifying its policies and operational procedures.

Let's assume that an entity is presented with another entity's certificate, which proceeds to verify it. The CPS tells the verifier how trustworthy the certificate is—in other words, how likely it is to belong to its named owner, and how likely is it that the owner is still authorized to use it. This is particularly important if your certificate users communicate with other organizations that need to trust that those certificates are genuine and valid.

The CPS should indicate points such as the following:

- How users are authenticated before being issued a certificate
- Physical and computer security of the CA server
- CA private key length, certificate lifetime and certificate renewal intervals
- Policies for revoking certificates
- CRL publication points and intervals

Of course, you should address the same issues in internal documentation.

Define Your CA Trust Strategies

You will need to decide which CAs your users and computers can trust. If you run your own CAs, you should consider arranging them in a hierarchy.

CA Hierarchies

In theory, you could only have issuing CAs, and have all your users and machines (and your communicating partners, if any) trust them. The issue here is that every time a CA renews or revokes its certificate or a new CA is introduced, you will have to modify those trust relationships.

One common solution is to have a hierarchy of CAs, with root CAs certifying intermediate CAs and the intermediate CAs certifying the issuing CAs. That way your users and partner will only have to establish trust in a small number of root CAs, and changes in the subordinate ones will not affect them. Note that to establish a common point of trust with other organizations, you can pick a commercial CA to root part of your hierarchy.

Root CAs need only issue intermediate CA certificates infrequently and periodically publish their CRLs. Therefore, you can operate them offline for added security. Typically you should use a standalone CA and not an enterprise CA for this purpose, since enterprise CAs can only certify other Microsoft CAs, and you can't operate them offline due to their integration with Active Directory.

Figure 6-7 on the following page shows an example of a trust hierarchy.

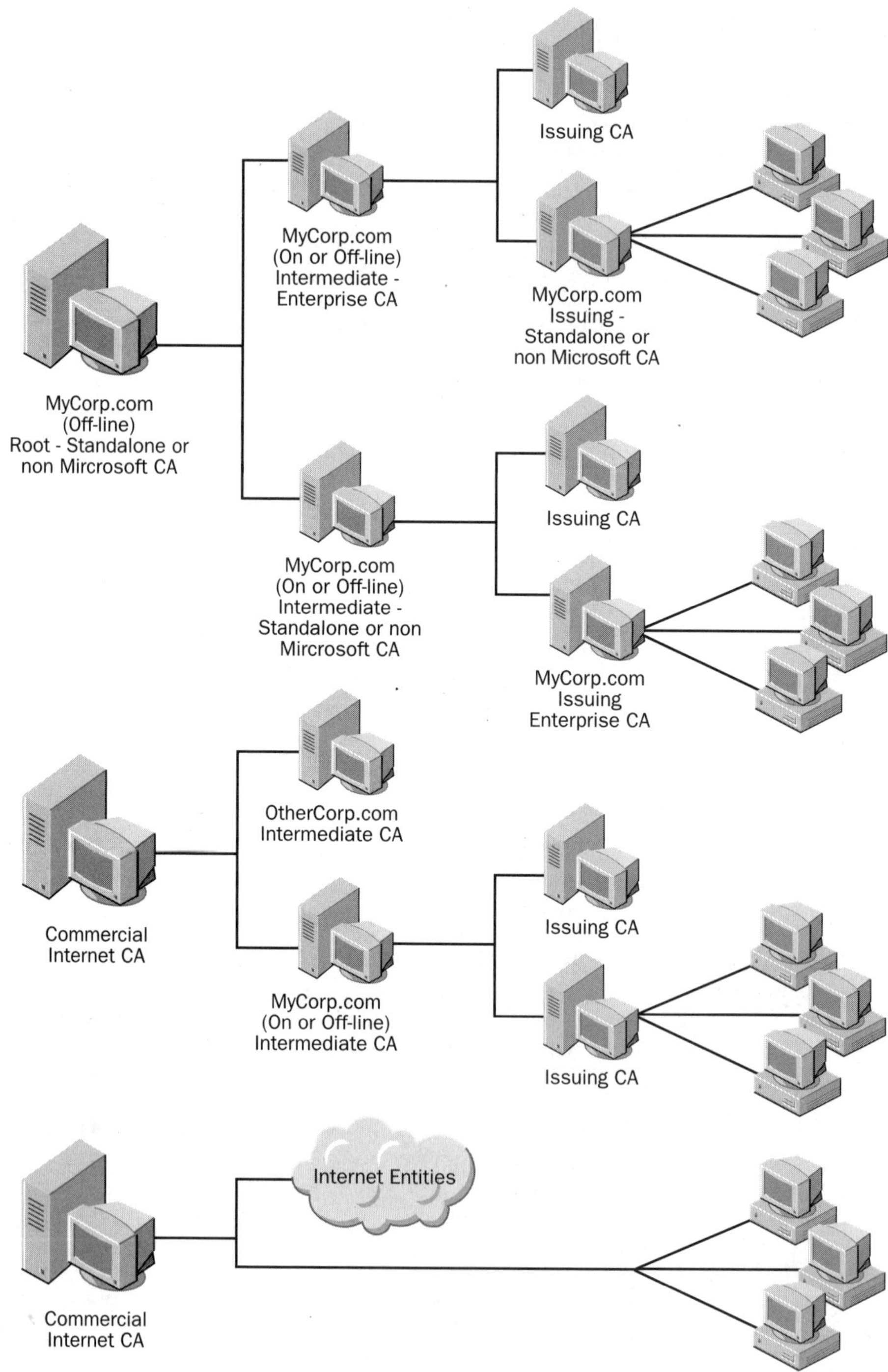

Figure 6-7. *Example of a CA trust hierarchy.*

Trust in CAs

Domain users and computers need to obtain the certificates of your root CAs, possibly the certificates of other organizations' CAs (not necessarily root ones), and perhaps the certificates of commercial CAs (because you want to trust them as they let your Web browsers visit secure Web sites). All these CAs can form part of your hierarchy.

Every Windows 2000 computer has a single store for CA certificates to be trusted by the machine and its users. Note that this comes preloaded with the certificates of a number of commercial CAs. It is also automatically populated with the Microsoft enterprise CAs you might have.

You add to this store through the Group Policy, using the Trusted Root CAs and Enterprise Trust containers under Computer Configuration, Windows Settings, Security Settings, Public Key Policies. The former container is used for your own non-enterprise CAs you unconditionally trust; the latter is for the foreign CAs.

In the Enterprise Trust container you can optionally restrict certificate usage—for example, if you want to restrict users to only accepting certificates for e-mail use—even if the CA can issue any kind of certificate. You can also use it with non-root CAs if you want to restrict your trust to only a part of a foreign hierarchy.

Define the CA Server Security Requirements

If you implement your own PKI, a large part of your organizational security depends on the security of your CAs and their keys. And if you implement a hierarchy, the CAs at the top are more valuable than the ones at the bottom.

You can take the following measures to secure your CAs:

- Use hardware CSPs (smart cards, for example) for the root keys.
- Operate root CAs—or even intermediate ones—offline.
- Physically protect the CAs.

Define Certificate Lifetimes

Normally certificate lifetimes are nested. In other words, an issued certificate (of a users or a CA) expires before the certificate of the CA that issued it. Otherwise, after the CA's expiration, the issued certificate becomes invalid, even if it hasn't expired itself. Microsoft CAs enforce this nesting in their certificate issuing, but other CA products don't necessarily do that.

Key lifetimes are set as a matter of policy, and Windows 2000 cannot (currently) enforce their expiration.

Certificate lifecycles typically look like this:

1. The CA certificate is issued.
2. The user certificate is issued.

3. The user certificate might be revoked.
4. The user certificate is renewed or expires. (They all expire some time).
5. The CA certificate is renewed or expires. (They all expire some time.)

When choosing the lifetimes for those keys and certificates, you should consider these points:

- **The length of user and CA private keys.** Longer keys are harder to mathematically attack and therefore support longer lifetimes.
- **Private key storage.** A more secure key supports longer lifetimes. Hardware storage provides more security than disk storage.
- **The security of the CA server.** More security means longer lifetime for its keys.
- **The security of the computer environment in which you store the keys of the issued certificates.**
- **The amount of administrative effort you are willing to devote to certificate renewal.** Shorter lifetimes mean that renewals will happen more often, which might require some administrative effort.
- **Certificate lifetime nesting.**

At the end of the day, you must strike a balance between the risks you are willing to accept (key theft or mathematical attack) against the administrative effort you are willing to make. You must also draw a procedure regarding key pair renewal that users should follow when they renew their certificates.

Table 6-3 offers some examples of certificate renewal administration.

Table 6-3. Certificate renewal.

Purpose of certificate	Certificate lifetime	Renewal schedule
Root certification authority (4096-bit key)	20 years	Renew every 9.5 years to ensure that you can certify issuing certification authorities for the full 10 years. Renew with a new key pair at least every 20 years to limit the key lifetime.
Intermediate certification authority (3072-bit key)	10 years	Renew every 4.5 years to ensure that you can certify issuing certification authorities for the full 5 years. Renew with a new key pair at least every 10 years to limit the key lifetime.
Issuing certification authority (2048-bit key)	5 years	Renew every 2.5 years to ensure that you can renew 2-year certificates for their full lifetimes. Renew with a new key pair at least every 5 years to limit the key lifetime.

(continued)

Table 6-3. *(continued)*

Purpose of certificate	Certificate lifetime	Renewal schedule
Normal users (512-bit keys)	1 year	Renew with a new key pair every year to limit the key lifetime.
Administrators (1024-bit keys)	2 years	Renew with a new key pair every 2 years to limit the key lifetime.
Computers (1024-bit keys)	2 years	Renew with a new key pair every 2 years to limit the key lifetime.

Define the Enrollment and Renewal Processes

You should define the procedures for enrollment and certificate renewal. As mentioned in the section on user keys earlier in this chapter, the following methods are available to interact with the Microsoft CAs:

- **Using the Certificate Request Wizard.** The Certificate Request Wizard, a part of the Certificates Snap-In, is only available to Windows 2000 entities accessing Microsoft enterprise CAs.
- **Using a browser with the CA Web interface.** This method is available to all kinds of entities.
- **Using automatic certificate enrollment.** This method is available to Windows 2000 computers only, as defined in the Group Policy.
- **Using smart card enrollment.** This method is only available to Windows 2000 entities accessing Microsoft enterprise CAs.
- **Using the Microsoft Enrollment Control.** This method is available for custom applications.

Web browsers also typically access non-Microsoft CAs.

Define the Revocation Policy

You should draw a revocation policy to define the circumstances under which certificates should be revoked. We discussed some reasons in the section on revocation earlier in this chapter. Note that revocation of a CA certificate implicitly means the revocation of all its subordinate CA certificates and issued user certificates. Those subordinate certificates will fail to validate when the verifying entities obtain a CRL showing the parent CA certificate as revoked.

Part of your policy should also define where and how frequently the CRLs are published. You should also specify—even within your system and application policies—how frequently the CRL should be downloaded by the verifying entities that accept the certificates as proof of identity.

Define the Maintenance and Disaster-Recovery Processes

You should draw procedures specifying how to back up, recover, and revoke your CAs.

If the CA fails, you can attempt to recover by fixing the computer problem affecting the server. If that is not feasible, you can replace the server and recover the CA keys and issued certificates from the backups. Microsoft CAs offer backup and recovery of that information.

If the CA is compromised, you should revoke its certificate as described in the previous section. This is quite a serious event, potentially affecting a large part of your infrastructure. Following the revocation you should proceed to inform your users, remove the certificate from the Group Policy (if the certificate is replicated through the Group Policy), replace the CA with a new one, and renew all the subordinate and issued certificates.

Document the Design

After you make all those decisions and draw the policies, be sure to document them!

We suggest that your Organizational Security Policy should reference a particular type of PKI. This high-level policy should reference a detailed PKI policy, which in turn should include a base certificate practice statement. You could establish the CPS of individual CAs on this base CPS.

Summary

This chapter introduced cryptography and the security services cryptography offers, as well as the public key functionality in Windows 2000 and the Windows 2000 Certificate Services. This public key functionality enables secure e-mail, secure Web browsing, strong authentication with smart cards, secure data storage, secure networking, secure software distribution, and efficient and scalable management of the necessary cryptographic keys. You can use the Windows 2000 Certificate Services together with Active Directory to implement your own PKI.

Chapter 7
Access Control Model

Windows 2000 security controls the use of system and network resources through two interrelated mechanisms: user authentication and authorization. Chapter 5 detailed how the operating system requires and receives user authentication from security credentials. Windows 2000 uses the access control model to implement the second phase of protecting resources: determining if an authenticated user has the correct authorization to access a resource.

Shared resources—resources available to users and groups other than the resource's owner—might be available for unauthorized use. In the Windows 2000 access control model, users and groups of users are assigned rights that inform the operating system what each user and group of users can and can't do. Additionally, shared resources are assigned permissions that enable resource managers to enforce access control in two ways: by restricting access to unauthorized users and by limiting the extent of access to authorized users. This chapter explores the fundamental components of the access control model.

Access Control: The Basics

In Windows 2000, as in Windows NT 4.0, access control is the model by which the operating system ensures authorized use of its objects by subjects, or *security principals*. Security principals include users, groups, and services. Security principals perform actions on files, folders, printers, registry keys, Active Directory entries, and other objects. The actions that a security principal can perform on an object—in other words, the type of access allowed—depend on the type of object. Files, for example, can be read, written to, modified, and executed.

Each object has an owner that grants permissions to security principals. Access control checks use these permissions to determine which security principals can access the object and how they can access it. One user could have read-only access to a file; another user could have permissions to read, execute, and write to that same file. The object's owner sets these permissions.

To make object management easier for complex systems, object owners generally grant permissions to security groups rather than to individual users. Users added to existing groups adopt the permissions of that group. Defining permissions for container objects, such as folders, also eases access control management. Permissions defined for container objects are inherited by all objects and subcontainers within that container.

Access Control Overview

To better understand how Windows 2000 implements access control, we need to examine the components that the operating system uses when determining who can access what shared resources and with what permissions. Although users are the ones who decide to delete batch files, print to printers, and read data from Active Directory accounts, programs actually perform the operations. More specifically, the executable program sequence within a process, called a thread, runs program instructions. Because a thread has its own registers, kernel stack, environment block, and user stack in the process's address space, different threads in a process can run concurrently on different processors.

Although only threads can act on system objects, threads do not carry their own security identifiers (SIDs). A thread assumes the rights and privileges of the security principal that initiated the process. When a user logs on, either locally or remotely, the system creates an access token for that user. This access token contains the user's SID, the SIDs for any groups the user belongs to, and the user's privileges. This token provides the security context for whatever actions the user executes on that computer.

When a user starts up an application, each thread that executes gets a copy of the access token. Acting as the user's agent, the thread presents the access token to the operating system each time that thread requests any level of access to a securable object. The operating system uses the token to perform an access check against the object's security information. This check ensures that the principal is authorized to access the object at the requested level.

A security descriptor defines the security information for the object. Along with the object owner's SID, the security descriptor contains lists of entries that specify the access rights allowed or denied to users and groups. For objects configured with permissions, the descriptor includes a discretionary access control list (DACL) made up of access control entries (ACEs). An ACE contains a set of bit flags in an access mask and the SID of the security principal that identifies to whom the permissions are granted. The operating system tries to match the user, and then groups SIDs in the access token with entries in the ACL to determine if the user is authorized for the requested access. Figure 7-1 shows a user's access token and object's security descriptor during an access check.

For objects configured with auditing (discussed in Chapter 10), the security descriptor additionally contains a system access control list (SACL). The SACL informs the security subsystem how to audit access attempts to the object.

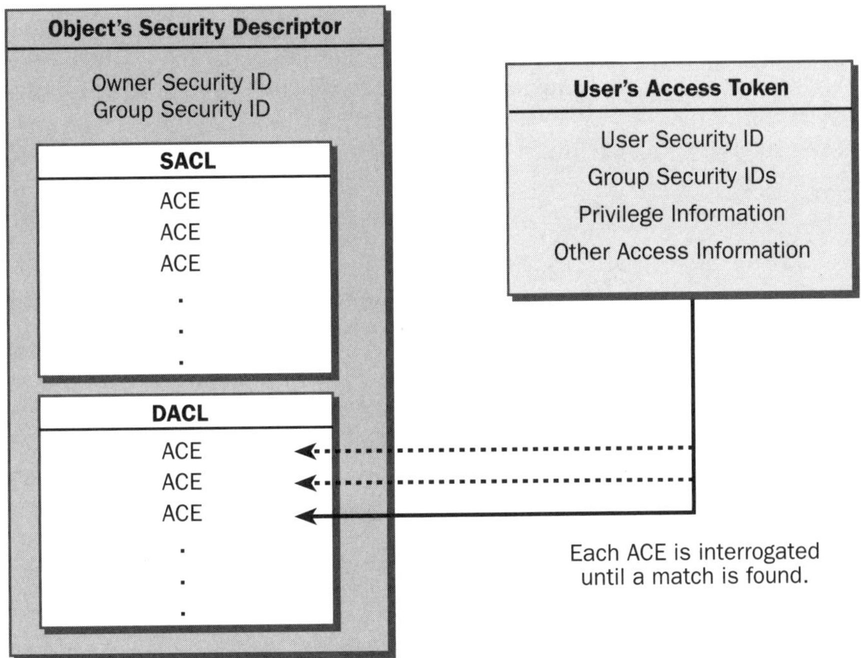

Figure 7-1. *Access token and security descriptor.*

Permissions

An object's owner grants permission to users and groups of users based on his or her desire to make the object available. Although setting permissions for individual users gives owners precise control of their resources, in reality users often have equivalent credentials and can be more efficiently managed as a group. And by setting group permissions rather than individual user permissions, users who require changes to their access control requirements can simply be deleted from one group and added to another.

In addition to permissions that reference an entire object, Active Directory directory service provides more exacting control over shared resources by letting owners allow or deny access to an object's individual properties. This feature provides a way for an owner to protect certain properties of an object while allowing users to manipulate or use the object's other properties. For instance, an owner can allow friends to view the pager and telephone number properties of an Active Directory object; allow business associates to view the pager number only; and deny read access to everyone else.

Resource access is restrictive by nature. Users (or groups of users) cannot touch an object with an ACL that is absent of user or group permissions. Unless the owner grants specific permission to a security principal (or permits unrestricted access to the object) the security principal is implicitly denied access. That is not to say, however, that permissions never need to be explicitly denied. An object's owner could allow read access to a sensitive file to all users in a group except one. In such a case, the owner explicitly grants read access to the group and also explicitly denies read access to the individual.

As you'll see later in the chapter, an object's ACL stores permissions based on the SID of the associated user or group. Each new authorization that an owner permits or denies updates the ACL with a new entry.

In the ACL, a bit mask of access rights specifies what actions a given user or group can perform on an object. Each bit denotes whether a specific operation or set of operations can be performed on the object. The bit mask is comprised of four separate types of access rights: generic, standard, SACL, and object-specific. Generic access rights have not changed since Windows NT 4.0 and apply to all objects. The generic access rights are as follows:

- GENERIC_EXECUTE allows execute access.
- GENERIC_READ allows read access.
- GENERIC_WRITE allows write access.
- GENERIC_ALL allows read, write, and execute access.

Standard access rights are more specific than generic access rights and apply to most object-type operations. The standard access rights are as follows:

- DELETE allows deletion of the object.
- READ_CONTROL allows reading of the object's security descriptor, not including the SACL.
- SYNCHRONIZE allows use of the object for synchronization.
- WRITE_DAC allows modification of the DACL in the security descriptor.
- WRITE_OWNER allows changes to the owner field in the security descriptor.

The SACL access right allows the reading or changing of the information that controls auditing of an object. Object-specific access rights vary, depending on the object type. Each object type defines its own set of access rights.

In addition to these access rights, some objects have custom actions or operations that aren't tied to any particular properties. Windows 2000 controls access to these actions with *extended rights*. Extended rights are identified by global unique identifiers (GUIDs) and—like other permissions—warrant an entry in an object's ACL.

Permission Inheritance

Permission inheritance is an NT control model characteristic that allows you to set permissions only once to control access to a container and all the objects and subcontainers created within it. If you set inheritable permissions on a container, any subordinate objects created will adopt the container's permissions. This allows you, for example, to set inheritable read and write access on a folder. Thanks to permission inheritance, the files (and folders) created within that folder will automatically have the same permissions.

In addition to granting permissions to newly created objects, permission inheritance affects existing objects. When you change a folder's access permissions, Windows 2000 uses the latest control mechanisms to update the existing files and folders within that container. This feature can alleviate much of the administrative burden of changing permissions for a collection of resources.

User Rights

User rights authorize security principals to perform operations on a computer rather than on a specific object. Thus, owners do not assign user rights; user rights are assigned as part of the computer's security policy. Windows 2000 divides authorization for computer access into two categories: First, the operating system controls how a security principal accesses the computer—either through an interactive logon, through a network connection, as a service, or as a batch job. This type of user right is called a *logon right*. The second type of user right involves the authorization required to manage system resources, such as loading device drivers and changing the system time. These rights are referred to as *privileges*.

Security Identifiers

Windows 2000 uses SIDs to uniquely identify security principals and security groups. A SID is generated when the principal's account or security group is created. The creator and scope of a SID depends upon the type of account. For user accounts, the Local Security Authority (LSA) generates SIDs that are unique for that system. The domain security authority generates the SID for domain accounts. Active Directory stores a domain account SID as an object attribute of the user or group the SID identifies. Domain account SIDs are unique within a domain or—when multiple domains exist in the same enterprise—within an enterprise. The uniqueness of SIDs, both locally and at the domain level, extends indefinitely—even after accounts are destroyed and groups are dissolved. SIDs appear in the following access control structures:

- Access tokens include a user's SID and the SIDs for the groups to which the user belongs.
- The security descriptor includes the SID of the owner of the object associated with the security descriptor.
- Each ACE in a security descriptor associates a SID with its respective access permissions.

Certain SIDs that identify generic users and generic groups are found on all systems and have constant values. For example, the generic group Everyone has a SID of S-1-1-0 on all systems and includes everyone that uses that computer. Windows NT and Windows 2000 use quite a few constant SIDs on every system. Here are some examples:

- **Dialup (S-1-5-1).** All members who log on to a system through a dial-up connection implicitly belong to this group.
- **Network (S-1-5-2).** All members who log on to a system through a network connection implicitly belong to this group.
- **Guests (S-1-5-32-546).** This built-in group contains, by default, only the Guest account.
- **Power Users (S-1-5-32-547).** This group is empty by default. Users added to Power Users can manage local accounts and printers, and install applications.
- **Print Operators (S-1-5-32-550).** Members in this group, which exists exclusively on domain controllers, can manage printers and document queues.

A quick look at the structure of a SID—such as the preceding SIDs, for example—demonstrates that the SID is hierarchical, and variable in length. High-level SIDs, such as the one used by the Everyone group, can be concise. Other SIDs are longer and more detailed. The SID for the Administrators group is (S-1-5-32-544). The general format of a SID is:

$S - R - X - Y^1 - Y^2 \ldots Y^{n-1} - Y^n$

This format breaks down as follows:

- **S,** shown as a textual *S*, indicates that the string is a SID.
- **R** refers to the version number of the SID structure. In Windows 2000, this version number is 1.
- **X** indicates the identifier authority, named thus because it's the highest-level authority that can issue SIDs. For the Administrator's group or any other specific Windows 2000 account or group, the identifier authority is NT Authority (identifier authority 5). The World Authority (identifier authority 1) issues SIDs for generic users and groups, such as the Everyone group.
- **$Y^1 - Y^{n-1}$.** The rest of a SID's elements indicate the subauthorities. All subauthority values, except for the very last one, identify the domain in an enterprise. These elements are important because they differentiate SIDs in one domain from SIDs in another. The domain identifier for the Administrators group is Builtin (32). The Everyone group doesn't include a domain identifier.
- **Y^n.** The last item in the series of subauthorities, known as the relative identifier, identifies the particular account or group in the domain. The relative identifier for the Administrators group is Administrators (544). The Everyone group has a null relative identifier.

Ownership

As described earlier in the chapter, every Windows 2000 object is owned by a security principal that has the right to allow or deny access to the object at its discretion. These objects include both Active Directory objects and objects on NTFS volumes. Object creation typically involves a user, rather than a computer or service. At creation time, the SID in the user's access token that is attached to the creating process is copied to the object's security descriptor. This user becomes the owner until another authorized user takes ownership or the object is destroyed. If the user who creates an object is a member of either the Administrators group or the Domain Admins group, the group SID—not the user's SID—is copied to the security descriptor. This process effectively gives ownership privileges to all users in that group.

You can also transfer ownership to other security principals. You can grant a user right that specifically allows a user or group to take ownership of any object on the system. When a user with the take ownership user right assumes ownership of an object, control of the object becomes that user's. Users in the built-in Administrators group on a computer have the take ownership right by default. This transferability of ownership allows the system administrator to clean up resources created and owned by other users who are no longer using the computer system.

Access Tokens

When a user logs on to a system, the LSA obtains from the logon process the SIDs for the user and groups that the user belongs to. The LSA uses these SIDs to create an access token for the user. Every process or thread that subsequently acts on the user's behalf gets a copy of the access token. When a thread tries to perform an action on a securable object or attempts to execute a controlled system task, the operating system uses the access token to ensure that the thread (which acts on the user's behalf) has the correct level of authorization. The operating system checks the SIDs in the access token for matching SID entries in the target object's security descriptor.

Each user and group SID in an access token can have exactly one attribute that indicates how the operating system should use the SID during an access check. The SID can be SE_GROUP_ENABLED, which means that the SID is enabled for access checks against both allow and deny entries in the security descriptor. Alternatively, in Windows 2000 only, you can set the SID as SE_GROUP_USE_FOR_DENY_ONLY. This attribute informs the operating system to only match the SID against deny entries in the security descriptor. In other words, a SID with the SE_GROUP_USE_FOR_DENY_ONLY attribute can only be used to exclude a user or group from object access.

In addition to SIDs, the access token includes a number of other fields that collectively describe the user's security context. The access token uses the following fields:

- **User** holds the SID for the user's account.
- **Groups** hold the list of SIDs for groups that the user belongs to.
- **Privileges** are a list of privileges that the user and user's groups have on the local computer.
- **Owner** holds the SID of the user or security group that becomes, by default, the owner of objects of which the user creates or assumes ownership.

- **Primary Group** holds the SID for the user's primary security group.
- **Default Discretionary Access Control List** is a built-in set of default permissions applied to objects created by the user if other access control information is unavailable.
- **Source** identifies the process for which the access token was created.
- **Type** indicates whether the access token is the primary token or is being used by an intermediate source for impersonation.
- **Impersonation Level** indicates to what extent a service can impersonate the client represented by this access token. (See the following section regarding impersonation for descriptions of the different impersonation levels.)
- **Statistics** includes information about the access token that the operating system uses internally.
- **Restricting SIDs** contains a list of SIDs that limit the authorization of threads to a level beneath the normal access of the user.
- **Session ID** indicates whether the access token represents the Terminal Services client session.

Impersonation

Windows 2000 supports impersonation, which allows servers to make requests to network services on behalf of clients. The network requests, however, should not be based on the privileges of the server that makes the request but rather on the privileges of the client for which the server acts. When a user connects to a network service, the service uses an authentication mechanism—such as Kerberos v5 or Secure Sockets Layer (SSL)—to establish a security context on the server that represents the client. The server then impersonates the client context when making network requests.

Specifically, impersonation allows threads to run in a different security context than that of the process that owns the thread. Depending on the client's permissions, the server impersonating the client might see upgraded or degraded access capabilities.

Under normal circumstances, a server runs under its own security context. Each thread that executes uses the primary access token that identifies the server's security context. When a client requests a service to act on its behalf and the service accepts, the client's access token is transferred to the server as an *impersonation token*. The server associates the impersonation token with the thread created to carry out the task. Whenever that thread tries to access resources, the operating system uses the client identity information found in the impersonation token to perform the access checks. Once the client operation is finished, the thread dismisses the impersonation token and returns to using the primary access token associated with the service's own security context.

When a client connects to a server and requests impersonation, the client can control the extent to which the server can act on its behalf by selecting an impersonation level. Windows 2000 supports four impersonation levels:

- **Anonymous.** This level allows the service to impersonate the client but doesn't let the service know anything about the client. Thus the impersonation token doesn't contain client-specific information.
- **Identify.** This level lets the service obtain the client's identity for its own use but doesn't allow the service to impersonate the client.
- **Impersonate.** Using this level allows the service to impersonate the client when accessing resources on the server's computer. If the server and client processes are on the same machine, the server can impersonate the client for access to network resources.
- **Delegate.** This level lets the service impersonate the client when accessing resources on both the server's computer and on other computers.

Access Control Lists

An ACL is a list of entries that defines the criteria that an operating system should use when protecting an object and that object's properties. It's easy to understand why the protection requires a list of entries rather than an all-inclusive setting or a simple per-user array. The Windows 2000 security subsystem allows for multidimensional, object-based access control. An object's owner can separately control access to each object, and also separately control access to each of the object's properties. For each object or object property, the owner can control access for each requesting user or group. For each requesting user or group, the owner can control the type of access requested. For each type of access requested, the owner can control whether that access type is allowed or denied. As you can imagine, an ACL can end up storing a lot of security information. The ACL partitions this information by storing permissions for each user or group in a separate entry. Because the list is processed from its first ACE to its last, the order of ACEs in the list is important. The earlier the ACE is in the list, the more likely it is to be enforced.

Two types of ACLs exist: The DACL specifies which security principals can access the object and how; the SACL specifies which access requests by which security principals should be audited. Each ACL includes the size and revision number of the data structure, a count of entries in the list, and an ordered list of zero or more ACEs.

Caution There is an important distinction between an empty DACL and an absent DACL. While the DACL provides for an empty list—a list of zero ACEs—the DACL itself can also be absent from the security descriptor. These two cases provide completely opposite accessibility to the object: A security descriptor without a DACL allows unconditional access to anyone that requests it; a security descriptor with an empty DACL allows access to no one.

Access Control Entries

Windows 2000 allows six types of ACEs for use within DACLs and SACLs. You can find three generic types in the ACL of any securable object. The other three types, called *object-specific* types, are present only within ACLs of Active Directory objects. The object-specific ACE types are new for Windows 2000. They are used for inheriting access permissions that apply to specific object types; they also provide a way to define permissions that apply to a specific attribute of a directory object.

The basic difference between generic and object-specific ACE types is the amount of control they provide for inheritance and object access. While generic ACEs offer limited control over the types of child objects that can inherit them, object-specific ACEs offer a finer level of granularity regarding which child objects can and can't inherit them. The ACE types are as follows:

- **Access-denied.** This generic type denies access in a DACL.
- **Access-allowed.** This generic type allows access in a DACL.
- **Access-denied, object-specific.** This type denies access to a property or set of properties and limits inheritance to child objects in a DACL.
- **Access-allowed, object-specific.** This type allows access to a property or set of properties and limits inheritance to child objects in a DACL.
- **System-audit.** This generic type logs access attempts in a SACL.
- **System-audit, object-specific.** This type logs attempts to access a property or set of properties and limits inheritance to child objects in a SACL.

In addition to a flag that specifies the ACE type, each generic ACE contains other access control data: A SID that identifies a user or group associated with the entry, an access mask that specifies the access rights permissible for that user or group, and a set of bit flags that controls the behavior of inheritance and (in the case of a SACL) auditing.

Generic ACEs are straightforward, but their simplicity creates a few drawbacks. Although generic ACEs have inheritance flags that specify propagation behavior, they have a limited ability to determine what type of child objects are allowed to inherit them. At best, generic ACEs can discriminate between container objects and noncontainer objects. Furthermore, the access that a generic ACE provides applies to an entire object, including all data and properties associated with that object.

Object-Specific ACEs

Object-specific ACEs are used in ACLs for Active Directory objects. Like generic ACEs, object-specific ACEs contain an ACE type, a SID, an access mask, and inheritance/audit flags. In addition, object-specific ACEs contain fields for an object type and an inherited object type. The object type contains a GUID that identifies a type of child object, a property, a property set, or an extended right. This GUID indicates what the object-specific ACE controls.

- If the GUID specifies a child object type, the user or group indicated by the ACE's SID can create that type of object in this container.
- If the GUID specifies a property or property set, the user or group indicated by the ACE's SID can read or write to that property or property set.
- If the GUID specifies an extended right, the user or group indicated by the ACE's SID has that extended right.

The inherited object type provides a way for the owner to specify which type of child objects can inherit this ACE. The inherited object type contains a GUID that indicates a child object type.

Object flags included in the ACE indicate whether an object type GUID is present (ACE_OBJECT_TYPE_PRESENT) or an inherited object type GUID is present (ACE_INHERITED_OBJECT_TYPE_PRESENT). If neither flag is specified, the object-specific ACE effectively acts as a generic ACE.

Security Descriptors

Just as access tokens inform the security subsystem of a user's rights and privileges, information contained in an object's security descriptor helps the subsystem regulate who can access the object and how it can be accessed. When a thread executing within the security context of an authorized user creates an object, the security descriptor gets populated with access control information. The access control information comes from one of three places: First, the executing thread (also known as the subject thread) can directly assign a security descriptor to the object. If the thread doesn't assign a security descriptor, the operating system checks the parent for inheritable access control information. If the parent doesn't have inheritable information available, the operating system reverts to the default access control information provided by the object's resource manager.

Resource managers—not to be confused with object owners—are responsible for the naming, security, allocation, and disposal of different groups of objects based on object type. For example, the registry manages and provides default access control information for registry keys; NTFS manages and provides default information for files and folders. Table 7-1 lists resource managers for common object types.

Table 7-1. Resource managers for Windows 2000 object types.

Resource Manager	Object Type
NTFS	Files and folders
Server Service	Shares
Active Directory	Active Directory objects
The registry	Registry keys
Service Control Manager	Services
Print Spooler	Printers
Windows Manager	Terminals, window stations, desktops, and windows

Subjects can also modify the security descriptors of existing objects. A thread operating in an object owner's security context, or the security context of a different user that has the owner's permission, can change access control information for that object. Specifically, the thread can add or remove explicit permissions to the object's DACL. An object's security descriptor can also be modified as a result of a change to the container to which the object belongs. When the permissions of a parent object change, the resource manager propagates all changes marked as inheritable to child objects. Permissions added to a security descriptor this way are called *inherited* permissions, while those set directly by the owner are called *explicit* permissions.

Although object owners can't change inherited permissions in an object, object owners can set explicit permissions to qualify any permissions passed down from the parent. An owner can explicitly allow or deny access for objects within containers that are (from the owner's viewpoint) too restrictive or too permissive. For example, suppose the inheritable permissions of a container object allow full access to users in three separate groups. The owner of a child object can qualify this level of access by denying access to one of the groups and allowing read-only access to another group. Because ACEs in the DACL are processed in order during an access check, explicit permissions appear before inherited permissions so that they can be processed first. We'll discuss inheritance in more detail later in this chapter.

Although the precise information found in the descriptor depends on the type of object and how the object was created, the security descriptor has a defined structure, which the following list breaks down piece by piece:

- **Header.** In addition to a revision number, the header includes a set of control flags that describes the security descriptor or its components. The control flags are bits that specify Boolean values, such as whether a DACL or SACL is included in the descriptor. Additionally, control flags in a Windows 2000 descriptor contain information about automatic propagation, such as whether inheritable permissions can modify the descriptor's DACL and SACL.
- **Owner.** This field holds the SID for the object's owner.
- **Primary Group.** This field contains the SID for the owner's primary group.
- **DACL.** Controlled by the object's owner, the DACL is a list of zero or more ACEs that regulate access to the object for specific users or groups. Each ACE pertains to one SID and includes information that specifies whether the entry allows or denies access and the operations associated with these types of access.
- **SACL.** The SACL is also a list with zero or more ACEs, but the SACL is used for auditing rather than controlling object access. Along with a user or group SID, the ACE in the SACL includes which operations to audit and whether success or failure (or both) triggered the event auditing.

Default Security Descriptors

As stated earlier in the chapter, the owner of an Active Directory object can specify a security descriptor at creation time. If the owner doesn't specify the security descriptor, the resource manager provides default security information that the operating system applies to the object. The fields of the default security descriptor that Active Directory provides depend on the creator's access token and the inheritable properties of the container in which the object was created. The following rules apply for the descriptor fields:

- The Owner field is set to the SID in the creator's access token, unless the access token includes a default owner. If it does, the owner field is set to the creator's default owner. However, if the creator is in the Domain Administrator's group, the owner field is set to the Domain Administrator's group SID.
- The Primary Group field is assigned to default primary group in the creator's access token, if one exists. If not, the primary group field is assigned a null SID.
- If an explicit DACL is provided, that DACL merges with any inheritable ACEs from the parent container's DACL and is set as the new object's DACL. If an explicit DACL is not provided but the Active Directory schema provides a default DACL, the default DACL is set as the new object's DACL. If a default DACL is not provided by Active Directory but is provided by the owner's access token, that default DACL is set as the object's DACL. Failing that, no DACL is assigned to the new object and all users receive unconditional access.
- Like the DACL, the SACL is set to the provided explicit SACL appended with any inheritable SACL ACEs from the parent container. If an explicit SACL is not provided, the Active Directory schema can provide a default SACL. If it doesn't, no SACL is assigned to the newly created object.

Inheritance

For the purpose of inheritance, Windows 2000 divides objects into two types: container objects and noncontainer objects. Inheritance is the process by which container objects pass access control information to the objects within them—both containers and noncontainers. Inheritance in this parent/child relationship occurs either when a new child object is created or when the DACL or SACL in the parent's security descriptor is modified.

ACLs can contain both inherited and explicitly set ACEs. One of the inheritance flags in the ACE identifies whether the ACE was inherited. Since inheritance functionally supports different propagation rules, the inheritance flags also indicate to the operating system what rules to apply to the ACE. For example, inheritance rules allow an ACE in a parent object to be marked for inheritance only, so that that object is skipped when processing access control on that parent. The operating system also allows for a scenario in which an ACE can be inherited by a child container but not by any children of the child. The inheritance rules, and the flags that indicate those rules, are synonymous in the DACL and SACL:

- **INHERITED_ACE.** This flag indicates whether the ACE was inherited from a parent container.
- **INHERIT_ONLY_ACE.** This flag specifies that the ACE should be propagated during inheritance, but not for access control processing of the object.
- **CONTAINER_INHERIT_ACE.** This flag qualifies the INHERIT_ONLY_ACE flag. If a container inherits an ACE with this flag set, the container turns off the INHERIT_ONLY_ACE flag and uses the ACE during access control processing. A noncontainer inheriting this ACE leaves the INHERIT_ONLY_ACE flag alone.
- **OBJECT_INHERIT_ACE.** This flag also qualifies the INHERIT_ONLY_ACE, but for noncontainers. A noncontainer receiving an ACE with this flag clears the INHERIT_ONLY_ACE flag and lets the authorization process use it. Container objects leave this ACE alone.
- **NO_PROPAGATE_INHERIT_ACE.** This inheritance flag indicates to a child container that the ACE can't be propagated to any subsequent children.

Since ACEs are processed in an ACL from first to last, the order of the ACEs in the ACL is important. While ACEs can actually appear in any order, Windows 2000 enforces a canonical order that ensures that explicit Deny and Allow ACEs take precedence over inherited ACEs. Specifically, all ACEs explicitly added by the object's owner appear before any inherited ACEs. This rule lets the owner, not the parent, dictate access control to the object. Following canonical order, the owner can add ACEs that qualify any inherited access control decision. For instance, suppose the owner of a parent object decides to restrict members of a specific group from accessing the object or the object's children. Even though the child object inherits that ACE, the owner of the child object can modify the effects of that ACE by adding an explicit ACE that allows access to a certain member of that group. Since explicit ACEs appear before inherited ACEs in the DACL, the explicit ACE gets processed first and the individual member receives access permission.

The second rule applies to all explicit ACEs. ACEs that deny access appear before ACEs that allow access. The first rule illustrated the ability to include an individual from an excluded group. This second rule ensures that a Deny ACE for a user or group will prevent the user or group from accessing a resource, regardless of more encompassing ACEs that allow access for the user or group. Suppose an owner decides to allow access to a group but deny access to one member of that group. If the individual Deny ACE arbitrarily occurred after the group Allow ACE, the group ACE would be processed first and the individual would have the same access to the object as the rest of the group. Thus, canonical order enforces explicit Deny ACEs.

The sequencing of all inherited ACEs depends on the order in which they were added to the list. ACEs handed down from one level—in effect, the parent level—are placed first in the list. ACEs inherited from two levels up the hierarchy are next. Third-level ACEs are next, and so on. This hierarchy ensures that ACEs inherited from parent objects take precedence over broader ACEs.

Figure 7-2 illustrates how ACEs are canonically ordered in a DACL or SACL.

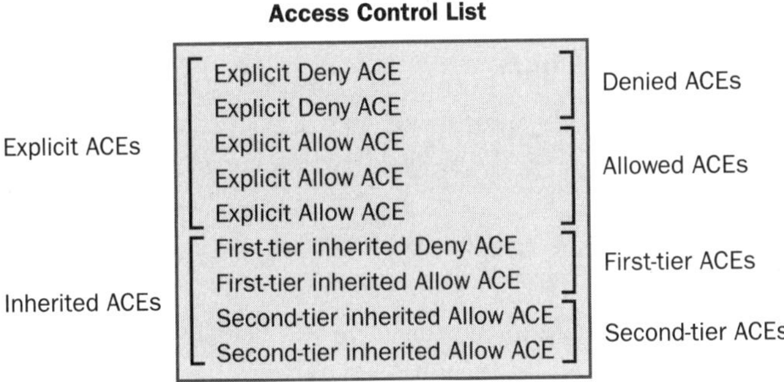

Figure 7-2. *Access control entry ordering.*

Access Checking

When a thread requests access to a resource, the resource manager checks the requestor's authorizations to determine whether it should generate auditing information for that thread. The function that makes the access determination compares the access token associated with the requesting thread against the object's security descriptor. The specific values it checks depend on the type of access requested by the thread. Remember that the operating system grants access to objects by specific operations rather than granting access to the object as a whole. The type of operation involves different access rights, such as permission to read, permission to execute, and permission to delete. Along with the access token, the thread also supplies an access mask that indicates the desired access rights the thread is requesting.

The access mask is actually just a 32-bit data structure. The subject thread sets a bit in the mask for each access right it wants. (The earlier section in this chapter regarding permissions details the four types of access rights found in the access mask.) Figure 7-3 shows the access mask format.

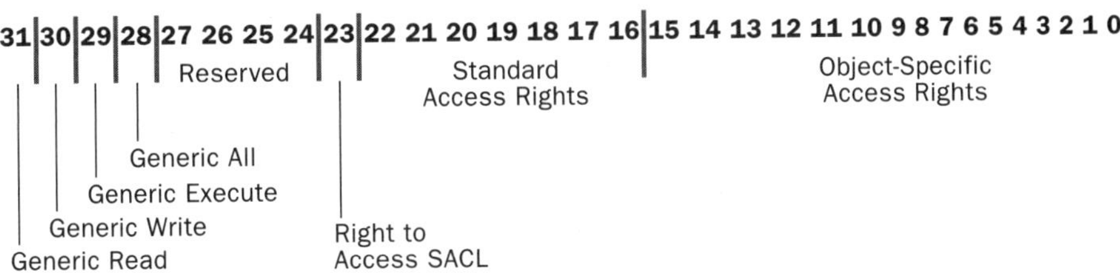

Figure 7-3. *Access mask.*

When the operating system completes the access check, a similar access mask is returned to the calling process. The returned access mask—known as the granted access mask—maps the same user rights to the same bits fields. The access-checking process turns on the appropriate bit in the granted access mask for each bit in the desired access mask that it authorizes. Unless all requested rights are granted, the granted access mask is cleared and access implicitly denied. The access-checking process steps through the following sequence to determine authorization:

1. If the DACL is absent in the security descriptor of the requested object, the desired access mask is copied to the granted access mask and the thread receives all requested access.
2. If the desired access mask is empty, the requesting thread doesn't receive any access.
3. If the desired access mask requests the right to access the SACL, the manage-auditing privilege is checked in the thread's access token. If this privilege exists, the corresponding bit in the granted access mask is turned on.
4. If the desired access mask requests read permissions, change permissions, or permission to modify the owner, the checking process compares the owner SID in the security descriptor to all user and group SIDs in the access token. If a match exists, the corresponding bits in the granted access mask are turned on.
5. The checking process interrogates each ACE in the DACL in order. If the inheritance flags of the ACE are marked INHERIT_ONLY or the SID in the ACE doesn't match any access token SID, the checking process skips that ACE. If a match is found and the ACE is the access-deny type, the rights denied in the ACE's mask are compared to the rights requested in the desired access mask. If the checking process finds any matches, the granted access mask is cleared and the thread receives no access. If the ACE is the access-allow type, the rights allowed in the ACE's mask are compared to the rights requested in the desired access mask. For each match found, the corresponding bit is turned on in the granted access mask. The checking process continues with the next ACE until all bits in the desired access mask are checked or until the checking process reaches the end of the DACL. If every ACE has been examined and some desired rights have still not been authorized, the granted access mask is cleared and the thread doesn't gain access to the object.

Audit Generation

Auditing an object means writing the successful or failed attempts to access the object to a security log. Like access control, the auditing process requires the requesting thread's access token and desired access mask. Instead of using the DACL from the target object's security descriptor, auditing uses the SACL information. Since events are audited based on the success or failure of an access, the auditing process uses the granted access mask to determine if the access was authorized. Because the granted access mask is needed for this step, auditing must take place after the access control check.

In normal object access control, the number of access control checks should greatly outnumber the number of audit events. Remember that each audit writes information to a security log that can continue to grow if not monitored. Using the process outlined in the following steps, the auditing interrogates each ACE in the SACL to determine if evidence of a request should be sent to the security log.

1. If the inheritance flags of the ACE are marked as INHERIT_ONLY, the ACE is skipped.
2. If the ACE's SID doesn't match any user or group SID in the access token, the ACE is skipped.
3. If the ACE's access mask includes a set bit that is not set in the desired access map, the ACE is skipped.
4. If the ACE type is access-success and corresponding bits are set in the ACE access mask and granted access mask, a successful access event is written to the security log.
5. If the ACE type is access-failure and a bit is set in the ACE but not set in the granted access mask, a failed access event is written to the security log.
6. Once all SACL entries are processed, audit checking stops.

Editing Access Control Settings

You can edit permissions for Active Directory and NTFS objects by using the graphical user interface tools to view or manage those resources. Use the Active Directory Users And Computers administrative tool to view or modify access permissions to Active Directory objects.

To view or modify access permissions to Active Directory objects

1. Choose Advanced Features from the View menu to see the security properties.
2. Select any object in the Active Directory namespace: Organizational Unit, User account object, or Group object, for example.
3. Right-click on the object and choose Properties from the context menu.
4. Click the Security tab to bring up the Security property page.

For objects on an NTFS partition, you can edit permissions that apply to users working on the machine where the file is stored and users accessing shared network files and folders. Additionally, you can set user-specific sharing permissions on network folders. Shared file permissions work in tandem with file and folder permissions.

To set access control permissions for files or folders on an NTFS partition

1. Right-click the object in Explorer and choose Properties.
2. Select the Security tab for basic and advanced permission editing.

Security Properties

The Security property page for Active Directory and NTFS objects shows the permissions for each user, group, and computer that the owner has authorized for object access. Figure 7-4 shows container permissions of a sample organizational unit (OU) labeled EngineeringPersonnel.

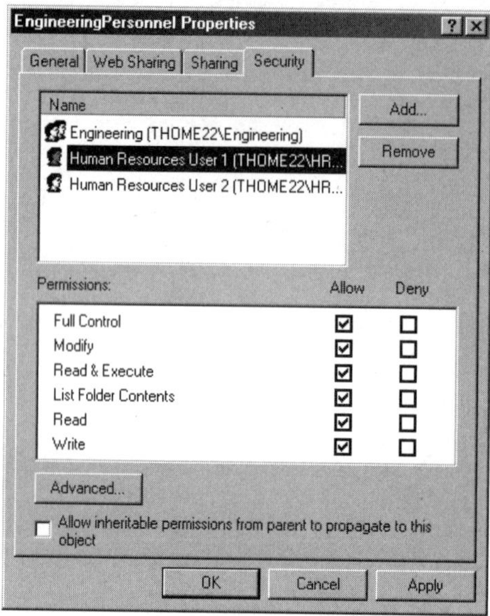

Figure 7-4. *Security permissions.*

As you can see, this OU has permissions configured for three security principals. The Engineering security principal represents a group, as indicated by the multi-person icon. The two user entries—Human Resources User 1 and User 2—complete the ACL. The Permissions frame displays the permissions for the currently selected user, Human Resources User 1. Notice that this user has been assigned full control—that is, allowable access for every operation. You can change permissions for any principal by highlighting that entry and setting or clearing the Allow and Deny check boxes. The Advanced button gives you more access to the security information stored in the object's security descriptor. As you'll see in the next section, you can change owners, modify inheritance behavior, set more granular permissions, and add auditing for users, groups, and computers. The check box at the bottom of the dialog enables this object to inherit permissions set by the parent. Clear the check box to disallow propagation of inheritable permissions.

To remove a specified user, group, or computer from being explicitly allowed or denied access to the object, highlight the group and click the Remove button. Clicking the Add button allows you to include a security principal in the ACL by displaying a select dialog similar to the one shown in Figure 7-5.

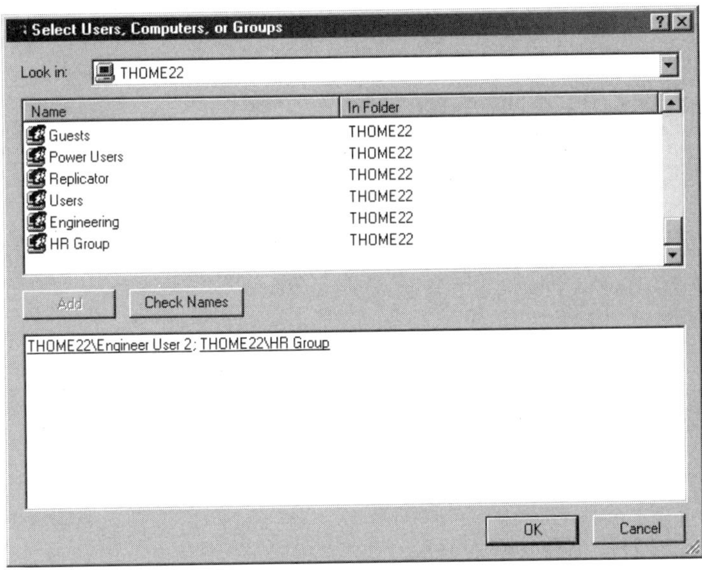

Figure 7-5. *Adding users, groups, and computers to the ACL.*

You can select a new candidate and click the Add button to display that entry in the bottom frame. Additionally, you can search different locations through the Look In drop-down list box or you can type names of users, groups, or computers in the bottom frame. The Check Names button is useful after you type entries and you want to verify the list of names. A warning appears for each name in the selection that doesn't correspond to a known user, group, or computer. In our example, we're adding a user (Engineering User 2) and a group (HR Group) to the ACL.

Advanced Access Control Settings

The Advanced button on the object properties' Security tab navigates to an access control settings dialog with three tabs: Permissions, Auditing, and Owner. This interface provides you with a way to modify the different fields of the object's security descriptor.

Permissions

Figure 7-6 shows the Permissions tab for an object's access control settings.

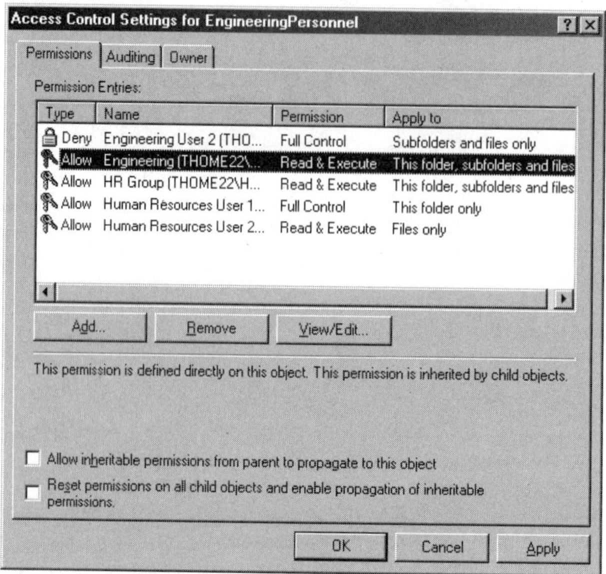

Figure 7-6. *The Permissions tab.*

Each entry in the list displays an entry type (either Allow or Deny), the security principal's name, a list of configured permissions, and the scope to which the permissions apply. You can sort the list according to any of these properties simply by clicking the field name. Don't forget the ACL rules for canonical order that specify the sequencing of ACEs in a list: Explicit ACEs appear before inherited ACEs and explicit Deny ACEs appear before explicit Allow ACEs. Clicking the Type field sorts the entries in this order.

The first check box at the bottom of the property sheet is a reiteration of the check box in the Security tab of the Properties dialog box. This check box enables you to propagate inheritable permissions from the parent object. The second check box appears for container objects and deals with permission inheritance for child objects. Setting this check box enables permission propagation to child objects.

The Properties dialog box uses the space above the check boxes for per-entry information. For the currently highlighted entry, the textual information tells whether the entry is an explicitly defined permission or is inherited from the parent object, and whether child objects inherit the permission. In our example, the Read & Execute permissions associated with the Engineering group are defined directly on the object and are inherited by child objects.

Three buttons provide the main interface for this property sheet: Enable the Remove button for explicitly defined permissions; disable the Remove button for inherited permissions; and click the Remove button to delete the currently highlighted entry. The Add button here works the same as the Add button on the Security property page: it allows you to add users, groups, and computers to the ACL. When you utilize the Add button, the editor responds with a Permission Entry dialog that allows you to immediately set individual allow and deny permissions. The Permission Entry dialog box is the same as the dialog box that appears when you highlight an entry and click the View/Edit button. Figure 7-7 shows this dialog for the HR Group entry.

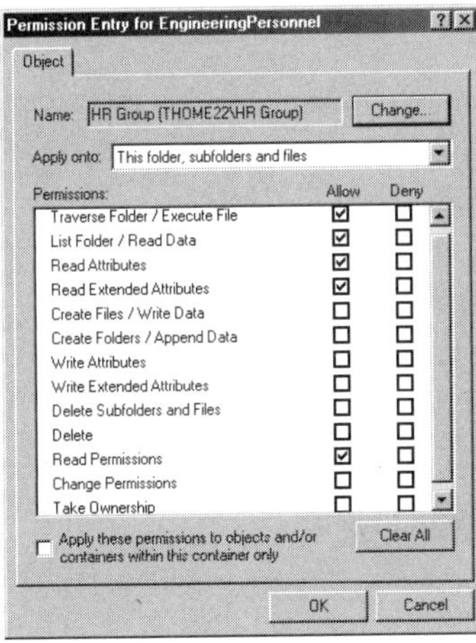

Figure 7-7. *Permission entry dialog box.*

The check boxes in this dialog box behave just like the permissions on the Security property page, although this dialog contains more extensive permissions. The Permission Entry dialog box also allows you to specify the scope of the inherited permissions through the Apply Onto drop-down list box. The available scopes for a container object are as follows:

- This Folder Only
- This Folder, Subfolders, And Files
- This Folder And Subfolders
- This Folder And Files
- Subfolders And Files Only
- Subfolders Only
- Files Only

In contrast, the only allowable scope for noncontainer objects is This Object Only.

Just as the Remove button is disabled on the Permissions property page for inherited entry, so too are the individual permissions unable to be edited. The Permission Entry dialog displays inherited permissions as viewable but disabled. You can edit permissions only at the object where they're defined.

The second tab on the Access Control Settings dialog configures auditing for this object. At first glance, the Auditing property page appears to be congruent to the Permissions page. The same buttons—Add, Remove, and View/Edit—allow you to manage entries in the list and set the acknowledged permissions for each. Similar check boxes at the bottom of the page influence inheritance behavior in the same way. Even the per-entry information displayed in the middle appears the same, indicating whether the owner explicitly defined the auditing entry and whether child objects inherit it.

The difference between the Auditing and Permissions tabs lies in the list entries. Instead of an entry for each user or group (as in the Permissions dialog box), specific events comprise the auditing list. Figure 7-8 shows a list of Success and Fail access attempts to audit.

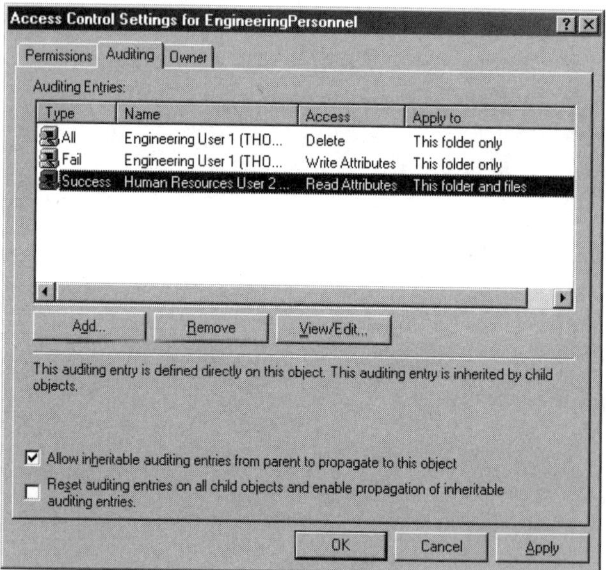

Figure 7-8. *Access control auditing.*

This dialog box contains three different access types for auditing. The first type specifies auditing for any Delete attempts made by Engineering User 1, either successful or unsuccessful. Also audited are failed Write Attribute attempts by Engineering User 1 and successful Read Attribute attempts by Human Resources User 2. In general, you'll want to limit the number of auditing entries to only critical access attempts. Each occurrence writes the event to the security log.

The final tab in the Access Control Settings dialog is for the Owner property page. You can use this page to assume ownership of the object. For a typical user, the take ownership permission must be explicitly granted to that user or the group the user is a member of. Otherwise, this sheet is grayed out and only read access is allowed. Users in the Administrators group on a computer have the right, by default, to assume ownership of any object on the computer. Figure 7-9 shows the Owner property page for the EngineeringPersonnel folder. HR User 1 is the currently logged-on user.

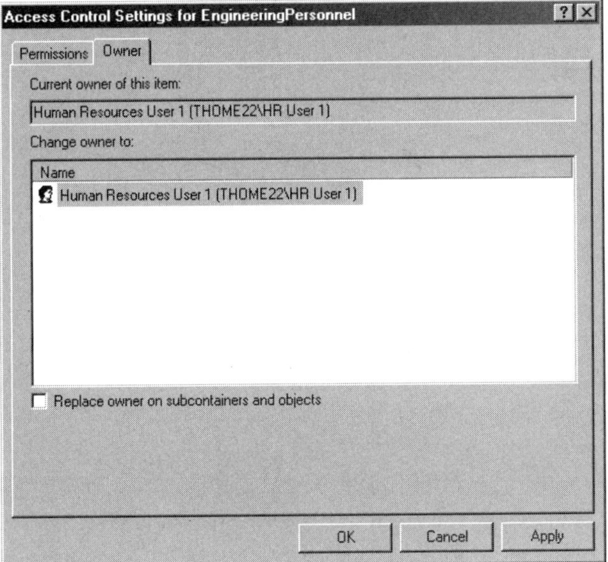

Figure 7-9. *Changing the object owner.*

The top edit box displays the current owner—in this case, the administrator. To take ownership, highlight the desired name and click the Apply button. This dialog box also allows you to assume ownership of child objects. To do this, set the Replace Owner on Subcontainers and Objects check box before hitting Apply.

NTFS Settings

In addition to file and folder access permissions, Windows 2000 includes other NTFS security features that you can apply on a per-user or per-group basis. Enabling folder sharing allows you to share information on your machine with other users on the network. The NTFS file system lets you set network restrictions that limit access to shared folders above and beyond the local access control settings.

As an administrator, you can also limit the amount of disk space each user is allowed on an NTFS volume. Use disk quotas to monitor disk usage on a per-user basis and set warning levels for auditing.

Folder Sharing

Folder sharing allows network users to access local data. The interface for this NTFS feature exists as a tab on each folder's properties dialog. In addition to setting access control properties for folders, you can set sharing permissions that target network access of specific users. The Permissions button on the Sharing property sheet evokes a Permissions dialog similar to the one in Figure 7-10.

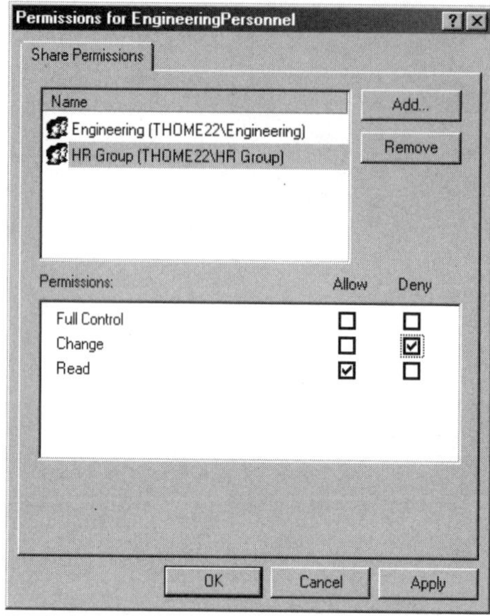

Figure 7-10. *Share permissions.*

Using this dialog, you can add and remove users and groups to your list and set access permissions for each. Figure 7-10 shows explicit Read permissions allowed and Change permissions denied for HR Group.

Disk Quotas

Disk quotas allow you to set thresholds and limits on the amount of disk space each user can consume. Though the cost of memory continues to drop, file servers and Web servers still operate on a finite amount of resources. If you don't set boundaries on resource consumption, you open the door for careless or malicious users to deplete available disk space and cause a possible denial of service to clients. Two values comprise a user's disk quota setting: The quota limit represents the maximum amount of space a user can allocate, and the threshold quota-warning level indicates the amount of disk space which, when exceeded, can log a system event warning in the Windows Event Log.

To set quotas for users on an NTFS volume in Windows Explorer, right-click the volume, select Properties, and then choose the Quota tab. This page lets you set disk quota properties—such as the default disk usage limits and warnings—and quota logging options. Click the Quota Entries button for user-specific settings. Figure 7-11 shows quota entries for the Administrators group and four users.

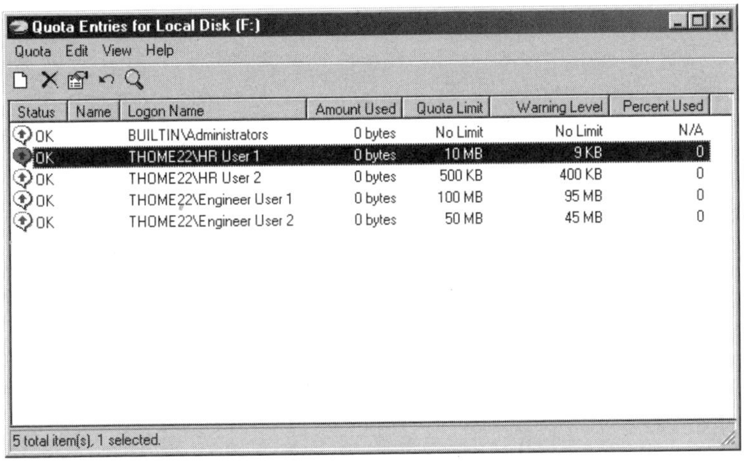

Figure 7-11. *Disk quota entries.*

Notice that the Administrators group has no limit set. Each of the user entries includes a Quota Limit and a slightly smaller Warning Level. The page also displays quota status and actual amount and percent used.

Be practical when setting warning limits, especially if using percentages. While event warnings for 90 percent consumption on a 5MB quota is appropriate, a user at 90 percent on a 500MB quota still has 50 MB to work with.

To add a quota entry, select New Quota Entry from the Quota drop-down menu. Use the subsequent Select Users dialog to choose an individual subject for the new entry. After you choose the user, the Add New Quota Entry dialog appears, as shown in Figure 7-12.

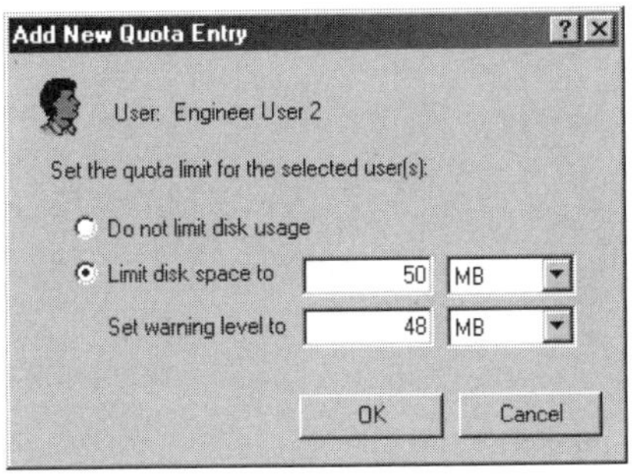

Figure 7-12. *Adding a disk quota entry.*

To set a limit and warning level, select the Limit Disk Space To radio button and fill the integer and byte unit levels.

Encrypting File System

EFS, which is covered in greater detail in Chapter 3, "Windows 2000 Security Model and Subsystems", provides protection for local data on NTFS volumes in the form of encryption. To do this, the operating system generates a per-file encryption key that it uses to protect the data. This key itself is encrypted with the user's EFS public key certificate. This encryption ensures that only the user with the associated EFS private key can decrypt this file. Additionally, a recovery agent can protect a copy of the file's encryption key. This redundant copy can be used in the event that the user's private key becomes unavailable and the user needs to recover the encrypted data.

To enable file encryption, you need only to set the encryption attribute of a file. The actual encryption and decryption of data occur transparently when you read data from and write data to the file. Since encryption involves an access-controlled object property, you'll need write permissions to the file to encrypt the file's data.

You can set the encryption attribute on folders as well as on files. Although actual folders don't get encrypted, EFS automatically encrypts any files created in or copied to an encrypted folder. Encrypting folders is good practice—folders are easier to manage than individual files. In addition, some applications create temporary files when manipulating user data files. Encrypting folders ensures that you're also protecting the information in temporary files.

To use Windows Explorer to encrypt a folder or file, right-click the object and choose Properties from the context menu. On the General tab, click the Advanced button to display the Advanced Attributes dialog, as shown in Figure 7-13.

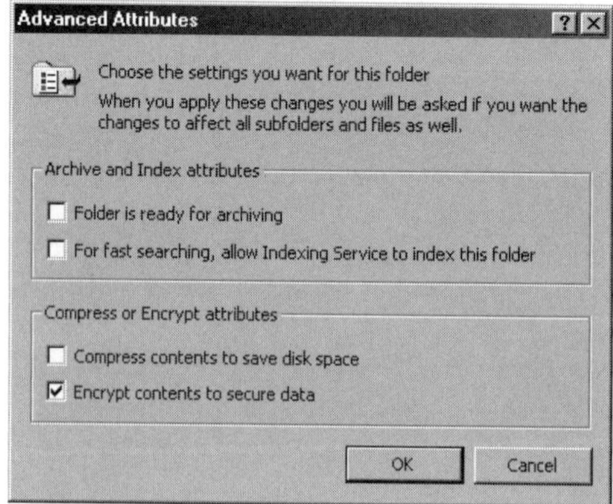

Figure 7-13. *Encrypting files and folders.*

To enable or disable encryption, set or clear the Encrypt Contents To Secure Data check box and click OK. Changes in a folder's encryption attribute will produce a confirm message box, allowing you to specify if you want the changes to apply to the folder only or to all subfolders and files.

Changing the name of an encrypted file does not alter its protection. Nor does moving or copying an encrypted file to a Windows 2000 NTFS destination. If the target volume is not NTFS, however, the moved or copied file will not remain encrypted.

Summary

Authorization checks, along with user authentication mechanisms, enable Windows 2000 to protect system and network resources from unauthorized users. Windows 2000 implements authorization with the access control model. This model allows object owners to assign separate permissions to users and groups of users. Permissions specify whether a user or group can access the object and how the object can be accessed.

Chapter 8
Group Policy

Windows 2000 introduces Group Policy to the suite of Windows management tools. Group Policy specifies options for managed desktop configurations for groups of computers and users. It includes options for registry-based policy settings, security settings, and other configuration settings. For example, users can use Local Group Policy to set ACLs for local hardware. Group Policy facilitates centralized and decentralized management of configuration settings throughout the enterprise.

Windows NT has been criticized for its lack of centralized security tools. Updating security policies on more than one computer usually meant that alterations had to be made directly on each computer. Another reported failing was the distribution of security tasks among the various administrative tools. For example, to establish an auditing policy, you had to use the User Manager for Domains; to enable auditing on specific objects, you had to use Windows Explorer, the Registry Editor, or Print Manager; to view the auditing results, you had to use Event Viewer.

Windows 2000 addresses these problems by taking the security facilities of many different administrative tools and placing them together in one tool. Windows 2000 also provides distributed security and application configuration across the enterprise, enabling centralized management of domains. To achieve this, Microsoft has developed the Microsoft Management Console (MMC) with a number of security-related snap-ins, allowing for the deployment of security across multiple systems from one centralized terminal.

Note Although we use the term "centralized" location here, we're actually referring to the use of a single machine located somewhere within the Active Directory infrastructure. This machine doesn't need to be logically or physically central to the company or network location.

In this chapter we'll focus on one of the MMC snap-ins—the Group Policy Snap-In. You can apply the Group Policy objects (GPOs) that the snap-in creates to a number of computers and users via Active Directory. You can also create GPOs that aren't linked to an Active Directory container, as well as apply policy in the form of Local Security Policy to a local machine. You can import Security Configuration Templates into Group Policy to further customize the use of Group Policy and aid deployment of Group Policy across the enterprise. You can use the Security Configuration Tool Set to edit or apply these templates, independently of the Group Policy if required . (Chapter 10 and Appendix B cover the Security Configuration Tool Set and Security Templates in detail.)

What Is Group Policy?

You create computer and user configurations by using the Group Policy Snap-In. Group Policy settings implement decisions about specific desktop or security configuration options.

The computer and user configurations are stored in a GPO, which is a collection of Group Policy settings containing both computer and user configurations for the given policy that can be applied to specific users or computers. The GPO contains the settings for a particular Active Directory container or containers. The Group Policy Snap-In then links the GPO to the Active Directory container.

The Group Policy Snap-In defines the Group Policy options for the following desktop settings, which we'll cover in more detail later in the chapter:

- Registry-based policies
- Security options
- Software installation and maintenance options
- Scripts options for startup/shutdown and logon/logoff options
- Folder redirection options

The benefits of using the Group Policy include the use of Active Directory services, which allow for centralized and decentralized management of policy options. Group Policy can handle a wide range of scenarios for implementation that are applicable to both small- and large-scale businesses. The Group Policy Snap-In provides an integrated tool with which to manage the Group Policy, and provides extensions to other MMC administrative tools, such as the Active Directory Users and Computers Snap-In.

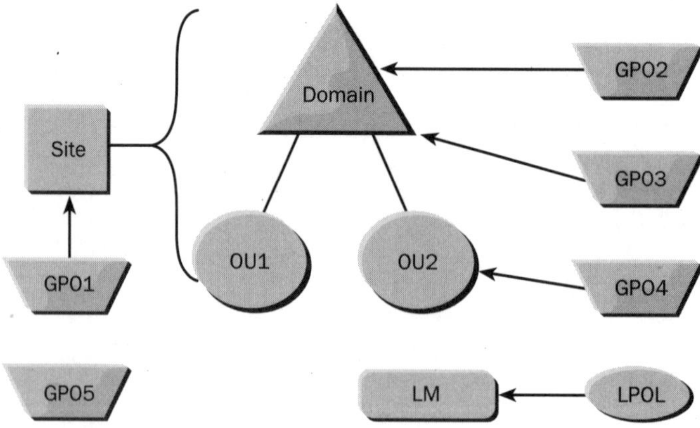

Figure 8-1. *A sample application of Group Policy objects.*

The example in Figure 8-1 shows four GPOs being applied to a fictitious enterprise structure. The Group Policy object GPO1 will filter down by default to be applied by the domain and both organizational units, OU1 and OU2.

GPOs OU2 and OU3 are then applied to the Domain. These will both filter down to OU1 and OU2. If GPO2 and GPO3 conflict, the following situations will occur:

- If one of the GPO's conflicting settings has been set to "no override," that setting will overwrite the other setting.
- The GPO that is applied last will overwrite the earlier GPO.

GPO4 is then applied to OU2, for example, to further tighten security settings. If this conflicts with the domain level settings, the GPO4 settings will be applied, since they will overwrite the Domain settings. We'll explain the process of applying GPOs and the order of precedence for GPOs in more detail later in this chapter. Table 8-1 illustrates which GPOs will be applied to the Active Directory containers.

Table 8-1. Active Directory containers and the GPOs applied to them.

Active Directory Container/Machine	Group Policy Object Application Order
Site	GPO1
Domain	GPO1, GPO2, GPO3
OU1	GPO1, GPO2, GPO3
OU2	GPO1, GPO2, GPO3, GPO4
LM	LPOL
None	GPO5

LPOL and GPO5 show less common uses for policy objects. LPOL is a policy object applied to a local machine (LM). In this instance, LPOL is not a GPO. LPOL is called a policy object because it contains the security settings for a machine. The LPOL represents the Local Computer Policy. GPO5 is a GPO that is not currently linked to any computers or Active Directory containers.

Group Policy Infrastructure

Group Policy settings are stored in GPOs associated with specific Active Directory containers, sites, domains, or OUs. As mentioned before, you can create GPOs by using the Group Policy Snap-In either as a standalone tool or as an extension to the Active Directory snap-ins. We recommend that you use the Group Policy Snap-In as an extension of the Active Directory snap-ins because it highlights the links between the Active Directory container and the relevant GPO or GPOs. To do this, right-click on the Active Directory container and choose Properties from the context menu. Click on the Group Policy tab. This allows you to search Active Directory for the required container and then define Group Policy on that container—and thus any objects within that container's scope.

Requirements for Using Group Policy

You can use Group Policy in one of two ways: You can use it to define the local policies on a local machine through the Local Group Policy settings. (This does not require the Active Directory infrastructure.) You can also use it to define the system configurations on a wider level when you must use the Active Directory infrastructure.

To use the Group Policy for a selected Active Directory container, you must install a Windows 2000 domain controller with read and write permission to access the system volume of domain controllers and the modify rights set for the currently selected directory container. You automatically create the system volume folder (%SYSTEMROOT%\Sysvol) when you install a Windows 2000 domain controller, or *promote* a server to domain controller. By default, Group Policy affects all computers and users in a selected Active Directory container, although the effects of the Group Policy can be filtered by the user's or computer's membership in Windows 2000 security groups. You can also use DACL permissions to delegate the use of the Group Policy Snap-In. You have a number of other Group Policy processing options; however, in most cases, administrators should be able to solve configuration challenges without using the special processing options.

You can use DACLs to filter the application of GPOs to Active Directory container units. Using security groups, DACLs can also filter the application of a GPO to specific security groups within a container, thereby ensuring faster processing of GPOs, since you can restrict the application of GPOs to certain groups while still allowing the Group Policy to be applied to Active Directory containers.

To achieve the highest level of policy settings security, activate the Registry Policy Processing option even if the GPOs have not changed policy for each of the Group Policy client-side extensions. This policy is located in the Computer Configuration node under Administrative Templates, System, and Group Policy. Each client-side extension has a policy setting for controlling the policy processing. By default, all Group Policy client-side extensions update the policy settings only when there are new or changed settings. Choosing this option ensures that the selected settings are applied at every logon to Active Directory. Selecting this option also negates the performance optimization achieved by skipping the application of policy settings when the policy settings have not changed. However, setting this option addresses the following security risk: If a computer is created in—or moved to—an OU, and the Group Policy is set to apply only GPOs to that OU, the new computer will by default not have the policy applied to it when there have been new or changed settings.

Consider a scenario in which users have the privileges to change some security settings on particular machines. Such privileges would enable them to change certain policies and settings on their own machines. In this case, it makes sense to reapply any domain security settings during logon, or to periodically refresh the Group Policy to maintain all computers with the same security configuration within that OU.

Group Policy MMC Snap-in Extensions

The nodes of the Group Policy tool are accessed through separate MMC snap-in extensions that cover the following areas:

- Administrative Templates
- Folder Redirection
- Scripts
- Security Settings
- Software Installation

All extensions are loaded by default when you start the Group Policy Snap-In. You can modify this default behavior by creating custom consoles or by setting policy settings for the use of the MMC itself. The policy settings are stored under the User Configuration\Administrative Templates\Windows Component\Microsoft Management Console node. By creating custom consoles, developers can create extensions to the MMC—thus expanding its capability to handle additional policy areas at a later date.

Windows NT 4.0 Policy vs. Windows 2000 Policy

Windows NT 4.0 introduced the System Policy Editor which enabled the administrator to specify user and computer configurations for the settings stored in the system registry. These settings were mainly related to a user's desktop environment. The System Policy Editor enabled the creation of system policies that contained specific registry settings and effectively controlled the user's work environment.

Windows 2000 introduces the Group Policy infrastructure and the Group Policy Snap-In for the MMC, extending the functionality of the System Policy Editor and enabling the creation of specific desktop configurations for a particular group of computers or users. The Group Policy Snap-In provides built-in features for creating a Group Policy setting that is then stored in a GPO. You can associate GPOs with Active Directory container units.

Some significant differences exist between the infrastructure and the facilities provided by the Windows NT System Policy and the Windows 2000 Group Policy. Windows NT 4.0 (and Windows 95/98) allows the specification of policies using the System Policy Editor. A policy created by the System Policy Editor has the following characteristics:

- It is applied to domains.
- It is controlled by user membership in security groups.
- It isn't secure. (A user can use the registry editor to change it.)
- It is persistent in users' profiles. The setting persists until the policy setting is reversed or until the user changes it via the registry.
- It is effectively limited to desktop lockdown.

Windows 2000 uses the Group Policy Snap-In and its associated extensions to control the GPOs; these are distributed using Active Directory. In Windows 2000 the Group Policy performs the following tasks:

- It represents the main method for maintaining centralized change and configuration management.
- It can be associated with sites, domains, and OUs.
- It affects all users and computers in the specified Active Directory container.
- It can be further controlled by user or computer memberships in security groups.
- It is secure, because only the Administrator can change the settings.
- Its default policy settings are not persistent. Two registry keys are cleaned when the GPO no longer applies: \Software\Policies and \Software\Microsoft\Windows\CurrentVersion\Policies.
- It can be used for expanded desktop lockdown and to enhance the users computing environment.

Group Policy Containers and Objects

The Group Policy uses a series of containers and objects to store its settings. These objects and containers are then distributed to the target systems using the Group Policy via Active Directory. It is important to note the difference between types of containers and objects to use them effectively.

Local and Nonlocal Group Policy Objects

GPOs are split into two kinds: local and nonlocal objects. Nonlocal objects are only available in an Active Directory environment, are identified using a globally unique identifier (GUID), and are stored at domain level. Nonlocal objects apply to users and computers in a site, domain, or OU with which the GPO is associated. Local objects, however, are stored on each computer that is running Windows 2000. These objects contain a subset of the available nonlocal GPO settings. If the settings conflict, the local GPO settings can be overwritten by nonlocal settings; otherwise, both apply.

Note For more information on the contents of local and nonlocal objects, please see the information about Group Policy in the Deployment Planning Guide volume of the *Microsoft Windows 2000 Server Resource Kit*.

Table 8-2 illustrates how GPOs are structured.

Table 8-2. The structure of Group Policy objects.

Computer Configuration	User Configuration
Computer's Registry Key	User's Registry Key
Computer's File System Path	User's File System Path
Computer's Directory Service Path	User's Directory Service Path

You can see that the Group Policy splits its settings into those that affect the computer and those that affect the user. If computer and user settings conflict, computer-related settings override user-related settings.

A GPO can be linked to one or more Active Directory containers, and multiple containers can be linked to the same GPO. A single container can also be linked to multiple GPOs. Within an Active Directory container, the administrator can use security groups to further limit the computers and users affected by a given GPO. You can adjust the security policy with the ACL Editor.

Each Windows 2000 computer has one local GPO, which is stored in the %SYSTEMROOT%\System32\GroupPolicy directory. Nonlocal GPOs consist of two parts that are stored separately—the Group Policy Container and the Group Policy Template. The Group Policy Container holds any small or infrequently changed piece of information, while any large or frequently changed piece of information is kept in the Group Policy Template. The Group Policy user interface keeps this separation of data transparent to the user.

Organizing Group Policy Objects

GPOs can be applied in a variety of ways. You should organize Group Policy carefully to avoid redundancy and redefinition of settings. By redundancy, we mean setting a particular security setting to the same value in more than one policy; by redefinition we mean configuring the same security setting differently by more than one GPO. An example would be setting the Password Policy at domain level, and then setting a tighter Password Policy for the Domain Controller OU. You should create individual GPOs to cover individual functional areas, such as Active Directory Policy, Audit Policy, EFS Policy, and so on.

To aid manageability, create and maintain Group Policy with an organized structure.

Note If a GPO contains an undefined setting, and it is allowed to inherit permissions and settings from its parent object, it will inherit the new settings. If it is set to block inheritance and the setting is defined in the Local Computer Policy, it will apply the local setting. If the GPO contains an undefined setting, and the setting is not defined in the Local Computer Policy, the setting will remain undefined.

However, these two objectives (reducing redundancy and ensuring manageability) conflict and thus require a compromise. To reduce redundancy, granular GPOs should be configured, but to maximize manageability, a small number of GPOs are required. A small number of GPOs also maximizes speed. Figure 8-2 illustrates this configuration.

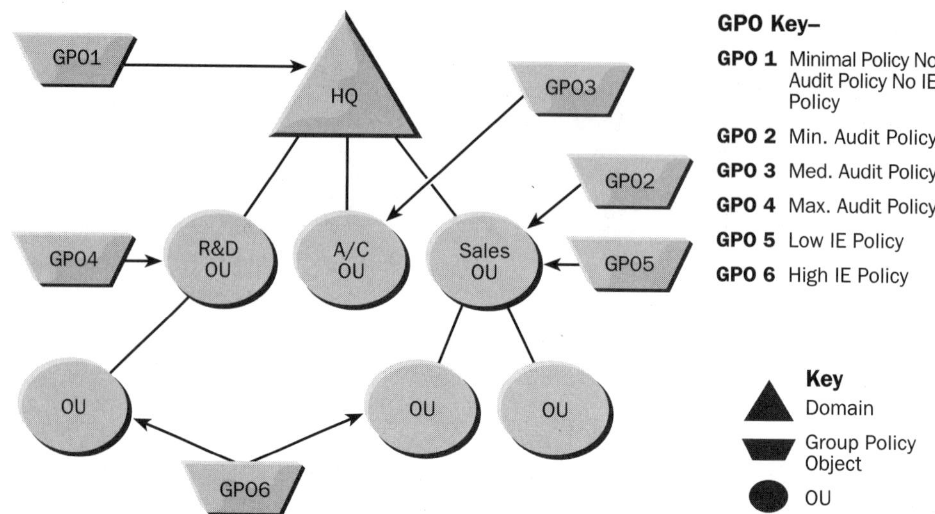

Figure 8-2. *A sample organizational structure of Active Directory containers and Group Policy objects.*

Figure 8-2 shows a fictitious organizational structure consisting of a domain with three higher-level OUs, two of which have child OUs beneath them. The figure also shows a series of GPOs.

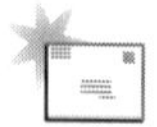

Note This scenario is purely for illustrative purposes. Plan carefully when designing an organizational hierarchy. We recommend that you consult a reliable reference guide, such as *Active Directory Services for Microsoft Windows 2000 Technical Reference* (Microsoft Press, 2000).

You can apply a security policy to the sample structure in two ways:

- Create a single GPO that covers all settings and apply it to the whole domain structure. Then apply additional policies, with any required settings for the OUs and child OUs. This would lead to redefinition within the policy settings.
- Create a series of GPOs, each of which contains a subset of security settings (for example, a specific policy for the implementation of EFS).

The second method allows a far more flexible approach to security configuration. It allows administrators to pick and choose security configurations and combine them, thus creating custom security configurations for each computer and user task.

In the preceding example, we have the HQ domain with a series of OUs organized in a hierarchy underneath. The three OUs at the top represent the Research & Development (R&D), Accounts (A/C), and Sales departments.

GPO1, which represents the basic domain policy, is applied to the HQ domain. This will filter down to all OUs in the hierarchy underneath it. This policy does not contain any auditing or Internet Explorer settings.

However, the organization requires different levels of auditing for each of its three higher-level departments, represented by GPO2, GPO3, and GPO4. Each presents a different level of auditing. GPO2 contains the minimum auditing policy, which is applied to the Sales OU. This will propagate down to the child OUs. GPO3 contains the medium auditing setting, which is then applied to the Accounts (A/C) OU. GPO4 represents the highest level of auditing and is applied to the R&D OU. This will also propagate down to the child OUs. Thus we have four GPOs, all covering auditing without redundancy or redefinition of any settings. The settings in GPO2, GPO3, and GPO4 will all overwrite the undefined settings for audit, which were set by GPO1 and its propagation throughout the organization.

GPO5 represents a low Internet Explorer security configuration, which is applied to the Sales OU. This configuration will propagate down to the child OUs—unless the lower OUs have the Block Policy Inheritance setting applied. GPO6 represents a more secure Internet Explorer setting for higher-risk computers and is applied to two of the child OUs. Note that both of these child OUs have different parent OUs. The settings in GPO6 will overwrite any Internet Explorer settings contained in GPO5. If GPO5 had block Policy Inheritance set, the settings would not be overwritten. In the Internet Explorer case, a redefinition of settings could be avoided by either applying GPO5 to the Sales OU and one of its child OUs, and setting the GPO not to propagate, or by using DACLs on specific security groups (if appropriate).

This example shows how the modularization of Group Policy settings allows flexible configuration of the users' and computers' settings. This flexibility allows you to easily change a setting, such as tightening Internet Explorer security after a security breach. All that is required is the modification to the appropriate Internet Explorer GPO and the reapplication of that GPO. This will produce less overhead than creating a new policy covering the entire configuration and then reapplying that policy to the domain structure.

Planning From a manageability standpoint, the more GPOs you create, the more difficult it might become to keep track of where particular settings are applied. The arrangement of links between the Active Directory containers and the GPOs will also rapidly become more complex. To balance the two objectives mentioned earlier (avoiding redundancy and redefinition), you must carefully plan the policy infrastructure. Keep in mind the following options:

- Split Group Policy settings into logical groupings (for example, an accounting GPO for all the accounts machines).

- Define a GPO for each logical computer grouping (for example, one account GPO for domains and one GPO for local accounts).
- Partition the computers into a hierarchical tree structure using OUs. (This partitioning should be role-based—a domain controller OU, for example.)
- Further customize policy through additional sub-OUs or by using security groups to determine which settings are applied to which computers.

Group Policy Containers

The Group Policy container is a Directory Service object that contains subcontainers for the Machine and User Group Policy information. It contains *version information* which ensures that the data in the container is synchronized with the Group Policy template information; *status information* which indicates whether the GPO is enabled or disabled for its Active Directory container; and a *list of components* that specify which extensions to the Group Policy have settings in the GPO. The Group Policy Container is stored in Active Directory and synchronized using a GUID.

Group Policy Templates

GPOs also store Group Policy information in a folder structure called the *Group Policy template* located in the system volume folder of domain controllers (%SYSTEMROOT%\Sysvol) in the \Policies subfolder. The Group Policy template is the container in which Administrative Template–based policies, Security Settings, applications available for Software Installation, and script files are stored.

When you modify a GPO, the directory name given to the Group Policy template is the GUID of the GPO that you modified, which is used to synchronize the Group Policy template and Group Policy container. For example, let's say you modified a GPO associated with a domain called Reading. The resulting Group Policy template folder would have a name similar to the following (the GUID would be different): %SYSTEMROOT%\sysvol\<SYSVOL>\Reading.iss.net\Policies\{47636445-af79-11d0-91fe-080036644603}. The second *sysvol* is shared as SYSVOL.

The Policy Template folder contains the following subfolders (These can vary depending on the configuration of the system.)

- **Adm** contains all the .adm files for this Group Policy template.
- **Scripts** contains all the scripts and script-related files for the Group Policy template.
- **User** includes a Registry.pol file that contains the registry settings to be applied to the users. When the user logs on, this Registry.pol file is downloaded and applied to the HKEY_CURRENT_USER portion of the registry.

- **User\Applications**, a subfolder of the User folder, contains the application advertisement scripts (AAS) used by the operating system–based Installation service. These scripts are applied to users at logon depending on the configuration of the Group Policy Software Installation Snap-In.
- **Machine** includes a Registry.pol file that contains the registry settings to be applied to computers. When the computer boots, this Registry.pol file is downloaded and applied to the HKEY_LOCAL_MACHINE portion of the registry.
- **Machine\Applications**, a subfolder of the Machine folder, contains the advertisement files (.aas) used by the operating system–based Installation service. These scripts are applied to the computers when the user logs on.

Gpt.ini File

At the root of each Group Policy template folder is a file called Gpt.ini. For local GPOs, the Gpt.ini file stores information indicating the following::

- Which client-side extensions of the Group Policy Snap-In contain User or Computer data in the GPO
- Whether the User or Computer portion is disabled
- Version number of the Group Policy Snap-In extension that created the GPO

Local Group Policy Objects

A local GPO exists on every computer. By default it contains only security policy. The local GPO is stored in %systemroot%\System32\GroupPolicy and has the following ACL permissions:

- Administrators: full control
- Operating system: full control
- User: read-only

Registry.pol Files

The Administrative Templates Snap-In extension of Group Policy saves information in the Group Policy template in ASCII files referred to as Registry.pol files. These files contain the customized registry settings that you specify (by using the Group Policy Snap-In) to be applied to the Machine (HKLM) or User (HKLU) portion of the registry.

Two Registry.pol files are created and stored in the Group Policy template: one for computer configuration, which is stored in the \Machine subdirectory, and one for user configuration, which is stored in the \User subdirectory.

Group Policy Areas

The root node of the Group Policy Snap-In is displayed as the name of the GPO and the domain that it belongs to, in the format GPO Name [domain.com] Policy. For example: Default Domain Policy [microsoft.com] Policy.

This namespace is then split into two parent nodes: Computer Configuration and User Configuration. These parent folders are used to configure specific desktop environments and to enforce Group Policy on groups of computers and users on the network. Computer Configuration includes all computer-related policies that specify operating system behavior, desktop behavior, and so on (for example, the Disable Boot / Shutdown /Logon / Logoff setting contained in the \Computer Configuration\Administrative Templates\System node). Windows 2000 Server applies the computer-related Group Policy when you boot the computer and during the periodic Group Policy refresh cycle.

User configuration includes all user-related policies that specify operating system behavior (for example, the Disable registry editing tools setting stored in the \User Configuration\Administrative Template\System node). User configuration is applied when the users log on to the computer and during the periodic Group Policy refresh cycle—the same cycle used by the computer configuration settings.

As you can see in Figure 8-3, several child nodes are under the User Configuration and Computer Configuration parent nodes. These child nodes are all separate Group Policy Snap-In extensions. A Group Policy Snap-In extension can extend either or both user or computer configuration nodes. Most extensions extend these nodes, usually with different options.

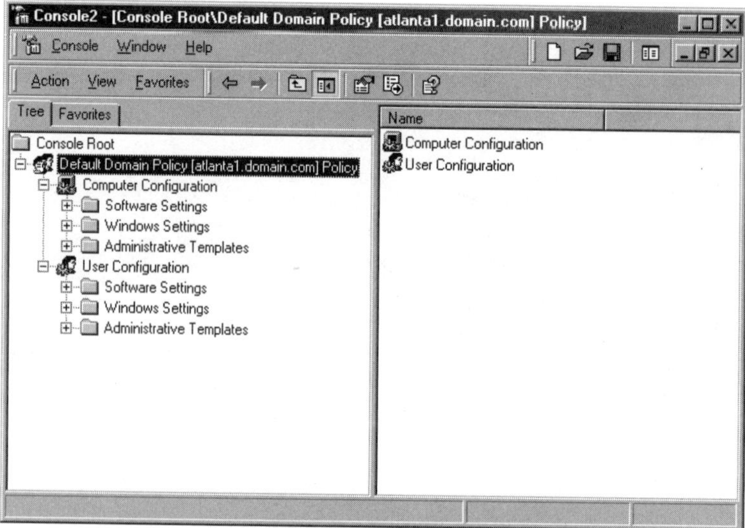

Figure 8-3. *Group Policy Snap-In showing Group Policy areas.*

Computer Configuration

Administrators use computer configuration to set the policies applied to computers regardless of who logs onto them. Typically, computer configuration contains the following subnodes, as shown in Figure 8-4. However, you can add and remove snap-in extensions, so the extensions on your machine might differ.

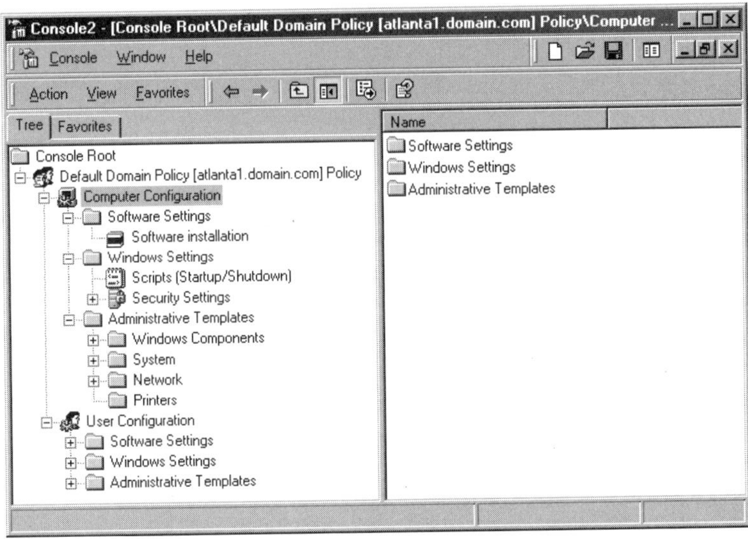

Figure 8-4. *Computer configuration nodes and subnodes.*

Software Settings

The \Computer Configuration\Software Settings node governs software settings that apply to all users who log onto the computer. This node commonly contains the Software Installation subnode, but since you can add or remove MMC extensions, the nodes available might vary.

Software Installation

The Software Installation subnode offers the ability to centrally manage your organization's software, enabling groups of users and computers to have software assigned and published. This subnode also enables you to associate an application with a particular Active Directory container from within a GPO. You can manage such an application in one of two modes:

- **Assigned mode.** Use assigned mode when everybody within a given set of computers has to have a specific application on his or her machine. A GPO is created to cover all the computers within the scope of the Active Directory container. When the administrator assigns the required software within the GPO, the server advertises the software on every machine within the object's scope. When a program is advertised, that program appears on the Start menu, and the registry is populated with the relevant file extensions—but the software is not actually installed on the machine. The first time the computer executes an application—or a file with the relevant file extension—the software will install on that machine. This happens whether the user selects the application from the Start menu or clicks on a data file associated with the application. Users cannot delete assigned applications. If the user attempts to delete the application, the application will be advertised the next time the user logs in to a computer running Windows 2000. This is because the policy will be refreshed at log on and hence the advertisement will be reapplied.

- **Published mode.** If, however, you want to make an application available to users within the scope of a given GPO, but make the installation discretionary, the application can be published. It is up to the user to decide whether to install a published application, which is achieved with the Add/Remove Programs option function in Control Panel.

Windows Settings

The \Computer Configuration\Windows Settings node contains the settings that apply to all users logging on to a particular computer. This node contains two subnodes: Scripts and Security Settings . Figure 8-5 shows these subnodes and their contents.

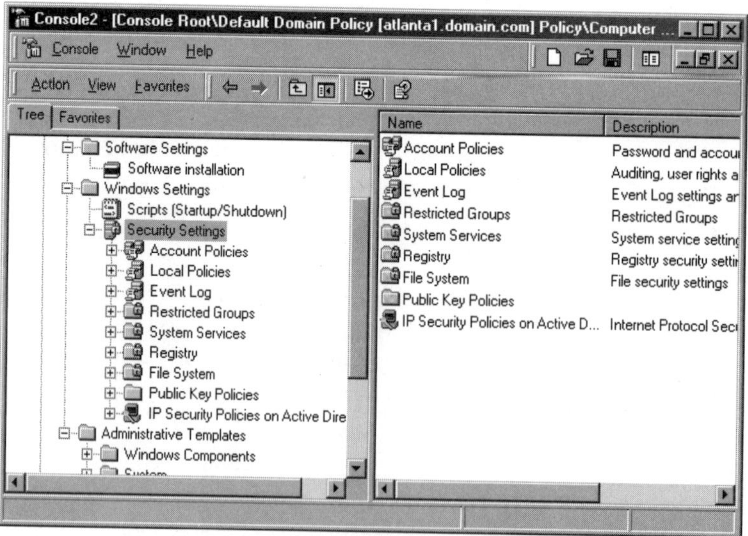

Figure 8-5. *The Scripts and Security Settings subnodes.*

Scripts

The \Computer Configuration\Windows Settings\Scripts node contains the information for the computer-specific scripts. These currently include the following:

- \Scripts\Startup and \Scripts\Shutdown specifies scripts that run when the computer starts up or shuts down and run as Local System.
- \Scripts\Logon and \Scripts\Logoff specifies scripts that run when the user logs on or logs off. These scripts run in user mode and not in privileged mode.

Security Settings

This extension defines security configuration for computers that fall within the scope of the GPO. The \Computer Configuration\Windows Settings\Security Settings node contains the security settings for all users who log on to the affected machine. Security settings can be defined at local, computer, domain, and network levels, and have four subnodes: Account Policy, Local Policies, Public Key Policies, and IP Security Policies On Local Machine.

On the Account Policy subnode, you can configure Password and Lockout Policies on member servers and workstations, since workstations and servers have their own local accounts database (the Security Account Manager, or SAM). Kerberos policies do not apply to local account databases, and thus are found only on domain controllers. The Account Policy subnode contains the following subnodes:

- Password Policy
- Account Lockout Policy
- Kerberos Policy

The Local Policies node enables you to configure security-relevant security options—including registry values. It includes the following subnodes:

- Audit Policy
- User Rights Assignments
- Security Options

Public key policies configure encrypted data-recovery agents for EFS and other PKI options, including certificate authorities.

Finally, the IP Security Policies On Local Machine subnode configures the Internet Protocol Security policies for computers within the given scope.

Administrative Templates

Administrative Templates are ASCII files used to generate user interface settings for Group Policy that are configurable by the administrator. They consist of a hierarchy of categories and subcategories. These categories define which options are displayed through Group Policy, as well as show the registry settings that can be modified through Group Policy. These settings include registry-based Group Policy settings that govern registry settings concerning the behavior and appearance of the desktop (including the operating system's components and applications). Computer configurations are stored in the HKLM registry hive and include settings for program policy settings and policy settings for Windows 2000 and its components.

The Administrative Templates node namespace is populated using .adm files or by using Group Policy extensions. The first time you use the Administrative Templates node, the .adm files are automatically installed. Any manual additions to the namespace should populate it using the same naming convention used in the registry: \CompanyName\product\version or \CompanyName\product&version.

The user interface displayed under these Administrative Templates is populated using the .adm files. Because of this, Windows 2000 ships with the following Administrative Templates:

- **System.adm.** This template is installed in Group Policy by default for Windows 2000 clients.
- **Inetres.adm.** This template is installed in Group Policy by default. It configures Internet Explorer policies for Windows 2000 clients.
- **Winnt.adm.** This template governs user interface options specific to Windows NT 4.0 for use with System Policy Editor.
- **Windows.adm.** This template governs user interface options specific to Windows 95/98 for use with the System Policy Editor.
- **Common.adm.** This template governs user interface options common to Windows NT 4.0 and Windows 95/98 for use with the System Policy Editor.

System.adm and Inetres.adm use the four reserved Group Policy registry areas:

- HKLM\Software\Policies (for computer policy)
- HKCU\Software\Policies (for user policy)

Note The following two older registry keys are also cleaned up. However, you should not use these keys in your new policies.

- HKCU and HKLM
- \Software\Microsoft\Windows\CurrentVersion\Policies

You should limit the use of the last three .adm files to the administration of earlier versions of Windows through the System Policy Editor, although you can load them into Group Policy. We don't recommend this practice, however, as it leads to persistent registry settings. When you add an .adm file to Group Policy (as we described earlier in the chapter) only the genuine Group Policy trees are visible in the console. Figure 8-6 shows the subnodes within an Administrative Template.

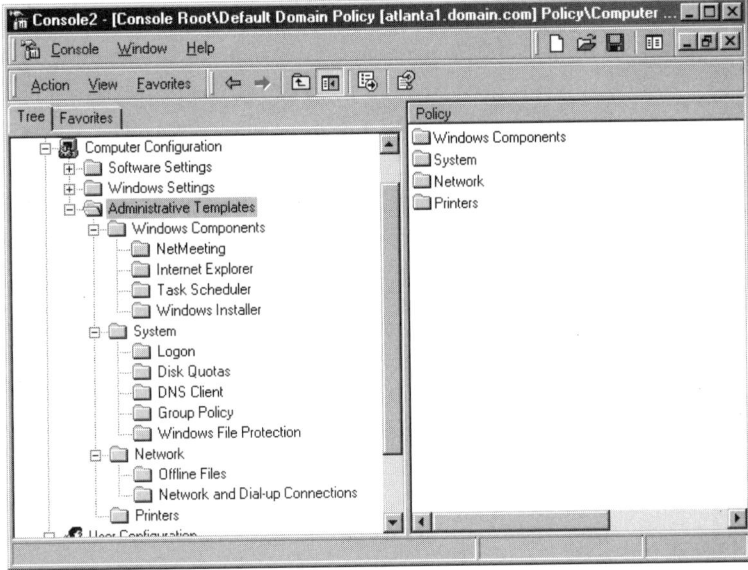

Figure 8-6. *Administrative Template subnodes.*

Windows Components

Windows Components is a subnode of the Administrative Template extension and typically contains the following subnodes, although they might vary depending on the configuration of your machine.

- **Internet Explorer** configures Security zones settings and autoinstall options.
- **Netmeeting** allows or disallows remote desktop sharing.
- **Task Scheduler** defines certain configuration options for the Task Scheduler.
- **Windows Installer** governs software configuration options for the Windows Installer package.

System Services

Security for system services is configured in the System subnode. This includes the startup options for the services and the access control required to start them. They include the following subnodes:

- **Logon.** This contains policy settings that control how logon and startup scripts are processed, as well as other settings that relate to the user logging on.
- **Disk Quotas.** These settings control the application of disk quotas, as well as configuring the logging of the disk quotas. Use the Disk Quotas options to

monitor and limit disk space use for NTFS volumes formatted as NTFS version 5.0. After you enable disk quotas, you can set options for disk quota limits and warnings.

- **DNS Client.** This allows you to set the primary DNS suffix on all computers in the subdomain.
- **Group Policy.** These settings configure the application of Group Policy, as well as define settings such as the default refresh interval for Group Policy updates.
- **Windows File Protection.** This controls how Windows 2000 interacts with anti-virus software and installation programs.

Networks

This configures the Offline file folder facilities of Windows 2000 and any dial-up connections; it typically contains the subnodes Offline Files and Network And Dial-up Connections.

Printers

This configures printers.

User Configuration

This node sets policies that apply to users regardless of which computer they log on to. Because of this node's nature as an MMC snap-in, you can install or remove snap-in extensions to customize its functionality. Figure 8-7 shows the User Configuration node.

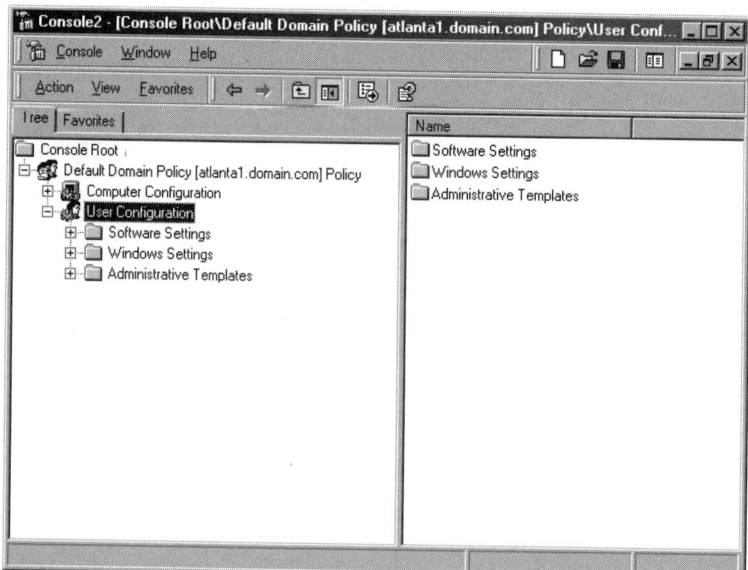

Figure 8-7. *Group Policy Snap-In showing the User Configuration node.*

Software Settings

The \User Configuration\Software Settings is for software settings that apply to users regardless of which computer they log on to. This node also has a Software Installation subnode, shown in Figure 8-8.

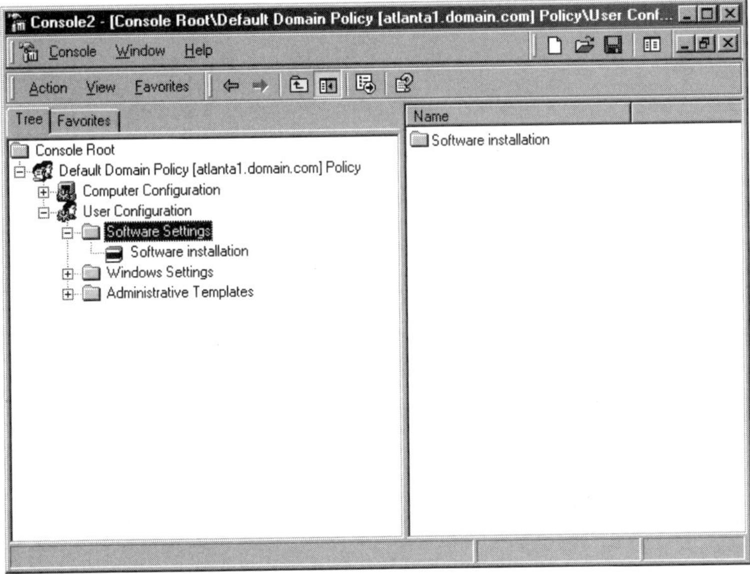

Figure 8-8. *Software Settings and Software Installation subnode.*

The \User Configuration\Software Settings\Software Installation subnode contains the settings that define how software is installed and maintained, regardless of the workstation that the user logs on to. (For more details, see the section on \Computer Configuration\Software Settings\Software Installation later in this chapter.)

Windows Settings

The \User Configuration\Windows Settings node contains the Windows settings that apply to users regardless of the machine they log on to. This node typically includes Folder Redirection, Security Settings, and Scripts subnodes.

However, depending on the configuration of the machine, other subnodes might be present. Figure 8-9 on the following page shows the Windows Settings node and its subnodes.

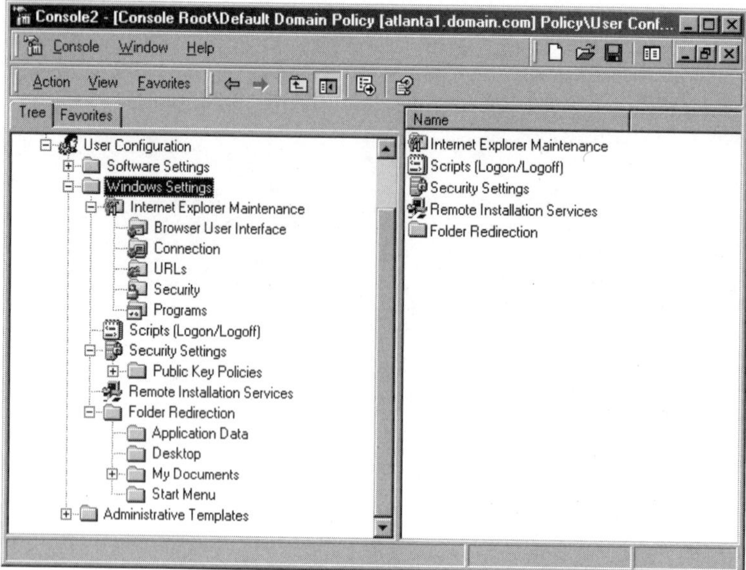

Figure 8-9. *The Windows Settings node and its subnodes.*

The \User Configuration\Windows Settings\Folder Redirection extension allows you to set the information needed for Windows 2000 to redirect certain special Windows 2000 folders to new network locations. Windows 2000 can redirect the following folders:

- **Application Data.** The Application Data folder is controlled by a Group Policy setting when client-side caching is enabled. In the Group Policy console, this folder is controlled by the \User Configuration\Administrative Templates\Network\Offline Files setting.
- **Desktop**
- **My Documents.** Redirecting the My Documents folder has many benefits, mostly because of its position within the roaming profile. This means that the directory and its contents are copied to and from the Local file store each time a user logs on and logs off. If this directory has a large number of files, this behavior will significantly affect performance.
- **My Documents\My Pictures**
- **Start Menu**

The Internet Explorer Maintenance subnode under Windows Settings configures options for the Internet Explorer Web browser, and contains the Browser User Interface, Connection, URLs, Security, and Programs subnodes.

The Scripts (Logon/Logoff) subnode is where any scripts are listed and configured.

The Security Settings subnode is blank by default in the user configuration.

The Remote Installation Services subnode contains a node called Choice Options that contains options available to users during client installation.

Administrative Templates

Administrative Templates nodes follow along similar lines to the \Computer Configuration\ Administrative Template settings, although here they apply to the user's settings or environment. Figure 8-10 shows the Administrative Templates node and its subnodes.

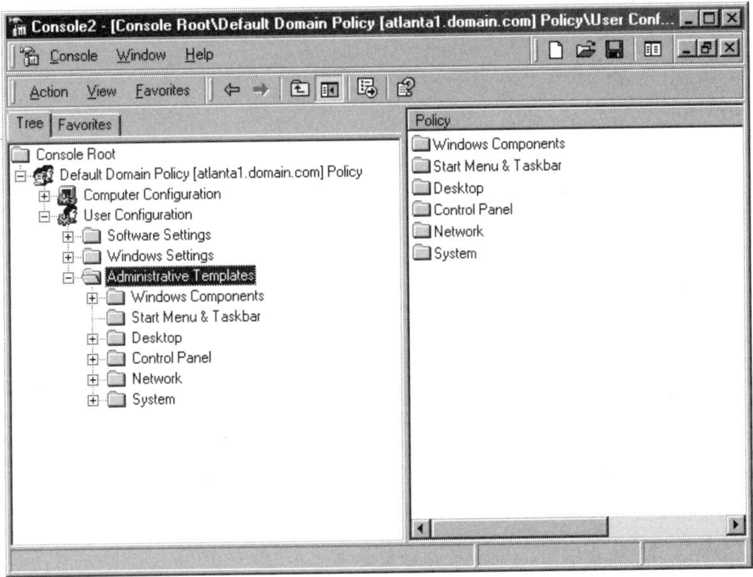

Figure 8-10. *The Administrative Templates node.*

Group Policy Application

As we mentioned previously, Group Policy is made up of two sections: the User Policy and the Computer Policy. These are both stored under the User Configuration and Computer Configuration nodes in Group Policy. The User Policy is obtained when the user logs on; Computer Policy loads when the machine boots. Users and Computers are the only type of Active Directory objects that receive policy. Security groups don't need to have policy applied to them. GPOs are applied in a specific order and overwrite previously applied policies when the GPO settings are inconsistent. When the settings in the different policies are mutually exclusive, however, they can combine to form an effective policy. The policies are applied in the following order:

1. **Windows NT4 Style Policies** (NTConfig.pol).
2. **Local Group Policy Object**. Each Windows 2000 computer has exactly one Group Policy Object stored locally.

3. **Site Group Policy Objects**. Any Group Policy Objects linked to the site are processed next.
4. **Domain Group Policy Objects.** These are processed in an order specified by the administrator.
5. **Organizational Unit Group Policy Objects.** These GPOs are processed from largest to smallest OU (parent to child OU), and in an administratively specified order at the level of each OU. The final GPOs to be processed are those linked to the OU that contains the user or computer.

Policy Inheritance and Precedence

GPOs are arranged hierarchically from the least restricted group (site) to the most restrictive group (OU). GPO settings are also cumulative in that child DS containers inherit GPO settings from parent DS containers. The processing of GPOs occurs in the following order: site, domain, OU. This means that any GPO applied to a high-level parent container propagates to all containers beneath it in the Group Policy hierarchy, including all users and computer objects. However, any GPO explicitly set for a child container will override the parent container's GPO.

You can also enforce Group Policy on child containers by using the No Override option at the GPO level, which prevents the subsequent application of Group Policies from overwriting that particular setting. If more than one object has been set to No Override, the highest one within the Active Directory hierarchy takes precedence. If a number of OUs are at the highest level, the OU that is specified as having the highest priority will take precedence.

GPOs can also be disabled, which means that their settings are not applied, although the GPOs still exist and are still linked to their parent container. No Override and Disabled are settings on GPO links, not the actual GPOs, and therefore apply to the whole GPO. This means that a GPO can be linked several times to the same OU and have independent No Override and Disabled settings for each link.

You can also prevent the inheritance of Group Policy from parent directory containers by selecting Block Policy inheritance for a given GPO. However, GPO links set to No Override are always applied. The Block Policy inheritance setting is applied directly to the Active Directory container and not to the GPOs or the GPO links. Thus, Block Policy inheritance deflects all Group Policy settings that would reach the domain or OU from above, regardless of the GPO they came from. Block Policy inheritance does not deflect Group Policy settings from GPOs that have been directly linked to the site, domain, or OU that has had Block Policy inheritance enabled.

Loopback provides alternatives to the default method of obtaining the ordered list of GPOs whose user configuration settings affect a user. By default, a user's settings come from a

GPO list that depends on the user's location in Active Directory. The ordered list goes from site-linked to domain-linked to OU-linked GPOs, with the inheritance determined by the location of the user in Active Directory. The administrator at each level specifies the order in which the system traverses the Active Directory hierarchy.

Loopback can be Not Configured, Enabled, or Disabled—as can any other Group Policy setting. In the Enabled state, loopback can be set to Merge or Replace. If the loopback is configured as Loopback with Replace, the GPO list for the user is replaced in its entirety by the GPO list already obtained for the computer at startup. The User Configuration settings from this list are applied to the user. If the Loopback is configured as Loopback with Merge, the GPO list is a concatenation. Notice that the GPO list obtained for the computer is applied later and therefore has precedence if it conflicts with settings in the user's list.

Note A computer that is a member of a workgroup processes only the local GPO.

If the local profile settings conflict with the Group Policy, the Group Policy settings take precedence. By examining how the Group Policy relates to the processes of computer startup and user logon, you can better understand the stage at which relevant Policy settings are loaded.

Security Policies Precedence

While the security policies usually follow the same order of precedence as the rest of the group policy, you'll find a few differences. The order, from lowest to highest precedence, is Local Policy, Domain Policy, OU Policy.

This hierarchy means that the local policy defined using the Local Security Policy tool has the least precedence, followed by that set out by the domain controller, configured with the Domain Security Configuration tool, followed finally by any policies defined at OU or child level.

In the case of the domain controller, the Default Domain Controllers Policy replaces the Local Computer Policy. The domain controllers are all contained with an OU class container object. This means that the Default Domain Controllers Policy—or any other GPO applied to the Domain Controllers OU—will be applied after the domain GPO.

Note The policies defined at the domain level take precedence over those set out at the local level. Notice that this is different from Windows NT 4.0. In Windows 2000, for example, when the domain controller configures the password policy, those password policies are applied to every computer in the domain, overwriting the local account password policy. In Windows NT 4.0, the domain password policy did not affect the password policy stored on the local account databases on member workstations or servers.

Startup and Logon

When the computer starts up and a user logs on successfully, the computer and user policies for that machine and user are loaded as described in the following steps:

1. The network starts, which in turn starts the Remote Procedure Call System Service (RPCSS) and Multiple Universal Naming Convention Provider (MUP).
2. An ordered list of GPOs is obtained, depending on the following:
   - Whether the computer is part of a Windows 2000 domain and therefore subject to Group Policy through the Active Directory infrastructure
   - Whether loopback is enabled and the setting of the loopback policy setting
   - The location of the computer object in Active Directory
3. The Computer Policy is applied systematically by default in the following order: Windows NT 4.0 System Policy, local, site, domain, OU, child OU, and so on. No user interface is displayed until all computer policies are loaded.
4. Startup scripts run, although this is hidden and sequential by default. Each script must complete or time out before the next one starts.

Note Startup scripts are sequential when executed singly, but synchronous in their execution among the GPOs in which they are deployed. This means that once a machine within this object has completed execution of the logon scripts, the settings defined within that script have been consistently deployed across the container.

5. The user presses Ctrl+Alt+Del to log on.
6. After the user is validated, the user profile loads, governed by the policy settings set by the current policy settings.
7. An ordered list of GPOs is obtained for the users. This list might depend on the following factors:
   - Whether the user is part of a Windows 2000 domain and therefore subject to Group Policy through Active Directory
   - Whether loopback is enabled and the state (Merge or Replace) of the loopback policy setting
   - The location of the user in Active Directory

   If the list of GPOs to be applied has not changed, no processing is done. You can use a policy setting to change this behavior. The check for GPO change is carried out on the domain controller.
8. User policy is applied. These are the settings under User Configuration from the gathered list. This occurs synchronously by default and in the following order: local, site, domain, OU, child OU, and so on. No user interface is displayed while user policies are being processed.

9. Logon scripts run. Unlike Windows NT 4.0 scripts, Group Policy–based logon scripts run hidden. The user object script runs last in a normal window.
10. The operating system user interface defined by Group Policy appears.

You can modify several of the settings in this list and set the policies to perform the following tasks:

- Reverse the synchronous or asynchronous defaults of running scripts or applying policy.
- Specify when the scripts time out. (The default for this is 600 seconds.)
- Specify whether the scripts run hidden, minimized, or in a normal window.

Windows NT 4.0 system policies are disabled by default, but you can enable them via a Group Policy setting.

Applications and Group Policy

The Group Policy Infrastructure can't force applications to use Group Policy. For example, if any applications have looked for entries in registry trees not covered by the Group Policy, they will continue to look there. The Group Policy doesn't copy registry settings from the Group Policy areas to Windows NT 4.0 System Policy areas, nor does it copy Windows NT 4.0 System Policy settings into the reserved Group Policies areas. The next section covers the process that application software goes through to obtain its registry keys.

Registry Initial State

When the computer has booted and the user has successfully logged on, the registry areas will have been wiped and rewritten to hold the cumulative settings from the Group Policy and Active Directory. If the Windows NT 4.0 system policy has been enabled (not recommended for Windows 2000 clients), other areas in the registry might have changed during logon.

Application Execution

When the user launches the application, it carries out the following process:

1. The user launches the application.
2. The application looks for the registry data in the following Group Policy Reserved areas:
   - HKLM\Software\Policies
   - HKLM\Software\Microsoft\Windows\CurrentVersion\Policies
   - HKCU\Software\Policies
   - HKCU\Software\Microsoft\Windows\CurrentVersion\Policies

   In each case, if the application finds what it needs, it stops and looks no further. If it does not find what it needs, it proceeds to the next stage.

Note Although the registry key HKCU\Software\Microsoft\Windows\CurrentVersion\Policies exists under Windows NT 4.0, it is not a part of the Group Policy reserved area, as Windows NT 4.0 does not implement the Group Policy. In this instance the registry key refers to the Windows NT 4.0 System Policy.

3. The application looks for the HKLM registry data outside the Group Policy reserved area. If it finds the data, it looks no further.
4. The application looks for the HKCU registry data outside the Group Policy reserved area; if it finds it, it looks no further.

The application uses its .ini file or default settings.

Applications that are newly authored with Windows 2000 in mind (native Windows 2000 applications, for example) never get past step 2. Any programs written to take advantage of the Windows 2000 Group Policy and Active Directory that remain compatible with earlier versions of Windows continue on to step 3 when they execute on older operating systems. Applications that predate Windows 2000 never see steps 1 and 2; they start execution at step 3.

This implies that for applications running on Windows 2000 clients, the Group Policy takes precedence over the Windows NT 4.0 System Policy. Older versions of applications that aren't aware of Active Directory and Group Policy continue to function on Windows 2000 computers as they did under Windows NT 4.0. Any settings contained within the HKLM registry hive take precedence over settings in the HK hive, as they did in Windows NT 4.0.

Software Installation and Group Policy

Windows NT 4.0 did not provide a centralized tool or service for installing individual Windows components, programs, and services. Windows 2000, however, includes the Software Installation application management utility, which is designed to be the main tool for managing software throughout its lifetime. Software Installation works in conjunction with Group Policy and Active Directory; however, it also relates to two other component services: Windows Installer, which installs software packaged in Windows Installer files; and Add/Remove Programs (in Control Panel), which users can use to manage software on their own computers.

You use the Software Installation Group Policy Snap-In to control access to the software for users who require it. This is achieved in one of two ways: you can assign software to computers or users, or the server can publish software to computers or users.

When you assign software to computers or users, it is not actually installed at that time. When you assign software to a user, the application is advertised to the user the next time he or she logs on to a workstation. This happens no matter which physical workstation the user logs on to. The application is installed to the hard drive the first time the user executes the program, or when the user selects a document associated with the program. When you assign the program to a computer, however, it is advertised on the systems, and the installation is carried out when it is safe to do so—usually during a period of low activity on the computer.

As we mentioned previously, the server can publish applications to computers. When the application is published to a user, the application does not appear on the user's computer. Neither is the application visible on the Start menu, and no changes are made to the registry on the user's computer. The advertisement attributes are stored in Active Directory, including the application name and the associated file extensions. These attributes are then exposed to the users in the Active Directory container. The user is then able to install the application using the Add/Remove Programs option in Control Panel, or by clicking on a file associated with the application.

For every application that you assign or publish in a particular GPO, an Application Assignment Script (.aas) is created. This script is then stored in the GPO template on the GPO's parent domain. The Application Assignment Scripts contain the advertisement information about the application configuration.

Before you can use the Software installation, a Windows installer package must exist for the software you want to install. If the program does not have a Windows Installer package, you can use third-party tools to generate one. You must create a software distribution point that contains the packages, program files, and components. This is a network share with permission set so that users can read from it. Permissions must also be set so that the user can write to the destination device or share.

You can also manage programs with the Software Installation Snap-In. The management of a software package typically involves two lifecycle stages. It starts by going through an evaluation phase during which a few users or new users have the software assigned or published. During the rollout phase, the new program is made available to all users using the Group Policy via Active Directory and would become the default version of the program. Any new users would only be able to install this version of the program. However, certain users could be left out if installing new software would have a negative impact on their work. At the end of the software lifecycle, the software is removed from the system or systems. If an administrator wants to remove software using Group Policy, he or she can choose from two mutually exclusive options. One option is to select Immediately Uninstall, which requires that all users stop using this program. Those users who still have the program on their desktop receive an advertisement that removes the program.

The administrator's other option is to choose Just Prevent New Installations. Users continue using the software they already have, but any new users will be unable to install the new software.

Using Group Policy Tools

Several extensions—all of which plug into the MMC Group Policy—expand the snap-in's functionality. Windows 2000 also introduces two new tools from within the Administrative Tools folder on the Start menu. These are Domain Controller Security Policy and Domain Security Policy, which set aspects of Group Policy that specifically relate to security configurations for the domain controller and domain. On workstations or member servers, the Local Security Policy tool replaces these tools.

The Group Policy tool set consists of the Group Policy Snap-In, the extensions to Active Directory Users and Computers, and Active Directory Sites And Services snap-ins. You can use all these tools to configure different aspects of the computer's security. The easiest approach is to create a customized MMC with the relevant snap-ins loaded.

Configuring a Domain Security Structure Using Group Policy

In the next few sections, we'll explain how to use Group Policy to configure a domain's security. Our example contains a single domain with multiple OUs reflecting a company's business model. The machines within this domain are a mix of workstations and servers that require two policies—one for each type of computer. In the following scenario, we will create OUs as required and create security groups to separate the workstations and servers. The security groups will filter the application of the policies. We will start by covering the creation and editing of GPOs.

Configuring a Custom Console

To carry out the following scenario, you must use the MMC with a number of snap-ins loaded. The following section describes how to load the MMC and the relevant snap-ins.

To configure a custom console

1. Log on to the domain server as an Administrator.
2. From the Start menu, click Run.
3. In the Run dialog box, type *mmc* and click OK.
4. Click the MMC Console menu item.
5. Click Add/Remove Snap-In. The Add/Remove Snap-In dialog box appears.
6. Click Add. The Add Standalone Snap-In dialog box displays.
7. In the Available Standalone Snap-Ins list box, click Active Directory Users and Computers.
8. Click Add, and then click Group Policy.

9. When prompted, ensure that the Group Policy Snap-In has the Local Computer selected, and click Finish.
10. Click Close.
11. Click the Extensions tab. Ensure that the Add All Extensions check box is checked for each primary extension added to the MMC console. (These are checked by default.) Click OK.

    Figure 8-11 shows how the snap-ins and extensions will be added to the saved console.

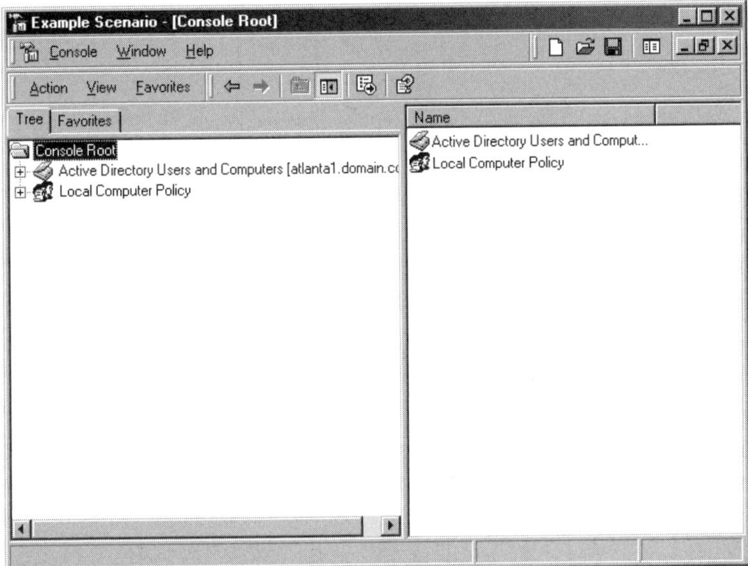

Figure 8-11. *Microsoft Management Console with associated Group Policy Snap-Ins loaded.*

12. Save the Example.msc console.

Accessing Group Policy

You can use the appropriate Active Directory tools to access Group Policy while focused on any site, domain, or OU. To access a particular GPO, right-click on any site, domain, or OU and choose Properties from the context menu. Then click on the Group Policy tab, shown in Figure 8-12 on the following page.

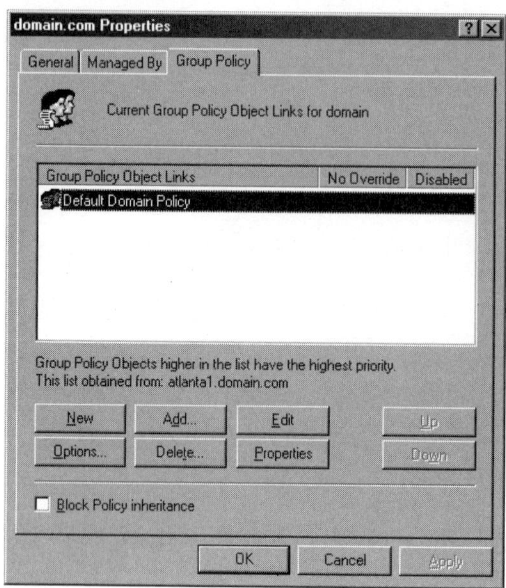

Figure 8-12. *The Group Policy tab for a sample network.*

To access a GPO scoped to a specific computer (or the local computer), you must load the Group Policy Snap-In into the MMC console namespace specifically targeted at the individual computer (or local computer). There are two major reasons for these differences. One reason is that sites, domains, and OUs can have multiple GPOs linked to them; you need an intermediate property page to manage them. The second major reason is that a GPO for a specific computer is stored on that computer and not in Active Directory. Only one such GPO or Local Group Policy can exist.

Active Directory Snap-in Extensions

The Active Directory Snap-In extensions cover aspects of Group Policy that expand across the domain structure using Active Directory. This involves the propagation of Security settings across the domain using Security Templates.

Scoping a Domain or OU

Scoping a domain or OU defines the scope that the GPO attached to that domain or OU will have. To scope the domain or OU, use the example MMC console that you saved earlier.

To scope Group Policy for a domain or OU

1. Open the Example.msc console.
2. Click on the plus sign next to Active Directory Users and Computers to expand the tree.

3. Click on the plus sign next to your domain name to expand the tree (KSTEST.ISS.NET in the example shown in the following figures).
4. Right-click the domain and choose Properties from the context menu.
5. Click the Group Policy tab to see the property page for the GPOs associated with the chosen container. This page allows you to add, remove, disable, specify "no override," change the order of the associated GPOs, and edit the GPOs. Clicking Edit starts the Group Policy Snap-In.

Note The Computers and Users containers are not OUs, and thus cannot have Group Policy applied directly to them. Users or computers in these containers receive policies from GPOs scoped to the domain and site objects only. The domain controller container is an OU, and Group Policy can be applied directly to it.

Scoping Local or Remote Computers

To access a GPO for a local or a remote computer, load the Group Policy Snap-In into the MMC and focus it on a specific computer or the local computer. To access the Group Policy settings for the local computer, open the example console you created earlier, and select the Local Computer Policy. You can add other computers to the console namespace by clicking the Browse button when you add the Group Policy Snap-In. When you expand the links for the local policy, they appear as shown in Figure 8-13.

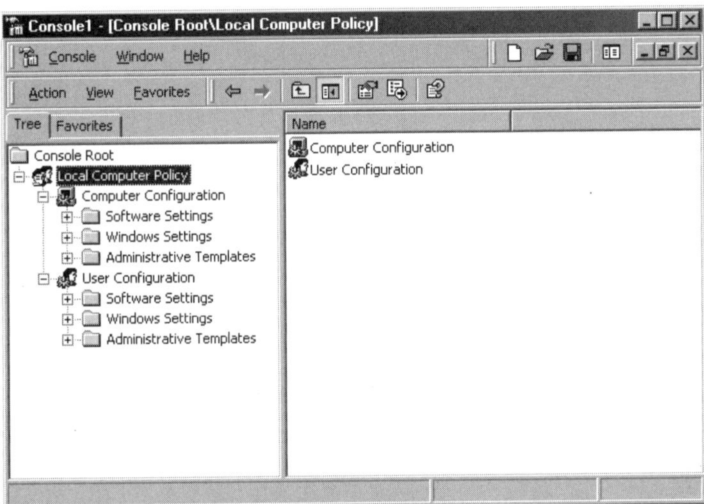

Figure 8-13. *The Local Policy MMC Snap-In.*

Note Some extensions are not loaded when you run Group Policy against a local GPO.

Creating an Active Directory Container

The Group Policy settings you create are contained in a GPO that in turn is associated with selected Active Directory containers such as sites, domains, or OUs.

To create an Active Directory container

1. Select the domain in the right pane of the MMC window.
2. Choose New from the MMC Action menu. This brings up the submenu shown here.

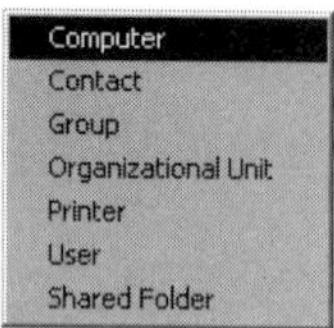

This submenu contains the list of objects that can be created. We will start by creating the OUs for the business structure.

To create an Organizational Unit

1. Select Organizational Unit from the submenu. This brings up the New Object – Organizational Unit dialog box, shown in Figure 8-14.

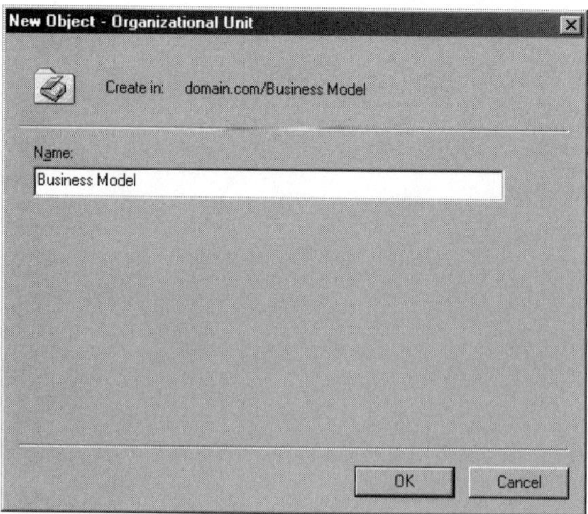

Figure 8-14. *New Object – Organizational Unit dialog box.*

2. Enter the name for the OU. In our example, we'll enter *Business Model.*
3. Click OK.

We will now repeat the process by creating two more OUs: Sales and Administration within the Business Model OU. We do this by clicking on the Business Model OU and right-clicking within the pane on the right side of the MMC window, then selecting New, and then choosing Organizational Unit from the context menu. We now need to create the two security groups for the Workstations and Servers.

To create a security group

1. Click on the OU (Business Model in this example).
2. Choose New from the MMC Action menu, and choose Group from the submenu. This brings up the New Object – Group dialog box, shown in Figure 8-15.

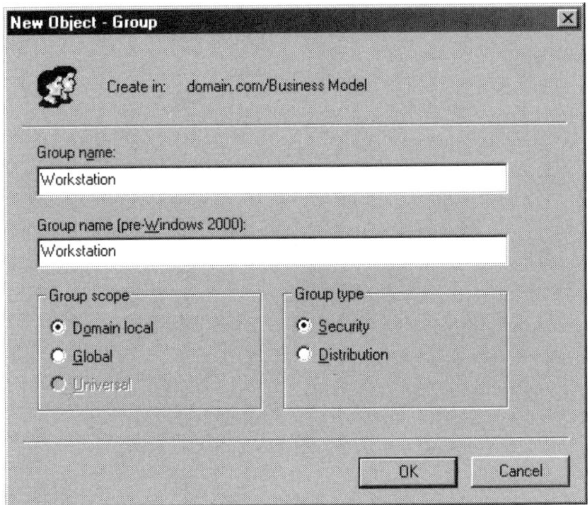

Figure 8-15. *New Object – Group dialog box.*

3. Enter the group name. The dialog box will also show the corresponding Group name for pre-Windows 2000 machines, which you can alter by highlighting the option and retyping the required group name. We will enter *Workstation*.
4. Select whether the scope of the group should be local to the domain or global across the domain structure. In our example the scope will be domain-local.
5. Select the Group Type. Groups can be either security groups or distribution groups. We want security groups to filter the Group Policy application. (For more details on security groups and distributed groups, see Chapter 4, "Active Directory.")
6. Click OK.

Now repeat the process for a domain-local security group named Servers.

Populating the GPOs

Now that we have created the OU and the security groups, we need to populate them. We'll start with the security groups.

➲ To populate the security group

1. Navigate to the OU containing the security group.
2. Right-click on the required security group and choose Properties from the context menu to open the dialog box shown in Figure 8-16. This dialog box has a number of tabs; we need the Members tab.

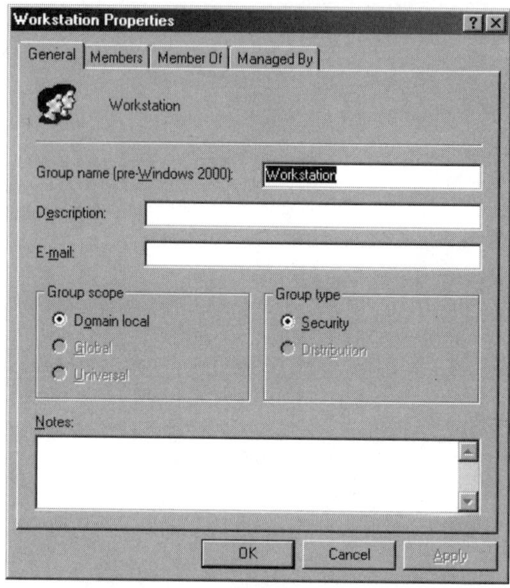

Figure 8-16. *Workstation Properties dialog box.*

3. Click on the Members tab.
4. To add computers or users to the group, click Add. This brings up the Select Users, Contacts, Computers Or Groups dialog box.
5. Select the domain you want from the Look In drop-down list, and then select the names of the users or groups in the Name list.
6. Click Add.
7. If the name is not automatically underlined, click on the Check Names button to verify the name.
8. Click OK.

Using the preceding procedure, we will add two machines to the Workstation security group: ATLANTA2 and ATLANTA3. When we've added the machines, the Members page will be updated to show the name of the user or computer and the Active Directory folder it comes from, which should be similar to Figure 8-17.

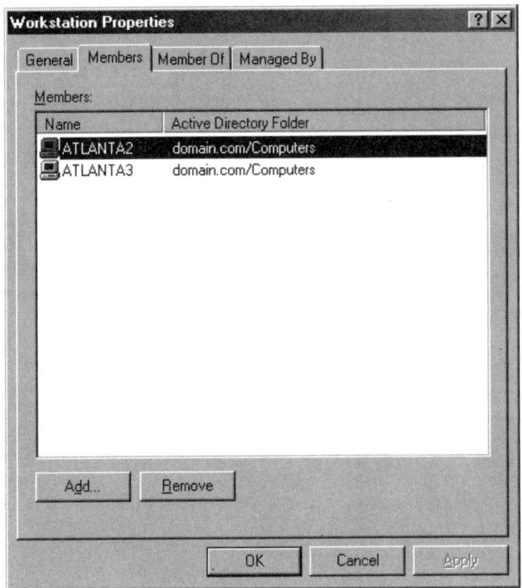

Figure 8-17. *Members tab.*

Using the security group Properties tab, you can also set child groups to be members of the security group, as well as delegate control of the security group to a specified user.

Now repeat steps 3 through 8 for the Servers security group and add ATLANTA4 and ATLANTA5.

More Info The computers ATLANTA2, ATLANTA3, ATLANTA4, and ATLANTA5 were created as Active Directory objects. For more information on how to create computers within Active Directory, see Chapter 4.

Now that we have created and populated the security groups, it is time to populate the OUs. This procedure is similar to the procedure for security groups. The main difference is that while you can place new Active Directory objects, including users and computers, within the OU, you can also move Active Directory objects into place from other OUs or other Active Directory containers.

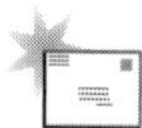

Note If an Active Directory object is taken from a container to be placed in a new container, it is removed from the first container. For example, Move performs as a Cut operation as opposed to a Copy operation.

To assign a computer to the OU, either create a new object within the OU or carry out the following steps to move an existing Active Directory object to the new OU.

To populate the OUs

1. Navigate to the Active Directory object you want to move.
2. Right-click on the object and select Move from the context menu.
3. The Move dialog box will appear, as shown in Figure 8-18.

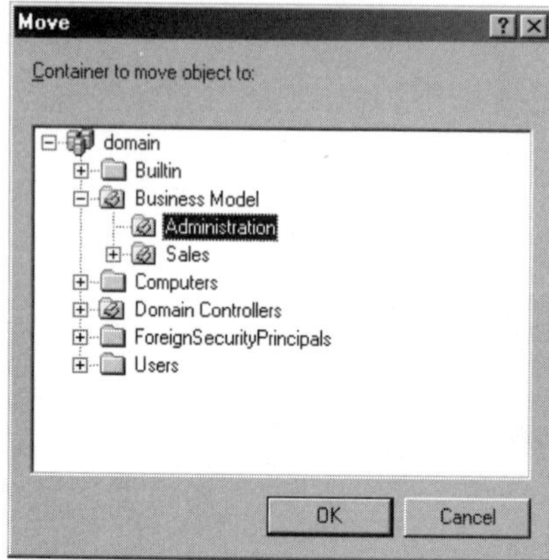

Figure 8-18. *The Move dialog box.*

4. Expand the domain tree so that the OU to which you want to move the GPO appears.
5. Select the OU and click OK.

You will see that the Active Directory object disappears from the original container and reappears in the new container. We will move ATLANTA3 and ATLANTA4 to the Administration OU.

We will then move ATLANTA5 and ATLANTA2 to the Sales OU.

Figure 8-19 offers a visual summary of what we've done so far.

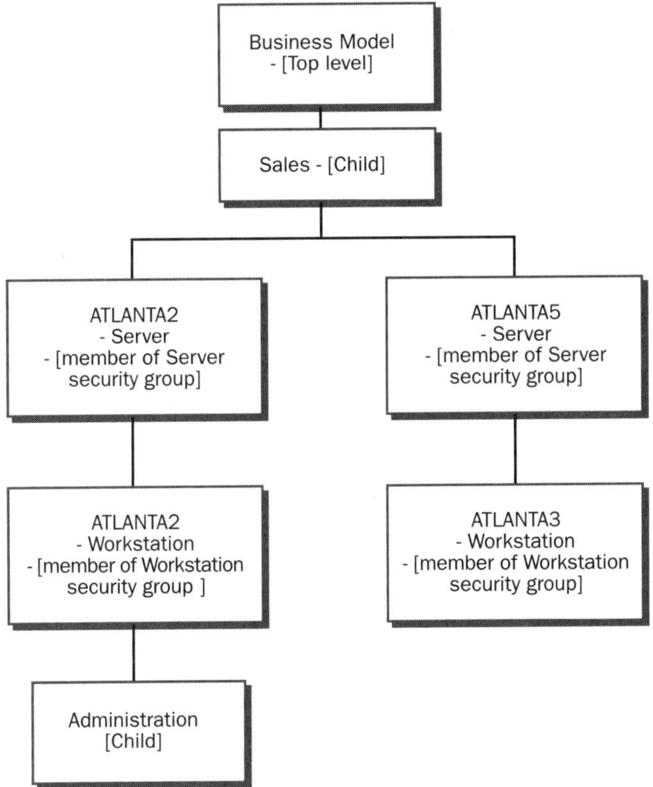

Figure 8-19. *GPO hierarchy.*

Managing Group Policy Objects

To manage GPOs, you need to right-click a site, domain, or OU, choose Properties from the context menu, and then click the Group Policy tab. The Group Policy tab displays any GPOs that have been associated with the current site, domain, or OU.

The Group Policy tab contains an ordered list of GPO links with the highest priority GPO at the top. You can change the order by selecting a GPO and then using the Up or Down buttons.

To link a new GPO, click the Add button. To edit an existing GPO in the list, select the object and click the Edit button, or just double-click the object. This starts the Group Policy

Snap-In, which is how the GPO is modified. (We'll describe this procedure in more detail later in the chapter.) To permanently delete a GPO from the list, select it from the list and click the Remove button. Take care when deleting an object—the GPO might be associated with another site, domain, or OU. If you merely want to remove a GPO from the list, use the Disabled check box.

To determine what other Active Directory containers are associated with a given GPO, right-click the GPO and choose Properties from the context menu. Then click the Links tab.

The No Override check box marks the selected GPO as one whose policies cannot be overridden by another GPO.

Note You can enable the No Override check box on more then one GPO. If you do so, the GPO with the higher priority wins and is applied.

The Disabled check box simply disables the GPO without removing it from the list. To remove it from the list, use the Remove button. You can also disable only the User or Computer portion of the GPO. Right-click the GPO and choose Properties from the context menu. You'll see the available options on the General tab.

The Block Policy Inheritance check box has the effect of negating all GPOs that exist higher in the hierarchy. However, it cannot block any GPOs that are enforced using the No Override check box. Those are always applied.

Note Policy settings contained within the local GPO that are not specifically overridden by Domain-based policy settings are also always applied.

To create a new policy

1. Right-click on the Policy Organizational Unit you want to create the policy for and choose Properties from the context menu. Then click the Group Policy tab.
2. Click New. You will be prompted to type a new name for the policy.
3. If you then want to configure the policy, click Edit to change the settings or click Properties to control how the policy is deployed.

All Group Policy functionality is derived from the snap-in extensions. In this exercise, we've enabled all these extensions. Using standard MMC methods, you can restrict the extension snap-ins loaded for any given snap-in. There are also Group Policy settings to restrict the use of snap-in extensions. (See the Administrative Templates\System\Group Policy node.) Use the Explain tab to learn more about the use of these policy settings. (We'll cover the Explain tab in more detail later in this chapter.)

If you have more than one GPO associated with an Active Directory container, check that the order of GPOs is correct. The higher the GPO is in the list, the higher its precedence.

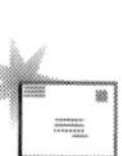

Note GPOs higher in the list are processed last, which is what gives them a higher precedence.

GPOs in the list are objects, and as such have context menus that allow you to view the properties of each GPO. You can use the context menus to obtain and modify general information about a GPO. This general information includes setting DACLs and the other site, domain, or OUs to which this GPO is linked. (We cover DACLs in the Securing Group Policy section of this chapter.)

Adding or Browsing a Group Policy Object

The Add/Browse dialog (shown in Figure 8-20) shows GPOs currently associated with domains/OUs, sites, or all GPOs regardless of their current associations (links).

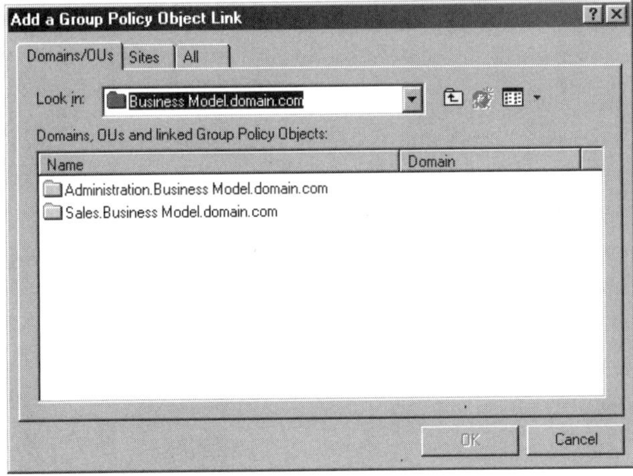

Figure 8-20. *Add/Browse dialog box.*

GPOs are stored in each domain. The Look In drop-down box allows you to select a different domain to view, and the list box on the Domains/OUs tab displays the sub-OUs and GPOs for the currently selected domain or OU. To navigate the hierarchy, double-click a sub-OU.

To add a GPO to the currently selected domain or OU, either double-click the object or select it and click OK. Alternatively, you can create a new GPO by doing the following: Click the All tab, and either right-click in the open space and choose New from the context menu, or click the Create New GPO toolbar button. (The Create New GPO toolbar button is only active in the All tab.) To create a new GPO and link it to a particular Active Directory container, use the New button on the Group Policy tab of the GPO's property sheet.

Note You can create two or more GPOs with the same name. This is by design and is possible because the GPOs are actually stored as GUIDs and the name shown is a friendly name stored in Active Directory.

The Sites tab (shown in Figure 8-21) displays all GPOs associated with the selected site. Use the drop-down list to select another site. There is no hierarchy of sites.

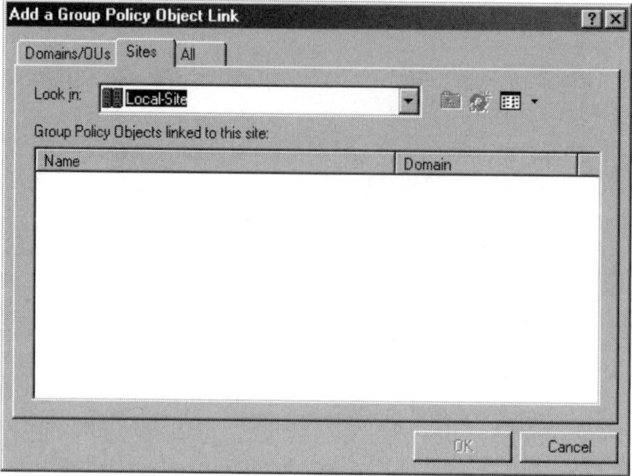

Figure 8-21. *The Sites tab.*

The All tab (shown in Figure 8-22) shows a flat list of all GPOs stored in the selected domain. This is useful when you want to select a GPO that you know by name rather than by its current association. This is also the only place to create a GPO that does not have a link to a site, domain, or OU.

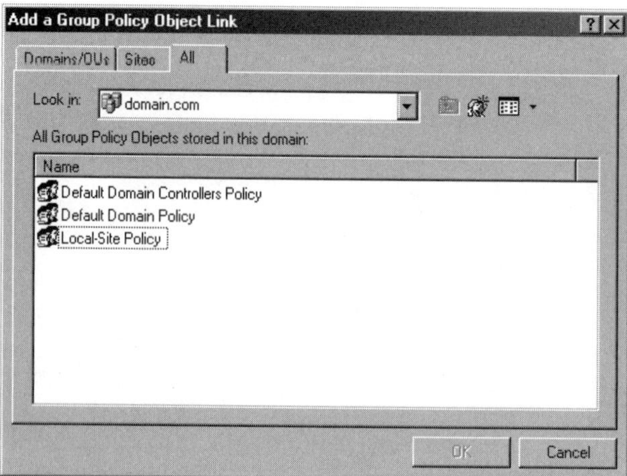

Figure 8-22. *The All tab on the Add A Group Policy Object Link dialog box.*

To create an unlinked GPO, open the Add/Browse dialog box for any site, domain, or OU. Click the All tab, click the Create New GPO toolbar button (or right-click the white space and choose New from the context menu). Name the new GPO, and then click Cancel—do not click OK. Clicking OK links the new GPO to the current site, domain, or OU. Clicking Cancel creates an unlinked GPO.

You can also use the Example.msc console we created earlier to edit GPOs.

To edit a GPO

1. If you have not already done so, log on to the domain controller as an Administrator.
2. From the Start menu, point to Programs, then Administrative Tools, then choose Example.msc (saved earlier and automatically placed here and in the recent documents list).
3. Click the plus sign next to Active Directory Users And Computers, and navigate through to the domain containing the object you want to edit. Right-click the container, choose Properties from the context menu, and then click the Group Policy tab.
4. Click Edit. This brings up the Group Policy window shown here, which you can then use to edit the required setting.

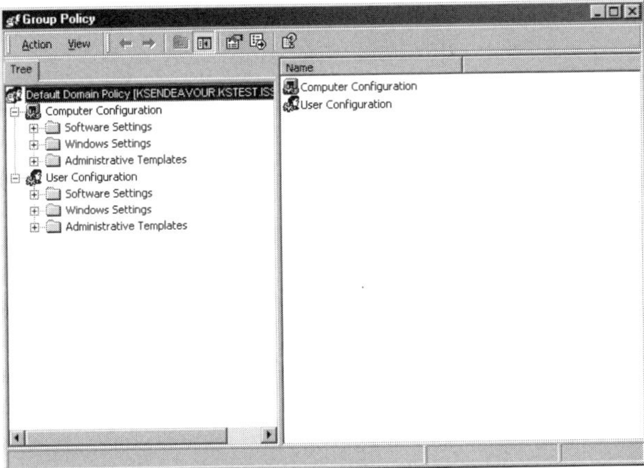

5. Navigate through the tree structure until you find the required policy setting.
6. Either double-click the setting or right-click the setting and choose Security from the context menu to bring up the Policy Setting dialog box, shown in Figure 8-23.

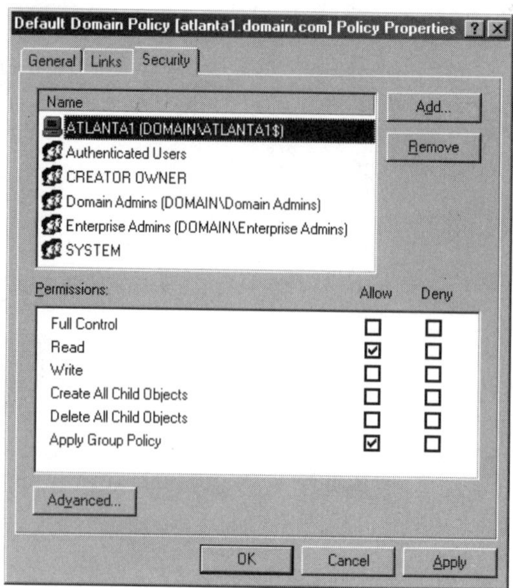

Figure 8-23. *The Security tab of the Policy Setting dialog box.*

This Policy Setting dialog box displays a series of users and groups and the permissions allocated for them. Six permissions can be allowed or denied for each user or security group. Any permission that you deny to a user or security group will overrule the permission if you've granted it elsewhere. The permissions are as follows:

- **Full Control.** This permission allows the user or group full access to the GPO, meaning they can read, write modify and delete the GPO and its settings, as well as change access permissions.
- **Read.** This permission allows the user or group to read the GPO settings but not modify them.
- **Write.** This permission allows the user or group to write settings to the GPO.
- **Create All Child Objects.** This permission permits the user to create child objects within the GPO.
- **Delete All Child Objects.** This permission permits the user to delete any child objects.
- **Apply Group Policy.** This permission allows the user or group to apply the GPO. To apply the GPO, the user or group must have the Read and Apply Group Policy permissions set to Allow.

7. Ensure that the Define This Policy setting check box is checked if applicable. (If you want to disable the setting, clear the check box.)
8. Certain GPOs might require you to enter a user or group name for the ACLs. To do this, click Add. You will be prompted to enter a user or group name. Alternatively, click on the Browse button. This brings up the Select Users, Computers Or Groups dialog box, shown in Figure 8-24.

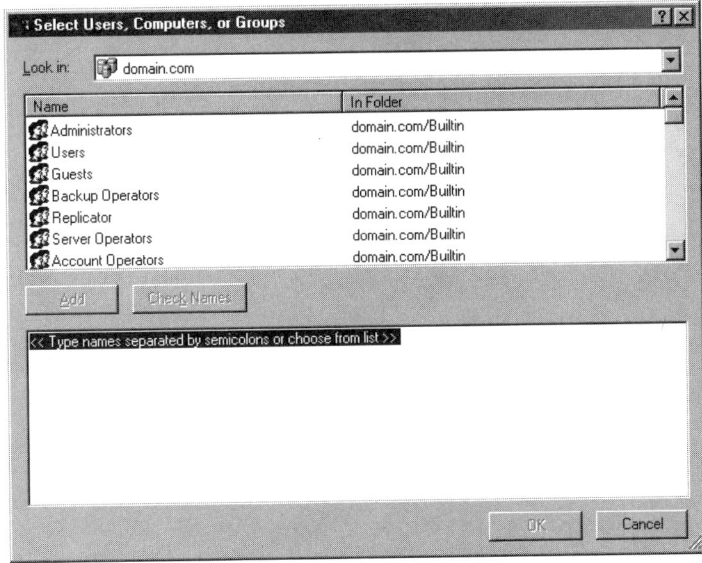

Figure 8-24. *Select Users, Computers, Or Groups dialog box.*

9. Select the domain you want to use.
10. Select the names of the users or groups.
11. Click Add.
12. If the name is not automatically underlined, click Check Names to verify the name.
13. Click OK, then click OK again.
14. To remove a user or group, select the user or group name and click Remove.
15. Once the correct users are displayed, click OK to return to the Group Policy window.

Applying Group Policies to the Example Scenario

Now that we have created the Group Policy infrastructure, we can create the policies to be applied to the OUs. We will create two new Policies for this example: Workstation Policy and Server Policy.

To create an OU policy

1. Right-click the Business Model OU and choose Properties from the context menu.
2. Click the Group Policy tab. You should see the property page shown in Figure 8-25.

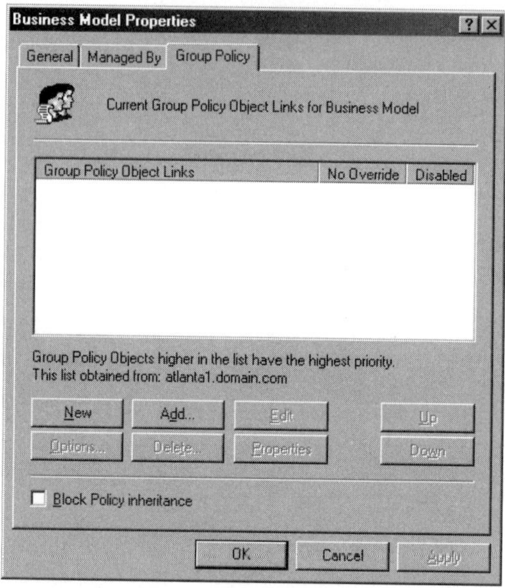

Figure 8-25. *Group Policy tab of the Properties dialog box.*

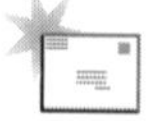

Note Since we're creating a new object, there are no Group Policy links to the object, but if you're working with an existing object, you might have existing links.

We will now create the Workstation and Server policies. We are then going to edit the group policies to include a custom text message for users who log on to the domain.

To edit group policies to include a custom message

1. Click New.
2. Enter *Workstation Policy* for the name and press Enter.
3. Click New.
4. Enter *Server Policy* for the name and press Enter.

   Two new policies have now been created, although currently they are not populated with any settings.

5. Select the Workstation Policy and click Edit.
6. Navigate to the Computer Configuration\Windows Settings\Security Settings\Local Policies\Security Option node.
7. Right-click the Message Text For Users Attempting To Log On setting and choose Security from the context menu. Make sure that the Define This Policy Setting check box is checked, and type *Workstation Policy being applied here.* into the text box shown in Figure 8-26.

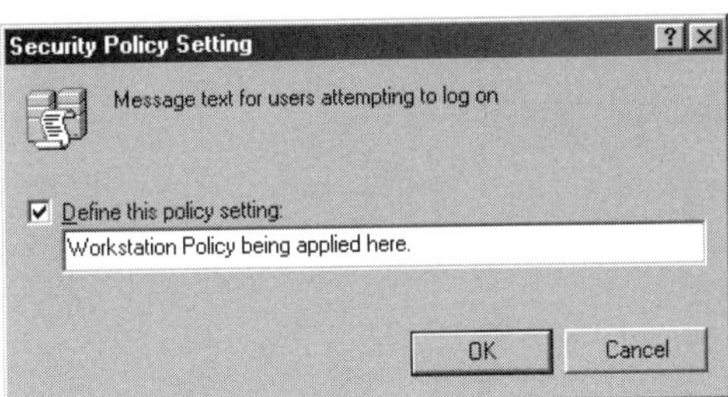

Figure 8-26. *Security Policy setting.*

8. Click OK to save the message. You should see a screen similar to Figure 8-27.

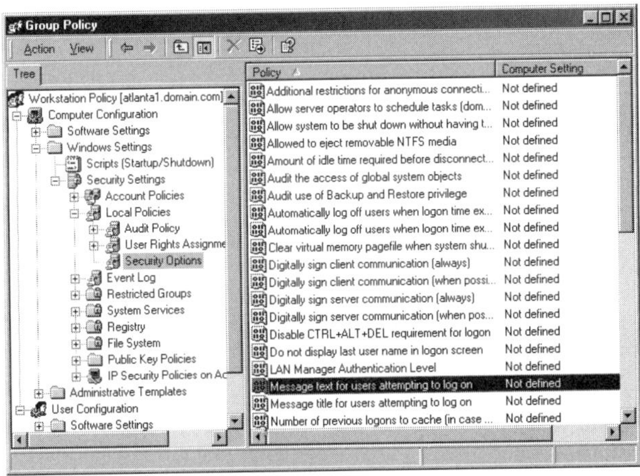

Figure 8-27. *Domain Security Policy for the OU with custom logon message.*

9. To force the system to refresh the policy, navigate to the Computer Configuration\Administrative Templates\System\Group Policy node. You'll have three options for controlling the time deployment of the Group Policy:
   - **Disable Background Refresh Of Group Policy.** This setting controls whether the group policy is applied to users' computers while they are logged on.

- **Group Policy Refresh Interval For Computers.** This setting controls the interval between the refresh of Group Policy on nondomain controller machines. The default interval is 90 minutes but the setting is disabled by default. This means that by default the Group Policy will only refresh at startup. You can also configure an offset value to prevent or minimize the chances of two machines requesting a group policy update at the same time.
- **Group Policy Refresh Interval For Domain Controllers.** This setting controls the interval between the refresh of group policy on domain controller. The default interval is 5 minutes but the setting is disabled by default. This means that by default the Group Policy will only refresh at startup. You can also configure an offset value to prevent or minimize the chances of two machines requesting a group policy update at the same time.

We are now going to configure our test machines as follows: We will set the background refresh interval for Group Policy to 2 minutes with a 1-minute offset.

10. Double-click Disable Background Refresh Of Group Policy. The dialog box shown in Figure 8-28 will appear.

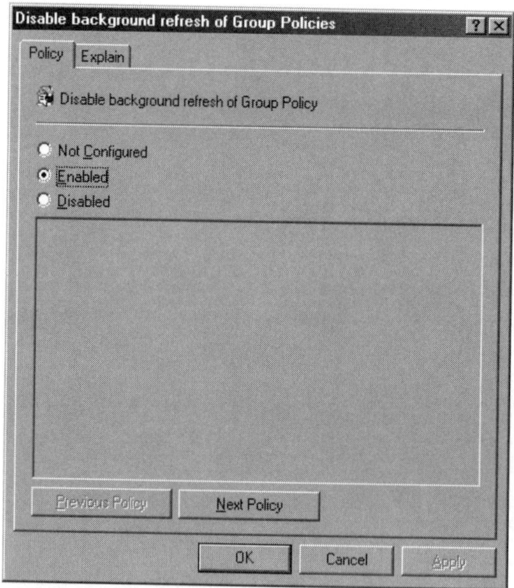

Figure 8-28. *Disable Background Refresh of Group Policy Properties dialog box.*

11. Select Disabled.
12. Click Apply.
13. Click OK.

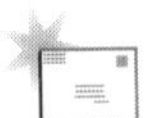

Note The Disable Background Refresh Of Group Policy setting is somewhat confusing. If the Disable Background Refresh Of Group Policy setting is enabled, the Group Policy will only refresh when the user logs on or the computer starts up. If this setting is disabled, the Group Policy will refresh using the interval specified within the Group Policy.

14. Select Group Policy Refresh Rate For Computers, set the rate to Enabled, and enter 2 minutes for the interval with 1 minute for the offset. To do this, double-click the Group Policy Refresh Interval For Computers setting. This will bring up the dialog box shown in Figure 8-29.

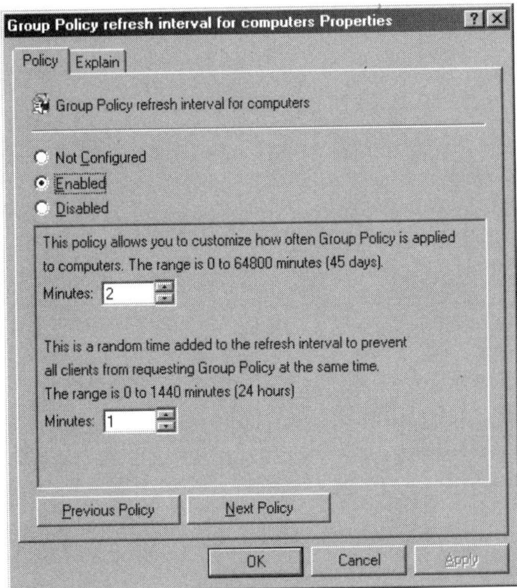

Figure 8-29. *Group Policy Refresh Interval For Computers Properties dialog box.*

15. If you are unsure about the settings that you want to apply—or you want an explanation of the options available, click on the Explain tab. An explanation similar to that shown in Figure 8-30 on the following page will appear.
16. When you've set the correct delay, click Apply.
17. Click OK.

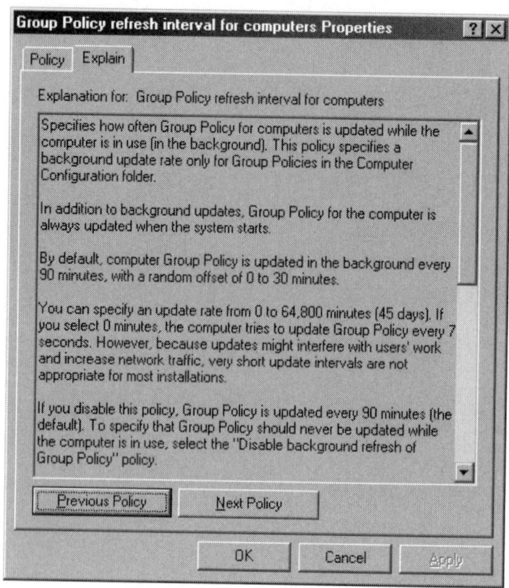

Figure 8-30. *Explanation tab for Group Policy Refresh Interval For Computers setting.*

We will now repeat the process from step 5 through step 17 for the Server Policy. However, this time we will enter *Server Policy being applied here.* for the Message Text For Users Attempting To Log On setting in \Computer Configuration\Windows Settings\Security Settings\Local Policies\Security Options. We will use the same values for the refresh rates for this policy.

Once we've configured the correct settings within the policy, we then have to control the deployment. We will do this using the security groups we created earlier. We will assign the Workstation Policy to the Workstation security group and the Server Policy to the Server security group. We will then apply both policies to the Business Model OU and allow the security groups to filter the Policy deployment to the correct machines.

To apply the Security Filter to the policies

1. Right-click the Business Model node in the MMC window and choose Properties from the context menu. Click the Group Policy tab in the Business Model Properties dialog box.
2. Right-click Workstation Policy in the list and choose Properties from the context menu to open the Workstation Policy Properties dialog box.
3. Click the Security tab, which should look like Figure 8-31.
4. Click Add to add a security group.

   The Select Users, Computers Or Groups dialog box appears.
5. Scroll down until you find Workstations, and then select it.
6. Click Add.

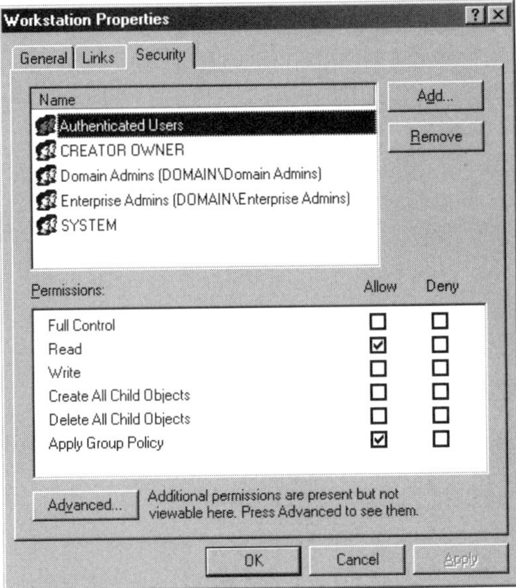

Figure 8-31. *The Security tab.*

7. Click OK.

   The Workstation Policy Properties menu should have changed to the settings shown in Figure 8-32.

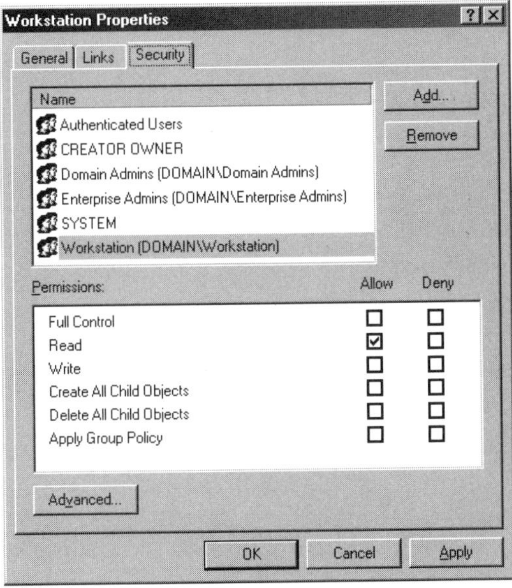

Figure 8-32. *Workstation Policy Properties.*

We now need to configure the Policy so that the security settings will be applied. To do this select Workstations and ensure that Read and Apply Group Policy are checked in the Allow column. The permissions should look like Figure 8-33.

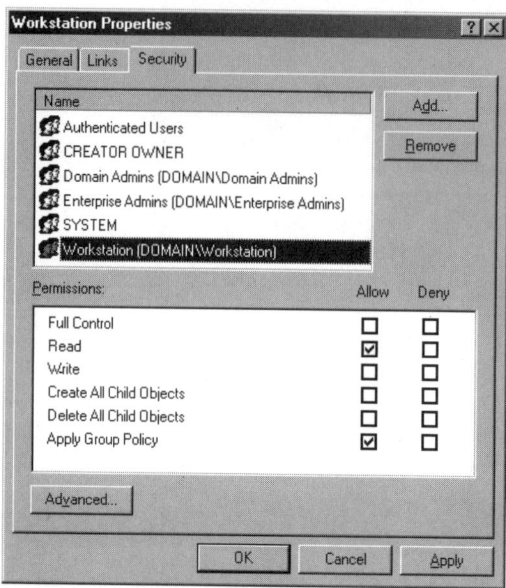

Figure 8-33. *Updated Workstation Policy properties.*

8. Click Apply and then click OK.

Note By default, the Authenticated Users setting has the Apply Group Policy box in the Allow column checked, which means that property is applied to all "computers" within the Authenticated Users group. To rectify this, clear the Apply Group Policy box in the Allow column for the Authenticated Users setting.

Now we have to set the permission for the Server Policy.

To set the permission for the Server Policy

1. Right-click Server Policy in the Business Model Properties dialog box and then choose Properties from the context menu to open the Server Policy Properties dialog box.
2. Click the Security tab, which should look like Figure 8-34.
3. Click Add to add a security group. This shows the Select Users, Computers Or Groups dialog box.
4. Scroll down until you find Servers, and select it.
5. Click Add.

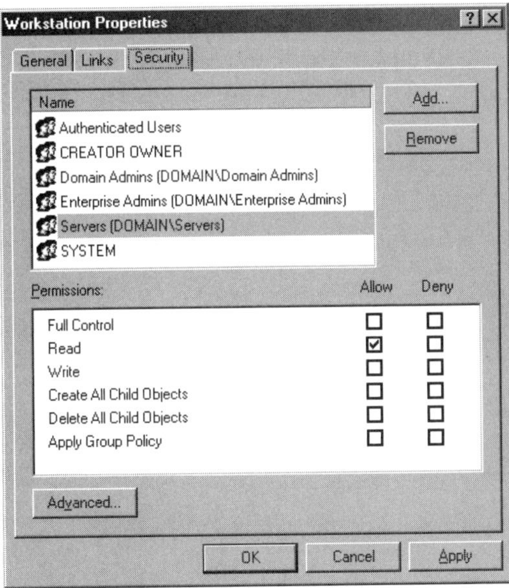

Figure 8-34. *Server Policy Properties.*

6. Click OK. The Server Policy Properties menu should have changed to those shown in Figure 8-35.

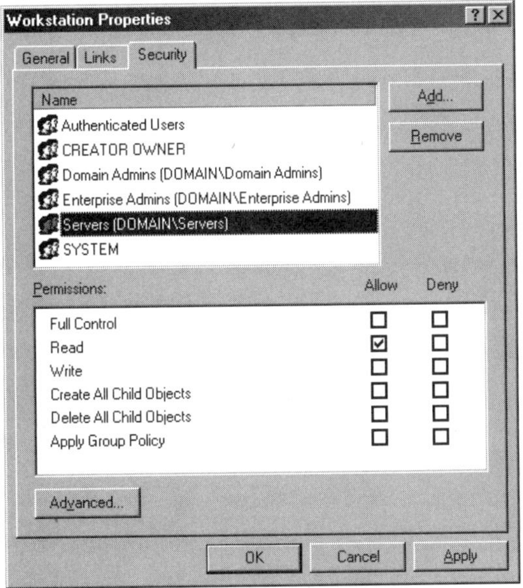

Figure 8-35. *Updated Server Policies.*

We now need to configure the Policy security settings so that it will apply the setting Select Server and ensure that Read and Apply Group Policy are both checked in the Allow column. Once again, ensure that the Authenticated User permission for Apply Group Policy is cleared in the Allow column.

7. Click Apply and then click OK.

   The Policy must then be refreshed both on the controllers and on the Local machines for the new settings to take effect.

Note Since, in the procedure above, we have not configured the User Configuration settings, we could disable these settings to enhance performance. To do so, right-click Workstation Policy on the Group Policy tab of the Business Model Properties dialog box and choose Properties from the context menu. Then click the Disable User Configuration Settings check box on the General tab of the Workstation Policy Properties dialog box and click OK. Repeat this procedure for the Server Policy.

Security Policies Tools

Windows 2000 includes tools to make the job of configuring the security within a Windows 2000 domain more manageable. The Local Security Policy Tool ships on all versions of Windows 2000. Its job is to configure the security settings within the Local Group Policy. The domain controller and domain Security Policy Tools are included to configure the security of the domain controller and the domain through the Group Policy.

Viewing Domain Security Policies

Whenever a new domain is created, a new domain security policy is created. This policy contains the following default settings:

- Password Policy
- Lockout Policy
- Kerberos Policy

To view a domain-wide security policy

1. Click on Programs from the Start menu.
2. Click on Administrative Tools, then Active Directory Users And Computers.

   This will load the Active Directory Users And Computers Snap-In into the MMC.
3. In the pane on the left of the MMC window, right-click the name of your domain and choose Properties from the context menu.

   The Properties dialog box appears.
4. Click the Group Policy tab, select Default Domain Policy, and then click Edit.

   The Group Policy Editor appears.

5. Expand the Computer Configuration node from within the Group Policy Editor and navigate to Windows Settings, Security Settings, and then Account Policies.
6. Select Password Policy and make changes to any of the settings in the right pane of the MMC window.

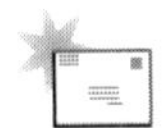

Note The password policy, lockout policy, and Kerberos policy are all configured by default in the domain GPO and therefore apply to all machines within that domain.

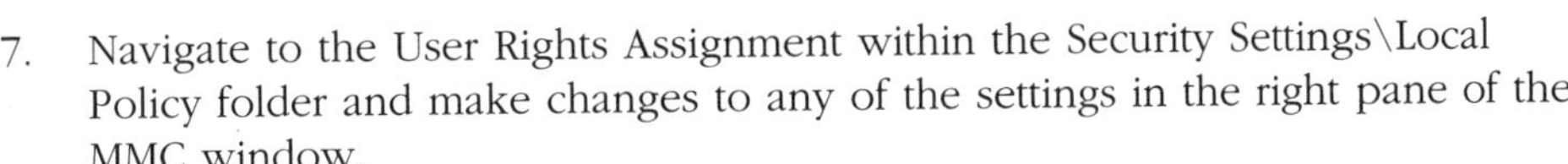

7. Navigate to the User Rights Assignment within the Security Settings\Local Policy folder and make changes to any of the settings in the right pane of the MMC window.

   Notice that none of the user rights are configured in the default domain GPO. While these user rights are defined for the machines in the domain, they are not defined within the default domain GPO. User rights for the domain controller computers are defined with the domain controllers security policy.

Viewing Domain Controller Security Policies

In this section we'll cover the default configuration for domain controllers, which is applied to all machines within the Domain Controllers OU. We will use the Group Policy Snap-In as opposed to the Active Directory Users And Computers Snap-In, and the path to the default Domain Controllers GPO.

To load the default Domain Controllers GPO

1. On the Start menu, click Run. In the Open text box type *mmc* and then click OK.
2. Choose Add/Remove Snap-In from the Console menu, and click Add.
3. From the list of Standalone Snap-Ins, select Group Policy and click Add.
4. In the select Group Policy Object dialog box, click Browse to find the Domain Controllers OU.
5. The dialog box that opens shows you all the GPOs linked to the current container. (The default GPO selected when you add the Group Policy Snap-In is the one for the local computer.)
6. In the Browse For A Group Policy Object dialog box, double-click the folder containing the GPOs for the Domain Controllers OU.
7. Select Default Domain Controllers Policy and click OK.
8. In the Select Group Policy Object dialog box, click Finish.
9. In the Add Standalone Snap-In dialog box, click Close
10. In the Add/Remove Snap-In dialog box, click OK.

You can review the security policies in the same way as the domain policy; however, there will be some differences. For example, Password policy is not defined for the default domain controller's policy as it is defined for the entire domain by the default domain policy. In addition, the User Rights Assignment is configured, whereas in the default domain policy it was left undefined.

General Points Regarding Account Policies

We can see that account policies such as those covering passwords and lockouts are defined for the entire domain in the default domain GPO. The default domain controller section covers local policies, including auditing user rights and security options for domain controllers. Settings defined in the default domain controller GPO have higher precedence than those set in the default domain GPO. Thus if a user right was altered in the default domain GPO, it would not affect domain controllers.

However, the account policy is treated slightly differently. All domain controllers within the domain receive their policy from the GPO defined at the domain node—in other words, the default domain GPO. This is true regardless of where the computer object for the domain controller is.

This scheme allows for the consistent application of account policies, which are enforced for all domain accounts. All non–domain controller computers in the domain follow the normal GPO hierarchy. By default, the workstations and member servers will enforce the account policy settings, which are configured by the default domain GPO. However, if another GPO at a lower scope overrides the default settings, those settings will take effect.

Local Security Policy

All versions of Windows 2000 provide a tool that enables you to configure the security settings of the local machine within the Group Policy. When loaded, it contains the following default nodes:

- Account Policies
- Local Policies
- Public Key Policies
- IP Security Policies On A Local Machine

All these nodes are initially configured. These relate to the Windows Settings\Security Settings node.

These settings relate to the corresponding nodes within a Security Template. The main difference for a Security Policy for a local computer is the addition of the Effective Policy setting (in the Effective Setting column), shown in Figure 8-36.

The MMC displays the settings configured in the Local Security Policy and the settings actually enforced according to the Group Policy precedence rules. Domain controllers do not have a Local Security Policy. Instead, they use the Default Domain Controller Security Policy.

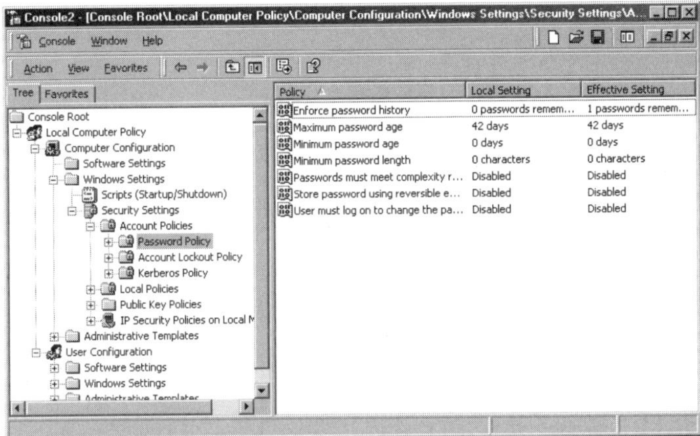

Figure 8-36. *Effective Policy settings alongside the Local Policy settings.*

Domain Controller Security Tool

The Domain Controller Security Tool contains the following security settings nodes, which are again related to the corresponding nodes with the Security Templates.

- Account Policies
- Local Policies
- Event Log
- Restricted Groups
- System Services
- Registry
- File System
- Public Key Policies
- IP Security Policies On A Local Machine

Since these settings relate only to the domain controller machine, they only display the settings for the domain controllers. They do not list the effective settings. The setting in the Policy for the domain controller is the setting applied.

Domain Security Policy Tools

As in the case of the Local Security Policy and the Domain Controller Security Tool, Domain Security Policy Tools also relate to security templates. They also cover the same security areas as the Domain Controller Security Tool. (See the preceding list.) Since these settings are applied to the domain, they do not have an effective settings option. The settings contained within this policy are applied to the whole domain, regardless of machine used. The only exception to this is the domain controller. The policy is applied to the domain controller, and then the domain controller policy is applied. In the event of any conflicts, the domain controller policy will override the domain policy.

Managing Group Policy

As you've already seen, the Group Policy can be used for local machine configuration, but it is designed for network configuration at the network and enterprise levels. To achieve this with minimum Total Cost of Ownership (TCO), certain facilities are built into the Group Policy to ease management and the securing of the Group Policy itself.

Administering Group Policy in the Network

The Group Policy is best applied across a network environment. It includes certain features to lower the administrative overhead involved.

Group Policy in Replicated Environments

In a domain containing more than one domain controller, Active Directory information takes time to propagate from one domain controller to another. In this section we'll describe the replication mechanism as it relates to Group Policy.

An administrator using the Active Directory Users And Computers Snap-In can create an OU on any domain controller. By default, GPOs are created or edited only on the domain controller that is holding the master token for primary domain controller emulator operations. An OU must be replicated to the domain controller holding the token before the GPO created there can be linked to it, allowing the Group Policy settings to be applied. These considerations are more significant if the intradomain links are slow.

Options governing the selection of a domain controller

The Group Policy View menu contains an entry named DC Options that opens the Options For Domain Controller Selection dialog box, which you can use to specify a domain controller to use for editing Group Policy. The following options are available for this dialog box:

- **The One With The Operations Master Token For The PDC Emulator.** This is the default and preferred option, and is safest from the standpoint of data safety.
- **The One Used By The Active Directory Snap-ins.** It uses the same domain controller as the utility from which the Group Policy console was invoked, if Group Policy was started in this way.
- **Use Any Available Domain Controller.** This allows the Group Policy Snap-In to choose any available domain controller. This is the least safe option, because different administrators could theoretically edit a GPO simultaneously with indeterminate outcome.

Domain controller selection set through Group Policy

In addition to the View menu option described previously, there is also a Group Policy setting for domain controller selection. This is part of the System.adm template that is loaded into the Group Policy by default. To access this setting, click the Group Policy node in the console tree (\User Configuration\Administrative Templates\System\Group Policy). In the details pane, double-click the Group Policy Domain Controller selection icon and select the appropriate setting from the drop-down list.

Group Policy over Slow Links

Group Policy is applied remotely, provided the computer is a member of the domain that the Routing And Remote Access server belongs to or is trusted by. This is true whether logging on via Routing And Remote Access or logging on with cached credentials and then establishing a Routing And Remote Access connection.

Group Policy is not applied to computers that are members of a foreign domain (a domain not containing the computer and not in a trust relationship with the computer's domain), or a workgroup. Although the connection can still be made, access to domain resources might be adversely affected because of mismatched IPSec security.

By default, registry-based polices are always applied; you cannot turn them off. Over a slow link, the security settings are applied by default. However, the other settings are not applied by default. For all but the registry settings, you can toggle the default behavior to apply or not.

A remote access connection is not necessarily a slow link, nor is a local area network (LAN) necessarily a fast link. By default, the fast or slow status of a link is based on a test ping to the server. If it takes less than 2000 milliseconds (two seconds), it's considered a fast link; if it takes longer it's considered a slow link. You can set this value using the Group Policy setting Slow Network Connection Timeout for user profiles Properties (\Group_policy_object_name\Computer Configuration\Administrative Templates\System\Logon).

Group Policy on Sites

GPOs applied to Active Directory site objects affect all computers in the site. Directory information is replicated among—and available between—all the domain controllers in the site and to any domain controllers in sites for which a site link has been established. Therefore, any GPO linked to a site is applied to all computers in that site, regardless of which domain (in the forest) contains the computers.

This behavior allows multiple domains within a forest to get the same GPO and included policies. The GPO is stored only on a single domain and must be read from that domain whenever the affected clients read their site-linked Group Policy. If child domains are set up across wide area network (WAN) boundaries, the site setup should take this into account. If not, any computers in a child domain will have to access a site-linked GPO across a WAN link, thus increasing the processing time for Group Policy.

Securing Group Policy

In this section we'll cover steps you can use to secure the Group Policy against accidental damage or tampering. Remember that these steps on their own are not sufficient to secure GPOs against a determined attack.

Default Permissions

Table 8-3 outlines the default permissions on GPOs.

Table 8-3. GPO default permissions.

Security group	Default settings
Authenticated users	Read, Apply Group Policy (AGP)
Local system	Full Control (includes AGP)
Domain administrators	Read, Write, Create Child, Delete Child, AGP
Administrators	Read, Write, Create Child, AGP

The administrator cannot delete the Default Domain Policy Group Policy Object, by default, thereby preventing the accidental deletion of this GPO, which contains important and required settings for the domain. If it truly needs to be deleted—for example, because the policies have been set in other GPOs—the Delete access control entry (ACE) must be given to the appropriate group.

Using Security Groups to Filter Group Policy

Because Group Policy can apply settings from more than one GPO to a site, domain, or OU, you can add GPOs that are either associated with other Active Directory containers or GPOs that are currently unlinked. You can also declare the priority for how these GPOs affect the directory object that they are applied to. In Windows 2000, computers can belong to security groups, and administrators can use security groups to further refine which computers and users a particular GPO influences. Administrators can filter the effect of any GPO on computers that are members of specified security groups. This filtering occurs using the standard ACL Editor. Administrators can also use the ACL Editor to delegate who can modify the GPO.

Delegating Control of Group Policy

To delegate control of Group Policy, first create and save Group Policy Microsoft Management Console (.msc) files. Next, determine which users and groups have access permissions to the GPO and the site, domain, and OU.

Setting Read and Write Permission for Group Policy

The security ACL Editor tab for a GPO is hosted in that GPO's Properties form. To access the ACL Editor, right-click the root node of Group Policy and choose Properties from the context menu, and then click the Security tab. You use the Security property page to set permissions on a selected GPO. These permissions allow or deny specified groups access to the GPO.

Your organization's top network administrators (members of the Domain Administrators group) can also use the ACL Editor to determine which administrator groups can modify policies in GPOs. To do this, the network administrator can define groups of administrators (for example, Accounting Administrators), and then provide them with read/write access to selected GPOs. In this way, the network administrator can delegate control of the GPO policies.

Note A user or administrator who does not have write access (but does have Read access) to a GPO cannot use the Group Policy Snap-In to see the settings that it contains. Every extension to Group Policy assumes that it has write access to the GPO storage locations. Therefore, Group Policy does not open a GPO when the current user does not have write access to it.

Policy for Microsoft Management Console

Several Group Policy settings provided in System.adm govern use of the MMC. This is significant—saving previously configured consoles is a way to delegate administrative rights. To set an administrative Group Policy setting that governs use of an extension in an MMC console, select the required Group Policy in the Console Root of the Group Policy MMC Snap-In. Navigate to the Administrative Templates, Group Policy leaf, as shown in Figure 8-37, and double-click each extension to Group Policy for which you want to set a restriction.

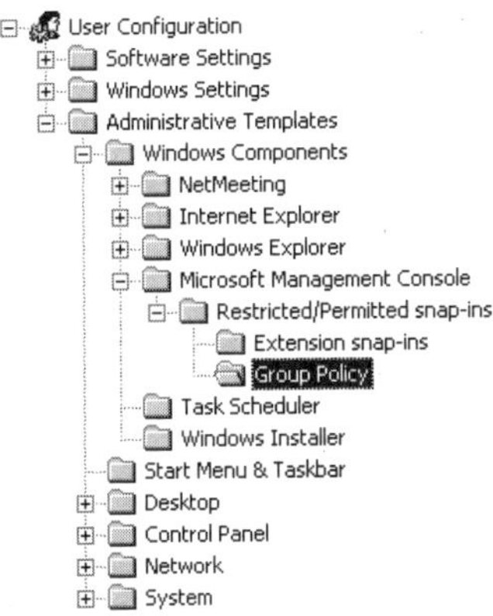

Figure 8-37. *Controlling use of extensions in an MMC Console.*

Migration Issues

It is likely that at some point during its lifecycle your corporate network will operate in mixed-domain mode, in which the network is composed of Windows NT 4.0 or legacy boxes as well as Windows 2000 workstations or servers. It is important that Windows 2000 be able to handle a variety of client machines for the mixed-domain networks. We can also reverse the situation—Windows 2000 computers can form part of a Windows NT 4.0 domain. In this situation, although a limited amount of Group Policy can be introduced to the Windows 2000 machines, the Windows 2000 machines would require a separate security configuration and policy to ensure maximum security. Since Windows NT 4.0 does not support Active Directory, any policy created for the Windows 2000 machines would have to be local in nature. The easiest way to configure the security on the Windows 2000 machines would then be through the use of scripts and the Security Configuration Tool Set's command line tool, secedit.exe. We'll discuss this procedure in more detail in Chapter 9, "Security Configuration and Monitoring."

Client Operating Systems

Let's take a look at how the different client operating systems interact with Windows 2000.

- **Windows 2000 Server.** Computers running Windows 2000 Server can either be ordinary member servers of Active Directory or domain controllers. Group Policy fully supports both.
- **Windows 2000 Professional.** Group Policy fully supports client computers running Windows 2000 Professional.
- **Windows NT 4.0 Workstation and Server.** These clients continue to be fully supported by Windows NT 4.0 System Policy, for which the System Policy Editor (Poledit.exe) is provided. The administrator uses Poledit.exe to write Windows NT 4.0–style .adm files. Windows NT 4.0 does not use Active Directory. Because computers running Windows NT 4.0 do not have local GPOs, Group Policy does not apply.
- **Windows 95 and Windows 98.** Windows 95/98 clients should run System Policy Editor (Poledit.exe) on the local computer. This ensures that the Config.pol file created will be compatible with those operating systems. Copy the resultant Config.pol file to the %SYSTEMROOT%\SysVol folder of the Windows 2000 Server domain controller. Group Policy does not apply.
- **Windows NT 3.51, Windows 3.1, and MS-DOS.** Group Policy does not apply to these operating systems.

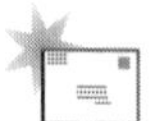

Note Exactly one local GPO exists on each computer running Windows 2000, and the User Configuration settings it contains are the same for each user of that computer. Administrators can handle multiple user configurations using policy on a computer running Windows 2000 that is subject to only a single GPO because it is not part of a Windows 2000 domain (for example, a standalone computer). To do so, the administrator uses System Policy through System Policy Editor. Poledit.exe is run on the local computer to create a correctly formatted .pol file. User profiles provide individually configured desktops for individual users if neither System Policy nor Group Policy is used.

The Role of Administrative Templates

Windows 2000 continues the tradition of using Administrative Templates with the .adm filename extension, as they did in Windows NT 4.0. However, the roles for which they are used are somewhat different.

In previous versions of Windows, Administrative Templates were ANSI-encoded text files. They created a namespace within System Policy Editor for convenient editing of the profiles for each user. The registry is organized in a treelike hierarchical structure made up of keys and subkeys, hives, and value entries. Administrative Templates provided a friendlier GUI than the bundled Microsoft Registry Editor (Regedit.exe). They also added a degree of safety by only exposing the keys used in the .adm file, as opposed to Regedit.exe and Regedt32.exe, which expose all keys and provide no protection for accidental alteration of the keys.

Windows 2000 also includes the .adm files listed earlier in this chapter. Additional .adm files can also be created with the new version of the .adm language as a superset of the previous version. This means that while older templates can create and populate a user interface in Group Policy, you cannot use new templates to create user interfaces in the Windows NT 4.0 System Policy Editor.

The Role of System Policy Editor

While the Group Policy MMC Snap-In has largely replaced the System Policy Editor (Poledit.exe), the latter is still useful under certain circumstances:

When managing computers running Windows 95 or Windows 98, you must run the Windows 2000 version of the System Policy Editor locally to create Config.pol files compatible with the local operating system.

You can also use System Policy Editor to manage computers running Windows NT 4.0 Workstation and Windows NT 4.0 Server. These computers also need their own style of .pol file: NTConfig.pol.

A standalone computer running Windows 2000 is not subject to nonlocal Group Policy by way of Active Directory. The only Group Policy that applies to such a computer is Local Group Policy, which contains settings for only one user. To provide settings for multiple users, use System Policy Editor to write a Registry.pol file. Only the Windows 2000 version of System Policy Editor is compatible with Windows 2000.

Although earlier versions of System Policy Editor worked only with ASCII-encoded .adm files, the Windows 2000 version also supports Unicode-encoded .adm files.

Windows NT 4.0 System Policies

If a Windows NT 4.0 client computer managed by a Windows 2000 server is upgraded to Windows 2000, the computer receives only Computer Configuration Group Policy and not Windows NT 4.0 machine System Policy. The policy received by the user who logs on will be User Configuration Group Policy if the user account is in Active Directory. If a Windows NT 4.0 domain controller manages the user account, the user gets Windows NT 4.0 user System Policy.

Policies included with Windows 2000 only set registry keys and values in one of following four reserved trees:

- HKLM\Software\Policies
- HKCU\Software\Policies
- HKLM\Software\Microsoft\Windows\CurrentVersion\Policies
- HKCU\Software\Microsoft\Windows\CurrentVersion\Policies

The first two are preferred. All four trees are secure, and cannot be modified by a user who is not an administrator. When Group Policy changes for any reason, these trees are wiped clean and the new policies are then rewritten.

Windows NT 4.0 policies do not respect these special trees and can write to any part of the registry. After such a policy is applied, it persists until the value is intentionally reversed, either by a counteracting Windows NT 4.0–style policy or by editing the registry.

Summary

This chapter introduced the Group Policy framework to set user and computer settings across Active Directory. Group Policy provides a means for centralized and decentralized system configuration, as well a way to delegate administrative rights to localized teams of administrators.

The next chapter will cover the Security Configuration Tool Set and how you can use it to create customized security configurations that you can then import into GPOs for distribution across Active Directory.

Chapter 9
Security Configuration and Monitoring

Windows NT has always provided a range of tools to manage the various security features of the operating system. However, each particular feature had its own tool. For example, to establish an auditing policy, you first had to enable auditing via the User Manager For Domains tool, and then enter the Event Viewer to set the audit behavior for each of the security, system, and application logs. Similarly, you used a different tool to set file system security; the tool required you to set security on the registry. The tools were even invoked in completely different ways (a legacy from Windows NT Version 3.5*x*). The introduction of many additional security features in Windows 2000 raised the possibility that even more tools would be required.

With Windows 2000, Microsoft has attempted to rationalize the tools required to manage the security of the system and for the first time has tried to provide additional functionality to simplify the construction and deployment of appropriate security configurations across multiple systems. The tools are scalable, to a degree, and you can apply the security policies you create to individual systems or deploy them via Group Policy objects (GPOs) across domains or organizational units (OUs). You can also export the policies from one domain and import them into another. Therefore, once you centrally develop a particular policy, you can roll it out throughout the enterprise.

The rapid expansion of the Internet and the increasing trend for users to access corporate resources via Remote Access Service (RAS), coupled with the increase in telecommuting, makes the job of administering security across an enterprise increasingly difficult. Historically, as companies expanded and spread their offices globally, the security administration required to manage and monitor the systems grew proportionally. What was needed was a method of defining a security policy for an enterprise and then applying it from a centralized location throughout the organization to all employees, regardless of their method of connection to the corporate network or their physical location. Windows NT offered no built-in tools to enable this, nor did any third-party product adequately provide this functionality.

Windows 2000 introduces the Security Configuration Tool Set, which together with GPOs allows you to centrally define one or more security policies and then automatically apply them selectively across the enterprise. The Security Configuration Tool Set also provides functionality to analyze a given system's security configuration against that defined in a specified security policy.

With the inclusion of a command-line tool, this functionality can be taken further to allow the generation of automated scripts that include security configuration or analysis options. This enables the administrator to schedule security tasks for quiet periods, thereby minimizing network disruptions, and also allows periodic redistribution of the policy to all Windows 2000 computers on the network via tools such as Microsoft Systems Management Server if group policy is not used.

The Security Configuration Tool Set consists of a series of Microsoft Management Console (MMC) snap-ins and a command-line tool designed to provide a central interface for security-related administrative tasks, enabling administrators to simplify and centralize security configuration management and to perform security analysis tasks when necessary. To this end, the Security Configuration Tool Set allows the configuration and analysis of the security areas we'll discuss in this chapter.

The Security Configuration Tool Set

The Security Configuration Tool Set allows the configuration and analysis of the following security areas:

- **Account Policies.** These include password policy, lockout policy, and domain Kerberos Policy.
- **Local Policies.** These include audit policy, user-rights assignment, and numerous security-relevant operational parameters.
- **Event Logs.** These enable settings for the Event Logs.
- **Restricted Groups.** These control membership of specific groups that have sensitive capabilities assigned to them (for example, administrators and backup operators).
- **System Services.** This enables configuration of security for different services that have been installed, including startup options, and access control on these services.
- **System Registry.** This enables security settings for registry keys.
- **File System Store.** This enables the configuration of security for local system file volumes and directory trees.

Security settings are stored in text-based .inf template files; the Tool Set's configuration engine parses the information they contain. This architecture supports the creation of new sections, enabling you to specify and analyze new areas of security as the system evolves. Predefined security templates are included as a starting point for customized security policies. Microsoft has designed the Security Configuration Tool Set to be extendable, adding extensions either as new areas of configuration and analysis or as new attributes within existing areas.

Microsoft designed the Security Configuration Tool Set to reduce costs associated with security administration. As such, it must be easy to learn and use. To that end, the graphical user interface (GUI) is uniform across the Tool Set and uses the standardized context menus and views supported by the MMC.

Security Configuration Tool Set Components

The Security Configuration Tool Set consists of the following components, shown in Figure 9-1 on the following page. These components form the core engine of the Security Configuration Tool Set, which runs on every Windows 2000–based system and is responsible for all security configuration and analysis functionality.

- **Security Templates Snap-In.** This MMC snap-in enables you to create, edit, and save security configurations to a security template. The template can later be imported into the Security Configuration And Analysis Snap-In.
- **Security Configuration And Analysis Snap-In.** This MMC snap-in tool allows you to import one or more security templates into a database. You can then apply this database to the computer or use it to analyze the current system configuration against the composite configuration stored in the database.
- **Security Settings extension to the Group Policy editor.** This snap-in tool extends the Group Policy editor (the Group Policy snap-in) and allows you to define security configurations as part of a GPO. You can then assign these GPOs to a specific computer, domain, or other OU scope described in Active Directory, so that the changes can be propagated to all computers within that scope. These machines then import the policy to the local computer-policy database. Policy propagation is done periodically to ensure that the system adheres to the designated policy.
- **Secedit.exe command-line tool.** This command-line tool allows you to perform configuration and analysis functions without a GUI.

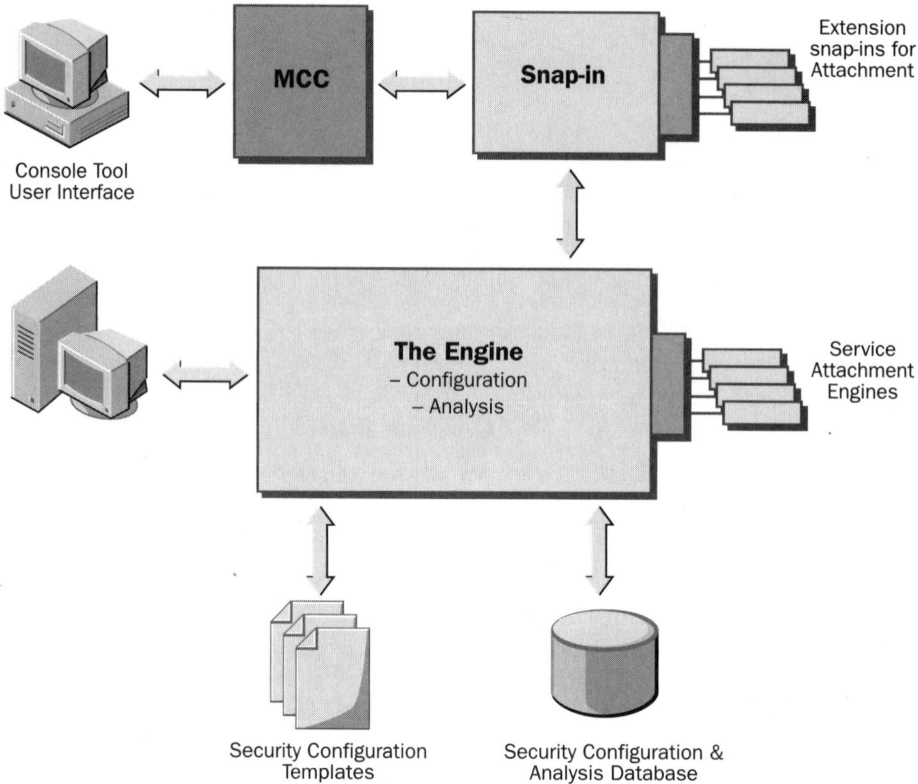

Figure 9-1. *Security Configuration Tool Set architecture.*

Security Configuration Tool Set User Interfaces

As you've just learned, the Security Configuration Tool Set is a set of MMC snap-ins and a command-line utility. The GUI supports the functions described in this section.

Defining Security Templates

The Security Templates Snap-In, shown in Figure 9-2, enables you to define, edit, and save security templates. Since you save the templates as text-based files, you can read them using any text-based editor. However, Microsoft does not recommend using a text editor to alter these templates, as you could inadvertently change the format of the file, rendering it unable to be parsed by the Security Configuration Service Engine.

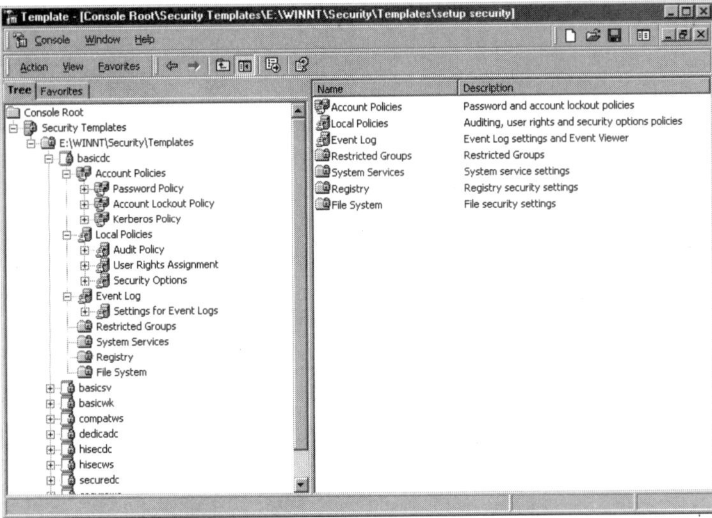

Figure 9-2. *Security Templates Snap-In.*

Configuring System Security

To configure a Windows 2000 system, use one of the options described in this section.

Security Settings Extension to the Group Policy Editor

You can use the Security Settings extension to Group Policy to apply entire security policies to machines contained in the Active Directory. You can also use it to set specific security settings in real time on individual machines. The Security Configuration Engine resolves any conflicts between domain-level and local policies using the precedence rules defined by Group Policy. Specifically, domain-level security policies always override local security policies. The OU, which contains a machine, has the highest precedence of all domain-level policies. (See Chapter 8, "Group Policy," for further details.) Two default security policies are created for every Active Directory–based domain: the default domain policy and the default domain controller's policy. Shortcuts to both of these policies are available via the Administrative Tools Start Menu on any domain controller machine.

To create a new security policy and associate it with an Active Directory container, use the Active Directory Users And Computers Snap-In: Right-click on the scope you are interested in, choose Properties from the context menu, and then click the Group Policy tab. The same security areas available in the Security Templates Snap-In are available under the Computer Configuration\Windows Settings\Security Settings node. Thus you can also import a template created via the Security Templates Snap-In directly into the GPO.

To modify specific security settings on an individual machine interactively, start the Group Policy editor, open the Computer Configuration node, open the Windows Settings node, and then open the Security Settings node, as shown in Figure 9-3. This allows you to modify the local security policy. The local security policy is then combined with the applicable domain-level policies, conflicts are resolved, and the effective policy is applied to the local machine. A local security policy shortcut is also available on the Administrative Tools Start menu if you enable the Display Administrative Tools settings for the Start menu properties.

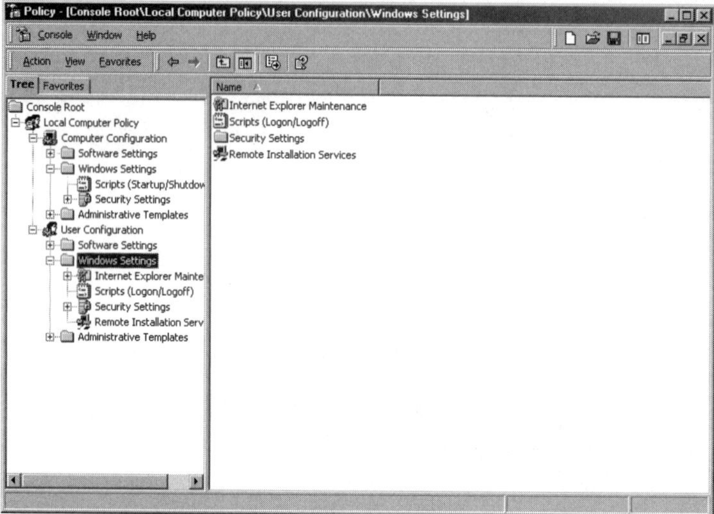

Figure 9-3. *Security Settings extension for Group Policy editor.*

Security Configuration And Analysis Snap-In

The Security Configuration And Analysis Snap-In, shown in Figure 9-4, is useful for configuring an individual machine with the security settings defined in one or more security templates. This is accomplished by importing the desired templates into a database, then using that database to configure the system. You can also perform a security analysis against the database to reveal mismatches between the database settings and the actual system settings.

Secedit Command-Line Tool

The command-line tool shown in Figure 9-5 allows you to perform security configuration and analysis operations without a GUI. This is useful when scheduling or scripting operations, or when used in combination with other tools—such as remote console environments—or with other management infrastructures, such as Microsoft Systems Management Server.

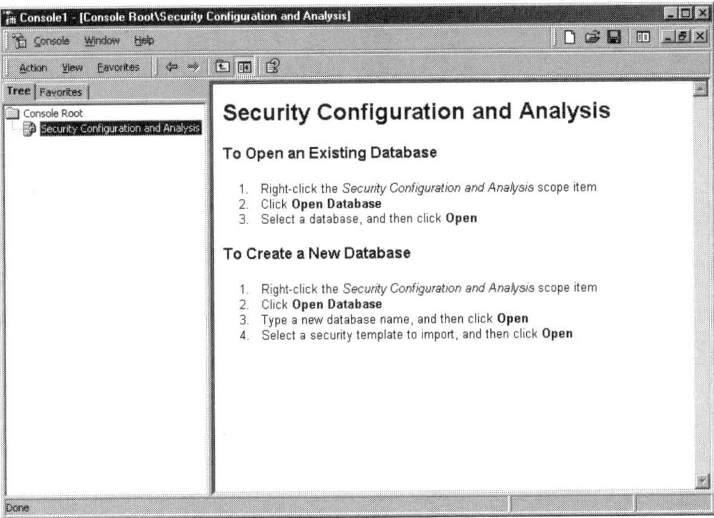

Figure 9-4. *Security Configuration And Analysis Snap-In.*

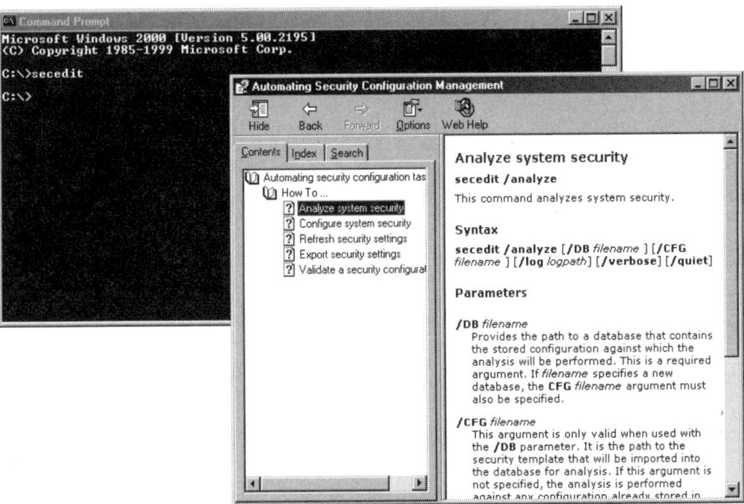

Figure 9-5. *The command-line tool Secedit.exe.*

Analyzing System Security

To analyze system security, either click Analyze on the context menu within the Security Configuration And Analysis Snap-In or use Secedit.exe.

Viewing Analysis Data

The Security Configuration And Analysis Snap-In allows the user to view security analysis information in each security area. Baseline settings (defined in a database) are displayed alongside current system settings, with any mismatches highlighted. This can serve to highlight changes that a proposed security policy would impart to a given system if it were applied, or it can highlight violations to a policy already in use. You can adjust database settings based on the analysis results, if necessary, and apply them to the system if desired.

Security Templates, Databases, and Policies

The Security Configuration Service relies on the presence of security configurations, security databases, and security templates to define system and OU security. In this section we'll try to clear up any confusion surrounding these topics. We'll also explain their properties and how they are stored within a system.

Security Templates

Security templates are text-based files that include security settings for any or all of the security areas listed here and shown in Figure 9-6.

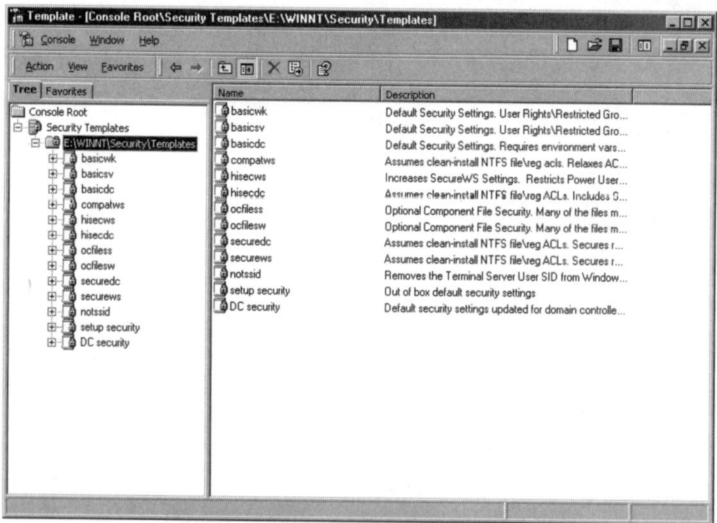

Figure 9-6. *Predefined security templates.*

- **Account Policies.** These policies cover areas of security regarding users and their accounts. Domain controllers receive their account policies from the default domain policy even if there are account policies specified for the Domain

Controllers OU. This is because a domain can have only one account policy for all domain accounts, and that domain policy is enforced by the domain controllers in the domain. Account Policies include the following areas:

- **Password Policy.** This policy includes restrictions on password length, age, uniqueness, and so on. You can modify this policy to meet the specific requirements of your organization. You can also set requirements for users to use complex passwords and prevent the reuse of passwords, or variants of simple passwords.
- **Account Lockout Policy.** This policy gives the rules on Account Lockout, including duration, reset by time or administrator, and so on. You can set users' accounts to lock out after a certain number of failed logon attempts. You can also specify the duration of lockout.
- **Kerberos Policy.** This policy governs the security settings for Kerberos authentication, such as settings for Kerberos ticket lifetimes. Kerberos settings are domain-wide settings enforced by domain controllers; thus the Kerberos settings are defined in the default domain controller GPO.

- **Local Policies.** These include the following security areas:
  - **Audit Policy.** Windows 2000 can record a variety of security events ranging from system-wide events to local file access. This area contains the overall audit policy settings. Specific audit settings are configured in other areas.
  - **User Rights Assignment.** You can specify rights for user accounts and security groups through these settings, including the rights for users and groups to perform a variety of security-related tasks.
  - **Security Options.** A wide range of security options are controlled via specific registry keys and govern such diverse issues as the welcome dialog message, Server Message Block signing, and the right to eject removable NTFS-formatted media.
- **Event Log.** This governs the configuration of the event logs, including settings such as maximum log size and log overwriting policy.
- **Restricted Groups.** This allows administrators to control who should and should not belong to a given group. When a restricted group policy is applied to a machine, only the restricted groups that are local to that machine will be configured.
- **System Services.** This controls the startup mode for each service (auto, manual, or disabled), together with the level of access available to users. This defines whether a user can start, stop, pause, or delete a service, or is restricted to read or write access only. You can also set audit levels for the services to aid in detecting intruders.
- **Registry.** This allows you to configure the permissions granted to registry keys. It can also specify the types of accesses for which auditing is desired.

- **File System.** This allows configuration of the permissions granted to file system objects (folders, subfolders, and files); it can also specify the types of accesses for which auditing is desired.

Predefined Security Templates

Windows 2000 includes several predefined security templates. These are split into two categories: basic and incremental templates. We do not recommend that you apply these templates to production-environment computers without first verifying that the correct level of system and network functionality will be retained following the application.

Basic Templates

Basic templates specify default Windows 2000 security settings for all security areas with the exception of user rights and groups, and are designed to reverse changes to system security that result in unwanted system behavior.

- **Basicwk.inf** (for computers running Windows 2000 Professional)
- **Basicsv.inf** (for computers running Windows 2000 Server)
- **Basicdc.inf** (for domain controllers running Windows 2000 Server)
- **OCFiless.inf** (for standalone or member servers—not domain controllers)
- **OCFilesw.inf** (for computers running Windows 2000 Professional)

User rights and group modifications are not affected, as these are often modified by applications to allow successful execution of the applications by different levels of users. It is not the intent of the basic templates to undo such changes. The OCFiles templates contain default security settings for all optional component files that might or might not be installed during or after setup. Since not all of the files specified in the OCFiles templates can exist on a given system, you might receive numerous warning messages in the log file generated by the configuration. This merely indicates that a file did not exist and thus security could not be set on it.

Incremental Templates

Windows 2000 also includes incremental templates to modify default security settings. This means that these templates are intended for machines already running the default security settings. They do not include the default settings plus the modifications.

Compatws.inf

This template is for workstations or servers. The default Windows 2000 access permissions are assigned to three primary groups: Users, Power Users, and Administrators. The default permissions for the Users group have been considerably tightened over previous versions of Windows NT, providing for a more secure operating system environment. However, this will result in noncertified applications (including most legacy applications) failing to operate correctly. To run most noncertified applications on Windows 2000, end users will need to either be members of the Power Users group, or you'll have to loosen the permissions for the Users group. This "compatible" template loosens up the permissions for the Users group in a manner consistent with the requirements of most legacy applications. It is supplied for those customers who do not want their end users to be members of the Power Users group, as these users have slightly more permissions than members of the Windows NT 4.0 Users group had. Certified applications are required to run successfully under a User context and thus allow customers to secure their systems without sacrificing application compatibility.

Securews.inf and Securedc.inf

Securews.inf (for workstations and servers) and Securedc.inf (for domain controllers) provide increased security for areas of the operating system not covered by the default access permissions, including increased security settings for Account policy, Auditing, and some well-known security-relevant registry keys. Access control lists (ACLs) are not modified by the secure configurations, as they assume that default Windows 2000 security settings are in place and thus the secure configurations simply remove all members of the Power Users group.

Hisecws.inf and Hisecdc.inf

Hisecws.inf (for workstations and servers) and Hisecdc.inf (for domain controllers) provide increased security over the secure configuration, primarily for parameters that affect network communication protocols. As such, you should use this template only in pure Windows 2000 environments, and you should apply it to all machines in that environment. The high-security template also changes the access permissions for the Power User group to be equivalent to that of the Users group. This essentially makes any end users either Users or Administrators.

Security Databases

The Security Configuration Engine is database-driven. It is not aware of the existence of security templates. Thus, you must import template information into a database before the Security Configuration Engine can configure or analyze a system. The Security Configuration And Analysis Snap-In allows you to create a database and then import any number of templates into it prior to performing a configuration or an analysis. When performing an analysis, you can modify the database settings while viewing the analyzed results. This process updates the database, which can subsequently be applied to the system or exported back to a template. One special database (%windir%\security\database\secedit.sdb) is used to store the Local Security Policy, as we'll explain in the next section.

Security Policies

There are essentially two types of security policies: local security policies and domain-level security policies. Local security policies cover the Account Policies security area—which contains password and lockout settings—and the Local Policies security area, which contains Audit Policy, User Rights, and Security Options nodes. The local security policy settings are maintained in a database (%windir%\security\database\ secedit.sdb) on each Windows 2000 machine. Domain-level security policies can contain settings for all security areas and are defined in GPOs associated with containers in Active Directory. Domain-level security policies apply to all machines contained within the scope of the container; any domain-level security policy setting will override a conflicting local security policy setting, in accordance with Group Policy precedence rules.

You can see this hierarchy when viewing the security settings in the local Group Policy editor. You'll see that there are two columns: one for the local policy setting and one for the effective policy setting. If the effective policy setting is different from the local policy setting, it indicates that there is a domain-level security policy setting for that particular security parameter. Domain-level security policies are refreshed every time the machine is booted and approximately every 90 minutes thereafter. *Refreshed* means that the combined local and domain-level security policies are applied only if the domain-level security policy has changed since last applied. Additionally, the combined policy is computed and applied every time a change is made to the local security policy via the local Group Policy editor. Finally, the overall security policy is applied every 16 hours, whether or not there has been a domain-level or local security policy change. This covers situations in which local administrators modify security settings not covered by the local security policy (for example, file system ACLs) that might have domain-level security policy settings. You can generate a policy refresh using the command-line tool by including an option to force a policy propagation even when domain-level security policy has not changed. Accomplish this with the Secedit.exe command-line tool with the /refreshpolicy switch and the optional /enforce switch.

The Security Templates Snap-In

The Security Templates Snap-In is the central MMC snap-in for viewing, defining, and modifying existing security templates or creating new ones.

The Security Templates Snap-In allows you to create a text-based template file that contains security settings for all of the areas supported by the Security Configuration Tool Set. These template files are used to configure or analyze security using other tools, including the following:

- Importing a template file into the Security Settings extension for Group Policy to configure local, domain, or OU policy.
- Importing a template file into a Security Configuration And Analysis database.
- Specifying the template and database when using the Secedit.exe command-line tool to configure or analyze a system.

Loading the Security Templates Snap-In

The Security Templates Snap-In is the GUI used to create these template files; it is loaded into the MMC.

To install the Security Templates Snap-In

1. Choose Run from the Start menu, and then type *MMC* in the Open text box of the Run dialog box.
2. Choose Add/Remove Snap-In from the Console menu of the MMC.
3. Click Add in the Add\Remove Snap-In dialog box.
4. Select Security Templates in the list of available Standalone Snap-ins in the Add/Remove Snap-In dialog box.
5. Click Add, and then click Close.
6. Click OK.
7. Expand the Security Templates node.
8. Expand %systemroot%\Security\Templates.

Creating a New Template

You can create a new template with the same security areas as the other existing templates. However, none of the attributes will have defined settings.

To create a new template

1. Click on the %systemroot%\Security\Templates node.
2. Choose New Template from the Action menu.
3. Enter the name for the new template (*MySecure.inf*) and a description.
4. Click OK.

Modifying an Existing Template

Windows 2000 includes a range of default templates that you can use as the basis for a security configuration. You will most likely need to modify them to meet your particular organization's requirements. You can modify the templates using the Security Templates Snap-In.

Caution We don't recommend that you modify templates using a text editor: this can result in a loss of formatting and subsequently could result in the Security Configuration Service being unable to parse the templates' structure.

To modify an existing setting within the template, first locate the required setting or settings in the tree and then carry out the following steps. (In this example, we're going to modify the Allow To Eject Removable NTFS Media setting in the Local Policy\SecurityOptions node.) Figure 9-7 shows the original setting.

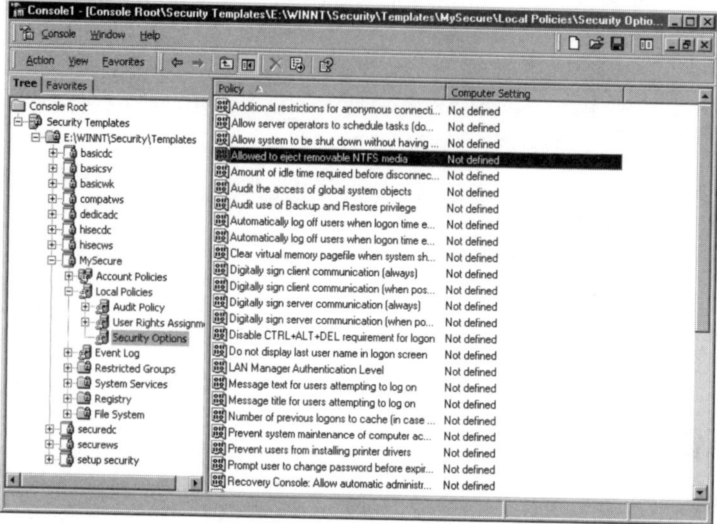

Figure 9-7. *MySecure Template before modification.*

To modify an existing setting

1. Double-click the setting you want to change.
2. Set or clear the Define This Policy Setting In The Template check box to change the setting.
3. Click OK.

The pane will then show the updated settings.

To save the new template

1. Either right-click the template name (MySecure.inf) in the left-hand pane and choose Save As from the context menu or click on the template name and choose Save As from the Action menu.
2. Enter a new name and then click Save.

This will then save the changes made to the template—as shown in Figure 9-8—enabling it to be exported to other machines.

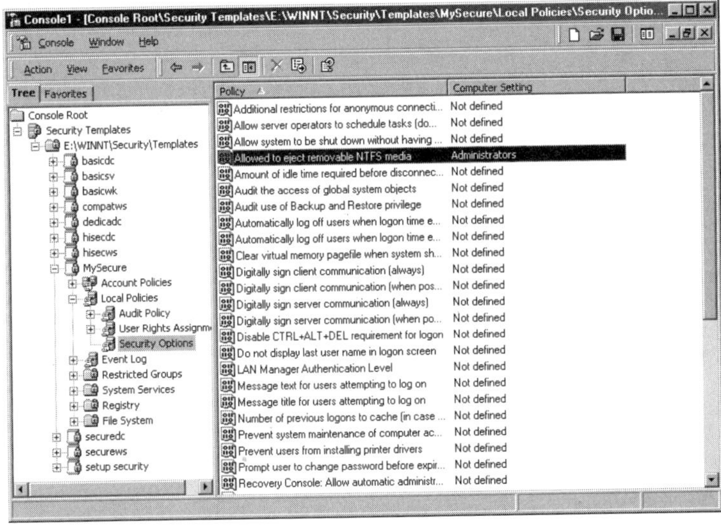

Figure 9-8. *MySecure template after modification.*

Modifying Account Policies

To modify any of the account policy settings, expand the Account Policy settings node. In the left-hand pane select either Password Policy, Account Lockout, or Kerberos Policy. This will display a list of settings in the right-hand pane. Figure 9-9 shows the Account Policy settings.

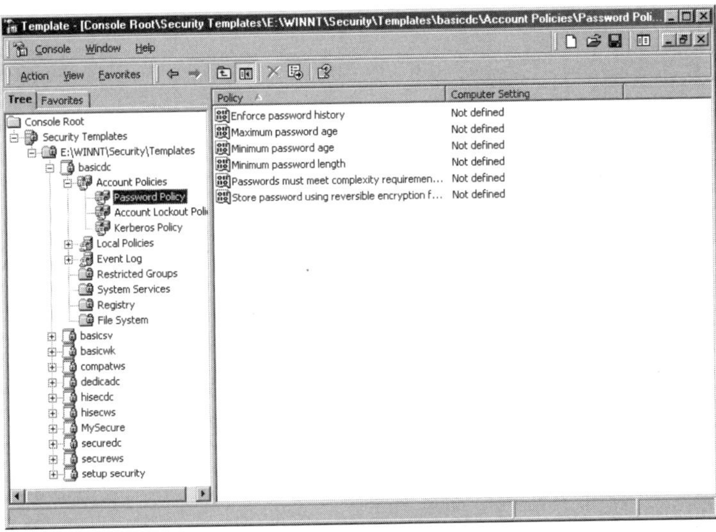

Figure 9-9. *Modifying the Account Policy settings.*

To change one of these settings

1. Double-click the setting you want to change.
2. Set or clear the Define This Policy Setting In The Template check box to change the setting.
3. Click OK.

Modifying Local Policies

To modify the Local Policy settings (Audit, User Rights, or Security Option), expand the Local Policies node, shown in Figure 9-10. In the right-hand pane select Audit Policy, User Rights Assignment, or Security Options . This will display a list of settings.

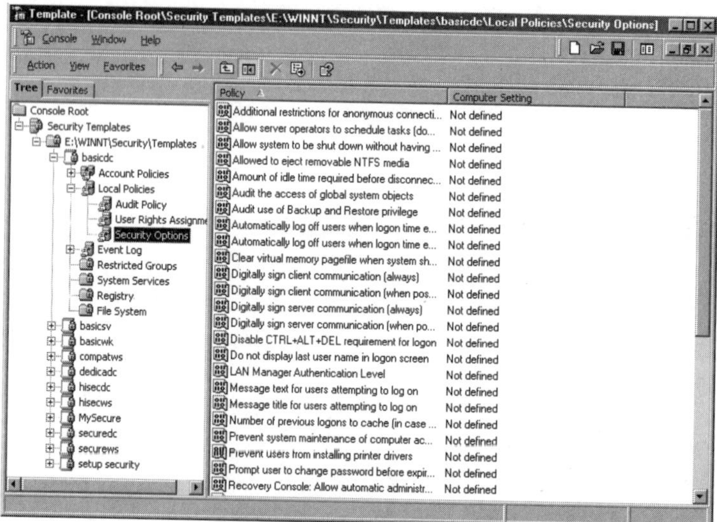

Figure 9-10. *Local Policy settings.*

To change one of these settings

1. Click the setting you want to change.
2. Set or clear the Define This Policy Setting In The Template check box, then change the setting.
3. Click OK.

Modifying Event Log Settings

To modify any of the event-log policy settings, expand the Event Log node. Select Settings For Event Logs in the left-hand pane. This will display a list of settings, as shown in Figure 9-11.

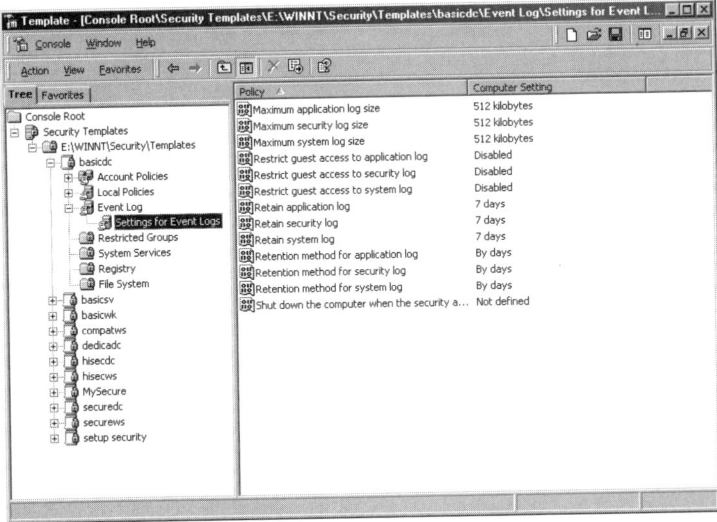

Figure 9-11. *Event Log settings.*

To change one of these settings

1. Double-click the setting you want to change.
2. Set or clear the Define This Policy Setting In The Template check box.
3. Click OK.

Creating a Restricted Group Policy

Restricted groups allow the administrator to define who should and should not belong to a specific group. When a template (or policy) that defines a restricted group is applied to a system, the Security Configuration Tool Set adds members to the group and removes members from the group to ensure that the actual group membership coincides with the settings defined in the template (or policy).

Members of the Restricted Groups typically include groups who by definition have access to—or are able to bypass—security areas and restrictions. This might include, for example, the Backup Users group, which can typically bypass file security in order to backup files.

In this example, we will define a restricted group policy for the Local Administrators group, in addition to the existing restricted group policy set up for local members of the Power Users group by the Securews.inf template.

To create the restricted group policy

1. Right-click the Restricted Groups node, and choose Add Group from the context menu.
2. Type *Administrators*.

3. Click OK. The local Administrators group is added as a restricted group in the right-hand pane of the Security Templates Snap-In.
4. Double-click Administrators in the right-hand pane to open the Configure Membership For Administrators dialog box. You can now define who should be a member of the Administrators group, and you can specify other groups that the Administrators group can be a member of. If no users are specified as members of a defined restricted group (the Members Of This Group list is empty), the Security Configuration Tool Set removes all current members of that group when the template is used to configure a system. If no groups are specified for a restricted group to belong to (the This Group Is A Member Of list is empty), no action is taken to adjust membership in other groups.
5. Click Add next to the Members Of This Group list, then click Browse in the Add Member dialog box. The Select Users Or Groups dialog box appears.
6. Select the Administrator user in the Select Users Or Groups dialog box. Click Add, click OK, and then click OK again.
7. Click OK until you return to the MMC window.

The restricted group policy you created states that only the local Administrator user can belong to the Administrators local group when the Securews.inf template is used to configure a Windows 2000 system. During configuration, the Tool Set removes all other users that belong to the Administrators local group at the time of configuration. Similarly, if (at the time of configuration) the local Administrator user does not belong to the Administrators local group, the Security Configuration Tool Set adds the local Administrator user to the Administrators local group.

Setting Permissions for the System Services

The System Services settings control the startup settings and access-control settings for each of the system services, such as DHCP server, TCP/IP, and so on.

Caution If you apply these settings through a policy on Active Directory, they will be propagated to all systems in the policy scope. Therefore, take care when applying the templates to ensure that the settings will not adversely affect the system they are applied to. This might be a particular issue if a system has a highly specialized role.

To configure the settings, click the System Services node in the left-hand pane. This will display a list of all services, their startup mode, and the permissions applied to them.

To change a setting

1. Double-click the setting you want to change.
2. Set or clear the Define This Policy Setting In The Template check box to change the setting. (If you have not previously configured the service, the Security

dialog box will appear when you check the Define This Policy Setting In The Template check box. The procedure for using this dialog box is covered in steps 2 through 6 of the next procedure.)

3. Select the required startup mode. You have three options:
   - **Automatic.** The service starts automatically at start time.
   - **Manual.** The service has to be started manually.
   - **Disabled.** Service is disabled.

To set the security permissions for the service

1. Click the Edit Security button to open the Security dialog box for the service. This displays a list of groups that have permission for that service. These permissions are also displayed.
2. To add a group, click Add. This opens the Select Users, Computers, Or Groups dialog box.
3. Select the location or domain you want to add the group from, using the Look In drop-down list box.
4. Select the names you want to add and click Add. Click Check Names to verify the names, and then click OK.
5. If you want to remove groups, select the user to remove and click Remove.
6. When all settings are complete, click OK until you return to the MMC window.

Configuring Registry Settings

The Registry node enables you to configure the access-control permissions and audit settings for certain registry keys.

To change these settings

1. Select the Registry node in the left-hand pane. This will bring up a list of registry settings in the right-hand pane. Note that this only occurs on certain templates. Templates that do not configure the Registry settings will not have this option.
2. Double-click the setting you want to configure.
3. Select Do Not Allow Permissions On This Key To Be Replaced if you want to disable policy changes for the selected registry setting. Otherwise select Configure This Key, and then select either Propagate Inheritable Permissions To All Subkeys or Replace Existing Permissions On All Subkeys With Inheritable Permissions.
4. Click Edit Security to select the access control permissions. You can change these just as you would the system services. However, under Advanced options, you'll see two more option tabs: Auditing and Owner. Auditing controls the audit permissions for the given object; Owner displays the current owner for the key or subkeys and allows you to change the owner.

Configuring Permissions for a File System Directory

You can use the Securews.inf to configure permissions for the file system as well.

To configure file system directory permissions

1. Right-click File System, and choose Add File from the context menu.
2. In the Add A File Or Folder dialog box, select the %systemroot%\repair directory. Click OK. The Access Control List (ACL) editor (which you normally view by using the Security tab in Windows Explorer) appears. This allows you to specify permissions for the %systemroot%\repair directory in the Securews.inf template.
3. Select the Everyone group, and click Remove.
4. Click Add to open the Add Users, Computers, Or Groups dialog box. Specify the Administrators group and click Add, then click OK. Give the Administrators group Full Control permissions.
5. Clear the Allow Inheritable Permissions From Parent To Propagate To This Object check box.
6. Click OK to accept the Administrator-only permissions defined for the %systemroot%\repair directory.
7. Select the inheritable permissions required for the directory.

Inheriting, Overwriting, and Ignoring Policy Changes

After you define permissions for a file system or registry object, the Security Configuration Tool Set asks you how the object's children should be configured.

If you select Propagate Inheritable Permissions To Subfolders And Files, normal Windows 2000 ACL inheritance procedures take effect. Specifically, any inherited permissions on child objects are adjusted according to the new permissions defined for this parent. Any explicit access control entries (ACEs) defined for a child object remain unchanged.

If you select Overwrite, Replace Existing Permissions On All Subfolders And Files With Inheritable Permissions, all explicit ACEs for all child objects (that are not otherwise listed in the template) are removed, and all child objects are set to inherit the inheritable permissions defined for this parent.

To prevent a child object from being overwritten by a parent, you can add the child object to the template and ignore it. If you add a child object to the template and ignore it, that child's inheritance mode and that child's explicit ACEs remain unaltered. Selecting Do Not Allow Permissions On This File Or Folder To Be Replaced for an object in a template makes sense only if a parent of that object is configured to overwrite children. If no parent exists in the template, ignoring an object has no impact. If a parent exists but is configured such that children inherit, ignoring a child has no impact.

In this example, the ACL configuration for the %systemroot%\repair directory in the Securews.inf template is defined as follows: Administrators have full control on the %systemroot%\repair directory. By default, these full control permissions apply to this folder, subfolders, and files. You specified this when you defined the Administrator permissions in the ACL Editor.

The %systemroot%\repair directory does not inherit any permissions from its parent. You specified this when you cleared the Allow Inheritable Permissions From Parent To Propagate To This Object check box in the ACL Editor.

All ACLs on all subfolders and files of the repair directory are configured to inherit the inheritable Administrators Full Control permission from this parent, regardless of their current configuration. You specified this when you selected the Overwrite mode of operation.

Note We'll cover importing templates into GPOs and other details concerning Group Policies later in this chapter and in Chapter 8, "Group Policy."

Security Template Management

Because of its integration with the MMC, the Security Templates Snap-In provides for routine maintenance of the templates.

To perform these modifications

1. If not already loaded, load the Security Templates Snap-In or load a previously saved MMC console with the security templates present.
2. By right-clicking the Security Templates node in the left-hand pane you can access the following options on the context menu:

Note The actual options visible will depend on the exact configuration of your machine, and might not match the following list exactly.

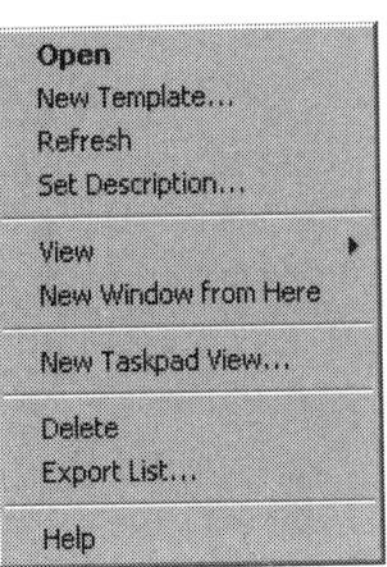

- **Open.** This selects the Security Templates node.
- **New Template Search Path.** This changes the default search path for the security templates.

- **View.** This alters the view configuration.
- **New Window From Here.** This opens a new MMC window rooted at the Security Templates node.
- **New TaskPad View.** This opens the New TaskPad View Wizard.
- **Delete**
- **Export List.** This exports the current list to file.
- **Help**

3. Click on the %systemroot%\Security\Templates node and then right-click on the security template to access further folder options on the context menu:
   - Open
   - New Template
   - Refresh
   - Set Description
   - New Window From Here
   - Delete
   - Help

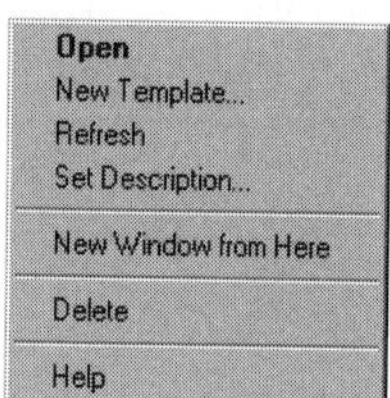

Saving the Template Console

Before exiting the Security Templates Snap-In, you should save the console to avoid having to reload it every time. When you reload this console at a later date, the Security Templates Snap-In will already be installed.

Security Configuration And Analysis Snap-In

The Security Configuration And Analysis tool is a standalone snap-in designed to work with the MMC. The management console does no actual processing or analysis; it only provides the GUI to the Security Configuration Service. The aim of this tool is to allow administrators to load security configurations into the computer and to check the systems for differences between the system's settings and those in the configuration. This analysis is useful for a number of reasons:

- To identify security weakness that might exist in the current configuration
- To identify changes that a potential security policy might impart to a system before the policy is actually deployed
- To identify deviations from a policy currently imposed on a system

In the following sections, we'll walk through performing a security analysis and configuring system security.

Installing the Security Configuration And Analysis Snap-In

In order to perform a security analysis, the Security Configuration And Analysis Snap-In (as shown in Figure 9-12) must be loaded.

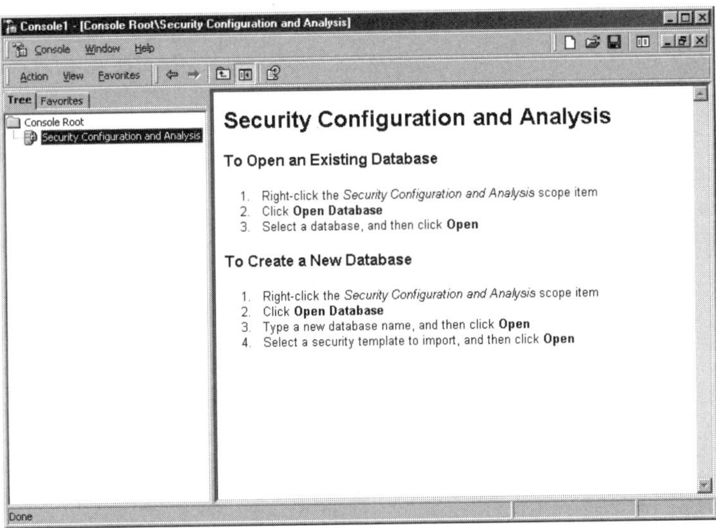

Figure 9-12. *Security Configuration And Analysis Snap-In.*

To load the snap-in (if not already present)

1. Choose Run from the Start menu, type *mmc* in the Run dialog box, then click OK.
2. Choose Add/Remove Snap-In from the MMC Console menu, and click Add.
3. Select Security Configuration And Analysis from the list of standalone snap-ins.
4. Click Add, then click Close.

Importing and Exporting Templates

The Security Configuration And Analysis Snap-In allows you to import and export templates to and from a working database. You can also merge templates into a single composite database that you can then use for analysis and configuration of a system. You can do this by importing each template into a working database. Once you've created a composite template, you can save it and export it for future analysis or to configure other systems. If there are conflicting settings, the last template imported takes precedence.

Creating the Database

Because all security configurations and analyses are database-driven, you must load a baseline analysis template into a database before the analysis can take place.

To create the database

1. Right-click the Security Configuration And Analysis node and choose Open Database from the context menu.
2. Type in a database name (for example, the system name).
3. Click Open.
4. Select the security template to import into the database. (In this example we'll use the MySecure.inf template.)
5. Set the Clear This Database Before Importing check box. If the database is new, this step will not be required.
6. Click Open.

The MMC window will now look as shown in Figure 9-13.

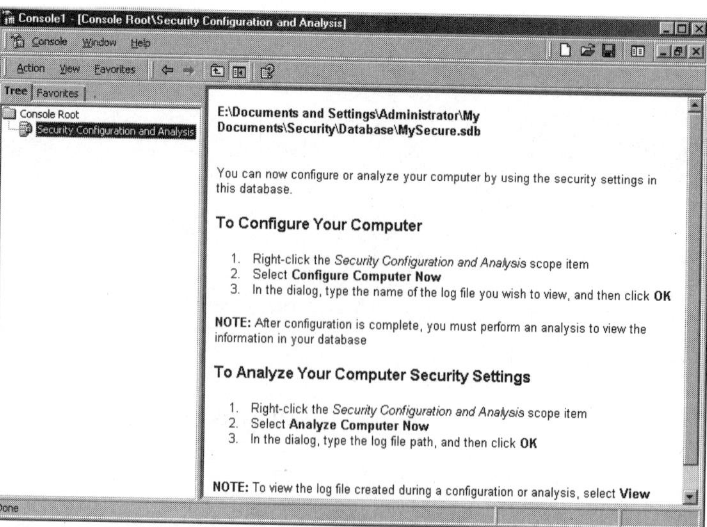

Figure 9-13. *Security Configuration And Analysis Snap-In startup screen.*

The name of the database is now displayed in the right-hand pane and there are several more options on the context menu for Security Configuration And Analysis.

Performing the Analysis

To perform the analysis, you'll compare the current state of the system to the security template that you imported. This template is used as a base configuration; it contains the recommended security settings for that system.

The snap-in queries system security settings for all of the areas covered in the base configuration. If the current system settings match the base configuration, they are assumed to be correct. If not, the mismatching attributes are flagged as potential problems requiring investigation.

To perform an analysis

1. Right-click Security Configuration And Analysis, and then choose Analyze Computer Now from the context menu.
2. Specify the log file you want to use. Click OK. A progress dialog box displays as the analysis proceeds.

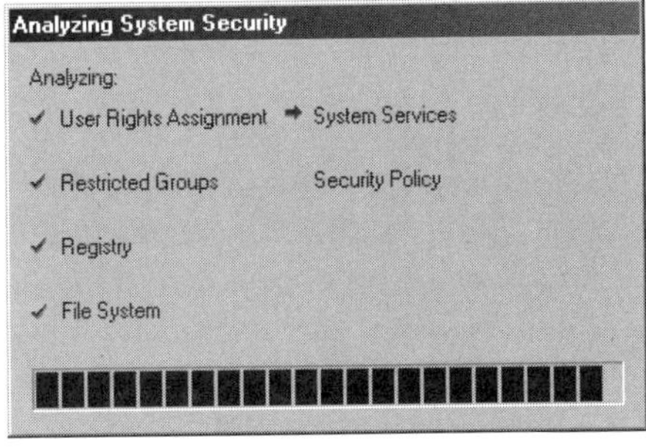

Reviewing the Analysis Results

After you've completed the analysis, the security areas are available under the Security Configuration And Analysis node. They are organized by security area, with flags used to highlight problem areas. For each attribute, the current system and base configuration settings are displayed.

To review the results of the analysis, expand the Security Configuration And Analysis node, expand the Local Policies node, and then select Security Options.

The right-hand pane—shown in Figure 9-14—displays both database settings and actual system settings for each object. Red flags highlight discrepancies; green flags highlight consistencies. If there are no flags or check marks, the security setting is not specified in the database (that is, the security setting was not configured in the template you imported). You can double-click any setting in the right-hand pane to investigate discrepancies further and modify database settings if desired.

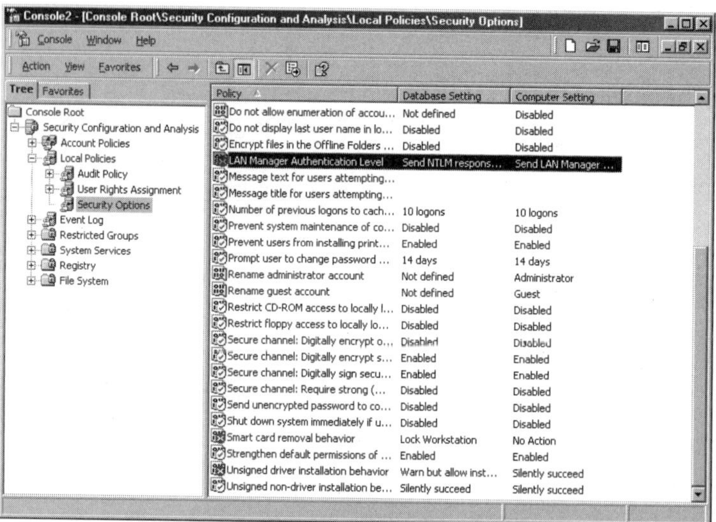

Figure 9-14. *The results of an analysis.*

When a template specifies a container object set to overwrite the existing settings (as was the case when we configured the repair directory), all children of that object are analyzed for compliance. Child objects that do not inherit from the parent are flagged as mismatched because Overwrite implies that all children (that is, all children not otherwise specified in the template) should inherit from the parent. Child objects inheriting from the parent (and containing no explicit ACEs of their own) are flagged as matches even if they currently inherit a different DACL than the one specified by the parent in the template. In this latter case, the relevant mismatch was flagged on the parent itself.

Modifying Baseline Analysis Settings

After you review the analysis results, you might decide to update the baseline database that you used to perform the analysis. This might be desirable if you have changed your mind about the relevancy of the security specification you originally defined for an object.

If there is a discrepancy between the database setting and that in the template, you have two options:

- Alter the database setting by right-clicking the object, clicking Security, and altering the attribute.
- Modify the underlying template to permanently modify that setting.

By altering the database setting you will reconfigure that setting for all machines that use that database to configure their security. If you alter the template, however, you will alter all machines that include that template in their security baseline, including those using templates applied with Group Policy.

In the previous example, you already clicked the Edit Security control. The ACL currently defined for the repair directory in the database could be modified, and future analyses or configurations using this database would then be based on the newly defined ACL. You can save such modifications to a template by choosing Export Template from the context menu of the Security Configuration And Analysis node.

Configuring System Security

Thus far, you have created a customized security template named MySecure.inf and analyzed the current system settings against this template. If you are comfortable with the security changes indicated by this template (as shown by the mismatches flagged in the analysis), you can now configure the system with these new security settings.

To configure the system with the new settings

1. Right-click the Security Configuration And Analysis node and choose Configure Computer Now from the context menu. A warning message is displayed, indicating that your security changes might be overwritten by the system configuration (Group Policy) database.
2. Click OK.
3. Specify the following as the path to the log file, where %systemroot% is the drive and path to your Windows directory (for example, c:\winnt):

   ```
   %systemroot%\security\logs\MySecure.log
   ```
4. Click OK. A progress dialog displays to indicate the security areas being configured. When the configuration is complete, your system is configured with the settings specified in MySecure.inf.
5. Click the Close button in the upper right corner of the Security Configuration And Analysis MMC Snap-In.

6. Click Yes to save the console settings.
7. Specify SCA as the filename, and save the file.

This allows you to start the Security Configuration And Analysis Snap-In without having to add it to a console in the future. You can add both the Security Templates Snap-In and the Security Configuration And Analysis Snap-In to the same console if you desire.

Viewing the Updated Settings

Changes made to local policy settings are automatically trapped by the Security Configuration Tool Set and stored in the local policy database. You can view these settings as you did earlier in this chapter.

To view the policy

1. Choose Run from the Start menu, type *Gpedit.msc* and click OK.
2. Expand the Computer Configuration node, expand the Windows Settings node, expand the Security Settings node, and then expand the Account Policies node.
3. Select Password Policy and examine the settings in the right-hand pane.

Note You must be an administrator to view the local policy. If you are not logged on as the local administrator, you might not be a member of the administrators group any more because of the Restricted Group policy you just applied to the system.

4. Expand the Local Policies node, select Security Options, and examine the settings in the right-hand pane.

This procedure is the same for viewing discrepancies for the settings in the Account Policies, Local Policies, Event Log, and System Services nodes.

Viewing Updated Registry Settings

After you've configured the computer, you can view the registry settings, their permissions, audit settings, and any discrepancies.

To view the registry settings

1. If you are not currently in the Security Configuration And Analysis Snap-In, load it and load the saved database.
2. Expand the Security Configuration And Analysis node, expand the Registry node, expand the Machine node, and select the Software node. This will display the registry settings in hierarchical format as shown in Figure 9-15.
3. To view keys and subkeys, click on the required node.

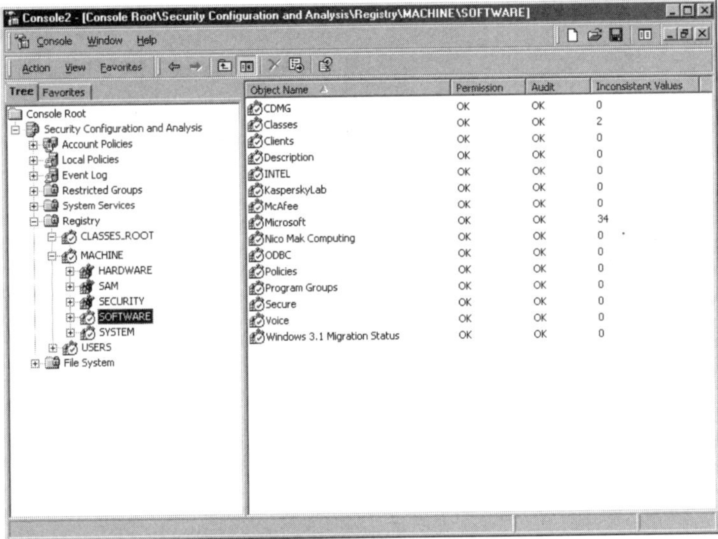

Figure 9-15. *Viewing updated registry settings.*

Viewing Updated File System Security Settings

Because file system settings are not local policies, you can verify the configuration of the repair directory through Windows Explorer.

To view file system security settings

1. Start Windows Explorer.
2. Expand %systemroot%.
3. Right-click the Repair directory and select Properties from the context menu.
4. Click the Security tab.
5. Click OK when you're finished viewing the settings.

Now that you've applied the customized security settings specified in MySecure.inf to the system, you can monitor any deviations from this security policy by periodically performing a system analysis against the database.

Security Settings Extension for Group Policy Snap-In

An important part of the Security Configuration Tool Set is the Security Settings extension, which integrates with the Group Policy Snap-In. The Group Policy infrastructure is developed for use with the Windows Administration Initiative, whose goal is to allow administrators to configure a large number of clients using a client-server model. The settings are set on the server and then automatically propagated to the clients. Active Directory allows the grouping of users and computers based on *scope*, and Group Policy makes extensive use of this. Scope is defined over three levels: sites, domain, and OU.

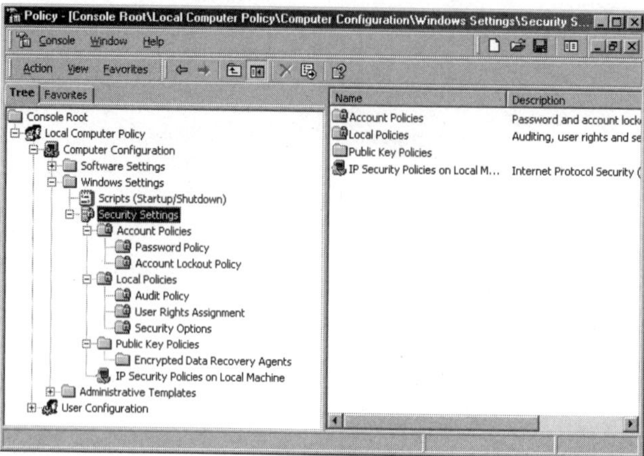

In addition to the security areas we've previously discussed, the following security areas are exposed under the Security Settings extension to Group Policy:

- **Internet Protocol (IP) Security Policy.** This configures the IPSec Policy Object in Active Directory. This policy defines encryption and signature requirements for IP packets between the source and destination computers.
- **Public Key Policies.** These include sub-policies used by the Public Key Infrastructure (PKI)–based technologies in Windows 2000.
- **Encrypted Key Recovery Agents.** These include a set of X509 version 3 certificates. The holder of the private key associated with each certificate can recover any file encrypted with the encrypting file system on any computer within the scope of the policy.
- **Root Certificates.** These include a series of self-signed X509 certificates that belong to various certificate authorities. Any certificate identified as root, with a given scope, represents the highest level of trust in that certificate authority. All certificate validation of end-entity certificates must terminate in a root certificate.
- **Certificate Trust Lists.** These include a series of non–self-signed X509 certificates that belong to certificate authorities. Certificate trust lists include additional information such as the purpose for which the CA is trusted. This enables administrators to limit the scope of the CA in terms of the kind of valid certificates they issue.

Installing the Security Settings Extension

The Group Policy Snap-In contains the Security Settings extension. Follow the procedures below to install first the Group Policy Snap-In and then the Security Settings extension.

To install the Group Policy Snap-In

1. Choose Run from the Start menu, type *mmc /s* and click OK.
2. Choose Add/Remove Snap-In from the Console menu, and click Add.
3. Select Group Policy from the list of standalone snap-ins.
4. Click Add, click Finish, then click Close.
5. Click the Extensions tab. Ensure that the Security Settings extension is selected to be installed, then click OK

If you already have the Group Policy Snap-In installed, but without the Security Settings extension, the extension must now be installed.

To install the Security Settings extension

1. Load the MMC.
2. Choose Add/Remove Snap-In from the Console menu.
3. Click Add and select Group Policy, (or Local Computer Policy, depending on how it is configured on your system).
4. Click Add and then click Finish.
5. Click the Extensions tab.
6. Select the Security Settings extension from the list of available extensions.
7. Click OK.
8. To select the security settings, expand the Group Policy node, expand the Computer Configuration node, expand the Windows Settings node, and then expand the Security Settings node.
9. Save the console. This will enable you to install the Group Policy Snap-In at a later date with the security settings already expanded.

Editing Settings Within the Security Settings Extension

Because the security settings are all based around the MMC, you edit them as you do the security templates. (For more information on editing values, please see the section on Security Templates earlier in this chapter.) However, there are certain additional features available as part of the Group Policy.

When editing a particular policy setting, a dialog box appears that contains two sections:

- **Effective Policy Setting.** This is the local and domain-level security policy settings combined.

- **Local Policy Setting.** This is the setting specified for the local machine. If there is no domain-level security policy, this setting will be the effective setting. If there is a domain-level security policy for this setting, the domain-level security policy will be the effective setting, and changing the local policy has no impact until you remove the domain-level security policy setting.

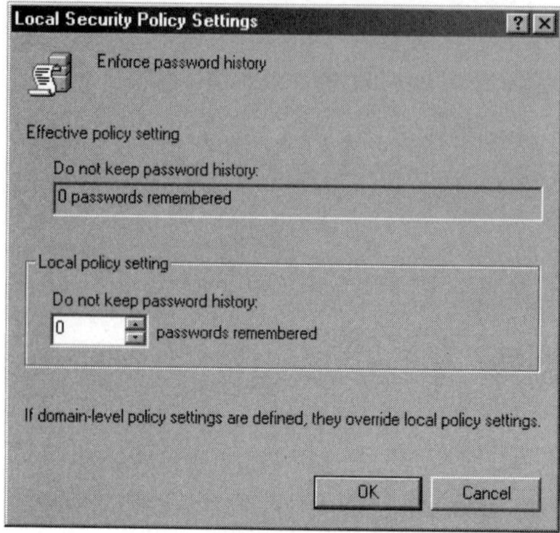

The Public Key Policies subtree contains only the Encrypted Data Recovery Agent node, which itself contains the list of Key Recovery Agent certificates currently in force. For details on how to manage these certificates, see Chapter 8, "Group Policy."

The final node, IP Security Policies On A Local Machine, enables you to apply specific IP security policies on the local machine. Three policies are displayed by default; you can create others by right-clicking the IP Security Policies On A Local Machine node. The three default policies are

- **Server (Request Security).** This is the lowest level of IP Security policy for a server that for all IP traffic will always request security using Kerberos trust. It will, however, allow unsecured communication with clients that do not respond to the request.
- **Secure Server (Require Security).** This is the higher-level IP Security policy for servers that will always require security using Kerberos trust for all IP traffic. It will not allow unsecured communication with clients that do not respond to the request.
- **Client (Respond Only).** This is the lowest level of IP Security policy for clients that allows them to communicate unsecured. Where servers request security, only the requested protocol and port traffic with that server is secured.

For full details on IP Security, see Chapter 11, "Network Security."

Secedit.exe Command-Line Tool

The Security Configuration Tool Set is designed to enable security configurations to be applied over a large number of machines or over a distributed network with minimal effort. This will typically be accomplished using the Group Policy infrastructure. However, if the Group Policy infrastructure is not appropriate, you can often use the command-line tool, perhaps in conjunction with other tools. Those other tools might include remote consoles, the Task Scheduler, and Microsoft Systems Management Server.

You can also perform the configuration and analysis operations available from the Security Configuration And Analysis user interface with the Secedit.exe command-line tool. Secedit.exe also provides some capabilities not available in the GUI.

To view detailed help on how to use Secedit.exe

1. Choose Run from the Start menu, type *cmd* and then click OK.
2. Type *Secedit*
3. Press Enter. This displays the Help menu shown in Figure 9-16.

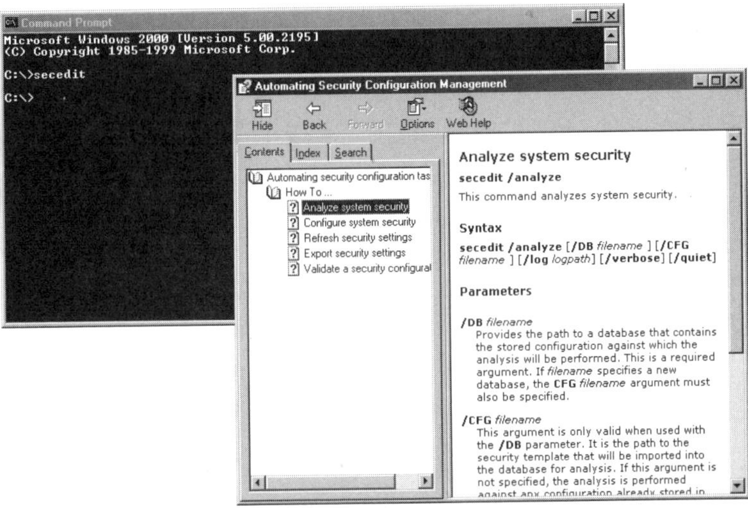

Figure 9-16. *Secedit.exe Help menu.*

The Secedit.exe command has five primary switches: /analyze, /configure, /export, /refreshpolicy, and /validate.

The /analyze and the /configure switches perform the same tasks available with the Security Configuration And Analysis Snap-In GUI.

The /export switch dumps database configuration information into a template (.inf) file. This feature is also available in the snap-in through the Security Configuration And Analysis context menu after a database has been opened.

The /refreshpolicy switch allows you to trigger a Group Policy propagation event which, by default, occurs whenever the machine boots, every 60 to 90 minutes thereafter, and when local security policy is modified using the Security Settings extension to Group Policy (as described earlier in this chapter). When a policy propagation event is triggered, pending policy changes are enforced by the corresponding Group Policy extensions (in this case, the Security Settings extension). To cause a refresh in policy regardless of whether there has been a change, use the /enforce switch in conjunction with /refreshpolicy.

The /validate switch verifies the syntax of a template created using the Security Templates Snap-In.

As we described earlier in this chapter, all configurations and analyses are database-driven. Therefore, Secedit.exe supports parameters for specifying a database (with the /db switch) as well as a configuration file (with the /cfg switch) to be imported into the database prior to performing the configuration. By default, the configuration file is appended to the database. To overwrite existing configuration information in the database, use the /overwrite switch. As with the snap-in, you can specify a log file (with the /log switch); however, Secedit.exe also allows you to record detailed log information (with the /verbose switch). Also note that while the snap-in always configures all security areas, Secedit.exe allows you to specify areas to be configured (with the /areas switch). Security areas not specified with the /areas switch are ignored even if the database contains security settings for those areas.

Configuring Security with Secedit.exe

The following example reapplies only the file system configuration specified by MySecure.inf.

To configure file system security with Secedit.exe

1. Change to the %systemroot%\security\database directory.
2. Type the following lines of code:

```
secedit /configure /db MySecure.sdb /areas FILESTORE /log
%systemroot%\security\logs\MySecure.log /verbose
```

where %systemroot% is the drive and path to your Windows directory.

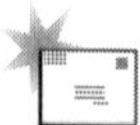

Note Since the database already existed and contained configuration information previously imported from MySecure.inf, you did not need to specify the /cfg switch. Notice also that paths for /db, /cfg, and /log—other than the current directory—must be absolute.

You will see a screen similar to Figure 9-17.

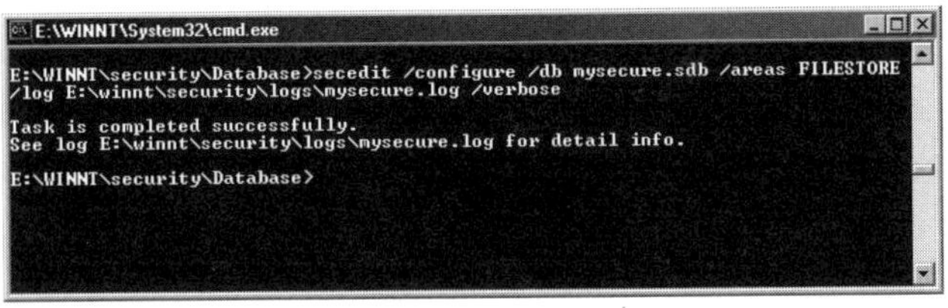

```
E:\WINNT\System32\cmd.exe
E:\WINNT\security\Database>secedit /configure /db mysecure.sdb /areas FILESTORE
/log E:\winnt\security\logs\mysecure.log /verbose

Task is completed successfully.
See log E:\winnt\security\logs\mysecure.log for detail info.

E:\WINNT\security\Database>
```

Figure 9-17. *Secedit configuration screen.*

3. Type the following line of code (replacing %systemroot% with the drive and path to your Windows directory):

   ```
   %systemroot%\security\logs\MySecure.log
   ```

Notice that previous configurations configure all security areas, while this configuration processed only the file security area.

Performing Security Analysis with Secedit.exe

Your system is currently configured according to the customized settings defined in MySecure.inf. You will now violate this policy, and then perform a command-line analysis to locate the violation.

Recall that MySecure.inf specifies a restricted Group Policy for the Administrators group such that only the administrator user should belong to the Administrators group. Violate that policy by adding Everyone to the administrators group. Type the following line of code at the command prompt, and press Enter:

```
Net LocalGroup Administrators Everyone /Add
```

Perform the analysis using MySecure.sdb as the baseline configuration. Type the following command at the command prompt:

```
secedit /analyze /db MySecure.sdb /Log Monitor.log /verbose
```

If you have access to a global regular expression print (Grep) tool, you can parse the log file to locate mismatches. Type the following line at the command prompt:

```
grep Mismatch Monitor.Log
```

Notice that the administrators group is flagged. Mismatches on registry values occur because these particular registry values are configured on the system but not in the database. The snap-in tool does not flag these types of mismatches.

Customizing the Security Configuration Tool Set

You can add your own security options that correspond to registry values and have those options exposed in the Security Configuration Tool Set UI under the Security Options node. The tool set can then edit, configure, and analyze these settings

Registry Extensions

The Security Configuration Tool Set exposes numerous security-relevant registry values under the Security Options node in the UI. These registry values appear in the UI with friendly names. For example, the security option exposed as Audit Use Of Backup And Restore Privilege corresponds to the following registry value:

```
HKLM\System\CurrentControlSet\Control\Lsa\FullPrivilegeAuditing
```

This predefined range of registry settings might not be complete for every organization. You might find that there is a security-relevant registry setting that you would like to manage that isn't exposed by the Security Configuration Tool Set interface by default. In this case, you can extend the Security Configuration Tool Set to support these registry settings.

Note Before editing the registry, be sure to make a rescue disk and a backup of the registry. For more information on how to do this, consult the Help file for regedit.exe or regedt32.exe.

Editing the Registry

The security options for the Security Configuration Tool Set are kept in the registry under the following key:

```
HKLM\SOFTWARE\Microsoft\Windows NT\CurrentVersion\SeCEdit\
```

RegValues

The subkeys under the RegValues key are named for the path to the registry value they are going to set. For example, the name of the subkey for

```
HKLM\System\CurrentControlSet\Services\EventLog\System\RestrictGuestAccess
```

is

```
MACHINE/System/CurrentControlSet/Services/EventLog/System/RestrictGuestAccess
```

The registry values in the subkey are

- **DisplayName:** *Reg_Sz.* This is where you enter the text to be displayed in the Security Configuration Tool Set under Local Policies\Security Options.
- **DisplayType:** *Reg_Dword.* As illustrated in Table 9-1, this determines the interface you see when modifying this setting.

Table 9-1. DisplayType.

Value	Interface
0	Enabled/Disabled check box (Enabled = 1, Disabled = 0)
1	Scroll box (Range from 0 through 999)
2	Text box
3	List box

- **ValueType**: *Reg_Dword*. This determines the data type of the value. Some of the common data types are listed in Table 9-2.

Table 9-2. ValueType: common data types.

Value	Data Type
1	REG_SZ
3	REG_BINARY
4	REG_DWORD

Modifying a Registry Value

Before you modify the registry, be sure to create a backup. In this example, we are going to create a registry setting that will allow or disallow the execution of the CD autoplay functionality. First we will modify the registry to enable the Security Template GUI to display the registry option and allow us to then set a value. Figure 9-18 shows the registry before modification. This option is not available by default.

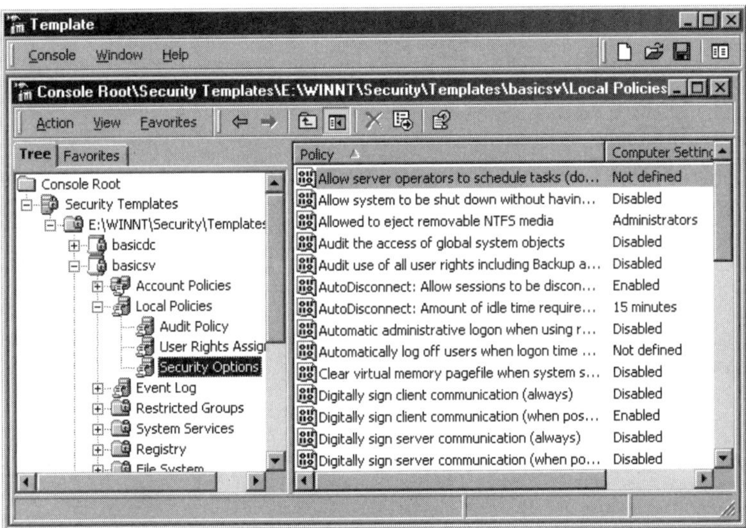

Figure 9-18. *Security template before modification.*

To modify the registry

1. Choose Run from the Start menu.
2. Type *Regedit* and press Enter.
3. Navigate to the following hive:

   `HKLM\SOFTWARE\Microsoft\Windows NT\CurrentVersion\SeCEdit\Reg Values`

   Figure 9-19 shows this subtree.

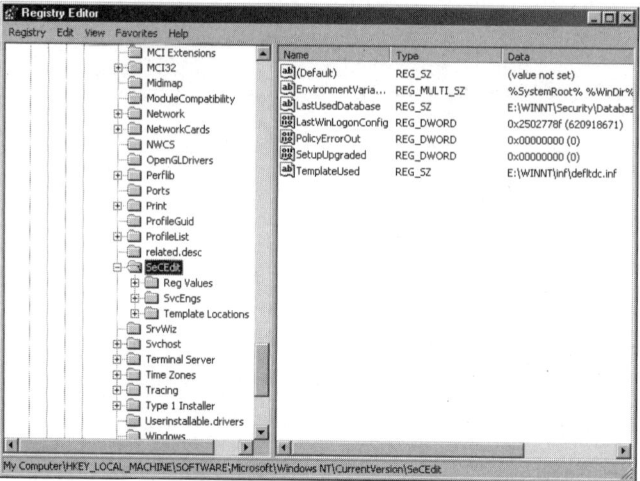

Figure 9-19. *SecEdit registry tree.*

4. Right-click on Reg Values to open the context menu.

5. Select New – Key.

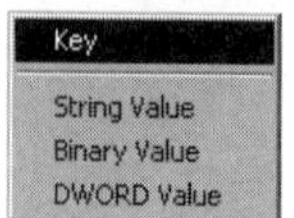

6. Type in the following for the name, and then press Enter:
   `MACHINE/System/CurrentControlSet/Services/CDRom/AutoRun`
7. Right-click on the newly created key. Select New – DWORD Value.
8. Enter ValueType for the name and press Enter.
9. Right-click the ValueType subkey and choose Modify from the context menu.
10. In the Value Data box, type *4* and click OK.

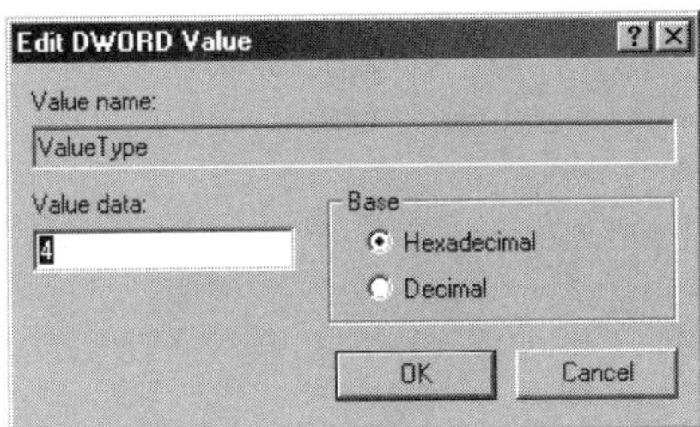

11. Right-click the AutoRun key. Select New – DWORD Value.
12. Enter DisplayType for the name and press Enter.
13. Right-click the DisplayType subkey and choose Modify from the context menu.
14. Type "0" in the Value Data box and click OK.
15. Right-click the AutoRun key. Select New - String Value.
16. Type DisplayName for the name of the subkey and press Enter.
17. Right-click the DisplayName subkey and choose Modify from the context menu. This brings up the Edit string dialog box.

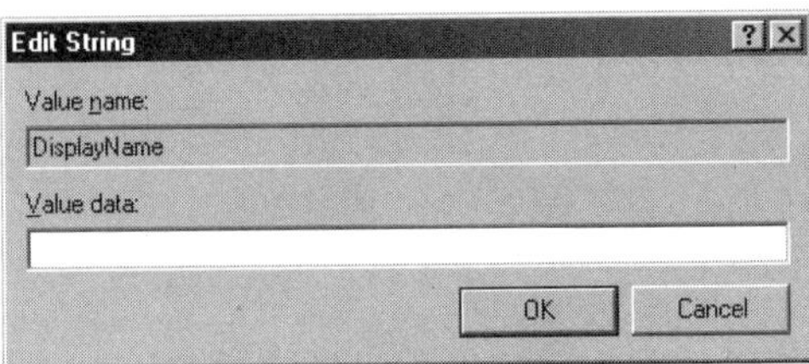

18. Enter Allow AutoPlay of CDs in the Value Data box and click OK. The record is now complete, as shown in Figure 9-20 on the following page.

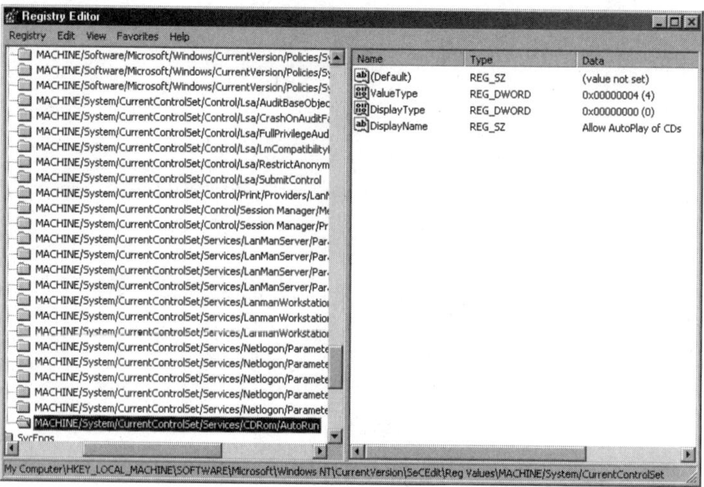

Figure 9-20. *Completed registry modification.*

19. Exit Regedit.exe.

Implementing the New Settings

This section offers some tips on changing the settings in the Security Templates Snap-In into the MMC.

To view the new setting and populate it

1. Select a template, such as Basicsv.inf, from the list of templates.
2. Expand the Local Policies node.
3. Select the Security Options node. The Allow AutoPlay of CDs setting should now be visible at the top of the list, as shown in Figure 9-21.
4. To populate the new setting, double-click it.
5. If it is not already checked, set the Define This Policy Setting In This Template check box.
6. Select the required setting and click OK.

You've now saved the setting in the current template. Close the console window and save the template file when prompted.

Open a new console window and load the Security Configuration And Analysis Snap-In into the MMC.

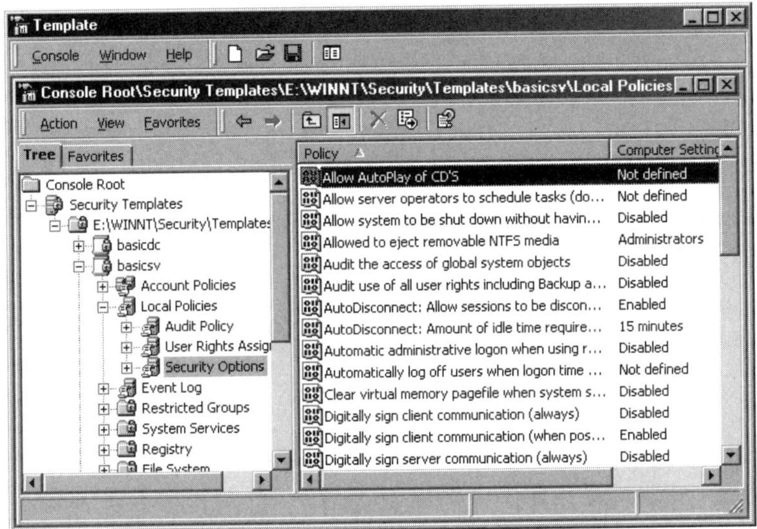

Figure 9-21. *Security template after modification.*

To configure a system using this new template

1. Load a database into the Security Configuration And Analysis Snap-In.
2. Import the saved template into the database; right-click the Security Configuration And Analysis node and choose Import Template from the context menu. Be sure to set the Clear This Database Before Importing box, then click Open.
3. Right-click the Security Configuration And Analysis node and choose Configure Computer Now from the context menu to apply the new setting to the computer.
4. Enter an error-log destination and click OK. A progress display will appear on screen.
5. You will then have to run an analysis to view the changes. To do this, right-click the Security Configuration And Analysis node and choose Analyze Computer Now from the context menu.
6. Once the analysis has completed, expand the Local Policies node and select the Security Options node. You will see the Allow AutoPlay of CDs setting in the right-hand pane.

Caution Beware of editing the database setting in the Security Configuration And Analysis Snap-In. If the template is not saved, the modification will be applied to the system but it will not be saved to the template and thus will not be applied to any computers that require the modification via a GPO.

As you have seen, once you've loaded the required keys into the registry, the Security Configuration Tool Set GUI will display the option to alter the new values. You can save the values into a template or configure them on the system immediately. If saved into a template that is then applied to another system, the new values will be set. However, unless the new registry keys that you added to the original system are also added to the new system, any analysis of the template (on a system without the appropriate registry keys) or the database of the new system will fail to show the state of the new registry keys. To correct this problem, any new Local Policies\Security Options registry keys added should be replicated to all systems on which a template or the local database can be analyzed. We therefore recommend that you make any changes via an automated script that you can apply to several systems if required.

In the previous example, you added the new registry key and values manually. To automate this process in a manner that can then be applied to additional systems and hence solve the problem of replicating the registry keys outlined above, use the Reg.exe program from the *Windows 2000 Resource Kit*. The syntax is as follows:

```
REG ADD RegistryPath=Value [DataType] [\\Machine]
RegistryPath [ROOTKEY\]Key\ValueName=Value
```

Table 9-3 shows the parameters to Reg.exe.

Table 9-3. Reg.exe parameters.

Name	Parameter
ROOTKEY	[HKLM | HKCU | HKCR | HKU | HKCC] [Optional default = HKEY_LOCAL_MACHINE] The Root key can be abbreviated as follows: HKEY_LOCAL_MACHINE HKLM HKEY_CURRENT_USER HKCU HKEY_CLASSES_ROOT HKCR HKEY_CURRENT_CONFIGURATION HKCC
Key	The full name of a registry key under the selected ROOTKEY
ValueName	The value to add under the selected Key
Value	The value to assign to the registry entry being added
DataType	[REG_SZ | REG_DWORD | REG_EXPAND_SZ | REG_MULTI_SZ] [Optional default = REG_SZ]
Machine	Name of remote machine (omitting defaults to current machine)

Therefore, to automate the example, you can create a small batch file containing the following code:

```
reg add "HKLM\SOFTWARE\Microsoft\Windows NT\CurrentVersion\
 SeCEdit\Reg Values\MACHINE/System/CurrentControlSet/Services/
 CDRom/AutoRun\DisplayName"=" Allow AutoPlay of CD's" REG_SZ
reg add "HKLM\SOFTWARE\Microsoft\Windows NT\CurrentVersion\
 SeCEdit\Reg Values\MACHINE/System/CurrentControlSet/Services/
 CDRom/AutoRun\DisplayType"=0 REG_DWORD
reg add "HKLM\SOFTWARE\Microsoft\Windows NT\CurrentVersion\
 SeCEdit\Reg Values\MACHINE/System/CurrentControlSet/Services/
 CDRom/AutoRun\ValueType"=4 REG_DWORD
```

Security Descriptor Definition Language

The Security Descriptor Definition Language (SDDL) converts security descriptors to and from text strings that are suitable for storage or transportation in a security template file. While it is not necessary to understand the SDDL for normal operation of the Security Configuration Tool Set, it is useful language to know if you need to troubleshoot a security template file directly. You can find more information about the Security Descriptor Definition Language in the Microsoft Developer Network.

Enterprise Configuration Rollout

The Security Configuration Tool Set allows you to define one or more security policies. When placed in a GPO, these policies can be automatically deployed across sections of the enterprise.

Windows 2000 ships with predefined security templates, each designed for a particular type of system. When Active Directory is used to propagate a GPO across a site, domain, or OU, the security configurations it contains will be applied to all machines within the given scope, regardless of type. This could result in a template designed to secure a workstation being applied to a server or domain controller or vice versa. Even when limited to servers, each template might have its specific use and hence security requirements, resulting in the application of inappropriate security configurations. This could lead to inadequate security enforcement or excessive security, and ultimately a loss of functionality.

The first step in reducing this problem is to carefully plan the structure of Active Directory. You can construct OUs to reflect the nature of the workstations and servers they contain. However, if you attempt to develop detailed security templates for specific systems, you might have to work out a compromise between the desirability of deploying these templates via GPOs and the complexity of the OUs required to do so. You will encounter other issues that bear on the design of OUs within a given domain. One solution might be to deploy highly specific security templates via the Secedit.exe command-line security configuration tool.

Summary

This chapter introduced the concepts of security templates and the Security Configuration Tool Set, and how you can use them to aid security. You have also seen how you can tie in security templates with Group Policy to enable large-scale enterprise scale deployment of consistent security configurations. In Chapter 10, we'll look at how you can use auditing to increase Windows 2000 security.

Chapter 10
Auditing

An effective security management regime relies on the relationship between the security status of a company's IT infrastructure and the requirements of a security policy. The security policy and associated controls must meet the company's overall business security policy objectives. Auditing is a useful tool for determining your company's security status. Auditing means different things to different people, but it generally falls into three main areas. The first area—known as vulnerability management—concerns checking the configuration of a system or systems against a defined baseline, and perhaps ensuring that the applied baseline meets current best-security practice recommendations. The second area—known as threat management—concerns the real-time detection of a threat or actual intrusion. The third area concerns collecting and analyzing data on events (generated by the system or its applications) that reveal security information related to the actual use or abuse of a given system or group of systems.

These three areas are interrelated: Checking a system's configuration against a baseline will reveal discrepancies, but is the baseline adequate or appropriate? Identifying threats allows you to take proactive measures—in most cases, directly against the threat. Thus, threat management and vulnerability management together provide the opportunity to both identify the threat and confirm a system's vulnerability to that threat. A particular threat becomes much more serious if you know that one or more of your systems are vulnerable to it.

Auditing events on a system complements both of these security approaches. Given that a high percentage of threats to an organization's security can come from inside the organization, auditing user activity also provides important information on how systems are run on a daily basis. It is notoriously difficult to identify all internal user behavior that should be considered a breach of security policy. An authorized user pushing the limits of his or her overall mandate is usually hard to spot.

Following a security incident, adequate and appropriate system and user auditing will help discover the extent of the incident and (one hopes) how it was able to occur. Auditing can also serve to provide evidence of the incident.

In this chapter we are going to look at the Windows 2000 auditing system. The Security Policy tools built into Windows 2000 provide a degree of security vulnerability management; Chapter 9, "Security Configuration and Monitoring," covers their use. Windows 2000 provides no threat management tools. You must obtain these from third parties who specialize in this area.

Auditing tracks the activities of users and processes by recording selected types of events in the logs of a server or workstation. An event is any significant occurrence in the system that requires notification. As mentioned earlier, auditing is necessary from a security perspective to provide the information required to spot attempted attacks, to investigate what happened when an incident has occurred, and to possibly provide evidence in support of an investigation. If your organization has no audit measures in place, finding out how your security was compromised can be difficult, if not impossible. You won't be able to fix the vulnerability, and the system might remain open to the same or a similar attack.

Effective Auditing

Auditing comes with a tradeoff: it provides information, but it also has an impact on system performance. How much information do you get in exchange for the impact on performance? That depends on how much auditing you turn on. How much do you need to turn on? That depends on why you want to perform auditing. Reasons for auditing differ between organizations as well as within an organization, depending on a system's role or the sensitivity of the data it contains. Before you turn on any auditing, you must understand why you are doing so and what results you expect to gain. Too little auditing in a given environment might not provide the information required to meet your goals; too much auditing will have an undesirable impact on your system and can hide significant events in the overall picture. Before we discuss the functionality provided by Windows 2000, think about what functionality you require.

Consider the following scenarios:

- **You are responsible for a Web site.** What are your auditing objectives? Per haps you want to be notified if your Web pages are defaced. You might decide that you need some auditing on the Web page files to find out if someone is altering them. What else do you need? If your site is hacked, you might want to know how the hacking occurred. If you don't investigate how the attack took place, the site can remain vulnerable to attack. Even reinstalling the site might not solve your problem, because the vulnerability exposed by the hacker can still be present in your rebuilt system. In the case of a Web server, how much auditing should the operating system do and how much can the Web server application do? Another issue to consider: When do you want to know that your site Web pages have been defaced, and is auditing write access to the files sufficient to detect this? A cryptographic checksum of the files might be more appropriate for this task. If you need to know immediately when a page changes, how will you generate that information, and to whom will you send it? When someone receives the information, what will the response be? As you can see, you need to consider many issues as part of the process of implementing an auditing strategy.

- **You are responsible for a Windows 2000 installation for a financial institution.** One or more major financial applications are running on your systems. Your systems hold sensitive data and you might have a regulatory requirement to hold audit data for extended periods. In this example, you might decide that your auditing priorities are to record access to particularly sensitive files on the system. This is not a significantly different requirement than the Web site's requirements, but your focus might be on long-term analysis. You also need to consider how you will collect auditing information from multiple systems in a way that will allow you to archive the information. Additionally, you might decide your financial application needs to audit internal events that Windows 2000 cannot see. Where will you record these events, and do you need to be able to consolidate them with operating system events? If you collect logs from multiple systems, do you need to cross-reference the logs? As in the first example, you'll need to resolve several issues as part of implementing an overall auditing strategy.

Auditing Strategy

The following list is not exhaustive, but it includes some of the questions that you need to answer as part of the process of choosing an auditing strategy. We'll discuss each question later in the chapter, when we examine the auditing functionality provided by Windows 2000.

- Why are you auditing?
- Do you need different auditing requirements for different systems?
- Who is responsible for log collection and archive, and should this archive be independent of the system backup?
- Who should have access to audit logs?
- Is the loss of some audit information acceptable?
- How long do you need to keep the logs?
- Who is responsible for reviewing audit logs?
- How often should the logs be reviewed?
- Are tools required to assist in the review of the logs?
- What is the escalation procedure when something suspicious is found?
- Does the discovery of some events require immediate notification?
- If you require immediate notification of events, who is going to respond and how?
- Do you need to collect audit logs centrally?
- Do you need to analyze logs from multiple systems simultaneously?

Auditing produces information concerning system use and abuse. When this information indicates that something serious has happened, you need to have a response preplanned. This is particularly true if you need to use auditing information to support legal or administrative action. In this case, your plans must include actions that need to be taken to preserve evidence, both in terms of current system configuration (which is outside the scope of this book) and the integrity of the audit logs.

Caution Normally, a company that does not plan for legal action before an incident occurs is usually unable to take legal action against an attacker after the incident, as there will be insufficient evidence to take the case to court. If you don't have a procedure for dealing with an incident once it occurs, knowing that it occurred in the first place is not very useful. Any response will be slow and inefficient.

Windows 2000 Auditing Functionality

Windows 2000 has the potential to audit a large number of events on the system, and for ease of use (and in the case of the Security log, for security reasons) events are divided among six logs. By default, all auditing to the Security log is turned off and must be enabled via the Group Policy if required. Additionally, you can enable other logs on the system that contain information of security interest.

The Windows 2000 auditing subsystem supports six logs. The first three—Application, System, and Security—are present on all Windows 2000 systems (and are also present on Windows NT 4.0). The other three—Directory Service, File Replication, and DNS Server—are present only if you've installed the appropriate service:

- **Application.** This log records events produced by applications or programs. For example, a virus scanner, which is configured to automatically install virus data updates, might generate an event in the application log when it has been successfully installed or if it finds a virus. Any application vendor can program an application to register itself with the auditing subsystem and record events to the application log. Thus the quantity and usefulness of information in this log depends entirely on the applications you install.
- **System.** This log contains events produced by Windows 2000 itself and by components such as drivers. For example, a device driver can produce a warning event that informs you of reduced performance or a particular configuration in the System log. A hardware failure, however, would produce an error event describing the hardware failure.
- **Security.** This log contains information regarding security events, including information relating to monitoring the activity of users and processes, as well as messages regarding security services, such as failure to start. Each auditable security event is classified as either a success or a failure. Only the system can write to the Security log to prevent rogue applications from flooding the log. Because of this limitation, applications often store security information in the other audit logs.

- **Directory Service.** This log contains information relating to the directory service. Notification that the directory database has been defragmented or messages concerning inter-site messaging are recorded here.
- **File Replication.** This log records events concerning file replication. These events include information that the service has started or stopped or that replication has completed successfully.
- **DNS Server.** This log contains information concerning the Domain Name System (DNS), including details of when the DNS service has started or stopped as well as any error or information messages relating to DNS zones.

You can independently set the configuration of each log in terms of maximum size and what should happen when the log reaches that size. In the case of the Security log only, you can also control what will be recorded in the log.

Audit Log File Policy

You can control audit log file properties via the Event Viewer MMC Snap-In, which is useful for controlling the local audit log settings or those of another individual system. The Event Viewer Snap-In offers the greatest range of control over the auditing log file configuration. Group Policy is the recommended means of setting audit log configuration for a range of systems. By default, you can control only the Application, System, and Security log settings via Group Policy.

To start the Event Viewer Snap-In, click Start, then select Programs, Administrative Tools, and Event Viewer. Figure 10-1 shows the Event Viewer dialog box for a domain controller with all six logs present.

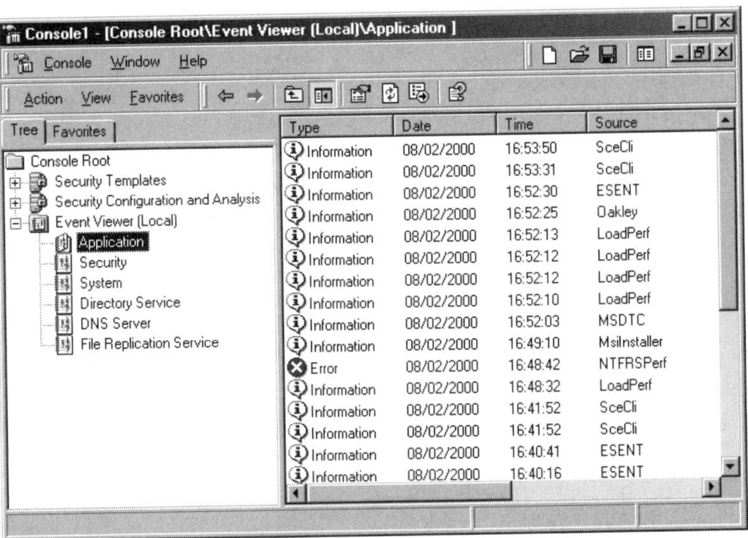

Figure 10-1. *The six Event Viewer logs.*

Selecting any of the logs and right-clicking allows you to select the log's properties dialog. Figure 10-2 shows this tabbed dialog.

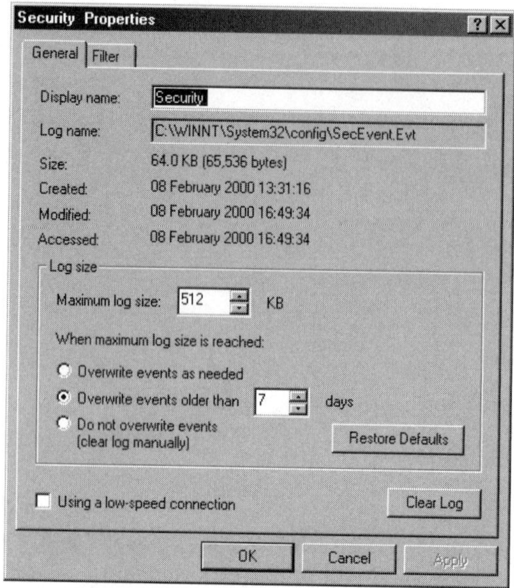

Figure 10-2. *The Application Log Properties tab.*

The first tab (General) displays information concerning the log file. The second tab (Filter) controls how the log's information will be displayed in the Event Viewer. The General dialog allows you to alter the log's display name and shows the file that holds the log, by default C:\WINNT\system32\config*xxxxxxxx*.evt. (You cannot alter this file via this dialog.) You can also configure the log size and overwriting policy via this dialog. You can set the maximum log size in 64 KB increments, with a minimum size of 64 KB. You should set the maximum log size in relationship to the overwriting option you select, the amount of disk space available, and the proposed frequency of collection. Three overwriting options govern the actions that the system will take when the log reaches maximum size:

- **Overwrite events as needed.** Enabling this setting means that when the logs reach the maximum permitted size, new audit events will start overwriting the oldest events. Therefore, this setting entails the risk that you will lose events if the logs have not been backed up before they reach their maximum size.
- **Overwrite events older than *x* days (7 days by default).** Similar to the first option, this setting dictates that should the event log reach the maximum size permitted, new audit events will start overwriting the oldest events, providing

that they are more than *x* days old. Again there is a risk that you'll lose events if you don't back up the log. If there are no allowable events to overwrite, no events will be written to the log and auditing will effectively stop.

- **Do not overwrite events (clear logs manually).** No events will ever be overwritten; however, this option will not permit the log to wrap. If the log reaches the maximum permissible size, no new audit events can be written, and auditing will effectively stop. While this is the most secure option, its security relies on the audit log being collected—and subsequently cleared—before the log reaches its maximum size. Windows 2000 provides no built-in functionality to detect when the log file is nearing its maximum size; therefore, you can deploy scripts to collect and clear the logs, but they must do so on a fixed-time basis. Logs configured not to overwrite must therefore be sized to prevent the possible loss of audit data between log collections. Third-party products are available to securely address this issue.

Halting the Computer When the Security Log Is Full

In the case of the Security log only, a third component exists for dealing with the log. Should the Security log reach the maximum size permitted, by default the system will stop auditing. If, given your auditing policy, this is not acceptable, you can set the system to stop if it is unable to continue auditing. Consider this option only in the highest of security environments, as it is aptly named CrashOnAuditFail: the system will crash (blue screen) if auditing fails. While this might sound drastic, it is a logical extension of what you have asked the system to do. To complete a graceful shutdown would require the system to be able to audit, but it is unable to do so. Enabling CrashOnAuditFail could result in a denial of service attack against your own system should the log ever become full. You can use Group Policy to set CrashOnAuditFail, or you can directly edit the registry key shown in Table 10-1. Once you set this option, the system will crash if unable to audit.

Table 10-1. Settings for CrashOnAuditFail.

Hive	HKEY_LOCAL_MACHINE\SYSTEM
Key	\CurrentControlSet\Control\Lsa
Name	CrashOnAuditFail
Type	REG_DWORD
Value	1

Once the system has crashed, registry value is set to 2, and an administrator is the only person allowed to log on to the system . An administrator should then back up and clear the audit log and reset the registry key value to 1 (You'll also need to change the registry key type back to REG_DWORD, as it gets set to REG_NONE at the same time as the registry value changes). You can then reboot the system and resume normal operation.

Event Log Security

Access to the event logs is controlled to prevent unauthorized modification or viewing. Access is normally determined by the account under which an application is running. Four types of accounts are used for the event log:

- **LocalSystem** is a special account that service application can use.
- **Administrator** is an account for administrators of the system.
- **ServerOperator(ServerOp)** is an account for domain server administrators.
- **Everyone** is an account for all users of all systems.

Each of these accounts will have a mixture of read, write, or clear permissions, as Table 10-2 illustrates.

Table 10-2. Event logs and accounts.

Log	Application	Access
Application	LocalSystem	Read, Write, Clear
	Administrator	Read, Write, Clear
	ServerOp	Read, Write, Clear
	Everyone	Read, Write
Security	LocalSystem	Read, Write, Clear
	Administrator	Read, Clear
	Everyone	
System	LocalSystem	Read, Write, Clear
	Administrator	Read, Write, Clear
	ServerOp	Read, Clear
	Everyone	Read

Only the LocalSystem account can write to the Security log, preventing applications from flooding the log. By default, Everyone can read the Application and System logs. On domain controllers these permissions extend to the three additional event logs. Administrators can only access Manage Auditing and Security Log if they have the necessary privileges, which they do by default. However, the administrator can remove these privileges.

Access to the Application and System audit logs can be further restricted by use of the registry key illustrated by Table 10-3. Setting the key to a value of 1 prevents guest accounts and null logons from viewing the relevant log. You must set the key for each log type to be protected.

Table 10-3. Settings for restricted access to the Application and System audit logs.

Hive	HKEY_LOCAL_MACHINE\SYSTEM
Key	\CurrentControlSet\Services\EventLog\[logname]
Name	RestrictGuestAccess
Type	REG_DWORD
Value	1

Backing up Audit Logs

Most auditing strategies require log backup for future reference or centralized examination. It is not unusual for a security incident to go unnoticed for some time. And even if the incident is detected, it's not unusual for there to be a requirement to confirm that it has not occurred in the past. Therefore, we strongly recommend the retention of audit logs. Since you can treat each log separately, your backup strategy can differ for each log type. You might decide to treat the Security log differently from the other logs, but as you will see later in the chapter, both the System and Application logs can also contain relevant information. In high-security environments, you might want to back up the logs to an alternative location—such as long-term secure storage media—on a daily basis. Audit logs are prime targets for hackers, who will usually try to alter or delete them in an attempt to cover their tracks.

Event Log Formats

Windows 2000 stores audit logs internally in an .evt format, which provides the most compact form of storage because all audit information is not stored in the log. To allow worldwide use of Windows 2000, the event log subsystem is designed to provide event logs in more than one language with little additional effort on the part of the programmer. When a programmer writes a program, he or she creates and stores event message strings for every language the program is intended to support. When a program writes an event to the event log, the program does not write a text string; instead, it writes a number representing that specific event. Every number and application combination maps to a specific text string. The logs are stored in this form and as such cannot be read directly. Event Viewer combines the stored audit data with the text strings to output the complete event information to the screen. You have three options when backing up the audit logs: event log format (.evt), text format (tab-delimited .txt), and comma-separated values format (comma-delimited .csv).

Of these formats, event log format is the most compact and the only one that the Event Viewer can view. You can view text format and comma-separated values formats directly and import them into a database if required. In certain circumstances, such as when evidential reasons mandate minimal log manipulation, you might prefer to back up the event logs in their native form (.evt).

Figure 10-3 shows the Event Viewer representation of the Directory Service log for a domain controller. Figure 10-4 shows that same information in a Unicode comma-separated values file.

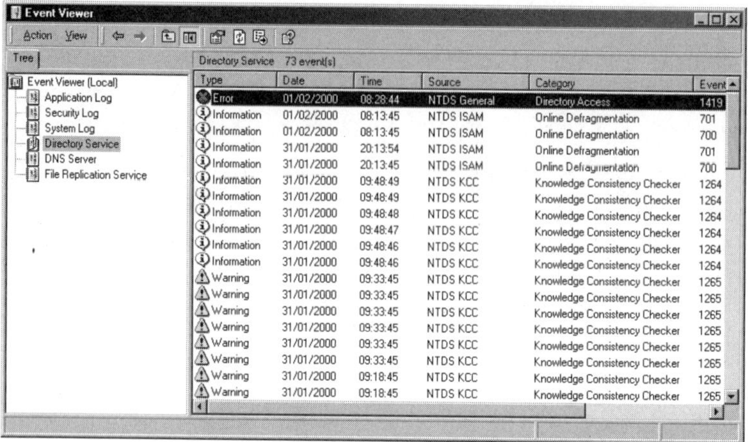

Type	Date	Time	Source	Category	Event
Error	01/02/2000	08:28:44	NTDS General	Directory Access	1419
Information	01/02/2000	08:13:45	NTDS ISAM	Online Defragmentation	701
Information	01/02/2000	08:13:45	NTDS ISAM	Online Defragmentation	700
Information	31/01/2000	20:13:54	NTDS ISAM	Online Defragmentation	701
Information	31/01/2000	20:13:45	NTDS ISAM	Online Defragmentation	700
Information	31/01/2000	09:48:49	NTDS KCC	Knowledge Consistency Checker	1264
Information	31/01/2000	09:48:49	NTDS KCC	Knowledge Consistency Checker	1264
Information	31/01/2000	09:48:48	NTDS KCC	Knowledge Consistency Checker	1264
Information	31/01/2000	09:48:47	NTDS KCC	Knowledge Consistency Checker	1264
Information	31/01/2000	09:48:46	NTDS KCC	Knowledge Consistency Checker	1264
Information	31/01/2000	09:48:46	NTDS KCC	Knowledge Consistency Checker	1264
Warning	31/01/2000	09:33:45	NTDS KCC	Knowledge Consistency Checker	1265
Warning	31/01/2000	09:33:45	NTDS KCC	Knowledge Consistency Checker	1265
Warning	31/01/2000	09:33:45	NTDS KCC	Knowledge Consistency Checker	1265
Warning	31/01/2000	09:33:45	NTDS KCC	Knowledge Consistency Checker	1265
Warning	31/01/2000	09:33:45	NTDS KCC	Knowledge Consistency Checker	1265
Warning	31/01/2000	09:33:45	NTDS KCC	Knowledge Consistency Checker	1265
Warning	31/01/2000	09:18:45	NTDS KCC	Knowledge Consistency Checker	1265
Warning	31/01/2000	09:18:45	NTDS KCC	Knowledge Consistency Checker	1265

Figure 10-3. *Event Viewer representation of the Directory Service log.*

Replicationlog - Notepad

File Edit Format Help

```
Type,Date,Time,Source,Category,Event,User,Computer
Error,01/02/2000,08:28:44,NTDS General,Directory Access ,1419,Everyone,KSJANEWAY
Information,01/02/2000,08:13:45,NTDS ISAM,Online Defragmentation ,701,N/A,KSJANEWAY
Information,01/02/2000,08:13:45,NTDS ISAM,Online Defragmentation ,700,N/A,KSJANEWAY
Information,31/01/2000,20:13:54,NTDS ISAM,Online Defragmentation ,701,N/A,KSJANEWAY
Information,31/01/2000,20:13:45,NTDS ISAM,Online Defragmentation ,700,N/A,KSJANEWAY
Information,31/01/2000,09:48:49,NTDS KCC,Knowledge Consistency Checker ,1264,N/A,KSJANEWAY
Information,31/01/2000,09:48:49,NTDS KCC,Knowledge Consistency Checker ,1264,N/A,KSJANEWAY
Information,31/01/2000,09:48:48,NTDS KCC,Knowledge Consistency Checker ,1264,N/A,KSJANEWAY
Information,31/01/2000,09:48:47,NTDS KCC,Knowledge Consistency Checker ,1264,N/A,KSJANEWAY
Information,31/01/2000,09:48:46,NTDS KCC,Knowledge Consistency Checker ,1264,N/A,KSJANEWAY
Information,31/01/2000,09:48:46,NTDS KCC,Knowledge Consistency Checker ,1264,N/A,KSJANEWAY
Warning,31/01/2000,09:33:45,NTDS KCC,Knowledge Consistency Checker ,1265,N/A,KSJANEWAY
Warning,31/01/2000,09:33:45,NTDS KCC,Knowledge Consistency Checker ,1265,N/A,KSJANEWAY
Warning,31/01/2000,09:33:45,NTDS KCC,Knowledge Consistency Checker ,1265,N/A,KSJANEWAY
Warning,31/01/2000,09:33:45,NTDS KCC,Knowledge Consistency Checker ,1265,N/A,KSJANEWAY
Warning,31/01/2000,09:33:45,NTDS KCC,Knowledge Consistency Checker ,1265,N/A,KSJANEWAY
Warning,31/01/2000,09:33:45,NTDS KCC,Knowledge Consistency Checker ,1265,N/A,KSJANEWAY
Warning,31/01/2000,09:18:45,NTDS KCC,Knowledge Consistency Checker ,1265,N/A,KSJANEWAY
Warning,31/01/2000,09:18:45,NTDS KCC,Knowledge Consistency Checker ,1265,N/A,KSJANEWAY
Warning,31/01/2000,09:18:45,NTDS KCC,Knowledge Consistency Checker ,1265,N/A,KSJANEWAY
Warning,31/01/2000,09:18:45,NTDS KCC,Knowledge Consistency Checker ,1265,N/A,KSJANEWAY
Warning,31/01/2000,09:18:45,NTDS KCC,Knowledge Consistency Checker ,1265,N/A,KSJANEWAY
Warning,31/01/2000,09:18:45,NTDS KCC,Knowledge Consistency Checker ,1265,N/A,KSJANEWAY
Warning,31/01/2000,09:03:45,NTDS KCC,Knowledge Consistency Checker ,1265,N/A,KSJANEWAY
Warning,31/01/2000,09:03:45,NTDS KCC,Knowledge Consistency Checker ,1265,N/A,KSJANEWAY
Warning,31/01/2000,09:03:45,NTDS KCC,Knowledge Consistency Checker ,1265,N/A,KSJANEWAY
Warning,31/01/2000,09:03:45,NTDS KCC,Knowledge Consistency Checker ,1265,N/A,KSJANEWAY
Warning,31/01/2000,09:03:45,NTDS KCC,Knowledge Consistency Checker ,1265,N/A,KSJANEWAY
Warning,31/01/2000,09:03:45,NTDS KCC,Knowledge Consistency Checker ,1265,N/A,KSJANEWAY
Warning,31/01/2000,08:48:45,NTDS KCC,Knowledge Consistency Checker ,1265,N/A,KSJANEWAY
Warning,31/01/2000,08:48:45,NTDS KCC,Knowledge Consistency Checker ,1265,N/A,KSJANEWAY
Warning,31/01/2000,08:48:45,NTDS KCC,Knowledge Consistency Checker ,1265,N/A,KSJANEWAY
Warning,31/01/2000,08:48:45,NTDS KCC,Knowledge Consistency Checker ,1265,N/A,KSJANEWAY
Warning,31/01/2000,08:48:45,NTDS KCC,Knowledge Consistency Checker ,1265,N/A,KSJANEWAY
Warning,31/01/2000,08:48:45,NTDS KCC,Knowledge Consistency Checker ,1265,N/A,KSJANEWAY
Warning,31/01/2000,08:33:45,NTDS KCC,Knowledge Consistency Checker ,1265,N/A,KSJANEWAY
```

Figure 10-4. *CSV file representation of the Directory Service log.*

If necessary—and to be able to view the logs on a system other than the system the logs were generated on—you'll also need to copy a number of supporting files. These files hold the messages required to complete the audit entries. The files are usually executables (.exe) or dynamic link libraries (.DLL). The list of applications that have been registered with the event log subsystem is under the HKEY_LOCAL_MACHINE\SYSTEM\CurrentControlSet\Services\EventLog\ registry key.

There are three subkeys under this key, one for each of the three main logs. To read event logs on a machine other than the machine they were created on, you have to ensure that the second machine has exactly the same applications loaded, or that all the files referred to by the EventLog registry key are also present on the second system. Figure 10-5 illustrates the process Event Viewer follows to display an event from an event log.

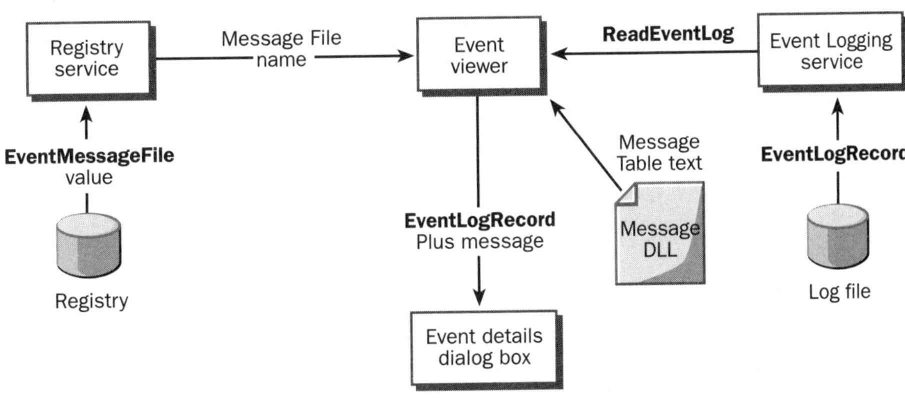

Figure 10-5. *How Event Viewer displays an event log record.*

The EventLog registry key (including subkeys and values) must also be copied into the registry of the system used to read the event logs. Although this might sound complicated, third-party utilities are available to complete this process automatically, while also backing up the logs to a central location for storage and subsequent review.

Configuring Audit Policy

Security auditing under Windows 2000 (and Windows NT) is a two-stage process. First you have to set a high-level auditing policy, and then you have to set auditing on specific objects. Once you've decided on your auditing objectives and have therefore chosen an appropriate level of auditing, your next task is to decide on the categories of events you want to audit, such as user logon and logoff and account management. The categories of events you select constitute your high-level audit policy. When you first install Windows 2000, no categories are selected, and therefore no audit policy is in force. You can choose from the following event categories:

- **Audit Account Logon Events.** This will record the success or failure of a user to authenticate to the local computer across the network.

- **Audit Account Management.** This audits the creation, modification, or deletion of user accounts or groups. It also audits any successful or unsuccessful attempts to change the user password. If you require a more granular level of auditing, you can use the Object Access category to set this category at the object level.
- **Audit Directory Service Access.** Administrators can monitor access to Active Directory, allowing successful and failed audit attempts to be logged in the Directory Service event log. This event log is present only on Windows 2000 domain controllers.
- **Audit Logon Events.** This records the success or failure of a user to interactively log on to the local machine.
- **Audit Object Access.** This records any successful or failed attempts by the user to access an object, including a directory, file, or printer. This is only performed for objects that have auditing set, allowing for a more granular approach to auditing.
- **Audit Policy Change.** Any successful or failed attempts to make high-level changes in the security policy—including privilege assignments and audit policy changes—are recorded under this category.
- **Audit Privilege Use.** This records all successful and failed attempts by users to use a privilege. This category also covers special privileges and informs you when these privileges are assigned, but not when they are used.
- **Audit Process Tracking.** This provides detailed tracking information for events such as process activation, handle duplications, indirect object access, and exits from processes.
- **Audit System Events.** This audits events—including both successful and failed attempts—that affect the security of the whole system.

If you choose to audit access to objects as part of your audit policy, you must turn on either the Audit Directory Service Access category (for auditing directory objects on a domain controller) or the Audit Object Access category (for auditing file system, registry, or printer objects). Once you have turned on the correct object access category, you can use each individual object's properties to specify whether to audit successes or failures for the permissions granted to each group or user.

As shown in Figure 10-6, you can enable auditing policy via either Local or Group Policy.

If you select either the Audit Directory Service Access category or the Audit Object Access category, you must determine the objects you want to monitor access to and modify their security descriptors accordingly. For example, if you want to audit any attempts by users to open a particular file, you can set a *Success* or *Failure* attribute directly on that file for that particular event.

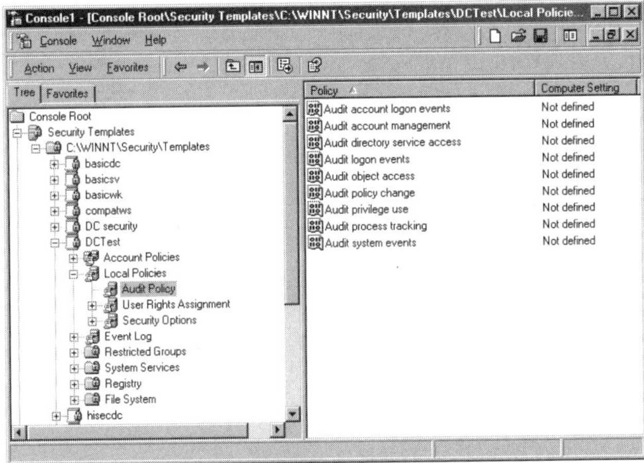

Figure 10-6. *Setting Audit Policy using the Group Policy Snap-In.*

Privileges Required to Set Audit Policy

To be able to configure and implement audit policy settings, you must have the following privileges set for your account. Members of the Administrators group have these privileges by default.

- **Generate Security Audits.** This allows a process to make entries in the Security log for object access auditing.
- **Managing Auditing And Security Log.** This allows a user to specify object access auditing options for individual resources such as files, Active Directory objects, and registry keys. Users with this privilege can also view and clear the Security log from Event Viewer.

Enabling Security Auditing on Standalone Systems

The procedure described in this section applies to Windows 2000 Professional computers as well as to Windows 2000 Server computers running as standalone servers. While you can configure auditing policy in the same manner for systems that are members of a domain, the security auditing policy of the domain or organizational unit (OU)—if enabled—will overwrite the local security auditing policy.

To set a security auditing policy

1. Open the Group Policy Snap-In for the local computer or the Administrative Tools option from the Control Panel.
2. In Local Computer Policy, click Audit Policy, which is located in \Computer Configuration\Windows Settings\Security Settings\Local Policies\Audit Policy. In the details pane, double-click the policy you want to set, or right-click and select Security.
3. In Local Security Policy Setting, click the options you want, and then click OK.

Note To set the policy, you must be logged on as the administrator or as a member of the Administrators group. Group Policy is available only to members of the Administrators group.

Unless these settings are overridden by a Group Policy applied to the domain or OU, the new auditing settings will take effect as soon as you close the console. The new settings will be apparent in the Effective Settings column the next time you view the Audit Policy.

Enabling Security Auditing on Domain Controllers

Auditing provides the ability to determine whether your system has been attacked, the method of attack, and when your system was attacked. It also allows you to troubleshoot security issues. As you can see, it's very important to have a security auditing policy for your domain controllers.

To set a security auditing policy for domain controllers

1. Open Active Directory Users And Computers Snap-In.
2. In the console tree, click Domain Controllers, which you'll find under the Active Directory Users And Computers\domain name\Domain Controllers node.
3. Choose Properties from the Action menu.
4. On the Group Policy tab, click the policy you want to change, and then click Edit.
5. In the Group Policy window in the console tree, click Audit Policy, which is located under Computer Configuration\Windows Settings\Security Settings\Local Policies\Audit Policy.
6. In the details pane, double-click the attribute or event you want to audit and make your changes. Click OK when you're done.
7. Repeat step 6 for other events you want to audit.

Enabling Security Auditing on Domain Systems

Security auditing for workstations, member servers, and domain controllers can be enabled remotely only by domain administrators as part of Group Policy. To do that, create an OU, add the desired machine account(s) to the OU, and then use Active Directory Users And Computers to create policy to enable security auditing. Alternatively, you can apply Group Policy by creating a Group Policy object (GPO) using the Group Policy Snap-In, and then using the Active Directory Users And Computers Snap-In to apply the GPO.

Configuring Object Auditing

Once most auditing policy categories are set for auditing of successful or failed events, you don't need to take further action. However, in the case of object auditing, enabling the policy is only the first step. Once you enable object auditing, you must set auditing on the individual objects. We'll discuss the various object types later in this section.

Each object has a security descriptor associated with it that details the groups or users that can access the object, and the types of access permissions granted to those users or groups. This part of the descriptor is called the discretionary access control list (DACL). The security descriptor also contains auditing information, which is known as the system access control list (SACL).

The types of access that you can audit depend on whether you are trying to audit files, folders, or directory objects.

Auditing Files and Folders

If a hard-disk volume is formatted using the NTFS file system, you can control and audit access to files and folders. However, if the disk volume is formatted using FAT, auditing is not possible. When you audit a file or folder, an entry is made in the Security log each time the particular file or folder is accessed in a specified way. You must specify the files or folders to audit, as well as the actions that will trigger an audit event. You can design these settings for a single specified user or for groups of users. To enable auditing of files or folders, you must also enable object auditing, and then use Windows Explorer to specify which types of access are audited for specific files or folders.

Table 10-4 lists the types of file and folder access that are auditable.

Table 10-4. Types of folder and file access.

Types of folder access	Types of file access
Displaying names of files in the folder	Displaying the file's data
Displaying the folder's attributes	Displaying the file's attributes
Changing folder attributes	Displaying the file's owner and permissions
Creating subdirectories and files	Changing the file
Going to the folder's subdirectories	Changing the file attributes
Displaying the folder's owners and permissions	Running the file
Deleting the folder	Deleting the file
Changing folder permissions	Changing the file permissions
Changing folder ownership	Changing file ownership

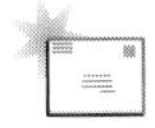

Note To audit files and folders, you must be logged on as a member of the Administrators group.

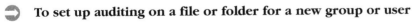

To set up auditing on a file or folder for a new group or user

1. Open Windows Explorer, and then locate the file or folder you want to audit.
2. Right-click the file or folder, choose Properties from the context menu, and then click the Security tab.
3. Click Advanced, and then click the Auditing tab.

4. Click Add. In the name field, type the name of the user you want, and then click OK to automatically open the Auditing Entry dialog box.
5. If necessary, in the Auditing Entry dialog box, select where you want auditing to take place in the Apply Onto list. The Apply Onto list is available only for folders.
6. Under Access, click Successful, Failed, or both for each access you want to audit.
7. If you want to prevent files and subfolders within the tree from inheriting these audit entries, select the Apply These Auditing Entries To Objects And/Or Containers Within This Container Only check box. Click OK when you're done.

Note To view or change auditing for an existing group or user, click the name in the Access Control Settings dialog box, and then click View/Edit. To remove auditing for an existing group or user, click the name in the Access Control Settings dialog box, and then click Remove.

Before Windows 2000 will audit access to files and folders, you must use the Group Policy Snap-In to enable the Audit Object Access setting in the Audit Policy. If you do not, you receive an error message when you set up auditing for files and folders, and no files or folders will be audited. Once you enable auditing in Group Policy, view the Security log in Event Viewer to review successful or failed attempts to access the audited files and folders.

Specifying Files and Folders to Audit

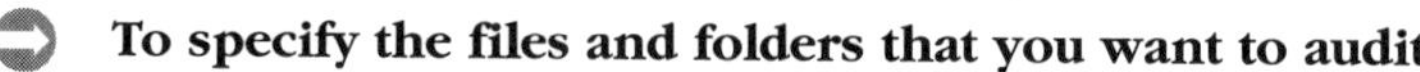

To specify the files and folders that you want to audit

1. In Windows Explorer, right-click the file or folder you want to audit, and then choose Properties from the context menu.

Note To open Windows Explorer, click Start, point to Programs, point to Accessories, and then click Windows Explorer. If the check boxes under Access are unavailable in the Auditing Entry dialog box, or if the Remove button is unavailable in the Access Control Settings dialog box, auditing has been inherited from the parent folder.

2. On the Security tab, click Advanced.
3. On the Auditing tab, click Add.
4. In the Select User, Computer, Or Group dialog box, click the name of the user or group whose actions you want to audit, and then click OK.
5. In the Auditing Entry dialog box, in Access, click Successful, Failed, or both for the actions you want to audit, and then click OK.

Caution You must log on as an administrator or as a member of the Administrators group to specify files and folders to audit. Otherwise, in step 2, the Security tab will not appear or will appear in read-only form.

Auditing Printers

As you can with most other objects, you can set auditing options for printers, and thereby monitor printer usage. The options for security print auditing are Success and Failure Of Print, Manage Printers, Manage Documents, Read Permissions, Change Permissions, and Take Ownership. Figure 10-7 shows these settings; the list that follows describes them.

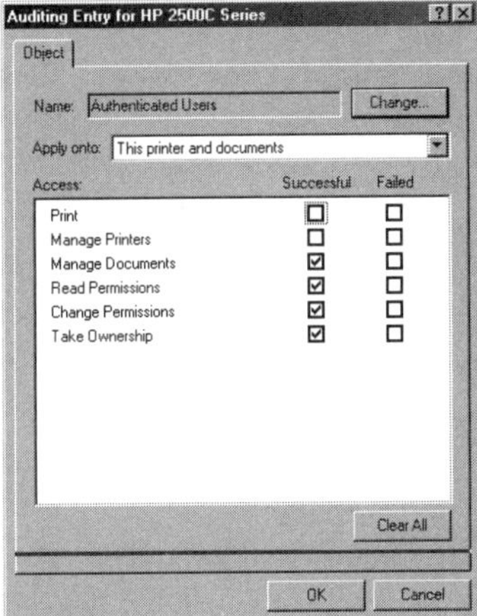

Figure 10-7. *Printer audit settings.*

- **Print.** Use this setting to generate an audit event every time a document is printed.
- **Managing Printer.** This setting covers auditing for sharing a printer, deleting a printer, or changing a printer's properties.
- **Managing Documents.** The setting includes changing job settings for documents and pausing, restarting, moving, or deleting documents from the print queue.
- **Change Permissions.** Use this setting to enable auditing for changing the printer permissions.
- **Take Ownership.** Use this setting to enable the auditing for the take ownership function.

To track printer usage

1. Open Printers.
2. Right-click the printer you want to audit, and then choose Properties from the context menu.
3. Click the Security tab, click the Advanced button, and then click the Auditing tab.

4. Click Add, and then click the user or group whose printer access you want to audit.
5. In the Access column, click the successful and failed printing events you want to audit, and then click OK twice.

Auditing Local Drives

You can audit drives in a similar manner to files and folders.

To set an audit policy on drives

1. Open Computer Management (Local).

Note To open Computer Management, click Start, point to Settings, and then click Control Panel. Double-click Administrative Tools, and then double-click Computer Management.

2. In the console tree, click Logical Drives, which you can find by clicking on Storage.
3. Right-click the drive you want to audit, choose Properties from the context menu, and then click the Security tab, shown in Figure 10-8.
4. Click Advanced, and then click the Auditing tab, shown in Figure 10-9.
5. To set audit entries for either a new user or a group, click Add. In Look In, choose the domain that the user or group is a member of. In Name, type the name of the user or group you want to set entries for, and then click OK to open the Audit Entry dialog box.

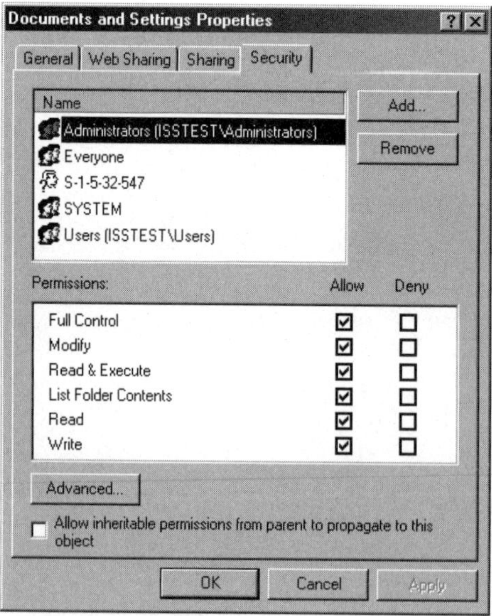

Figure 10-8. *Security tab.*

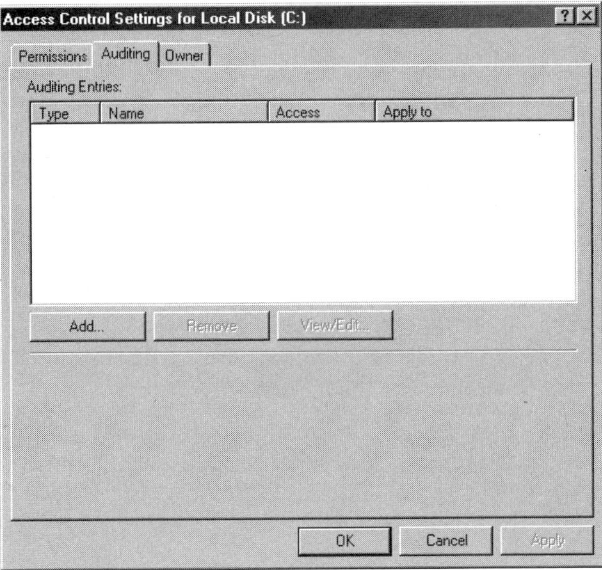

Figure 10-9. *Auditing tab.*

6. To change audit entries for an existing user or group, click the name of the user or group, and then click View/Edit.
7. To remove audit entries for an existing user or group, click the name, and then click Remove. Skip steps 8, 9, and 10.
8. In the Auditing Entry dialog box, select where you want auditing to take place in Apply Onto, if necessary. Figure 10-10 shows the Auditing Entry dialog box.

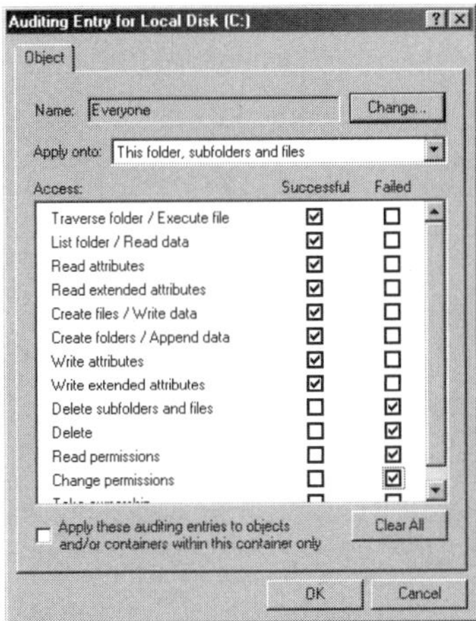

Figure 10-10. *Auditing Entry dialog box.*

9. In Access, click Successful, Failed, or both for each access you want to audit.
10. If you want to prevent files and folders from inheriting these audit entries, select the Apply These Auditing Entries To Objects And/Or Containers Within This Container Only check box.

Note The preceding procedure for setting auditing does not work on removable drives. Setting drive auditing this way is the same as setting auditing on the root directory of the local drive selected.

Once you enable auditing in Group Policy, use Event Viewer to review successful or failed attempts to access the audited files and folders. You can set or change audit entries only on computers for which you are an administrator or have been granted the Manage Auditing And Security Log right in Group Policy.

You can change audit entries on a remote computer or a local computer. To access a remote computer, right-click Computer Management (Local), click Connect To Another Computer, and then select the computer you want to connect to.

Auditing the Registry

You can audit registry keys, allowing you to monitor actions such as setting or modifying registry keys.

To audit activity on a registry key

1. Click the key you want to audit.
2. Choose Permissions from the Security menu.
3. Click Advanced, and then click the Auditing tab.
4. Double-click the name of a group or user you want to audit.
5. Under Access, select or clear the Successful and Failed check boxes for the activities that you want to audit or to stop auditing. Table 10-5 describes the role of each check box.

Table 10-5. Options for auditing registry keys.

Select	To Audit
Query Value	Attempts to read a value entry from a registry key
Set Value	Attempts to set value entries in a registry key
Create Subkey	Attempts to create subkeys on a selected registry key
Enumerate Subkeys	Attempts to identify the subkeys of a registry key
Notify	Notification events from a key in the registry
Create Link	Attempts to create a symbolic link in a particular key
Delete	Attempts to delete a registry object
Write DACL	Attempts to write a discretionary access control list on the key
Write Owner	Attempts to change the owner of the selected key
Read Control	Attempts to open the discretionary access control list on a key

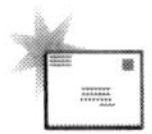

Note You must be logged on as an administrator or a member of the Administrators group to complete this procedure. If your computer is connected to a network, network policy settings can also prevent you from completing this procedure. You must first add users and groups before specifying the events to audit.

Auditing User Account Management

You can audit the success or failure of any user or group to perform an access to a file by enabling file auditing on object access and setting up given objects—such as directories, printers, or files—to generate audit events every time users access them. This allows you to audit the success or failure of any user or group to perform an access to a file.

To add users or groups to the Audit list

1. Click the key you want to audit.
2. Choose Permissions from the Security menu.
3. Click Advanced, click the Auditing tab, and then click Add.
4. In Look In, click the computer or domain of the users and groups you want to view.
5. Click the name of the user or group you want to add, and then click OK to open the Auditing Entry dialog box.

Note You must be logged on as an administrator or a member of the Administrators group to complete this procedure. If your computer is connected to a network, network policy settings can also prevent you from completing this procedure.

Using File System Objects to Audit File Access Operations

The file accesses that you can audit are as follows:

- **Traverse Folder/Execute File.** An attempt was made to open a folder or execute a file.
- **List Folder/Read Data.** An attempt was made to list the contents of a folder or read the data contained in a file.
- **Read Attributes.** An attempt was made to read the attributes of a file or folder.
- **Read Extended Attributes.** An attempt was made to read the extended attributes of a file or folder.
- **Create Files/Write Data.** An attempt was made to create new files in a folder or write data to a file.
- **Create Folders/Append Data.** An attempt was made to create a new folder or append data to an existing file.
- **Write Attributes.** An attempt was made to modify the attributes.
- **Write Extended Attributes.** An attempt was made to modify the extended attributes of a folder or file.

- **Delete Subfolders and Files.** An attempt was made to delete a folder or a file.
- **Delete.** An attempt was made to delete an object.
- **Read Permissions.** An attempt was made to read the attributes on a file or folder.
- **Change Permissions.** An attempt was made to change the permissions on a file or folder.
- **Take Ownership.** An attempt was made to take ownership of an object.

Audit Log Categories

Regardless of which log is viewed, the auditing system places every event into one of five categories, which Table 10-6 describes.

Table 10-6. Categories of audit events.

	Error	Indicates significant events, such as a loss of functionality or data. A service failure during startup will usually generate an error.
	Warning	Indicates an event that is not immediately significant, but might cause future problems. For example, resource consumption events are usually indicative of future problems. If the application can recover from the event without a loss of functionality or data, the event is classified as a warning event.
	Information	Indicates a successful operation, such as that of an application, service, or driver. The use of this event type is usually restricted to major server services, as it would be inappropriate for a desktop application to generate an event every time it starts.
	Success Audit	Indicates an event that occurs when an attempt to audit is successful. A user's successful attempt to log on to the system will generate a success audit if logon/logoff auditing is enabled.
	Failure Audit	Indicates an event that occurs when an attempt to audit fails. A user's attempt to access an object to which he or she is denied access—and which is subject to auditing—will generate a failed audit event.

Full-Privilege Auditing

By default, a number of privileges are not audited under the Use Of Privileges audit policy option. This option enables you to audit the backup and restore privileges and is enabled by setting the registry key described in Table 10-7.

Table 10-7. Settings for full-privilege auditing.

Hive	HKEY_LOCAL_MACHINE\SYSTEM
Key	\CurrentControlSet\Control\Lsa
Name	fullprivilegeauditing
Type	REG_BINARY
Value	1

However, keep in mind that the following rights are not audited, even with full-privilege auditing enabled:

- Bypass traverse checking
- Generate security audits
- Create a token object
- Debug programs
- Create a new security context

Note Enabling the security context setting will generate a large amount of audit information, so it should only be set on high-security machines.

This security context setting causes an audit event to be generated for every occasion that a privilege is invoked—for example, when a file is backed up or restored.

Setting Up Permissions for Auditing

You set up permissions for auditing by viewing the security properties of files, folders, shared folders, printers, and Active Directory objects.

When you set up permissions, you specify the level of access for groups and users. For example, you can let one user read the contents of a file, let another user make changes to the file, and prevent all other users from accessing the file. You can set similar permissions on printers so that certain users can configure the printer while other users can only print from it.

You set up auditing to detect and record security-related events, such as a user's attempt to access a confidential file or folder. When you audit an object, an entry is written to the Windows 2000 Security log whenever a user accesses that object in a certain way. Each entry in the Security log includes information such as the user's name and the action he or she performed. You determine which objects to audit, whose actions to audit, and exactly what types of actions to audit. Once you set up auditing, you can identify and analyze security breaches when users access certain objects. The audit trail can show you who performed each action, and who tried to perform actions that are not permitted.

If your computer is connected to a network, network policy might restrict or disable security logging. The Security log is limited in size, so carefully select the events to audit, taking into consideration the amount of disk space you are willing to devote to the Security log.

If security auditing is enabled on a remote machine, you can view the event logs remotely with Event Viewer. Open an MMC console in author mode (use the *mmc /a* command), and add Event Viewer to the console. When prompted to specify which computer the snap-in will manage, click Another Computer and enter the name of the remote computer.

Only domain administrators can remotely enable security auditing for workstations, member servers, and domain controllers. To do this, create an OU, add the desired machine account or accounts to the OU, and then use Active Directory Users And Computers to create a policy to enable security auditing.

Auditing and Group Policy

Auditing is only useful if you analyze the logged audit events on a regular basis. This kind of analysis is difficult to do using Event Viewer, so the data is usually exported to a database. Working with a database permits you to execute more advanced queries against the data, and allows the automatic creation of detailed reports.

Before you or your organization create an audit policy, you must make audit decisions about what areas of the system to audit, and in how much detail. In a situation in which large amounts of audit data are generated, it is often appropriate to use a supplementary program to import the data automatically and perform analyses. These specialized programs can usually perform scheduled analyses of the audit logs and generate alerts for specified incidents.

Local and Group Policy

You can use either Local Policy or Group Policy to enable auditing. If the machine is on a domain, the Group Policy for that domain can override any decisions made on the local machine, depending on decisions made in the Group Policy.

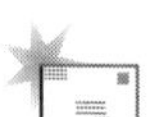

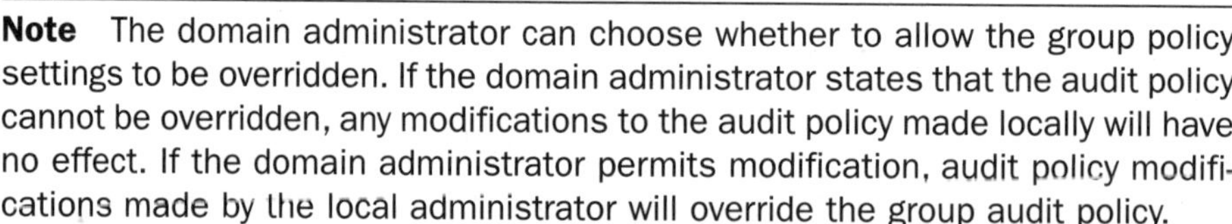

Note The domain administrator can choose whether to allow the group policy settings to be overridden. If the domain administrator states that the audit policy cannot be overridden, any modifications to the audit policy made locally will have no effect. If the domain administrator permits modification, audit policy modifications made by the local administrator will override the group audit policy.

The Group Policy Snap-In allows you to set success and failure traps for the security events listed in Table 10-8.

Table 10-8. Auditing success and failure events.

Policy	Success
Account logon events	An attempt has been made to interactively authenticate to the system.
Account management	A user or group account was created, modified, or deleted; or a password was successfully changed.
Directory service access	An attempt has been made to gain access to an object in Active Directory.
Logon events	An attempt was made to authenticate with the system
Object access	An attempt was made to gain access to a directory, printer, or file that is set for auditing.

(continued)

Table 10-8. *(continued)*

Policy	Success
Policy change	An attempt was made to change the user rights or audit policies.
Privilege use	A privileged operation was attempted.
Process tracking	This policy provides detailed tracking information for events such as program activation, some forms of handle duplication, indirect object access, and process exit.
System events	An internal process has occurred. Examples include a trusted logon process registering, or an authentication package loading.

Event Log Subsystem

The event log is a single collection of important hardware and software events that you can view using the Event Viewer Snap-In.

Event Record

When an event is generated it is sent to the relevant Event Viewer log. Depending on the type of event that has been generated, the contents of the event might vary slightly. The event consists of two parts: the Event Header and the Event Description.

Table 10-9 describes the Event Header in more detail.

Table 10-9. The Event Header.

Information	Meaning
Date	The date the event occurred.
Time	The (local) time the event occurred.
User	The username of the user on whose behalf the event occurred. This name is the client ID if the event was actually caused by a server process or the primary ID if impersonation is not taking place. Where applicable, a Security log entry contains both the primary and impersonation IDs. (Impersonation occurs when Windows 2000 allows one process to take on the security attributes of another.)
Computer	The name of the computer on which the event occurred. The computer name is usually your own, unless you are viewing an event log on another Windows 2000 computer.
Event ID	A number identifying the particular event type. The first line of the description usually contains the name of the event type. For example, 6005 is the ID of the event that occurs when the Event log service is started. The first line of the description of such an event is "The Event log service was started."

(continued)

Table 10-9. (continued)

Information	Meaning
Source	The software that logged the event, which can be either an application name, such as SQL Server, or a component of the system or of a large application, such as a driver name. For example, Elnkii indicates the EtherLink II driver. Product support representatives can use both the Event ID and the Source to troubleshoot system problems.
Type	A classification of the event severity: Error, Information, or Warning in the system and application logs; Success Audit or Failure Audit in the Security log. In Event Viewer's normal list view, these classifications are represented by symbols.
Category	A classification of the event by the event source. This information is primarily used in the Security log. For example, for security audits, Category corresponds to one of the event types for which success or failure auditing can be enabled in the User Manager For Domains Audit Policy dialog box.

The Event Description

Right-clicking an event in the log brings up an Event Properties window. This window gives a more detailed event description than the description that appears in the log. Record Data contains data relevant to the specific application. The data field, if used, contains information generated by the application that generated the log entry. This data is specific to the application and can be displayed as either bytes or words (though either way, it is usually only understood by a support engineer). Figure 10-11 shows the event description.

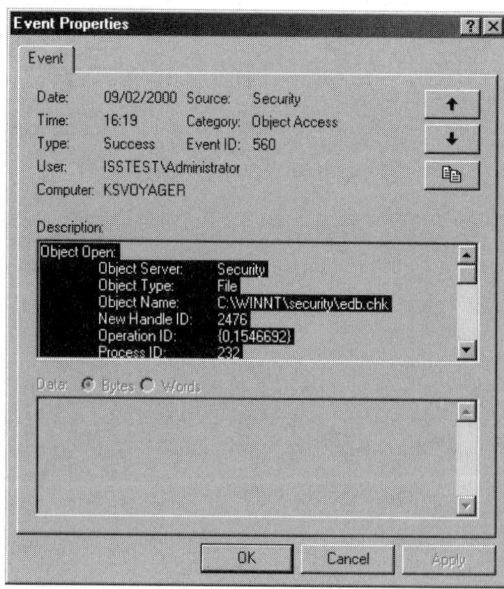

Figure 10-11. *Event description.*

Event Log Properties

Event log properties contain important information about how the computer maintains the log. This information includes the maximum size the log should be, and what to do when the log becomes full. You need to consider both of these items carefully. It is not unusual to keep logs for three to six months. These logs often become large, so it's necessary to clear them from time to time. Because a successful attack on a machine can go unnoticed for some time, it is best to save the log to some form of backup device before you clear the log. A good policy is to back up each log once a month and then erase the contents of the log from the machine. It's also a good policy to keep backups of your logs for three to six months in case you need to examine a previous log for evidence of an attack.

It is generally considered bad practice to set the log up to overwrite events after a given period of time or when it becomes full. For this reason, the log size should be adequate for the rate at which the logs are produced, and you should set the log to never write over events. However, in certain circumstances this is unhelpful. With the exception of high-security environments, keeping large logs for workstations is excessive. Therefore, the easiest solution is to set the log to a suitable size and let it overwrite events as needed. On a server, you are best off adopting a more proactive approach to keeping long-term logs and backing them up, as mentioned earlier. The maximum log size that you should set depends entirely on the system and how busy it is. This information is only available by examining how quickly the machine generates events. A server with 50 users connecting to its resources across the network generates considerably more logon events than a single workstation, and as such needs an appropriately larger log file. The destination to which the log file is written is contained in the log name text box of the log's properties.

Caution If the log is set not to overwrite events, and the log reaches its maximum size, the system might halt until the log is erased.

Filtering Events

By clicking the Filter tab in the properties window of a given log, you can use a variety of conditions to filter the log. For example, you can use a filter to view log information between certain dates and times. This kind of filter might be useful for examining system activity around the time of a particular incident or just prior to a hardware failure. To filter in a date-restricted field, you need to change the From and To tabs from First Event or Last Event to Events On, then enter the date and time required in the text boxes available. You can filter events based on type, such as information, warning, error, success audit, or failure audit. You can also use any combination of these types to form a filter. Figure 10-12 on the following page shows the Filter tab.

The lower half of the Filter tab presents much more detailed filtering controls. These include permitting filtering for events that pertain to a specific computer, a specific user, a specific event ID, or a specific source. You might find it useful to filter for a specific source when investigating a problem with the setup of a service. Filtering for a given user makes it easier to monitor the activities of a given account.

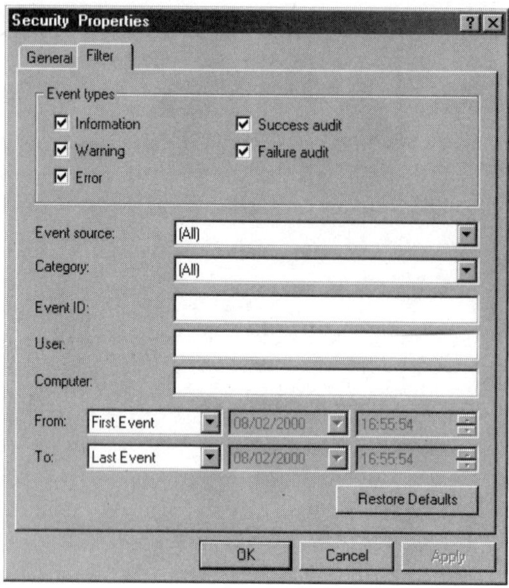

Figure 10-12. *The Filter tab.*

Security Event Records

Auditing a local object creates an entry in the Security log. For events concerning access to objects, the entries in the Security log also depend on the audit settings defined for each object.

Viewing Security Logs

The security entries that appear in the Security log depend on the auditing categories selected for your auditing policy. For example, if your auditing policy specifies auditing of files and folders, and a file's properties specify that failed deletions of that file should be audited, each failed attempt by a user to delete the file will appear in the Security log. You can use the Event Viewer to view the Security log.

The Size of the Security Log

Because the Security log is limited in size, you should carefully select the categories of events to be audited. You should also consider the amount of disk space you are willing to devote to the Security log.

Events that Can Be Audited

When you examine the Security log, you will see events according to the event category to which they pertain. You can audit the following events:

- Account disabled
- Account expired
- Assign special privilege

- Audit log cleared
- Audit policy change
- Authentication package loading
- Close handle
- Domain local group changed
- Domain local group created
- Domain local group member added
- Domain local group member deleted
- Domain local group member removed
- Domain changed
- Duplicate handle
- Failed logon
- Global group member added
- Global group member removed
- Indirect reference
- Invalid workstation
- Logoff
- Logon successful
- Logon type restricted
- Number of audits discarded
- Open object
- Password expired
- Privilege assigned
- Privileged object access
- Privileged service
- Process created
- Process exit
- Registered logon process
- System restart
- System shutdown
- Time restricted logon failure
- Unknown user name or password
- User changed
- User created
- User deleted

Finding Specific Logged Events

Searches can be useful when you view large logs. For example, you can search for all Warning events related to a specific application, or search for all Error events from all sources. To search for events that match a specific type, source, or category, choose Find from the View menu.

The options available in the Find dialog box are described in Table 10-10.

Filter Events

Event Viewer lists all events recorded in the selected log. To view a subset of events with specific characteristics, go to the View menu, click Filter, and then on the Filter tab, specify the criteria you want.

Filtering has no effect on the actual contents of the log; it changes only the view. All events are logged continuously, whether the filter is active or not. If you archive a log from a filtered view, all records are saved, even if you select a text format or comma-delimited text format file.

Table 10-10 describes the Filter options available in the Log Properties dialog box.

Table 10-10. Log Properties and Filter options.

Use	To Filter For
View Events From	Events after a specific date and time. By default, this is the date of the earliest event in the log file.
View Events To	Events up to and including a specific date and time. By default, this is the date of the latest event in the log file.
Information[1]	Infrequent significant events that describe successful operations of major services. For example, when a database program loads successfully, it might log an Information event.
Warning[1]	Events that are not necessarily significant but indicate possible future problems. For example, a Warning event might be logged when disk space is low.
Error[1]	Significant problems such as a loss of data or loss of functions. For example, an Error event might be logged if a service was not loaded during Windows 2000 startup.
Success Audit[1]	Successful audited security access attempts. For example, a user's successful attempt to log on to the system might be logged as a Success Audit event.
Failure Audit[1]	Failed audited security access attempts. For example, if a user tried to access a network drive and failed, the attempt might be logged as a Failure Audit event.
Source[2]	A source for logging events, such as an application, a system component, or a driver.

(continued)

Table 10-10. *(continued)*

Use	To Filter For
Category[3]	A classification of events defined by the source. For example, the security event categories are Logon and Logoff, Policy Change, Privilege Use, System Event, Object Access, Detailed Tracking, and Account Management.
User[3]	A specific user that matches an actual user name. This field is not case-sensitive.
Computer[3]	A specific computer that matches an actual computer name. This field is not case-sensitive.
Event ID[2]	A specific number that corresponds to an actual event.

Notes:

[1] This option is not available for LAN Manager 2.*x* servers.

[2] This option is not available for audit logs on LAN Manager 2.*x* servers.

[3] This option is not available for error logs on LAN Manager 2.*x* servers.

By default, Event Viewer sorts events by date and time of occurrence from the newest to the oldest. To specify a sort order, choose Newest First or Oldest First from the View menu. The default sort order is Newest First. When a log is archived, the default sort order is saved.

View Details about Events

The Event Properties dialog box shows a text description of the selected event and any available binary data. Binary data, which appears in hexadecimal format, is information generated by the program that is the source of the event record. A support technician familiar with the source program can interpret the data's meaning. Not all events generate binary data.

To control the types of security events that are audited: in Group Policy, go to Computer Configuration\Windows Settings\Security Settings\Local Policies\Audit Policy. To control the auditing of files and folders, display the Properties of a file or folder.

Auditing Dynamic Host Configuration Control Protocol

Windows 2000 Dynamic Host Configuration Control Protocol (DHCP) servers include several new logging features and server parameters that provide enhanced auditing capabilities. You can now specify the following features:

- The directory path in which the DHCP server stores audit log files
- A maximum size restriction (in megabytes) for the total amount of disk space available for all audit log files created and stored by the DHCP service

- An interval for disk checking that is used to determine how many times the DHCP server writes audit log events to the log file before checking for available disk space on the server
- A minimum size requirement (in megabytes) for server disk space that is used during disk checking to determine if sufficient space exists for the server to continue audit logging
- Selective enabling or disabling of the audit-logging feature at each DHCP server

Only the directory path in which the DHCP server stores audit log files can be modified using the DHCP console.

To set the audit log path

1. Select the applicable DHCP server in the console tree.
2. Choose Properties from the Action menu.
3. Click the Advanced tab and edit Audit Log File Path as necessary.

Adjust the other audit logging parameters in the preceding list through registry-based configuration changes.

How Audit Logging Works

The audit-logging behavior discussed in this section applies only to the DHCP Server service provided with Windows 2000 Server, and replaces the DHCP logging behavior used in earlier versions of Windows NT Server, which do not perform audit checks and use only a single log file named Dhcpsrv.log for logging service events.

The formatted structure of DHCP server logs and the level of reporting maintained for audited logging are the same as in earlier DHCP server versions provided with Windows NT Server.

Naming Audit Log Files

The DHCP Server service bases the name of the audit log file on the current day of the week, as determined by checking the current date and time at the server. For example, if the DHCP server starts when the current date and time is Wednesday, March 5, 1998, 04:56:42 P.M., the server audit log file is named DhcpSrvLog.Wed

Starting a Daily Audit Log

When a DHCP server starts or a new weekday begins (in other words, the local time on the computer is 12:00 A.M., the server writes a header message in the audit log file indicating that logging has started. Then, depending on whether the audit log file is a new or existing file, the following actions occur:

- If the file already existed without modification for more than a day, it is overwritten.

- If the file already existed but was modified within the previous 24 hours, the file is not overwritten. Instead, new logging activity is appended to the end of the existing file.

Disk Checks

After audit logging starts, the DHCP server performs disk checks at regular intervals to ensure the ongoing availability of server disk space, and also to ensure that the current audit log file does not become too large or that log-file growth does not occur too rapidly.

The DHCP server performs a full disk check whenever either of two conditions occurs: A set number of server events are logged, or the date changes on the server computer.

By default, the DHCP server performs a periodic disk space check for every 50 events it writes to the audit log. The DHCP server can also detect a date change when the server computer reaches 12:00 A.M. on its locally set Date/Time clock.

Each time the server completes a disk check, it determines whether disk space is filled. The disk is considered full if either of the following conditions is true:

- **Low disk space.** The server considers the disk full when disk space on the server computer is lower than the required minimum amount for DHCP audit logging. By default, if the amount of disk space remaining on the server disk drops below 20 megabytes, audit logging halts.
- **Audit log file too large.** If the current audit log file is larger than 1/7 of the maximum allotted space or size for the combined total of all audit logs currently stored on the server, the server considers the disk full. At the time of the disk check, the DHCP server compares the exact size (in megabytes) of the current audit log file with a value obtained by dividing the combined maximum allotted space for all audit logs currently stored on the server by the current value for the maximum number of log files the server permits to be stored simultaneously before overwriting and discarding older log files. By default, seven is the maximum number of log files the server permits to be stored—one for each day of the week. Assuming the default is set, the largest size that the current audit log file can reach is 1 MB.

In either case, if the disk is full, the DHCP server closes the current file and ignores further requests to log audit events until either 12:00 A.M. or until disk status is improved and the disk is no longer full.

Even if audit-logged events are ignored because a disk is full, the DHCP server continues disk checking every 50 events (or the currently set interval) to determine whether disk conditions have improved. If subsequent disk checks determine that the required amount of server disk space is now available, the DHCP server reopens the current log file and resumes logging.

Ending a Daily Audit Log

At 12:00 A.M. local time on the server computer, the DHCP server closes the existing log and moves to the log file for the next day of the week. For example, if the day of the week changes at 12:00 A.M. from Wednesday to Thursday, the log file named DhcpSrvLog.Wed is closed and the file named DhcpSrvLog.Thu is opened and used for logging events.

Analyzing Server Log Files

Windows 2000 DHCP server log files are designed to use audit logging to permit log files to remain enabled for use without requiring added monitoring or administering to manage log file growth or conserve disk resources.

The following section outlines the format of these log files and how you can use them to gather more information about DHCP Server service operations on the network.

DHCP Server Log File Format

DHCP server logs are comma-delimited text files; each log entry represents a single line of text. The following fields appear (in this order) in a log file entry: *ID, Date, Time, Description, IP Address, Host Name, MAC Address.*

Table 10-11 describes each of these fields in detail.

Table 10-11. DHCP server log fields.

Field	Description
ID	A DHCP server event ID code
Date	The date on which this entry was logged on the DHCP server
Time	The time at which this entry was logged on the DHCP server
Description	A description of this DHCP server event
IP Address	The IP address of the DHCP client
Host Name	The host name of the DHCP client
MAC Address	The media access control address used by the network-adapter hardware of the client

Auditing for Message Queuing

You can use auditing to record which users attempt to access Message Queuing objects, the type of operation attempted, and if the attempt succeeded or failed. The security descriptor for an object specifies the various access events to be audited for the object. As we mentioned earlier in the chapter, this part of the security descriptor is known as a SACL. More specifically, a SACL specifies the following:

- The users or groups to audit when accessing the object
- The access events to audit for each user or group

- A *Success* or *Failure* attribute for each access event, based on the permissions granted to each user or group in the object's DACL

Configuring Auditing

Before you implement auditing, you must first establish an auditing policy. An auditing policy specifies categories of security-related events you want to audit. When you establish the auditing policy for a Message Queuing server, you must grant the Manage Auditing And Security Log permission for the Message Queuing server that will perform the audited operation.

Next you select the object access category and set auditing options for specific objects. Once you set the object access category, you can use the Properties page for individual Message Queuing objects to specify whether to audit successes or failures for the permissions granted to each user or group.

If you specify audit options for a Message Queuing object, but you haven't established an audit policy on the Message Queuing server that carries out the operation, an audit message is not created. You might receive an error message stating that auditing is not enabled. This indicates either that auditing is disabled or no auditing policy has been established on the computer that you are using; it does not mean that auditing is not enabled on the computer to which you are trying to audit access.

Audit Messages

Audit messages are created in the Windows 2000 Security log on the computer that performs the operation, which is not necessarily the computer that owns the object. Because of this arrangement, audit messages for a single Message Queuing object can be scattered across a network. For example, as shown in Figure 10-13, if the test queue located on client 1 in the San Francisco site is deleted by client 2 in the Seattle site, the audit message is created on server 2 of the Seattle site.

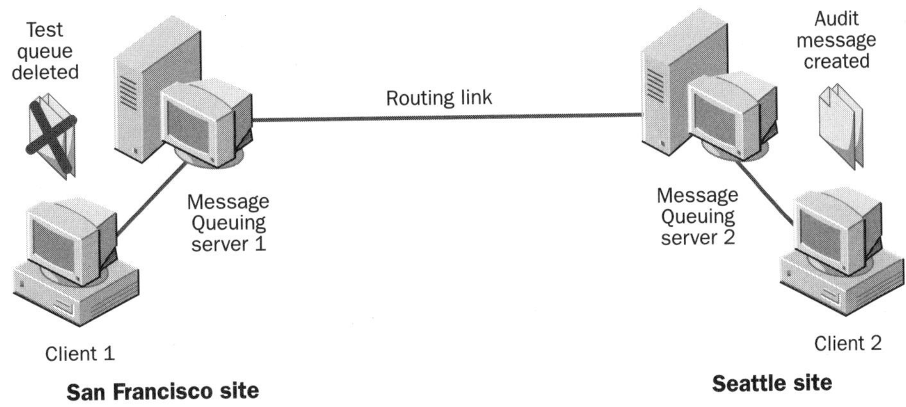

Figure 10-13. *Audit messages can be scattered across a network.*

When a queue is accessed, the audit message for this operation is always created on the computer on which the queue resides. Because a Message Queuing server performs all queue operations except the Receive Message and Peek Message operation, audit messages are created on the Message Queuing server that carries out the operation. Audit messages are created only when a queue is accessed, not each time a message is received or sent.

Each audit message has an Open entry and a Close entry in the Windows 2000 Security log. When a queue is accessed for a Receive Message or Peek Message operation, the Close audit entry is written to the log immediately after the Open entry is written to the log.

IP Security Audit Log

An event is defined as any significant occurrence in the system that requires notification. Event logging starts automatically each time you start Windows 2000. Use Event Viewer to view the System log for troubleshooting problems with the policy agent. You should also check the Security log for Oakley informational messages—the protocol that determines the key to be used by Internet Protocol security (IPSec)—and messages regarding failed IPSec communications.

For example, to determine why one of the services is not running, you can filter the System log to display only messages pertaining to the Policy Agent. You can also display a particular type of Policy Agent event message. You can use the same filtering on the Security log for Oakley messages by following these steps:

1. Expand the Event Viewer folder to display the System and Security logs.
2. Use the Action menu to apply filtering.

Verifying IPSEC Security

You can use IPSec Monitor to verify that the assigned policy is active.

To verify that the assigned policy is active

1. Choose Run from the Start menu.
2. Type "ipsecmon *ComputerName*" and click OK.

When IPSec Monitor opens, you will see a message in the lower right corner indicating whether IP Security is enabled on the computer. Figure 10-14 shows the IPSec Monitor.

To enable IP Security, you must assign a policy. However, no policies will be listed in the IPSec Monitor Security Association list unless a security association (SA) with another computer is currently active.

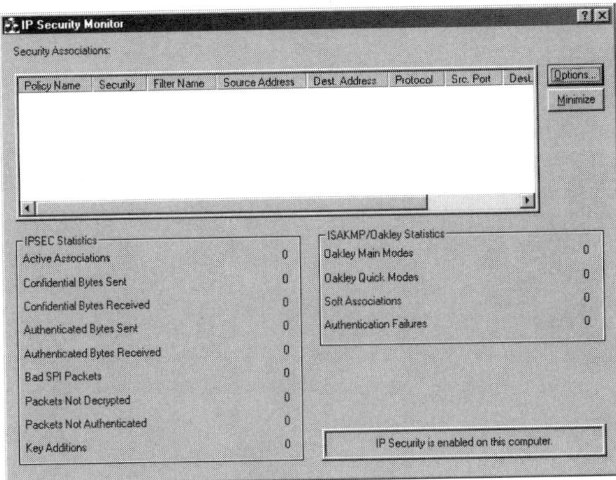

Figure 10-14. *IP Security Monitor.*

Event Viewer and the Security Audit Log

The IPSec Policy Agent indicates the source of its policy by making entries in the System log. The Policy Agent also indicates the polling interval as specified by the active policy for checking for policy changes in Active Directory. Administrators who edit the active IPSec policy on the local computer cause the changes to take effect immediately.

You can also see whether the computer is using Local Policy or policy from Active Directory by viewing the Event Log (specifically, by viewing the System log informational entry by the IPSec Policy Agent).

TCP/IP Properties

By displaying the properties for TCP/IP, you can see the active IPSec policy. If the computer is running local IPSec policy, the computer's name will be displayed in an editable form. If the computer is running policy assigned through Group Policy, the name will be unavailable and cannot be edited.

Event Identifications and Descriptions

Table 10-12 provides a reference for identifying events, shows which log records those events, shows the source of the log, indicates the type of event audited, and gives a brief description of the event.

Table 10-12. Event IDs and descriptions.

Event ID	Event Log	Source	Event Type	Details
512	Security	Security	Success	Windows 2000 is starting up.
513	Security	Security	Success	Windows 2000 is shutting down.
514	Security	Security	Success	An authentication package has been loaded by the LSA and will be used to authenticate logon attempts. Authentication packages are responsible for validating user identification and authentication information collected by logon processes during logon.
515	Security	Security	Success	A trusted logon process has registered with the LSA and will be trusted to submit logon requests. Logon processes are trusted components responsible for collecting identification and authentication information from external devices, such as terminals and networks. They use LSA services to log on these users.
516	Security	Security	Success	Internal resources allocated for the queuing of audit messages have been exhausted, leading to the loss of some audit data. This message indicates that audit event messages have been discarded, either because they were overwritten by later messages, or because of a cessation of auditing dependent on the audit policy in force.
517	Security	Security	Success	The audit log has been cleared. This event is always recorded, regardless of audit policy.
518	Security	Security	Success	A notification package has been loaded by the security accounts manager (SAM) and will be notified of any account or password changes. The name of the notification package will be given. The notification package is a trusted process and any change in authorized packages should be investigated immediately.
528	Security	Security	Success	A successful logon has occurred.
529	Security	Security	Failure	A logon failure has occurred because of an unknown user account or because of a known user account with an invalid password. An unexpected increase in the number of these messages can indicate an attempt by someone to gain unauthorized access to the system.

(continued)

Table 10-12. *(continued)*

Event ID	Event Log	Source	Event Type	Details
530	Security	Security	Failure	A logon failure has occurred because the user attempted to log on outside the hours he or she was authorized to do so.
531	Security	Security	Failure	A logon failure has occurred because the account has been disabled.
532	Security	Security	Failure	A logon failure has occurred because the user's account has expired.
533	Security	Security	Failure	A logon failure has occurred because the user isn't authorized to log on to this system.
534	Security	Security	Failure	A logon failure has occurred because the user has not been granted the requested logon type at this machine.
535	Security	Security	Failure	A logon failure has occurred because the user's password has expired.
536	Security	Security	Failure	A logon failure has occurred because the NetLogon service is not active.
537	Security	Security	Failure	A logon failure has occurred for reasons other than those specifically identified in other failed audit events.
538	Security	Security	Success	A user has logged off.
539	Security	Security	Failure	A logon failure has occurred because the account was locked out after exceeding the account lockout policy settings.
540	Security	Security	Success	A successful network logon has occurred.
541	Security	Security	Success	An IP Security Exchange has been established. A return of (Mode == Key Exchange (Main Mode)) indicates that a peer has been successfully authenticated, and Key Exchange security established. A return of (Mode == Data Protect (Quick Mode) means that a Data Protection security association over a given filter has been established.
542	Security	Security	Success	An IP Security Exchange (IKE) security association (quick mode) has been torn down (ended).
543	Security	Security	Success	An IP Security Exchange (IKE) security association (main mode) has been torn down (ended).

(continued)

Table 10-12. *(continued)*

Event ID	Event Log	Source	Event Type	Details
544	Security	Security	Failure	An IKE security association establishment failed because peer could not authenticate and the certificate trust could not be established.
545	Security	Security	Success	An IKE peer authentication has failed. The identity of the peer could not be confirmed or the authentication parameters were incorrect. The cause of this audit message depends on authentication type; the message can be caused by IPSec configuration problems, by Kerberos issues, or by corrupt or incorrectly loaded certificates.
546	Security	Security	Failure	An IKE security association establishment failed because peer sent an invalid proposal (for example, it was impossible to agree on the security attributes necessary for protecting the traffic). The audit message will identify which attribute was in contention, what was expected, and what value the peer sent.
547	Security	Security	Failure	An IKE security association negotiation failed. The audit message will identify the mode (Main or Quick), the filter, where the failure occurred (Local or Peer), and will give an explanation of the failure together with likely causes.
560	Security	Security	Success	An object identified by the given handle has been successfully opened, or an attempt to open it has been rejected. The only way to know what happened to the object is to look at the object name in the audit log. If this event is associated with a file containing sensitive data, there might be security implications.
561	Security	Security	Success	A handle to an object has been allocated.
562	Security	Security	Success	A handle to an object has been closed.
563	Security	Security	Success	An object has been opened with the intent to delete it. This message does not mean that the object has been deleted; the only way to know what happened to the object is to look at the object name in the audit log. If this event is associated with a file containing sensitive data, there might be security implications.

(continued)

Table 10-12. *(continued)*

Event ID	Event Log	Source	Event Type	Details
564	Security	Security	Success	An object, identified by the given handle, has been deleted.
565	Security	Security	Success	An object, identified by the given handle, has been opened.
566	Security	Security	Success	An attempt to access an LSA secret has failed.
576	Security	Security	Success	A privilege that is not auditable on an individual basis has been assigned to a user's security context at logon. For example, bypass traverse checking (SeChangeNotifyPrivilege) is a privilege assigned to all users by default and falls into this category.
577	Security	Security	Success	An attempt has been made to use a privilege to access a privileged system service.
578	Security	Security	Success	An attempt has been made to use a privilege to perform a privileged object operation.
592	Security	Security	Success	A new process has been created.
593	Security	Security	Success	A process has exited.
594	Security	Security	Success	A handle to a kernel object has been duplicated. This event record indicates that a handle has been duplicated for the same or less access than previously granted. If the source handle is closed, a separate Handle Closed audit record is generated.
595	Security	Security	Success	Indirect access to an object has been obtained. The audit message will give details of the Primary and Client ID and username.
608	Security	Security	Success	A specific user right has been assigned to a user.
609	Security	Security	Success	A specific user right has been withdrawn from a user.
610	Security	Security	Success	The user identified has created a new trust relationship with the identified domain.
611	Security	Security	Success	The identified user has removed a trust relationship within the specified domain.

(continued)

Table 10-12. *(continued)*

Event ID	Event Log	Source	Event Type	Details
612	Security	Security	Success	The audit policy has been changed. The audit message details the actual changes. Any unexpected changes to audit policy should be investigated immediately.
613	Security	Security	Success	IPSec Policy Agent has started.
614	Security	Security	Success	IPSec Policy Agent is disabled.
615	Security	Security	Success	IPSec Policy Agent has changed.
616	Security	Security	Success	IPSec Policy Agent encountered a potentially serious failure.
617	Security	Security	Success	Kerberos policy has been changed.
618	Security	Security	Success	The encrypted data recovery policy has been changed.
619	Security	Security	Success	The quality-of-service policy has been changed.
620	Security	Security	Success	Trusted domain information has been modified.
624	Security	Security	Success	A new user account has been created.
625	Security	Security	Success	A user account type has been changed.
626	Security	Security	Success	A user account has been enabled.
627	Security	Security	Success	An attempt to change a password has been made. The audit message will indicate the account name and target domain.
628	Security	Security	Success	A person with administrative rights on the system has set a user password.
629	Security	Security	Success	The specified user has disabled the identified user account.
630	Security	Security	Success	A user account has been deleted.
631	Security	Security	Success	A Global group has been created.
632	Security	Security	Success	The user has been added to a Security Enabled Global group.
633	Security	Security	Success	The user has been removed from a Security Enabled Global group.
634	Security	Security	Success	A Security Enabled Global group has been deleted.
635	Security	Security	Success	A Security Enabled Local group has been created.

(continued)

Table 10-12. *(continued)*

Event ID	Event Log	Source	Event Type	Details
636	Security	Security	Success	A user has been added to a Security Enabled Local group. This event will also occur when a new user is created and added to the None group used internally by Windows 2000.
637	Security	Security	Success	A user has been removed from a Security Enabled Local group. This event will also occur when a user account is deleted and automatically removed from the None group used internally by Windows 2000.
638	Security	Security	Success	A Security Enabled Local group has been deleted.
639	Security	Security	Success	A Security Enabled Local group has changed.
640	Security	Security	Success	The general account database has changed.
641	Security	Security	Success	A Security Enabled Global group has changed (other than Group membership).
642	Security	Security	Success	A user account has changed.
643	Security	Security	Success	The domain policy has changed. The audit message will identify the user, computer, and domain. Changing the domain policy can have security implications and should be investigated.
644	Security	Security	Success	The named account has been automatically locked out. This usually occurs because of repeated authentication failures.
645	Security	Security	Success	A computer account has been created.
646	Security	Security	Success	A computer account has been changed.
647	Security	Security	Success	A computer account has been deleted.
648	Security	Security	Success	A Security Disabled Local group has been created
649	Security	Security	Success	A Security Disabled Local group has changed (other than Group membership).
650	Security	Security	Success	A user has been added to a Security Disabled Local group.
651	Security	Security	Success	A user has been removed from a Security Disabled Local group.
652	Security	Security	Success	A Security Disabled Local group has been deleted.

(continued)

Table 10-12. *(continued)*

Event ID	Event Log	Source	Event Type	Details
653	Security	Security	Success	A Security Disabled Global group has been created.
654	Security	Security	Success	A Security Disabled Global group has changed (other than Group membership).
655	Security	Security	Success	A user has been added to a Security Disabled Global group.
656	Security	Security	Success	A user has been removed from a Security Disabled Global group.
657	Security	Security	Success	A Security Disabled Global group has been deleted.
658	Security	Security	Success	A Security Disabled Universal group has been created.
659	Security	Security	Success	A Security Disabled Universal group has changed.
660	Security	Security	Success	A user has been added to a Security Disabled Universal group.
661	Security	Security	Success	A user has been removed from a Security Disabled Universal group.
662	Security	Security	Success	A Security Disabled Universal group has been deleted.
663	Security	Security	Success	A Security Enabled Universal group has been created.
664	Security	Security	Success	A Security Enabled Universal group has changed.
665	Security	Security	Success	A user has been added to a Security Enabled Universal group.
666	Security	Security	Success	A user has been removed from a Security Enabled Universal group.
667	Security	Security	Success	A Security Enabled Universal group has been deleted.
668	Security	Security	Success	A change has been made to the status of a Security Enabled/Disabled group, or a Group is made into a Universal Group.
669	Security	Security	Success	Security identifier (SID) history was added to an account. This allows one account to have access to the resources that belong to another account, usually an old account of the same user. The audit message will list both accounts. Any unexpected SID history changes should be investigated.

(continued)

Table 10-12. *(continued)*

Event ID	Event Log	Source	Event Type	Details
670	Security	Security	Success	An attempt to add SID history to an account failed.
672	Security	Security	Success	An authentication ticket has been granted. The audit message will give details of the ticket.
673	Security	Security	Success	A ticket-granting ticket (TGT) has been granted.
674	Security	Security	Success	A ticket has been renewed.
675	Security	Security	Success	Pre-authentication failed.
676	Security	Security	Success	An authentication ticket request failed.
677	Security	Security	Success	A TGT request failed.
678	Security	Security	Success	A specified client has been mapped to the specified account.
679	Security	Security	Success	At attempt to map a specified client to an account failed.
680	Security	Security	Success	An account was used for a logon. This audit message will be generated on the authentication server—which is a domain controller for domain accounts—or on the local machine for local accounts.
681	Security	Security	Success	An attempt to log on failed. This audit message will be generated on the authenticating server—which is a domain controller for domain accounts—or on the local machine for local accounts.
682	Security	Security	Success	A logon session was reconnected. This audit message will be generated on the authenticating server—which is a domain controller for domain accounts—or on the local machine for local accounts.
683	Security	Security	Success	A logon session was disconnected. This audit message will be generated on the authenticating server—which is a domain controller for domain accounts—or on the local machine for local accounts.

DHCP Server Log: Common Event Codes

DHCP server audit log files use reserved event ID codes to provide information about the type of server event or activity logged. Detailed information about DHCP event codes can be found in the Windows 2000 Server online help. The information found there applies to both Windows 2000 DHCP servers and to servers running earlier versions of Windows.

Summary

This chapter introduces the comprehensive auditing functionality provided by Windows 2000. To optimize the benefits of auditing, you need to spend some time developing a sound and appropriate auditing policy. Likewise, there is little point in auditing if you aren't going to allocate resources for correlating and examining the resultant audit records.

Chapter 11
Network Security

As you've seen throughout this book, Windows 2000 includes profound improvements to the operating system security model. However, we haven't yet discussed how to protect data as it is being transmitted over the network. You can secure the file system on a Windows 2000 machine by applying permissions to it and even encrypting it, but when an authorized user accesses files from another system, those files are transmitted over the network in an unprotected form and can easily be intercepted by unauthorized users.

This chapter examines the technologies incorporated into Windows 2000 that enable you to secure data as it is transmitted over the network, and protect systems and services from unauthorized access through the network. These technologies include:

- **IPSec.** Internet Protocol security, or IPSec, is a public standard defining the use of end-to-end encryption at the Open Systems Interconnection (OSI) model's network layer, thus protecting all network communication generated by participating systems.
- **Dynamic DNS.** You can secure the Windows 2000 DNS server so that only authenticated systems can access and dynamically update their resource records.
- **DHCP Security.** Authorizing DHCP servers prevents rogue servers from issuing inaccurate TCP/IP configuration data and incorrect DHCP response messages.
- **Remote Access.** Accessing a network from a remote location is a useful but inherently dangerous capability. Windows 2000 includes several mechanisms to ensure that remote users are properly authenticated and that their data is protected.

Securing IP Communications

Many traditional security mechanisms used by network operating systems are based on usernames and passwords. Windows 2000 adds several new features, such as an encrypting file system and smart card authentication, but these technologies are designed to provide security at the workstation. They do nothing to protect data as it travels over the network. For example, network administrators can protect sensitive files by carefully applying strict access permissions, but when an authorized user accesses one of these files from a remote system, the data is completely unprotected as it is transmitted over the network. Even if the file is encrypted, the server system decrypts it before sending it to the client.

Physical protection of the network is one possibility. You can prevent intruders from accessing the network by denying them access to the cable itself, but this requires extraordinary measures, such as installing cables within metal conduits and carefully restricting access to wall plates and wiring closets. For networks requiring extremely high security, such as government installations, this might be a possibility, but it's usually not practical for the average consumer.

Therefore, supposedly protected data can be compromised while in transit and used in a variety of ways to damage your network or your business. Networks today are much larger than they used to be, and threats to network security do not all originate outside the firewall. The following sections describe some of the most common techniques for compromising a network from the inside.

Packet Capturing

A network analyzer, or "sniffer," is a device that connects to the network and captures data as that data travels between systems. By putting its network interface into what is known as *promiscuous mode*, the sniffer reads all packets on the network, not just those addressed to a specific computer. The analyzer can be a portable device or a software program running on a computer. Microsoft's Systems Management Server includes a network analyzer called Network Monitor, and many similar products are available. These tools can read the contents of each packet, including any data found there, such as part of a confidential file. Any information transmitted over the network as clear text is vulnerable to this type of attack.

Data Modification

Once an intruder is able to access the data in captured packets, that intruder can also alter the data and send the packets on to the intended recipients. The recipients of the packets will not be able to detect that any modifications have taken place.

Spoofing

Every packet on a TCP/IP network contains the IP addresses of the source and destination systems. Intruders can gain access to information they are not authorized to access by using the IP address of another system and pretending to be that system. This is called *spoofing*. In a typical communication session between a client and a server, the two systems establish a connection by using the Transmission Control Protocol (TCP), and then they exchange packets, each of which contains a sequence number. To impersonate one of the systems involved in the connection, the intruder captures some of the packets, uses the IP address of one of the systems, and transmits his or her own packets using the same range of sequence numbers. At the same time, the intruder might initiate a denial of service attack against the system being impersonated, preventing that system from transmitting its own packets. Once the impostor has successfully assumed the role of the victim, he or she can receive any data originally meant for that system, and even send messages of his or her own. This type of attack not only compromises the data transmitted over the network, but can also allow the intruder to do further damage by accessing files still stored on the drives to which he or she now has access.

Password Compromise

Most network administrators do not enforce strict password policies. As a result, an intruder can often find it ridiculously easy to obtain passwords. Surprisingly, a great many passwords are compromised by an intruder simply calling a user, pretending to be someone else, and asking the user for the passwords. However, intruders can also crack passwords with software designed for that purpose, or intercept passwords using a sniffer. Although operating systems and applications often encrypt passwords before transmission, some, such as FTP, do not. This is why network support personnel are encouraged not to use their administrative accounts for routine tasks such as FTP file transfers. Intruders who obtain passwords with sufficient rights can not only access protected files, but can also perform even more damaging acts, such as modifying network or system configuration settings and creating bogus accounts for use later, after the intrusion is discovered.

Denial of Service Attacks

By flooding a computer or a network with useless traffic, an intruder can disrupt normal operations, prevent users from accessing network resources, shut down overburdened systems and applications, and distract administrators from other types of attacks on specific systems. There are several types of denial of service attack, most of which take advantage of regular TCP/IP features and procedures. For example, an intruder might send repeated messages to a system requesting the opening of new TCP connections. The intruder thus fills the target system's queue with unfulfilled requests, and legitimate attempts by other systems to open connections on the network fail.

Key Compromise

As with a password compromise, an intruder who is able to obtain a key used to encrypt or otherwise secure data can access protected resources, intercept communications that are believed to be secure, and assume the identity of another user.

Application Layer Attack

In many cases, the security of applications running on network systems is imperfect, enabling intruders to compromise the system by modifying operating system, application, or data files; introducing unauthorized software such as viruses or Trojan horses; or disrupting the access control mechanisms in the application or operating system. These types of exploitation are especially prevalent in applications such as Web servers that are designed to provide services to Internet clients.

You can use IPSec to prevent all the types of attack on Windows 2000 systems described thus far. IPSec is a protocol designed to secure network transmissions by encrypting individual Internet Protocol (IP) packets before they are transmitted. IP is a connectionless protocol that operates at the network layer of the OSI reference model. Virtually all the other TCP/IP protocols use IP as the "envelope" when sending messages to other systems on the network. If you encrypt the data carried in this envelope, intruders might be able to intercept the packet, but they won't be able to read its contents.

As Figure 11-1 illustrates, the OSI reference model splits a computer's networking processes into seven layers. The network layer is the third layer, just above the data-link layer and physical layer that define the protocol used by the LAN on which the computer is located (such as Ethernet or Token Ring). Network layer protocols such as IP are the primary end-to-end delivery systems for internetwork communication. This means that only the system generating the packet and the packet's ultimate recipient are privy to the data carried inside. Intermediate systems, such as the routers used to connect LANs together, process the packets only as high as the network layer to forward them on to their next destination.

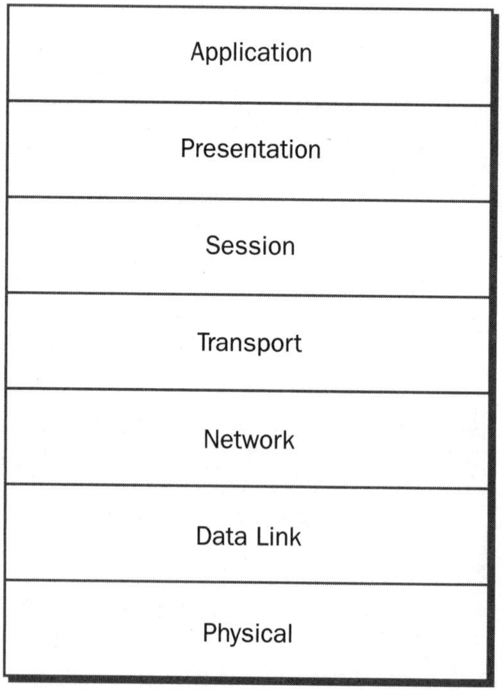

Application
Presentation
Session
Transport
Network
Data Link
Physical

Figure 11-1. *The OSI reference model.*

When you use IPSec to protect data, the sending system encrypts each individual packet and transmits it in the normal manner. Decryption doesn't occur until the packet reaches its final destination. This way, anyone intercepting the packet during its journey through the network can only capture the encrypted version, which is useless to unauthorized users. This practice also means that the intermediate systems that forward the packets don't have to support IPSec, thus enabling you to deploy IPSec on LANs, over WAN connections, and on remote access connections using dial-up or virtual private network connections (VPNs). Encryption operating at the data-link layer only protects the data on each intermediate link. Every router processing the packets would have to decrypt the packets on receipt and encrypt them again before forwarding them, which would not only increase the processing overhead of the routers but would also limit you to the use of routers that support IPSec.

Network layer encryption also means that the protection that is applied to all the workstation's outgoing traffic, no matter what application or process generates it. This is in direct contrast to encryption protocols that operate at higher layers of the OSI model. The Secure Sockets Layer (SSL) protocol used to secure World Wide Web client/server communications, for example, operates at the application layer—which is the top layer of the model—so that both the client and the server applications must support the protocol for it to function properly. IPSec is completely transparent to all processes running above the network layer, meaning that all the protocols carried within IP datagrams, such as TCP, the User Datagram Protocol (UDP), and the Internet Control Message Protocol (ICMP), are automatically protected. IPSec also doesn't require any modification to the applications running on the communicating systems, as SSL does, because the data is encrypted after it leaves the application layer of the transmitting system and is decrypted before it arrives at the application layer on the receiving system.

In addition to the encryption of individual packets, IPSec provides a number of additional security services for participating systems, including the following services:

- **Non-repudiation.** Using digital signatures and public key technology, IPSec verifies that a message actually originated from the sender, and not from an impostor. The sender cannot deny having generated the message, nor can a third party generate a message on the sender's behalf.
- **Authentication.** IPSec supports various authentication methods that enable systems to verify the identity of another party before communicating with the other party, including preshared key authentication, Kerberos authentication, and digital signatures based on public key certificates.
- **Encryption.** To encrypt the packet data, the IPSec implementation in Windows 2000 uses the Data Encryption Standard (DES) algorithm or the Triple Data Encryption Standard (3DES) algorithm. DES and 3DES are symmetric encryption algorithms, meaning that both systems possess the key used to encrypt and decrypt the data. These algorithms encrypt the data in 64-bit blocks, with 3DES processing each block three times for additional security.

- **Anti-replay.** In some cases, intruders can make use of intercepted packets even if they can't read the packet contents. For example, an intruder can deduce that the initial exchange of messages between a client and a server contains authentication information, and by resending the same packets at a later time, the intruder might be able to gain access to the server. IPSec uses a technique called cipher block chaining (CBC), which—when used together with DES or 3DES and a unique initialization vector (IV)—makes each encrypted packet appear different, even when two packets carry exactly the same data. This prevents intruders from using traffic-analysis techniques to intuit the contents of a packet, even when they can't penetrate the encryption.
- **Integrity.** IPSec can create hash message authentication codes (HMACs) to digitally sign each packet before transmission. This signature, also called a cryptographic checksum or a message integrity code (MIC), is based on a single key shared by the two systems involved, which differentiates it from other digital signatures that use public key technology. HMACs are also called *message digests* because they summarize the contents of the packet, and *one-way transforms* because while you can create a digest out of the message, you can't recreate the message from the digest. The sending system computes the HMAC by running the packet data through a hashing algorithm, such as Message Digest 5 (MD5) or Secure Hash Algorithm 1 (SHA1), and then attaches it to the packet. When the receiving system processes the packet, the system performs the same computation. If any modifications have been made to the data in transit, the HMAC results will differ from the signature included in the packet.

The protection provided by IPSec can prevent intruders from compromising the network using any of the attacks listed earlier. If you encrypt the data in the packets, intruders can't read the packet contents. Even though IPSec does not prevent capture of the packets, it does prevent intruders from using the data. This encryption, along with two-way authentication that establishes trusts between systems, also prevents intruders from intercepting passwords and keys, spoofing identities, and compromising applications. In addition to encrypting individual packets, IPSec's cryptographic checksum prevents anyone from modifying packet data before it reaches the recipient. IPSec can also provide packet-filtering capabilities that enable administrators to regulate communication based on IP addresses, protocols, or ports. This filtering can prevent many types of denial of service attacks by causing systems to discard packets that arrive from unauthorized sources.

IPSec Standards

IPSec is based on a series of standard documents in the process of ratification by the Internet Engineering Task Force (IETF) that are designed to provide various security services for systems using either the current IPv4 or the future IPv6 protocol. RFC 2411—known as the IP Security Document Roadmap—explains how the protocols defined in the various documents work together. At the time of this writing, most of the Requests for Comments (RFCs) that define the various elements of IPSec are proposed standards, meaning that the documents are completed but have not yet been ratified as Internet standards. The IPSec implementation included in Windows 2000 is based on these documents, but the specifications might change before the documents are ratified. This means that Windows 2000's IPSec support might eventually have to be modified to conform to the standards. The RFCs pertaining to IPSec are as follows:

- **RFC 2411** IP Security Document Roadmap
- **RFC 2401** Security Architecture for the Internet Protocol
- **RFC 2402** IP Authentication Header
- **RFC 2403** The Use of HMAC-MD5-96 within ESP and AH
- **RFC 2404** The Use of HMAC-SHA-1-96 within ESP and AH
- **RFC 2405** The ESP DES-CBC Cipher Algorithm With Explicit IV
- **RFC 2406** IP Encapsulating Security Payload (ESP)
- **RFC 2407** The Internet IP Security Domain of Interpretation for ISAKMP
- **RFC 2408** Internet Security Association and Key Management Protocol (ISAKMP)
- **RFC 2409** The Internet Key Exchange (IKE)
- **RFC 2410** The NULL Encryption Algorithm and Its Use With IPSec
- **RFC 2412** The OAKLEY Key Determination Protocol

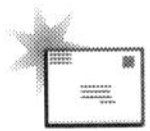

Note Unlike many other networking standards, the RFCs published by the IETF are in the public domain and freely available for downloading. To search for specific RFCs by number or by keywords, see *http://www.rfc-editor.org/rfcsearch.html.*

IPSec Protocols

IPSec uses two different protocols to provide systems with varying levels of security: IP Authentication Header (AH) and IP Encapsulating Security Payload (ESP). The following sections describe these two protocols.

IP Authentication Header

The IP Authentication Header (AH) protocol, as defined in RFC 2402, provides a relatively modest amount of additional security, with a proportionately small amount of overhead. AH provides authentication, anti-replay, and integrity services for the entire packet (that is, the IP header plus the data that follows it), but does not encrypt the data. When you use AH alone, the operators of the communicating systems are assured that the data they receive is unmodified and really did originate from the other user, but there is no guarantee that the message was not intercepted and its data compromised.

Note You can use AH by itself or in cooperation with the ESP protocol, as outlined later in this chapter.

AH adds another header to a standard IP datagram. This header follows the original IP header and precedes the next header, which can be for a transport layer protocol (TCP or UDP) or the ICMP, and the data generated by the application that created the packet, as shown in Figure 11-2.

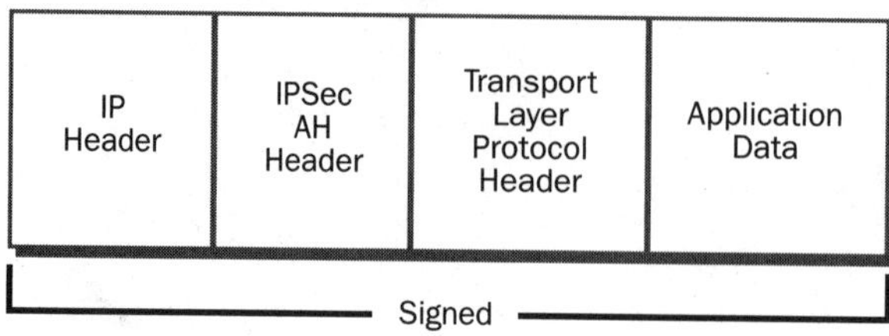

Figure 11-2. *An IP datagram with an AH header.*

If the packet contains other IPSec protocols (such as ESP), their headers come immediately after the AH header. The *Protocol* field in the IP header must identify the next header that appears in the packet. Normally, this would be the TCP or UDP header, and the value for the *Protocol* field would be 6 or 17, respectively. In a packet with an AH header, however, the *Protocol* field value is 51 and the *Next Header* field value in the AH header identifies the transport layer protocol header. Figure 11-3 shows the format for the AH header.

1 2 3 4 5 6 7 8	1 2 3 4 5 6 7 8	1 2 3 4 5 6 7 8 1 2 3 4 5 6 7 8
Next Header	Payload Length	Reserved
Security Parameters Index		
Sequence Number		
Authentication Data		

Figure 11-3. *The AH header format.*

The functions of the fields are as follows:

- ***Next header* (8 bits).** This field identifies the header that immediately follows the AH header, using the standard values defined in the Assigned Numbers RFC. If the system uses the ESP protocol in addition to AH, the value is 50. If not, the value of this field is 6 in the case of a TCP packet and 17 in the case of a UDP packet.

- ***Payload length* (8 bits).** This field specifies the length of the AH header, in 32-bit words minus two.
- ***Reserved* (16 bits).** This field is reserved for future use; the field contains a value of 0.
- ***Security Parameters Index* (32 bits).** This field contains an arbitrary value that—in combination with the destination IP address and the security protocol (AH, in this case)—identifies the security association for the datagram. A *security association* (SA) is an agreement between two computers on the security measures they will use to protect the information they transmit. The values 0 through 255 are reserved for future uses.
- ***Sequence Number* (32 bits).** This field contains a value that begins with 1 and increments for every packet using a particular SA. This field provides the protocol's anti-reply service. The receiving system checks to see if it has already received a packet with the same sequence number and SA values; if so, the system discards the packet.
- ***Authentication Data* (variable).** This field contains the Integrity Check Value (ICV) that the transmitting system calculates for all IP header fields that are immutable in transit or predictable in value; the entire AH header, including the Authentication Data field (which is set to a value of zero for this purpose); and the upper-level protocol header and data that follow the AH field. The receiving system uses the ICV to verify the packet's integrity by performing the same calculation and comparing the results with this value. The length of the value must be a multiple of 32 bits; the field can contain padding to bring its length up to the next 32-bit boundary.

IP Encapsulating Security Payload

The IP Encapsulating Security Payload protocol (ESP) provides encryption of the data carried in IP packets, as well as authentication, integrity, and anti-replay services. Unlike AH, which simply adds a header to the IP packets, ESP actually encapsulates the data within its protocol structure, as Figure 11-4 illustrates.

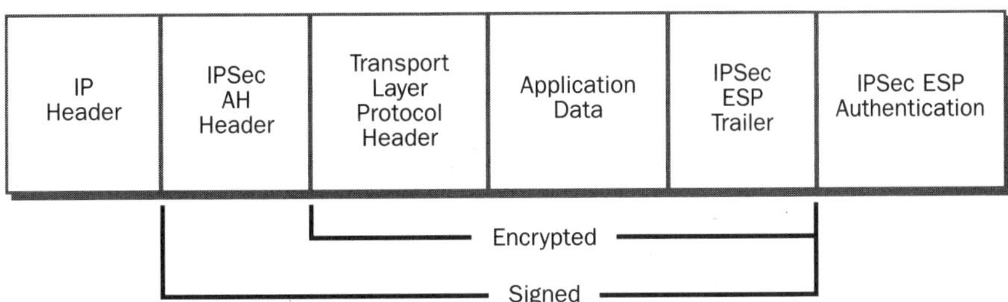

Figure 11-4. *An IP datagram with the ESP header.*

All data following the ESP header up to and including the ESP trailer—which includes the original transport layer (or ICMP) header and the application data—is encrypted for protection against unauthorized use. The information used to compute the integrity signature runs from the beginning of the ESP header to the end of the ESP trailer. Unlike the AH protocol, ESP does not include the packet's original IP header in the signature, which means that, unbeknown to the recipient, an intruder can conceivably modify the contents of this header. To avoid this, you can use both the AH and ESP protocols simultaneously to provide the greatest amount of protection.

As with the AH protocol, the *Protocol* field in the IP header does not identify the transport layer header, but instead identifies the ESP header with a value of 50.The *Next Header* field in the ESP trailer specifies the appropriate value for the transport layer header. Figure 11-5 shows the ESP packet format, which includes the transport layer header and the application data.

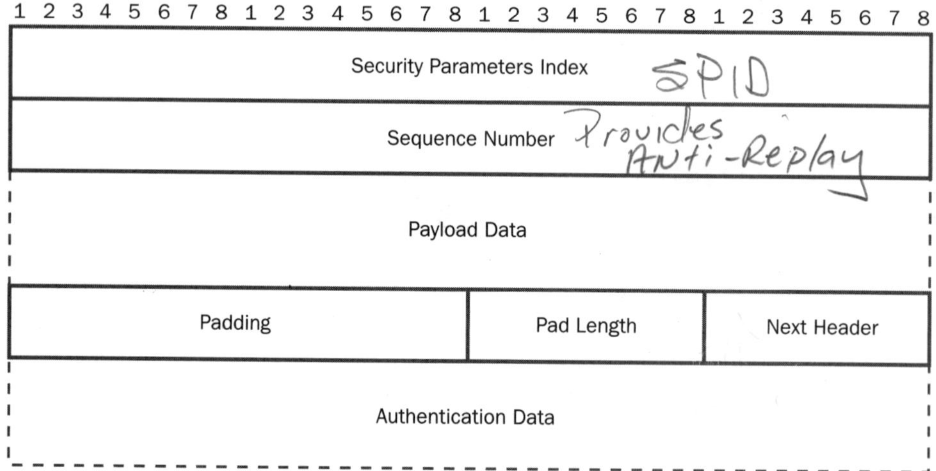

Figure 11-5. *The ESP packet format.*

The functions of the fields are as follows:

- ***Security Parameters Index* (32 bits).** This field contains an arbitrary value that, in combination with the destination IP address and the security protocol (AH in this case), identifies the SA for the datagram. The values 0 through 255 are reserved for future uses.
- ***Sequence Number* (32 bits).** This field contains a value that begins with 1 and increments for every packet using a particular SA. This field provides the protocol's anti-reply service. The receiving system checks to see if it has already received a packet with the same sequence number and SA values; if so, the system discards the packet.
- ***Payload Data* (variable).** This field contains the original transport layer (or ICMP) header from the packet before ESP was applied, plus the application data.

- ***Padding* (0–255 bytes)**. This field contains sufficient padding to satisfy the needs of some encryption algorithms that can only work with data blocks of a specific length and to ensure that the *Pad Length* and *Next Header* fields that follow are right-aligned in a 32-bit word. This ensures that the *Authentication Data* field can begin on a 32-bit boundary.
- ***Pad Length* (8 bits).** This field specifies the number of bytes of padding that immediately precede this field.
- ***Next Header* (8 bits).** This field identifies the header that immediately follows the ESP header, using the standard values defined in the Assigned Numbers RFC. The value of this field is 6 in the case of a TCP packet, and 17 for a UDP packet.
- ***Authentication Data* (variable).** This is an optional field that contains the ICV calculated by the transmitting system for all the fields from the beginning of the ESP header to the end of the ESP trailer (excluding the original IP header and the ESP *Authentication Data* field itself). The receiving system uses the ICV to verify the packet's integrity by performing the same calculation and comparing the results with this value. This field must begin on a 32-bit boundary.

Transport Mode and Tunnel Mode

Both packet formats described in the previous sections for AH and ESP define the protocols running in transport mode. *Transport mode* is used for client-to-client security between systems that are on the same LAN or connected by private WAN links. In transport mode, both of the end systems must support IPSec, but the intermediate systems don't have to support IPSec because they simply forward the packets in the normal manner.

Tunnel mode is intended for gateway-to-gateway links, such as those used for virtual private networking through the Internet that require the maximum amount of security. In tunnel mode, the transmitting system encapsulates the entire IP datagram by creating a completely new IP header. The ESP protocol encrypts the entire datagram, including the original IP header, and the AH protocol generates a signature for the entire packet, including both the original IP header and the new one. In effect, the encapsulation and encryption processes create a secure tunnel through an inherently insecure network, such as the Internet. Figure 11-6 displays the packet formats for both ESP and AH in tunnel mode.

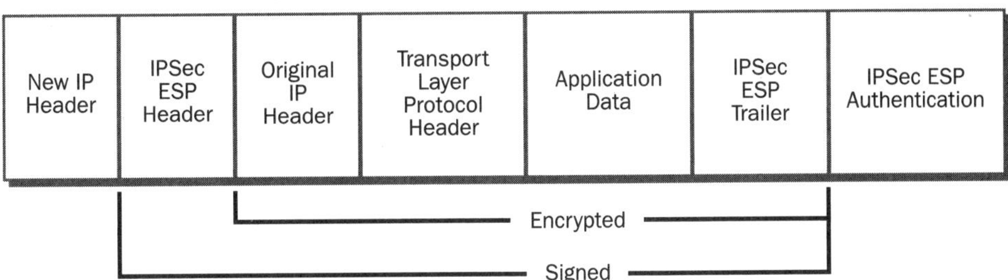

Figure 11-6. *ESP and AH tunnel mode packet formats.*

In tunnel mode, only the gateways providing the security services must support IPSec. In a case in which the tunnel connects two networks through the Internet, the systems that are the ultimate source and destination of the packets do not have to support IPSec; indeed, they do not even have to run TCP/IP. The system originating the message transmits packets to a gateway on the local network, which encapsulates the packets in IP datagrams with IPSec security and transmits them over the Internet to a gateway on another network, as illustrated by Figure 11-7. The remote gateway receives the packets, decrypts the data and performs integrity checks as needed, and then sends the data on the destination system using a normal IP datagram or any other network layer protocol.

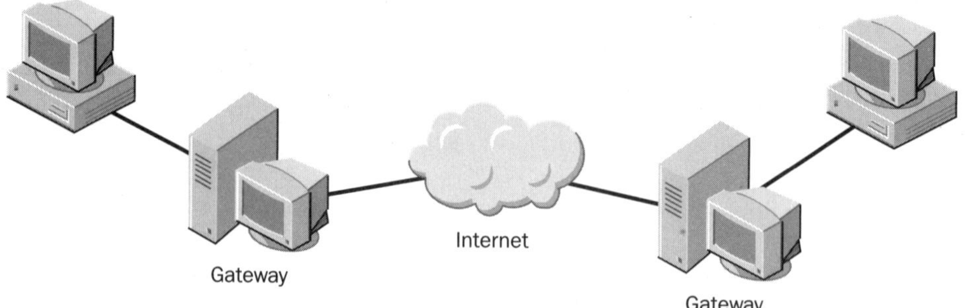

Figure 11-7. *You can use IPSec tunneling for virtual private network connections.*

L2TP Tunneling

When you create tunnels in the manner shown in Figure 11-7, you can use IPSec itself as the tunneling protocol, or you can use the Layer 2 Tunneling Protocol (L2TP) to create the tunnel, with IPSec providing the data encryption. L2TP is a protocol—defined by the IETF in RFC 2661—that is a combination of the Point-to-Point Tunneling Protocol (PPTP) and Cisco Systems' Layer 2 Forwarding protocol (L2F). L2TP is designed to encapsulate Point-to-Point Protocol (PPP) frames—such as those used by Dial-up Networking and WAN connections—inside UDP datagrams, as shown in Figure 11-8. UDP is the TCP/IP transport layer protocol that provides connectionless service. Whether the original data sent through the tunnel uses TCP or UDP at the transport layer, each separate datagram is packaged in yet another UDP datagram before transmission.

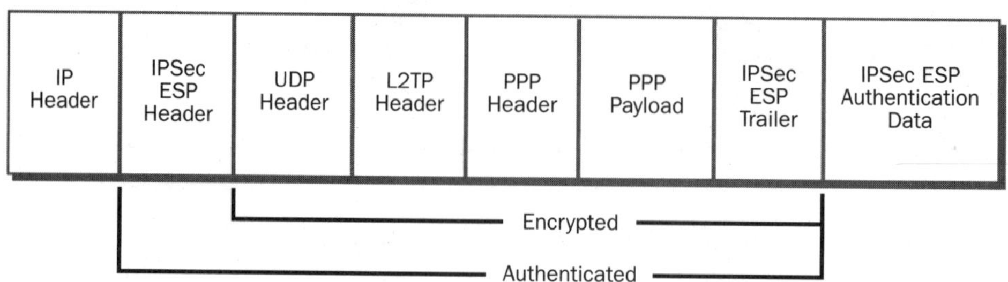

Figure 11-8. *The L2TP packet format.*

L2TP does not provide its own encryption service; it uses IPSec's ESP protocol to encrypt and authenticate the entire UDP datagram, thereby protecting it from compromise by unauthorized users. You can create L2TP tunnels without encryption, but this is technically not a VPN connection because the data is not protected.

To use L2TP, you'll need an L2TP server and an L2TP client that are connected by an IP internetwork. This connection can already exist when you create the tunnel, or the client might have to initiate a dial-up into a Network Access Server (NAS). The communication process begins with the creation of PPP frames in the normal manner. PPP frames can contain IP, IPX, or NetBEUI frame data. The PPP frame is then passed to the L2TP driver, which adds an L2TP header containing appropriate values identifying the tunnel through which the packet will be sent. The L2TP driver then passes the frame to the TCP/IP protocol driver, which encapsulates the L2TP frame into a UDP datagram, after which the correct IPSec policy is applied. IPSec then encrypts the UDP datagram, calculates the authentication signature, and adds the appropriate ESP header and trailer fields. Finally, the entire packet structure, which now consists of a PPP frame within an L2TP frame within a UDP datagram within an ESP frame within an IP frame, is encapsulated yet again in a PPP frame and passed to the appropriate WAN miniport driver for transmission.

IPSec Components

The IPSec implementation in Windows 2000 is composed of administrative and run-time elements. The administrative components are as follows:

- **IPSec Policies**. IPSec uses policies to store configuration data for the various security services it provides. These policies enable administrators to implement IPSec security by selecting the types of communication that should be permitted and deciding how to protect that communication. The administrator can then associate the policies with users, groups, or other Active Directory directory service structure objects.
- **IPSec Policy Management.** This is a snap-in for the Microsoft Management Console application that you use to create and manage IPSec policies.

The run-time components—that is, the elements involved in the secured communications process on an IPSec system—are as follows:

- **IPSec Policy Agent Service.** This service, which runs on each system that supports IPSec, accesses the IPSec policy information stored in Active Directory or the local system registry and forwards the information to the IPSec driver.
- **Internet Key Exchange (IKE).** The IKE is a protocol for the creation of an SA and the exchange of keys between two systems. RFC 2409 defines a two-phase process for the IKE. The first phase consists of the establishment of the Phase 1 SA: a secure, authenticated communication channel between the systems. Establishing the Phase 1 SA involves negotiating the encryption algorithm, hashing algorithm, and authentication method that the systems will use, followed by the authentication process itself. The second phase is the establishment of

two Phase 2 SAs for the IPSec service, one inbound and one outbound, including the negotiation of the IPSec protocol (AH and/or ESP), the hash algorithm (MD5 or SHA1), and the encryption algorithm (DES or 3DES), as well as exchanging or refreshing authentication and encryption key material.

- **IPSec Driver.** This driver receives the IP filter list from the IPSec policy that is currently active and monitors communication on the network. When the driver detects outbound packets that match an entry in the filter list, the driver commands the IKE to begin the key exchange process with the destination system. Once the SAs have been established with the other system, the driver inserts the appropriate values in the IPSec protocol header fields and performs any necessary encryption tasks. For incoming packets, the driver checks the signatures by duplicating the computations performed by the sending system and decrypts the packet data, if necessary.

Thus, once the IPSec policies are in place, a typical exchange of communication proceeds as follows:

1. The user on Workstation A is working in an application that generates a message to be sent to a particular user at Workstation B.
2. The IPSec driver on Workstation A compares the message's destination IP address or protocol against the IP filter list in the currently active IPSec policy.
3. If the IPSec policy specifies that the communication between the systems should be secure, the IPSec driver instructs the IKE to commence negotiations with Workstation B.
4. Workstation B's IKE receives a message from Workstation A's IKE requesting a secure negotiation.
5. The two systems negotiate a Phase 1 SA and two Phase 2 SAs—one inbound and one outbound.
6. Using the parameters agreed upon for the outbound Phase 2 SA, the IPSec driver on Workstation A computes the integrity signature for the outgoing data, encrypts the data, and constructs the IPSec packets by adding the appropriate header fields to the IP datagrams.
7. Workstation A transmits the completed packets to Workstation B, which passes them to its own IPSec driver.
8. Using the parameters of the inbound SA, Workstation B's IPSec driver decrypts the data and verifies the packet's integrity by recomputing the signature and comparing it to the results in the packet.
9. The IPSec driver on Workstation B passes the decrypted data to the TCP/IP stack, which in turn passes it up to the application that is the original destination of the message.

Deploying IPSec

The first step in deploying IPSec on your network is to determine what communication needs to be secure. You won't be surprised to learn that securing communication with IPSec imposes an additional burden on your network in several ways. Encryption procedures and integrity calculations increase the processor burden on both the sending and receiving systems, while the IKE negotiations and IPSec protocol headers added to each packet generate additional network traffic. You could conceivably use the maximum amount of security that IPSec provides on all your network communication, but the additional burden on your systems and your network could produce a palpable performance degradation.

In most cases, the best course of action is to select specific computers or networks that you want to secure. IPSec security polices are based on filters that use IP addresses to decide whether specific packets should be secure. If, for example, you have a database server that hosts extremely sensitive information, you can configure it to require IPSec security for all its client communication by creating a filter that specifies all IP addresses. In the same way, you can create a filter that calls for the use of IPSec security only when the system communicates with specific systems or specific networks. You can also specify in a policy whether IPSec security should be optional or mandatory. Remember that Windows 2000 is currently the only version of Windows that supports IPSec. If you have Windows 95, 98, or NT systems on your network, or if you use other computing platforms such as UNIX or Macintosh, IPSec communication is not possible. In addition, you must decide how much security you want to provide. In some cases, you might only want to ensure the integrity of your network communication, while other cases call for encryption as well.

One of the most important factors to consider is the security policy you use on the systems that host important network services such as DHCP, DNS, and WINS. If you have workstations on your network that do not support IPSec, you cannot use a policy such as Secure Server—which requires that all communication be secure—because those workstations will not be able to access the services.

Running IPSec Policy Management

To deploy IPSec on Windows 2000 systems, you create policies using the IP Security Policy Snap-In for Microsoft Management Console. By default, Windows 2000 includes IP Security Policies on Local Machine in the Local Security Settings console, accessible by selecting Local Security Policy from the Administrative Tools program group in the Start menu. You can also open the console manually by running Mmc.exe and adding the IP Security Policy Management Snap-In. When you select IP Security Policies On Local Machine in the scope pane (on the left, as shown in Figure 11-9 on the following page), you see the three policies created on the system by default.

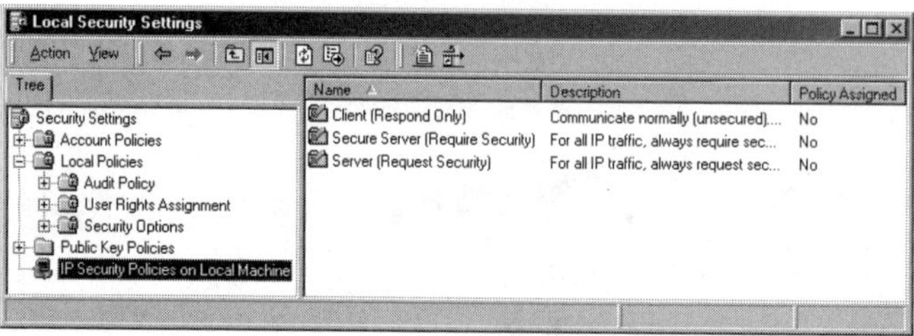

Figure 11-9. *The IP Security Policies console.*

The three default policies are as follows:

- **Client (Respond Only).** This policy configures the system to use IPSec security only when requested by another system. The system never requires security, and initiates a negotiation only in response to another system's request. This policy is intended for client systems that you want to use additional security whenever another system needs it, such as when the client is connecting to a server that contains sensitive information.
- **Secure Server (Require Security).** This policy configures the system to require IPSec security for all communication and to deny all connections to systems that do not support IPSec. This policy is intended for a server that contains extremely sensitive information, or for a gateway system used to establish VPN connections.
- **Server (Request Security).** This policy configures the system to request—but not require—the use of IPSec security from all other systems. The typical use for this policy would be for a server that you want to use IPSec whenever possible, but which also has to service clients that don't run Windows 2000 and therefore do not have IPSec capabilities.

All the policies listed in the result pane (on the right in Figure 11-9) are, by default, not assigned (deactivated). You can activate them by highlighting a policy and clicking the Assign button on the toolbar or by selecting Assign from the Action menu.

To configure the system to use IPSec, you can activate one of the default policies as is, modify its properties, or create new policies for your own use. When you select Create IP Security Policy from the Action menu, the console launches a wizard that leads you through the process of configuring a policy from scratch. In the same way, many of the individual elements of a policy link to wizards that help you modify that policy's properties.

IPSec policies are composed of three basic elements: rules, IP filter lists, and filter actions. A rule is a combination of an IP filter list and a filter action that determines when and how security will be used. A filter list is a selection of IP addresses, protocols, and ports that identify the systems for which the rule is to be applied. A filter action defines the type of security that will be imposed when the rule is applied. For example, the Server (Request Security) policy contains the rules shown in Figure 11-10.

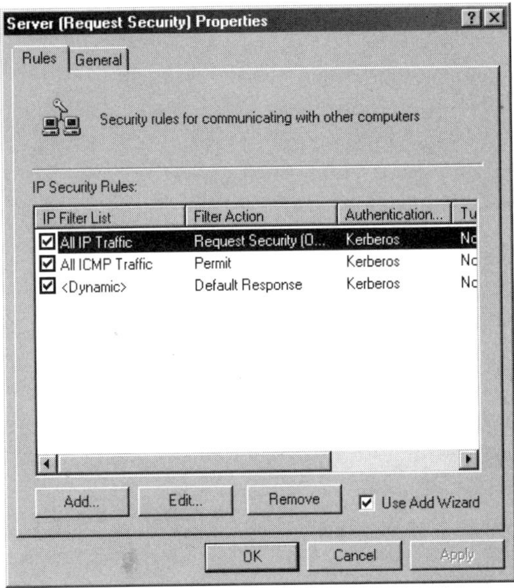

Figure 11-10. *The Server (Request Security) Properties dialog box.*

The first filter list specifies that all IP traffic should have this rule imposed on it, and the filter action for the rule calls for the system to request (but not require) the use of IPSec security. You can modify the filter list to apply the rule only to specific IP addresses, and you can modify the filter action to require security instead of only request it. You can configure other parameters to modify the security measures that the rule invokes.

The following sections examine the processes for creating and modifying these various elements.

Creating a Policy

When you elect to create a new policy, the IP Security Policy Wizard prompts you for a name and description for the policy, and asks whether you want to activate the default response rule. This rule causes the system to respond to computers that request security. You then specify the authentication method that you want the policy to use, as shown in Figure 11-11 on the following page.

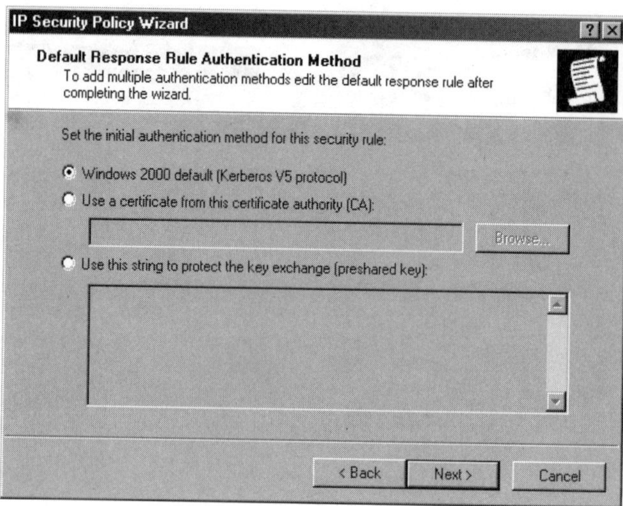

Figure 11-11. *The Default Response Rule Authentication Method dialog box.*

By default, Windows 2000 IPSec policies use Kerberos v5 for authentication, but you can also elect to use certificates obtained from an authority or an alphanumeric string that will function as a preshared key for the two systems involved in security negotiations. To use a preshared key, you must configure all the computers that will communicate with the system on which you're creating the policy with the same key. This method is intended for use when negotiating with systems that aren't running Windows 2000 and therefore do not support the Kerberos protocol. Once you've selected an authentication method, the console creates the new policy, and you can proceed to configure it with rules, filter lists, and filter actions.

Creating a Rule

When you click the Add button on the Rules page of a policy's Properties dialog box, the console invokes the Security Rule Wizard by default. (You can also bypass the wizard and create rules directly by clearing the Use Add Wizard check box.) The wizard begins by producing the Tunnel Endpoint dialog box, shown in Figure 11-12, in which you can specify whether the rule is for a system that will function as one end of a tunnel. If so, you must furnish the IP address for the network interface that will function as the connection to the tunnel.

Next you specify whether the rule should apply to all the system's network connections, to LAN connections only, or to remote access connections only. You also must select an authentication method for the rule, using the same dialog box as that shown in Figure 11-11. The final two steps of the rule creation process are the selection or creation of IP filter lists and the selection of filter actions. In both cases, you can use one of the default options provided, modify the options to your specifications, or create your own lists and actions.

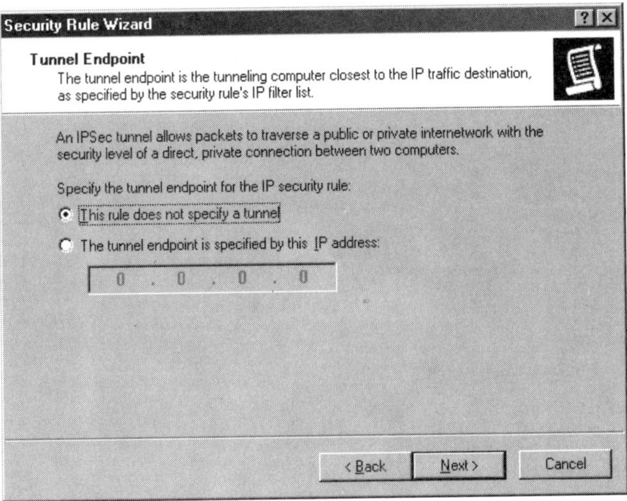

Figure 11-12. *The Tunnel Endpoint dialog box.*

Note The creation of filter lists and filter actions can be part of the rule-creation process, or you can perform each procedure separately, after you've created the rule. The following sections contain more information on these procedures.

You can create as many rules in a policy as needed—and activate or deactivate them as needed—by using the check boxes in the policy's rules list. More than one rule can be active at the same time, enabling you to define different security scenarios for different types of communication.

Creating a Filter List

Each rule in a particular policy has its own Properties dialog box, such as the one shown in Figure 11-13 on the following page. You can use this dialog box to configure the parameters by which the rule is applied. The filter lists define which communication the rule should secure, and the IP Filter List page of the dialog box contains two default filters: All IP Traffic and All ICMP Traffic. Unless you want to apply the rule to all the system's IP or ICMP traffic, you should create new filter lists (or modify the existing ones).

Note You maintain filter lists independently of the rules that use them. When you create a new filter list for a rule, or when you modify an existing one, the list becomes available to all other rules on your system. Thus, the changes that you make to the existing filter lists affect all the rules that use those lists. Consider this fact carefully before you modify the default filter list parameters.

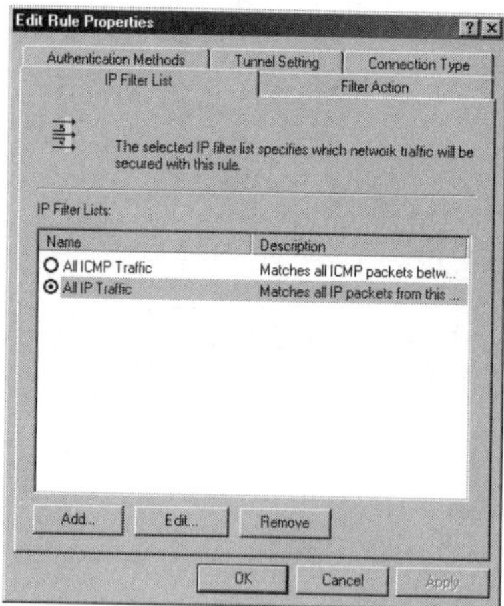

Figure 11-13. *The Properties dialog box for a rule.*

When you click the Add button or edit an existing filter list, you see the IP Filter List dialog box shown in Figure 11-14. This dialog box summarizes all the filter list's properties. You select the types of communication that you want to secure by adding entries to the Filters box using either the Add Filter Wizard or a Filter Properties dialog box, depending on whether the Use Add Wizard check box is selected.

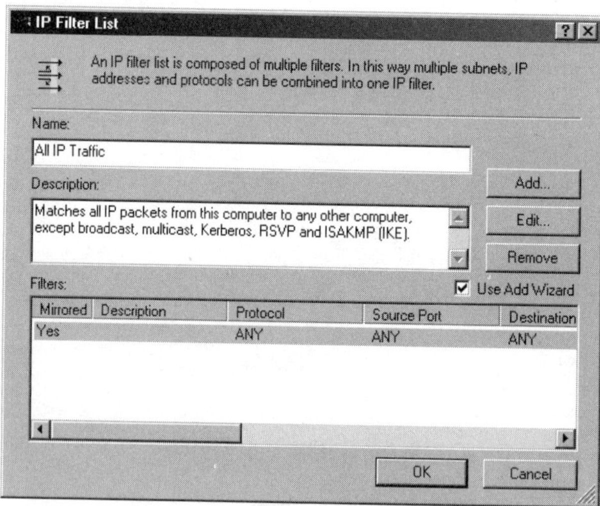

Figure 11-14. *The IP Filter List dialog box.*

The Add Filter Wizard automatically creates mirrored filters, which are filters that apply to traffic moving in both directions. If you want to create separate rules for the traffic traveling in each direction, you can either use the wizard to create the filter and then remove the mirroring feature, or you can manually create the filter without mirroring. The wizard prompts you to specify the IP addresses for the systems that you want to secure and the protocol generating the traffic that you want to secure. This simplified procedure offers less flexibility than manually creating a filter.

When you create a filter without the wizard, you see a Filter Properties dialog box like that shown in Figure 11-15.

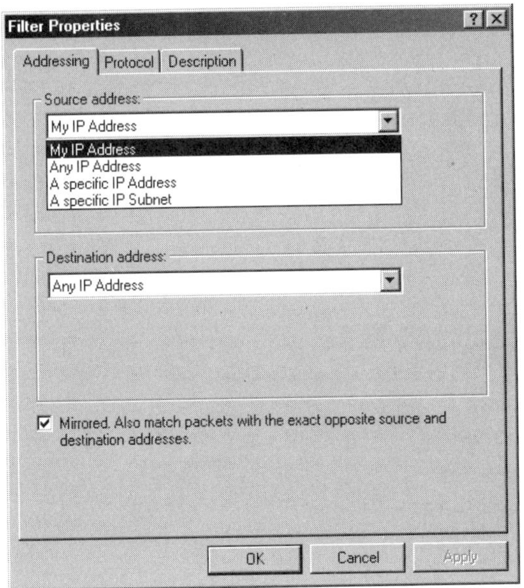

Figure 11-15. *The Filter Properties dialog box.*

On the Addressing page, the Mirrored check box enables you to specify whether the filter should operate symmetrically. You then identify the systems involved in the communication you want to secure by specifying any of the following parameters for the source and destination systems:

- **My IP Address.** This refers to the system's current IP address, enabling you to secure all traffic to or from the system.
- **Any IP Address.** This refers to any valid IP address, enabling you to secure the traffic to or from any address.
- **A Specific DNS Name.** This enables you to specify the name of a DNS server, allowing you to secure all traffic to or from that server.
- **A Specific IP Address.** This enables you to specify a particular IP address, allowing you to secure all traffic to or from that address.
- **A Specific IP Subnet.** This enables you to specify a particular network address, allowing you to secure all the traffic to or from that network.

On the dialog box's Protocol page, you specify the type of traffic that you want to secure. By default, the filter causes all traffic to be secured, but you can select a specific protocol to limit the security to certain applications. When you select the TCP or UDP protocol, you can also specify certain port numbers to be secured. If, for example, you want to secure all Internet communication, select the TCP protocol and port number 25, which is the well-known port number for the Simple Mail Transport Protocol (SMTP) used by Internet e-mail clients. The Description page enables you to specify a test description for the filter.

Once you create the filter, it appears in the IP Filter List dialog box with a summary of the properties you specified. You can create multiple filters in a list. Each of these filters is applied when you select that filter list to be used by the rule that you associated it with.

Tip Every TCP/IP system maintains a list of well-known ports and the protocols they support in a text file called Services. On Windows 2000 systems, the default location of this file is the C:\Winnt\system32\drivers\etc directory.

Creating a Filter Action

Once you've created a filter list, you have to create a filter action that specifies the type of security the rule should apply to the traffic that conforms to the list. Once again, you can use a wizard to create the filter action, or you can do it manually. The Filter Action page of the rule's Properties dialog box lists three filter actions that are created by default:

- **Permit.** This action allows the traffic specified by the filter list to proceed without requesting security of any kind.
- **Request Security (Optional).** This action requests security for the traffic specified by the filter list, but enables the traffic to proceed even if the client doesn't support IPSec.
- **Require Security.** This action requires security for the traffic specified by the filter list, thereby refusing communication with untrusted clients.

Using the Filter Action Wizard

Although you can create a filter action manually, the IP Security Filter Action Wizard provides additional guidance and explanation that simplifies the process. The wizard first prompts you for a name and description for the new filter action, and then you choose the general filter action behavior from among the following three options:

- **Permit.** This option allows any communication between the systems specified in the IP filter list to occur without IPSec security or negotiation of any kind.
- **Block.** This option prevents all security negotiation and all communication from occurring between the systems specified in the IP filter list.
- **Negotiate Security.** This option enables the systems specified in the IP filter list to negotiate a common set of security parameters.

The wizard then asks you whether the rule should permit communication only with systems that support IPSec or allow unsecured communication with non-IPSec systems. Select the latter option if you have systems on your network that aren't running Windows 2000 and must access your secured resources. Next the wizard prompts you to select a security method: high security uses the ESP protocol and medium security uses AH. If you select Custom, you can select one or both protocols and specify the algorithms used to calculate the packet integrity signatures and encrypt the data.

Manually Creating Filter Actions

To create a filter action without using the wizard, clear the Use Add Wizard check box on the Filter Action page of the rule's Properties dialog box and click the Add button to display the New Filter Action Properties dialog box shown in Figure 11-16. On the Security Methods page, you can choose one of the same three options listed previously for the general behavior of the filter action: Permit, Block, or Negotiate Security.

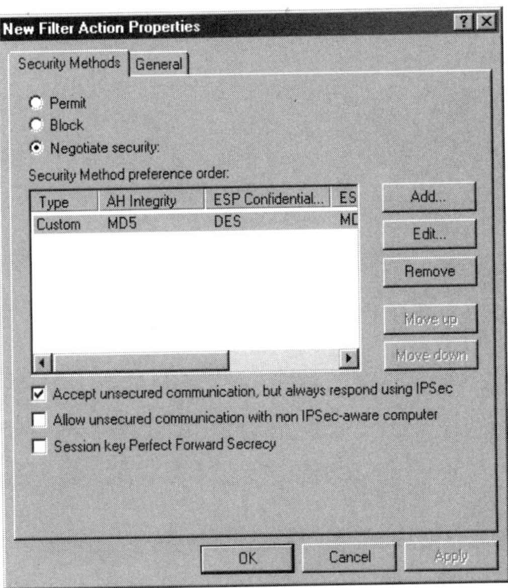

Figure 11-16. *The New Filter Action Properties dialog box.*

If you choose Negotiate Security, you can create a series of security methods for the filter action. These security methods are combinations of protocols and algorithms that the system will offer to other computers during the IKE negotiation process, in the order in which they appear, until the systems agree on a common set of parameters. The number of security methods you create should depend on the different IPSec implementations you use on your network and the amount of security you think your data requires.

When you create a security method, you can select either the AH or ESP protocol in the wizard, or you can select your own custom method by using the Custom Security Method Settings dialog box shown in Figure 11-17. In this dialog box, you can choose either protocol or both protocols, and you also specify the integrity algorithm (MD5 or SHA1) and the encryption algorithm (DES or 3DES) that the system should use. You can also specify how often the communicating systems should generate new keys, based on the number of kilobytes transmitted or the elapsed time.

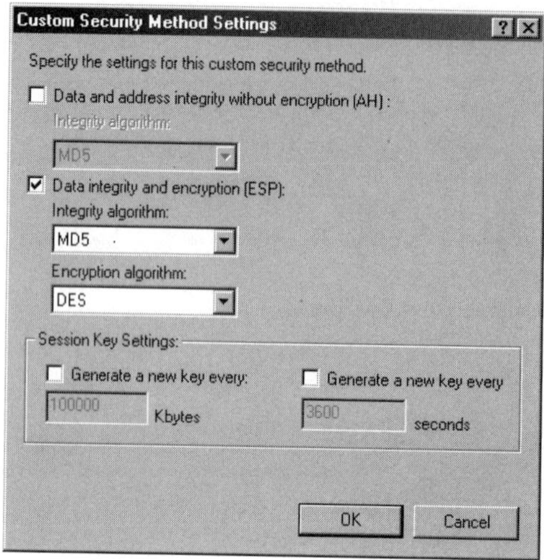

Figure 11-17. *The Custom Security Method Settings dialog box.*

The two check boxes at the bottom of the Security Method page of the New Filter Actions Properties dialog box enable you to restrict communication to other IPSec systems only or allow unsecured communication. The third check box, Session Key Perfect Forward Secrecy, prevents the system from reusing secret keys after their lifetimes expire. This method of creating filter actions differs from the wizard in that you can create multiple security methods with different algorithms.

Once you've completed creating and configuring the rules, filter lists, and filter actions for your system, you are ready to activate them. Be sure that the appropriate filter list is associated with each rule you plan to use, and that you activate the rules you want to use for each policy by filling the check boxes in the rules list of the policy's Properties dialog box. Finally, you must activate your policies by assigning them with the Assign button on the MMC toolbar or with the Assign menu item.

DHCP Security Issues

The Dynamic Host Configuration Protocol (DHCP) is an important service that automatically provides TCP/IP configuration settings to network workstations. Without DHCP, administrators would have to manually assign an IP address to each computer on the network and then physically travel to each machine to configure its TCP/IP client. When a workstation boots, it sends out broadcast messages in search of DHCP servers on the local network. The servers respond by offering IP addresses and other configuration data (in the form of DHCP options) to the workstation, which chooses one of the offered addresses and rejects the others. After configuring itself, the workstation uses the parameters assigned by the DHCP server until a predetermined lease period expires or is renewed.

DHCP is a public Internet standard—ratified by the IETF—that you can use on any type of TCP/IP network. Windows 2000 Server products include a DHCP server application that can support TCP/IP clients running on many different computing platforms, not just Windows. Similarly, other DHCP server products can support various client platforms. The Windows 2000 DHCP server has security features, however, that make it more suitable for use on enterprise networks.

DHCP and IPSec

Because Windows 2000 supports the IPSec security protocol, you can use its DHCP server to service client systems that require all communication to be secure. As mentioned earlier, however, you have to be aware of the types of workstations on your network when you configure the IPSec policies on the system running the DHCP server program. If all your workstations run Windows 2000, you can configure the server to secure all its communications. However, if the DHCP server must service clients running other versions of Windows or other operating systems that don't support IPSec, you can configure the server to use IPSec wherever possible, but you must leave the system open to unsecured communication as well. Otherwise, your non-IPSec workstations will not be able to receive TCP/IP configuration parameters from the server.

Rogue DHCP Servers

DHCP was designed primarily to support large TCP/IP networks, because these are the environments in which manually configuring TCP/IP clients is the greatest burden. In many cases, an enterprise network will have multiple DHCP servers, both for reasons of fault tolerance and to provide load balancing. Another security-related issue associated with DHCP is the possible introduction of a rogue DHCP server onto the network. A rogue DHCP server is an unauthorized system running DHCP server software, which might configure clients with incorrect IP addresses or prevent them from renewing their leases with the authorized servers on the network. A client with an incorrect IP address could fail to locate the domain controller it needs to log on to the network, and a client whose lease renewal is rejected might be unable to obtain a new address in a timely manner. The presence of a rogue server could be malicious, or it could just be a case of someone mistakenly installing the software without understanding its function.

Windows 2000 includes a feature in Active Directory that prevents rogue DHCP servers from negatively affecting the network. This feature takes the form of an Active Directory object type called *DhcpServer*, which stores as one of its attributes a list of IP addresses identifying the systems that are authorized to perform DHCP services on the network. This authorization makes it impossible for rogue servers to start providing DHCP services.

Note Because the DHCP server authorization process requires Active Directory to function, you must install the first DHCP server on your network on either a domain controller or a member server, not on a workgroup server. The installation of this first server creates the *DhcpServer* object and enables other servers to be authorized. This reliance on Active Directory also means that DHCP server authorization applies only to the Windows 2000 DHCP Server. DHCP servers running on Windows NT or other platforms can neither be authorized nor detected.

DHCP Server Authorization

The authorization process begins when the DHCP service attempts to load on a Windows 2000 server. The service generates packets using a message type called DHCPInform and transmits the packets as broadcasts to the local network. These messages are intended to locate other DHCP servers on the network and contain special, vendor-specific DHCP options that cause them to function as queries for information about the directory service enterprise root. The other DHCP servers, upon receiving a DHCPInform message, respond with a DHCPAck message containing the requested information about the directory service enterprise root.

If no other DHCP servers respond, the new server is permitted to initialize and begin providing DHCP services. However, the server continues to transmit DHCPInform messages every five minutes to determine if any other DHCP servers have appeared on the network. If other servers do respond, the new server uses the information in their replies to query the directory service to determine if its IP address is included in the list of authorized servers. If the server is authorized, it completes the initialization process and begins providing DHCP services. If the server is not authorized, the DHCP service shuts down.

Authorizing DHCP Server

If you install DHCP on a domain controller, the system is automatically authorized when you add it to the list of servers in the DHCP console. When this occurs, the server appears in the list of Authorized DHCP Servers, as shown in Figure 11-18.

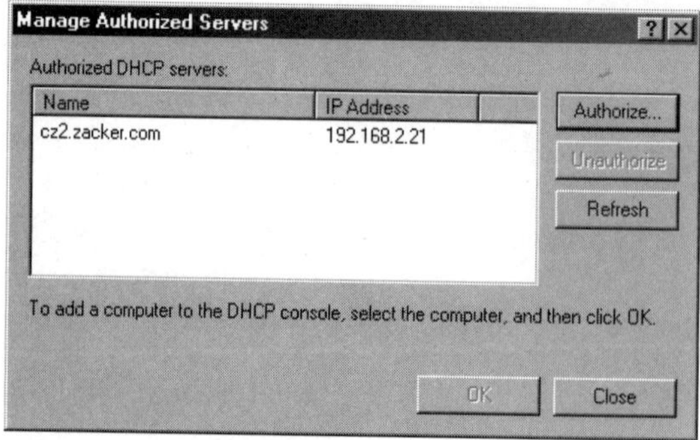

Figure 11-18. *The Manage Authorized Servers dialog box.*

However, when you install DHCP on a system that isn't a domain controller, you must first add it to the list.

To add DHCP to the list of Authorized DHCP Servers

1. Open the DHCP console, highlight DHCP at the root of the tree display in the scope pane, and choose Manage Authorized Servers from the Action menu.
2. Click the Authorize button in the Manage Authorized Servers dialog box.
3. Specify the name or IP address of the server you want to authorize in the Authorize DHCP server dialog box.
4. Click OK to add the specified system to the list of authorized DHCP servers.

Securing Dynamic DNS

The Domain Name System (DNS) is far more important to Windows 2000 than it was to Windows NT. Active Directory relies on DNS for the structure of its namespace and for the storage of information about its domain controllers and other network systems. Originally, DNS was designed to facilitate the dissemination of information, not the receipt of it. Administrators had to manually create the resource records that contain the names and IP addresses of systems on the network. One reason why Windows NT has always relied on NetBIOS names and its own NetBIOS name server—the Windows Internet Naming Service (WINS)—to resolve system names into IP addresses is that the name and address information for new systems could automatically be registered into the name server.

Eventually, however, the IETF recognized the need to automatically create, modify, and delete resource records in a DNS server, and developed a standard published as RFC 2136, "Dynamic Updates in the Domain Name System." One requirement for running Active Directory is access to a DNS server that supports dynamic update, so that domain controllers can register their existence with the name server by creating (or updating) SVR resource records. In addition, DHCP clients and servers can send updates to DNS servers, so that the A and PTR resource records for standard workstations are always current. Depending on the clients' capabilities, the clients either transmit the updates to the DNS server themselves or rely on the DHCP server to do it on their behalf. Without dynamic update, administrators would find it difficult or impossible to keep the DNS namespace updated with the correct IP addresses because DHCP address assignments can change frequently.

DNS Security Standards

Because of the importance of DNS and its data to a Windows 2000 network, the ability to perform dynamic updates presents a security issue. If unauthorized systems are permitted to modify DNS records, the efficacy of the name service could be compromised. For this reason, the Windows 2000 DNS server also supports the use of secured dynamic updates, as defined in an IETF Internet draft document "GSS Algorithm for TSIG (GSS-TSIG)."

Secured dynamic updates work just like dynamic updates, except that only authorized users are permitted to submit changes to the DNS records.

Note Internet drafts are working documents defining technologies that have not yet begun the IETF standard ratification process, which starts when a document is published as an RFC. Draft documents are subject to change before ratification as Internet standards.

Several different standards define mechanisms for securing dynamic DNS updates, including RFC 2137, "Secure Domain Name System Dynamic Update," and RFC 2535, "Domain Name System Security Extensions." Windows 2000 doesn't use either of these, relying instead on Generic Security Service Application Programming Interface (GSS-API) defined in RFC 2078. This standard defines a security service that is independent of the protocol that actually provides the security. This service enables DNS to use Windows 2000's standard Kerberos v5 protocol as the underlying security mechanism.

To perform secure dynamic updates, DNS clients and servers establish a security context by exchanging tokens that negotiate the use of a particular protocol and exchange key. Once the security context has been established, the messages exchanged between the two systems contain a transaction signature that verifies their authenticity. The tokens and transaction signatures are packaged as two special resource records called TKEY and TSIG, respectively. You'll find the formats for these records in two additional Internet draft documents: "Secret Key Establishment for DNS (TKEY RR)" and "Secret Key Transaction Signatures for DNS (TSIG)." TKEY and TSIG have resource record type codes of 249 and 250, respectively, and are known as *meta-resource records* because they don't appear in zone files and are not cached by DNS servers.

The Secured Dynamic Update Procedure

Only DNS zones that are integrated into Active Directory support secured dynamic updates. Standard primary zones support dynamic updates but not secured dynamic updates. This is because the ACLs of the *dnsZone* and *dnsNode* objects specify which users and groups are permitted to modify the resource records contained in those objects. You can modify the permissions for these objects by using either the DNS or Active Directory Users And Groups console, just as you would modify the permissions for any other type of object.

The process by which a DNS client performs a secured dynamic update is as follows:

1. Dynamic updates must be performed to the DNS server that is the authoritative source for the record you are adding, modifying, or deleting. Therefore, the client sends a query to its local DNS server to discover which server is authoritative for its name. The local server responds with the name of the zone that contains the record and the name of the server that is authoritative for the zone.
2. The client attempts to perform an unsecured update by sending a dynamic update request to the authoritative server. If the zone containing the name to

be updated is configured to accept secured updates only, the server rejects the client's request.

3. After receiving the server's rejection of the unsecured dynamic update request, the client begins the secured dynamic update process by transmitting a message containing a TKEY resource record. The server responds with its own TKEY message, enabling the two systems to negotiate the use of a common security mechanism. If both systems are running Windows 2000, they both propose the use of Kerberos v5 as the security protocol. Using Kerberos, the two systems exchange messages that verify each other's identities and then establish a security context, which includes an exchange of keys.
4. Once the security context is established, the client re-sends the dynamic update request to the server, except this time the request message includes a TSIG resource record containing a key generated by using the security context. The server uses the TSIG key and the security context previously established to verify the identity of the message's sender.
5. The server performs the dynamic update requested by the client by modifying the appropriate Active Directory objects, assuming that the client has the permissions needed to add, delete, or modify the resource record in question, and that all the usual prerequisites for a dynamic update have been met.
6. The server transmits a message to the client, again including a TSIG resource record, confirming that the update has been completed successfully.

Changing DNS Server Security Defaults

By default, all Active Directory–integrated zones are configured to accept only secured dynamic updates. If you create a standard primary zone and then decide to convert it to an Active Directory–integrated zone, you must manually configure the zone to accept secured dynamic updates. To do this, open the Properties dialog box for the zone you want to configure in the DNS console by right-clicking it and selecting Properties from the context menu. You'll see the dialog box shown in Figure 11-19 on the following page. Using the Allow Dynamic Updates field on the General page, you can enable or disable the dynamic update feature for the zone, or configure it to accept only secured dynamic updates.

In this same dialog box, you can also click the Security tab to display the standard Windows 2000 permissions controls, which enable you to specify which users and groups should be able to modify the properties of the *dnsZone* object. By default, the Authenticated Users group is granted the Create All Child Objects permission, enabling its members to use dynamic updates to create *dnsNode* objects in the zone. The user who creates the new object also becomes the object's owner, and is granted full control over the object. You can also modify the permissions for a specific resource record by clicking Security on the record's Properties dialog box.

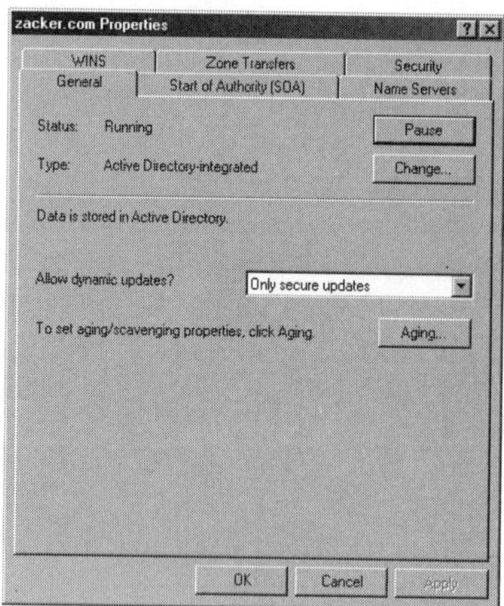

Figure 11-19. *A DNS zone's Properties dialog box.*

Note You can access the *dnsZone* and *dnsNode* objects in the DNS MMC console or in Active Directory Users And Groups, but to do the latter, you must first select Advanced Features from the View menu and navigate down to MicrosoftDNS in the System container.

Changing DNS Client Security Defaults

By default, the DNS client in a Windows 2000 system first attempts to perform an unsecured dynamic update, and if this fails, attempts a secured dynamic update. You can change this behavior in DNS client systems by adding a new value called *UpdateSecurityLevel* to the following registry key:

```
HKEY_LOCAL_MACHINE\SYSTEM\CurrentControlSet\Services\Tcpip\Parameters
```

The possible values for *UpdateSecurityLevel* are as follows:

- **0.** This value causes the system to attempt an unsecured dynamic update first and attempt a secured dynamic update if the unsecured attempt fails. This is the default value.
- **16.** This value causes the system to use unsecured dynamic updates only.
- **256.** This value causes the system to use secured dynamic updates only.

The only reason to change the default behavior of this registry value, however, is if you want to completely secure the DNS update process. If you configure systems to use unsecured dynamic updates only, they will be unable to update records in zones that have been secured.

Using Downlevel Clients

Windows 2000 DHCP clients are capable of dynamically updating their resource records in the DNS because they support a DHCP option that enables them to receive a fully qualified domain name (FQDN) from the DHCP server. The DHCP clients in previous versions of Windows and in other operating systems do not support this option, and therefore cannot update their own records. However, the Windows 2000 DHCP server can update the resource records for them. You control this capability from the DNS page of a DHCP server's Properties dialog box, as shown in Figure 11-20.

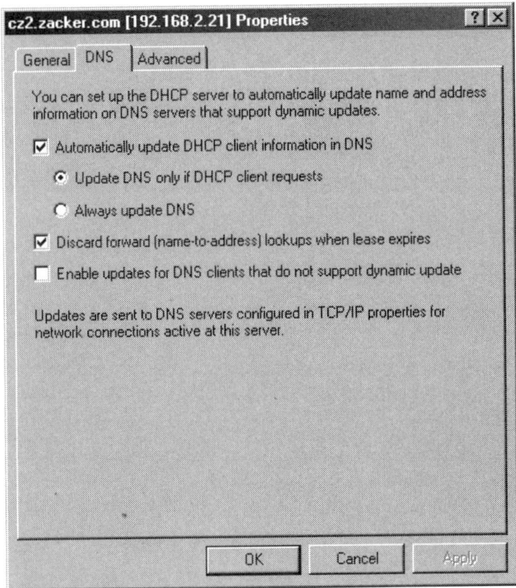

Figure 11-20. *A DHCP server's Properties dialog box.*

The problem with having DHCP servers dynamically update the resource records for downlevel clients, however, is that the server becomes the owner of the newly created objects. If, at a later time, a different DHCP server should attempt to update the object, the process will fail because that server does not own the object. To work around this problem, you can add your DHCP servers to a special security group in the Active Directory called DNSUpdateProxy. Objects created by the members of this group have no security, enabling any authenticated user to take ownership of them. The DNSUpdateProxy group is created in Active Directory by default and placed in the Users container. You add the computer objects representing the systems on which you are running the DHCP service in the usual manner—by accessing the group's member list and selecting objects from the Active Directory tree display.

DFS Security

The Windows 2000 Distributed File System (DFS) is a server tool that enables you to combine shared files and directories from different systems into a single continuous namespace. Instead of accessing resources in shares located on different computers all over the network, users can access a single share on a server running DFS. The DFS service creates a virtual root directory that contains the directory structures of shares located on different machines. The resources that make up the DFS directory structure can be located on NTFS or FAT drives on any Windows machine accessible to the network, and even on NetWare servers. Though users view the DFS structure as a single share, they are actually accessing the individual shares on various systems.

You might think this arrangement presents a security problem, because the same shared resources appear in two different places: the original shared drive and the DFS share. However, Windows 2000 successfully addresses this problem by doing essentially nothing. Rather than adding another access control mechanism, DFS relies completely on ACLs for the original shares that together make up the DFS share. If users have permission to access a resource in its individual share, they also have permission to access it through the DFS share.

There are several reasons for this course of action, including the fact that the individual shares can be on different types of drives and therefore use different access control mechanisms. Also, because DFS is designed only to provide a measure of additional convenience to users, the original individual shares continue to be accessible, even after they are added to the DFS share. If DFS included its own access control mechanism, administrators would have to maintain separate sets of permissions in two places to control access to the shared data.

Remote Access Security

Earlier in this chapter, you saw how Windows 2000 systems use IPSec to secure network communication—both the communication between systems on a LAN and systems at remote sites. Remote access clients can dial in to a server and work with network resources as though they were physically connected to the LAN, and encrypt the data passing over the phone line to prevent unauthorized users from compromising it. The remote access encryption mechanism only secures the actual link between the remote access client and the remote access server, however. For end-to-end encryption, you must use IPSec. By both encrypting and encapsulating PPP traffic, you can create a tunnel between two systems connected by a public IP network—such as the Internet—that provides a completely secure communication conduit. However, before you can establish that conduit, the two end systems intending to communicate must be able to authenticate each other.

Clients can authenticate themselves to a remote access server simply by using the Password Authentication Protocol (PAP) to transmit a username and password, but this provides only a minimum amount of security. An intruder that intercepts the data passing over the remote access link can compromise the user's password, endangering not only the transmitted data, but also any other data on the network that is accessible with that password. Windows 2000's Remote Access Service (RAS) includes a number of alternatives to using clear text passwords that provide far more secure authentication methods. These include secure user authentication methods—in which the server must authenticate a client before remote access is granted—and mutual authentication methods, in which each system must authenticate the other for a connection to be established successfully. These mechanisms can use encryption to transmit authentication data securely, or even smart cards to verify users' identities.

Extensible Authentication Protocol Support

Previous versions of RAS in Windows NT relied on protocols such as the Challenge Handshake Authentication Protocol (CHAP) and the Shiva Password Authentication Protocol (SPAP) to authenticate remote access clients using encryption. SPAP transmits the user's password in encrypted form, while CHAP uses the client's password to create a one-way hash of a challenge string sent by the server. The server performs the same calculation and compares its results to those transmitted by the client in order to authenticate the user. MS-CHAP v2 is a variation on the CHAP principle that adds the ability to perform two-way authentications using a similar hashing process.

The Extensible Authentication Protocol (EAP) is a PPP authentication protocol defined in RFC 2284 that supports multiple authentication mechanisms. During the establishment of a PPP connection, the two systems involved (optionally) negotiate the use of a particular authentication protocol. This negotiation occurs during the link-establishment phase of the connection, and it is at this time that traditional authentication protocols such as PAP and CHAP are chosen. EAP provides an alternative to this process: the systems agree to use EAP during the link establishment phase, but the selection of the actual authentication method is deferred until the authentication phase of the connection process actually begins. Once the authentication phase begins, the two systems negotiate the use of a particular EAP type. The idea behind this method is that EAP can easily be adapted to support new authentication methods, simply by defining additional types. Windows 2000 support two EAP types, EAP-MD5 and EAP-TLS, which we discuss in the remainder of this chapter.

EAP-MD5

EAP-MD5 uses the same authentication mechanism as CHAP, but defers its selection until the authentication phase of the connection begins. At this point the server requests the client's user ID with an EAP-Request message and the client replies with an EAP-Response containing the name. The server then transmits an MD5 challenge string to the client, which performs the hashing operation and returns the results to the server. Once the server has verified the information, the connection establishment process continues.

EAP-TLS

EAP-TLS is an EAP implementation of the TLS protocol (defined in RFC 2246). The use of TLS with EAP is defined in RFC 2716. TLS is based on the SSL protocol and provides support for additional security services such as two-way authentication and encryption algorithm negotiation. The authentication procedures performed by EAP-TLS are based on the exchange and verification of public key certificates. During two-way authentication the client system submits a user certificate—which you can store on the client system or on a smart card—and the server sends a machine certificate. This way, the server verifies that the client should be permitted access to the network, and the client is assured it has reached the expected servers.

Summary

As you have seen, Windows 2000 includes components that enable you to implement much greater security for your network communications than Windows NT components did. IPSec allows you to encrypt data transmissions at the OSI model's network layer, thereby preventing intervening systems from intercepting sensitive data. The Microsoft DHCP server now includes protection from the introduction of rogue servers and unauthorized systems that accidentally or maliciously supply incorrect TCP/IP settings to clients. The Microsoft DNS server can secure the dynamic resource record updates performed by domain controllers. By implementing these technologies, you can make your network a much safer place for data that should be protected from falling into the wrong hands.

Chapter 12
Terminal Services

Operating systems have historically been split between peer-to-peer and client/server models. Traditionally, however, peer-to-peer and client/server computing models rely on relatively powerful client machines acting as workstations. By implementing Terminal Services and utilizing thin clients, you can use considerably less powerful client computers and minimize your Total Cost of Ownership (TCO).

Terminal Services permit centralized processing, software and data storage, software installation, configuration, and administration. You can install applications onto the server and execute them via the server, thereby negating the need for powerful client machines. All processing—including data handling and storage—is performed on the server. Because you install the software on the server, you can make any global changes to the software just once on the server, and those changes will affect all clients that connect to Terminal Services. In a normal peer-to-peer or client/server environment, making changes to the software requires installing and configuring the software on each machine. The centralized administration of software reduces network administration costs and assists in providing a uniform working environment to users, independent of the platform or location used to log on to Terminal Services. Other benefits from a Terminal Services implementation include:

- Cheaper initial purchase because of lower prices for client or less powerful desktop hardware.
- Reduced need for hardware upgrades, because the server handles any requirements for more memory or processing power by the application, thereby benefiting all users.
- Central virus scanning and removal, as all data and applications are stored centrally.
- Reduced chance of client hardware problems, since the client machines tend to be simpler—usually consisting of a terminal or low-power computer. However, a server failure will affect all users, so redundancy is usually required.
- Increased security, because software and data is held centrally, enabling easy auditing and backup. Because there is little local data storage, users will have a hard time removing data maliciously.
- User and WAN access is incorporated via Terminal Services.

Windows NT 4.0 supports the typical client/server model, which allows full administration at the server and only limited administration elsewhere, regardless of access control rights.

Windows 2000 integrates Terminal Services into the core server services, enabling the deployment of Windows 2000 in a fully server-centric mode. (*Server-centric* means all applications run on the server.) Thus you can install or upgrade Windows 32-bit software onto the server without needing to install or upgrade the software on all workstations. Terminal Services running on a Windows 2000 server enable all client application execution, data processing, and data storage to occur on the server. The client's terminal emulation software sends keystrokes and mouse movements to the server. Terminal Services then perform all data manipulation locally and passes the results back to the client. This approach allows the remote control of servers and centralized management of applications, minimizing the bandwidth requirements between the server and client.

Terminal Services are optional services that you can use on Windows 2000 Server, Advanced Server, and Datacenter Server. Previously, Terminal Services were only available in the Windows NT 4.0 Terminal Server Edition. Terminal Services support a host of clients, including clients running on platforms other than Windows, as well as a variety of connection types, including TCP/IP and Remote Desktop Protocol (RDP). (We will discuss RDP later in the chapter.)

In this chapter we will look at Terminal Services, and how you can use them to effectively administer large-scale networks without compromising security.

Modes of Operation

A server running Terminal Services can be deployed in one of two modes: Application Server or Remote Administration.

In Application Server mode, applications are deployed and managed from a central location. This saves administrators initial development and deployment time, as well as maintenance and upgrade time and costs. Once an application is installed on the server, you can access it several ways:

- Remote access connection
- Local area network (LAN)
- Wide area network (WAN)

The clients can be Windows-based, Windows CE–based or non-Windows–based. If a Terminal Services–enabled server is deployed as an application server, each client must have a Terminal Services Client Access License (CAL) as well as a Windows 2000 Server CAL. A CAL is necessary regardless of the client's operating system or the connection protocol used to connect to Terminal Services. Windows 2000 Professional includes a Terminal Services CAL, but doesn't include a Windows Server 2000 CAL. Anyone upgrading from earlier versions of Windows NT—as well as clients using other operating systems—must purchase a Terminal Services CAL and Windows 2000 Server CAL or purchase the appropriate upgrade license.

Application Server Mode

Application Server mode is the original mode, and is similar in usage to Windows NT Server 4.0 Terminal Server Edition. This mode is designed to supply many users with Windows-based applications run from a server. Application Server mode configures Terminal Services in a number of specific ways, including:

- Memory and CPU utilization geared toward interactive applications
- Terminal Services application compatibility enhancements to aid applications that are not aware of the Terminal Services environment
- License allocation for each device that connects to a Terminal Services session

Terminal Services are also optimized to handle many sessions, thereby increasing the service overhead. These configurations are not required when you use Terminal Services in Remote Administration mode. Although the performance costs of using Application Server mode are reasonable on a server dedicated to application serving, they can be detrimental on a mission-critical server. Similarly, specialized installation and device licensing are critical to an application server, but cumbersome and unnecessary in a focused operations environment.

Terminal Services Licensing is a required component that licenses clients on Terminal Services in Application Server mode. We recommend that to avoid possible performance degradation, you do not enable Terminal Services Licensing on the same computer with Terminal Services.

Remote Administration Mode

Remote Administration mode is a new Terminal Services feature for Windows 2000, and is designed to provide operators and administrators with remote access to servers and domain controllers that run Microsoft BackOffice. The administrator has access to the GUI–based tools available in the Windows environment, even if he or she is not using a Windows-based computer to administer the server. Remote Administration mode allows this access without affecting server performance or application compatibility.

Note Terminal Services client software for 16-bit and 32-bit Windows-based computers is included with Windows 2000 Server. Clients using an operating system other than Windows require a third-party add-on.

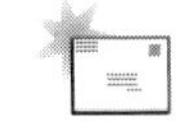

In addition to the console session, Terminal Services support up to two remote administrative sessions. Since using Terminal Services in Remote Administration mode is meant as a single-user remote access solution, no Terminal Services Client Access License (CAL) is required to use Remote Administration mode.

Remote Administration Benefits

The Remote Administration mode of Terminal Services includes the following features and benefits:

- Graphical administration of Windows 2000 servers from any Terminal Services client
- Remote upgrades, reboots, promotion, and demotion of domain controllers
- Access to servers over low-bandwidth connections, with up to 128-bit encryption
- Roaming disconnect support, allowing data-sensitive or time-consuming tasks to be completed successfully if the remote session is disconnected deliberately or because of network problems
- Remote application installation and execution, with fast access to local disks and media
- Console session unaffected while Remote Administration takes place, eliminating eavesdropping
- Negligible performance impact on the server; no impact on application compatibility
- No Terminal Services Client Licensing requirements
- Remote Desktop Protocol (RDP) feature set, including local printing, clipboard operations, and support for any RDP virtual channel applications, such as local drive mapping

In addition to the preceding features, two remote administrators can share a session for collaboration purposes. Used properly, Terminal Services operating in Remote Administration mode can simplify the remote administration of a network. However, as with all tools, this mode is open to abuse and vulnerable to problems that can arise through accidental misuse. Remote Administration mode is not meant to provide a managed multiuser experience. While it is possible for more than one administrator to remotely administer a Terminal Services–enabled server, you should avoid simultaneous administration. This eliminates the possibility of two administrators attempting to simultaneously modify the same resources, as in the case of two administrators altering a user's profile. You can check for the presence of other administrators by using the Terminal Services Manager utility (Programs/Administrative Tools) or the *quser* command-line utility.

The default permissions on Terminal Services objects are categorized into classes, as shown in Table 12-1. We'll describe these permissions in more detail later in the chapter.

Table 12-1. Default permissions for Terminal Services objects.

Group	Permission
Administrators	Full Control
System	Full Control
Users	User Access
Guests	Guest Access

You can alter the default permissions to restrict individual users and groups from performing certain tasks, such as logging off a user from a session or ending a session. Use the Terminal Services Configuration tool to manage permissions . You must have administrative privileges to set permissions. By default, there are three types of permissions which you can configure by setting permissions for which users or groups can use a specific task. Table 12-2 lists the permissions that you can set.

Table 12-2. Terminal Services permissions.

Permission	Description
Query Information	Query sessions and servers for information.
Set Information	Configure connection properties.
Reset	End a session. Be aware that ending a session without warning can result in loss of data at the client.
Remote Control	View or actively control another user's session.
Logon	Log on to a session on the server.
Logoff	Log off a user from a session. Be aware that logging off a user without warning can result in loss of data at the client.
Message	Send a message to another user's session.
Connect	Connect to another session.
Disconnect	Disconnect a session.
Virtual Channels	Use virtual channels.

Terminal Services Integration

Terminal Services are tightly integrated into the kernel and are available on every Windows 2000 Server installation. Enabling Terminal Services in Remote Administration mode requires no additional disk space and has minimal performance impact, requiring only about 2MB of server memory and making a negligible impact on CPU usage. The performance cost of running a remote session is similar to that of running the console. The server is affected only when the remote session is logged on.

Remote Desktop Protocol

As in Windows NT 4.0 Terminal Server Edition, Windows 2000 Terminal Services run by using the Remote Desktop Protocol (RDP), which is based on the T-120 protocol family. RDP is a multichannel-capable protocol, which allows for separate virtual channels for carrying serial device communication and presentation data from the server, as well as encrypted data from the client's mouse and keyboard. RDP also permits real-time data distribution from an application to multiple users. Data to be transmitted from an application or service is passed down through the protocol stacks, sectioned, directed to a Multipoint Communication Service (MCS) channel, encrypted, wrapped, framed, packaged onto the network protocol, and finally addressed and sent over the wire to the client.

The return data works the same way but in reverse: the packet is stripped of its address, then unwrapped, decrypted, and so on, until the data is presented to the application for use.

Preparing for Terminal Services

Before you deploy Terminal Services, you'll need to consider the security-relevant factors discussed in the following sections.

Security Auditing

The auditing within Terminal Services–enabled servers is the same as the auditing within a normal server. However, for certain events—such as logon or logoff—the Event description contains extra details.

Firewalls

If Terminal Services are available across a firewall, you'll need to determine the type of firewall. Packet-level firewalls are easier to configure for new protocols. If you decide to use an application-level firewall, you should obtain a filter for RDP from the vendor.

WAN and Remote Access Considerations

RDP supports TCP/IP-based connections between the Terminals Services client and server. You can make that connection through Network And Dial-up Connections, on the local LAN, or through a wide-area VPN connection.

Users can also use Layer 2 Tunneling Protocol (L2TP) or Point-to-Point Tunneling Protocol (PPTP) to gain access to Terminal Services. By implementing encryption, either tunneling protocol provides secure access to a private network for users operating over a public or insecure network.

Networks that implement WAN topologies typically have a number of firewalls or routers within the network. The filters on these routers and firewalls might prevent clients from accessing Terminal Services. Check the filters and firewall rules to ensure that the RDP port (port 3389) is not blocked. You should also ensure that access to specific corporate segments of the network is not limited to Internet Protocol or Internetwork Packet Exchange (IPX) network addresses. If any of these blocks exist, check them to ensure that they do not prevent remote connection.

Group Policy and Terminal Services

You learned in Chapter 9 that Group Policy is an effective mechanism for configuring and applying security policy to machines on the network. You can also use Group Policy to control certain Terminal Services in the network environment. If your organization uses both Windows 2000 Professional and Terminal Services, take care when applying Group

Policy, as both servers use the same policies. It is good practice to apply a separate policy to servers running Terminal Services by placing all of the computers running Terminal Services in a separate organizational unit (OU). You can use Group Policy to control access to Terminal Services applications in two ways:

- **Create mandatory profiles.** Mandatory profiles allow the application to specify which applications are visible to the user.
- **Create Group policies.** You can use Group policies to prevent users from opening applications through Windows Explorer or the Run command. Because policies are domain–based, they can affect the user's own computer as well as the user's Terminal Services session. The user policy for the domain is applied first, and then merged with the computer policy. If the administrator creates and implements a policy based on a user ID or a security group, the policy applies to that user (or group) regardless of whether he or she uses a computer or a Terminal Services client.

Terminal Services come with a set of user rights that you can modify to provide additional security. For example, to log on to a server running Terminal Services, the user must have local logon rights to the server. If Terminal Services have been configured in Remote Administrator mode, rights are granted only to administrators on the computer. If the server is configured as an Application Server, rights are granted to all members of the Users group. Because Windows 2000 includes all domain users in the Users group, all users can log on to Terminal Services in Application Server mode. You can use the Terminal Services Configuration tool to alter permissions for groups and users to log on.

Users who have been granted access to Terminal Services using the RDP protocol and who interactively log on to a Terminal Services–enabled server are automatically included in the Terminal Services Users local group. (This local group is built and created when you first configure Terminal Services.) However, users only belong to this group while they are interactively logged on to the server. This group gives the administrators the ability to control the resources that Terminal Services users can access.

You should not enable Terminal Services Application Server mode on domain controllers, because the user-rights policy will then apply to all domain controllers in the domain. For example, to use Terminal Services in application-sharing mode, users must be able to log on locally. If the server running Terminal Services is a domain controller, users will be able to log on locally on all domain controllers in the Terminal Services domain.

Members of the Administrators group on a server running Terminal Services can control the users that have access to the Terminal Server, the rights these users have, and the applications these users can run. When Terminal Services are run, these rights are extended to include the following areas:

- **Server Management.** This right enables administrators to use the Terminal Services Configuration tool to set user permissions and session activity, as well as the ability to disconnect actions and session capabilities.

- **User Control.** This right allows administrators to set users permissions on Terminal Services through the Terminal Services Configuration tool. Terminal Services profile information can be set through User manager extensions.
- **Session Control.** This feature allows administrators to monitor active users, sessions, and processes; to shadow sessions; and to force disconnects.
- **Application Installation.** When running Application Server mode, only the administrator can install applications on the server running Terminal Services. This restriction does not apply to Remote Administration mode.

You should also consider how users will access Terminal Services. If a user only needs access to a single application, you can place that user directly into the application upon the completion of the logon scripts during startup. You can configure this access by using the Client Connection Manager. You can distribute this configured client to a group of users, allowing all users in the group access to that particular application. You can also configure Terminal Services to allow anyone who has logon rights to access a particular application; use the Terminal Services Configuration tool to achieve this configuration.

You can also allow users to connect without entering usernames and passwords. Use Client Connection Manager to configure this on a per-user basis, or use Terminal Services Configuration or the User Manager extension to configure this access on a per-server basis. Deploy this feature with care, because it allows anyone to log on to Terminal Services. Ideally, you should restrict this feature to configurations in which an application that requires a password loads directly after the Terminal Services Client loads.

Terminal Services also make secondary logon possible, allowing users to execute applications that use a different security context. Users can log on by using a basic user account, and then performing a secondary logon to run any applications that require a higher level of security. To set this feature, run the *runas* command to start applications under a different context without having to log off.

You should also consider the following factors when planning a Terminal Services solution:

- **Smart cards or other hardware authentication devices.** Keep in mind that these means of authentication are not available to Terminal Services.
- **Network security.** Remember that remote access does not limit access to Terminal Services users. If a user establishes a modem or VPN link to the Internet, every user on Terminal Services can use that link.
- **File Transfer Protocol.** Remember to disable anonymous FTP to prevent unsecured access to the system.
- **Unused services.** Be sure to remove unused services—such as the OS/2 or POSIX subsystems—to prevent users from deploying them to circumvent security precautions.

Enabling Terminal Services

You have two ways to enable Terminal Services. The first way is to install Terminal Services components when you install the operating system. The Windows Components Wizard then runs during the installation process.

The other way to enable Terminal Services is to use the Windows Components Wizard on an existing Windows 2000 installation. The Windows Components Wizard follows the same procedure as it does during an installation of the operating system.

To enable Terminal Services using the Components Wizard

Note If you're installing Terminal Services components as you install the operating system, skip to Step 3 when the Windows 2000 Setup program asks you to select Windows components.

1. Open Add/Remove Programs in Control Panel.
2. Click Add/Remove Windows Components to open the Windows Components Wizard.
3. In the Windows Components screen, select the Terminal Services check box as shown in Figure 12-1.

   By default, the various Terminal Services client software is installed in the %systemroot%\system32\clients\tsclient directory. In large server farms you might want to prevent the client software from being installed on every server. To do this, select Terminal Services, click Details, clear the Client Creator Files check box, and click OK. Click Next to move to the next screen.

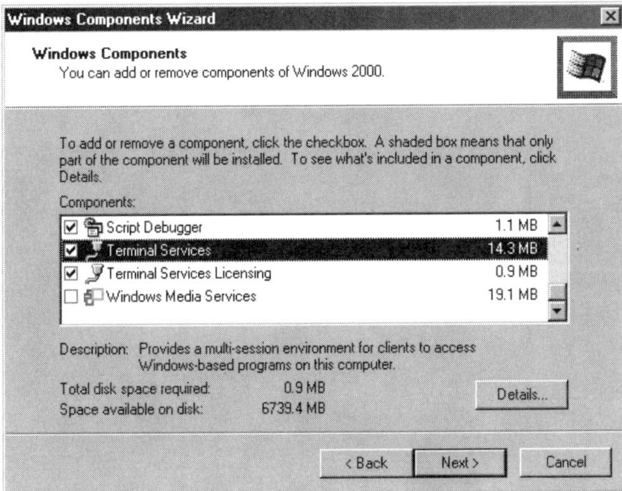

Figure 12-1. *Selection of the Terminal Services check box in the Windows Components Wizard.*

4. In the Terminal Services Setup screen, shown in Figure 12-2, click either Remote Administration Mode or Application Server Mode, and then click Next.

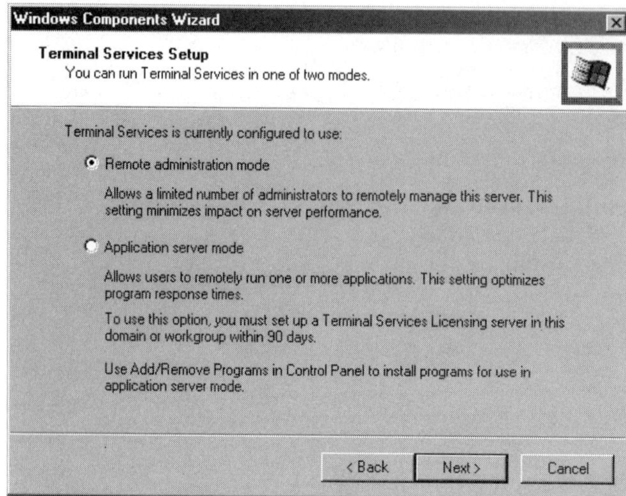

Figure 12-2. *Terminal Services Setup choices.*

5. Now the wizard might display a list of programs that will not work properly when you enable Terminal Services. After you enable Terminal Services, you'll need to use Add/Remove Programs to reinstall these programs for multisession access. Click Next.
6. In the next screen, specify whether you want permissions to be compatible with Windows 2000 Users or with Terminal Server 4.0 Users. Select the former option for the most secure environment in which to run applications.

Note When you select the Windows 2000–compatible setting, certain legacy applications might not work. You can resolve this by placing users into the Power Users group, which has built-in permissions to run legacy applications. You should then restrict the Power Users group to Terminal Services users, thereby placing the Terminal Services users built-in group into the Power Users group, which will be effective only while the users are connected to Terminal Services. When users are not connected to Terminal Services, their normal group permissions will take effect.

7. In Terminal Services Licensing Setup, specify whether you want the license server to serve your entire enterprise or your domain/workgroup, and then provide the directory location for the database. Click Next, and then click Finish.

The required files are copied to your hard disk. If you installed Terminal Services components on an existing Windows 2000 installation, you'll need to restart the system before you can use the Terminal Services software.

Terminal Services Configuration Tool

The Terminal Services Configuration tool allows you to reconfigure properties of existing connections, create new connections, and delete old connections. When you open the Terminal Services Configuration tool, a RDP connection will already be configured. RDP is usually the only connection that you need to configure for clients to use Terminal Services. You can only configure one RDP connection for each network adapter. To configure additional RDP connections, you need to add network adapters. You can set some connection properties on a per-user basis; you can set others on a per-server basis. Settings configured on a per-user basis are usually configured using extensions to the Local Users And Groups MMC Snap-In. Set per-server settings by using the Terminal Services Configuration tool. You can also configure settings that relate to the server by using the Terminal Services Configuration tool.

You can either access the Terminal Services Configuration tool through the Start\Programs\Administrative Tools menu, through the Administrative Tools icon in the Control Panel, or you can load it as a snap-in to the Microsoft Management Console. The Terminal Services Configuration tool enables you to remotely configure session, user, and connection properties.

Figure 12-3 shows the Terminal Services Configuration tool.

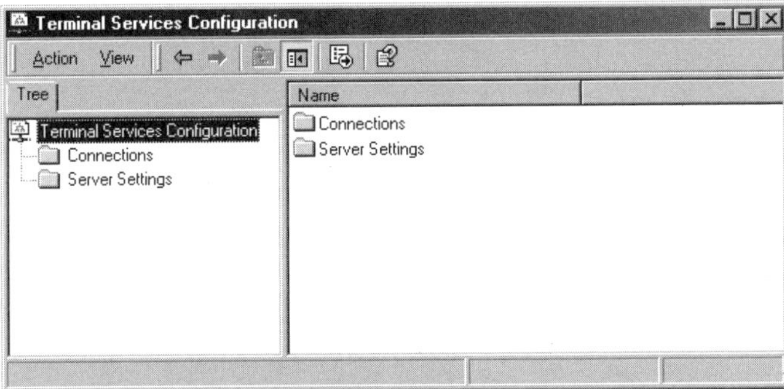

Figure 12-3. *Terminal Services Configuration tool.*

You'll see two nodes in the left pane. The top node is labeled Connections and contains connection settings and properties. The bottom node is labeled Server Settings and covers settings for the server only.

Configuring Connections

You can use the Terminal Services Configuration tool to configure the connections between the client and server.

To create a new connection

1. Open Terminal Services Configuration.
2. In the console tree, click Connections. This displays the available connections, as shown in Figure 12-4.

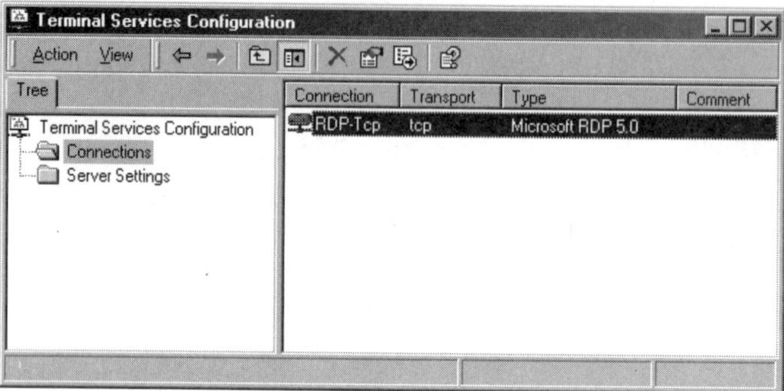

Figure 12-4. *Terminal Services Configuration: Connections node.*

3. Choose Create New Connection from the Action menu. The Terminal Services Connection Wizard will then appear. Click Next.
4. Select the type of connection from the Connection Type drop-down list. Click Next.
5. The Data Encryption screen shown in Figure 12-5 will appear. You will be asked to enter the required encryption settings for the connection. At this point you can also choose to use standard Windows authentication.

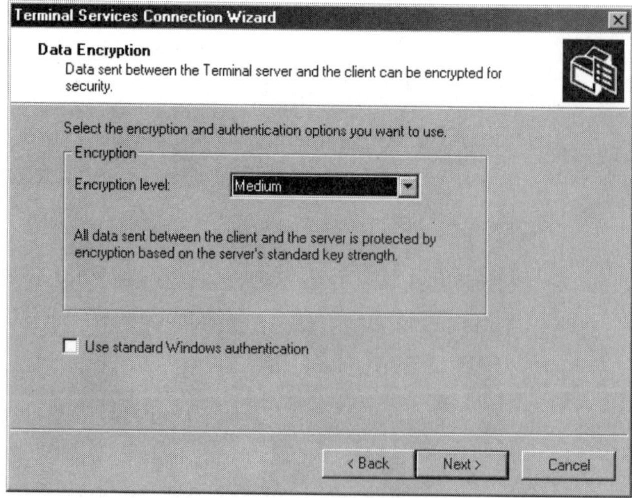

Figure 12-5. *The Data Encryption screen.*

4. Click Yes to confirm that you want to delete the connection.

   The connection is permanently deleted from the server.

Caution If there are active sessions on the server, you are warned that these sessions will end if you delete the connection. Ending an active session without warning can result in loss of data at the user's session.

To specify a maximum number of sessions that can connect to the server

1. Open Terminal Services Configuration.
2. In the console tree, click Connections.
3. In the details pane, right-click the connection for which you want to specify the maximum number of sessions, and then choose Properties from the context menu.
4. On the Network Adapter tab (shown in Figure 12-8), click Maximum Connections, type the maximum number of sessions that can connect to the server, and then click Apply.

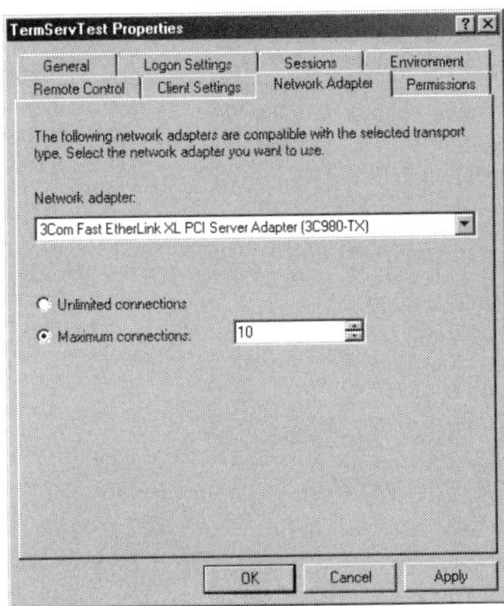

Figure 12-8. *Terminal Services Connection Properties dialog box: Network Adapter tab.*

By default, the connection is configured to allow an unlimited number of sessions to connect to the server. Restricting the number of sessions improves performance, since fewer sessions are demanding system resources.

Setting Connection Properties

Once you've created a connection, you can set or adjust its properties by double-clicking on it, which will display the Terminal Services Connection Properties dialog box.

General Settings

The General tab allows you to set the encryption level used to encrypt the data sent between the client and the server.

To change the level of encryption

1. Open Terminal Services Configuration.
2. In the console tree, click Connections.
3. In the details pane, right-click the connection you want to modify, and then choose Properties from the context menu. On the General tab you'll see a drop-down list box for selecting the encryption level. You can choose from three levels of encryption: low, medium, and high.

Low-level encryption uses either a 40-bit or 56-bit key to encrypt the data sent from the client to the server only. A Windows 2000 server running Terminal Services uses a 56-bit key when Windows 2000 clients connect to it and a 40-bit key when earlier versions of the client connect to it. This input-only encryption protects sensitive data such as user passwords.

Medium-level encryption uses either a 40-bit or 56-bit key to encrypt data both to and from the server. This level of encryption is typically used to secure sensitive data as it travels over the network for display on remote clients.

Recently MS decided to ship the 128-bit encryption version of Windows 2000 in its export version as well as the internal version. The high level setting encrypts data sent from client to server and from server to client by using strong 128-bit encryption.

Caution Raising the encryption level increases the client/server CPU requirements for each active remote session.

You can also make the connection by using standard Windows authentication, even if another authentication package has been installed on the server. Simply click the Use Standard Windows Authentication check box.

Logon Settings

This page controls the logon details used when starting a Terminal Service client. You have two options. The first option is to use information provided by the client; the second option is to provide the information beforehand. The latter option allows an automatic logon to the server or allows you to always use the same account to access Terminal Services.

To configure Terminal Services to allow a user to log on to the server automatically

1. Open Terminal Services Configuration.
2. In the console tree, click Connections.
3. In the details pane, right-click the connection through which you want to allow a user to log on automatically, and then choose Properties from the context menu.

4. On the Logon Settings tab, click Always Use The Following Logon Information. This enables you to configure logon information for a user.
5. In User Name, type the name of the user you want to allow to log on to the server automatically.
6. In Domain, type the name of the domain to which the user's computer belongs.
7. In both Password and Confirm password, type the user's password.
8. Click Always Prompt For Password to ensure that the user is always prompted for a password before logging on to the server.

Sessions Settings

For a Terminal Services connection, you can limit the number of active, disconnected, and idle sessions that remain on the server. Sessions that run indefinitely on the server consume valuable system resources. When an active or idle session reaches a session limit, you can either disconnect the user from the session or end the session. A user who is disconnected from a session can reconnect to the same session at a later time. When a session ends, it is permanently deleted from the server and any running applications are forced to shut down, which can result in loss of data at the client. When a disconnected session reaches a session limit, the session ends, permanently deleting it from the server. You can also allow sessions to continue indefinitely.

Session limits configured in Terminal Services Configuration apply to all sessions that use the connection to log on to the server. You can also configure session limits on a per-user basis by using the Terminal Services Extension to the Local Users And Groups and Active Directory Users And Computers Snap-Ins. Figure 12-9 shows the snap-in.

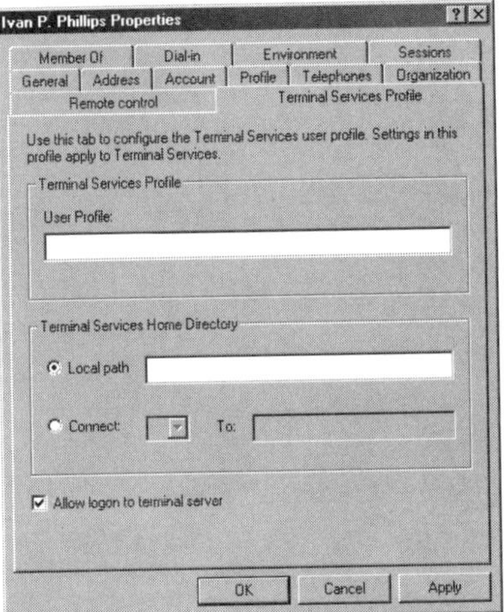

Figure 12-9. *Active Directory Users And Computers Snap-In: Terminal Services Profile tab.*

A connection can be broken by request, through connection error, or when the active or idle session limit is reached. By default, Terminal Services allow you to reconnect to a disconnected session from any computer. If set to Reset On Broken, all processes running in that session will abruptly terminate, a process similar to stopping an application by using End Task. If an administrator loses his or her connection, the previous session still runs, and might need to be manually terminated. However, you can restrict users to reconnecting only from the computer where the session originated. This option is supported only for clients that provide a serial number when connecting, such as Citrix ICA-based clients.

Use the Sessions tab to configure the time-out and reconnection delays and actions. You can use this tab to create rules that will override the user's own settings.

To set time-out settings for disconnected, active, and idle sessions

1. Open Terminal Services Configuration.
2. In the console tree, click Connections.
3. In the details pane, right-click the connection for which you want to modify time-out settings, and then choose Properties from the context menu. This displays the Sessions tab shown in Figure 12-10.

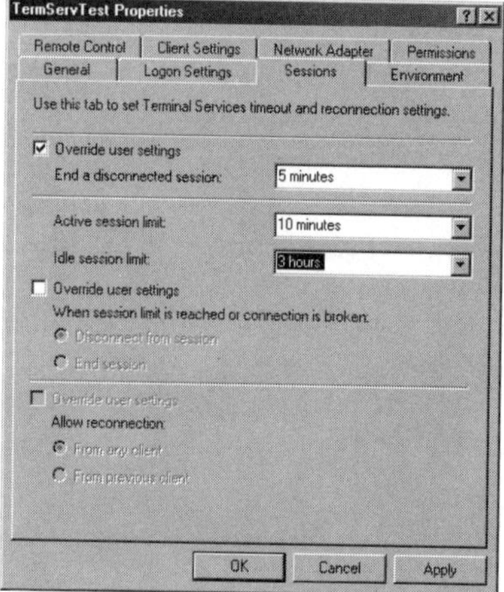

Figure 12-10. *Terminal Services Configuration Connection Properties dialog box: Sessions tab.*

4. On the Sessions tab, above End A Disconnected Session, select the Override User Settings check box. This allows you to configure time-out settings for the connection.
5. Configure the End A Disconnected Session, Active Session Limit and Idle Session Limit settings as appropriate. Select the maximum amount of time that a disconnected session, user section, and idle session remain on the server. When the

time limit is reached, the session ends (or the user is disconnected from the session). When a session ends, it is permanently deleted from the server. Select Never to allow the session to remain on the server indefinitely.

6. Click OK.

To change settings when a session limit is reached or connection is broken

1. Open Terminal Services Configuration.
2. In the console tree, click Connections.
3. In the details pane, right-click the connection you want to modify, and then choose Properties from the context menu.
4. On the Sessions tab, above When Session Limit Is Reached Or Connection Is Broken, select the Override User Settings check box. This allows you to configure these settings for the connection.
5. Under When Session Limit Is Reached Or Connection Is Broken, do one of the following:
   - Click Disconnect From Session to disconnect the user from the session, allowing the session to be reconnected.
   - Click End Session to end the session. When a session ends, it is permanently deleted from the server. Any running applications are forced to shut down, which can result in loss of data at the client.
6. Click OK.

To change settings for reconnecting disconnected sessions

1. Open Terminal Services Configuration.
2. In the console tree, click Connections.
3. In the details pane, right-click the connection you want to modify, and then choose Properties from the context menu.
4. On the Sessions tab, above Allow Reconnection, select the Override User Settings check box. This allows you to configure reconnection settings for the connection.
5. Under Allow Reconnection, do one of the following:
   - Click From Any Client to allow the user to reconnect to a disconnected session from any computer.
   - Click From Previous Client to allow the user to reconnect to a disconnected session only from the client computer where the session originated.

Note This option is supported only for Citrix ICA-based clients.

By default, you can reconnect to a disconnected session from any computer.

Environment settings

To specify a program to start automatically when a user logs on

1. Open Terminal Services Configuration.
2. In the console tree, click Connections.
3. In the details pane, right-click the connection for which you want to specify an initial program, and then choose Properties from the context menu.
4. On the Environment tab, under Initial Program, select the Override Settings From User Profile And Client Connection Manager Wizard check box. This enables you to configure an initial program for the connection. Figure 12-11 shows an example of a user setting.

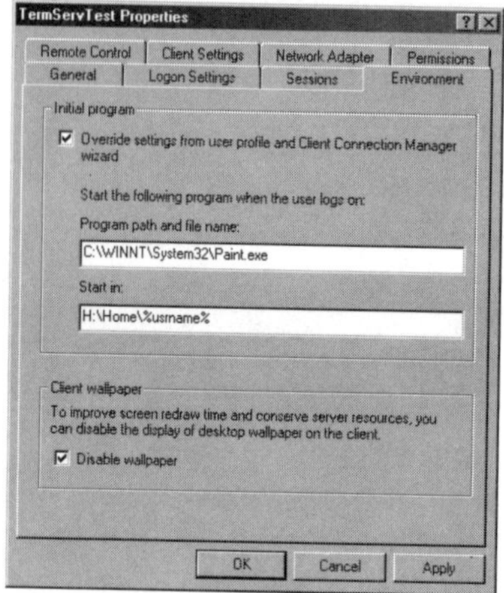

Figure 12-11. *Terminal Services Configuration Connection Properties dialog box: Environment tab.*

5. In Program Path And File Name, type the path and filename of the program that you want to start when the user logs on to Terminal Services.
6. In Start In, type the working directory path for the program.

Remote Control

You can monitor the actions of a client logged on to Terminal Services by remotely controlling the user's session from another session. Remote control allows you to either observe or actively control another session. If you choose to actively control a session, you will be able to input keyboard and mouse actions to the session. You can display a message on the client session asking permission to view or take part in the session before the session is remotely controlled. If no message is included, the user has no indication that the session is being watched. Of course, if the user who is remotely controlling the session interacts with the session, it will become apparent that the session is being remotely controlled. Use Terminal Services Configuration to configure remote control settings for a connection; use Terminal Services Manager to initiate remote control on a client session.

You can also configure remote control on a per-user basis by using the Terminal Services Extension to Local Users And Groups and Active Directory Users And Computers. The console session cannot remotely control another session, and a client session cannot remotely control the console session. The computer used as the client must be capable of supporting the server's screen resolution or the operation will fail.

To configure remote control settings

1. Open Terminal Services Configuration.
2. In the console tree, click Connections.
3. In the details pane, right-click the connection for which you want to configure remote control, and then choose Properties from the context menu.
4. On the Remote Control tab, click Use Remote Control With The Following Settings to configure remote control for the connection.
5. To display a message on the client asking permission to view or take part in the session, select the Require User's Permission check box.
6. Under Level Of Control, click View The Session to specify that the user's session can be viewed only, or click Interact With The Session to specify that you can actively control the user's session with your keyboard and mouse.

You initiate remote control on another user's session from Terminal Services Manager. Configuring remote control on a per-connection basis affects all sessions that use the connection. You can configure remote control on a per-user basis by using the Terminal Services Extension to Local Users And Groups and Active Directory Users And Computers.

To disable remote control

1. Open Terminal Services Configuration.
2. In the console tree, click Connections.
3. In the details pane, right-click the connection for which you want to disable remote control, and then choose Properties from the context menu.
4. On the Remote Control tab, click Do Not Allow Remote Control.

Client Settings

To connect client drives and printers while logging on

1. Open Terminal Services Configuration.
2. In the console tree, click Connections.
3. In the details pane, right-click the connection to which you want to connect client drives and printers, and then choose Properties from the context menu.

4. On the Client Settings tab, under Connection, clear the Use Connection Settings From User Settings check box. This allows you to configure these settings for the connection. Figure 12-12 shows these settings.

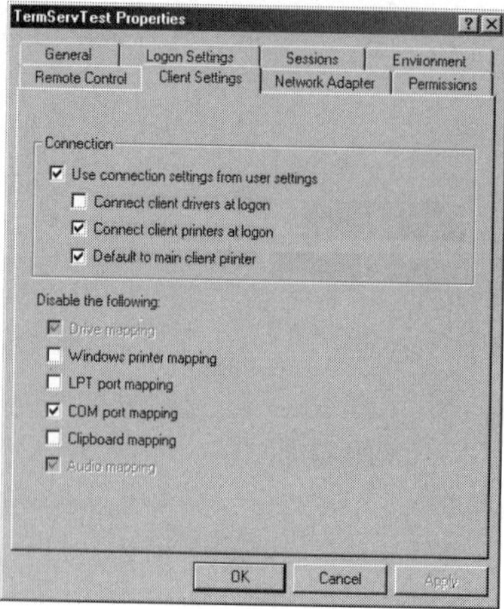

Figure 12-12. *Terminal Services Configuration Connection Properties dialog box: Client Settings tab.*

5. Choose from the following options:
   - Select the Connect Client Drives At Logon check box to automatically reconnect to all mapped client drives while logging on. This option is supported only for Citrix ICA-based clients.
   - Select the Connect Client Printers At Logon check box to automatically reconnect to all mapped local client printers while logging on.
   - Select the Default To Main Client Printer check box to automatically print to the default printer of the client. Otherwise, the default printer of the server is the default printer for all client sessions.

Be aware that automatically reconnecting to client drives and printers affects all clients that use the connection to log on to Terminal Services. If you want to define settings on a per-user basis, use the Terminal Services Extension to Local Users And Groups and Active Directory Users And Computers.

Because client sessions can establish multiple data channels between client and server, users can map to local devices, such as drives and printers. By default, drive and printer mappings that a user sets in a client session are temporary, and won't be available the next time the user logs on to the server. However, by using Terminal Services Configuration, you can specify that client mappings are automatically restored whenever the user logs on. In addition, you can disable specific client devices so that a user cannot map the device. Users can map the following devices:

- Audio (this option is supported only for Citrix ICA-based clients)
- Clipboard
- COM ports
- Drives (this option is supported only for Citrix ICA-based clients)
- LPT ports
- Windows printers

To configure settings for mapping client devices

1. Open Terminal Services Configuration.
2. In the console tree, click Connections.
3. In the details pane, right-click the connection for which you want to configure client device mappings, and then choose Properties from the context menu.
4. On the Client Settings tab, under Disable The Following, select the appropriate check box (or boxes):
   - **Drive Mapping.** Select this to disable client drive mapping. By default, this option is enabled. This option is supported only for Citrix ICA-based clients.
   - **Windows Printer Mapping.** Select this to disable client Windows printer mapping. By default, this feature is enabled. When enabled, clients are able to map Windows printers and all client printer queues are automatically reconnected at logon. However, when both LPT and COM port mappings are disabled, you will be unable to manually create printers. When disabled, clients are unable to map Windows printers, and client printer queues are not reconnected at logon. However, you will be able to manually reconnect printers if LPT port mapping or COM port mapping is enabled.
   - **LPT Port Mapping.** Select this to disable client LPT port mapping. By default, this feature is enabled. When enabled, client LPT ports are automatically mapped for printing and are available in the port list of the Add Printer Wizard. You need to use the Add Printer Wizard to manually create the printer to the LPT port. When disabled, client LPT ports are not automatically mapped. You will be unable to manually create printers using LPT ports.
   - **COM Port Mapping.** Select this to disable client COM port mapping. By default, this feature is disabled. When enabled, client COM ports are automatically mapped for printing and are available in the port list of the Add Printer Wizard. You will need to use the Add Printer Wizard to manually create the printer to the COM port. When disabled, client COM ports are

not automatically mapped. You will be unable to manually create printers to COM ports.

- **Clipboard Mapping.** Select this to disable client clipboard mapping. By default, this feature is enabled.
- **Audio Mapping.** Select this to disable client audio mapping. By default, this feature is disabled. This option is supported only for Citrix ICA-based clients.

Permissions

Use the Permissions tab to configure the permissions for users and groups to use Terminal Services.

To add users and groups to permission lists

1. Open Terminal Services Configuration.
2. In the console tree, click Connections.
3. In the details pane, right-click the connection for which you want to configure permissions, and then choose Properties from the context menu.
4. On the Permissions tab shown in Figure 12-13, click Add to open the Select Users, Computers, Or Groups dialog box.

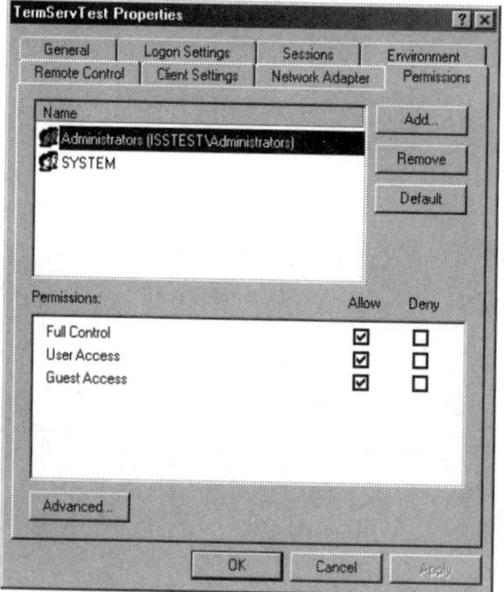

Figure 12-13. *Terminal Services Configuration Connection Properties dialog box: Permissions tab.*

5. Under Name, select from the list of objects, and then click Add.

6. Click OK. The object you selected is added to the Name list box on the Permissions tab.

Note Once you add a user or group, default permissions are applied.

To change the permissions a user or group has to a connection

1. Open Terminal Services Configuration.
2. In the console tree, click Connections.
3. In the details pane, right-click the connection for which you want to change permissions, and then choose Properties from the context menu.
4. On the Permissions tab, click Advanced to open the Access Control Settings dialog box shown in Figure 12-14.

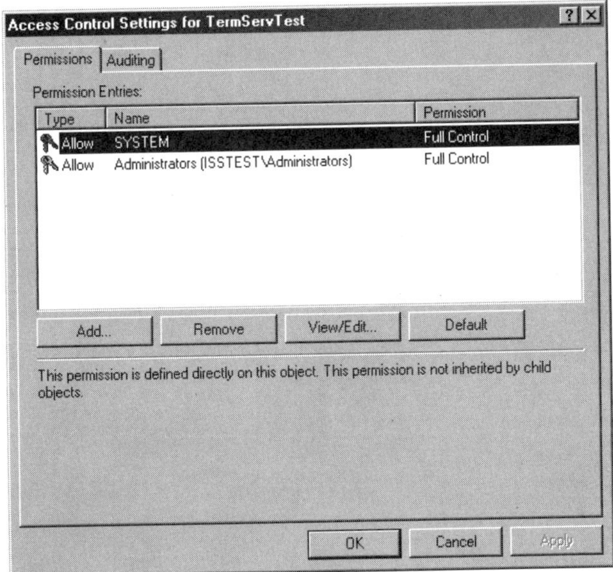

Figure 12-14. *Access Control Settings dialog box.*

5. In Permission Entries, select the user or group for whom you want to change permissions, and then click View/Edit to open the Permission Entry dialog box shown in Figure 12-15 on the following page.
6. In Permissions, select or clear (as appropriate) the Allow or Deny check boxes next to the permissions you want to set for the group.

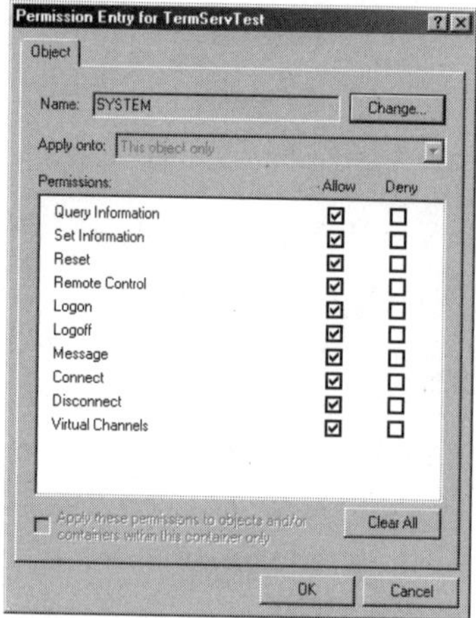

Figure 12-15. *Permission Entry dialog box.*

To remove a user or group from permission lists

1. Open Terminal Services Configuration.
2. In the console tree, click Connections.
3. In the details pane, right-click the connection for which you want to change permissions, and then choose Properties from the context menu.
4. On the Permissions tab, in Name, select the user or group you want to remove, and then click Remove.

Configuring Server Settings

Use the Server Settings node to configure settings for Terminal Services.

To view Terminal Server mode

1. Open Terminal Services Configuration.
2. In the console tree, click Server Settings.
3. In the details pane, right-click Terminal Server Mode, and then choose Properties from the context menu. The Terminal Services dialog box shown in Figure 12-16 opens, displaying information about the mode in which Terminal Services is currently running.

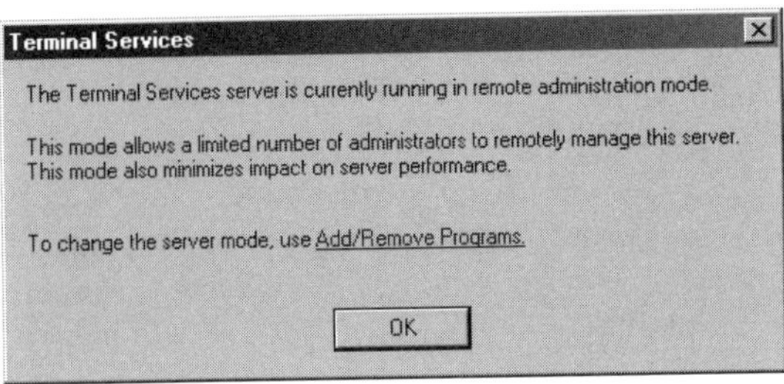

Figure 12-16. *Terminal Services dialog box.*

Using Temporary Folders with Terminal Services

By default, a server running Terminal Services creates a separate temporary folder for each new session on the server, enabling each user to store individual temporary files. To save disk space, these temporary folders are automatically deleted when the user logs off from a session. If you want to change these default settings for Terminal Services, use Terminal Services Configuration to modify them.

To delete or retain temporary folders when exiting

1. Open Terminal Services Configuration.
2. In the console tree, click Server Settings.
3. In the details pane, right-click Delete Temporary Folders On Exit, and then choose Properties from the context menu. The Delete Temporary Folders dialog box appears.
4. Click Yes to automatically delete temporary folders when a user logs off from a session; click No to retain temporary folders.

To use separate temporary folders for each session

1. Open Terminal Services Configuration.
2. In the console tree, click Server Settings.
3. In the details pane, right-click Use Temporary Folders Per Session, and then choose Properties from the context menu. The Use Temporary Folders Per Session dialog box appears.
4. Click Yes to create a separate temporary folder for each new session; click No if you do not want to create temporary folders for each new session.

To enable or disable Internet Connector licensing

1. Open Terminal Services Configuration.
2. In the console tree, click Server Settings.
3. In the details pane, right-click Internet Connector Licensing, and then choose Properties from the context menu. The Internet Connector Licensing dialog box appears.
4. Click Enable or Disable. By default, Internet Connector licensing is disabled.

To enable or disable Active Desktop

1. Open Terminal Services Configuration.
2. In the console tree, click Server Settings.
3. In the details pane, right-click Active Desktop, and then choose Properties from the context menu. The Active Desktop dialog box appears.
4. Select or deselect the Disable Active Desktop check box.

To change permission compatibility settings

1. Open Terminal Services Configuration.
2. In the console tree, click Server Settings.
3. In the details pane, right-click Permission Compatibility, and then choose Properties from the context menu. If you are running in Remote Administration mode, Terminal Services will tell you that you must switch to application mode before you can change permission compatibility settings. If you're running in Application Server mode, the Permission Compatibility dialog box appears.
4. Select Permissions Compatible With Windows 2000 Users to provide the most secure environment; select Permissions Compatible With Terminal Server 4.0 Users to provide an environment that is compatible with most legacy applications.

If you select Permissions Compatible With Windows 2000 Users, users will have the same permissions as members of the Users group and might not be able to run many legacy applications.

If you select Permissions Compatible With Terminal Server 4.0 Users, all users will have full access to critical registry and file system locations. This configuration is necessary if users need to run many legacy applications.

Terminal Services User Configuration

Terminal Services user configuration is essentially the same as configuration for local or Active Directory users. When Terminal Services are installed on a machine, two additional properties tabs—Remote Control and Terminal Services Profile—appear on the user's property page. In Chapter 4, "Active Directory," we covered how to create and manage users both at a local level and through Active Directory. In this chapter we will cover only the aspects pertinent to Terminal Services.

User Permissions

You control how users and groups access Terminal Services by setting access control permissions. Before adding users and groups to the permissions lists, consider what types of access each individual user or group requires. You can add any user, group, or computer in your network to the permissions lists. If your server belongs to a domain, you can also add user accounts and global groups from both the local domain and trusted domains.

Full Control

Full control allows users to

- Query information about a session.
- Modify connection parameters.
- Reset (or end) a session.
- Remotely control another user's session.
- Log on to a session on the server.
- Log off a user from a session.
- Send a message to another user's session.
- Connect to another session.
- Disconnect a session.
- Use virtual channels, which provide access from a server program to client devices.

User Access

User access allows users to

- Log on to a session on the server.
- Query information about a session.
- Send messages to other users' sessions.
- Connect to another session.

Guest Access

Guest access allows users only to log on to a session on the server.

Terminal Services Active Directory Users And Computers Extension

You can use the Terminal Services extension for the Active Directory Users And Computers Snap-In to view or modify access permissions to Active Directory objects.

Note The Terminal Services Active Directory Users And Computers Extension is already included in Local Users And Groups if Terminal Services is enabled on the server.

To add the Terminal Services Extension to Local Users And Groups

1. Click Start, and then click Run.
2. In Open, type *mmc*, and then click OK.

   A new Microsoft Management Console (MMC) appears.
3. Choose Add/Remove Snap-In from the Console menu.

   The Add/Remove Snap-In dialog box appears.
4. Click Add.

   The Add Standalone Snap-In dialog box appears.
5. Select Local Users And Groups, and then click Add.

   The Choose Target Machine dialog box appears.
6. Select the computer to which to add this console, and then click Finish.
7. In the Add Standalone Snap-In dialog box, click Close.
8. In the Add/Remove Snap-In dialog box, click the Extensions tab.
9. Click Terminal Services - Extension, and then click OK.
10. Choose Save from the Console menu.

    The Save As dialog box appears.
11. Enter a filename and path to use to store the console, and then click Save.

To change a user's Terminal Services profile path, choose from the following (depending on the account type)

1. For a domain user account, open Active Directory Users And Computers in the console tree, expand the domain node, and then click the folder in which users are located.
2. For a local user account, open Computer Management.
3. In the console tree, click Users (\Computer Management\System Tools\Local Users And Groups\Users).
4. Double-click the user whose profile path you want to change.

5. On the Terminal Services Profile tab (shown earlier in Figure 12-9), under User Profile, type the new path to the user's profile, and then click OK.

To change the path to a user's home directory, choose from the following (depending on the account type)

1. For a domain user account, open Active Directory Users And Computers.
2. In the console tree, expand the domain node, and then click the folder where users are located.
3. For a local user account, open Computer Management.
4. In the console tree, click Users (Computer Management\System Tools\Local Users And Groups\Users).
5. Double-click the user whose home directory you want to change.
6. On the Terminal Services Profile tab, do one of the following:
   - If the Terminal Services home directory is on the local server, click Local Path, and then type the path to the profile.
   - If the Terminal Services home directory is on a network share, click Connect, select a drive to connect, and then type the network path.
7. Click OK.

To allow a user to log on to Terminal Services, choose from the following (depending on the account type)

1. For a domain user account, open Active Directory Users And Computers.
2. In the console tree, expand the domain node, and then click the folder where users are located.
3. For a local user account, open Computer Management.
4. In the console tree, click Computer Management\System Tools\Local Users And Groups\Users.
5. Double-click the user for whom you want to change settings.
6. On the Terminal Services Profile tab, select the Allow Logon To Terminal Server check box, and then click OK.

To set the maximum duration of an active session, choose from the following (depending on the account type)

1. For a domain user account, open Active Directory Users And Computers.
2. In the console tree, expand the domain node, and then click the folder where users are located.
3. For a local user account, open Computer Management.
4. In the console tree, click Computer Management\System Tools\Local Users And Groups\Users.

5. Double-click the user that you want to change.
6. Under Active Session Limit on the Sessions tab (shown in Figure 12-17), select the amount of time to wait before the connection times out, and then click OK.

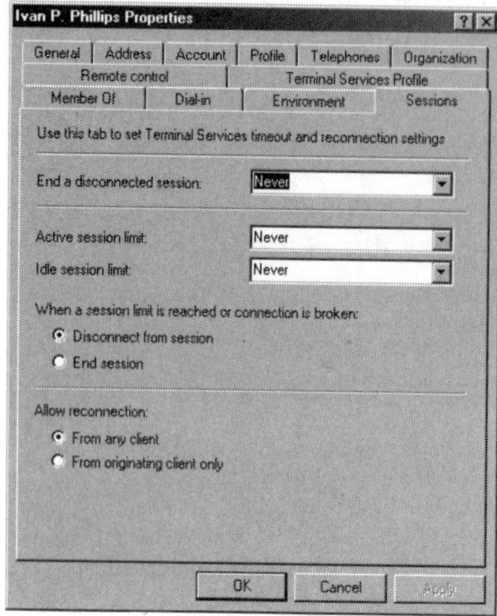

Figure 12-17. *Active Directory Users And Computers Snap-In User properties: Sessions tab.*

To set the maximum time a disconnected session remains active, choose from the following (depending on the account type)

1. For a domain user account, open Active Directory Users And Computers.
2. In the console tree, expand the domain node, and then click the folder where users are located.
3. For a local user account, open Computer Management.
4. In the console tree, click Computer Management\System Tools\Local Users And Groups\Users.
5. Double-click the user for whom you want to change settings.
6. On the Sessions tab, in End A Disconnected Session, select the amount of time you want to elapse before the disconnected session is reset, and then click OK.

To set the maximum idle time for a session, choose from the following (depending on the account type)

1. For a domain user account, open Active Directory Users And Computers.
2. In the console tree, expand the domain node, and then click the folder where users are located.

3. For a local user account, open Computer Management.
4. In the console tree, click Computer Management\System Tools\Local Users And Groups\Users.
5. Double-click the user for whom you want to change settings.
6. On the Sessions tab, in Idle Session Limit, select the amount of time you want to elapse before the idle session times out, and then click OK.

To change settings for when a session limit is reached or a connection is broken, choose from the following (depending on the account type)

1. For a domain user account, open Active Directory Users And Computers.
2. In the console tree, expand the domain node, and then click the folder where users are located.
3. For a local user account, open Computer Management.
4. In the console tree, click Computer Management\System Tools\Local Users And Groups\Users.
5. Double-click the user for whom you want to change settings.
6. On the Sessions tab, under When A Session Limit Is Reached Or Connection Is Broken, click Disconnect From Session to allow the session to be reconnected.
7. Alternatively, click End Session to end the session.
8. Click OK.

To change settings for reconnecting disconnected sessions, choose from the following (depending on the account type)

1. For a domain user account, open Active Directory Users And Computers. In the console tree, expand the domain node, and then click the folder where users are located.
2. For a local user account, open Computer Management.
3. In the console tree, click Computer Management\System Tools\Local Users And Groups\Users.
4. Double-click the user for whom you want to change settings.
5. On the Sessions tab, under Allow reconnection, click From Any Client to allow connection to that session from any client computer.
6. Or, click From Originating Client Only to allow only the client computer where the session was created to reconnect to that session. This option is only supported for Citrix ICA clients.
7. Click OK.

To specify a program to start on session connection, choose from the following (depending on the account type)

1. For a domain user account, open Active Directory Users And Computers.
2. In the console tree, expand the domain node, and then click the folder where users are located.
3. For a local user account, open Computer Management.
4. In the console tree, click Computer Management\System Tools\Local Users And Groups\Users.
5. Double-click the user for whom you want to change the starting program.
6. On the Environment tab, under Starting Program, select the Start The Following Program At Logon check box, shown in Figure 12-18.

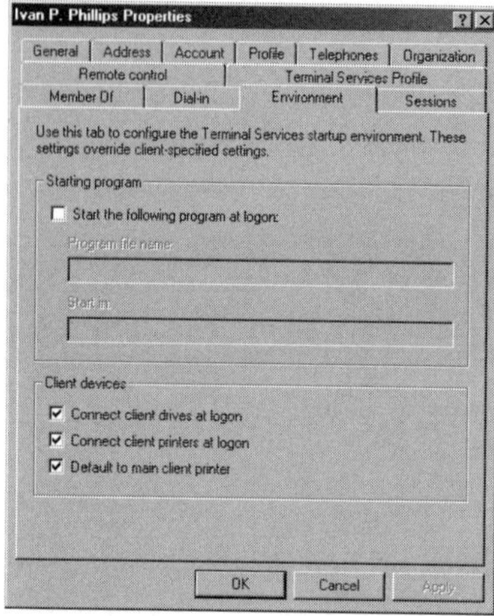

Figure 12-18. *Active Directory Users And Computers Snap-In User properties: Environment tab.*

7. In Program File Name, type the name of the program to start when the user logs on. You can also specify a working directory by typing the path in Start In.
8. Click OK.

To connect client printers at logon, choose from the following (depending on the account type)

1. For a domain user account, open Active Directory Users And Computers.
2. In the console tree, expand the domain node, and then click the folder where users are located.
3. For a local user account, open Computer Management.

4. In the console tree, click Computer Management\System Tools\Local Users And Groups\Users.
5. Double-click the user for whom you want to connect client printers.
6. On the Environment tab, under Client devices, select the Connect Client Printers At Logon check box, and then click OK.

To enable remote control, choose from the following (depending on the account type)

1. For a domain user account, open Active Directory Users And Computers.
2. In the console tree, expand the domain node, and then click the folder where users are located.
3. For a local user account, open Computer Management.
4. In the console tree, click Computer Management\System Tools\Local Users And Groups\Users.
5. Double-click the user for whom you want to enable remote control.
6. On the Remote Control tab shown in Figure 12-19, select the Enable Remote Control check box, and then click OK.

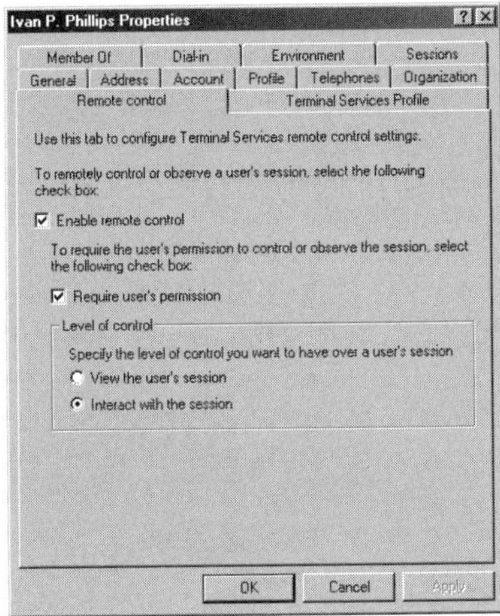

Figure 12-19. *Active Directory Users And Computers Snap-In User properties: Remote Control tab.*

To require user's permission to observe or control sessions, choose from the following (depending on the account type)

1. For a domain user account, open Active Directory Users And Computers.
2. In the console tree, expand the domain node, and then click the folder where users are located.

3. For a local user account, open Computer Management.
4. In the console tree, click Computer Management\System Tools\Local Users And Groups\Users.
5. Double-click the user whose permission you want to require.
6. On the Remote Control tab, select the Require User's Permission check box, and then click OK.

To set the level of control over a user's sessions, choose from the following (depending on the account type)

1. For a domain user account, open Active Directory Users And Computers.
2. In the console tree, expand the domain node, and then click the folder where users are located.
3. For a local user account, open Computer Management.
4. In the console tree, click Computer Management\System Tools\Local Users And Groups\Users.
5. Double-click the user for whom you want to set the level of control.
6. On the Remote Control tab, under Level Of Control, click View The User's Session to allow only session observation.
7. Or, click Interact With The Session to allow full remote control of the session.
8. Click OK.

Terminal Services Client Configuration

Windows-based clients have two possible installation methods. The first is to use the Terminal Services Client Creator utility, available under Programs/Administrative Tools. This utility creates floppy disks for the various PC client types; each client requires two floppy disks. The second option is to share the %systemroot%\system32\clients\tsclient directory; the installation then occurs over the network.

Installing a Terminal Services Client

Terminal Services Client will run on a PC with 8 MB of available RAM. A new installation does not require you to reboot the PC. You can install Terminal Services Client with as little as 1.5 MB available disk space.

The Terminal Services Client programs are installed by default in %systemdrive%\Program Files\Terminal Services Client; you'll find shortcuts in Programs\Terminal Services Client. In the following sections, we'll examine the two methods of using the Terminal Services Client to connect to a Windows 2000 Server-based computer.

Connecting to a Server Running Terminal Services

The Terminal Services Client program mstsc.exe, shown in Figure 12-20, allows for a quick connection to any server running Terminal Services.

Figure 12-20. *Terminal Services Client mstsc.exe.*

Simply type the name of the server (IP address, DNS name, or WINS name) into the Server box, and either press Enter or pick from the server from the available server list.

To connect to Terminal Services from a 32-bit client

1. Click Start, point to Programs, point to Terminal Services Client, and then click Terminal Services Client. The Terminal Services Client dialog box appears, as shown in Figure 12-20.
2. In Server, type either the name of a server running Terminal Services or a TCP/IP address. You can also select a server from Available Servers.
3. In Screen Area, select a Terminal Services Client window size.
4. Click Connect. The Logon Information dialog box appears.
5. Type your username, password, and (if required) domain, and then click OK.

If you previously disconnected from Terminal Services without ending the session, Terminal Services Client automatically reconnects to that session. This feature depends, however, on the connection you configure for reconnection of disconnected sessions.

Terminal Services Client Configuration Manager

You use Terminal Services Client Configuration Manager to configure connections between the client and the server from the client side. On the server side, you'd use the Terminal Services Configuration and Terminal Services Manager tools.

To create a new connection

1. Click Start, point to Programs, and then click Client Connection Manager. The window shown in Figure 12-21 appears.

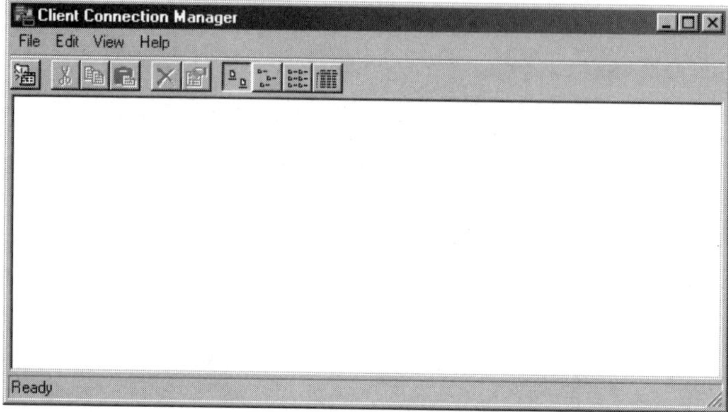

Figure 12-21. *Client Connection Manager window.*

2. Choose New Connection from the File menu to open the Client Connection Manager Wizard. Click Next.
3. Fill in a name for the connection and the server name or the IP address of the server running Terminal Services. Click Next.
4. Select the Log On Automatically With This Information check box and fill in your username, password, and the domain to which you'd like to connect. If you do not select the check box, you are prompted for your username, password, and domain each time you make a connection. Click Next.
5. You are then asked to choose the screen resolution for the client software. You can also choose to run the client software full screen. Make your selections and click Next.
6. You will then be asked to choose the connection properties. On a low-bandwidth connection, you can select data compression and bitmap caching to speed up the data transfer between client and Terminal Services. After you have chosen connection options, click Next.
7. As with the Terminal Services Configuration tool, you have the option of specifying a program to execute when the connection is made between client and Terminal Services. Enter the program path and filename for the program and any starting directory for the user and click Next.

8. The Icon and Program Group screen will then appear. Select the icon and program group for the connection and click Next.
9. To finish creating the connection, click Finish.

Changing the Target Server and Logon Information for Connection

To change the target server

1. Click Start, point to Programs, and then click Client Connection Manager.
2. Click the connection you want to change and choose Properties from the File menu.
3. Click the General tab. In Server Name Or IP address, type the name or TCP/IP address of the server, or click Browse to look for a server. Click OK when you've finished.

To change logon information

1. Click Start, point to Programs, and then click Client Connection Manager.
2. Click the connection you want to change and choose Properties from the File menu.
3. Click the General tab. Under Logon Information, type a new username, password, and domain name and then click OK.

To change connection options

1. Click Start, point to Programs, and then click Client Connection Manager.
2. Click the connection you want to change and choose Properties from the File menu.
3. Click the Connection Options tab.
4. Under Screen Area, click the size you want to use for the client window.
5. Click Full Screen if you want the client window to open full screen.
6. Select Enable Data Compression if you want the client to use data compression.
7. Select Cache Bitmaps To Disk if you want the client to cache bitmaps to disk.
8. Click OK when you've finished.

To change the starting program, the connection icon, or the program group

1. Click Start, point to Programs, and then click Client Connection Manager.
2. Click the connection you want to change and choose Properties from the File menu.
3. Click the Program tab.
4. Click Start The Following Program and type the program path and filename. If you do not specify a program to start, the connection will start at the Windows 2000 desktop.

5. Click Change Icon to change the icon. Click Use Default if you want to use the default icon associated with the program; click Browse to look for a new icon. Click OK when you're satisfied.
6. In Program Group, you can either type a new program group name or select a group from the list.
7. Click OK.

To delete a connection

1. Click Start, point to Programs, and then click Client Connection Manager.
2. Click the connection you want to delete.
3. On the File menu, click Delete.

To export a connection to a file

1. Click Start, point to Programs, and then click Client Connection Manager.
2. Click the connection you want to export and then choose Export from the File menu. (Choose Export All from the File menu to export all connections to a file.) The Export As dialog box appears.
3. Select the file you want to export the connections to, and then click Save.

If you export to an existing file, the connections are appended to the file. Exporting to an existing file does not automatically overwrite the contents of the file.

In the program group in which you installed the client software, Terminal Services Client is a default connection. When you use this connection to access a server, this default connection saves the information you supply (server name, resolution, user name, and domain). The Terminal Services Client connection does not appear in Client Connection Manager, but it is exported with all the connections listed in Client Connection Manager if you export all the connections. When the Terminal Services Client connection is imported, it overwrites the existing default connection and might transfer undesired information to another computer.

To import connections from a file

1. Click Start, point to Programs, and then click Client Connection Manager.
2. Choose Import from the File menu. The Import From dialog box appears.
3. Select the file to import and click Open.

Terminal Services Manager Tool

Administrators use the Terminal Services Manager administrative tool to view information on a server running Terminal Services within trusted domains. The Terminal Services Manager tool can monitor users, sessions, and applications that are running on each server running Terminal Services, and it allows remote managing of that server.

Any sessions connecting to Terminal Services from a client appear on the Session list in Terminal Services Manager. The name of the user who logs on using the session appears in the Users list, and you can monitor any applications that run from the user sessions on the Processes list. Therefore, you can oversee all users, sessions, and processes on servers running Terminal Services from one location.

The following sections describe the different types of sessions within the Terminal Services Manager.

Console Session

In Terminal Services Manager, the system console session automatically appears in the Session list when you connect to Terminal Services. Console is defined as the keyboard, mouse, and video monitor of the computer on which you install Terminal Services. You can log on to Terminal Services using the console session just as you would log on from a client session. Though you can send a message to the console session, you cannot perform any other administrative actions on it.

Listener Session

Listener sessions are different from regular sessions. These types of sessions listen for and accept new RDP client connections, thereby creating new sessions for the client requests. If you have configured more than one connection in Terminal Services Configuration, you will notice several listener sessions. You have the option to reset a listener session. However, we don't recommend this—doing so resets all sessions that use the same Terminal Services connection. Resetting a user's session without warning can result in loss of data at the client.

Idle Session

To optimize the performance of Terminal Services, the server automatically initializes idle sessions before making client connections. These sessions are available to clients for connection. Two idle sessions are created by default.

Using Terminal Services Manager

Terminal Services Manager monitors the sessions, users, and processes on servers running Terminal Services in trusted domains. In addition to monitoring, you can manage Terminal Services by using the actions provided by Terminal Services Manager. Table 12-3 describes these actions, which you'll find on the Actions menu. Performing most actions requires special privileges.

Table 12-3. Terminal Services actions.

Action	Description	Permission Level Required
Connect	Enables a user to connect to another session. Be aware that connecting to a session currently being used by another user might result in loss of data for the user. When you connect to another session, you are disconnected from your previous session. If you create more than one session on a server, you can use this option to switch between sessions. You cannot connect to another session from the system console.	User Access or Full Control
Disconnect	Disconnects a user from a session. The session remains attached to Terminal Services in the disconnected state; currently running applications continue to run. When you attempt to reconnect to the server, you are reconnected using the same session from which you disconnected, even if you are reconnecting from a different computer. Applications left open when you disconnect keep running when you reconnect to the session, with no loss of data. This option is useful if you change locations often (for example, from work to home).	Full Control
End Process	Enables you to end a process that is running at a user's session. This option is useful when an application stops responding. Be aware that ending a process without warning can result in loss of data at the user's session.	Full Control
Log Off	Enables you to log off a user from a session on the server. Be aware that logging off a user without warning can result in loss of data at the user's session. When you log off a user, all processes end and the session is deleted from the server.	Full Control
Remote Control	Enables a user to observe or remotely control another user's session. This option allows you to monitor the activities at the session and interact with it as needed. Before you begin monitoring a user's session, you can warn the user. You can either configure remote control with Terminal Services Configuration, or—on a per-user basis—with the Terminal Services Extension to Local Users and Groups and Active Directory Users and Computers. You cannot remotely control another session from the console.	Full Control

(continued)

Table 12-3. *(continued)*

Action	Description	Permission Level Required
Reset	Enables you to delete a session instantly. Be aware that resetting a user's session without warning can result in loss of data at that session. You should reset a session only when it malfunctions or appears to have stopped responding. Resetting a listener session resets all sessions that use the connection.	Full Control
Send Message	Enables a user to send a message to another user's session. For example, an administrator might want to send a message to a user before disconnecting or logging off the user from a session.	User Access or Full Control
Status	Enables you to monitor session-related counters, such as incoming and outgoing bytes and frames. You cannot view status information for console and listener sessions.	User Access or Full Control

Viewing the Users on a Server or Domain

With Terminal Services Manager, you can view information about the user's session, the state of the session, and other properties for each user on Terminal Services. To view user information on Terminal Services, click the server or domain in the navigation pane, and then click the Users tab. Table 12-4 describes each field on the Users tab.

Table 12-4. Fields on the Users tab.

Field	Description
Server	Displays the servers that users are logged on to. This field is shown only when you click a domain in the navigation pane.
User	Displays all users associated with the server or domain.
Session	Displays the sessions associated with a server or all servers in the domain. All sessions are displayed, regardless of status.
ID	Displays the numeric ID that identifies the session to the server.
State	Displays the current status of a session. Session states include *active*, *conn*, *connq*, *shadow*, *listen*, *disc*, *idle*, *down*, and *init*.
Idle Time	Displays the number of minutes that have elapsed since the last keyboard or mouse input from a session.
Logon Time	Displays the time when the user logged on, if applicable.

Viewing the Sessions Associated with a Server or Domain

With Terminal Services Manager, you can view information about the user, state, and other properties of each session on Terminal Services. To view a session on Terminal Services, click the server or domain in the navigation pane, and then click the Sessions tab, as shown in Figure 12-22.

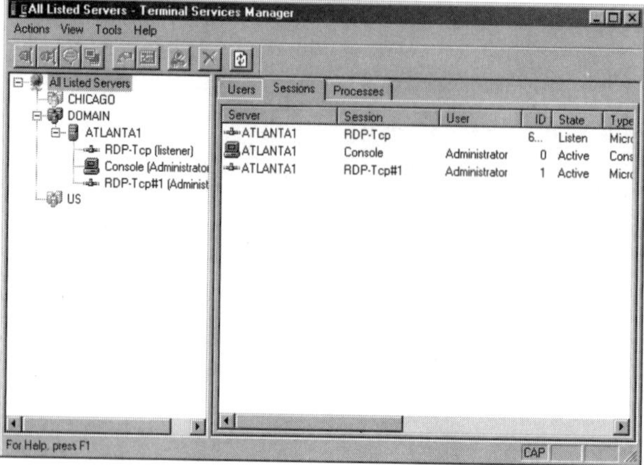

Figure 12-22. *Terminal Services Manager: Sessions tab.*

Table 12-5 describes each field on the Sessions tab.

Table 12-5. Fields on the Sessions tab.

Field	Description
Server	Displays the servers associated with the sessions. This field is shown only when you click a domain in the navigation pane.
Session	Displays the sessions associated with a server. All sessions are displayed, regardless of status.
User	Displays the users associated with the server or domain.
ID	Displays the numeric ID that identifies the session to the server.
State	Displays the current status of a session. Session states include *active*, *conn*, *connq*, *shadow*, *listen*, *disc*, *idle*, *down*, and *init*.
Type	Specifies the type of client using the session or whether the session is the system console.
Client Name	Specifies the name of the client computer using the session, if applicable.
Idle Time	Displays the number of minutes that have elapsed since the last keyboard or mouse input from a session.
Logon Time	The time at which the user logged on, if applicable.
Comment	Provides additional information about the session, such as its location. This field is optional.

Viewing the Processes Associated with a Server or Domain

With Terminal Services Manager, you can view current information about all processes on Terminal Services. To view the processes, click the server or domain in the navigation pane, and then click the Processes tab, as shown in Figure 12-23.

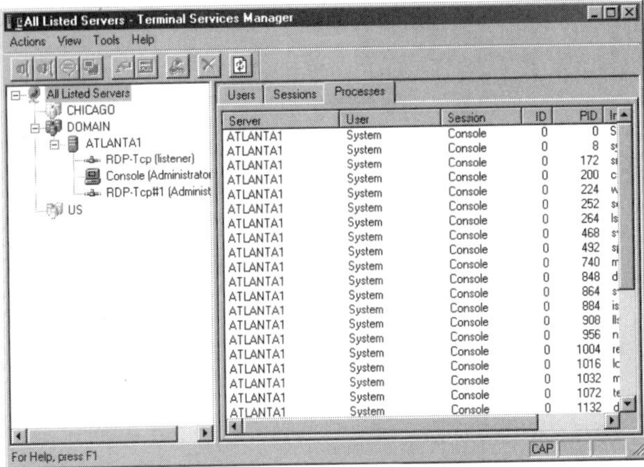

Figure 12-23. *Terminal Services Manager: Processes tab for servers or domains.*

Table 12-6 describes each field on the Processes tab.

Table 12-6. Fields on the Processes tab.

Field	Description
Server	Displays the servers associated with the processes. This field is shown only when you click a domain in the navigation pane.
User	Displays the users associated with the processes.
Session	Displays the sessions associated with the processes. All sessions are displayed, regardless of status.
ID	Displays the numeric ID that identifies the session to the server.
PID	Displays the numeric ID that identifies the process to the server.
Image	Specifies the executable program that created the process.

Viewing the Processes Associated with a Session

With Terminal Services Manager, you can view current information about all processes associated with a particular session. To view the processes, click the session in the navigation pane, and then click the Processes tab. Table 12-7 describes each field on the Processes tab.

Table 12-7. Fields on the Processes tab for sessions.

Field	Description
ID	Displays the numeric ID that identifies the session to the server
PID	Displays the numeric ID that identifies the process to the server
Image	Specifies the executable program that created the process

Viewing Client Information

With Terminal Services Manager, you can view client information about a particular session. To view client information, click the session in the navigation pane, and then click the Information tab, as shown in Figure 12-24.

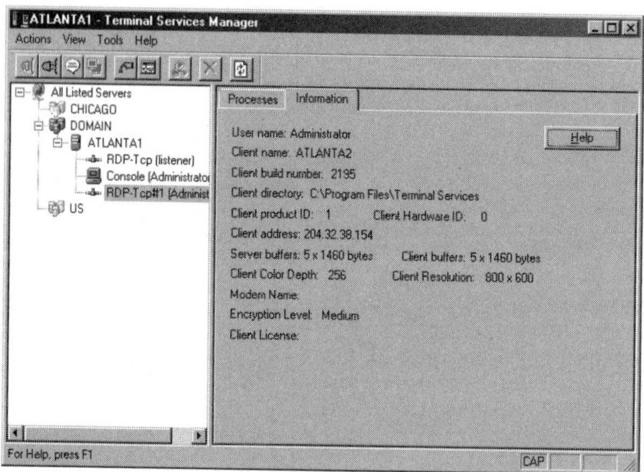

Figure 12-24. *Terminal Service Manger Connection Information.*

Managing Sessions

Sessions between the Terminal Server and remote console have a number of different states, and are controlled by the Terminal Server Manager tool. The following sections cover sessions in more detail and explain how to manage them.

Session States

Table 12-8 describes each possible state of a session.

Table 12-8. Session states.

Session state	Description
Active	The session is connected, and a user is logged on to the server.
Connected	The session is connected, but no user is logged on to the server.
ConnectQuery	The session is in the process of connecting. If this state continues, there is a problem with the connection.
RemoteControl	The session is in the process of remotely controlling another session.
Listen	The session is ready to accept a client connection.
Disconnected	The user is disconnected from the session, but the session is still attached to the server and can be reconnected at any time.
Idle	The session is initialized and ready to accept a connection. To optimize the performance of a server, two default (idle) sessions are automatically initialized before any client connections are made.
Down	The session failed to initialize correctly or could not be terminated, and is not available. If this state continues, there is a problem with the connection of the session.
Init	The session is in the process of initializing.

➲ To connect to another session

1. Right-click the session you want to connect to.
2. Choose Connect from the context menu. You are connected to the new session and disconnected from your previous session.

You can always connect to a session to which you are logged on with the same user account. To connect to another user's session, you must have either Full Control or User Access permission. You can only connect to another session from a session as long as the session you want to connect to is either active or disconnected. You must open Terminal Services Manager—or use the *tscon* command—from inside of a session to be able to connect to another session. If you are using the console session, you cannot connect to another session.

➲ To disconnect from a session

1. Open Terminal Services Manager.
2. Right-click the session you want to disconnect, and then choose Disconnect from the context menu.

You can always disconnect from your own sessions, but you must have Full Control permission to disconnect a session belonging to another user. When you disconnect a session, the session remains attached to the Terminal Services in the disconnected state and any applications that are running continue to run. The applications keep running when the session is reconnected, with no loss of data.

Users are automatically reconnected to the same session they disconnected from. If a user has logged on using more than one session on the server, Terminal Services displays a list of all sessions to which the user can reconnect.

You can also use the *tsdiscon* command to disconnect a session. You can reset a session that is in the disconnected state, thereby deleting the session from the server. You must have Full Control permission to reset a session.

To log off a user from a session

1. Open Terminal Services Manager.
2. On the Users tab, right-click the user you want to log off from a session, and then click Log Off.

You can always log off from your own sessions, but you must have Full Control permission to log off another user from a session. Logging off a user from a session without warning can result in loss of data at the user's session. Use Send Message on the Actions menu to send the user a warning message before you take this action.

When you log off a user, all processes end and the session is deleted from the server. You can also use the *logoff* command to log off a user from a session. You cannot log off a user from the console session.

To send a message to a user

1. Open Terminal Services Manager.
2. Right-click the session or user to which you want to send a message, and then choose Send Message from the context menu. The Send Message dialog box appears.
3. In Message Title, type the title of the message.
4. In Message, type the information you want to send to the user. To start a new paragraph, press Ctrl+Enter.
5. To send the message, click OK. The message will appear on the user's machine in a pop-up message box.

You must have either User Access or Full Control permission to send a message to a user. Use this feature to notify users of impending disconnection, server status, or other system information.

You can send messages only to those users whose sessions are in active or connected states, including the console session. Sending a message to a connected session is useful for warning users before they log on that the server will reboot shortly. You can also use the *msg* command to send messages to users.

Best Practices You cannot view server console messages when using Terminal Services to log on. Therefore, it is good practice to check the Server event logs, rather than to rely on a pop-up message box.

To reset a session

1. Open Terminal Services Manager.
2. Right-click the session you want to reset, and then choose Reset from the context menu. The session is immediately deleted from the server.

You can always reset your own sessions, but you must have Full Control permission to reset a session belonging to another user. If you reset a user's session with a warning, the user might lose data in the session. Thus, you should reset a session only when it malfunctions or appears to have stopped responding. If you reset a listener session, all sessions using the connection will be reset. You can also use the *reset session* command to reset a session.

To view status information for a session

1. Open Terminal Services Manager.
2. Right-click the session for which you want status information, and then choose Status from the context menu.
3. You'll see the session's status information about counters related to the session, as shown in Figure 12-25.

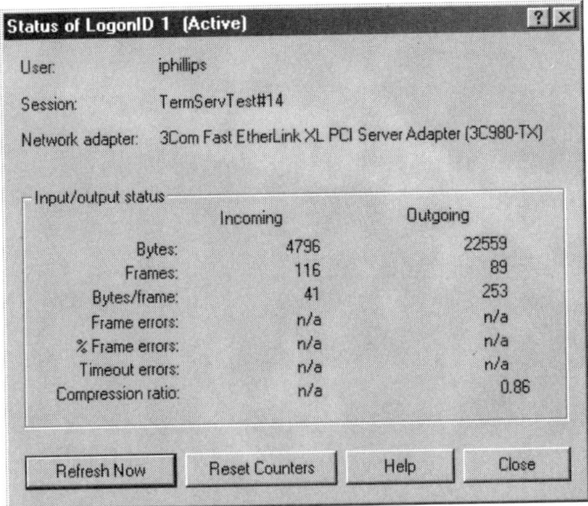

Figure 12-25. *Status Properties page.*

4. To refresh this information, click Refresh Now.
5. To reset counters, click Reset Counters.

You can always view status information for your own sessions, but you must have either Full Control or User Access permission to view status information for a session belonging to another user. You cannot view status information for the console or listener sessions.

To remotely control a session

1. Open Terminal Services Manager.
2. Right-click the session you want to monitor, and then choose Remote Control from the context menu. The Remote Control dialog box appears.
3. In Hot Key, select the keys you want to use to end a remote control session, and then click OK. The default hot key is Ctrl+*. (Use * from the numeric keypad only.)
4. When you want to end remote control, press Ctrl+* (or whatever hot key you have defined).

To remotely control another session, you must have Full Control permissions. To configure remote control settings for a connection, use Terminal Services Configuration. You can also configure remote control on a per-user basis by using the Terminal Services Extension to Local Users And Groups and Active Directory Users And Computers.

Before monitoring begins, the server warns the user that the session is about to be remotely controlled, unless you've disabled this warning. Your session might appear to be frozen for a few seconds while it waits for a response from the user.

When you enter the remote control session, your current session shares every input and output with the session you are monitoring. Your session must be capable of supporting the video resolution used at the session you are remotely controlling, or the operation will fail. The console session cannot remotely control another session, nor can another session remotely control the console session. You can also use the shadow command to remotely control another session.

To end a process

1. Open Terminal Services Manager.
2. On the Processes tab, under the User column, right-click the process you want to end, and then choose End Process from the context menu.

You can also use the *tskill* command to end a process. You might need to end a process because the application is not responding. Be aware that ending a process without warning can result in loss of data at the user's session.

To connect to a server running Terminal Services

1. Open Terminal Services Manager.
2. Expand the domain containing the servers you want to connect to.
3. Do one of the following:
   - To connect to a specific server, right-click the server, and then choose Connect from the context menu.
   - To connect to all servers running Terminal Services in the domain, right-click the domain, and then choose Connect To All Servers In Domain from the context menu.
   - To connect to all servers in all domains in your network, right-click All Listed Servers and then choose Connect To All Servers from the context menu.

Note We recommend that you connect only to one server running Terminal Services at a time. When a server is connected, Terminal Services Manager starts querying the server for information about its sessions and processes. Connecting to more than one server at a time can overload system resources.

To disconnect a session from a server running Terminal Services

1. Open Terminal Services Manager.
2. Expand the domain containing the servers you want to disconnect from.
3. Do one of the following:
   - To disconnect from a specific server, right-click the server, and then choose Disconnect from the context menu.
   - To disconnect from all servers running Terminal Services in the domain, right-click the domain, and then choose Disconnect From All Servers In Domain from the context menu.
   - To disconnect from all servers in all domains in your network, right-click All Listed Servers, and then choose Disconnect From All Servers from the context menu.

To find all servers running Terminal Services in a domain

1. Open Terminal Services Manager.
2. Right-click the domain whose Terminal Servers you want to find, and then choose Find Servers In Domain from the context menu.

Summary

This chapter explained how you can use Terminal Services to remotely administer a Windows 2000 Server. We also considered the security implications of running Terminal Services in both Application Server and Remote Administration modes. Using Terminal Servers to remotely administer domains and distribute software across an enterprise is vital to the centralized administration model within Windows 2000 and lowers TCO.

Chapter 13
Internet Information Services 5.0 and Internet Explorer 5.0

In this chapter we describe the potential security threats facing Internet Information Services (IIS) 5.0 Web servers and Internet Explorer 5.0 Web browsers. Then we'll explain the security requirements that you can implement to counter these threats and the mechanisms that you can employ to meet those requirements.

Internet Information Services

IIS 5.0 is the Web and File Transfer Protocol (FTP) server that comes with Windows 2000 Server and Advanced Server.

The function of the Web server is to accept input from Web browsers and serve content to them. Examples of such content are HTML (Web) pages, images, sounds, and executable files, as well as active content intended to run on a Web browser. This content can derive from static files, from the execution of scripts run by IIS, and from the execution of fully fledged programs; the latter two also process the user's input. Web servers implement the Hypertext Transfer Protocol (HTTP), and are also known as HTTP servers.

IIS 5.0 also implements the Web Distributed Versioning and Authoring (WebDAV) extensions to HTTP 1.1 that allow Web browsers to treat Web resources as file systems. Users can now modify, delete, and upload files on the Web server.

The function of the FTP server in IIS is simply to allow FTP clients to upload and download static files.

IIS Security Requirements

This section presents a sample list of security requirements you might want to impose on your Web server. Your individual requirements depend on the environment your server operates in (Internet or intranet) and its functionality, such as serving unclassified or sensitive information or performing monetary transactions.

We have divided the requirements into those that affect the Web connection across the network and those that affect the server itself.

Connection Requirements

You'll typically impose the connection requirements listed here on a per-directory basis, so some parts of your server content might be served with certain controls in place and other parts with none.

- **Confidentiality.** You might want to ensure that some or all of the data exchanged between the server and its clients is inaccessible to eavesdroppers.
- **Integrity.** You might want to ensure that active attackers cannot modify the data.
- **Authorized access.** You might want to ensure that some server content is made available only to authorized users. Or, you might want to authenticate users only for demographic and content customization purposes.

Server Security Requirements

Server security requirements relate to your Web server, as well as any other file servers from which it serves pages.

- **Authorized access.** You want to ensure that any access to the server(s) is authorized. In particular, you want to ensure that the server running IIS does not become an additional entry point for unauthorized access into the Windows 2000 host.
- **Confidentiality and integrity.** You might want to ensure that some of your Web content, user data, and configuration information remains confidential and correct.
- **Availability.** You might want to ensure service continuity after a disaster; you might also want to ensure that malicious acts do not compromise service availability. You might want to address reliability and nonmalicious interruptions elsewhere.

What's New

This section describes a number of new security features in Windows 2000 that can be beneficial to servers running IIS.

Inherited Permissions

Discretionary access control lists (DACLs) specified against a directory or registry key are inherited by its contents, so applying DACLs under Windows 2000 is much easier and less error-prone.

Security Templates

A lot of security settings, including user rights, file system and registry DACLs, and restricted group membership are now collected into security template files. You can use those templates to enforce a machine's local security policy. You can also test a machine's current configuration against a template for compliance. (See Chapter 9, "Security Configuration and Monitoring," Chapter 10, "Auditing," and Appendix B, "Security Tool Set Templates" for details.)

Active Directory Directory Services

The mutual and transitive trust among Windows 2000 domains allows Active Directory to serve as the organization's single account database. Servers running IIS can automatically authenticate users from this database, just by participating in Active Directory's domain forest. You can also give accounts in Active Directory to customer and partner users who access servers running IIS over the Internet.

Certificate Services

Windows 2000 offers a comprehensive Public Key Infrastructure (PKI). Domain users can now automatically obtain certificates and use them to access resources on servers running IIS. Active Directory automatically maps certificates to user accounts.

Kerberos Authentication

This protocol, new in Windows 2000, can potentially improve the efficiency of servers running IIS. In contrast to NTLM, Kerberos doesn't require a connection to the domain controller for each user authentication. Kerberos also supports the (multiple) delegation of user credentials, and makes access to back-end databases and other resources easier and cleaner to implement.

IPSec

This protocol provides confidentiality, integrity, and authentication services between hosts at the IP level. You can implement IPSec on intranets or over the Internet to offer virtual private networks. IIS services offered over such networks can benefit from those security services transparently, without any further configuration.

High Encryption Pack

Microsoft has recently obtained a license allowing Windows 2000 to be exported internationally with strong 128-bit cryptography. Applications such as IIS 5.0 and Internet Explorer 5.0 running on Windows hosts with the High Encryption Pack installed are now capable of strong encryption.

IIS Security Checklist

This section presents a concise checklist of settings that you can use to improve the security of a server running IIS. We've split these settings into the Windows 2000 settings that we discuss throughout this book, and IIS settings, which we discuss in the first half of this chapter.

Windows Security

The default Windows 2000 security settings provide a flexible work environment for users, but this flexibility can compromise system security. You can take several measures to tighten system security. Table 13-1 shows the default security settings.

Table 13-1. Default Windows security settings.

Action	Explanation
Use NTFS.	Lets you implement Discretionary Access Control on the file system.
Disable IP routing.	Is off by default. If enabled, a server running IIS sitting on the firewall could act as a router between the Internet and your intranet.
Run minimal services.	Be sure to run only the services that are absolutely necessary for your purposes. Each additional service that you run presents a possible entry point for malicious attacks. You'll find a list of services that you can disable in the *secureinternetwebserver* security template in the *Microsoft Windows 2000 Resource Kit*.
Enable auditing.	Auditing is a valuable tool for tracking logons and access to files. You can also use auditing for tracking server events, such as a change in your security policy. You can archive audit logs for later use. For more information, see the section on auditing later in this chapter.
Use isolated domain controllers as servers.	If you need to run IIS on a domain controller, make sure you isolate its domain from other corporate domains. If the server is compromised, any mutually trusted domains are also at risk.
Use directory DACLs to limit anonymous and authenticated user(s) to Web/FTP content only.	Limit the access remote users have to your computer.
Grant Local and Network privileges according to the authentication mechanisms used.	IIS authentication mechanisms perform either Interactive (Local) or Network logons. Make sure accounts have the logon privileges they need, but no more.

(continued)

Table 13-1. *(continued)*

Action	Explanation
Limit membership of the Administrators (and any other privileged) group.	Make sure only authorized personnel have Administrator access to the server.
Choose difficult passwords.	Passwords are more difficult to guess if they are at least six characters long and contain numbers and symbols. Use the password complexity security policy to enforce them.
Capture server security settings in a Security Template. Review periodically.	Security Templates describe a computer's Security Policy (see Chapter 9 and Appendix B), including directory DACLs, account privileges, and group membership. You can compare templates to actual settings and reapply them at will. Consult the two IIS templates in the *Microsoft Windows 2000 Server Resource Kit*.
Assign a strong password to the Administrator account.	This is the most important account on a server.
Back up vital files and the registry often.	No security effort can guarantee data safety. A well planned and tested backup strategy is essential to support ongoing system availability.
Run virus checks regularly.	You want to ensure that the content you serve is virus-free. For example, areas in your site that permit upload might contain infected files.
Run vulnerability-scanning software regularly.	From time to time, new vulnerabilities are discovered in software. It is better to find and patch them before attackers can exploit them.
Apply latest Service Packs and hotfixes available from Microsoft.	Review all Service Packs and hotfixes for their relevance to your installation and apply those necessary after testing.
Remove all net shares.	A server running IIS shouldn't need to export any shares.
Remove untrusted CA certificates from your certificate trust list (CTL).	Normally the CTL should only contain the CAs that this server needs to trust.
Use different Administrator accounts.	You should give each individual who has administrative privileges a distinct user account and password. This will make it easier to track each administrator's changes
Periodically change passwords of privileged accounts.	To lower the risk of user account information being compromised, change the passwords of personnel with Administrator or other high-level privileges.
Quickly delete unused accounts.	This will lower the risk of a disgruntled former employee or vendor gaining access to your network.

Internet Information Services Security

As with Windows 2000, you can perform a number of steps to increase the security of IIS 5.0. Table 13-2 shows the initial IIS 5.0 security settings.

Table 13-2. IIS 5.0 security settings.

Action	Explanation
Use most secure form of authentication possible.	Use the most secure form of authentication that your clients support. For example, integrated Windows authentication and digest authentication are more secure than basic authentication. You can also use client certificates for highly secure authentication. For more information, see the section on authentication later in this chapter.
Store executable files in a separate directory that is not in the IIS 5.0 directory tree.	This makes it easier to assign access permissions and auditing.
Synchronize Web and NTFS permissions.	If Web and NTFS permissions are not synchronized, use the more restrictive of the two. You can synchronize manually by modifying either of the two sets of permissions. You can also use the Permissions Wizard to apply predefined templates of such permissions. For more information, see the sections on authentication and access control later in the chapter.
Use the most restrictive permission possible.	For example, if your users utilize your Web site only for viewing information, assign only Read permissions. If a directory or site contains ASP applications, assign Scripts Only permissions instead of Scripts and Executables permissions. For more information, see the section on access control later in the chapter.
Write and Scripts and Executable permissions.	Use this combination with extreme caution. It can allow someone to upload potentially dangerous executable files to your server and run them. For more information, see the section on access control later in the chapter.
Use encryption if administering your computer remotely.	Typically, remote administration involves the exchange of sensitive information, such as the password for the Administrator's account. To protect this information over open networks, use Secure Sockets Layer (SSL) encryption. For more information, see the section on encryption later in the chapter.
Lock the desktop when away.	When you are not at the computer, lock the desktop by pressing Ctrl + Alt + Delete and selecting Lock Workstation.
Use a password-protected screen saver.	The time delay should be short so that no one can use the computer after you leave. The screen saver should be blank; animated screen savers can decrease server performance.

And of course it's also a good idea to keep your equipment as safe as possible. Lock each server in a secure room to reduce the chance of access by malicious individuals.

IIS Security Features

IIS 5.0 offers the following security features to address some of the security threats your server faces: authentication, access control, encryption, certificates, and auditing. This section describes how each feature functions and how the administrator can configure them.

Resource Hierarchy and Property Inheritance

The Property Inheritance feature of IIS affects the configuration of most of its features. Web and FTP resources in IIS are structured as follows:

- Master site
  - Web/FTP site
    - Virtual Directory
      - Directory
        - File

A child resource inherits a lot of resource properties from a parent resource. This automatic inheritance breaks when you edit a child's properties. After that, whenever you change the properties of a parent resource, IIS will ask you whether you want to replicate those changes to that child resource. Think of this as bringing the child resource in line with the rest of the resource hierarchy. You can also achieve this (for authentication and access control properties only) by running the Permissions Wizard and forcing the child to inherit the properties of its parent resource.

Authentication

The IIS authentication mechanisms optionally ask users accessing Web and FTP resources to authenticate themselves, and always map them to Windows user accounts. IIS then impersonates those Windows users to access the content it will serve. The Web server access permissions, the file system (NTFS) permissions, and the network address or hostname of the client host all serve to further control access. Those access control mechanisms (discussed in the next section), together with some input from the authentication mechanisms, determine which client user can access what files.

You can request authentication against a whole Web site, a directory, or a file—or against a whole FTP site. Once a user uses a mechanism to authenticate himself or herself to a Web resource, the browser caches that user's credentials, and automatically presents them to other resources on the same site that employ the same authentication mechanism.

Unauthenticated (public) access is called anonymous authentication. If anonymous Web authentication fails because of insufficient NTFS permissions, IIS will use another selected mechanism; otherwise, access is denied. If any other mechanism fails because of NTFS permissions (including FTP mechanisms), access is denied. IIS performs client authentication using certificates, if selected, independently of other mechanisms. Certificate mapping always takes precedence over other authentication mechanisms, if selected.

Some authentication mechanisms impersonate Windows accounts with an interactive logon, while others do so with a network logon. This means that the impersonated Windows account will need either the Log On Locally or the Access This Computer From The Network right. Two of the mechanisms—anonymous authentication without password synchronization and basic authentication—are known as Clear Text logons. By default these are interactive logons, and you can change them to network or batch logons (requiring the Log On As A Batch Job right), using the *LogonMethod* metabase property on a service, site, directory, or file basis. Knowledge Base article Q207671 has more information about this issue. (You can access the Knowledge Base at *http://search.support.microsoft.com/kb/c.asp*). The type of logon in turn affects the ability of IIS to access content on other hosts on behalf of the impersonated accounts.

Table 13-3 summarizes these authentication methods.

Table 13-3. Authentication methods.

Method	Security Level	Server Requirements	Client Requirements	Comments
Anonymous	None	IUSR_*computername* account (configurable)	Any browser	Used for public areas of sites
Basic	Low	Valid accounts	Any browser	Transmits password unencrypted (use with SSL)
Digest	High	Domain accounts in Active Directory with a plaintext (reversibly encrypted) copy of every password	Compatibility (currently only Internet Explorer 5.0)	Useable across proxy servers and firewalls
Integrated Windows	High	Valid accounts	Compatibility (Internet Explorer 5.0 to negotiate Kerberos)	Used for private areas of intranets (unusable across Web proxies)
Certificates	High	Server certificate and CTLs	Compatibility (Internet Explorer 3 or later and others) and client certificate	Widely used for secure transactions over the Internet
FTP Anonymous	None	IUSR_*computername* account (configurable)	None	Used for public areas of FTP sites
FTP Basic	Low	Valid accounts	None	Transmits password unencrypted (cannot use with SSL)

Anonymous Authentication

Anonymous authentication means no authentication at all. When a user accesses a resource configured for anonymous authentication, IIS maps the user to a local account. By default this is IUSR_*computername*, where *computername* is the name of the computer IIS runs on.

IIS is by default configured for password synchronization—in other words, it controls this account's password. In this mode it impersonates the account by performing a network logon, so the account needs to have the Access This Computer From The Network right. If password synchronization is turned off, IIS performs a Clear Text logon, which by default is an interactive one, and hence requires the Log On Locally right. You can redefine the Clear Text logon type, as described in "Configuring the *LogonMethod*" later in this chapter.

When you create IUSR_*computername*, you give it those rights and it becomes a member of the Guests group, to limit its access to the file system. You must replicate these settings if you use other accounts for anonymous access.

Basic Authentication

Basic authentication is a standard mechanism for collecting username and password information. The Web browser prompts the user for a username and password, which it transmits to IIS Base64 encoded. IIS uses the information to impersonate the user to Windows 2000. If the server rejects the logon information, the browser repeatedly prompts the user until he or she closes the dialog box. The username can optionally include a domain name in the form *domain\username*.

Basic authentication has the advantage of being part of the HTTP standard and therefore implemented by most browsers. It has the severe disadvantage, however, of exposing the logon information to eavesdropping. If you have strong security requirements, you might want to use this mechanism only over a secure network; or you might want to protect the network connection using SSL/TLS.

Basic authentication is known as a Clear Text logon, which by default is an interactive one, and hence requires that impersonated user accounts have the Log On Locally right.

Digest Authentication

Digest authentication is a challenge-response mechanism that proves the user's knowledge of the password without transmitting it in the clear. You'll find a definition in the Internet Engineering Task Force (IETF) RFC 2069 document. We discussed cryptography and Challenge-Response authentication in Chapter 6, "Cryptography and Microsoft Public Key Infrastructure."

Digest authentication works as follows:

1. The server sends some information (the challenge) to the browser.
2. The browser prompts the user for a username and password, as with basic authentication.

3. The browser hashes the password with the challenge, produces a digest, and sends it to the server along with the challenge.
4. The server also hashes its copy of the user password with the challenge, and compares the result with the digest it received.
5. Authentication only succeeds if the two digests are identical.

The challenge includes the client computer's identity, the domain (or realm), and the time, to prevent attackers from replaying the response.

Digest authentication is a new HTTP 1.1 feature and not yet supported by all browsers. If the server requires such authentication and the browser does not support it, authentication will fail, and the user might be repeatedly prompted for a username and password.

Digest authentication requires that users have accounts in a Windows 2000 domain, and that the Windows 2000 domain controller stores those passwords in a reversibly encrypted form. This is because in the hashing process described above, the browser uses the plaintext version of the password, and not the hashed password normally stored in the domain controllers. Therefore, if you choose to implement digest authentication, you will want to impose strict security requirements on your domain controllers to protect the reversibly encrypted passwords. You will also need to force your users to change their passwords to enable reversibly encrypted passwords, as described later in the chapter.

Using this authentication mechanism, IIS impersonates users with a network logon; the user accounts must therefore have the Access This Computer From The Network right.

This authentication protocol is usable across proxies and firewalls, and is also available to WebDAV.

Integrated Windows Authentication

Integrated Windows authentication is comprised of Kerberos v5 and a Challenge-Response authentication protocol (formerly known as NTLM)—the mechanisms normally used for authentication on Windows networks, here implemented over HTTP. As with digest authentication, those protocols prove the user's knowledge of a password without transmitting it in the clear. As an added bonus, there are no parameters to configure for integrated Windows authentication.

Kerberos v5 is preferable to the challenge-response protocol. It requires that both the Web server and browser have a relationship with a Key Distribution Center (KDC) and are Directory Services–compatible, which is the case when the two hosts are in Windows 2000 domains.

Integrated authentication proceeds as follows:

1. Internet Explorer will attempt to use the user's credentials if the user has logged onto a domain.

2. If this fails—because the user is not logged on or is logged onto another domain, for example—Internet Explorer will prompt for a username and a password until the user either enters a valid account or closes the dialog box.

Although integrated Windows authentication is secure, it is has some limitations:

- It is available only on Internet Explorer 2 or later; Kerberos negotiation is available only on Internet Explorer 5.0.
- It does not work over HTTP proxies.
- Kerberos Authentication is available only to client hosts participating in Windows 2000 domains.

This authentication mechanism is therefore best suited to intranet environments.

Using this mechanism, IIS impersonates users using a network logon; the user accounts must therefore have the Access This Computer From The Network right.

Certificates

IIS can also authenticate users by using their certificates, and optionally map those users to Windows accounts.

Certificate Authentication

IIS implements the SSL/TLS protocols that offer confidentiality, integrity, and mutual authentication services to the browser-Web server link. This secure link is known as the HTTPS interface, as opposed to the normal HTTP interface. IIS can make a Web resource available on either or both interfaces.

You can use the client authentication feature of the SSL protocol to authenticate users using their certificates over the HTTPS interface. This takes place at the TCP session layer, independently of the other IIS authentication mechanisms.

To start, users need to obtain a certificate from a certificate authority (CA) trusted by the Web server. Then, when accessing a part of the server requiring client authentication, the browser presents the certificate and proves its possession of the private key using a challenge-response protocol (part of the SSL/TLS negotiation). You can map each certificate to a separate account or you can map many of them into a single account. This account mapping overrides the mapping of the other IIS authentication mechanisms; you can use them in parallel.

SSL/TLS, as implemented in IIS, requires the server to possess a certificate and the associated private key to prove its identity to browsers. This prevents active man-in-the-middle attacks, in which an attacker masquerades as the IIS host. You should obtain this certificate from a CA that is already trusted by the browsers accessing the server, otherwise the CA's certificate should be distributed to the browsers.

Certificate Mapping

After authentication, you can map certificates to Windows accounts in a number of ways.

In IIS, you can define the following:

- **One-to-one mapping**. Certificates are individually mapped to accounts. You can do this manually by entering certificate files and their associated Windows accounts, consisting of usernames and passwords. The certificate presented by the Web user is compared bit-for-bit (as opposed to comparing some fields) with the ones stored in IIS to map it to an account. This process takes precedence over many-to-one mapping.
- **Many-to-one mapping.** This is also known as wildcard matching. Certificates are mapped to static accounts according to some rules. Rules simply match the contents of the Web user's certificate fields—holder's name, holder's organization, or issuer's name, for example—and then map it to a predefined account.

In Active Directory, there is an automatic mapping between certificates issued by the domain's Microsoft Enterprise CAs and user accounts. This happens through the User Principal Name stored in the certificate. You can create additional one-to-one mappings for certificates issued by third-party CAs. Note that there is no need for the account's password in this case. You can only enable Active Directory mapping against all Web sites on a server running IIS, and doing so disables IIS mapping.

Authentication and Mapping Scenarios

Certificate authentication, certificate account mapping, SSL, and the conventional IIS authentication mechanisms can combine to offer a number of authentication options to the administrator. Some common combinations are

- **Require Certificate Authentication and Enable Mapping.** If other mechanisms are enabled, they must also be satisfied by the user for authentication to succeed, but their account mappings will be ignored in favor of the certificate mapping.
- **Enable Certificate Authentication and Enable Mapping.** This works like the previous scenario, except that users with no certificates are mapped to Windows accounts by the conventional authentication mechanisms.
- **Enable Certificate Authentication but Disable Mapping.** Here, certificate authentication will ensure that a trusted authority issued the user a certificate, but a conventional mechanism will map the user to a Windows account.

Anonymous and Basic FTP Authentication

The FTP protocol always prompts for a username and password. The authentication settings determine which usernames are acceptable. You can configure authentication only against the FTP service (all FTP sites on a server) and against specific FTP sites, but not against directories or files.

Anonymous FTP authentication operates similarly to anonymous authentication for Web access. Users can log on anonymously or use ftp with any password. They are actually prompted to enter their e-mail addresses as passwords, for statistical purposes.

Basic FTP authentication operates in a similar way to basic authentication for Web access. At the logon prompt, the user can either enter a username or a domain\username. If IIS is running on a domain controller, the two username forms are equivalent. On a standalone or member server, the first form corresponds to local accounts.

Note that all FTP data transmitted over the wire, including the username and password information, is sent in the clear. IIS 5.0 does not support the SSL/TLS protocol for the FTP service and neither do Internet Explorer, Netscape Navigator, and other FTP clients. You should consider using the Web service instead to provide authenticated access to resources.

Configuring Web Authentication

This section explains the common steps in configuring the Web authentication mechanisms. You can select multiple authentication mechanisms for each Web site, virtual directory, or file.

1. Create any extra user accounts you might want to use with your selected authentication mechanisms, such as the anonymous authentication and certificate authentication in combination with many-to-one mapping. If IIS serves content residing on other hosts, we recommend that you use domain accounts, although replicating local accounts is also an option. (Make sure they all have the same password.) Enter the account details into the configuration of the IIS authentication mechanism that uses it. If appropriate, add the account to a group with reduced privileges, such as Guests. At installation, IIS creates the IUSR_*computername* local account on its server (or domain account if on a domain controller), adds the account to the local Guests group, sets the account's password, and keeps a copy of it.
2. Make sure that the account or accounts that IIS will need to impersonate have the local or network logon rights, depending on the authentication mechanisms you use. If serving content from other servers, make sure the authentication mechanism is capable of impersonating the user on those servers, and that the users have network logon rights on those servers. Grant rights by editing the Local Policy and Group Policy objects. Note that by default, domain users do not have the Log On Locally right on domain controllers, while IUSR_*computername* gets this right at installation.
3. Configure the NTFS permissions on the directories and files from which IIS serves content, to give appropriate access to the impersonated accounts. (For more information consult the next section, "Access Control.")
4. Use the IIS Snap-In to access the Properties page of a site, directory, or file.

5. Visit the Directory Security or File Security page and edit the Anonymous Access and Authenticated Access settings, as shown in Figure 13-1.

Note When you attempt to change the properties for a site or a virtual directory, the snap-in will ask whether you want to replicate those changes to individual directories and files under that site or directory.

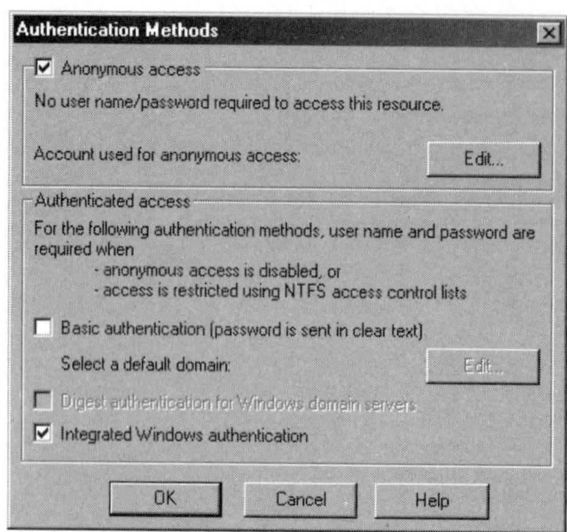

Figure 13-1. *The Authentication Methods dialog box.*

Configuring Anonymous Authentication

The Anonymous Access settings allow you to change the user account that IIS impersonates to serve Web content (by default IUSR_*computername)* as shown in Figure 13-2. Make sure that the user account meets the conditions described in steps 1 and 2 above.

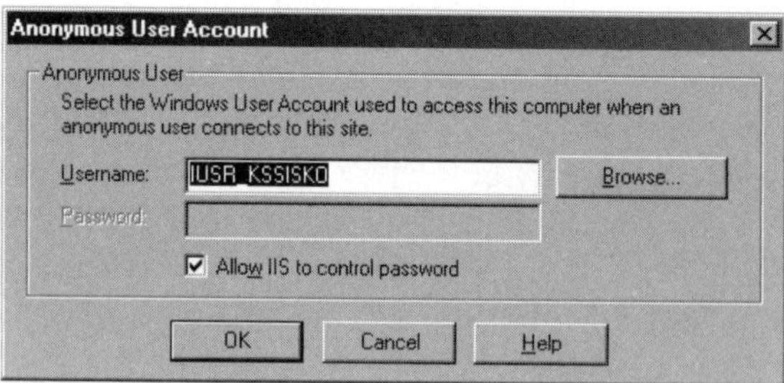

Figure 13-2. *Defining and controlling the account used for anonymous authentication.*

In the password field you can change the password that IIS uses to impersonate the user. You will first have to clear the Allow IIS To Control Password check box. By selecting the check box again, you can optionally make this password the actual account's password. This is known as password synchronization, and you should use it only with the server's local accounts—or domain accounts if on a domain controller. Note that if the account is local, and you have replicated it to other content-serving hosts, you must manually change the password there, too.

Configuring Basic Authentication

For basic authentication you can define a default domain against which IIS makes authentication requests. IIS uses basic authentication when users enter a *username* when prompted by the browser, rather than a *domain\username*. By default, authentication is made against the domain the server running IIS belongs to.

Configuring Digest Authentication

There are no parameters to configure for digest authentication, but you need to configure the domain controller to store user passwords in clear text.

You can do that in one of two ways:

- **On individual domain accounts.** Run the Active Directory Users And Computers Snap-In, then bring up a user's Properties page, view the Account page, and select the Store Password Using Reversible Encryption option.
- **Across a domain.** Enable the Store Password Using Reversible Encryption For All Users In The Domain option under Domain Security Policy, Security Settings, Account Policies, Password Policy.

Enabling the reversible encryption option will cause only new passwords to be reversibly encrypted—therefore, you need to force a password change on the accounts with which you want to use digest authentication. Again, you have two choices:

- **Change passwords manually.** Run the Active Directory Users And Computers Snap-In, right-click on a user, and choose Reset Password from the context menu.
- **Force a domain user to change his or her password.** Run the Active Directory Users And Computers tool, bring up the Properties page for a user, click the Account tab, and enable the User Must Change Password At Next Logon option.

Configuring Certificates

To enable certificate authentication you need to enable SSL on IIS first, as shown in Figure 13-3 on the following page. To do that, you need to generate a key pair and obtain a server certificate, as described in the encryption section later in the chapter.

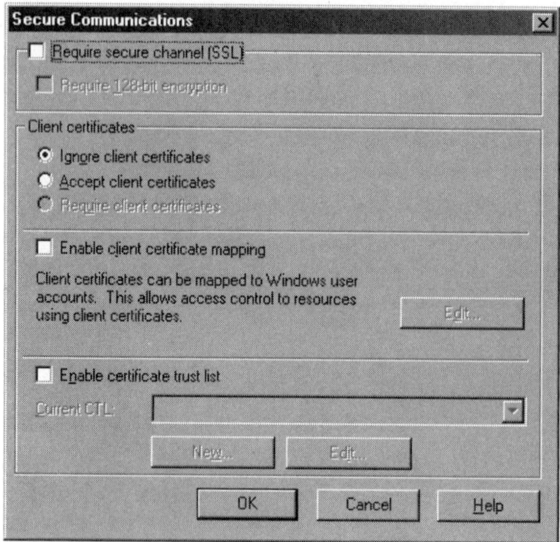

Figure 13-3. *Configuring Secure Communications and Certificate Client Authentication.*

With SSL enabled, you can enable and configure authentication by clicking Edit under Secure Communications at the Directory Security tab of a resource's Properties page. Here, you can choose from the following options:

- **Require Secure Channel (SSL)**. This makes the resource available only over the HTTPS interface.
- **Enable Client Certificate Mapping.** This maps certificates to Windows user accounts. These mappings take precedence over any mapping resulting from the conventional authentication mechanisms. You can edit those mappings in two ways:
  - **One-to-one mapping.** Supply a certificate in a .cer, .crt, .spc or .key file and specify the Windows account it is mapped into. Specify the account by entering a username (optionally in the *domain\username* form) and its password. You can also use the Browse button to choose the username from Active Directory.
  - **Many-to-one mappings.** Create rules on the following fields for a certificate Subject (the owner) or Issuer: Organization, Organizational Unit, Common Name, Country, State/Province, and Locality. For Subjects only: Initials, Given Name, Title, and E-mail. The matching criterion can be a static string or a string containing wildcards.
- **Configure Client Authentication**. The available options are
  - **Accept Client Certificates**. This means that if the user accesses the resource over the HTTPS interface and presents a certificate, IIS will use the certificate. This option is meaningful when you also enable mapping, so that certificate

owners will be mapped to accounts according to their certificate, and the rest according to the conventional authentication mechanisms in place.

- **Require Client Certificates**. This means that users will need to present a valid certificate to access the resource. This option is available only when you also enable the Require Secure Channel (SSL) option; otherwise, users could bypass this control by accessing the HTTP interface instead.
- **Ignore Client Certificates.** This means IIS will not request any certificates from the user. You can enable Active Directory one-to-one certificate mapping.

To load the IIS Snap-In into the Microsoft Management Console (MMC)

1. Right-click on the server name and choose Properties from the context menu.
2. Click Edit next to WWW Service Master Properties, click the Directory Security tab, and select the Enable The Windows Directory Service Mapper check box. This action will automatically map any certificates issued by a Microsoft Enterprise CA in this domain to the respective user accounts, by matching User Principal Name entries.

To establish further mappings from certificates issued by third-party CAs that don't contain UPNs

1. Load the Active Directory Users And Computers Snap-In into the MMC.
2. Choose Advanced Features from the View menu.
3. Right-click on a user, and select Name Mappings. In the Security Identity Mapping dialog box you can add certificates files to associate with the user account. Unlike the respective one-to-one IIS mapping, you don't need to enter the user's password.

Caution Active Directory mapping will disable any IIS certificate mapping anywhere on the server running IIS.

Configuring FTP Authentication

You can only set FTP authentication at the site level, as shown in Figure 13-4 on the following page.

1. Follow steps 1 through 3 from the earlier section on configuring Web authentication.
2. Load the IIS Snap-In into the MMC.
3. Right-click the entry for the FTP site and choose Properties from the context menu.
4. Click the Security Accounts tab.
5. You can enable anonymous authentication by selecting the Allow Anonymous Connections check box. (Configuration is the same as for anonymous Web

authentication, described in the Configuring Anonymous Authentication section above.) You can enable basic authentication by enabling anonymous authentication and then clearing the Allow Only Anonymous Connections check box, or by disabling anonymous authentication altogether.

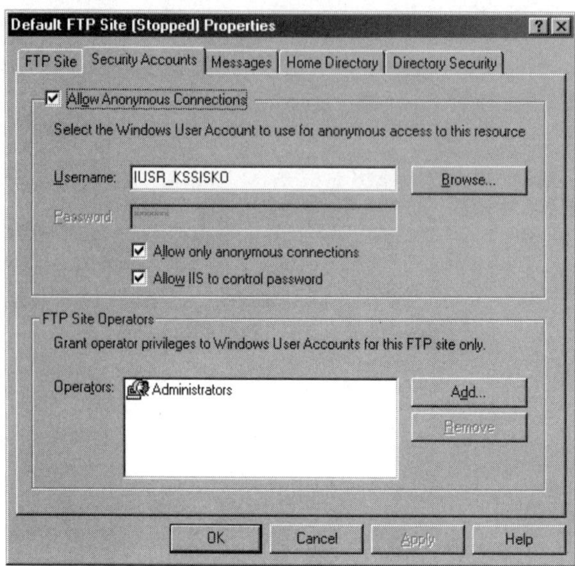

Figure 13-4. *Configuring authentication mechanisms for an FTP site.*

Configuring the *LogonMethod*

The Clear Text logon (used by the basic and anonymous authentication methods without password synchronization) defaults to an interactive (local) logon, but can be redefined as a batch or network logon. You do this by setting the *LogonMethod* IIS metabase property for a service, site, directory, or file.

The following sample VBScript will change the *LogonMethod* for the first Web site on a server called TestServer to a network logon.

```
Dim oIIS
Const LOGON_LOCAL = 0
Const LOGON_BATCH = 1
Const LOGON_NETWORK = 2
Set oIIS = GetObject("IIS://TestServer/W3SVC/1")
oIIS.LogonMethod = LOGON_NETWORK
oIIS.SetInfo
Set oIIS = Nothing
```

For further details, consult the Active Server Pages Guide, Administering IIS Programmatically section of the IIS 5.0 online documentation. You can also find more on this topic in the Knowledge Base article Q207671.

Access Control

As discussed earlier, access control mechanisms determine which client user can access what file, with some input from the authentication process. Those access control filters are the Web server access permissions, the file system (NTFS) permissions, and the network address of the client host.

In this section we will describe the combined authentication and access control process, how each mechanism works, and how to configure the mechanisms. We'll describe the Permissions Wizard that helps the administrator configure authentication and access control for common scenarios; we'll also discuss controlling access to a database that sits behind IIS.

Access Control Flow

Access control and authentication combine in the following manner:

1. The client requests a Web or FTP resource from IIS.
2. IIS, according to its configuration, might or might not require the client to authenticate itself. (For details, see the previous section on authentication.)
3. IIS checks the IP address and the DNS name (for Web access only) of the client host against the restrictions specified in IIS. A failed Web request returns a "403 Access Forbidden" message.
4. IIS checks that the user account specified in the Authentication process, if any, is valid and that the password is correct. Otherwise, in the case of a Web request, IIS returns a "403 Access Forbidden" message.
5. IIS checks that the Web or FTP access permissions are compatible with the type of access requested by the client (read, write, or other access). Otherwise, in the case of a Web request, IIS returns a "403 Access Forbidden" message.
6. IIS calls any third-party security modules specified by the administrator.
7. IIS checks that the NFTS permissions for the resource are compatible with type of access requested. Otherwise, in the case of a Web request, IIS returns a "401 Access Denied" message.
8. If all the above tests succeed, IIS fulfills the client request.

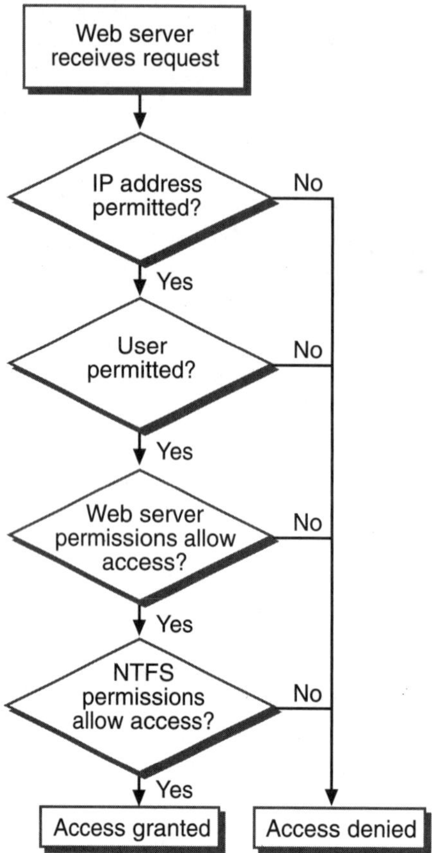

Network Address Access Control

You can instruct IIS not to serve certain IP addresses, ranges of IP addresses, hosts described by their fully qualified domain names (FQDNs), and DNS subdomains (the latter two are available only to the Web service).

Web Server Permissions

The Web and FTP server permissions define the operations allowed on each resource. They apply to all client users and are independent of the underlying NTFS permissions. If the two sets of permissions disagree, the most restrictive permissions apply. Again, the child container inherits those properties from its parent.

NTFS Permissions

IIS checks the permissions on the file system last, and they are the ones that ultimately enforce access control by users to resources. Such access control lists (ACLs) are only available in the NTFS (not the FAT) file system.

As a rule, the authentication settings, Web permissions, and NTFS permissions should agree. Here are some guidelines to use for these permissions.

- For the resources that allow anonymous access, make sure that the anonymous account (such as IUSR_*computername*) has appropriate permissions. Insufficient permissions will cause IIS to request authentication from the user if a non-anonymous mechanism is enabled for the resource.
- For resources that need authenticated access, make sure that only the intended user accounts have access. Microsoft additionally recommends that Administrators, the Creator/Owner, and the System group have the Full Control permission.
- In general, remove the Everyone group and other generic groups from the ACLs and replace them with the accounts and group that specifically need access.
- Use the permission inheritance feature of Windows 2000 to easily configure permissions across large directory structures.

We fully document NTFS ACLs in Chapter 7, "Access Control."

Permissions Wizard

The Permissions Wizard lets you apply predefined templates for authentication, Web/FTP access permissions, network address access control, and NTFS permissions to any Web site, FTP site, or directory. You can also use the wizard to inherit properties from a parent container (a master service, site, or directory) to a child container (site or directory). There are two Web site templates.

Public Web Site

This template is suitable for public access in an intranet or on the Internet. It sets authentication to anonymous, Web permissions to Read and Scripts Only, and NTFS permissions to Full Access for the Administrators group and Read, Read & Execute, and List Folder Contents for the Everyone group.

Secure Web Site

This template is suitable for private access in an intranet or on the Internet. It sets authentication to basic, digest, and integrated windows; it sets the rest of the properties as with a Public Web Site.

There is one template for an FTP site: Public FTP Site, which sets authentication to anonymous only, sets FTP permissions to Read, and NTFS permissions to Full Access for the Administrators group and Read for the Everyone group.

Delegation and Accessing Network Shares

IIS can serve Web and FTP content from servers other than the one on which it runs. One way of achieving this is by setting up a Virtual Directory and pointing it to a network share rather than to a local directory. IIS (versions 4 and 5) will then prompt for a username and password that it will use to access this share.

This is not very useful from an access control point of view, since the share is not accessed by the user who authenticated himself or herself to IIS, and hence IIS can use no DACLs to allow or deny access to the user.

IIS 5.0 can impersonate the user's account (the one resulting from the authentication process) to access the share if the authentication method supports it:

- Anonymous authentication without password synchronization and basic authentication, when defined as interactive logons, support a single-hop delegation, from IIS to the network resource only. If redefined as network logons, anonymous authentication without password synchronization and basic authentication don't support delegation.
- Anonymous authentication with password synchronization, digest authentication, NTLM and certificate mapping through Active Directory do not support delegation.
- Kerberos v5 supports multiple delegations. IIS impersonates the user to the network resource, which can in turn further impersonate the user to other servers.

Delegation also requires that the server running IIS is trusted for this purpose by the KDC residing in the domain controller. This trust is specified by the Trust Computer For Delegation flag in the computer's object in Active Directory. If you want to use multiple delegations with Kerberos, the KDC will also need to trust all impersonating servers. Individual user accounts can be exempt from delegation by having the Account Is Sensitive And Cannot Be Delegated flag set in the user object in Active Directory. Furthermore, Active Directory gives control over those two Active Directory flags to the users specified in the Enable Computer And User Accounts To Be Trusted For Delegation Security Policy, which defaults to domain administrators.

Finally, IIS 5.0 will attempt to impersonate the user when accessing the network share if the virtual directory's *UNCAuthenticationPassThrough* metabase property is set to True. If this impersonation fails, IIS will attempt to access the resource with the username and password specified against the virtual directory.

Another method for accessing resources on other servers is through *named pipes*, such as Remote Procedure Calls and DCOM communications. You'd also use delegation in this context.

Database Access Control

You can use a variety of techniques to effectively restrict access to your database files. These techniques can range from configuring your database software's security features to setting NTFS permissions for database files.

You can configure your database software's security features. With the security features provided by some databases, you can control user access to database files with a high degree of granularity. For example, with Microsoft SQL Server security features, you can control how users access a particular database file, including how those users access specific tables, records, and fields. For more information, consult your database software documentation.

Secure the database files and directories by setting appropriate NTFS permissions. Make sure that trusted users who need to update database files have appropriate permissions. For more information, see the section concerning NTFS permissions earlier in the chapter.

Use the appropriate NTFS permissions to secure .asp files containing scripts that pass username and password information to databases.

Tip Consider converting your ASP database scripts, especially those containing username and password information, into secure COM server components. For more information, see the Microsoft Internet Information Services Software Development Kit (SDK).

Select an appropriate Web server authentication method for identifying users who attempt to access your database. Database user authentication can depend greatly on the protocol used for connecting to a database. For example, if you decide to use the Named Pipes default connection protocol for SQL Server, authentication of Windows user account credentials will occur in addition to SQL Server authentication. You should carefully consult your database software documentation for guidelines regarding the integration of disparate authentication methods.

Configuring Network Address Access Control

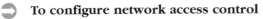

To configure network access control

1. Right-click on a resource (FTP site or directory and Web site, directory, or file) in the MMC.
2. Choose Properties from the context menu.
3. Click the Directory/File Security tab, and click Edit in the IP Address And Domain Name restrictions area.

   You'll see a dialog box similar to the one shown in Figure 13-5 on the following page.
4. Select Granted Access or Denied Access to define the default behavior.

   In the lower half of the dialog box you can define the exceptions, which can be:

   - **Single computer**, defined by an IP address. Use the DNS Lookup box to find a host's IP address given its FQDN.
   - **Group of computers**, defined by an IP address and a subnet mask. To evaluate this rule, IIS compares the bits—indicated by the mask—of the IP address with the client host's IP address. For example, an IP address of 1.2.0.0 and a mask of 255.255.255.0 match all addresses starting with 1.2.0.

- **Domain name**, defined either by a machine's FQDN or a subdomain with a wildcard in the form *.subdomain.com. This option is not available for the FTP service.

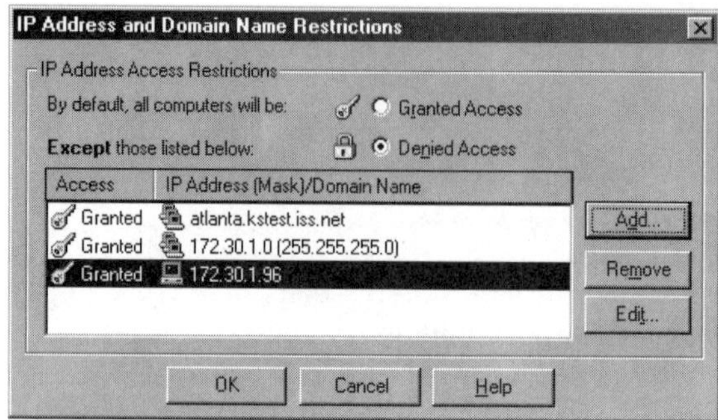

Figure 13-5. *Restricting access according to a client's network address.*

Notice that child containers inherit those properties from their parent containers. Also, if you change any properties to a container, IIS will prompt you to replicate them to any child containers that also define those properties.

Configuring Web Server Permissions

To configure Web permissions, as shown in Figure 13-6, open the Properties page of a resource (FTP site or directory and Web site, directory, or file), and then click the Home Directory, Virtual Directory, Directory, or File tab to choose options.

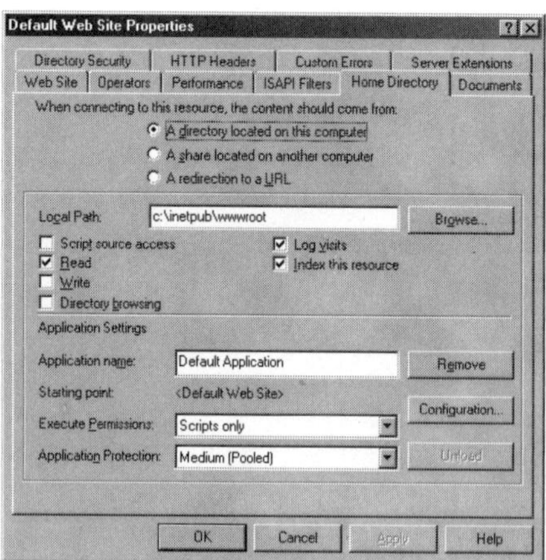

Figure 13-6. *Editing a site's Web permissions.*

Notice that with the WebDAV extensions to HTTP 1.1 now implemented in IIS, you can treat Web resources as file systems. Users can now upload files and directories and view their properties.

Configuring NTFS permissions

Remember the following guidelines when you configure NTSF permissions:

- If the disk partition you serve content from is in FAT format, convert it to NTFS with the Windows Convert utility.
- Use the Computer Management Snap-In or the Active Directory Users And Computers Snap-In (on domain controllers) to create and modify user accounts and groups.
- Use Windows Explorer to edit the permissions of files and directories.

Using the Permissions Wizard

You can run the Permissions Wizard by right-clicking on a site or directory, selecting All Tasks, and then selecting Permissions Wizard.

In addition to choosing between inheriting properties and applying templates, you will also be prompted to set NTFS permissions. Your choices are as follows:

- **Replace Directory And File Permissions With The Template Permissions.** Choose this option if you don't want to keep the current NTFS permissions on the files.
- **Leave The Current Permissions Intact, And Add The Template Permissions.** Choose this option when you have already set custom NTFS permissions you want to keep.
- **Leave The Current Permissions Intact, And Do Not Apply The Template Permissions.** Choose this option if you want to set the NTFS permissions manually, without the help of the wizard.

Configuring Delegation

To set the Trust Computer For Delegation and Account Is Sensitive And Cannot Be Delegated flags, use the Active Directory Users And Computers Snap-In.

To modify the Enable Computer And User Accounts To Be Trusted For Delegation Security Policy on a server, use the Local Security Policy tool or the Domain Controller Security Policy tool.

Here is a sample VBScript for enabling impersonation to a virtual directory named Content on a server called TestServer.

```
Dim oVdir
Set oVdir = GetObject("IIS://TestServer/W3SVC/1/Root/Content")
OVdir.UNCAuthenticationPassThrough = True
OVdir.SetInfo
Set oVdir = Nothing
```

For further details, consult the Active Server Pages Guide, Administering IIS Programmatically section of the IIS 5.0 online documentation.

Encryption and Certificates

The encryption features in IIS 5.0 provide confidentiality, integrity, and mutual authentication to the link between the Web browsers and the server. This section describes those features and how to configure them.

Transport Layer Security and Secure Sockets Layer

TLS and its predecessor, SSL, are protocols designed to provide confidentiality, integrity, and mutual authentication to TCP sessions. Most Web servers (including IIS) implement them, as do most Web browsers, including the latest versions of Internet Explorer.

An HTTP (Web) service offered over SSL/TLS is known as the HTTPS interface. IIS can serve Web content over both HTTP (typically on port 80) and HTTPS (typically on port 443). The protocol makes use of certificates to optionally authenticate the two communicating parties. SSL/TLS is a hybrid cryptographic protocol and works as follows:

1. The user's Web browser establishes a connection to the HTTPS interface on IIS.
2. The browser and the server negotiate the strength of encryption and the algorithm to use.
3. The server sends its certificate (which includes its public key) to the browser. The browser verifies the validity of the certificate using the issuing CA's certificate, which should be embedded into the browser or the operating system. In Windows 2000, those certificates are maintained in the local computer's CTL.
4. The browser generates a symmetric session key. It encrypts some information needed to generate this key with the server's public key, and sends the ciphertext to the server.
5. The server recovers this information using its private key, and generates the same symmetric session key.
6. Optionally, if the server requires certificate authentication, it sends a challenge, which the browser signs with its private key and sends back along with its certificate. The server then will verify the signature on the challenge. It will also verify that the user's certificate is valid and was indeed issued by a CA in the server's CTL. (We described this method of authentication earlier in this chapter.)
7. The browser and server start exchanging HTTP (Web) traffic, encrypting and cryptographically signing it with the session key.

Cryptographic Keys

The cryptographic keys employed by IIS in the above protocol are the server's key pair, the client's key pair (optionally), the server's CTL, and the generated session key.

The Server's Key Pair

Windows 2000 manages the private-public key pair and certificate of the server running IIS. You should be aware that the private key is normally stored unprotected in the registry. If something compromises the server, an attacker could steal this key and have another host masquerade as your Web server.

Windows 2000 also supports Fortezza PCMCIA cards for key storage (for use by the U.S. government); you might want to use them for the physical protection they offer to the private key.

The Symmetric Session Key

The symmetric session key is generated for each HTTPS session. Its most important property is its strength, which is typically 40, 56, or 128 bits, and in Microsoft products is regulated by U.S. cryptographic export restrictions. A complete discussion of the export of Microsoft products containing cryptography is available at *http://www.microsoft.com/exporting/*.

With the exception of nine countries restricted by a U.S. embargo, Microsoft has obtained approval to ship Windows 2000 internationally with strong 128-bit encryption. You enable strong encryption by applying the High Encryption Pack available on CD-ROM and through the Microsoft Web page. Once installed, this pack cannot be uninstalled. If you are located outside North America, make sure that your country allows the import and use of encryption products.

During the SSL negotiation phase, the browser and the server will agree to use the largest key length possible. Without the High Encryption Pack, IIS can negotiate a key of up to 56 bits in length. With the Pack, it can negotiate 128 bits with the browsers that support it. Currently, this includes only North American versions of browsers, but with the relaxation of export controls, most browsers will soon support strong encryption. Note that all session keys are 128 bits in length; 56 bit keys have 72 bits set to known, constant values.

IIS supports the Server Gated Cryptography (SGC) technology, which you enable by installing an SGC certificate. This allows the international version of IIS to use 128-bit keys, and was designed to exempt financial institutions from export controls. With the international availability of the High Encryption Pack, this IIS feature is now obsolete.

The Client's Key Pair

The client's key pair is used in client certificate authentication, as described earlier in this chapter. Note that IIS only needs copies of the users' certificates, if you choose to implement IIS one-to-one account mapping.

The Server's Certificate Trust List

The Certificate Trust List is a feature of Windows 2000 utilized by IIS. It is a list of certificates of CAs whose issued client certificates you can use to access the Web server. For example, you can configure your extranet server running IIS serving your clients to accept only certificates issued by your organization's own CA.

Configuring Encryption

The HTTPS functionality in IIS requires the server to have a key pair and certificate to authenticate itself to Web browsers.

The Server Key Pair and Certificate

You manage the server's key pair and certificate using the Web Server Certificate Wizard found in IIS and the Certificates Snap-In found in Windows 2000. Note that there can be only one certificate per Web site, since the name (and typically the domain name) of the server is part of the certificate. Also, since SSL encrypts the HTTP headers, multiple Host Header identities are not available to Web sites, and neither are multiple Web sites per server.

To access the wizard from the IIS Snap-In

1. Right-click the Web site and choose Properties from the context menu.
2. Click the Directory Security tab, and click Server Certificate in the Secure Communications area. The wizard allows the administrator to generate a new key pair and obtain a certificate from a CA, renew the existing certificate, or remove it. Note that a renewed certificate will be used only after the old one expires.

When the Web site doesn't yet have a certificate assigned, you have the following options:

- Obtain a certificate from a Microsoft Enterprise CA immediately, or generate a certificate request file for manual submission to CA. This operation is similar to the one described in the host keys section of Chapter 7. In the latter case, you will need to submit the Pending Request file to a CA, and obtain a certificate in text format that you copy to a file on the server running IIS. The next time you run the wizard, you will have the option of importing the certificate from this file or deleting the Pending Request file. Remember that for certificates assigned to computers, the Common Name field should be filled with the host's FQDN.
- Choose an existing key pair from the host's key store. The key pair must be one with server authentication in its intended purposes. The key store can include smart cards and Fortezza PCMCIA cards attached to the host. The cards must remain attached while IIS is operational; otherwise, you might need to restart the Web service.
- Import a certificate from a Key Manager backup file.

When the Web site does have a certificate assigned, the available options are as follows:

- Renew the current certificate, either automatically or manually, as in the first option above.
- Remove the current certificate.
- Replace the current certificate from an existing key pair from the host's key store, as described in the second option above.

Next to the wizard, you can find the View Certificate button, which brings up the standard Windows 2000 certificate viewer. Note that SGC certificates might indicate "The certificate has failed to verify for all of its intended purposes," which doesn't necessarily mean that the certificate does not work properly.

You can use the Certificates Snap-In to manage the key pair, as described in Chapter 7. For example, you can use it to make a backup copy of the private key and the certificate with the Export facility.

Upon generating a key pair and installing a certificate, IIS will immediately start serving a Web site's content on the HTTPS interface. To make sure that a resource (a site or directory) is available only over SSL, click the Directory Security tab of the Properties page of the site or directory, and click Edit in the Secure Communications area. To make sure that IIS only uses strong encryption (if available to your version of IIS), select Require 128-bit Encryption. Note that this will currently exclude international Web browsers, unless your certificate is an SGC certificate.

Certificate Trust List

You can access the CTL Wizard only from the Directory Security tab of a Web site's Properties page. Click Edit in the Secure Communications area, then under Enable Certificate Trust List, click New/Edit. You can choose to add CA certificates from a file or the local certificate store, which by default includes the certificates of many commercial CAs.

Auditing

Auditing or logging is an important security service that helps you hold your users accountable for their actions, as well as troubleshoot your server. You can use auditing to enforce accountability by tracking accesses to your resources. You can also use auditing to detect unauthorized attempts to access your resources.

You have three auditing options available to you:

- Auditing accesses to files and directories on the NTFS partitions from which IIS serves content
- Auditing server-wide events, such as logon attempts to the operating system
- Logging accesses and requests to IIS resources

Configuring File System Auditing

As shown in Figure 13-7 on the following page, you can configure file system auditing simply by using Windows Explorer to access a file's or directory's Properties page, and then clicking the Security tab, clicking Advanced, and clicking the Auditing tab. There you can specify to log certain types of accesses by users or groups. You can also set auditing on directories to include subdirectories. Note that the Audit Object Access under Security Settings, Local Policies, Audit Policy must be enabled on the host.

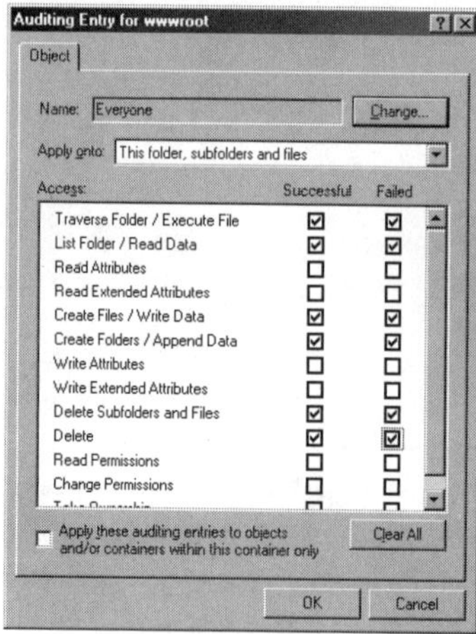

Figure 13-7. *Setting up auditing on a file or folder.*

Notice that file system auditing consumes a lot of system resources; use it with caution. Log entries are generated in the Security Log, which you can browse with the Event Viewer Snap-In.

Configuring Server Auditing

As shown in Figure 13-8, you can configure server auditing using the Local Security Policy and selecting the Audit Policies node of the Local Policies node. Make sure that the local policy is not overridden by Group Policies applied to the Site, Domain, or Organizational Unit.

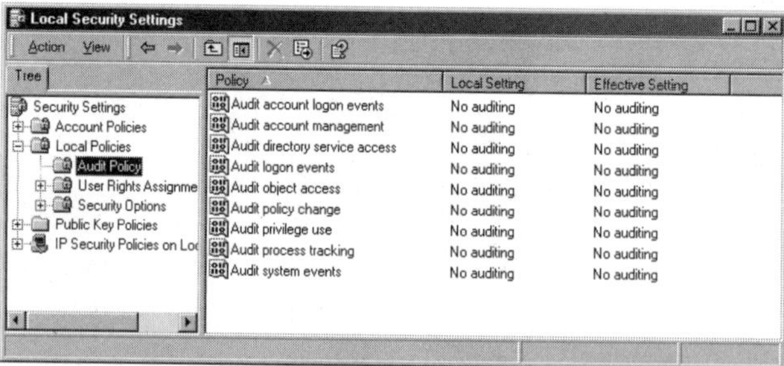

Figure 13-8. *Enabling auditing at the Local Security Policy.*

Configuring Web and FTP Auditing

You can configure Web and FTP auditing—which is enabled by default—at the Properties page for every IIS resource. The log file location is specified at the site level.

Internet Explorer 5.0

This section describes some common security threats facing IE users, some security requirements you might want to impose on the browsers, the security features Internet Explorer 5.0 offers, and how to configure those features.

Internet Explorer 5.0 is the Web browser integrated into the Windows 2000 desktop. In addition to browsing intranet and Internet Web and FTP sites, it can also browse the client host's file system and network shares found on your intranet. In this section, we sometimes refer to the former two as HTTP and FTP traffic, and the latter as Common Internet File System (CIFS) traffic.

IE Security Threats

This section describes the various security threats that face IE5 users.

Malicious Active Content

Active content is code that comes in the form of ActiveX controls, Java applets, and scripts that are downloaded from Web servers and executed by the browser. The latter two are run in a *sandbox*, a secure environment within the browser. ActiveX controls run in the user's environment, typically after the identity of their author has been verified, and on the understanding that they will not violate the user's or organization's security objectives. Signed Java applets can also have access outside the sandbox. Security concerns frequently arise with active content downloaded from the Internet because a) the security of the sandbox cannot be guaranteed; b) signed code can break its "promise to behave" and misuse its extended privileges; or c) someone can configure the browser to run unsigned code. Such malicious code can break your security objectives in many ways, starting with obtaining unauthorized access to the client host.

Executable Files and Documents

You can use Internet Explorer 5.0 to download executable files and Microsoft Office documents carrying macro code from within or outside your organization to your local hosts. You can also use the floppy drive, the CD-ROM drive, and the e-mail client to introduce code; it is just easier or even more tempting to do so with a Web browser. Just like malicious active content, the unauthorized execution of files and opening of documents can easily violate your security objectives, including the use of unlicensed software.

Confidentiality and Integrity

HTTP, FTP, and CIFS traffic, unless otherwise protected, normally travels in the clear and with little or no integrity control. It is possible for data to be eavesdropped or (though less likely) altered when traveling over insecure networks such as the Internet.

Password Confidentiality

Some authentication mechanisms—notably basic Web and FTP authentication—send user passwords in the clear. If no confidentiality mechanisms—such as SSL or IPSec—are in place, passwords can be eavesdropped.

Server Masquerading

When a browser attempts to connect to a Web or an FTP address, it relies on the DNS and network routing infrastructures to lead it to the correct host. On the Internet and on some intranets, that infrastructure might be outside an organization's control. Tampering with DNS and routing might enable a rogue host to masquerade as another to collect passwords and other confidential information sent to it, as well as to serve misleading content.

Cookie Privacy

Cookies are small pieces of data stored by the browser on behalf of Web sites. They enable sites to identify a) users who perform Web transactions that span multiple HTTP sessions, as in electronic shopping cart applications; b) users who have registered for an account with them, so the users don't have to log in at every visit; and c) users who visit repeatedly, to compile visitor profiles—even across multiple Web sites—for commercial and advertising purposes. It is this last use of cookies that poses a privacy threat to users.

Accessing Inappropriate Content

Users might access Internet content deemed inappropriate or that has no business value. Similarly, at home, children might access content that is not age-appropriate.

Internet Explorer Security Requirements

Against the threats described in the previous section, an organization might want to place security requirements, such as those described here, on the way users access intranet and Internet resources. You can meet some of those requirements at the desktop, by the security features of Internet Explorer 5.0, or centrally, at your firewall and Web proxy.

Authorized Access (Execution) of Code to the Browser

You might want to restrict the active content originating from the Internet that can run on the browser. You might also want to prevent users from downloading executable files from the Internet.

Authorized Access to Content

You might want to restrict the type of content your users (or your children) can access, according to a content-rating system.

Session Integrity and Confidentiality

You might want to protect the integrity and confidentiality of data submitted to Web sites (the security of downloaded data is controlled at the server end).

User Privacy

You might want to control the use of cookies in your organization. Users can control which personal data to make available to sites.

Internet Explorer 5.0 Security Features

Internet Explorer 5.0 offers a number of security features that help users and administrators meet the browser security requirements.

We will discuss each of those features in detail—including how to enable and configure them—in the following sections.

Security Zones

Internet Explorer can classify Web sites into *security zones* according to their network addresses. Those zones have different security requirements, and Internet Explorer 5.0 applies different security settings when accessing them. A fifth zone, My Computer, is not configurable from within Internet Explorer.

Internet Explorer includes four predefined zones: *Internet*, *Local Intranet*, *Trusted Sites*, and *Restricted Sites*, into which you can group Web sites according to the level of trust you place in a particular site.

Each zone then has a number of zone security settings configured against it. To simplify this configuration, Internet Explorer has four predefined templates of those settings, known as the Low, Medium-Low, Medium, and High Security Levels. We'll discuss zone security settings in the next section.

Note Zones and their configuration are also shared with the Microsoft Outlook Express and Microsoft Outlook e-mail clients.

Internet Zone

This zone contains Web sites not assigned to any other zone, including sites identified by their IP addresses—rather than their DNS names—that are not included in other zones. The default security level is Medium.

Local Intranet Zone

This zone should include all sites within an organization's firewall. Since there is no obvious method for identifying these sites, Internet Explorer can use the following rules:

- Include sites that don't have a dot in their address (*http://intranetsite/*, for example) and are also not listed in any other zone.
- Include sites that bypass the Web proxy. This rule is only useful if you configure Internet Explorer to bypass the intranet Web proxy for local sites.
- Include all sites that are referenced using a UNC path (*\\intranetsite\ share*, for example). Note that in certain CIFS configurations, you can use such addresses to specify Internet content.

You can also manually specify a list of intranet sites and domains. Optionally, you can also configure Internet Explorer 5.0 to use the HTTPS interface only to access those sites, which means that only sites authenticated with a certificate can be accessed.

All of the preceding rules are selected by default. The default security level is Medium-Low.

Trusted Sites Zone

This zone should contain sites that you trust to be safe, such as those of corporate subsidiaries or other established companies in whom you have confidence. You can manually specify those trusted sites and domains and whether users must access them over HTTPS. By default there are no sites assigned to this zone, and the security level is Low.

Restricted Sites Zone

This zone contains Web sites that you don't trust and believe threaten the security of your desktop. You can manually specify the untrusted sites. By default, no sites are assigned to this zone, and the security level is High.

My Computer Zone

This zone includes everything on the client computer, usually including the contents of the hard disk and any removable media drive contents. The zone excludes cached Java classes in the Temporary Internet Files Folder. You cannot configure the My Computer zone from within Internet Explorer; however, you can do so using the Internet Explorer Administration Kit (IEAK) and the Group and Local Policies. The default security level for this zone is custom-set to allow all actions.

Zone Security Settings

The security settings that you can configure on a per-zone basis are called *zone security settings*. These include controls on ActiveX and Java active content, file download, HTTP and CIFS authentication, and cookies. In this section we describe the security settings that you can configure against each zone, as well as the values assigned to each of the default security levels.

ActiveX Controls and Plug-ins

These options dictate how Internet Explorer approves, downloads, runs, and scripts ActiveX controls and plug-ins.

Note If a user downloads an ActiveX control from a site that is different from the page on which it is used, Internet Explorer applies the more restrictive of the two sites' zone settings. For example, if a user accesses a Web page within a zone that is set to permit a download, but the code is downloaded from another zone that is set to prompt a user first, Internet Explorer uses the prompt setting.

Download Signed ActiveX Controls

This option determines whether users can download signed ActiveX controls from a page in the zone. This option has the following settings:

- **Disable**, which prevents all signed controls from downloading.
- **Enable**, which downloads valid signed controls without user intervention and prompts users about whether to download invalid signed controls—that is, controls that have been revoked or have expired.
- **Prompt**, which prompts users about whether to download controls signed by untrusted publishers, but still silently downloads code validly signed by trusted publishers.

Download Unsigned ActiveX Controls

This option determines whether users can download unsigned ActiveX controls from the zone. This code is potentially harmful, especially when coming from an untrusted zone. This option has the following settings:

- **Disable**, which prevents unsigned controls from running.
- **Enable**, which runs unsigned controls without user intervention.
- **Prompt**, which prompts users about whether to allow the unsigned control to run.

Initialize And Script ActiveX Controls Not Marked As Safe

ActiveX controls are classified as either trusted or untrusted. This option controls whether a script can interact with untrusted controls in the zone. Untrusted controls are not meant for use on Internet Web pages, but in some cases you can use them with pages that you can absolutely trust not to use the controls in a harmful way. You should enforce object safety unless you can trust all ActiveX controls and scripts on pages in the zone. This option has the following settings:

- **Disable**, which enforces object safety for untrusted data or scripts. ActiveX controls that you can't trust are not loaded with parameters or scripted.

- **Enable**, which overrides object safety. ActiveX controls are run, loaded with parameters, and scripted without setting object safety for untrusted data or scripts. We do not recommend this setting except for secure and administered zones. This setting causes both untrusted and trusted controls to be initialized and scripted and ignores the Script ActiveX Controls Marked Safe For Scripting option.
- **Prompt**, which attempts to enforce object safety. However, if ActiveX controls cannot be made safe for untrusted data or scripts, users are given the option of allowing a Web page to load the control with parameters or allow scripts to use the control.

For more information about how to make ActiveX controls safe, see the MSDN site at *http://msdn.microsoft.com*.

Run ActiveX Controls And Plug-ins

This option determines whether Internet Explorer can run ActiveX controls and plug-ins from pages in the zone. This option has the following settings:

- **Administrator Approved**, which runs only those controls and plug-ins that you have approved for your users. To select the list of approved controls and plug-ins, use the IE Profile Manager or the Group and Local Policies.
- **Disable**, which prevents controls and plug-ins from running.
- **Enable**, which runs controls and plug-ins without user intervention.
- **Prompt**, which prompts users about whether to allow the controls or plug-ins to run.

Script ActiveX Controls Marked Safe For Scripting

This option determines whether an ActiveX control marked safe for scripting can interact with a script. This option has the following settings:

- **Disable**, which prevents script interaction.
- **Enable**, which allows script interaction without user intervention.
- **Prompt**, which prompts users about whether to allow script interaction.

This option is ignored when you set Initialize And Script ActiveX Controls That Are Not Marked Safe to Enable, because that setting bypasses all object safety. You cannot script unsafe controls while blocking the scripting of the safe ones.

Cookies

These options determine the settings for per-session cookies (text files that store the user's preferences) and cookies stored on the client computer.

Allow Cookies That Are Stored On Your Computer

This option determines whether cookies are stored on the hard drive for future browsing sessions. For example, this setting can allow a list of preferences or a user's name to be retained for the user's next browsing session. This option has the following settings:

- **Disable**, which prevents the creation of persistent cookies. If you disable persistent cookies, some Web sites will not retain their settings when users return to the sites.
- **Enable**, which automatically accepts persistent cookies.
- **Prompt**, which prompts users before the creation of persistent cookies.

Allow Per-Session Cookies (Not Stored)

This option determines how long cookies are stored when users browse a Web site. For example, this setting can allow the creation of a "virtual shopping cart" while a user shops online. Per-session cookies do not remain on the hard disk. They are in effect only for the specific browsing session. This option has the following settings:

- **Disable**, which prevents the creation of cookies. If you disable per-session cookies, some Web site information might not be displayed properly.
- **Enable**, which automatically accepts cookies.
- **Prompt**, which prompts users before the creation of cookies.

Downloads

The following options specify how Internet Explorer handles downloads.

File Download

This option controls whether file downloads are permitted within the zone. Note that this option is determined by the zone of the page that contains the download link, not the zone from which the file originated. This option has the following settings:

- **Disable**, which prevents the downloading of files from the zone.
- **Enable**, which allows the downloading of files from the zone.

Font Download

This option determines whether Web pages within the zone can download HTML fonts. This option has the following settings:

- **Disable**, which prevents HTML fonts from downloading.
- **Enable**, which downloads HTML fonts without user intervention.
- **Prompt**, which prompts users about whether to allow HTML fonts to download.

Miscellaneous

These options control whether users can access data sources across domains, submit unencrypted form data, launch applications and files from IFRAME elements, install desktop items, drag and drop files, copy and paste files, and access software channel features from this zone.

Access Data Sources Across Domains

This option specifies whether components that connect to data sources should be allowed to connect to a different server to obtain data. This option has the following settings:

- **Disable**, which allows database access only in the same domain as the Web page.
- **Enable**, which allows database access to any source, including other domains.
- **Prompt**, which prompts users before allowing database access to any source in other domains.

Drag And Drop or Copy And Paste Files

This option controls whether users can drag and drop or copy and paste files from Web pages within the zone. This option has the following settings:

- **Disable**, which prevents users from dragging and dropping or copying and pasting files from the zone.
- **Enable**, which enables users to drag and drop or copy and paste files from the zone without being prompted.
- **Prompt**, which prompts users about whether they can drag and drop or copy and paste files from the zone.

Installation Of Desktop Items

This option controls whether users can install desktop items from Web pages within the zone. This option has the following settings:

- **Disable**, which prevents users from installing desktop items from this zone.
- **Enable**, which enables users to install desktop items from this zone without being prompted.
- **Prompt**, which prompts users about whether they can install desktop items from this zone.

Launching Applications And Files In An IFRAME

This option controls whether users can launch applications and files from an IFRAME element (containing a directory or folder reference) in Web pages within the zone. This option has the following settings:

- **Disable**, which prevents applications from running and files from downloading from IFRAME elements on pages in the zone.

- **Enable**, which runs applications and downloads files from IFRAME elements on the pages in the zone without user intervention.
- **Prompt**, which prompts users about whether to run applications and download files from IFRAME elements on pages in the zone.

Software Channel Permissions

This option controls the permissions given to software distribution channels. This option has the following settings:

- **High safety**, which prevents users from being notified of software updates by e-mail, prevents software packages from being automatically downloaded to users' computers, and prevents software packages from being automatically installed on users' computers.
- **Low safety**, which notifies users of software updates by e-mail, allows software packages to automatically download to users' computers, and allows software packages to be automatically installed on users' computers.
- **Medium safety**, which notifies users of software updates by e-mail and software packages to be automatically downloaded to (but not installed on) users' computers. The software packages must be validly signed—the user is not prompted about the download.

Submit Non-Encrypted Form Data

This option determines whether HTML pages in the zone can submit forms to or accept forms from servers in the zone. Forms sent with SSL encryption are always allowed; this setting affects only data submitted by non-SSL forms. This option has the following settings:

- **Disable**, which prevents the submitting of information from forms on HTML pages in the zone.
- **Enable**, which allows information from forms on HTML pages in the zone to be submitted without user intervention.
- **Prompt**, which prompts users about whether to allow the submitting of information from forms on HTML pages in the zone.

Userdata Persistence

This option determines whether a Web page can save a small file of personal information associated with the page to the computer. This option has the following settings:

- **Disable**, which prevents a Web page from saving a small file of personal information to the computer.
- **Enable**, which allows a Web page to save a small file of personal information to the computer.

Scripting

These options specify how Internet Explorer handles scripts.

Active Scripting

This option determines whether Internet Explorer can run script code on pages in the zone. This option has the following settings:

- **Disable**, which prevents scripts from running.
- **Enable**, which runs scripts without user intervention.
- **Prompt**, which prompts users about whether to allow the scripts to run.

Allow Paste Operations Via Script

This option determines whether a Web page script can cut, copy, and paste information from the clipboard. This option has the following settings:

- **Disable**, which prevents a Web page script from cutting, copying, and pasting information from the clipboard.
- **Enable**, which allows a Web page script to cut, copy, and paste information from the clipboard without user intervention.
- **Prompt**, which prompts users about whether to allow a Web page script to cut, copy, or paste information from the clipboard.

Scripting Of Java Applets

This option determines whether scripts within the zone can use objects that exist within Java applets. This capability allows a script on a Web page to interact with a Java applet. This option has the following settings:

- **Disable**, which prevents scripts from accessing applets.
- **Enable**, which allows scripts to access applets without user intervention.
- **Prompt**, which prompts users about whether to allow scripts to access applets.

User Authentication

This option controls how HTTP user authentication is handled.

Logon

With this option you can determine whether Internet Explorer will prompt the user for a username and password during the authentication process. This option has the following settings:

- **Anonymous Logon,** which disables HTTP authentication and uses the guest account only for CIFS.
- **Automatic Logon Only In Intranet Zone,** which prompts users for user IDs and passwords in other zones. After Internet Explorer prompts users, these values can be used silently for the remainder of the session.

- **Automatic Logon With Current User Name And Password,** which attempts logon using Windows NT Challenge Response (also known as NTLM authentication), an authentication protocol between the client computer and the application server. If the server supports NTLM, the logon uses the network username and password for logon. If the server doesn't support NTLM, users are prompted to provide their user name and password.
- **Prompt For User Name And Password,** which prompts users for user IDs and passwords. After users are prompted, these values can be used silently for the remainder of the session.

Java

These options control the permissions that are granted to Java applets when they are downloaded and run in this zone. Different sets of permissions are assigned to unsigned (conventional) applets and signed ones.

Note If a user downloads a Java applet from a different site than the page on which the applet is used, Internet Explorer applies the more restrictive of the two sites' zone settings. For example, if a user accesses a Web page within a zone that is set to allow a download, but the code is downloaded from another zone that is set to prompt a user first, Internet Explorer uses the prompt setting.

Java Permissions

This option has the following settings:

- **Custom**, which controls permissions settings individually.
- **Disable Java**, which prevents any applets from running.
- **High Safety**, a predefined set of permissions that prompts the user when signed applets request access privileges outside the Java sandbox. Unsigned applets are given only sandbox privileges. Those permissions include:
  - Allow Thread Access In The Current Execution Context
  - Open Network Connections To The Applet Host
  - Create A Top-Level Pop-Up Window With A Warning Banner
  - Access Reflection APIs For Classes From The Same Loader
  - Read Base System Properties
- **Medium Safety**, which is predefined as above, and in addition automatically permits signed applets to a) access local files that the user selects in file dialog box; and b) use a secure scratch memory space. Unsigned applets are given only sandbox privileges.
- **Low Safety**, which is predefined to automatically permit signed applets to perform all operations. Unsigned applets are given only sandbox privileges.

In the next sections we will describe each of those permissions, along with the settings for each of the predefined safety levels.

Java Permissions for Signed and Unsigned Content

In this section we'll describe the permissions that you can give to Signed and Unsigned Content. First we examine the two options specific to those categories, and then we look at the common permissions.

Run Unsigned Content

This option is specific to Unsigned Content. You can configure this option to the following settings:

- **Run In Sandbox**, which runs unsigned Java applets for this zone in the Java sandbox. You can further enable or disable individual Java permissions.
- **Disable**, which disables running unsigned applets for this zone.
- **Enable**, which enables running unsigned applets for this zone. All Java permissions are enabled.

Run Signed Content

This option is specific to Signed Content. You can configure this option to the following settings:

- **Prompt**, which sets individual options in the Additional Signed Permissions category to Prompt. You can disable or enable each individual option.
- **Disable**, which disables running signed applets for this zone.
- **Enable**, which enables running unsigned applets for this zone. All Java permissions are enabled.

Note The Prompt setting is only available to Signed Content options.

Access To All Files

This option determines whether applets can have read access to all the files on the users' systems. This option has the following settings:

- **Prompt**, which prompts users before signed applets can have read access to all the files on the users' systems.
- **Disable**, which prevents applets from having read access to all the files on the users' systems.
- **Enable**, which allows applets to have read access to all the files on the users' systems.

Access To All Network Addresses

This option determines whether applets can access network addresses other than the address of the host from which they were downloaded. This option has the following settings:

- **Prompt**, which prompts users about whether signed applets can access network addresses.
- **Disable**, which prevents applets from accessing network addresses.

- **Enable**, which allows applets to access network addresses.

Execute

This option determines whether applets can run other applications. This option has the following settings:

- **Prompt**, which prompts users about whether signed applets can run other applications.
- **Disable**, which prevents applets from running other applications.
- **Enable**, which allows applets to run other applications.

Dialogs

This option determines whether applets can create file dialog boxes. This option has the following settings:

- **Prompt**, which prompts users about whether signed applets can create file dialog boxes.
- **Disable**, which prevents applets from creating file dialog boxes.
- **Enable**, which allows applets to create file dialog boxes.

System Information

This option determines whether applets can read system properties. This option has the following settings:

- **Prompt**, which prompts users about whether signed applets can read system properties.
- **Disable**, which prevents applets from reading system properties.
- **Enable**, which allows applets to read system properties.

Printing

This option determines whether applets can access printer resources. This option has the following settings:

- **Prompt**, which prompts users about whether signed applets can access printer resources.
- **Disable**, which prevents applets from accessing printer resources.
- **Enable**, which allows applets to access printer resources.

Protected Scratch Space

This option determines whether applets can use storage space on the hard drive. This option has the following settings:

- **Prompt**, which prompts users about whether signed applets can use storage area on the hard disk.
- **Disable**, which prevents applets from using storage area on the hard disk.
- **Enable**, which allows signed to use storage area on the hard disk.

User-Selected File Access

This option determines whether applets can access selected files. This option has the following settings:

- **Prompt**, which prompts users about whether signed applets can access selected files.
- **Disable**, which prevents applets from accessing any files (users are not prompted for permission).
- **Enable**, which prompts users about whether applets can access selected files.

Predefined Java Security Levels

Tables 13-4 and 13-5 define the high, medium, and low safety settings for the Java Permissions option described earlier.

Table 13-4. Java safety settings for unsigned content.

Java Custom Option	High Safety	Medium Safety	Low Safety
Run Unsigned Content			
Run Unsigned Content	Run in sandbox	Run in sandbox	Run in sandbox
Additional Unsigned Permissions			
Access to all files	Disable	Disable	Disable
Access to all network addresses	Disable	Disable	Disable
Execute	Disable	Disable	Disable
Dialog	Disable	Disable	Disable
System information	Disable	Disable	Disable
Printing	Disable	Disable	Disable
Protected scratch space	Disable	Disable	Disable
User-selected file access	Disable	Disable	Disable

Table 13-5. Java safety settings for signed content.

Java Custom Option	High Safety	Medium Safety	Low Safety
Run Signed Content			
Run Signed Content	Prompt	Prompt	Enable
Additional Signed Permissions			
Access to all files	Prompt	Prompt	Enable
Access to all network addresses	Prompt	Prompt	Enable
Execute	Prompt	Prompt	Enable
Dialog	Prompt	Prompt	Enable
System information	Prompt	Prompt	Enable
Printing	Prompt	Prompt	Enable
Protected scratch space	Prompt	Enable	Enable
User-selected file access	Prompt	Enable	Enable

Predefined Security Levels

Table 13-6 shows the values assigned to the predefined Security Levels.

Table 13-6. Predefined Security Level values.

Security Option	Low	Medium-low	Medium	High
ActiveX controls and plug-ins				
Download signed ActiveX controls	Enable	Prompt	Prompt	Disable
Download unsigned ActiveX controls	Prompt	Disable	Disable	Disable
Initialize and script ActiveX controls not marked as safe	Prompt	Disable	Disable	Disable
Run ActiveX controls and plug-ins	Enable	Enable	Enable	Disable
Script ActiveX controls marked safe for scripting	Enable	Enable	Enable	Disable
Cookies				
Allow cookies that are stored on your computer	Always	Always	Always	Disable
Allow per-session cookies (not stored)	Always	Always	Always	Disable
Downloads				
File download	Enable	Enable	Enable	Disable
Font download	Enable	Enable	Enable	Prompt
Java				
Java permissions	Low safety	Medium safety	Medium safety	High safety
Miscellaneous				
Access data sources across domains	Enable	Prompt	Disable	Disable
Drag and drop or copy and paste files	Enable	Enable	Enable	Prompt
Installation of desktop items	Enable	Enable	Prompt	Disable
Launching applications and files in an IFRAME	Enable	Enable	Prompt	Disable
Software channel permissions	Low safety	Medium safety	Medium safety	High safety
Submit non-encrypted form data	Enable	Enable	Prompt	Prompt
Userdata persistence	Enable	Enable	Enable	Disable
Scripting				
Active scripting	Enable	Enable	Enable	Enable
Allow paste operations via script	Enable	Enable	Enable	Disable
Scripting of Java applets	Enable	Enable	Enable	Disable
User authentication				
User Authentication - Logon	Automatic	Automatic	Prompt	Prompt

Secure Client and Server Communications

Internet Explorer 5.0 implements a number of industry standard protocols for securing the communications between the browser and Web servers. The Web server normally offers or demands secure communications, and Internet Explorer 5.0 merely implements the technology required to take advantage of those protocols. A number of security settings (not configurable against zones) are available to enable those features.

Security services are enabled by the use of certificates that enable server-to-client authentication, a prerequisite for any kind of secure communication. Optionally, you can use certificates for client-to-server authentication. Internet Explorer 5.0 makes full use of the Windows 2000 certificate and key stores discussed in Chapter 7. For example, certificate verification uses the CA certificates found on the host's local store. For client authentication, the user will be prompted to use a certificate found in his or her profile or any attached hardware devices.

Secure Channels

Internet Explorer 5.0 implements the standards SSL 2.0 and 3.0, TLS 1.0, and Microsoft's Private Communications Technology 1.0 (PCT). These offer the following security services:

- **Client authentication.** This service verifies the identity of the client to the server using a client certificate. Not available with SSL 2.0.
- **Server authentication.** This service verifies the identity of the server to the client using a server certificate.
- **Session confidentiality.** This service encrypts the exchanged information so only the communicating parties can read it.
- **Session integrity.** This service verifies the integrity of the exchanged information, ensuring it has not been modified en route.

Note Encrypting all traffic over secure channels is processor-intensive for both the client and the server, and is therefore typically used only for the exchange of sensitive information.

To connect to Web resources available over SSL and TLS and PCT, use the *HTTPS://* URL prefix instead of *HTTP://*. When connected, hovering the mouse pointer over the lock icon on the status bar will display the strength of the symmetric encryption algorithm used. Double-clicking the icon will display the Web server's certificate and allow the user to save it to the local host's certificate store.

At the client's end, configuration is limited to which protocols to use and which CAs to trust to issue certificates to Web servers.

When validating a Web server's certificate against the certificate of its issuing CA, Internet Explorer uses the local host's CA certificate store. Therefore, by controlling the contents of this certificate store, an organization can control which CAs it trusts to issue Web server certificates. Those CA certificates are identified by the Server Authentication value under Enhanced Key Usage and Certificate Purposes. Internet Explorer 5.0 can now also check for server certificate revocation, as described later in this section.

Server Gated Cryptography

Normally, Windows 2000 without the High Encryption Pack applied is limited to using 56-bit symmetric algorithms to provide session confidentiality. If the Web server though authenticates itself with an SGC certificate, Internet Explorer 5.0 is capable of using 128-bit-strong encryption. With the international availability of the High Encryption Pack, however, this technology is rendered obsolete.

CryptoAPI 2.0 and Cryptographic Service Providers

CryptoAPI 2.0 provides the underlying security services for certificate management, secure channels, and code signing and verification (Authenticode technology) to Internet Explorer 5.0. Cryptographic service provider (CSP) modules interface with CryptoAPI and perform several functions, including key generation and exchange, data encryption and decryption, hashing, creation of digital signatures, and signature verification.

That means Internet Explorer 5.0 can obtain cryptographic keys for client authentication from any hardware device attached to the host that has a CSP module installed. Windows 2000 comes preinstalled with CSP for Gemplus GemSAFE and Schlumberger smart cards.

Fortezza Support

Internet Explorer 5.0 also supports Fortezza cards for storing the user's cryptographic keys. These are PCMCIA cards designed for use in secure communications by the U.S. government. When in Fortezza mode, Internet Explorer 5.0 displays an "F" over the lock icon.

For this functionality to be available to Internet Explorer 5.0, the manufacturer's CSP must be installed.

Server Certificate Revocation

Internet Explorer 5.0 can now verify Web server certificates for revocation. It does that by visiting the certificate revocation list (CRL) that the URL specified in the certificate itself. If verification is required, and the URL is unresponsive, Internet Explorer 5.0 cancels the connection to the Web server.

Note Outlook Express also includes certificate revocation, which is controlled through a separate option within the e-mail program.

Publisher's Certificate Revocation

Internet Explorer 5.0 also adds support for Authenticode Publisher certificate revocation.

Authenticode

Authenticode is a Microsoft technology that allows Internet Explorer to authenticate the publisher or author of downloaded software and verify that the software hasn't been tampered with since publication. Authenticode is commonly used with ActiveX controls (.ocx), cabinet files (.cab), Java applets, and generic executable files (.exe).

Authenticode works as follows:

1. The software publisher digitally signs the distribution file using the private part of a private-public key pair. The publisher also obtains a certificate for the public key from a Certification Authority. The file is made available (for example, on the Internet or the organization's intranet) with the digital signature and the certificate attached to it.
2. Internet Explorer detects such a signature after downloading a signed file, and depending on the Download Signed ActiveX Controls setting, it might
   - Cancel the download.
   - Proceed with the download without checking if the publisher is designated as trusted. Internet Explorer prompts the user only if the publisher's certificate has expired or been revoked or if the signature fails to verify because the file has been tampered with.
   - Prompt the user as above, as well as if the publisher is not designated as trusted.

Trusted publishers are the ones that have explicitly been designated as such. See the next section for information on how to specify trusted publishers.

When validating a publisher's certificate against the certificate of its issuing CA, Internet Explorer uses the local host's CA certificate store (as it does when verifying a Web server's SSL certificate). Therefore, by controlling the contents of this certificate store, an organization can control which CAs it trusts to issue publisher certificates. Those CA certificates are identified by the Code Signing value under Enhanced Key Usage and Certificate Purposes.

Internet Explorer also consults its own trusted publishers certificate store for CA certificates.

Internet Explorer 5.0 can now also check for publisher certificate revocation, as described in the section about secure client and server communication later in this chapter.

Content Ratings

You can use the *content ratings* feature to control access to rated content, such as content containing explicit language, nudity, sex, and violence. Internet Explorer 5.0 implements the Platform for Internet Content Selection (PICS) standard. You can collect content ratings from the content sites themselves or from rating bureaus on the Internet. You can configure rules through the IE user interface, by importing a PICS Rules file, or by using the IE Administration Kit and the Group Policy.

This standard defines a language for rating services. Internet Explorer 5.0 is installed with the PICS-based Recreational Software Advisory Council on the Internet (RSACi) system. This system rates sites in four labels using five values, as explained in Table 13-7.

Table 13-7. PICS-based ratings.

Level	Violence rating	Nudity rating	Sex rating	Language rating
4	Rape or wanton, gratuitous violence	Frontal nudity qualifying as provocative	Explicit sexual acts or sex crimes	Crude, vulgar language or extreme hate speech
3	Aggressive violence or death of humans	Frontal nudity	Non-explicit sexual acts	Strong language or hate speech
2	Destruction of realistic objects	Partial nudity	Clothed sexual touching	Moderate expletives or profanity
1	Injury to a human being	Revealing attire	Passionate kissing	Mild expletives
0	None of the above	None of the above	None of the above or innocent kissing; romance	None of the above

There are four important concepts in content rating:

- **Labels.** These are the categories in which sites are rated. RSACi has the above four categories and a scale from 0 to 4, but every PICS system has its own labels and value scales.
- **Site ratings.** You can obtain these from the sites themselves (they are embedded into the HTML code) or from rating bureaus on the Internet.
- **Rules.** These define the maximum rating (for each label) that the user is permitted to see. You can enter rules into Internet Explorer 5.0 through its Graphical User Interface or by importing a PICS Rules file. They can also be centrally controlled using the IEAK and Group Policy. You configure the rules for every Rating System independently, and the most restrictive apply. An option controls whether unrated sites are blocked or permitted by default.
- **Approved/disapproved sites.** These sites are exempt from scrutiny by the Content Rules. You can specify sites using wildcards.

The rules, as well as the rest of the Content Ratings setup, are protected by a Supervisor (administrator or a parent) password. Optionally, a supervisor can use this password to temporarily permit the viewing of blocked content.

Internet Explorer Administration Kit and Group Policy

You can use the Internet Explorer Administration Kit (IEAK) to roll out Internet Explorer 5.0 across an organization, and (with the Group and Local Policies) to centrally configure certain IE security settings across the organization's desktops. Those tools are:

- **The Customization Wizard.** This wizard is included in the IEAK. You can use it to configure Internet Explorer once and then install it across an organization. The configuration can be *locked down* to prevent users from changing their browser's settings.
- **The Profile Manager.** You can use the profile manager—which is also included in the IEAK—to centrally configure browsers that use Internet Explorer's automatic (remote) configuration feature. Automatic configuration can be enabled in the first place either locally by the user, by the Customization Wizard at installation, or by the Group and Local Policy.
- **The Group and Local Policy.** You can use this to centrally manage certain portions of the IE configuration, as well as manage the host CA certificate stores.

The configurable security settings are

- **Security Zones And Content Ratings.** You can use these settings to define the Security Zone settings and the Content Rating rules for a set of users. In Group Policy you'll find this setting under User Configuration, Windows Settings, Internet Explorer Maintenance, Security. In the Profile Manager it is under Wizard Settings.
- **Authenticode Settings.** Use these settings to define the trusted publishers for a set of users, and whether those users are allowed to define their own trust in publishers. In Group Policies you'll find this setting under User Configuration, Windows Settings, Internet Explorer Maintenance, Security. In the Profile Manager it is under Certificate Settings.
- **Automatic Browser Configuration.** Use this configuration to configure Internet Explorer so as to periodically receive its configuration from a URL. The IE Profile Manager then provides this configuration. In Group Policy you'll find it under User Configuration, Windows Settings, Internet Explorer Maintenance, Connection; and also under Connection Settings in the same policy container. In the Profile Manager it is under Wizard Settings; and under Wizard Settings, it is under Connection Settings.
- **Internet Settings (Advanced Settings).** You can use these settings to define some of the Secure Communications and Other Security Settings (described in the next section). In Group Policy you'll find it under User Configuration, Windows Settings, Internet Explorer Maintenance, Advanced, Internet Settings. In the Profile Manager it's under Internet Settings.
- **Administrator Approved (ActiveX) Controls.** Use these in conjunction with the Run ActiveX Controls And Plug-Ins Zone Security Setting to define which

controls can be run. In Group Policy you'll find this setting under User Configuration, Administrative Templates, Internet Explorer. In the Profile Manager it's under Control Management.

- **Trusted Root CAs and Enterprise Trust.** Use these to control which CA certificates populate the certificate stores of computers. In Group Policy you'll find these under Computer Configuration, Windows Settings, Security Settings, Public Key Policies. In the Profile Manager they are under Certificate Settings.

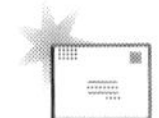

Note Windows 2000 applies Group Policies under User Configuration on sets of users; it applies policies under Computer Configuration on sets of computers.

Other Security Settings

A couple of Internet Explorer security features do not belong to any of the above categories:

- **Empty Temporary Internet Files Folder When Browser Is Closed.** This will protect the user's privacy from parties with access to the host's file system.
- **Warn If Forms Submittal Is Being Redirected.** This indicates if the form is redirected from the site the form (the Web page) was downloaded from to another site.

These settings are not configured against security zones.

Profile Assistant

Profile Assistant lets the user enter personal information, such as name and address, into an IE Profile once. This information can then be given—with the user's consent—only to sites that request it.

The information can include first, middle, and last name, title, nickname, e-mail address, home address and phone numbers, work address and phone numbers, family names, gender, birthday, anniversary, and more.

When a site requests information from the user's Profile, the Profile Assistant dialog box shows the following:

- The Requester Name, the individual, or the organization making the request.
- The URL of the site.
- Profile Information requested, with a checkbox against each one, letting the user choose which pieces of information to consent to share.
- Edit Profile, which lets the user edit the information sent to this Web site.
- Privacy, showing whether the information will be secure when sent over the Internet, as well as a statement describing how the requester intends to use the information.

You can disable or enable the Profile Assistant altogether. In the latter case, the Profile is not made available to sites at all.

Configuring Security Zones and Settings

You can configure IE zones by choosing Internet Options from the Tools menu, and then clicking the Security tab.

If the zone allows it, you can click Sites to specify which sites and domains belong to the zone. The options available to each zone are described in the section on security zones earlier in the chapter.

By clicking the slider on the left, if available, you can choose a predefined security level for this zone. The Default Level button resets this back to the default value for this zone. The Custom Level button allows you to make custom settings. You can see these features in Figure 13-9.

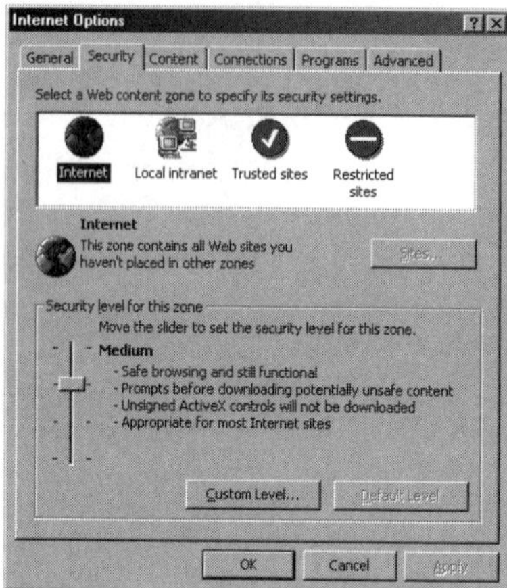

Figure 13-9. *Configuring security zones.*

Configure Java permissions like any other zone security setting—by using the Custom Level button. You can make custom settings by setting Java Permissions to Custom and clicking the Java Custom Settings button. In this window you'll see the following:

- The Edit Permissions tab, which allows editing for the Java permissions discussed previously.
- The View Permissions tab, which shows the same current settings at a lower level. For further information consult the Microsoft Software Development Kit for Java. Java settings are displayed in three windows:
  - Permissions Given To Unsigned Content
  - Permissions That Signed Content Are Allowed and given without prompting.
  - Permissions That Signed Content Are Denied or require user prompting.

Figures 13-10 and 13-11 illustrate the View and Edit tabs.

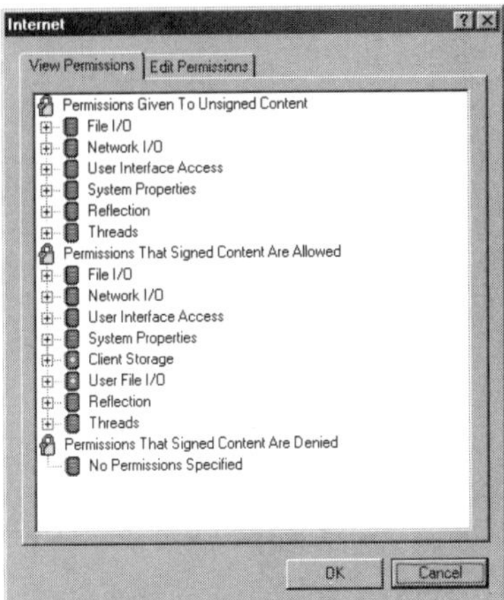

Figure 13-10. *Viewing the Custom Java security settings.*

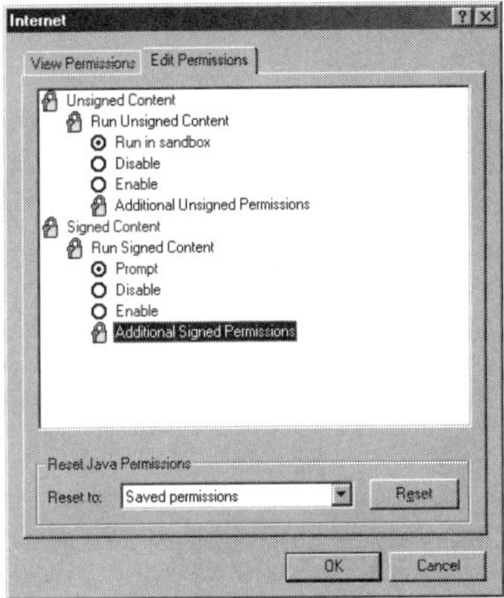

Figure 13-11. *Editing the Custom Java security settings.*

The same security settings can be made using the Internet Explorer Customization Wizard, the IEAK Profile Manager, and Group and Local Policy. Those tools can additionally configure the My Computer security zone.

Configuring Secure Client and Server Communications

You can use the following security settings to enable the Secure Client and Server Communications features. You'll find these settings under Tools, Internet Options, Advanced, Security.

- Check For Publisher's Certificate Revocation
- Check For Server Certificate Revocation
- Do Not Save Encrypted Pages To Disk, meaning that pages downloaded over an HTTPS link are not cached.
- Use Fortezza
- Use PCT 1.0
- Use SSL 2.0
- Use SSL 3.0
- Use TLS 1.0
- Warn About Invalid Site Certificates
- Warn If Changing Between Secure And Not Secure Mode, meaning that a warning will be displayed when a site directs the user from an HTTP page to an HTTPS one and vise versa.

You can view these settings in Figure 13-12.

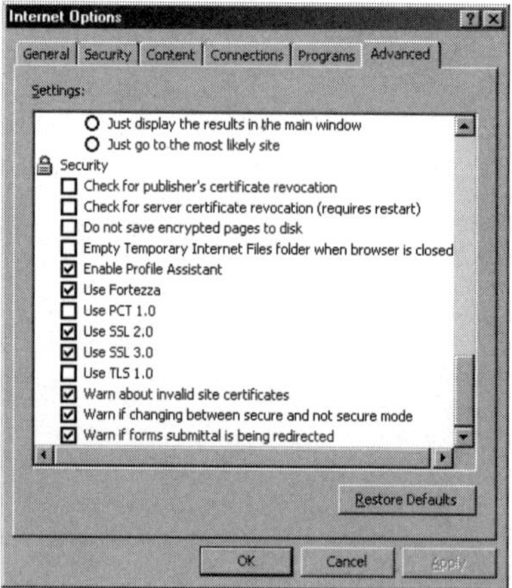

Figure 13-12. *Configuring the Secure Communications options.*

You can view and manage user keys and CA certificates with the Certificates tool found at Tools, Internet Options, Content, Certificates. Figure 13-13 shows this tool. Specifically, the user can do the following:

- View, import, and export his or her own key pair and certificate.
- View, import, and export the certificates of other people (to exchange secure e-mail).
- View, import, and export certificates of Web servers and Certification Authorities. Import might be restricted by the Group and Local Policies, the IE Customization Wizard, or the IE Profile Manager.

Similar functionality is available through the Certificates Snap-In..

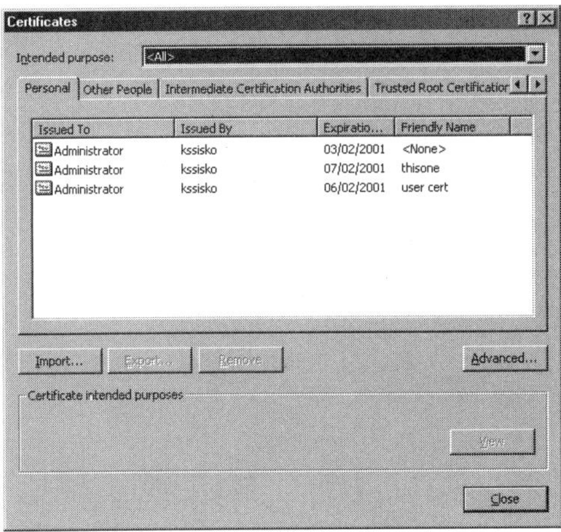

Figure 13-13. *Managing personal and CA certificates.*

Configuring Authenticode

The settings relevant to Authenticode are as follows:

- The Check For Publisher's Certificate Revocation setting under Tools, Internet Options, Advanced, Security.
- The Download Signed ActiveX Controls setting under Security Zones.
- The Trusted Publishers And Issuers Of Credentials (CAs issuing Code Signing certificates to publishers) under Tools, Internet Options, Content, Publishers. This window permits browsing and deleting of certificates. Publishers can only become trusted and their certificates added to this store after Internet Explorer downloads a file signed by them, in which case the user will be prompted on whether to trust the publisher in the future.

You can also use the local host's CA certificate store to specify those issuers of credentials. That can be populated in a number of ways, including Internet Explorer's Certificates tool, the Certificates Snap-In, and the Group and Local Policies.

Configuring Content Ratings

You can enable and disable content ratings under Tools, Internet Options, Content, Content Advisor, Enable/Disable, and by entering the Supervisor password. Configure content ratings using the Settings button and entering the Supervisor password, as shown in Figure 13-14.

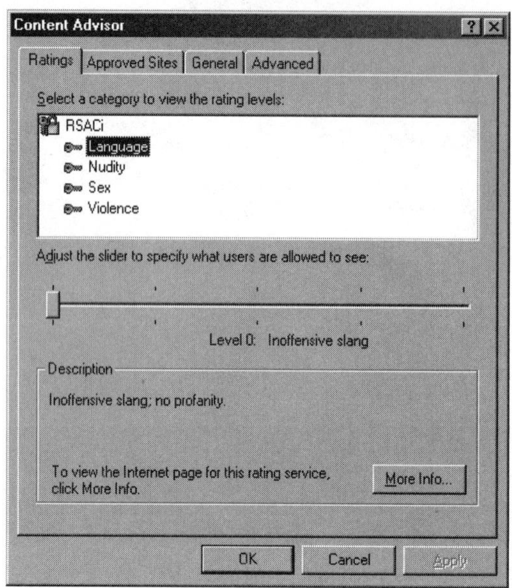

Figure 13-14. *Configuring permitted Content Ratings.*

In this screen, the available pages are as follows:

- **Ratings.** Here you specify the Content Rules. A slide bar sets a level for each of the rating labels, up to which the user is allowed to view Web content. This page displays the labels for each of the installed rating services (only RSACi, by default). The More Info button brings up the Web page of the selected rating service.
- **Approved sites.** Here you specify the exempt sites. Simply enter a site (using wildcards to specify sets of sites) and press Always to make a site always approved or Never to make a site disapproved. Selecting Remove deletes the selected entry from the list.
- **General.** Here the following options are available:
    - **Users Can See Sites That Have No Rating** defines the default behavior in the absence of any ratings for a site.

  - **Supervisor Can Type A Password To Allow Users To View Restricted Content** allows exactly that.
  - **Change Password** modifies the Supervisor password that protects all the content ratings settings and can be used to temporarily permit restricted content.
  - **Find Rating Systems** brings up a Microsoft Web page with rating systems available for use with Internet Explorer.
  - **Rating Systems** shows the currently installed Rating Systems (only RSACi, by default) and allows you to add new ones (using .rat files) and remove any of the existing ones.
- **Advanced.** Here you can select from the following:
  - A **Ratings Bureau** (an Internet site) that will be queried for a rating every time a Web site is accessed. The list of bureaus, if any, is compiled from the .rat files that define the installed Rating Systems. By default, the RSACi system is configured with no Bureau.
  - The **PICSRules**, which can programmatically define rules for permitting or restricting access to rated content. Those rules are equivalent to the ones entered through the user interface under the ratings page. The available options are Import a PICSRules (.prf) file, Remove a PICSRules file, or adjust the order in which they are evaluated.

Configuring Internet Explorer Administration Kit and Group Policy

Consult the *Microsoft Windows 2000 Server Resource Kit* for documentation on the IE Customization Wizard and the IE Administration Kit Profile Manager. Consult Chapter 9 for information on how to edit Group and Local Policy.

Configuring Other Security Settings

You can find other security settings under Tools, Internet Options, Advanced, Security, along with the Secure Communications options. There, you can set the Empty Temporary Internet Files Folder When Browser Is Closed and the Warn If Forms Submittal Is Being Redirected options described previously.

Configuring Profile Assistant

You can enable the Profile Assistant with the Enable Profile Assistant option under Tools, Internet Options, Advanced, Security.

You can configure the Profile Assistant under Tools, Internet Options, Content, My Profile. When using the Profile Assistant for the first time, the user will be prompted to either create a new, empty Profile, or use an existing contact from the Address Book of the default mailer (assuming the user has added his or her own address to the Address Book).

The user then can fill in a profile, as shown in Figure 13-15.

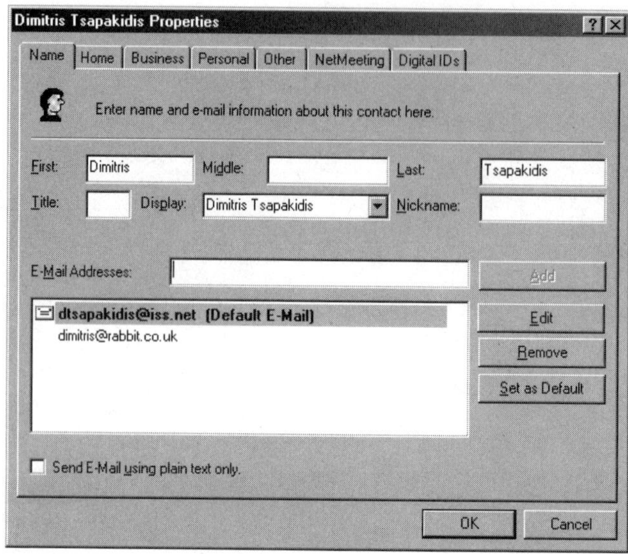

Figure 13-15. *Editing the user's profile.*

Summary

This chapter introduced the security features of the Internet Information Services 5.0 and Internet Explorer 5.0, the standard Windows 2000 tools for publishing and browsing content on your intranet and the Internet. We also explained how to best use those features, as well as the security features of the underlying Windows 2000 operating system, to secure your organization's Web servers and browsers.

Appendix A
Microsoft Windows 2000 Resource Kit Tools

The following Resource Kit command-line and GUI-based tools are available on the *Microsoft Windows 2000 Server Resource Kit* CD-ROM. You can use these tools to complement the security management tools included with Windows 2000. You'll find further information on how to use these tools, including the full syntax and description of the switches, on the Tools help pages included with the Resource Kit. The Resource Kit highlights the tools that are new to Windows 2000 and not included in the *Microsoft Windows NT 4.0 Server Resource Kit.*

Appsec.exe: Application Security

The Application Security tool is new for Windows 2000; you'll find it in the Computer Management Tools folder. This tool is a GUI-based application that allows an administrator in a multiuser environment to restrict the access of ordinary users to predefined applications on the network. Figure A-1 shows the Application Security dialog box.

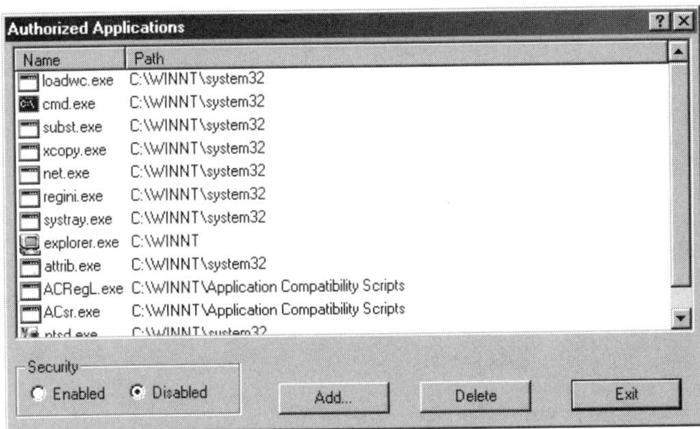

Figure A-1. *Application Security dialog box.*

The Application Security tool causes the system to reject any attempts by unauthorized users to execute programs that they are not permitted to use. The tool increases security by preventing the user from running an executable file even through the command line or from within another application. You can use this tool in conjunction with Group Policy to disable and hide restricted programs.

The tool also has a tracking feature that allows you to track the executable files required for a permitted set of actions by performing those actions as a user would. This feature enables you to discover applications that users are invoking from other applications. For example, Microsoft Outlook invokes Microsoft Word for editing e-mail.

The tool restricts the file based on the full path name. Only the named executable in the designated location can be run, thereby preventing users from running other versions of the same executable file from alternate locations. The tool is typically used to restrict access to users on a Terminal Services Application Server deployment. This restriction allows important tools to be available on the computer—or accessible on the network—for use by administrators. The restriction also limits the applications a user can run.

The Application Security tool supports two levels of security: Admin and Non-admin. Admin can always run any executable file, even when the tool's security is enabled. Non-admin restricts access to only the allowed executable list. These settings apply to the computer; there is no per-user configuration. The settings also cover only 32-bit executables and not DLLs. By default, users are restricted from running 16-bit applications when the tool's security is enabled.

When you first enable the Application Security tool, users who are already logged on to the Terminal Server will not be affected; they will continue to be able to run applications that aren't on the authorized list. To be restricted to the applications allowed by the tool, such users must first log off and log back on. You can enforce this restriction by stopping the session.

Auditpol.exe: Audit Policy

You'll find the Audit Policy tool in the Diagnostic Tools folder. This tool was also present in the Windows NT 4.0 Resource Kit.

Audit Policy is a command-line tool. The tool enables the user to modify the audit policy of the local computer or of any remote computer. To run the Audit Policy tool, the user must have administrator privileges on the target computer.

Dsstore.exe: Directory Services Store

The Directory Services Store tool is new for Windows 2000. You'll find it in the Security Tools folder. The tool assists in managing Enterprise Public Key Integration.

This tool includes functionality necessary for several deployment scenarios, including listing, verifying, and checking information about a given computer.

Dumpel.exe: Dump Event Log

The Dump Event Log tool was present in the Windows NT 4.0 Resource Kit; you'll find it in the Diagnostic Tools folder. Dump Event Log is a command-line tool that dumps an event log for a local or remote system into a tab-separated text file. You can also use this tool to filter certain event types.

Efsinfo.exe: Encrypting File System Information

The Encrypting File System Information tool is new for Windows 2000; you'll find it in the Security Tools folder. This command-line tool displays information about files and folders that have been encrypted with Encrypting File System (EFS) on NTFS partitions.

Users can encrypt and decrypt files, thereby helping to keep files safe from intruders who might gain unauthorized physical access data (for example, by stealing a laptop or an external disk drive). The Cipher command-line tool included with the Windows 2000 operating system can also encrypt or decrypt a file or folder.

Elogdmp.exe: Event Log Dump

The Event Log Dump tool is new for Windows 2000; you'll find it in the Computer Management Tools folder. Event Log Dump is a command-line tool that dumps information from a selected event log. This tool locally or remotely displays the application, system, or security logs. When you use the tool in conjunction with the FindStr.exe tool that is included with Windows 2000, you can search for specific event log messages to display. To view the contents of the system or security log on any remote computer, you must be a domain administrator or be part of the local administrator's group on that computer.

Floplock.exe: Lock Floppy Disk Drives

Lock Floppy Disk Drives is a service that allows you to control access to the floppy drives of a computer. You can use this service to help prevent unauthorized software installation or the introduction of viruses via floppy disks.

If the service is started on Windows 2000 Professional, only members of the Administrators and Power Users groups can access the floppy drives. When the service is started on Windows 2000 Server, only members of the Administrators group can access floppy drives.

The service works by assigning a discretionary access control list (DACL) to a floppy drive. When the service locks the floppy drives on a machine, only users in the Administrators group can use the floppy drive (or drives). If you configure the service to start automatically, the lock stays in place even after the computer is restarted.

You must install FloppyLock separately, after installing the Resource Kit tools. (See the online help for details.) Once you install FloppyLock, you control it in the same manner as you control other services. FloppyLock was also part of the Windows NT 4.0 Resource Kit.

Gpolmig.exe: Group Policy Migration

The Group Policy Migration tool is new for Windows 2000. You'll find it in the Deployment Tools folder. This command-line tool helps to migrate Windows NT 4.0 System Policies files to Windows 2000 Group Policy object structure.

The location of the registry settings that implement software policy has changed in Windows 2000; therefore, the migration might not have an effect on some applications and components.

Gpotool.exe: Group Policy Verification Tool

The Group Policy Verification tool is new for Windows 2000; you'll find it in the Network Management Tools folder. This command-line tool allows you to check the health of the Group Policy objects (GPOs) on domain controllers. The tool performs the following functions:

- **Check GPOs for consistency**. The tool reads mandatory and optional directory services properties (version, friendly name, extension GUIDs) and SYSVOL (system volume) data, compares directory services and SYSVOL version numbers, and performs other consistency checks. Functionality version must be version 2.0 and user/computer version must be greater than 0 if the extensions property contains any GUIDs.
- **Check GPO replication**. The tool reads GPOs from each domain controller and compares them.
- **Display information about a particular GPO.** This information includes properties that you can't access through the Group Policy MMC Snap-In, such as functionality version and extension GUIDs.
- **Browse GPOs**. A command-line option can search policies based on friendly name or GUID. The tool also supports partial matches for both name and GUID.
- **Set preferred domain controllers**. By default, the tool will use all available domain controllers in the domain; you can overwrite this default with the list of domain controllers supplied by the command line.
- **Provide cross-domain support.** A command-line option is available for checking policies in different domains.

- **Run in verbose mode**. If all policies are fine, the tool displays a validation message; in case of errors, information about corrupted policies is printed.

Gpresult.exe: Group Policy Results

The Group Policy Results tool is new for Windows 2000; you'll find it in the Network Management Tools folder.

This command-line tool displays the following information about the result that the Group Policy had on the current computer and logged-on user:

- **Operating system.** This information includes type (Professional/Server/Domain Controller) and build number (if the operating system is a Terminal Server) and the mode the operating system is using.
- **User information**. This information includes username and Active Directory location (if applicable), domain name and type, site name, profile type and location (local or roaming), security group membership, and security privileges.
- **Computer information**. This information includes computer name and Active Directory location (if applicable), domain name and type, and site name.

The Group Policy Results tool also provides the following information about Group Policy:

- Last time policy applied, and DC for that policy, user, and computer
- Complete list of GPOs and details
- Registry settings that were applied and their details
- Folders that are redirected and their details
- Software management information detailing assigned and published applications
- Disk quota information
- IP Security settings
- Scripts

Ipsecpol.exe: Internet Protocol Security Policies Tool

The Internet Protocol Security Policies Tool is new for Windows 2000; you'll find it in the Network Management Tools folder. This command-line tool configures Internet Protocol Security (IPSec) policies in the directory service, local registry, or remote registry.

The tool has the same functionality as the IPSec MMC Snap-In. This tool has two mutually exclusive modes: static and dynamic. The default mode is dynamic.

Dynamic mode applies policy to the Policy Agent, which is active only for the lifetime of the Policy Agent service. (For example, after reboot—or when the service is stopped—the agent is no longer active.) The benefit of dynamic mode is that the policy can coexist with directory service–based policies, which override any local policy not plumbed by the tool.

Static mode creates or modifies stored policy. The policies you create will last the lifetime of the store. The IPSec MMC Snap-In uses static mode. The -w flag indicates static mode. The flags listed for static mode in the syntax listing are valid only for static mode.

You can use the tool to create scriptable ways of creating large or complex IPSec policies by placing commands into a batch file. The Internet Protocol Security Policies Tool facilitates just-in-time policy with its batch ability. If someone wants a secured channel with your server, simply send him or her the tool binaries and the command line or batch file to run.

If your computer uses directory service policy and you want to add rules that will allow you to speak IPSec to computers not covered in the directory service policy, use the tool's dynamic mode. Specific privileges must be present for dynamic and static modes to run: For static mode, you must enable read/write access to the storage that you write. For dynamic mode, you must have administrator privileges on the computer to which you are plumbing the dynamic policy.

Logevent.exe: Event Logging Utility

The Event Logging Utility tool was also present in the Windows NT 4.0 Resource Kit; you'll find it in the Diagnostic Tools folder. This tool, which you should install on the computer you use to view the event log, makes entries to the event log on either a local or remote computer from the command prompt or a batch file. The tool is useful for storing historical information from the execution of batch programs run from login scripts or the AT command.

The ability to store entries into the event log of other computers allows you to centrally collect data, if required. The application installs automatically when you use the tool for the first time.

Klist.exe: Kerberos List

The Kerberos List tool is new for Windows 2000; you'll it find in the Network Management Tools folder. Kerberos List is a command-line tool that enables you to view and delete Kerberos tickets granted to the current logon session. To use this tool, and see any tickets, you must join your Windows 2000 computer to a Windows 2000 domain.

Running Kerberos List from a client machine shows information about:

- Ticket-granting tickets (TGTs) sent to a Windows Kerberos key distribution center (KDC).
- Ticket-granting tickets sent to Ksserver on UNIX.

Caution Deleting Kerberos tickets can disable the full functionality of Windows 2000 for the current logon session.

Kerbtray.exe: Kerberos Tray

The Kerberos Tray tool is new for Windows 2000; you'll find it in the Network Management Tools folder.

Kerberos Tray is a GUI tool that displays Kerberos ticket information for a computer running the Kerberos protocol. When you start the tool it places an icon in the status area of your desktop. You can use the Kerberos Tray icon to view and purge the ticket cache. Positioning your mouse cursor over the Kerberos Tray icon will display the time left on your initial TGT (received when you first logged on to the Windows 2000 domain, before the ticket expires). The icon will also change in the last hour of life before the Local Security Authority (LSA) renews the ticket.

Double-clicking on the Kerberos Tray icon brings up a list of tickets you have obtained since logon. Right-clicking the icon brings up a context menu. Choosing List Tickets from this menu displays the same dialog box as a double click, as shown in Figure A-2.

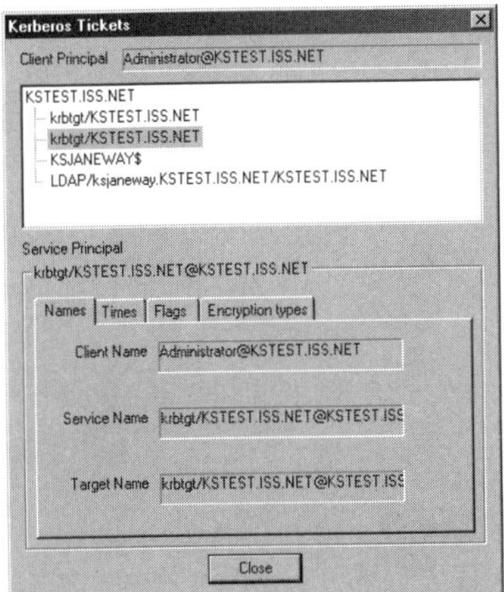

Figure A-2. *Kerberos Tickets dialog box.*

The Kerberos Tickets dialog includes the following sections:

- The top section lists the name of your Kerberos client principal associated with your Windows 2000 account.
- The scrolling list contains domains and tickets for services that you have used since logon. If you select an item here, its properties are displayed in the remaining sections of the dialog box.

- The middle section lists the service principal. This name is the target principal name for the selected ticket from the domain list.
- The bottom section is a set of property pages (Names, Times, Flags, and Encryption Types) that describe attributes of the ticket selected in the scrolling list. Only unexpired tickets show attributes.

Purge Tickets destroys all tickets that you have cached. Use this option with caution. It can stop you from being able to authenticate to resources. If you find yourself unable to authenticate, log off and log on again. You'll acquire new tickets the next time you use Kerberos services.

Netset.exe: NetSet

The NetSet tool is new for Windows 2000; you'll find it in the Network Management Tools folder. The tool helps you to configure a variety of network parameters from the command prompt.

The NetSet tool can list, install, configure, and uninstall networking components, making this tool useful for automating post-setup network configurations. NetSet can also facilitate unattended resetting of network parameters on individual computers when recovering from user errors or hardware failures. For operations other than listing network components, you must provide an answer file, which is a text file that describes the actions you want to perform.

Sectemplates.mmc: Security Configuration And Analysis Tool IIS Templates

The IIS templates are new for Windows 2000. You can find them in the Internet Information Services Tools folder. In Windows 2000, you can easily use security templates to standardize and implement security policies. Templates are a file representation of a security configuration. The Windows 2000 Resource Kit includes two IIS-specific security templates: Secure Internet Web Server template and Secure Intranet Web Server template. These templates are designed for use with the Security Configuration And Analysis Snap-In.

Tracelog.exe: Trace Log

The Trace Log tool is new for Windows 2000; you'll find it in the Computer Management Tools folder. Trace Log is an event-tracing command-line tool that starts, stops, or enables trace logging.

The tool first creates a circular buffer and enables tracing. The Windows Management Instrumentation (WMI) provider (such as the operating system) or an application (such as the directory service) starts tracing events. These traces are written to the buffer. You can view the results of event logging with either the Trace Dump or the Reduce Trace Data tool. When the tool fills the buffer, it writes the data to a log file and empties the buffer. If real-time mode is set, you can view the results of event logging with the Trace Dump tool or another application directly from the buffer. Table A-1 details the Trace Log display.

Table A-1. Trace Log display.

Name	Description
Logger Name	Name of the logging instance. For the kernel, this name is either NT Kernel Logger or the default that you provide.
Logger Id	ID of the logger.
Logger Thread Id	Thread ID of the logger.
Buffer Size	The size of the buffer allocated.
Maximum Buffers	The maximum buffers in pool.
Minimum Buffers	The number of buffers to preallocate.
Number of Buffers	The number of buffers currently in use.
Free Buffers	The number of buffers in the free list.
Buffers Written	The number of buffers that have already been written to.

Tracedmp.exe: Trace Dump

The Trace Dump tool is new for Windows 2000; you'll find it in the Computer Management Tools folder. Trace Dump is an event-tracing command-line tool that produces a summary of event log items.

Trace Dump can either process a trace log file or poll real-time trace buffer data generated by the Trace Log tool, which Trace Dump converts to a .csv file. This output provides you with a view of event trace results. Trace Dump gives you several ways to view event-tracing data:

- **Summary.txt file.** This file gives you a summary of the events traced.
- **A .csv (comma-separated value) file.** Events traced are saved in chronological order. A .csv file gives you a more detailed view for each event.
- **Real-time tracing.** You can also use Trace Dump for real-time event tracing. Trace Dump will read directly from the buffer instead of from a Trace Log file.

Usrtogrp.exe: Add Users To A Group

The Add Users To A Group tool is also present in the Windows NT 4.0 Resource Kit; you'll find it in the Network Management Tools folder. This command-line tool adds users to a local or global group according to information contained in a user-specified input text file.

The specified group is created if it does not already exist. For each user in the file, the tool searches to locate the user account. If you are adding users to a local group, the tool searches trusted domains for the account. If you are placing users in a global group, the tool searches only the specified domain. Once the tool finds the account, it places it in the group. If the username exists in multiple domains, only the first occurrence is placed in the group.

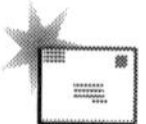

Note The Add Users To A Group tool does not create user accounts. All users specified must already exist. This tool is useful for granting membership in a group to large numbers of users—up to a maximum of 1000. This tool is especially useful if you don't know which trusted domain contains the user accounts you're looking for.

Appendix B
Security Tool Set Templates

The following three tables detail the main security settings enforced by the respective Security Configuration Tool Set Templates. We haven't included file system, system services, or individual registry settings unless these are specifically set under the security options section. The title of each setting is shown in the Security Configuration Tool Set GUI, the accompanying title in parentheses is that contained in the security template. Where the setting configures a registry key, the key details are given in italics.

Table B-1. Domain Controller Template security settings.

	Basic Domain Controller	Secure Domain Controller	High-Security Domain Controller
Account Policies			
Password Policy			
Enforce password history (PasswordHistorySize)	Not defined	24 passwords remembered	24 passwords remembered
Maximum password age (MaximumPasswordAge)	Not defined	42 days	42 days
Minimum password age (MinimumPasswordAge)	Not defined	2 days	2 days
Minimum password length (MinimumPasswordLength)	Not defined	8 characters	8 characters
Passwords must meet complexity requirements (PasswordComplexity)	Not defined	Enabled	Enabled
Store password using reversible encryption for all users in the domain (ClearTextPassword)	Not defined	Disabled	Disabled
Account Lockout Policy			
Account lockout duration (LockoutDuration)	Not defined	30 minutes	0
Account lockout threshold (LockoutBadCount)	Not defined	5 invalid logon attempts	5 invalid logon attempts

(continued)

Table B-1. *(continued)*

	Basic Domain Controller	**Secure Domain Controller**	**High-Security Domain Controller**
Reset account lockout counter after (ResetLockoutCount)	Not defined	30 minutes	30 minutes
Local Policies			
Audit Policy			
Audit account logon events (AuditAccountLogon)	Not defined	Failure	Success/Failure
Audit account management (AuditAccountManage)	Not defined	Success/Failure	Success/Failure
Audit directory services access (AuditDSAccess)	Not defined	Failure	Success/Failure
Audit logon events (AuditLogonEvents)	Not defined	Failure	Success/Failure
Audit object access (AuditObjectAccess)	Not defined	None	Success/Failure
Audit policy change (AuditPolicyChange)	Not defined	Success/Failure	Success/Failure
Audit privilege use (AuditPrivilegeUse)	Not defined	Failure	Success/Failure
Audit process tracking (AuditProcessTracking)	Not defined	None	None
Audit system events (AuditSystemEvents)	Not defined	None	Success/Failure
Security options			
Additional restrictions for anonymous connections *MACHINE\System\CurrentControlSet\Control\Lsa\RestrictAnonymous*	Not defined	Do not allow enumeration of SAM accounts and shares	No access without explicit anonymous permissions
Allow server operators to schedule tasks (domain controllers only) *MACHINE\System\CurrentControlSet\Control\Lsa\SubmitControl*	Not defined	Disabled	Disabled

(continued)

Table B-1. *(continued)*

	Basic Domain Controller	Secure Domain Controller	High-Security Domain Controller
Allow system to be shut down without having to log on *MACHINE\Software\Microsoft\Windows\CurrentVersion\Policies\System\ShutdownWithoutLogon*	Not defined	Disabled	Disabled
Allowed to eject removable NTFS media *MACHINE\Software\Microsoft\Windows NT\CurrentVersion\Winlogon\AllocateDASD*	Not defined	Administrators	Administrators
Amount of idle time required before disconnecting session *MACHINE\System\CurrentControlSet\Services\LanManServer\Parameters\AutoDisconnect*	Not defined	15 minutes	15 minutes
Audit the access of global system objects *MACHINE\System\CurrentControlSet\Control\Lsa\AuditBaseObjects*	Not defined	Disabled	Disabled
Audit use of Backup and Restore privilege *MACHINE\System\CurrentControlSet\Control\Lsa\FullPrivilegeAuditing*	Not defined	Disabled	Disabled
Automatically log off users when logon time expires *MACHINE\System\CurrentControlSet\Services\LanManServer\Parameters\EnableForcedLogOff*	Not defined	Enabled	Enabled
Automatically log off users when logon time expires (local) [Not in the Registry]	Not defined	Enabled	Enabled
Clear virtual memory pagefile when system shuts down *MACHINE\System\CurrentControlSet\Control\Session Manager\Memory Management\ClearPageFileAtShutdown*	Not defined	Disabled	Enabled

(continued)

Table B-1. *(continued)*

	Basic Domain Controller	Secure Domain Controller	High-Security Domain Controller
Digitally sign client communication (always) *MACHINE\System\CurrentControlSet\Services\LanmanWorkstation\Parameters\RequireSecuritySignature*	Not defined	Disabled	Enabled
Digitally sign client communication (when possible) *MACHINE\System\CurrentControlSet\Services\LanmanWorkstation\Parameters\EnableSecuritySignature*	Not defined	Enabled	Enabled
Digitally sign server communication (always) *MACHINE\System\CurrentControlSet\Services\LanManServer\Parameters\RequireSecuritySignature*	Not defined	Disabled	Enabled
Digitally sign server communication (when possible) *MACHINE\System\CurrentControlSet\Services\LanManServer\Parameters\EnableSecuritySignature*	Enabled	Enabled	Enabled
Disable Ctrl+Alt+Del requirement for logon *MACHINE\Software\Microsoft\Windows\CurrentVersion\Policies\System\DisableCAD*	Not defined	Disabled	Disabled
Do not display last username in logon screen *MACHINE\Software\Microsoft\Windows\CurrentVersion\Policies\System\DontDisplayLastUserName*	Not defined	Disabled	Enabled
LAN Manager Authentication Level *MACHINE\System\CurrentControlSet\Control\Lsa\LmCompatibilityLevel*	Not defined	Send NTLM response only	Send NTLMv2 response only\refuse LM & NTLM

(continued)

Table B-1. *(continued)*

	Basic Domain Controller	Secure Domain Controller	High-Security Domain Controller
Message text for users attempting to log on *MACHINE\Software\Microsoft\Windows\CurrentVersion\Policies\System\LegalNoticeText*	Not defined		
Message title for users attempting to log on *MACHINE\Software\Microsoft\Windows\CurrentVersion\Policies\System\LegalNoticeCaption*	Not defined		
Number of previous logons to cache (in case domain controller is not available) *MACHINE\Software\Microsoft\Windows NT\CurrentVersion\Winlogon\CachedLogonsCount*	Not defined	10 logons	10 logons
Prevent system maintenance of computer account password *MACHINE\System\CurrentControlSet\Services\Netlogon\Parameters\DisablePasswordChange*	Not defined	Disabled	Disabled
Prevent users from installing printer drivers *MACHINE\System\CurrentControlSet\Control\Print\Providers\LanMan Print Services\Servers\AddPrinterDrivers*	Not defined	Enabled	Enabled
Prompt user to change password before expiration *MACHINE\Software\Microsoft\Windows NT\CurrentVersion\Winlogon\PasswordExpiryWarning*	Not defined	14 days	14 days
Recovery Console: Allow automatic administrative logon *MACHINE\Software\Microsoft\Windows NT\CurrentVersion\Setup\RecoveryConsole\SecurityLevel*	Not defined	Disabled	Disabled

(continued)

Table B-1. *(continued)*

	Basic Domain Controller	Secure Domain Controller	High-Security Domain Controller
Recovery Console: Allow floppy copy and access to all drives and all folders *MACHINE\Software\Microsoft\Windows NT\CurrentVersion\Setup\RecoveryConsole\SetCommand*	Not defined	Disabled	Disabled
Rename administrator account [Not in the Registry]	Not defined	Not defined	Not defined
Rename guest account [Not in the Registry]	Not defined	Not defined	Not defined
Restrict CD-ROM access to locally logged-on user only *MACHINE\Software\Microsoft\Windows NT\CurrentVersion\Winlogon\AllocateCDRoms*	Not defined	Enabled	Enabled
Restrict floppy access to locally logged-on user only *MACHINE\Software\Microsoft\Windows NT\CurrentVersion\Winlogon\AllocateFloppies*	Not defined	Enabled	Enabled
Secure channel: Digitally encrypt or sign secure channel data (always) *MACHINE\System\CurrentControlSet\Services\Netlogon\Parameters\RequireSignOrSeal*	Not defined	Disabled	Enabled
Secure channel: Digitally encrypt secure channel data (when possible) *MACHINE\System\CurrentControlSet\Services\Netlogon\Parameters\SealSecureChannel*	Not defined	Enabled	Enabled
Secure channel: Digitally sign secure channel data (when possible) *MACHINE\System\CurrentControlSet\Services\Netlogon\Parameters\SignSecureChannel*	Not defined	Enabled	Enabled

(continued)

Table B-1. *(continued)*

	Basic Domain Controller	Secure Domain Controller	High-Security Domain Controller
Secure channel: Require strong (Windows 2000 or later) session key *MACHINE\System\CurrentControlSet\Services\Netlogon\Parameters\RequireStrongKey*	Not defined	Disabled	Enabled
Secure system partition (for RISC platforms only) [Not in the Registry]	Not defined	Not defined	Not defined
Send unencrypted password to reversible connect to third-party SMB servers *MACHINE\System\CurrentControlSet\Services\LanmanWorkstation\Parameters\EnablePlainTextPassword*	Not defined	Disabled	Disabled
Shut down system immediately if unable to log security audits *MACHINE\System\CurrentControlSet\Control\Lsa\CrashOnAuditFail*	Not defined	Disabled	Disabled
Smart card removal behavior *MACHINE\Software\Microsoft\Windows NT\CurrentVersion\Winlogon\ScRemoveOption*	Not defined	Force Logoff	Force Logoff
Strengthen default permissions of global system objects (e.g. Symbolic Links) *MACHINE\System\CurrentControlSet\Control\Session Manager\ProtectionMode*	Not defined	Enabled	Enabled
Unsigned driver installation behavior *MACHINE\Software\Microsoft\Driver Signing\Policy*	Not defined	Do not allow installation	Do not allow installation
Unsigned non-driver installation behavior *MACHINE\Software\Microsoft\Non-Driver Signing\Policy*	Not defined	Warn but allow installation	Silently succeed

(continued)

Table B-1. *(continued)*

	Basic Domain Controller	Secure Domain Controller	High-Security Domain Controller
Event Log			
Settings for Event Logs			
Maximum application log size (MaximumLogSize)	512 kilobytes	Not defined	Not defined
Maximum security log size (MaximumLogSize)	512 kilobytes	5120 kilobytes	10240 kilobytes
Maximum system log size (MaximumLogSize)	512 kilobytes	Not defined	Not defined
Restrict guest access to application log (RestrictGuestAccess)	Disabled	Enabled	Enabled
Restrict guest access to security log (RestrictGuestAccess)	Disabled	Enabled	Enabled
Restrict guest access to system log (RestrictGuestAccess)	Disabled	Enabled	Enabled
Retain application log (RetentionDays)	7 days	Not defined	Not defined
Retain security log (RetentionDays)	7 days	Not defined	Not defined
Retain system log (RetentionDays)	7 days	Not defined	Not defined
Retention method for application log (AuditLogRetentionPeriod)	By days	Not defined	Not defined
Retention method for security log (AuditLogRetentionPeriod)	By days	As needed	As needed
Retention method for system log (AuditLogRetentionPeriod)	By days	Not defined	Not defined
Shut down the computer when the security audit log is full (CrashOnAuditFull)	Not defined	Not defined	Not defined

Table B-2. Server Template security settings.

	Basic Server	Secure Server	High-Security Server
Account Policies			
Password Policy			
Enforce password history (PasswordHistorySize)	0 passwords remembered	24 passwords remembered	24 passwords remembered
Maximum password age (MaximumPasswordAge)	42 days	42 days	42 days
Minimum password age (MinimumPasswordAge)	0 days	2 days	2 days
Minimum password length (MinimumPasswordLength)	0 characters	8 characters	8 characters
Passwords must meet complexity requirements (PasswordComplexity)	Disabled	Enabled	Enabled
Store password using reversible encryption for all users in the domain (ClearTextPassword)	Disabled	Disabled	Disabled
Account Lockout Policy			
Account lockout duration (LockoutDuration)	Not defined	30 minutes	0
Account lockout threshold (LockoutBadCount)	0 invalid logon attempts	5 invalid logon attempts	5 invalid logon attempts
Reset account lockout counter after (ResetLockoutCount)	Not defined	30 minutes	30 minutes
Local Policies			
Audit Policy			
Audit account logon events (AuditAccountLogon)	No auditing	Success/Failure	Success/Failure
Audit account management (AuditAccountManage)	Not defined	Success/Failure	Success/Failure
Audit directory services access (AuditDSAccess)	Not defined	Not defined	Not defined
Audit logon events (AuditLogonEvents)	No auditing	Failure	Success/Failure

(conrinued)

Table B-2. *(continued)*

	Basic Server	Secure Server	High-Security Server
Audit object access (AuditObjectAccess)	No auditing	No auditing	Success/Failure
Audit policy change (AuditPolicyChange)	No auditing	Success/Failure	Success/Failure
Audit privilege use (AuditPrivilegeUse)	No auditing	Failure	Success/Failure
Audit process tracking (AuditProcessTracking)	No auditing	No auditing	No auditing
Audit system events (AuditSystemEvents)	No auditing	No auditing	Success/Failure
Security options			
Additional restrictions for anonymous connections *MACHINE\System\CurrentControlSet\Control\Lsa\RestrictAnonymous*	None. Rely on default permissions	Do not allow enumeration of SAM accounts and shares	No access without explicit anonymous permissions
Allow server operators to schedule tasks (domain controllers only) *MACHINE\System\CurrentControlSet\Control\Lsa\SubmitControl*	Not defined	Not defined	Not defined
Allow system to be shut down without having to log on *MACHINE\Software\Microsoft\Windows\CurrentVersion\Policies\System\ShutdownWithoutLogon*	Disabled	Not defined	Not defined
Allowed to eject removable NTFS media *MACHINE\Software\Microsoft\Windows NT\CurrentVersion\Winlogon\AllocateDASD*	Administrators	Administrators	Administrators
Amount of idle time required before disconnecting session *MACHINE\System\CurrentControlSet\Services\LanManServer\Parameters\AutoDisconnect*	15 minutes	15 minutes	15 minutes
Audit the access of global system objects *MACHINE\System\CurrentControlSet\Control\Lsa\AuditBaseObjects*	Disabled	Disabled	Disabled

(conrinued)

Table B-2. *(continued)*

	Basic Server	Secure Server	High-Security Server
Audit use of Backup and Restore privilege *MACHINE\System\CurrentControlSet\Control\Lsa\FullPrivilegeAuditing*	Disabled	Disabled	Disabled
Automatically log off users when logon time expires *MACHINE\System\CurrentControlSet\Services\LanManServer\Parameters\EnableForcedLogOff*	Not defined	Not defined	Not defined
Automatically log off users when logon time expires (local) [Not in the Registry]	Enabled	Enabled	Enabled
Clear virtual memory pagefile when system shuts down *MACHINE\System\CurrentControlSet\Control\Session Manager\Memory Management\ClearPageFileAtShutdown*	Disabled	Disabled	Enabled
Digitally sign client communication (always) *MACHINE\System\CurrentControlSet\Services\LanmanWorkstation\Parameters\RequireSecuritySignature*	Disabled	Disabled	Enabled
Digitally sign client communication (when possible) *MACHINE\System\CurrentControlSet\Services\LanmanWorkstation\Parameters\EnableSecuritySignature*	Enabled	Enabled	Enabled
Digitally sign server communication (always) *MACHINE\System\CurrentControlSet\Services\LanManServer\Parameters\RequireSecuritySignature*	Disabled	Disabled	Enabled
Digitally sign server communication (when possible) *MACHINE\System\CurrentControlSet\Services\LanManServer\Parameters\EnableSecuritySignature*	Disabled	Enabled	Enabled

(conrinued)

Table B-2. *(continued)*

	Basic Server	Secure Server	High-Security Server
Disable Ctrl+Alt+Del requirement for logon *MACHINE\Software\Microsoft\Windows\CurrentVersion\Policies\System\DisableCAD*	Disabled	Disabled	Disabled
Do not display last user name in logon screen *MACHINE\Software\Microsoft\Windows\CurrentVersion\Policies\System\DontDisplayLastUserName*	Disabled	Disabled	Enabled
LAN Manager Authentication Level *MACHINE\System\CurrentControlSet\Control\Lsa\LmCompatibilityLevel*	Send LM & NTLM responses	Send NTLM response only	Send NTLMv2 response only\refuse LM & NTLM
Message text for users attempting to log on *MACHINE\Software\Microsoft\Windows\CurrentVersion\Policies\System\LegalNoticeText*			
Message title for users attempting to log on *MACHINE\Software\Microsoft\Windows\CurrentVersion\Policies\System\LegalNoticeCaption*			
Number of previous logons to cache (in case domain controller is not available) *MACHINE\Software\Microsoft\Windows NT\CurrentVersion\Winlogon\CachedLogonsCount*	10 logons	10 logons	10 logons
Prevent system maintenance of computer account password *MACHINE\System\CurrentControlSet\Services\Netlogon\Parameters\DisablePasswordChange*	Disabled	Disabled	Disabled
Prevent users from installing printer drivers *MACHINE\System\CurrentControlSet\Control\Print\Providers\LanMan Print Services\Servers\AddPrinterDrivers*	Enabled	Enabled	Enabled

(conrinued)

Table B-2. *(continued)*

	Basic Server	Secure Server	High-Security Server
Prompt user to change password before expiration *MACHINE\Software\Microsoft\Windows NT\CurrentVersion\Winlogon\PasswordExpiryWarning*	14 days	14 days	14 days
Recovery Console: Allow automatic administrative logon *MACHINE\Software\Microsoft\Windows NT\CurrentVersion\Setup\RecoveryConsole\SecurityLevel*	Disabled	Disabled	Disabled
Recovery Console: Allow floppy copy and access to all drives and all folders *MACHINE\Software\Microsoft\Windows NT\CurrentVersion\Setup\RecoveryConsole\SetCommand*	Disabled	Disabled	Disabled
Rename administrator account [Not in the Registry]	Not defined	Not defined	Not defined
Rename guest account [Not in the Registry]	Not defined	Not defined	Not defined
Restrict CD-ROM access to locally logged-on user only *MACHINE\Software\Microsoft\Windows NT\CurrentVersion\Winlogon\AllocateCDRoms*	Disabled	Disabled	Disabled
Restrict floppy access to locally logged-on user only *MACHINE\Software\Microsoft\Windows NT\CurrentVersion\Winlogon\AllocateFloppies*	Disabled	Disabled	Disabled
Secure channel: Digitally encrypt or sign secure channel data (always) *MACHINE\System\CurrentControlSet\Services\Netlogon\Parameters\RequireSignOrSeal*	Disabled	Disabled	Enabled

(conrinued)

Table B-2. *(continued)*

	Basic Server	Secure Server	High-Security Server
Secure channel: Digitally encrypt secure channel data (when possible) *MACHINE\System\CurrentControlSet\Services\Netlogon\Parameters\SealSecureChannel*	Enabled	Enabled	Enabled
Secure channel: Digitally sign secure channel data (when possible) *MACHINE\System\CurrentControlSet\Services\Netlogon\Parameters\SignSecureChannel*	Enabled	Enabled	Enabled
Secure channel: Require strong (Windows 2000 or later) session key *MACHINE\System\CurrentControlSet\Services\Netlogon\Parameters\RequireStrongKey*	Disabled	Disabled	Enabled
Secure system partition (for RISC platforms only) [Not in the Registry]	Not defined	Not defined	Not defined
Send unencrypted password to connect to third-party SMB servers *MACHINE\System\CurrentControlSet\Services\LanmanWorkstation\Parameters\EnablePlainTextPassword*	Disabled	Disabled	Disabled
Shut down system immediately if unable to log security audits *MACHINE\System\CurrentControlSet\Control\Lsa\CrashOnAuditFail*	Disabled	Disabled	Disabled
Smart card removal behavior *MACHINE\Software\Microsoft\Windows NT\CurrentVersion\Winlogon\ScRemoveOption*	No Action	Lock Workstation	Lock Workstation

(conrinued)

Table B-2. *(continued)*

	Basic Server	Secure Server	High-Security Server
Strengthen default permissions of global system objects (e.g. Symbolic Links) *MACHINE\System\CurrentControlSet\Control\Session Manager\ProtectionMode*	Enabled	Enabled	Enabled
Unsigned driver installation behavior *MACHINE\Software\Microsoft\Driver Signing\Policy*	Not defined	Warn but allow installation	Do not allow installation
Unsigned non-driver installation behavior *MACHINE\Software\Microsoft\Non-Driver Signing\Policy*	Not defined	Silently succeed	Silently succeed
Event Log			
Settings for Event Logs			
Maximum application log size (MaximumLogSize)	512 kilobytes	Not defined	Not defined
Maximum security log size (MaximumLogSize)	512 kilobytes	5120 kilobytes	10240 kilobytes
Maximum system log size (MaximumLogSize)	512 kilobytes	Not defined	Not defined
Restrict guest access to application log (RestrictGuestAccess)	Disabled	Enabled	Enabled
Restrict guest access to security log (RestrictGuestAccess)	Disabled	Enabled	Enabled
Restrict guest access to system log (RestrictGuestAccess)	Disabled	Enabled	Enabled
Retain application log (RetentionDays)	7 days	Not defined	Not defined
Retain security log (RetentionDays)	7 days	Not defined	Not defined
Retain system log (RetentionDays)	7 days	Not defined	Not defined

(conrinued)

Table B-2. *(continued)*

	Basic Server	Secure Server	High-Security Server
Retention method for application log (AuditLogRetentionPeriod)	By days	Not defined	Not defined
Retention method for security log (AuditLogRetentionPeriod)	By days	As needed	As needed
Retention method for system log (AuditLogRetentionPeriod)	By days	Not defined	Not defined
Shut down the computer when the security audit log is full (CrashOnAuditFull)	Disabled	Not defined	Not defined

Table B-3. Workstation Template security settings.

	Basic Workstation	Secure Workstation	High-Security Workstation
Account Policies			
Password Policy			
Enforce password history (PasswordHistorySize)	0 passwords remembered	24 passwords remembered	24 passwords remembered
Maximum password age (MaximumPasswordAge)	42 days	42 days	42 days
Minimum password age (MinimumPasswordAge)	0 days	2 days	2 days
Minimum password length (MinimumPasswordLength)	0 characters	8 characters	8 characters
Passwords must meet complexity requirements (PasswordComplexity)	Disabled	Enabled	Enabled
Store password using reversible encryption for all users in the domain (ClearTextPassword)	Disabled	Disabled	Disabled
Account Lockout Policy			
Account lockout duration (LockoutDuration)	Not defined	30 minutes	0
Account lockout threshold (LockoutBadCount)	0 invalid logon attempts	5 invalid logon attempts	5 invalid logon attempts

(continued)

Table B-3. *(continued)*

	Basic Workstation	Secure Workstation	High-Security Workstation
Reset account lockout counter after (ResetLockoutCount)	Not defined	30 minutes	30 minutes
Local Policies			
Audit Policy			
Audit account logon events (AuditAccountLogon)	No auditing	Success/Failure	Success/Failure
Audit account management (AuditAccountManage)	No auditing	Success/Failure	Success/Failure
Audit directory services access (AuditDSAccess)	Not defined	Not defined	Not defined
Audit logon events (AuditLogonEvents)	No auditing	Failure	Success/Failure
Audit object access (AuditObjectAccess)	No auditing	No auditing	Success/Failure
Audit policy change (AuditPolicyChange)	No auditing	Success/Failure	Success/Failure
Audit privilege use (AuditPrivilegeUse)	No auditing	Failure	Success/Failure
Audit process tracking (AuditProcessTracking)	No auditing	No auditing	No auditing
Audit system events (AuditSystemEvents)	No auditing	No auditing	Success/Failure
Security options			
Additional restrictions for anonymous connections *MACHINE\System\CurrentControlSet\Control\Lsa\RestrictAnonymous*	None: Rely on default permissions	Do not allow enumeration of SAM accounts and shares	No access without explicit anonymous permissions
Allow server operators to schedule tasks (domain controllers only) *MACHINE\System\CurrentControlSet\Control\Lsa\SubmitControl*	Not defined	Not defined	Not defined
Allow system to be shut down without having to log on *MACHINE\Software\Microsoft\Windows\CurrentVersion\Policies\System\ShutdownWithoutLogon*	Enabled	Not defined	Not defined

(continued)

Table B-3. *(continued)*

	Basic Workstation	Secure Workstation	High-Security Workstation
Allowed to eject removable NTFS media *MACHINE\Software\Microsoft\Windows NT\CurrentVersion\Winlogon\AllocateDASD*	Administrators	Administrators	Administrators
Amount of idle time required before disconnecting session *MACHINE\System\CurrentControlSet\Services\LanManServer\Parameters\AutoDisconnect*	15 minutes	15 minutes	15 minutes
Audit the access of global system objects *MACHINE\System\CurrentControlSet\Control\Lsa\AuditBaseObjects*	Disabled	Disabled	Disabled
Audit use of Backup and Restore privilege *MACHINE\System\CurrentControlSet\Control\Lsa\FullPrivilegeAuditing*	Disabled	Disabled	Disabled
Automatically log off users when logon time expires *MACHINE\System\CurrentControlSet\Services\LanManServer\Parameters\EnableForcedLogOff*	Not defined	Not defined	Not defined
Automatically log off users when logon time expires (local) [Not in the Registry]	Enabled	Enabled	Enabled
Clear virtual memory pagefile when system shuts down *MACHINE\System\CurrentControlSet\Control\Session Manager\Memory Management\ClearPageFileAtShutdown*	Disabled	Disabled	Enabled
Digitally sign client communication (always) *MACHINE\System\CurrentControlSet\Services\LanmanWorkstation\Parameters\RequireSecuritySignature*	Disabled	Disabled	Enabled

(continued)

Table B-3. *(continued)*

	Basic Workstation	Secure Workstation	High-Security Workstation
Digitally sign client communication (when possible) *MACHINE\System\CurrentControlSet\Services\LanmanWorkstation\Parameters\EnableSecuritySignature*	Enabled	Enabled	Enabled
Digitally sign server communication (always) *MACHINE\System\CurrentControlSet\Services\LanManServer\Parameters\RequireSecuritySignature*	Disabled	Disabled	Enabled
Digitally sign server communication (when possible) *MACHINE\System\CurrentControlSet\Services\LanManServer\Parameters\EnableSecuritySignature*	Disabled	Enabled	Enabled
Disable Ctrl+Alt+Del requirement for logon *MACHINE\Software\Microsoft\Windows\CurrentVersion\Policies\System\DisableCAD*	Not defined	Disabled	Disabled
Do not display last username in logon screen *MACHINE\Software\Microsoft\Windows\CurrentVersion\Policies\System\DontDisplayLastUserName*	Disabled	Disabled	Enabled
LAN Manager Authentication Level *MACHINE\System\CurrentControlSet\Control\Lsa\LmCompatibilityLevel*	Send LM & NTLM responses	Send NTLM response only	Send NTLMv2 response only\refuse LM & NTLM
Message text for users attempting to log on *MACHINE\Software\Microsoft\Windows\CurrentVersion\Policies\System\LegalNoticeText*			

(continued)

Table B-3. *(continued)*

	Basic Workstation	Secure Workstation	High-Security Workstation
Message title for users attempting to log on *MACHINE\Software\Microsoft\Windows\CurrentVersion\Policies\System\LegalNoticeCaption*			
Number of previous logons to cache (in case domain controller is not available) *MACHINE\Software\Microsoft\Windows NT\CurrentVersion\Winlogon\CachedLogonsCount*	10 logons	10 logons	10 logons
Prevent system maintenance of computer account password *MACHINE\System\CurrentControlSet\Services\Netlogon\Parameters\DisablePasswordChange*	Disabled	Disabled	Disabled
Prevent users from installing printer drivers *MACHINE\System\CurrentControlSet\Control\Print\Providers\LanMan Print Services\Servers\AddPrinterDrivers*	Disabled	Enabled	Enabled
Prompt user to change password before expiration *MACHINE\Software\Microsoft\Windows NT\CurrentVersion\Winlogon\PasswordExpiryWarning*	14 days	14 days	14 days
Recovery Console: Allow automatic administrative logon *MACHINE\Software\Microsoft\Windows NT\CurrentVersion\Setup\RecoveryConsole\SecurityLevel*	Disabled	Disabled	Disabled
Recovery Console: Allow floppy copy and access to all drives and all folders *MACHINE\Software\Microsoft\Windows NT\CurrentVersion\Setup\RecoveryConsole\SetCommand*	Disabled	Disabled	Disabled

(continued)

Table B-3. *(continued)*

	Basic Workstation	Secure Workstation	High-Security Workstation
Rename administrator account [Not in the Registry]	Not defined	Not defined	Not defined
Rename guest account [Not in the Registry]	Not defined	Not defined	Not defined
Restrict CD-ROM access to locally logged-on user only *MACHINE\Software\Microsoft\Windows NT\CurrentVersion\Winlogon\AllocateCDRoms*	Disabled	Disabled	Disabled
Restrict floppy access to locally logged-on user only *MACHINE\Software\Microsoft\Windows NT\CurrentVersion\Winlogon\AllocateFloppies*	Disabled	Disabled	Disabled
Secure channel: Digitally encrypt or sign secure channel data (always) *MACHINE\System\CurrentControlSet\Services\Netlogon\Parameters\RequireSignOrSeal*	Disabled	Disabled	Enabled
Secure channel: Digitally encrypt secure channel data (when possible) *MACHINE\System\CurrentControlSet\Services\Netlogon\Parameters\SealSecureChannel*	Enabled	Enabled	Enabled
Secure channel: Digitally sign secure channel data (when possible) *MACHINE\System\CurrentControlSet\Services\Netlogon\Parameters\SignSecureChannel*	Enabled	Enabled	Enabled
Secure channel: Require strong (Windows 2000 or later) session key *MACHINE\System\CurrentControlSet\Services\Netlogon\Parameters\RequireStrongKey*	Disabled	Disabled	Enabled
Secure system partition (for RISC platforms only) [Not in the Registry]	Not defined	Not defined	Not defined

(continued)

Table B-3. *(continued)*

	Basic Workstation	Secure Workstation	High-Security Workstation
Send unencrypted password to connect to third-party SMB servers *MACHINE\System\CurrentControlSet\Services\LanmanWorkstation\Parameters\EnablePlainTextPassword*	Disabled	Disabled	Disabled
Shut down system immediately if unable to log security audits *MACHINE\System\CurrentControlSet\Control\Lsa\CrashOnAuditFail*	Disabled	Disabled	Disabled
Smart card removal behavior *MACHINE\Software\Microsoft\Windows NT\CurrentVersion\Winlogon\ScRemoveOption*	No Action	Lock Workstation	Lock Workstation
Strengthen default permissions of global system objects (e.g. Symbolic Links) *MACHINE\System\CurrentControlSet\Control\Session Manager\ProtectionMode*	Enabled	Enabled	Enabled
Unsigned driver installation behavior *MACHINE\Software\Microsoft\Driver Signing\Policy*	Not defined	Warn but allow installation	Do not allow installation
Unsigned non-driver installation behavior *MACHINE\Software\Microsoft\Non-Driver Signing\Policy*	Not defined	Silently succeed	Silently succeed
Event Log			
Settings for Event Logs			
Maximum application log size (MaximumLogSize)	512 kilobytes	Not defined	Not defined
Maximum security log size (MaximumLogSize)	512 kilobytes	5120 kilobytes	10240 kilobytes
Maximum system log size (MaximumLogSize)	512 kilobytes	Not defined	Not defined
Restrict guest access to application log (RestrictGuestAccess)	Disabled	Enabled	Enabled

(continued)

Table B-3. *(continued)*

	Basic Workstation	Secure Workstation	High-Security Workstation
Restrict guest access to security log (RestrictGuestAccess)	Disabled	Enabled	Enabled
Restrict guest access to system log (RestrictGuestAccess)	Disabled	Enabled	Enabled
Retain application log (RetentionDays)	7 days	Not defined	Not defined
Retain security log (RetentionDays)	7 days	Not defined	Not defined
Retain system log (RetentionDays)	7 days	Not defined	Not defined
Retention method for application log (AuditLogRetentionPeriod)	By days	Not defined	Not defined
Retention method for security log (AuditLogRetentionPeriod)	By days	As needed	As needed
Retention method for system log (AuditLogRetentionPeriod)	By days	Not defined	Not defined
Shut down the computer when the security audit log is full (CrashOnAuditFull)	Not defined	Not defined	Not defined

Index

A

B

C

D

G

H

I

J

K

L

N

R

S

T

John Hayday John has more than 24 years of experience in all aspects of security. For the last ten years he has concentrated on issues of information technology security.

He is currently Director of Knowledge Services at Internet Security Systems, Inc. (*www.iss.net*). He is responsible for the production of technical security training courses, and the provision of long-term security research and support for a range of multinational organizations. John has authored a number of security guides on Windows NT and Windows 2000. He is also responsible for the ISS SAVANT Security Service, providing customers with the latest in Windows security information.

The manuscript for this book was prepared and submitted to Microsoft Press in electronic form. Text files were prepared using Microsoft Word 97 and Word 2000 for Windows. Pages were composed by J & L Publishing using Adobe PageMaker 6.52 for Windows, with text in Garamond and display type in Franklin Gothic. Composed pages were delivered to the printer as electronic prepress files.

Cover Designer: Tim Girvin Design, Inc.
Cover Illustrator: Glenn Mitsui
Interior Graphic Designer: James D. Kramer
Interior Illustrator: David Holter
Project Manager: Linda Robinson
Manuscript Editor: Rebecca McKay
Principal Compositor: Linda Robinson
Principal Proofreader: Paul Vautier
Indexer: Kari J. Kells